MAX-PLANCK-INSTITUT
FÜR AUSLÄNDISCHES ÖFFENTLICHES RECHT
UND VÖLKERRECHT

Beiträge zum ausländischen öffentlichen Recht und Völkerrecht

Begründet von Viktor Bruns

Herausgegeben von
Armin von Bogdandy • Anne Peters

Volume 299

Henner Gött

The Law of Interactions Between International Organizations

A Framework for Multi-Institutional Labour Governance

Springer

ISSN 0172-4770 ISSN 2197-7135 (electronic)
Beiträge zum ausländischen öffentlichen Recht und Völkerrecht
ISBN 978-3-662-62388-6 ISBN 978-3-662-62389-3 (eBook)
https://doi.org/10.1007/978-3-662-62389-3

This Springer imprint is published by the registered company Springer-Verlag GmbH, DE, part of Springer Nature.
The registered company address is: Heidelberger Platz 3, 14197 Berlin, Germany

For my family

Preface

International organizations interact with each other. In labour governance, this phenomenon is ubiquitous. The International Labour Organization, equipped with a mandate to pursue social justice and decent work for all, interacts with a wide range of economic, financial, human rights and other organizations, all of which work on labour issues as well. These interactions vary in shape and form and can substantially affect all interacting organizations' work. For this reason, they are of significant structural relevance for labour governance as a whole.

For the organizations themselves, interactions are an ambivalent matter: through interactions, each organization can promote its own model of labour governance, thus enhancing its effectiveness and legitimacy. Yet, interactions simultaneously expose each organization to adverse influence from others, compromising its efforts and jeopardizing its goals. In this context, it becomes critical to ensure that interactions take place in a structured and predictable manner.

This book enquires how international law addresses interactions between international organizations in labour governance. Based on detailed case studies of mutual influence between the International Labour Organization, the World Bank and the Council of Europe's human rights bodies, it provides a systematic analysis of the law of inter-organizational interactions as it stands at present. It identifies key challenges and envisions a (more) developed law of inter-organizational interactions as a normative framework structuring interactions and enhancing the effectiveness and legitimacy of multi-institutional labour governance.

The book is based on my doctoral thesis I defended at the Law Faculty of Georg-August-University Göttingen in summer term 2019. The thesis was awarded the Faculty Prize for the best dissertation.

I am indebted to a remarkable community of teachers, colleagues and friends. Above all, I express my sincere gratitude and appreciation to my supervisor Peter-Tobias Stoll for his unwavering support, patience, trust and guidance. He gave me the freedom and inspiration to pursue this project and included me into an exceptional academic environment at the Göttingen Institute of International and European Law.

I also thank Andreas Paulus, who agreed to serve as second examiner and provided many thoughtful and critical comments on the thesis.

Armin von Bogdandy and Anne Peters accepted this book into the prestigious *Beiträge zum ausländischen öffentlichen Recht und Völkerrecht* series of the Max Planck Institute for Comparative Public Law and International Law in Heidelberg, for which I am much obliged. I also gratefully acknowledge the German National Academic Foundation (Studienstiftung des deutschen Volkes) for supporting me with a doctoral scholarship.

As my research proceeded, I had the opportunity to present work in progress at a series of conferences, workshops and seminars in Göttingen, at ELTE Budapest, the University of Oslo and the German National Academic Foundation's annual doctoral forum. I am grateful for the comments and feedback I received.

Throughout the entire duration of this project, I was fortunate to receive support, understanding and encouragement from many knowledgeable colleagues and dear friends. Pars per toto, I thank Till Patrik Holterhus and Patrick Abel for their continuous intellectual engagement with my work and for an outstanding and inspiring time in Göttingen.

I dedicate this book to my family, especially my parents Gisela and Rainer and my brothers Kristoff and Steffen.

Göttingen, Germany
May 2020

Henner Gött

Summary Contents

Table of Contents

Part III The Silence of Inter-Organizational Law

Abbreviations

ACABQ	Advisory Committee on Administrative and Budgetary Questions (UN)
ACC	Administrative Committee on Coordination (UN)
AoA	Articles of Agreement
ASEAN	Association of Southeast Asian Nations
BVerfGE	Entscheidungen des Bundesverfassungsgerichts
CAS	Conference Committee on the Application of Standards (ILO)
CDF	Comprehensive Development Framework (World Bank)
CEACR	Committee of Experts on the Application of Conventions and Recommendations (ILO)
CEB	Chief Executives Board for Coordination (UN)
CESCR	Committee on Economic, Social and Cultural Rights
CETS	Council of Europe Treaty Series
CFA	Committee on Freedom of Association (ILO)
CJEU	Court of Justice of the European Union
CM	Committee of Ministers (CoE)
CoE	Council of Europe
CPC	Committee for Programme and Coordination
CPIA	Country Policy and Institutional Assessment
DARIO	Draft articles on the responsibility of international organizations
EBRD	European Bank for Reconstruction and Development
ECB	European Central Bank
ECHR (in case references)	European Court of Human Rights, Reports of Judgments and Decisions
ECHR	European Convention on Human Rights
ECOSOC	Economic and Social Council (UN)
ECR	European Court Reports
ECSR	European Committee of Social Rights
ECtHR	European Court of Human Rights
EEC	European Economic Community

EHRR	European Human Rights Reports
EIB	European Investment Bank
ESC	European Social Charter
ESM	European Stability Mechanism
EU	European Union
EWI	Employing workers indicator
FAO	Food and Agriculture Organization of the United Nations
GATT	General Agreement on Tariffs and Trade
HLCM	High-Level Committee on Management (UN)
HLCP	High-Level Committee on Programmes (UN)
HRC	Human Rights Committee
IACtHR	Inter-American Court of Human Rights
IBRD	International Bank for Reconstruction and Development
IBRD-AoA	Articles of Agreement of the International Bank for Reconstruction and Development
ICAO	International Civil Aviation Organization
ICFTU	International Confederation of Free Trade Unions
ICJ	International Court of Justice
ICSID	International Centre for Settlement of Investment Disputes
IDA	International Development Association
IEG	Independent Evaluation Group (World Bank)
IFAD	International Fund for Agricultural Development
IFC	International Finance Corporation
ILC	International Law Commission (UN)
ILO	International Labour Organization
ILOAT	Administrative Tribunal of the International Labour Organization
IMO	International Maritime Organization
IO	International organization
IOCC	Inter-Organization Coordinating Committee
ISPA	Inter-Agency Social Protection Assessment
ITLOS	International Tribunal for the Law of the Sea
ITUC	International Trade Union Confederation
MDG/MDGs	Millennium Development Goal(s)
MERCOSUR	Mercado Común del Sur/Southern Common Market
MIGA	Multilateral Investment Guarantee Agency
MoU	Memorandum of understanding
NGO	Non-governmental organization
OECD	Organisation for Economic Co-operation and Development
OHCHR	Office of the High Commissioner for Human Rights (UN)
PACE	Parliamentary Assembly of the Council of Europe
PCIJ	Permanent Court of International Justice
PRSP	Poverty Reduction Strategy Paper (World Bank)
RESC/(R)ESC	(Revised) European Social Charter

RIAA	Reports of International Arbitral Awards
SADC	Southern African Development Community
SCR	Supreme Court of Canada Reports
SDG/SDGs	Sustainable Development Goal(s)
SPIAC-B	Social Protection Inter-Agency Cooperation Board
UDHR	Universal Declaration of Human Rights
UN-HABITAT	United Nations Centre for Human Settlements
UN	United Nations
UNAIDS	Joint United Nations Programme on HIV/AIDS
UNCTAD	United Nations Conference on Trade and Development
UNDCP	United Nations International Drug Control Programme
UNDG	United Nations Development Group
UNDP	United Nations Development Programme
UNESCO	United Nations Educational, Scientific and Cultural Organization
UNGA	General Assembly (UN)
UNICEF	United Nations Children's Fund
UNIDO	United Nations Industrial Development Organization
UNMIK	United Nations Interim Administration Mission in Kosovo
UNOPS	United Nations Office for Project Services
UNSC	Security Council (UN)
UNTS	United Nations Treaty Series
UNWTO	World Tourism Organization
USA	United States of America
USAID	United States Agency for International Development
USSR	Union of Soviet Socialist Republics
VCLT	Vienna Convention on the Law of Treaties
VCLT-IO	Vienna Convention on the Law of Treaties between States and International Organizations or between International Organizations
WBG	World Bank Group
WHO	World Health Organization
WIPO	World Intellectual Property Organization
WTO	World Trade Organization
YILC	Yearbook of the International Law Commission

1. Introduction

A. Multi-Institutional Labour Governance

Since well over a century, improving labour conditions worldwide has been a concern of international law and policy. From the second half of the nineteenth century onwards, states, trade unions, employers' associations and further domestic, inter-, supra- and transnational actors have engaged in what today would be called labour governance:[1] They launched initiatives, convened meetings and conferences, created networks, established private associations and public international organizations (IOs), drafted political and legal documents, and engaged in the dissemination, implementation and further development of the policies and instruments thus created.[2]

Among the many actors involved in labour governance, the International Labour Organization (ILO) is perhaps the most important institutional actor on the international plane.[3] Since its inception in 1919, it has been a principal forum for

[1]In the political and social sciences, variations and other terms are also being used, such as e.g. "global labour governance", "international labour governance" or "transnational labour governance", see e.g. Anke Haasel, 'The Evolution of a Global Labor Governance Regime' (2008) 21 Governance 231, 235; Guglielmo Meardi and Paul Marginson, 'Global Labour Governance: Potential and Limits of an Emerging Perspective' (2014) 28 Work, Employment and Society 651, 651; Rüdiger Krause, 'The Promotion of Labour Standards Through International Framework Agreements' in Henner Gött (ed), *Labour Standards in International Economic Law* (Springer 2018) 334. Without taking a stance on the merits of these proposals, this study will use the term 'labour governance' without further qualifying adjectives.

[2]On these developments see Jean-Michel Servais, *International Labour Law* (4th edn, Kluwer Law International 2014) 19 et seqq.

[3]As to the global level, the Commission on Global Governance observed that "governance has been viewed primarily as intergovernmental relationships, but it must now be understood as also

H. Gött, *The Law of Interactions Between International Organizations*, Beiträge zum ausländischen öffentlichen Recht und Völkerrecht 299,
https://doi.org/10.1007/978-3-662-62389-3_1

developing, negotiating, adopting and monitoring international labour policies and instruments. Despite recurring prophecies of doom regarding its relevance and future, the ILO's overall track record is impressive. At the time of writing, the ILO has adopted over 400 instruments containing international labour standards. Moreover, it has created a comprehensive *acquis* of policies, official documents and reports, technical assistance programmes, research and expertise, and a sophisticated institutional practice with a long tradition and a high reputation both inside and outside the organization. On the occasion of the ILO's 75th anniversary in 1994, Stephen M. Schwebel famously remarked that

> it is clear that, if the ILO did not exist, it would have to be invented.[4]

Despite the many challenges of labour governance that remain unresolved, and despite the undeniable fact that the ILO has not always lived up to its full potential and to the expectations put in it, Schwebel's observation is no less accurate in 2020, one year past the organization's centenary.

Yet, notwithstanding its importance, the ILO is not the *only* IO engaging in labour governance. The end of the Second World War marked the rapid emergence of other regional and universal IOs which, pursuant to their mandates and their practice, qualify as actors in labour governance.[5] Many of them complement the ILO's efforts, and some have even been designed with the ILO in mind. Nevertheless, each of these other IOs has its own approach to labour issues, as laid down in its respective legal foundations and as shaped by its institutional practice. The result is that labour governance, even to the extent it is conducted by public international institutions, does not follow *one universal* model. Rather, despite resemblances and similarities, each IO deals with labour issues in its own distinct manner. Consequently, the ILO is

---

involving non-governmental organizations (NGOs), citizens' movements, multinational corporations, and the global capital market (…)", Commission on Global Governance, *Our Global Neighbourhood: Report of the Commission on Global Governance* (Oxford University Press 1995) 2.

[4]Stephen M Schwebel, 'The Prescience and Pertinence of the ILO' in International Labour Office (ed), *Visions of the Future of Social Justice: Essays on the Occasion of the ILO's 75th Anniversary* (ILO 1994) 257 et seq. His colleague at the International Court of Justice Mohammed Bedjaoui seconded: "One can only rejoice at the immense amount of work that has been accomplished by the ILO since 1919, and ... realize the extent to which it has developed international legislation for the protection of workers", Mohammed Bedjaoui, 'For a "World Charter of Human Labour and Social Justice"' in International Labour Office (ed), *Visions of the Future of Social Justice: Essays on the Occasion of the ILO's 75th Anniversary* (ILO 1994) 26.

[5]Besides governmental actors, there is of course also a broad spectrum of non-governmental actors that are highly relevant in labour governance (and global governance in general), which however will not be addressed further in this study. See e.g. Janelle M Diller, 'Pluralism and Privatization in Transnational Labour Regulation: Experience of the International Labour Organization' in Adelle Blackett and Anne Trebilcock (eds), *Research Handbook on Transnational Labour Law* (Edward Elgar Publishing 2015). For the relevance of non-governmental actors in general see also Peter-Tobias Stoll, 'Global Governance and the Private Sector' in Joachim Ahrens, Rolf Caspers and Janina Weingarth (eds), *Good Governance in the 21st Century Conflict, Institutional Change, and Development in the Era of Globalization* (Edward Elgar Publishing 2011).

confronted with (at times rather self-confident) co-habitants, each of which contributes to what may be termed multi-institutional labour governance.

B. The Neglected Relevance of Inter-Organizational Interactions

Multi-institutional labour governance, however, does not mean that the ILO and the other IOs operate in clinical isolation from each other. Rather, virtually all IOs involved in labour governance influence each other continuously and in manifold ways. This study will refer to this mutual influence as inter-organizational interactions, a term further unfolded below.[6] Such inter-organizational interactions occur frequently, are highly diverse in shape and form, and can have a significant impact on each IO's work. As far as the ILO is concerned, inter-organizational interactions have induced important organizational developments. For example, they have led to the creation of a new supervisory procedure for freedom of association[7] and have informed constitutional amendments[8] and reformulations of the ILO's mandate and capacity.[9] They have also time and again resulted in challenges[10] and have even played a part in an ongoing and potentially existential constitutional crisis within the ILO.[11] At the same time, the ILO has influenced other IOs, e.g. by inducing them to incorporate the ILO's core strategic objectives into their own agendas[12], or by making significant contributions to the drafting of treaties and further instruments adopted by them.[13]

---

[6]See Chap. 3 B.

[7]The creation of the special supervisory procedure, including the FFCC and the CFA, was the result of a complex interaction between the ILO and the UN, particularly ECOSOC. For a detailed account of the events see Antony Evelyn Alcock, *History of the International Labour Organization* (Palgrave Macmillan 1971) 253 et seqq.; Lee Swepston, 'Human Rights Law and Freedom of Association: Development Through ILO Supervision' (1998) 137 International Labour Review 169, 171; Henner Gött, 'Interactions between International Organizations - Approaching a Neglected Governance Dimension' (2020) 17 International Organizations Law Review 75, 81 et seqq.

[8]See the competence to evaluate other IOs' economic and financial policies in the 1944 Philadelphia Declaration, discussed in Chap. 8 B. IV.

[9]In the Declaration on Social Justice for a Fair Globalization (International Labour Conference, 97th session, 10 June 2008) XCI ILO Official Bulletin Ser A No 2 58 (2008 Declaration), Part II C.

[10]Francis Maupain, 'A Second Century for What? The ILO at a Regulatory Crossroad' (2019) 16 International Organizations Law Review 1, 16 et seq.

[11]See Chap. 2 D. III.

[12]See the mainstreaming of the ILO's Decent Work Agenda in the UN System, discussed in Chap. 14 C.

[13]On the drafting of the ESC see below, Chap. 6 B. For a further example, see the ILO's influence on the social rights enshrined the ICESCR, Philip Alston, 'The United Nations' Specialized Agencies and Implementation of the International Covenant on Economic, Social and Cultural Rights' (1979) 18 Columbia Journal of Transnational Law 79, 82 et seqq.

The ubiquity and impact of interactions urge to assess their relevance for the effectiveness and legitimacy of both each IO's work and labour governance as a whole. This task goes beyond empirically determining and acknowledging interactions' factual shape, scale and effects: in order to properly assess interactions, it must also be determined what shape, scale and effects inter-organizational interactions *ought to* have.

This normative question has mostly been treated as a matter of international policy. Both inside and outside the interacting IOs, there have been countless calls for policy coherence and inter-institutional cooperation, derived from arguments of political imperatives, soundness and preference.

However, the question how inter-organizational interactions ought to occur also has a profoundly complex *legal* dimension. For one part, there is no reason to believe that the relevant normative propositions can only and exclusively be derived from political imperatives. On the contrary, how inter-organizational interactions ought to occur may and must as well be answered by referring to pertinent legal norms. What is more, given the frequency, complexity and impact of inter-organizational interactions, and given the fact that labour governance is a politically highly contentious field, there is a genuine interest in exploring this legal dimension in search for more suprapartisan normative guidance. In other words, beyond political standpoints, there is a need to ascertain to what extent the ILO may legally influence other IOs—and to what extent these other IOs may influence the ILO.

Yet, surprisingly, international legal scholarship has given little attention to this legal dimension of inter-organizational interactions. Insofar as scholars addressed inter-organizational interactions and their legal ramifications at all, they mostly did so as an also-ran of other phenomena. Notably, instead of focusing on inter-organizational interactions proper, there is a tendency to centre on their effects on the interacting IOs' member states or their ultimate beneficiaries, i.e. in the case of labour governance workers or employers. By contrast, only very few contributions examine what the respective rights and duties of the interacting IOs themselves are, or, more generally, how and pursuant to which premises and principles international law regulates mutual influence among IOs.[14]

C. Purpose and Outline of the Study

In response, this study places inter-organizational interactions and their regulation by international law at the centre of attention. At the heart of its interest lies the ILO's model of labour governance (a term defined shortly), which can on the one hand be influenced, altered and even thwarted, but on the other hand also be promoted and

[14]In recent years, inter-organizational interactions have increasingly sparked academic interest, which is to be welcomed, Gött (n 7) 76.

reinforced through interactions.[15] Whether and to what extent this is legally permissible has a direct bearing on the ILO's performance, accountability, legitimacy and eventual success. Thus, the questions addressed in this study are not only fundamental for the ILO itself, but also for its members and its ultimate beneficiaries, i.e. workers, employers, and society as a whole. In addition, they are no less fundamental for the IOs the ILO interacts with and for our understanding of relations between IOs in general.

The study approaches inter-organizational interactions between the ILO and other IOs from the perspective of positive international law as it stands at present. It endeavours to identify pertinent international legal norms that either protect or promote the ILO's model of labour governance vis-à-vis other IOs. This comprises norms that either regulate other IOs' influence on the ILO or define and secure a role for the ILO in the work of other IOs. In consequence, the focus will be on corresponding international legal rights the ILO (and international legal obligations other IOs) might possess. The principal interest of this study is not to determine if such norms *can* or *should* be in place,[16] but if they *are*.

By pursuing this agenda, the study accomplishes two things: Firstly, it examines and evaluates in detail the legal regulation of inter-organizational interactions between the ILO and two other highly relevant IOs engaging in labour governance: the World Bank and the Council of Europe (CoE) with its two main human rights bodies, the European Court of Human Rights (ECtHR) and the European Committee of Social Rights (ECSR).

Secondly, in doing so, it also explores the law of inter-organizational interactions as such: most of this study's findings are relevant well beyond interactions between the ILO, the World Bank and the CoE. They also allow conclusions on interactions between the ILO and further IOs, as well as on interactions between IOs in general. By examining the many different layers of norms in the context of their application to concrete situations, the study provides an inductive approach to inter-organizational interactions and their regulation by international law. It revisits and re-evaluates positions previously taken in international institutional law and general international law literature and contributes to understanding the inter-organizational constellation as a distinct field of contemporary international legal research.

The study is divided into five parts. Part I lays the foundation by introducing the ILO's model of labour governance (Chap. 2), as well as the concept and a tentative taxonomy of inter-organizational interactions (Chap. 3). Subsequently, it presents three case studies of interactions between the ILO on the one side and the World Bank and the CoE, respectively, on the other (Chaps. 3, 4 and 5). These case studies are then used as reference points to extrapolate the structural relevance of inter-organizational interactions for the ILO and its model of labour governance (Chap. 7).

---

[15] In Chap. 7, it will be argued that this ambiguity results in a dilemma for the ILO.

[16] These questions will still be addressed, notably in Part IV.

The following two parts are dedicated to the actual legal analysis. For reasons of illustration, exemplification and verification, this legal analysis has recourse to the three case studies presented in Part I.

Part II focuses on legal norms emanating from the the ILO's, World Bank's and CoE's institutional laws,[17] i.e. their respective constituent instruments, relevant further instruments adopted under their auspices, and established organizational practice (Chaps. 7 and 8). The analysis shows that each of the examined IOs' institutional laws sets its own standards and takes its own specific perspective on inter-organizational interactions. Each examined IO is given the competence to engage in inter-organizational interactions, to cooperate and to compromise. That being said, each IO must at all times fully abide by its constitutional objectives and its institutional, procedural and substantive provisions, regardless of any repercussions on the other IOs. Thus, the World Bank's and CoE's institutional laws relativize the ILO's governance model in favour of their respective own; they are 'structurally egocentric'. Moreover, this structural egocentrism is subject to dynamic development (Chap. 10).

In search for ways to mitigate the ILO's relativization, Part II then examines the prospects of interpreting the examined IOs' laws (more) coherently (Chap. 11). In addition, it enquires whether the ILO's member states are obliged to exert influence on the other examined IOs in order to enhance the ILO's role and relevance (Chap. 12).

Part III then turns to the legal norms defining the inter-organizational legal relationships between the ILO, the World Bank and the CoE, a body of law referred to in this study as inter-organizational law. In a first step, Part III examines inter-organizational treaties between the ILO and the other examined IOs, comprising both stand-alone bilateral agreements (Chap. 13) and, as far as the ILO and the World Bank are concerned, the relevant components of the UN System's legal framework (Chap. 14). It then turns to customary inter-organizational law and general principles of law (Chap. 15). The analysis reveals that inter-organizational law only governs certain types of the ILO's interactions with the other IOs, and that the pertinent norms hardly protect or promote the ILO's model of labour governance. As to several types of interactions, there are hardly (if any) discernible established norms at all. Ultimately, inter-organizational law does not even define what will be

[17]So far, no established term has emerged in scholarship or practice that could safely be used as a common generic term for these legal norms. For clarity, the term 'institutional law' is understood here as a non-technical term not connected to a particular theory or concept of IOs. For present purposes, the decisive point is that these norms create international rights and obligations between the IO and its respective member states, and among the different states becoming members of the IO, but not between two interacting IOs. For a useful disambiguation see Fernando Lusa Bordin, *The Analogy Between States and International Organizations* (Cambridge University Press 2019) 8 et seqq. See also Andreas L Paulus, 'The International Legal System as a Constitution' in Jeffrey L Dunoff and Joel P Trachtman (eds), *Ruling the World? Constitutionalism, International Law, and Global Governance* (Cambridge University Press 2009) 76; Tobias Winkler, *Die Vereinten Nationen im Gefüge der internationalen Organisationen* (Nomos 2019) 225 et seqq.

called a general legal default rule, i.e. a closure rule that applies between the ILO and the other examined IOs in cases in which no more specific rules exist (Chap. 16).

Part IV evaluates the results of the preceding parts. It argues that the law of inter-organizational interactions is underdeveloped, because it has never truly been conceptualized and 'explored' before. As a consequence of this underdevelopment, inter-organizational interactions are structured according to the rationalities of political and other non-legal factors, and the ILO finds itself in an 'inter-organizational power play' (Chap. 17). This diagnosis is then discussed against the backdrop of contemporary international law narratives and selected arguments, pursuing the question whether the legal status quo resembles an adequate way of regulating the ILO's inter-organizational interactions. The study argues that a more elaborate legal framework structuring inter-organizational interactions in labour governance would be preferable over the legal status quo (Chap. 18).

The concluding Part V explores perspectives for law in inter-organizational interactions in labour governance. The study envisions a more evolved law of inter-organizational interactions as a normative framework structuring interactions and enhancing the efficiency and legitimacy of multi-institutional governance. Although there is no merit in regulatory enthusiasm, there is a realistic potential for developing the legal framework for inter-organizational interactions further. However, to tap this potential, it is not sufficient to engage in political or conceptual debates about which developments would be desirable to properly situate the ILO and its model of labour governance vis-à-vis other IOs. Therefore, this study proposes to include the specific perspective of legal doctrine and to elaborate a normative scaffold capable of accommodating an advanced law of inter-organizational interactions (Chap. 19).

D. Preliminary Remarks on Terminology

Speaking of governance models and inter-organizational interactions necessarily involves a certain degree of terminological abstraction. This study will explain terms as they become relevant during the course of the analysis. The central concept of 'inter-organizational interaction', tentatively sketched above, will be explained in the necessary depth in Chap. 3. At this point, some preliminary remarks on another central term of this study are warranted: the ILO's 'model of labour governance'.

In its 1995 report "Our Global Neighbourhood", the Commission on Global Governance defined 'governance' as

> the sum of the many ways individuals and institutions, public and private, manage their common affairs. It is a continuing process through which conflicting or diverse interests may be accommodated and co-operative action may be taken. It includes formal institutions and regimes empowered to enforce compliance, as well as informal arrangements that people and institutions either have agreed to or perceive to be in their interest.[18]

[18] Commission on Global Governance (n 3) 2.

'Labour governance' is the application of this understanding to the field of labour, i.e. it is the sum of the many ways in which individuals and institutions, public and private, manage their common affairs regarding labour issues. In a manner of speaking, labour governance resembles 'the way in which labour issues are planfully dealt with'.

In this context, it needs emphasis that 'labour governance' is not understood here as requiring actors to be *exclusively or primarily* concerned with labour issues. Rather, "the many ways individuals and institutions, public and private, manage their common affairs" also involves actors who only peripherally deal with labour issues, while centring on other issues. This encompassing understanding of 'labour governance' is important in the context of IOs. As will be unfolded below, there are numerous IOs that frequently address labour issues and have a profound impact on how these issues are dealt with, although these IOs are primarily pursuing other objectives. Pertinent examples are financial institutions and institutions concerned with the protection and promotion of human rights.

By the 'ILO's model of labour governance', this study understands the specific way in which the ILO engages in labour governance. This includes not only the ILO's objectives, institutional structure, processes and procedures, but also its output, notably ILO conventions, recommendations, declarations, supervisory practice, promotional activities and technical assistance programmes. Thus, whenever this study speaks of the ILO's model of labour governance, these aspects are understood to be included. The reason for the inclusion is that, with regard to the ILO (and arguably also with regard to most other IOs), objectives, institutional structure, process and output cannot truly be separated and regarded in isolation from each other.[19]

Just as the ILO has its model of labour governance, other IOs have their respective objectives, institutional structure, procedures and outputs, all of which determine how they address labour matters. Therefore, whenever this study speaks of any other IO's model of labour governance, it refers to the specific goals, institutional structure, processes, procedures and outputs of that other IO.

This study uses the term *model* of labour governance. A model is a system that is empirically being used and normatively ought to be pursued and maintained.[20] 'Model of governance' means, therefore, a system of governance that is in use and at the same time, according to a corresponding normative proposition, ought to be

---

[19]For instance, as will be seen, the ILO's particular tripartite structure and working method is permanently grafted onto ILO labour conventions and remains relevant for them even after their adoption and ratification, see Chap. 2 C. II. 2. For a comprehensive overview see Anne Trebilcock, 'The International Labour Organization' in Michael J Bowman and Dino Kritsiotis (eds), *Conceptual and Contextual Perspectives on the Modern Law of Treaties* (Cambridge University Press 2018). On a similar note, the ILO's supervisory practice has been borne and decisively shaped by tripartite consensus and is, figuratively speaking, 'owned' by the ILO's tripartite constituents, see Chap. 2 C. III. 3.

[20]Collins English Dictionary - Complete & Unabridged (13th edn, Harper Collins Publications 2018) entry 'model'.

pursued. As will be shown in this chapter, this double nature is precisely what qualifies the ILO's model. On the one hand, the ILO actually uses and adheres to its model. On the other hand, the model has always served as a normative ideal that the ILO has actively promoted vis-à-vis both its constituents and other actors, including other IOs. This is notably true for the fundamental choice in favour of universal tripartite social dialogue.

Besides terminology, some preliminary remarks on the citation of certain instruments are necessary. For reading convenience only, this study cites the 1969 Vienna Convention on the Law of Treaties[21] (VCLT) consistently with regard to all treaties concluded between states, irrespective of the fact that the VCLT only applies to treaties which are concluded by states for which the VCLT has already entered into force (Art. 4 VCLT). In cases in which, pursuant to Art. 4 VCLT, the VCLT does not apply, the citation is intended to refer to the respective rule of customary international law. In the same manner, the study consistently cites the 1986 Vienna Convention on the Law of Treaties between States and International Organizations or between International Organizations[22] (VCLT-IO) and the ILC's 2011 Draft Articles on the Responsibility of International Organizations[23] (DARIO), none of which resemble legally binding instruments, in lieu of the respective norms of customary law. In all these cases, differences between the cited instruments and customary law are indicated where they exist. If an institution's name is spelled differently in titles of official documents, titles of publications and literal quotes, the original spelling remains unchanged.

E. Preliminary Remarks on the Analytical Perspective

Finally, two brief preliminary remarks on this study's choice of perspective are warranted.

The first remark concerns the chosen 'IO-centric' focus. While this study focuses on IOs and their interactions with one another, it cannot ignore that the prevailing understanding of IOs and their conduct is still a functionalist one: IOs are widely regarded as agents acting at the disposal and under the firm control of their respective member states. The latter, by contrast, are often seen as autonomous and unitary actors wielding the actual power behind IOs.[24] At first sight, it might thus appear

[21]Vienna Convention on the Law of Treaties (adopted 23 May 1969, entered into force 27 January 1980) 1155 UNTS 331 (VCLT).

[22]Vienna Convention on the Law of Treaties between States and International Organizations or between International Organizations (adopted 21 March 1986, not yet in force) UN Doc A/CONF.129/15 (VCLT-IO).

[23]ILC, 'Draft Articles on the Responsibility of International Organizations' [2011] UN Doc A/CN.4/L.778.

[24]For a (critical) overview see Jan Klabbers, 'The EJIL Foreword: The Transformation of International Organizations Law' (2015) 26 European Journal of International Law 9, 24 et seqq.

more worthwhile to adopt a state-centric perspective on inter-organizational interactions, understanding them as a form of interaction between states that is merely channelled and mediated by IOs as institutionalized fora of international relations.

It is indeed true that IOs are to a significant extent controlled by their constituents. The same is arguably true, mutatis mutandis, for every other incorporated legal person. However, this does not mean that it would be futile to examine IOs and their mutual interactions in their own right.

To begin with, it is questionable that adopting a state-centric perspective on IOs would be appropriate regarding the institutions examined here. The ILO has a tripartite constituency including independent and powerful groups of employers' and workers' represenatives, and the ECtHR and ECSR operate as independent judicial or quasi-judicial bodies within the CoE.

Furthermore, a legal study examining inter-organizational interactions only from the perspective of member states would run the risk of confusing a *factual* dominance of member states with IOs' distinct *legal* existence. International law defines the ILO and other IOs involved in labour governance as separate legal subjects capable of having their own set of rights and obligations, being separate points of attribution of conduct, and being capable of incurring international responsibility independently of their member states. An enquiry into the legal regulation of inter-organizational interactions cannot afford to lose sight of this important distinction between the factual and the normative, the 'is' and the 'ought'. Therefore, this study, while having due regard to the factual and legal role of member states,[25] will centre on the ILO, the World Bank and the CoE as protagonists of inter-organizational interactions.

A second preliminary remark is due regarding the focus on positive law. This focus is inevitably taking less account of theory and policy, including theories and policies that emphasize the importance of certain goals or values and caution against an overly narrow focus on positive law alone.

Against this background, it needs mention that this study does not intend to discard the many theoretical or policy contributions aiming at enhancing the interplay between IOs in labour governance and beyond. Nor does this study intend to obstruct or discourage the many national, international or transnational efforts to promote social justice, decent work, the protection of fundamental rights at work, a fair globalization or sustainable development. Instead, this study seeks to complement these initiatives. Positive international law is an important point of reference for scholars of theory, for policy makers, and for legal practitioners working with or within IOs. In expounding the bases, content and limits of pertinent international legal norms, the study ascertains the relevance of law as a normative framework for multi-institutional labour governance. In doing so, it provides normative reference points for theorists, policy makers and legal practitioners across political camps, power structures and ideational divides.

---

[25] See especially Chap. 12.

Part I
The ILO and Inter-Organizational Interactions

Interactions between the ILO and other IOs are of significant importance for labour governance. They can considerably affect the ILO's model of labour governance by influencing the organization's structure, functioning and output. At the same time, through interactions, the ILO can have significant influence on other IOs.

In order to fully grasp the factual relevance of inter-organizational interactions for the ILO and for multi-institutional labour governance as a whole, it is necessary to examine in closer detail how the ILO approaches labour issues and how this approach is affected by interactions. This includes expounding the key features of the ILO's model of labour governance, the relevant factual characteristics and conceptual underpinnings of inter-organizational interactions, and the various ways how the ILO and its work are actually affected by such interactions in concrete situations.

2. The ILO's Model of Labour Governance

As this study centres on the relevance of inter-organizational interactions for the ILO's model of labour governance, it is imperative to first examine this model and its elements in the necessary depth. The ILO is perhaps most famous for its unique tripartite structure and for its comprehensive body of international labour standards. While these are essential elements of the ILO's model of labour governance, there are other important features, without which the ILO and its model cannot be understood properly.

A. The ILO: An Initial Overview

At the outset, it is convenient to give an initial overview on the ILO, including its objectives (Sect. I.), the activities and instruments through which it seeks to attain these objectives (Sect. II.), and its organizational structure (Sect. III.).

I. Objectives

The ILO's core objective is to promote social justice and decent work. The preamble of the 1919 ILO Constitution[1] specifies this objective to the effect that the ILO is mandated to promote workers' rights, improve working conditions, promote social

[1]Constitution of the International Labour Organisation (adopted 1 April 1919, entered into force 28 June 1919) 15 UNTS 40 (ILO Constitution).

H. Gött, *The Law of Interactions Between International Organizations*, Beiträge zum ausländischen öffentlichen Recht und Völkerrecht 299, https://doi.org/10.1007/978-3-662-62389-3_2

security and prevent a deregulatory 'race to the bottom' among states seeking to obtain comparative economic advantages by lowering labour standards.[2]

As part of a major constitutional revision in 1944–1946, the ILO revised its mandate through the 1944 Declaration Concerning the Aims and Purposes of the ILO,[3] better known as the Declaration of Philadelphia. The Declaration restated the ILO's mission and purview in generously broad terms, including e.g. by explicit mentioning the goal of full employment, the right to collective bargaining and policies concerning wages and occupational safety and health.[4] The restatement effectively enlarged the ambit of the organization.[5] In 1946, the Declaration of Philadelphia was annexed to the ILO Constitution and forms an integral part thereof.[6]

After the Declaration of Philadelphia had set the scene for the ILO's activities for the remainder of the twentieth century, another significant recalibration of the ILO's mandate occurred around the turn of the millennium, more particularly as a reaction to the end of the Cold War and accelerating globalization. In 1999, ILO Director-General Juan Somavia presented the Decent Work Agenda, which set forth interrelated strategic objectives and called for an integrated approach for their achievement. The objectives are the creation and promotion of standards and fundamental principles and rights at work, the creation of greater opportunities for women and men to decent employment and income, the improvement of coverage and effectiveness of universal social protection, the strengthening of tripartism and social dialogue, and the cross-cutting objective of promoting gender equality and non-discrimination.[7] Decent work has since become the leading paradigm for the ILO's activities. The Decent Work Agenda was institutionalized by the unanimous adoption of the ILO's 2008 Declaration on Social Justice for a Fair Globalization.[8] The 2008 Declaration is not (and was not intended to be) a formal amendment to the ILO Constitution.

[2]The PCIJ held early on that the employed language "could hardly be more comprehensive", *Competence of the International Labour Organization to Regulate, Incidentally, the Personal Work of the Employer (Advisory Opinion)* (1926) PCIJ Rep Series B No 13 7, 17.

[3]ILO, Declaration Concerning the Aims and Purposes of the International Labour Organisation (International Labour Conference, 10 May 1944) 15 UNTS 104 (Declaration of Philadelphia).

[4]Cf. Part III Philadelphia Declaration. See also Heiko Sauer, 'International Labour Organization', *Max Planck Encyclopedia of Public International Law* (Oxford University Press 2014) para 5.

[5]Francis Maupain, 'New Foundation or New Façade? The ILO and the 2008 Declaration on Social Justice for a Fair Globalization' (2009) 20 European Journal of International Law 823, 833. For this reason, Haas has termed the Philadelphia Declaration's reformulation "extraordinarily ingenious", Ernst B Haas, *Beyond the Nation State: Functionalism and International Organization* (Stanford University Press 1964) 159.

[6]Francis Maupain, *The Future of the International Labour Organization in the Global Economy* (Hart Publishing 2013) 70 et seq.

[7]Maupain, 'New Foundation or New Façade? The ILO and the 2008 Declaration on Social Justice for a Fair Globalization' (n 5) 833.

[8]Declaration on Social Justice for a Fair Globalization (International Labour Conference, 97th session, 10 June 2008) XCI ILO Official Bulletin Ser A No 2 58 (2008 Declaration).

Rather, it resembles an expression of the ILO's own contemporary understanding of its mandate, with a particular view to the challenges brought about by globalization.[9] In 2019, 100 years after its foundation, the ILO adopted the ILO Centenary Declaration for the Future of Work.[10] The Centenary Declaration aims to further update and adjust the ILO's mandate in light of transformative changes in the world of work, driven not only by globalization, but also by technological innovations, demographic shifts and climate change.

II. Activities and Principal Instruments

The ILO pursues its objectives through a variety of activities and means.

The first such activity is norm creation. The ILO engages in the drafting and adoption of international labour standards, primarily laid down in conventions and recommendations. ILO conventions are international treaties that require separate ratification by ILO member states. Once they have entered into force, they create binding legal obligations for all ratifying states.[11] By opposite, recommendations are legally non-binding guidelines and often designed to complement and specify ILO conventions ILO.[12]

The ILO's body of conventions and recommendations is vast. At the time of writing, the ILO has adopted 190 conventions and 205 recommendations. That being said, some of these instruments have not entered into force, while others have been withdrawn or closed for ratification. Furthermore, at several points in its history, the ILO has engaged in updates and revisions of conventions and recommendations. Notably, from 1995 to 2002, the ILO has surveyed its *acquis* to identify those instruments which are still up to date.[13] Moreover, the ILO has accorded a greater importance to some of its instruments. It accorded eight of its conventions the status of fundamental conventions.[14] In 1998, the ILO adopted the Declaration on

[9]ILO, *ILO Declaration on Social Justice for a Fair Globalization* (ILO 2008) 1.

[10]Centenary Declaration for the Future of Work (International Labour Conference, 108th session, 21 June 2019) <https://www.ilo.org/wcmsp5/groups/public/%2D%2D-ed_norm/%2D%2D-relconf/documents/meetingdocument/wcms_711674.pdf> accessed 26 April 2020.

[11]Jean-Michel Servais, *International Labour Law* (4th edn, Kluwer Law International 2014) 55.

[12]ibid 79.

[13]This work was undertaken by the Working Party on Policy regarding the revision of standards inserted by the Governing Body. For an overview on the Cartier Working Party's results see ILO, 'Working Party on Policy Regarding the Revision of Standards (Cartier Working Party)' (2002) - Information Note on the Progress of Work and Decisions Taken Concerning the Revision of Standards' (2002) <https://www.ilo.org/wcmsp5/groups/public/%2D%2D-ed_norm/%2D%2D-normes/documents/genericdocument/wcms_125644.pdf> accessed 26 April 2020.

[14]These are the Freedom of Association and Protection of the Right to Organise Convention, 1948 (No 87) (adopted 9 July 1948, entered into force 4 July 1950) 68 UNTS 17, the Right to Organise and Collective Bargaining Convention, 1949 (No 98) (adopted 1 July 1949, entered into force 18 July 1951) 96 UNTS 257, the Forced Labour Convention, 1930 (No 29) (adopted 28 June 1930,

Fundamental Principles and Rights at Work,[15] which affirmed this status, stated that all member states, regardless of whether they are parties to the fundamental conventions or not, are bound to respect the principles underlying these conventions solely by virtue of ILO membership, and installed a special follow-up procedure. These principles are freedom of association and the effective recognition of the right to collective bargaining, the elimination of forced or compulsory labour, the abolition of child labour and the elimination of discrimination in respect of employment and occupation.[16] The prioritization as 'fundamental' did not alter the legal status of the respective conventions, but was meant to focus the ILO's and its member states' activities and resources on their ratification and implementation and to help define a common set of "rules of the game".[17] Four other conventions were classified as governance conventions, which likewise emphasized their relevance as compared to the remaining conventions.[18]

As a further means besides conventions and recommendations, not explicitly provided for in its Constitution, the ILO has issued seven declarations. These notably include the aforementioned 1944 Declaration of Philadelphia, the 1998 Declaration on Fundamental Principles and Rights at Work, the 2008 Declaration on Social Justice for a Fair Globalization and the Centenary Declaration for the Future of

---

entered into force 1 May 1932) 39 UNTS 55, the Abolition of Forced Labour Convention, 1957 (No 105) (adopted 25 June 1957, entered into force 16 January 1959) 320 UNTS 291 the Minimum Age Convention, 1973 (No 138) (adopted 26 June 1973. entered 19 June 1976) 1015 UNTS 297, the Worst Forms of Child Labour Convention, 1999 (No 182) (adopted 17 June 1999, entered into force 19 November 2000) 2133 UNTS 161, the Equal Remuneration Convention, 1951 (No 100) (adopted 29 June 1951, entered into force 23 May 1953) 165 UNTS 303, and the Discrimination (Employment and Occupation) Convention, 1958 (No 111) (adopted 25 June 1958, entered into force 15 June 1960) 362 UNTS 31.

[15]ILO, Declaration on Fundamental Principles and Rights at Work and its Follow-up (Labour Conference, 86th session, 18 June 1998) (Annex revised 15 June 2010) LXXX ILO Official Bulletin Ser A 73 (1998 Declaration).

[16]No 2 1998 Declaration; Servais (n 11) 50.

[17]Maupain, *The Future of the International Labour Organization in the Global Economy* (n 6) para 53. Critical Philip Alston, '"Core Labour Standards" and the Transformation of the International Labour Rights Regime' (2004) 15 European Journal of International Law 457.

[18]This category comprises the Labour Inspection Convention, 1947 (No 81) (adopted 11 July 1947, entered into force 7 April 1950) 54 UNTS 3, the Employment Policy Convention, 1964 (No 122) (adopted 9 July 1964, entered into force 15 July 1966) 569 UNTS 65, the Labour Inspection (Agriculture) Convention, 1969 (No 129) (adopted 25 June 1969, entered into force 19 January 1972) 812 UNTS 87, and the Tripartite Consultation (International Labour Standards) Convention, 1976 (No 144) (adopted 17 June 1976, entered into force 16 May 1978) 1089 UNTS 354. The category was initially named "priority conventions" and renamed in 2008, Franz Christian Ebert and Claire La Hovary, 'International Labour Law', *Max Planck Encyclopedia of Public International Law* (Oxford University Press 2013) para 7.

Work, which are also the most relevant ones for the purposes of the present study.[19] Declarations are sporadically used instruments addressing matters of great importance.[20]

Besides norm creation, the ILO also supervises the implementation of international labour standards by its member states. It does so through an elaborate system of bodies and procedures, discussed in more detail below. The ILO supervisory system examines states' reports, and, under certain conditions, cases brought before it. The ILO lacks 'hard' means of enforcement to ensure compliance. Rather, its system is built on persuasion, dialogue and public 'naming and shaming'.[21] That being said, the ILO's supervisory activities have played an important role, not least for the incremental further development and concretization of international labour law.

Apart from the creation and supervision of labour standards, the ILO is a central forum for the formulation and promotion of international policies, programmes and initiatives on labour and social issues.[22] Moreover, since the 1950s, the ILO has provided technical assistance and development cooperation to its constituents.[23] The core idea behind this is to create the necessary institutional, organizational and technical capacities at country level to foster ILO objectives and to implement its instruments and policies. For these purposes, the ILO has established field offices and cooperates with a broad variety of donors and development partner organizations.[24]

[19]Further declarations are the 1964 Declaration Concerning the Policy of "Apartheid" of the Republic of South Africa, Adopted by the International Labour Conference at Its 48th Session (1964) XLVII ILO Official Bulletin 1 (Apartheid Declaration), the 1975 Declaration on Equality of Opportunity and Treatment for Women Workers (1975) LVIII ILO Official Bulletin 96, and the Governing Body's 1977 Tripartite Declaration of Principles concerning Multinational Enterprises and Social Policy (amended in 2000 and 2006 and revised in 2017) (1977) reproduced in ILO, *Tripartite Declaration of Principles Concerning Multinational Enterprises and Social Policy* (ILO 2017) 1 (MNE Declaration).

[20]These can be either systemic questions, like the three aforesaid declarations, or particular matters, as was the case in the Apartheid Declaration, Servais (n 11) 80 et seq.

[21]As a (rather remote) means of last resort, the Governing Body may recommend to the Conference such action as it may deem wise and expedient to secure compliance (Art. 33 ILO Constitution). Besides, the ILO has occasionally had resort to other means in exceptional circumstances, such as the 'expulsion' of South Africa in the 1960s as a response to the latter's apartheid policy, see Chap. 14 B. II. 3.

[22]Servais (n 11) 318.

[23]See e.g. Daniel Roger Maul, 'The ILO, Asia and the Beginnings of Technical Assistance, 1945–60' in Jill M Jensen and Nelson Lichtenstein (eds), *The ILO from Geneva to the Pacific Rim: West Meets East* (Palgrave Macmillan 2016).

[24]ILO, 'Partnering for Development' (*ILO Website*) <https://www.ilo.org/pardev/lang%2D%2Den/index.htm> accessed 26 April 2020.

III. Organs and Other Bodies

The ILO has three main organs: The International Labour Conference (named the General Conference in the ILO Constitution), the Governing Body and the International Labour Office.

The International Labour Conference is the ILO's plenary organ and meets annually.[25] Both the plenary conference and most of its committees are composed in a tripartite manner.[26] The Conference, firstly, has important organizational functions. It adopts the biennial budget, elects the Governing Body and decides on general issues of policy.[27] Secondly, it has a central role in the ILO's norm-creating activities. Notably, it discusses and adopts ILO conventions and recommendations.[28] The Conference decides by simple majority of delegates present at the Conference (Art. 17(2) ILO Constitution), unless otherwise provided (such as e.g. a two-thirds majority for the adoption of labour conventions, Art. 19(2) ILO Constitution).[29]

The Governing Body is the ILO's executive organ, meeting three times per year. It is composed of 56 members from all tripartite groups.[30] The workers' and employers' members are autonomously elected by their respective groups in the International Labour Conference.[31] The Governing Body performs important executive functions.[32] It decides on matters of policy, sets the International Labour

---

[25]The sessions are held in Geneva and take place in June.

[26]Claire La Hovary, 'The ILO's Mandate and Capacity: Creating, Proliferating and Supervising Labour Standards for a Globalized Economy' in Henner Gött (ed), *Labour Standards in International Economic Law* (Springer 2018) 40.

[27]Sauer (n 4) para 9.

[28]ibid 12. The Conference's procedure is laid down in more detail in its Standing Orders.

[29]Pursuant to the quorum laid down in Art. 17(3) ILO Constitution, a vote is void unless the total number of votes cast is equal to half the number of the delegates attending the Conference. Since tripartite subcommittees use a 1:1:1 quota, workers' and employers' representatives have more weight there, La Hovary, 'The ILO's Mandate and Capacity: Creating, Proliferating and Supervising Labour Standards for a Globalized Economy' (n 26) 40.

[30]Ten government members, from states of "chief industrial importance" (currently, these are Brazil, China, France, Germany, India, Italy, Japan, the Russian Federation, the United Kingdom and the United States), have a permanent seat in the Governing Body, while the other government members are elected every three years by the International Labour Conference. The privileged membership of some states in the ILO Governing Body has further repercussions. One of the functions of the Governing Body is to elect the ILO Director-General (Art. 8(1) ILO Constitution). Hence, unequal access of states to the Governing Body is perpetuated in the election of a further organ, Christoph Möllers, *Gewaltengliederung: Legitimation und Dogmatik im Nationalen und Internationalen Rechtsvergleich* (Mohr Siebeck 2005) 289 et seqq.; Matthias Ruffert and Christian Walter, *Institutionalisiertes Völkerrecht* (2nd edn, C H Beck 2015) para 389.

[31]Claire La Hovary, 'A Challenging Ménage À Trois? Tripartism in the International Labour Organization' (2015) 12 International Organizations Law Review 204, 210.

[32]For a full list of duties, see ILO, *Compendium of Rules Applicable to the Governing Body of the International Labour Office* (ILO 2016) para 5 et seq.

Conference's agenda and adopts the draft budget. It also elects the ILO Director-General and directs the work of the International Labour Office (Art. 8 (1) ILO Constitution).[33] The Governing Body decides by consensus whenever possible.[34] Similar to the Conference, the Governing Body's procedure is further specified in its Standing Orders.

The International Labour Office is the ILO's secretariat. The Office is the only main organ without a tripartite structure. It is led by the ILO Director-General and employs around 2700 staff members in the ILO headquarters in Geneva, the ILO representation in New York and in around 40 field offices.[35] It executes the other organs' decisions, but also performs a broad range of further tasks, such as the preparation of reports, research and documentation, provision of assistance to the ILO member states to implement ILO instruments and policies, the administration of the ILO's technical cooperation programmes and projects and the administration of the ILO's relations to third parties, including other IOs.[36] The combination of these tasks makes the Office the focal point of the ILO's activities. At the same time, it endows the Office with important factual capacities to influence the ILO's work.

The ILO also comprises a range of subcommittees, regional bodies and conferences, and associated institutions, such as the International Institute for Labour Studies or the Administrative Tribunal of the ILO (ILOAT).[37] Apart from the ILO's supervisory committees, these other bodies will not be discussed further here.

B. The Two Fundamental Choices Underlying the ILO's Model

To fully grasp the questions examined in this study, it is important to recall not only the ILO's objectives, means and organizational structure, but also the underlying rationales behind them. The ILO's model was designed on the basis of two fundamental choices regarding the way the ILO was to function and pursue its objectives.[38] These choices are, firstly, to pick universal tripartite social dialogue as the preferred model of deliberation and decision-making (Sect. I.), and, secondly, to

---

[33]Sauer (n 4) para 10.

[34]ILO, *Compendium of Rules Applicable to the Governing Body of the International Labour Office* (n 32) para 46.

[35]ILO, 'International Labour Office' <https://www.ilo.org/global/about-the-ilo/who-we-are/international-labour-office/lang%2D%2Den/index.htm> accessed 26 April 2020.

[36]Sauer (n 4) para 11.

[37]ibid 8.

[38]Maupain called them "gambles", because of them being ambitious and their success being highly uncertain at the time of drafting, Maupain, *The Future of the International Labour Organization in the Global Economy* (n 6) 8.

confine the ILO to an exclusively persuasive model of regulating labour matters (Sect. II.).[39]

I. Universal Tripartite Social Dialogue

The first fundamental choice was to conduct labour governance in a specific setting, namely through tripartite social dialogue (Sect. 1.) that is universal (Sect. 2.).

1. Tripartite Social Dialogue

The ILO's founders chose tripartite social dialogue as the preferred means of labour governance. Tripartism is a model of governance in which governments, employers and workers deliberate and decide together and in principle on equal footing.[40]

Delving deeper into the ILO's constitutional framework, it does not take long to notice that tripartism is a fundamental organizational principle. As already mentioned, two of the three main organs and the vast majority of other committees and bodies are constituted in a tripartite manner.[41] Deliberations are conducted in a tripartite setting, and decisions are taken by tripartite consensus or by a majority of the three constituents. As will be explained in further detail below, tripartism permeates and dominates virtually all areas of ILO activity. The rationale for this permeation is twofold. Firstly, including workers and employers enables the ILO to tap these groups' specific perspectives, experience and expertise. Secondly, it assures that the ILO works on the basis of consensus, or at least majoritarian support, of both the governments and the social partners. This tripartite consensus provides the ILO with a unique source of legitimacy.[42]

Apart from being an organizational principle, tripartite social dialogue is also an ideal of how labour governance should be organized to begin with. Its embodiment in the ILO's organizational structure was a conscious decision in favour of that ideal. As has often been highlighted, endowing the ILO with a tripartite configuration was

---

[39]ibid 7.

[40]La Hovary, 'The ILO's Mandate and Capacity: Creating, Proliferating and Supervising Labour Standards for a Globalized Economy' (n 26) 38.

[41]A notable exception is the Financial Committee, which is composed solely of government representatives, Art. 13(2) lit. c ILO Constitution.

[42]See e.g. ILO, 'Towards the ILO Centenary: Realities, Renewal and Tripartite Commitment, Report of the ILO Director-General' (International Labour Conference, 102nd session, June 2013) ILC.102/I(A) paras 88 et seqq.; La Hovary, 'A Challenging Ménage À Trois? Tripartism in the International Labour Organization' (n 31); Lars Thomann, 'The ILO, Tripartism, and NGOs: Do Too Many Cooks Really Spoil the Broth?' in Jens Steffek, Claudia Kissling and Patrizia Nanz (eds), *Civil Society Participation in European and Global Governance. A Cure for the Democratic Deficit?* (Palgrave Macmillan 2008).

a response to the Bolshevik revolution in Russia, which had happened only two years before the ILO was founded, and to ongoing social unrest in many European countries at the time. Deciding in favour of tripartite social dialogue pitted the ILO against other available models of labour governance, especially the 'democratic centralism' of Soviet-type socialist states.[43] At the same time, it served to work as a "revolution insurance" by giving workers a say in labour governance rather than excluding them from the process.[44]

Moreover, the choice for tripartite social dialogue as a model for the ILO has served as an ideal and benchmark for social progress in its member states. When the ILO was founded, hardly any country had a tripartite model of industrial relations, and the ILO's structure was therefore truly pioneering.[45] Moreover, throughout its history, the ILO has actively promoted social dialogue in its member states. The ILO was of course not the sole reason for the proliferation of tripartite social dialogue, but certainly has reinforced respective developments in many states[46] and, as will be exemplified in Chap. 6, to some extent even in the work of some other IOs.

2. Universality

The ILO builds on its founders' vision of tripartite social dialogue being universal. This universality has two dimensions: Universality of membership and universality as to the labour-related topics the ILO deals with.

Firstly, the founders aimed at securing universal membership, so that the ILO could have a worldwide impact. This was based on two reasons. One reason is that the objective of pursuing social justice by ensuring humane working conditions itself

---

[43]Maupain, *The Future of the International Labour Organization in the Global Economy* (n 6) 8. Thus, in its early years, the ILO was under heavy attack by the Third Internationale and like-minded communist groups, who regarded the ILO as a "rallying point of the bourgeoisie", Antony Evelyn Alcock, *History of the International Labour Organization* (Palgrave Macmillan 1971) 128.

[44]Abdul-Karim Tikriti, *Tripartism and the International Labour Organization* (Almqvist & Wiksell International 1982) 155. Daniel Roger Maul, *Human Rights, Development and Decolonization: The International Labour Organization, 1940-70* (Palgrave Macmillan 2012) 3. The visible juxtaposition of models between the ILO and the Soviet bloc has remained relevant throughout the Cold War, and has secured the ILO a certain degree of enhanced support by employers and Western governments during that period, Claire La Hovary, 'Showdown at the ILO? A Historical Perspective on the Employers' Group's 2012 Challenge to the Right to Strike' (2013) 42 Industrial Law Journal 338, 360; Servais (n 11) 28.

[45]Jasmien van Daele, 'Engineering Social Peace, Peace: Networks, Ideas, and the Founding of the International Labour Organization' (2005) 50 International Review of Social History 435, 466. England and France were noteworthy exceptions, Torsten Landelius, *Workers, Employers and Governments: A Comparative Study of Delegations and Groups at the International Labour Conference, 1919–1964* (Norstedt & Söner 1965) 21.

[46]One example is the ILO's support for Solidarnosc and the free trade union movement in communist Poland in the 1980s, Maupain, *The Future of the International Labour Organization in the Global Economy* (n 6) 9.

implies that these objectives should be attained for everyone, not just workers in certain parts of the world.[47] The other reason is that universal membership mitigates competition among states over the most 'business-friendly' (i.e. least regulated) labour market. If the ILO did not have universal membership, members could incur a comparative disadvantage against non-members, as the latter would be free to lower levels of labour protection below those set by the ILO. The preamble of the ILO Constitution acknowledges this risk of a 'race to the bottom' by stating that

> the failure of any nation to adopt humane conditions of labour is an obstacle in the way of other nations which desire to improve the conditions in their own countries.[48]

Secondly, universality also refers to the subject-matters the ILO can address. Obviously, the ILO was established as an organization dealing with 'labour issues', which imposes a vague but nevertheless traceable limit on its ambit. Yet, very early on, the precise scope of this mandate was called into question. The ILO's contested competence to regulate agricultural labour, agricultural production methods, or the work of the employer, gave rise, inter alia, to several advisory opinions of the PCIJ.[49] In its *Agricultural Labour* and *Competence to Regulate the Personal Work of the Employer* opinions, the Court upheld the choice for universality, holding that the ILO was competent to regulate all forms of work and all categories of workers.[50] The ILO's competence was further expanded by the Philadelphia Declaration to cover all individuals, also including employers.[51] In subsequent practice, the ILO has time and again explored the 'frontiers' of this encompassing mandate, with ILO Convention No 169 Concerning Indigenous and Tribal Peoples in Independent Countries being a prominent (but not isolated) example.[52]

---

[47] Ebere Osieke, *Institutional Law and Practice in the International Labour Organization* (Martinus Nijhoff Publishers 1985) 52.

[48] Universal membership is an aim, but it is not a goal to be achieved at all costs, as is e.g. illustrated by the possibility of withdrawal of a member form the ILO, ibid.

[49] *Competence of the ILO in Regard to International Regulation of the Conditions of the Labour of Persons Employed in Agriculture* (Advisory Opinion) PCIJ Rep Series B No 2; *Competence of the ILO to Examine Proposal for the Organization and Development of the Methods of Agricultural Production* (Advisory Opinion) PCIJ Rep Series B No 3, *Competence of the International Labour Organization to Regulate, Incidentally, the Personal Work of the Employer* (Advisory Opinion) PCIJ Rep Series B No 13.

[50] *Competence of the ILO in Regard to International Regulation of the Conditions of the Labour of Persons Employed in Agriculture* (n 49) 27; *Competence of the International Labour Organization to Regulate, Incidentally, the Personal Work of the Employer* (n 49) 17.

[51] See e.g. Para. II lit. a Philadelphia Declaration.

[52] ILO Indigenous and Tribal Peoples Convention, 1989 (No 169) (adopted 27 June 1989, entered into force 5 September 1991) 1650 UNTS 383. See further Maria Victoria Cabrera Ormaza, *The Requirement of Consultation with Indigenous Peoples in the ILO: Between Normative Flexibility and Institutional Rigidity* (Brill Nijhoff 2018). In more recent times, the ILO's universal mandate for all forms of work has led to a new challenge, posed by the ever-diversifying world of work, see ILO 'Changing Patterns in the World of Work, Report of the Director-General' (International Labour Conference, 95th session, 2006) Report 1(C).

II. Effectuation Through Persuasion

The second fundamental choice was to curtail the ILO's means to give effect to its policies and instruments. The organization's only means of doing so is persuasion.[53] The ILO neither can enact immediately binding legislation, nor does it have any means of coercive enforcement at its disposal.[54] Instead, the ILO is bound to convince its members to adopt and implement its instruments and policies. Persuasion manifests itself in some of the ILO's central means of governance. For instance, member states are free to ratify ILO conventions or not. They are merely required to present adopted conventions and recommendations to their competent organs and to report on matters regarding unratified conventions (Art. 19(5) ILO Constitution).[55] In a similar manner, in case of violations of obligations, the ultimate 'sanction' is a form of public 'naming and shaming' by the ILO's supervisory bodies and the International Labour Conference.[56]

The limitation to persuasion has earned the ILO the image of a 'weak' institution. While the impetus for such critique may be understandable to some extent, the ILO's perceived 'weakness' must be seen in the light of the other fundamental choice for universal tripartite social dialogue. This other choice largely made persuasion the only available realistic modus of regulation. Stronger means of enforcement could have put a strain on such dialogue. They could have burdened or even jeopardized universal consensus-finding and the acceptability of results, induced the members to settle for the 'common lowest denominator', or even induced states not to join the ILO in the first place, or to withdraw from the organization.[57] The choice for persuasion was thus "risky but unavoidable".[58]

---

[53]Steve Charnovitz, 'The International Labour Organization in Its Second Century' (2000) 4 Max Planck Yearbook of United Nations Law 147, 171.

[54]Proposals to endow the ILO with the competence to adopt a directly binding international labour code were dropped during the negotiations leading to the adoption of the Constitution in 1919, James T Shotwell, *The Origins of the International Labour Organization, Volume 1: History* (Columbia University Press 1934) 145 et seqq.

[55]Charnovitz 'The International Labour Organization in Its Second Century' (n 53) 172.

[56]The 'enforcement' under Art. 33 ILO Constitution has attained utterly limited relevance, see Brian Langille, 'The Curious Incident of the ILO, Myanmar and Forced Labour' in Adelle Blackett and Anne Trebilcock (eds), *Research Handbook on Transnational Labour Law* (Edward Elgar Publishing 2015) 519. For an empirical analysis of the ILO's supervisory system see Faradj Koliev and James H Lebovic, 'Selecting for Shame: The Monitoring of Workers' Rights by the International Labour Organization, 1989 to 2011' (2018) 62 International Studies Quarterly 437.

[57]Maupain, *The Future of the International Labour Organization in the Global Economy* (n 6) 15 and 153.

[58]ibid 14. Moreover, the fact that the ILO is limited to persuasion can also be an asset, as it can facilitate compromise and social progress. It is easier to agree to trade-offs if there is no imminent threat of enforcement measures. All justified concerns notwithstanding, it must not be forgotten that the ILO has successfully persuaded states and other IOs to have regard to its instruments and policies in a number of cases. One example is the mainstreaming of the ILO's Decent Work Agenda within the UN System, now appearing inter alia in Goal 8 of the 2030 Sustainable Development

C. The Permeation of the Fundamental Choices, in Particular Tripartism

The relevance of the described fundamental choices for the ILO cannot be overstated. The fundamental choices permeate the ILO's constitutional configuration and the way it fulfils its mandate. It is convenient to exemplify this by looking at how the fundamental choice for universal tripartite social dialogue materializes in the composition of organs and bodies as well as the ILO's norm-setting and supervisory activities.

I. Tripartism in the Composition of Organs and Bodies

As mentioned before, two out of three main organs—the International Labour Conference and the Governing Body—and most other ILO bodies have a tripartite composition. Both the International Labour Conference and the Governing Body are composed by a 2:1:1 ratio of governments, workers and employers. The plenary Conference is composed of two government, one worker and one employer representative from each member state (Art. 3(1) ILO Constitution). Similarly, the Governing Body consists of 28 members of governments and 14 members of each workers' and employers' groups.[59] That being said, it has become established organizational practice that in all the Conference's and Governing Body's committees that have a tripartite composition (i.e. most of them), the ratio is 1:1:1, giving even more weight to employers and workers.[60] This has significant implications on the format in which the ILO takes decisions. Formally, committee decisions need to be adopted by the plenary Conference or the Governing Body, respectively. However, in practice, committee decisions are usually adopted without modifications. Hence, in substance, most decisions are effectively taken in a 1:1:1 format.[61]

Additionally, the ILO Constitution's provisions on the organs' composition contain additional safeguards intended to secure the independence of workers' and employers' representatives, which is a crucial prerequisite for the ILO's pluralist model of tripartite social dialogue. For example, employers' and workers' delegates

---

Goals (see the discussion in Chap. 14 C. I. Another example is – again – the ILO's influence on the drafting and implementation of the ESC, discussed in Chap. 6.

[59]La Hovary, 'The ILO's Mandate and Capacity: Creating, Proliferating and Supervising Labour Standards for a Globalized Economy' (n 26) 40.

[60]ibid. In consequence, in the committees, workers and employers could technically even outvote the governments. The 1:1:1 quota was established early on in the ILO's history, see e.g. Clarence Wilfred Jenks, 'The Significance for International Law of the Tripartite Character of the International Labour Organisation' (1936) 22 Transactions of the Grotius Society 45, 47.

[61]La Hovary, 'The ILO's Mandate and Capacity: Creating, Proliferating and Supervising Labour Standards for a Globalized Economy' (n 26) 40.

to the International Labour Conference are nominated by their governments, but this must happen in agreement with the most representative domestic organization (Art. 3 (5) ILO Constitution).[62] The nomination is supervised by the (tripartite) ILO Credentials Committee, which, by a two-thirds majority, may refuse to admit delegates which have not been nominated in accordance with the applicable constitutional provisions (Art. 3(9) ILO Constitution).[63] The Credentials Committee thus effectively exercises a tripartite gatekeeper function.[64] Once admitted to the Conference, each delegate may freely express views and may vote individually, i.e. is not subject to directions (Art. 4(1) ILO Constitution). Thus, employers' and workers' delegates may argue and vote against 'their' (and any other) government.[65]

In the Governing Body, the government members represent their own governments, but the workers' and employers' members represent their respective groups (Art. 7(4) ILO Constitution).[66] This strengthens the position of the workers' and employers' members in the Governing Body vis-à-vis the governments.[67]

Finally, as mentioned before, both the Conference and the Governing Body have the right to establish committees (Arts. 7(8) and 17 ILO Constitution)[68] and have done so on many occasions. The composition of these committees is not expressly

---

[62]Art. 3(5) ILO Constitution. On the interpretation of this provision see *Designation of the Workers' Delegate for the Netherlands at the Third Session of the International Labour Conference* (Advisory Opinion) PCIJ Rep Series B No 1 23 and 25.

[63]Credentials have thus become a subject of central relevance for the proper functioning of tripartism. The Credentials Committee has repeatedly had to decide on cases of alleged violations of constitutional nomination requirements. In this context, it has been confronted with incidental questions e.g. on the independence of workers' and employers' organizations, see Tikriti (n 44) 182 et seq.; Henne van der Kooy 'What is the Substance of Tripartism in the International Labour Organisation?: Criteria for the Verification of Credentials at the International Labour Conferences' (1977) 8 Netherlands Yearbook of International Law 73, 96 et seqq.

[64]Faina Milman-Silvan, 'Freedom of Association in Deliberative Spaces: The ILO Credentials Committee' in Adelle Blackett and Anne Trebilcock (eds), *Research Handbook on Transnational Labour Law* (Edward Elgar Publishing 2015) 204, 208. Its threshold of review has traditionally been low and focused on ensuring universal representation at the Conference. In recent years, however, the Credentials Committee has begun to take into account whether the nomination of the workers' and employers' delegates by their governments was compatible with freedom of association, Volker Rittberger and others, 'Inclusive Global Institutions for a Global Political Economy' in Volker Rittberger, Martin Nettesheim and Carmen Huckel (eds), *Authority in the Global Political Economy* (Palgrave Macmillan 2008) 21.

[65]Ibid.

[66]La Hovary Claire, 'A Challenging Ménage À Trois? Tripartism in the International Labour Organization' (n 31) 204, 206.

[67]Clarence Wilfred Jenks, *The International Protection of Trade Union Freedom* (Stevens and Sons 1957) 70.

[68]The Governing Body's right to establish committees is not explicitly mentioned in the ILO Constitution, but can be implied in its competence to set its own procedure. It is moreover explicitly laid down in Art. 4.2.1 of the Standing Orders of the Governing Body (reproduced in ILO, *Compendium of Rules Applicable to the Governing Body of the International Labour Office* (n 32) 14 et seqq.).

regulated by the Constitution.[69] Yet, it has been established practice that committees are in principle tripartite.[70]

II. Tripartism in Norm-Setting: The Example of ILO Labour Conventions

Norm creation is one of the ILO's foremost functions. In the following, the pivotal relevance of tripartism for norm-setting will be exemplified by the procedure leading to the adoption of a new labour convention (Sect. 1.). Subsequently, it will be shown that tripartism remains intrinsically connected to a convention after its adoption (Sect. 2.).

1. Tripartism in the Procedure Leading to the Adoption of Conventions

As all ILO activities, the creation of a labour convention takes place against the backdrop of the fundamental choices outlines above, more particularly the goal of universal acceptance and implementation of the convention-to-be and the need to achieve this solely by persuasion. As a consequence, drafting of new labour conventions is a thorough process that involves all three of the ILO's organs and reserves plenty of room for tripartite social dialogue. At all of its stages, there are extensive discussions, driven by the desire to achieve consensus or at least the largest degree of support attainable.[71]

The norm-setting procedure usually begins when the Governing Body includes the item of a new convention on the International Labour Conference's agenda.[72] In

[69]The Constitution merely regulates that the Financial Committee shall be composed of government representatives only, Art. 13(2) lit. c ILO Constitution.

[70]This principle also underlies the Standing Orders, see e.g. Art. 55(3) International Labour Conference Standing Orders and Arts. 4.2.2 and 4.2.3 of the Standing Orders of the Governing Body.

[71]This might include additional informal efforts that complement the formal procedure. For example, there was an informal tripartite meeting in preparation of the Worst Forms of Child Labour Convention, 1999 (No 182), one of the eight fundamental conventions. The Governing Body can also submit the issue to the International Labour Conference for a general discussion, see Art. 11ter of the Standing Orders of the International Labour Conference <https://www.ilo.org/dyn/normlex/en/f?p=NORMLEXPUB:62:0::NO::P62_LIST_ENTRIE_ID:3088520>, accessed 26 April 2020 (International Labour Conference Standing Orders). This means that the Conference discusses the need and desirability of adopting a new instrument, without this discussion directly aiming at the adoption of a convention text, Servais (n 11) 51. Consensus is not always reachable, and some (including some important) ILO instruments have not attained support from all tripartite groups, see the examples cited in La Hovary, 'A Challenging Ménage À Trois? Tripartism in the International Labour Organization' (n 31) 216 et seq.

[72]Technically, the Conference can also decide this itself, Art. 16(3) ILO Constitution.

doing so, it must consider proposals by a government or another IO, but also by employers' or workers' organizations (Art. 14(1) ILO Constitution).[73] Once the Governing Body has decided to include the issue of a new convention on the Conference's agenda, any government can formally object (Art. 16(1) ILO Constitution). However, such objection can be overcome if the Conference decides to keep the agenda item by a two-thirds majority (Art. 16(2) ILO Constitution).

From this point on, there are two possible ways forward to prepare the convention: The usual procedure is the so-called double discussion procedure.[74] The alternative single discussion procedure is only used in exceptional cases and will not be addressed further here.[75] Pursuant to the double discussion procedure, the International Labour Office prepares a report on the issue, which includes, inter alia, a detailed analysis of existing domestic laws and practices.[76] The Office's report is circulated to the governments for comments, requesting them to consult with 'their' most representative workers' and employers organizations.[77] On the basis of the replies, the Office prepares a second report, which outlines the principal points to be discussed at the Conference.[78] Both reports and other material are then transmitted to the next Conference for a first discussion, usually taking place in one of the Conference's (tripartite) technical committees.[79] Following this discussion, the Office then prepares one or more draft convention texts. These are then again transmitted to the governments, which again consult with 'their' social partner organizations.[80] Based on the governments' replies, the Office draws up a report with the draft text including necessary amendments.[81] This report is then placed before the next Conference for a second round of discussions. The draft is usually first discussed again in the technical committees before the full Conference adopts each of the provisions in turn. After the finalization by the Conference's Drafting

---

[73]Or a proposal of another IO, which has e.g. happened in the case of ILO Convention No 87. Furthermore, additional preparatory steps can be taken, such as the convening of tripartite technical conference by the Governing Body, No 5.1.3 of the Standing Orders of the Governing Body.

[74]On the double discussion procedure see Art. 39 International Labour Conference Standing Orders. Art. 5.1.4 Governing Body Standing Orders sets forth that this is the procedure unless indicated otherwise.

[75]On the single discussion procedure, see Art. 38 International Labour Conference Standing Orders.

[76]Art. 39(1) International Labour Conference Standing Orders.

[77]These are the same organizations that also send a delegate to the Conference in accordance with Art. 3 ILO Constitution, Art. 39(1) International Labour Conference Standing Orders.

[78]Art. 39(3) International Labour Conference Standing Orders.

[79]Art. 39(4) International Labour Conference Standing Orders, Servais (n 11) 52. It is worth noting that the modus is one of discussion, rather than negotiation, as would be the more common modus for international treaties, Nicolas Valticos and Geraldo W von Potobsky, *International Labour Law* (2nd edn, Kluwer 1995) 50.

[80]Art. 39(6) International Labour Conference Standing Orders. This is also the point when the Office consults with the UN and the specialized agencies, Art. 39bis International Labour Conference Standing Orders.

[81]Art. 39(7) International Labour Conference Standing Orders.

Committee, the plenary Conference casts the final vote on the convention's adoption.[82]

As mentioned before, the final adoption of a convention requires a two-thirds majority (Art. 19(2) ILO Constitution). Due to the plenary Conference's 2:1:1 composition, this means that governments cannot adopt a convention without support from either workers or employers.[83] At the same time, neither of the latter is in a position to unilaterally obstruct the adoption of a convention.

2. The Impact of Tripartism on Adopted Conventions

Tripartism remains intrinsically connected to an ILO convention after the latter has been adopted by the Conference. As one consequence of tripartism, the general law of treaties enshrined in the VCLT is applicable to ILO conventions only subject to a range of modifications, as established in ILO practice.[84] This section will exemplify these modifications by focusing on the topics of reservations to labour conventions and labour conventions' interpretation.[85]

The first modification to be discussed here is that it is impermissible for states to make reservations to labour conventions, unless and to the extent the convention itself allows them.[86] Under the general law of treaties, states are free to make reservations to a treaty up until its ratification, unless the treaty explicitly prohibits the reservation or if reservations would be incompatible with the object and purpose of the treaty (Art. 19 VCLT). By contrast, it became established ILO practice already during the 1920s that reservations were in principle inadmissible, and that the Office would refuse to register ratifications that contained reservations.[87] This happened because of two reasons. Firstly, as seen, labour conventions are discussed, developed

---

[82]See Art. 40 International Labour Conference Standing Orders.

[83]La Hovary, 'A Challenging Ménage À Trois? Tripartism in the International Labour Organization' (n 31) 216.

[84]The normative basis for such modifications is Art. 5 VCLT, discussed in Chap. 10.

[85]For amendments to conventions see Desiree LeClercq, 'Sea Change: New Rulemaking Procedures at the International Labour Organization' (2015) 22 ILSA Journal of International & Comparative Law 105. A further issue, which has mainly lost its relevance today and is thus not discussed here, was accession to ILO conventions by non-ILO member states. Such an accession, if negotiated between the non-member and the member governments alone, was considered inadmissible, Jenks, 'The Significance for International Law of the Tripartite Character of the International Labour Organisation' (n 60) 64.

[86]Under Art. 19 VCLT, reservations are admissible unless the reservation in question is prohibited by the treaty or the reservation is incompatible with the object and purpose of the treaty.

[87]The ILO practice is explained at length in the ILO's submissions to the ICJ in the *Prevention of Genocide* advisory proceedings, *Reservations to the Reservations to the Convention on the Prevention and Punishment of the Crime of Genocide* (Written Statement of the International Labour Organization) [1951] ICJ Pleadings 216, 235 et seq. See also Jenks, 'The Significance for International Law of the Tripartite Character of the International Labour Organisation' (n 60) 58 et seq.; Jan Klabbers, 'On Human Rights Treaties, Contractual Conceptions and Reservations' in Ineta

and adopted by tripartite bodies. If states, upon ratification, could subsequently alter the scope of their obligations under a convention previously agreed upon in a tripartite setting, this could undermine the tripartite consensus underlying the convention, especially since there is no procedure in place through which workers' and employers' representatives could object to such reservations.[88] Secondly, Art. 19 (3) ILO Constitution already requires the Conference to take due regard during the drafting process of special circumstances in countries which might require modifications.[89] This allows for similar flexibility but places the discussion thereon in the Conference.[90]

The second modification to be mentioned here is interpretation of labour conventions. There are numerous nuances concerning the interpretation of ILO conventions, many of which resemble modifications of the general rules laid down in Arts. 31–33 VCLT.[91] Some of these modifications can be directly traced back to tripartism. One such modification is that subsequent interpretative agreements between states (Art. 31(3) lit. a VCLT) and unilateral interpretative declarations (Art. 31(2) lit. b VCLT) are impermissible in the case of labour conventions.[92] The reason for this is that the ILO Constitution foresees a system of supervision and dispute settlement (discussed further below) involving tripartite bodies, and moreover envisages authoritative interpretations by the ICJ. This system could be sidelined if states could agree on interpretations of conventions among themselves without including workers and employers.[93] Another modification is the greater

---

Ziemele (ed), *Reservations to Human Rights Treaties and the Vienna Convention Regime: Conflict, Harmony or Reconciliation* (Martinus Nijhoff Publishers 2004).

[88]Jenks, 'The Significance for International Law of the Tripartite Character of the International Labour Organisation' (n 60) 59; La Hovary, 'A Challenging Ménage À Trois? Tripartism in the International Labour Organization' (n 31) 217; Anne Trebilcock, 'The International Labour Organization' in Michael J Bowman and Dino Kritsiotis (eds), *Conceptual and Contextual Perspectives on the Modern Law of Treaties* (Cambridge University Press 2018) 848, 860.

[89]Charnovitz 'The International Labour Organization in Its Second Century' (n 53) 173; Trebilcock, 'The International Labour Organization' (n 88) 860.

[90]An overview is provided by George P Politakis, 'Deconstructing Flexibility in International Labour Conventions' in Jean-Claude Javillier, Bernard Gernigon and George P Politakis (eds), *Les Normes Internationales du Travail: Un Patrimoine pour l'Avenir: Mélanges en l'Honneur de Nicolas Valticos* (ILO 2004). In addition, the ILO has developed other means to ensure flexibility, e.g. by including pertinent clauses into conventions, see Trebilcock, 'The International Labour Organization' (n 88) 860 et seq.

[91]See the meticulous analysis by Trebilcock, 'The International Labour Organization' (n 88) 864 et seqq.

[92]The sole exception being that the convention allows for such an agreement or declaration, ibid 872 et seq., citing an unpublished paper by Yemin, also regarding the further example of agreements made between the parties in connection with the conclusion of a treaty (Art. 31(2) lit a VCLT).

[93]Jenks, 'The Significance for International Law of the Tripartite Character of the International Labour Organisation' (n 60) 65, discussing the example of the 'conclusions' adopted by a number of ILO member states in 1926 regarding the Hours of Work (Industry) Convention, 1919 (No 1) (adopted 28 November 1919, entered into force 13 June 1921) 38 UNTS 17.

emphasis on preparatory works by some of the ILO's bodies involved in interpretation, notably the International Labour Office. The preparatory works include the Office's reports on consultations with governments and social partners and the conference materials. In its published interpretations, the Office refers to the preparatory works even in instances when the meaning of a provision seems clear. It has been argued that the reason for this was to enhance the tripartite constituents' "ownership" of labour conventions and their meaning.[94]

III. Tripartism in the Supervisory System

Finally, tripartite social dialogue also plays a central role in the ILO's supervisory system. Out of the four different existing ILO supervisory procedures,[95] the following paragraphs will only touch on the two procedures relevant for this study, namely the regular supervisory procedure and the special supervisory procedure concerning freedom of association, and the respective supervisory bodies involved in these two procedures.

1. The Regular Supervisory Procedure

The regular supervisory procedure is a reporting procedure in which ILO bodies examine periodical reports submitted by the member states. Member states have to submit:

- Reports on the implementation of ratified conventions (Art. 22 ILO Constitution).[96]
- Reports on non-ratified conventions, stating their domestic law and practice regarding the subject-matter of the convention, progress made towards ratification and any remaining difficulties for ratifying the convention (Art. 19(5) lit. e ILO Constitution).[97]

---

[94]Trebilcock, 'The International Labour Organization' (n 88) 871.

[95]There are four different procedures through which compliance with conventions and constitutional principles can be monitored: The regular supervisory procedure, the representation procedure (Arts. 24 and 26 ILO Constitution), the complaint procedure (Arts. 26-34 ILO Constitution) and the special supervisory procedure for freedom of association cases. In ILO law and practice, supervision is bestowed in no less than seven different bodies, some of which are standing, while others can be convened from time to time on an ad hoc basis. The CEACR, the CAS, the CFA, the FFCC, a Commission of Inquiry appointed pursuant to Art. 29 ILO Constitution, an ad hoc committee which can be appointed during a representation procedure, and the ICJ as an arbiter of last instance. Further, the ILO can establish an in-house tribunal pursuant to Art. 37(2) ILO Constitution.

[96]For fundamental and governance conventions, the reporting period is three years, for other conventions five years, subject to adjustment by the Governing Body.

[97]See for recommendations Art. 19(6) lit. c and d ILO Constitution.

In a first phase of the regular supervisory procedure, state reports and any comments on them by workers' and employers' organizations (Art. 23 ILO Constitution) are examined by the Committee of Experts on the Application of Conventions and Recommendations (CEACR). The CEACR is a standing subcommittee of the ILO Governing Body.[98] It is composed of 20 independent and impartial jurists appointed by the Governing Body.[99] The CEACR examines the member states' reports and issues an annual report.[100] It may also address direct requests at member states, which are of a more technical nature and do not form part of its annual report.

In the second phase of the regular supervisory procedure, the CEACR's annual report is examined by the Conference Committee on the Application of Standards (CAS). The CAS is a standing subcommittee of the International Labour Conference. It is the second central body in the regular supervisory procedure. Unlike the CEACR, the CAS is not composed of experts, but of representatives of the ILO's tripartite constituents. It discusses the CEACR's annual report in a tripartite setting. Due to the immense workload within the supervisory system, the CAS focuses on the worst cases of non-compliance.[101] For that purpose, it compiles and discusses a list of usually around 25 of the observations from the CEACR's annual report. The CAS issues a final report, in which it adopts conclusions on the cases discussed. The CAS's final report is formally adopted by the International Labour Conference, which marks the last step in the regular supervisory procedure.

At first glance, the regular supervisory procedure might seem to be less a tripartite undertaking than the work of independent experts within the CEACR. Indeed, the CEACR copes with the largest share of work by examining states' reports on the more than 8000 ratifications of labour conventions that currently exist, plus further reports on unratified conventions and recommendations.[102] Moreover, the impression of the experts' central role is reinforced by the fact that the CEACR's annual report is published before it is discussed by the CAS.[103] At this first stage, tripartism manifests itself only indirectly, in that the CEACR members are appointed and the

[98]Established in 1926 to handle the increasing workload resulting from state reports on the implementation of their obligations under ILO instruments.

[99]La Hovary, 'The ILO's Mandate and Capacity: Creating, Proliferating and Supervising Labour Standards for a Globalized Economy' (n 26) 43.

[100]The CEACR's annual report is composed of three parts:

1) A general report on member states' compliance,
2) Observations on fundamental questions concerning the application of ratified conventions by particular ILO Member States.
3) A topic-specific General Survey on a topic chosen by the Governing Body, to assess the overall impact of ILO instruments, detect problems and recommend solutions. The General Survey draws on reports on both ratified and non-ratified conventions, ibid.

[101]ibid.

[102]Between 1919 and 2016, there were 8,059 ratifications of ILO conventions in total, Frank Hendrickx and others, 'The Architecture of Global Labour Governance' (2016) 155 International Labour Review 339, 343.

[103]On current difficulties, see below, Sect. D. III.

committee's mandate is defined by the (tripartite) Governing Body. That being said, tripartism moves centre-stage in the second phase. While the CAS only discusses a relatively small number of cases, it nevertheless acts much like a tripartite follow-up on the CEACR's observations and offers an opportunity for the tripartite constituents to formally comment on the experts' findings and to introduce 'second thoughts' where deemed necessary. The tripartite constituents can choose which cases (not) to discuss and to adopt conclusions on. This puts them in control of the ILO's capacity to publicly 'name and shame' perpetrators. Moreover, a tripartite condemnation of non-compliance may have more political weight than expert statements. Thus, eventually, the outcome of the regular supervisory procedure is in many ways determined by (and its function is dependent on) tripartite social dialogue.

2. The Special Supervisory Procedure Regarding Freedom of Association

The special supervisory procedure for freedom of association is not explicitly provided for in the ILO Constitution. It was established in 1950/1951 to reinforce the ILO's efforts in the central field of freedom of association.[104] As part of the new procedure, the Governing Body created the Committee on Freedom of Association (CFA) as a standing tripartite subcommittee. The CFA is composed of three members from each of the tripartite groups and is chaired by a neutral academic. It is mandated to deal specifically with alleged violations of freedom of association, brought before it by workers' and employers' organizations.[105] The CFA examines the cases in dialogue with the ILO member state concerned, irrespective of whether that member state has ratified the pertinent ILO conventions on freedom of association or not.[106] It issues a report to the ILO Governing Body, in which it draws conclusions on the case and may make recommendations to the state concerned on ways to improve the situation.[107]

The CFA has decided over 3200 cases, from which the ILO has distilled a broad range of principles of freedom of association. This 'case-law' issued by a tripartite body has had an overwhelming impact on the development and contouring of freedom of association, both within the ILO and beyond.[108]

[104] Alcock (n 43) 253 et seqq.

[105] Technically, cases can also be submitted by other actors, which, however, rarely ever happens.

[106] In case of non-ratification, the CFA's standard of review is 'principles' of freedom of association, derived from the ILO Constitution, rather than specific provisions of the two conventions.

[107] As a follow up, the CFA may also propose to establish a direct contacts mission with the Member State.

[108] La Hovary, 'The ILO's Mandate and Capacity: Creating, Proliferating and Supervising Labour Standards for a Globalized Economy' (n 26) 44.

3. 'Internalization' of Interpretation and 'Soft Law Jurisprudence' as a Tripartite Constitutional Compromise

Besides, and more fundamentally, tripartism has also been the reason for significant systemic transformations of the ILO's supervisory system as such. A case in point is the question of interpretation of the ILO Constitution and ILO conventions.

There is a disparity between the ILO Constitution's 'black letter law' on the one hand and established practice regarding interpretation of the ILO Constitution and of ILO conventions on the other hand. Art. 37(1) ILO Constitution vests the competence to decide any questions or disputes on the interpretation of the ILO Constitution and ILO conventions in the ICJ. It has always been common ground that, due to Art. 37 ILO Constitution, none of the ILO supervisory bodies can interpret ILO instruments in a formally binding manner.[109]

However, Art. 37(1) ILO Constitution has only been activated six times and only during the interwar period to request advisory opinions from the PCIJ. The provision has remained inactive since 1932.[110] What is more, no use has ever been made of Art. 37(2) ILO Constitution, a provision introduced in 1946, which enables the ILO to establish an own in-house dispute settlement tribunal that could adopt authoritative interpretations in lieu of the ICJ.[111]

Instead, ILO practice has witnessed an 'internalization' of interpretation. In the course of their respective activities, the ILO supervisory bodies have each elaborated on a regular basis on the scope and content of obligations arising under ILO instruments. For instance, the CEACR has expressed its understanding of the content of ILO conventions in its observations and its General Survey.[112] The same is true for the CFA in its reports on freedom of association cases.[113] Additionally, incidental interpretations of ILO instruments are rendered and officially published by the International Labour Office, notably on the occasion of assisting ILO member states in implementing ratified ILO conventions.[114] These interpretations are naturally

---

[109]Claire La Hovary, 'The ILO and the Interpretation of Fundamental Rights at Work: A Closer Look at Establishing a Tribunal under Article 37(2)' in Paul van der Heijden (ed), *Ensuring Coherence in Fundamental Labor Rights Case Law: Challenges and Opportunities* (SJEC 2016) 51.

[110]ibid.

[111]ibid.

[112]Servais (n 11) 67; Claire La Hovary, "The ILO Supervisory Bodies' 'Soft Law Jurisprudence" in Adelle Blackett and Anne Trebilcock (eds), *Research Handbook on Transnational Labour Law* (Edward Elgar Publishing 2015) 318 et seqq.

[113]The ILO also publishes an own digest of CFA decisions and principles on freedom of association, ILO, *Digest of Decisions and Principles of the Freedom of Association Committee of the Governing Body of the ILO* (5th edn, ILO 2006).

[114]It has become an established practice that these interpretations are published in the ILO Official Bulletin and – if no member objects – add to the ILO's *acquis* of informal soft law jurisprudence. In the same manner, the International Labour Office has also issued interpretations in legal memoranda on other matters than supervision. For an example, see e.g. ILO, 'Notice of Withdrawal Required Under Article 1, Paragraph 5 of the Constitution of the International Labour Organisation From Any

polyform in origin, context, form and content: The interpreting bodies, working on different tasks in tripartite, civil service or neutral/expert compositions, issue different interpretations for different purposes.[115] Nevertheless, the joint result of the committees' and the Office's activities is a body of "soft law jurisprudence", i.e. an incidentally and incrementally created *acquis* of interpretation of ILO instruments that has gained substantial influence on the development of international labour law.[116] Despite the formally non-binding nature of interpretations given by these bodies, it had been accepted for decades that the rendering of 'soft' interpretations constituted a proper exercise of the functions of the aforesaid bodies, namely to assist in the implementation of ILO instruments and to assess compliance, to the extent that it has been considered an established developed intra-organizational "custom".[117]

Against the backdrop of these developments, the non-use of either of Art. 37 ILO Constitution's two sections must be understood as a deliberate choice by the ILO's tripartite constituents: Proposals in favour of referrals to the ICJ under Art. 37 (1) ILO Constitution or the establishment of an in-house tribunal pursuant to Art. 37(2) ILO Constitution have recurrently been made on various occasions during the ILO's history. Yet, so far, the ILO's constituents have at all times preferred the 'internalized' soft law jurisprudence over both external review by the ICJ and internal but authoritative interpretation by an in-house tribunal. Besides certain procedural questions, one main argument raised against referrals to the ICJ was that the ICJ would be ill-suited and fail to have due regard to the specifics of tripartism.[118] The non-establishment of an in-house tribunal, for its part, was to a large extent the result of significant practical difficulties to come up with a model satisfying all tripartite groups.[119] By contrast, while the 'softness' of interpretations by the supervisory bodies and the Office undoubtedly contains an element of uncertainty, it offers a well-tested, flexible and generally accepted mode of dispute resolution, or at least a pragmatic form of 'dispute handling'. Moreover, avoiding authoritative interpretations has the advantage of keeping interpretations 'open' and in flux, so that they could be settled (and, if needed, re-opened) by tripartite dialogue.

State Member Intending to Withdraw From the Organisation - Question Whether an Extension of the Notice Is Legally Permissible' [1977] United Nations Juridical Yearbook 248.

[115]It was one of the employers' concerns that this polyform nature and the underlying reasons for it tends to be neglected by other institutions which interact with the ILO, see below, Sect. D. III. 2.

[116]La Hovary, "The ILO Supervisory Bodies' 'Soft Law Jurisprudence" (n 112).

[117]La Hovary, 'The ILO and the Interpretation of Fundamental Rights at Work: A Closer Look at Establishing a Tribunal under Article 37(2)' (n 109) 51. The tripartite constituents accepted this practice early on, see e.g. the Governing Body's reaction to the Office's early interpretations of ILO conventions, reproduced in Conley Hall Dillon, *International Labour Conventions: Their Interpretation and Revision* (University of North Carolina Press 1942) 135.

[118]Dillon (n 117) 135. La Hovary, 'The ILO and the Interpretation of Fundamental Rights at Work: A Closer Look at Establishing a Tribunal under Article 37(2)' (n 109) 52.

[119]While the employers wished to retain (and possibly to expand) social partners' involvement in interpretation, the workers sought to avoid additional costs and did not see the necessity to change a system they felt was working, La Hovary, 'The ILO and the Interpretation of Fundamental Rights at Work: A Closer Look at Establishing a Tribunal under Article 37(2)' (n 109) 54 et seq.

This underlines the fundamental role that tripartite social dialogue has for the nature and the 'ownership' of interpretations of ILO instruments.

IV. Conclusions

The fundamental choices for universal tripartite social dialogue and for governance by persuasion are deeply engrained in the ILO's constitutional configuration. The preceding survey has exemplified this with regard to tripartism, which materializes at virtually every level of ILO activity. Tripartism predefines the composition of most organs, it governs the creation of labour standards by the ILO and remains intrinsically connected to them even after their ratification and entry into force. Moreover, tripartism governs the ILO's supervisory practice and even has significant transformative power, as the example of the 'internalization' of ILO instruments' interpretation illustrates.

D. The Model's Fragility

The ILO's model of labour governance has proven remarkably resilient. However, it has time and again faced significant and sometimes existential challenges. Some of these challenges resulted from the changing economic, social and political environment, while others were a consequence of changing attitudes or sentiments of the ILO's constituents.[120] In many cases, both causes coincided.

The issues addressed by this study cannot fully be understood and estimated without taking into account these challenges and the vulnerability of the ILO's model to external influence, not least because many of them were directly or indirectly connected to other IOs' activities. This section will in turn shed light on challenges to universality, to persuasion and to tripartite social dialogue.

---

[120]For an example of changes of the economic environment, ILO drafters assumed economic interdependence as a corollary of open markets and free trade. This can be seen from the Preamble of the 1919 ILO Constitution. This assumption proved wrong throughout most parts of the 20th century. In the interwar period, states had recourse to protectionism. After the Second World War, market liberalization was only pursued among certain, predominantly Western countries, while explicitly opposed by the socialist bloc and others. It eventually became a reality after 1989 and the 'new globalization', Maupain, *The Future of the International Labour Organization in the Global Economy* (n 6) 12. For a historical account see Peter-Tobias Stoll, 'International Economic and Social Dimensions: Divided or Connected?' in Henner Gött (ed), *Labour Standards in International Economic Law* (Springer 2018) 11.

I. Challenges to Universality

For a significant period of ILO history, universality of membership was either simply non-existent or at least under latent threat. This can be illustrated by the case of the USSR and the USA.

Both the USA and the USSR only joined the ILO in 1934, 15 years after the latter had been established.[121] In 1940, the USSR was expelled from the League of Nations for its attack on Finland and thus lost its ILO membership pursuant to Art. 387 Treaty of Versailles.[122] This absence effectively put the organization in the camp of the Western states during the early Cold War years, for which it was the reified counter-model to the Stalinist 'centralized' (i.e. totalitarian) model of labour governance.[123] The USSR's return in 1954 posed a new challenge to universality, as the former and the emergent number of developing countries began to question Western dominance in the organization.[124]

In 1977, the USA withdrew from the ILO on grounds of a perceived politicization of the organization,[125] only to rejoin in 1980 when the ILO began to support free trade unions in communist countries. While the USA's absence was relatively short, it caused severe budgetary cuts and a significant loss of reputation. The withdrawal gave rise to several actors contemplating establishing mechanisms for tripartite social dialogue at regional organizations, e.g. the OAS or the OECD, as an alternative (and direct institutional competition) to the ILO.[126]

After 1989, the ILO attained quasi-universal membership. At the time of writing, the ILO counts 187 member states. However, challenges to universality persist, albeit coming from a different direction. During the last decades, non-governmental organizations have proliferated and diversified. At the same time, work relations themselves have diversified, with phenomena such as informal work, domestic work, hired work, etc. As a corollary, organized labour has been on the

---

[121] Yves Beigbeder, 'The United States' Withdrawal from the International Labor Organization' (1979) 34 Relations industrielles / Industrial Relations 223, 225. The reason for the then isolationist USA to join was to overcome the US Supreme Court's resistance against domestic labour regulations, see Edward C Lorenz, 'The Search for Constitutional Protection of Labor Standards, 1924-1941: From Interstate Compacts to International Treaties' (2000) 23 Seattle University Law Review 569, 587 et seqq.

[122] Beigbeder (n 121) 225. It has been subject to debate whether Russia withdrew or was expelled from the League, see Thomas D Grant, *Admission to the United Nations - Charter Article 4 and the Rise of Universal Organization* (Martinus Nijhoff Publishers 2009) 267 et seq.

[123] Alcock (n 43) 253 et seqq.

[124] Beigbeder (n 121) 225.

[125] Osieke (n 47) 35 et seqq.

[126] Francis Blanchard, *L'Organisation Internationale Du Travail - De La Guerre Froide à Un Nouvel Ordre Mondial* (Seuil 2004) 139 et seq.; Maupain, *The Future of the International Labour Organization in the Global Economy* (n 6) 9.

decline and the level of unionization of workers has been decreasing.[127] This has given rise to claims that the ILO's tripartite structure, dependent on the existence of representative associations of workers and employers, would no longer be sufficient for truly universal representation of non-governmental actors.[128] However, the ILO, while endorsing cooperation with other non-governmental organizations,[129] has consistently shown resistance against reforming the tripartite model. As the ILO Director-General put it in his 2013 report to the Conference:

> Clearly, and importantly, the representative function in the world of work belongs – and can only belong – to governments, with their democratic mandate, and to representative and independent organizations of employers and workers. The same principle has always applied to all decision-making structures in the ILO and will continue to do so. There can be no dilution of that tripartite mandate; it cannot be shared with other organizations, however visible or expert they may be, and however aligned with the objectives of the ILO. That implies no adverse appreciation of their value and standing, but rather a recognition of their distinctive character.[130]

That being said, the new challenge to universality persists. Newly emerging machinery for participation and inclusion of non-governmental organizations, e.g. in bilateral or regional economic agreements, go beyond tripartism and include further actors, including in labour matters.[131] Such machinery manifests an alternative model of universality which deviates from the ILO's.

II. Challenges to Persuasion

Throughout its history, the fundamental choice for governance by persuasion has faced challenges. Many of the ILO's conventions only achieved a small number of ratifications, some of them so few that they never entered into force. Similarly, the persuasive value of public shaming in the ILO's supervisory system is regularly named as an example for 'toothlessness' in critical comments on the ILO's capacity

[127] On this and other relevant developments see ILO, 'Changing Patterns in the World of Work, Report of the Director-General' (n 52).

[128] See ILO, 'Towards the ILO Centenary: Realities, Renewal and Tripartite Commitment, Report of the ILO Director-General' (n 42) para 88 et seqq.; Milman-Silvan (n 64) 205 et seqq.

[129] See Part II A of the 2008 Declaration on Social Justice for a Fair Globalization, ILO, 'Towards the ILO Centenary: Realities, Renewal and Tripartite Commitment, Report of the ILO Director-General' (n 42) para 98.

[130] ibid 97.

[131] See Jan Orbie, Lore van den Putte and Deborah Martens, 'Civil Society Meetings in European Union Free Trade Agreements: The Purposes Unravelled' in Henner Gött (ed), *Labour Standards in International Economic Law* (Springer 2018). See further Henner Gött, '"Legitimation durch den, den es Angeht?" - Die Einbindung der Zivilgesellschaft in die Transatlantische Regulierungszusammenarbeit aus demokratischer Perspektive' in Sinthiou Buszewski, Stefan Martini and Hannes Rathke (eds), *Freihandel vs. Demokratie* (Nomos 2016).

to effectively regulate labour issues.[132] Notwithstanding the fact that a persuasive model was perhaps the only viable option to make the ILO's vision of universal tripartite social dialogue work in reality, and notwithstanding the undeniable positive results of the ILO's work in many areas, the generally perceived underperformance of persuasion contributed to a nimbus of weakness. Persuasion, it seems, is simply 'not enough' to improve labour conditions.

Partly as a consequence thereof, a major—albeit somewhat indirect—challenge to the ILO's persuasive model came with the famous 'social clause' debate in the 1990s.[133] The establishment of the WTO in 1995 had brought about a new and powerful IO with an adjudicatory dispute settlement system and the possibility to impose 'trade sanctions' (suspension of trade benefits) as a means of enforcement.[134] The WTO's inception reinvigorated demands for a 'social clause', i.e. to integrate labour standards into WTO law, thus making these standards enforceable through the 'hard' WTO dispute settlement system.[135] The underlying premise of this proposal was that the ILO's own mechanisms were insufficient.

As is well-known, the idea of a social clause in the WTO eventually failed.[136] Yet, the idea of trade-labour linkages has survived and experienced a certain revival in the context of bilateral and regional trade agreements. The USA, the EU and other economies now regularly include labour chapters in their respective agreements.[137]

---

[132] For example, Reed and Yates contend that the ILO "has at best a symbolic role to play in improving labour rights and minimum working conditions", Austina Reed and Charlotte Yates, 'The ILO Declaration on Fundamental Principles and Rights at Work: The Limitations to Global Labour Standards' in Maureen Irish (ed), *The Auto Pact: Investment, Labour, and the WTO* (Kluwer Law International 2004) 243.

[133] For an account see e.g. Virginia A Leary, 'The WTO and the Social Clause: Post-Singapore' (1997) 8 European Journal of International Law 118; Friedl Weiss, 'Trade and Labor I' in Patrick FJ Macrory, Arthur E Appleton and Michael G Plummer (eds), *The World Trade Organization: Legal, Economic and Political Analysis* (Springer 2005).

[134] On WTO dispute settlement, see Peter-Tobias Stoll, 'World Trade Organization, Dispute Settlement', *Max Planck Encyclopedia of Public International Law* (Oxford University Press 2014) and Michael Koebele, 'World Trade Organization, Enforcement System', *Max Planck Encyclopedia of Public International Law* (Oxford University Press 2011), with further references.

[135] Christian Barry and Sanjay G Reddy, *International Trade and Labor Standards: A Proposal for Linkage* (Columbia University Press 2008).

[136] WTO Ministerial Conference, Singapore Ministerial Declaration (13 December 1996) WT/MIN (96)/DEC, para 4; Charnovitz, 'The International Labour Organization in Its Second Century' (n 53) 159 et seq.; Peter-Tobias Stoll, 'International Economic and Social Dimensions: Divided or Connected?' in Henner Gött (ed), *Labour Standards in International Economic Law* (Springer 2018) 11, 27; Simon Pahle, 'The Rise and Demise of the "Social Clause" Proposal in the 1990s: Implications of a Discourse Theoretical Reading' (2010) 51 Labor History 389.

[137] For an overview see ILO, *The Social Dimensions of Free Trade Agreements* (ILO 2013); ILO, *Assessment of Labour Provisions in Trade and Investment Arrangements* (ILO 2016). Furthermore, labour provisions are also included in Generalized Systems of Preferences on enhanced market access for developing countries, see e.g. Jeffrey Vogt, 'A Little Less Conversation: The EU and the (Non)Application of Labour Conditionality in the Generalized System of Preferences (GSP)' (2015) 31 The International Journal of Comparative Labour Law and Industrial Relations 284.

Some of them, notably the USA and Canada, have consistently included mechanisms for inter-state arbitration which can, as a last resort, result in suspensions of trade benefits or the payment of fines.[138] The relevance of these developments has been overshadowed by the general underperformance of the respective mechanisms.[139] That being said, labour chapters are likely to remain a feature of future agreements, and discussions as to their improvement are ongoing.[140] From the ILO's perspective, one of the most central questions is how to reconcile them with its own persuasive approach.[141]

III. Challenges to Tripartite Social Dialogue: The Post 2012 Constitutional Crisis

Finally, and perhaps most significantly, tripartite social dialogue has come under pressure, too. The historical challenge, the centralized model of labour governance employed by socialist states as the 'reified antithesis' to the pluralist ILO model, has already been mentioned above. However, the end of the Cold War and the vanishing of the socialist model did not put the challenges to tripartism to an end. Instead, the challenges merely started to come from a different direction. This section will exemplify the persisting challenges to tripartism by focusing on a crisis of the tripartite model that escalated within the ILO in 2012. The relevance of this crisis both for the ILO in general and for this study in particular merits a closer analysis.

[138] Patrick Abel, 'Comparative Conclusions on Arbitral Dispute Settlement in Trade-Labour Matters Under US FTAs' in Henner Gött (ed), *Labour Standards in International Economic Law* (Springer 2018) 174 et seq.

[139] For an empirical account see e.g. Rainer Dombois, Erhard Hornberger and Jens Winter, *Internationale Arbeitsregulierung in der Souveränitätsfalle - Das Lehrstück des NAALC* (LIT Verlag 2004); Rainer Dombois, 'Sozialklauseln Im US-Freihandelsabkommen: Ein Wirksames Mittel Internationaler Arbeitsregulierung?' (2006) 13 Industrielle Beziehungen 238.

[140] See e.g. Axel Marx, Franz Christian Ebert and Nicholas Hachez, 'Dispute Settlement for Labour Provisions in EU Free Trade Agreements: Rethinking Current Approaches' (2017) 5 Politics and Governance 49; Henner Gött, 'An Individual Labour Complaint Procedure for Workers, Trade Unions, Employers and NGOs in Future Free Trade Agreements' in Henner Gött (ed), *Labour Standards in International Economic Law* (Springer 2018).

[141] Jordi Agustí-Panareda, Franz Christian Ebert and Desirée LeClercq, 'Labour Provisions in Free Trade Agreements: Fostering Their Consistency with the ILO Standards System' (2014) Background Paper Social Dimensions Of Free Trade Agreements 5. For a detailed textual proposal see Peter-Tobias Stoll, Henner Gött and Patrick Abel, 'A Model Labour Chapter for Future EU Trade Agreements' in Henner Gött (ed), *Labour Standards in International Economic Law* (Springer 2018).

1. From Cold War to Crisis

During the Cold War, there had been a kind of tacit truce between employers and workers within the ILO. There have always been tensions and disagreement between the two groups. However, facing communism as a realistic systemic alternative, employers were more eager to make concessions within the ILO in order not to jeopardize social peace in the 'Western' pluralistic social model.[142] As part of this truce, the employers had accepted over decades that the International Labour Office and the ILO's supervisory bodies would render interpretations and 'soft law jurisprudence' which interpreted ILO conventions in an dynamic and at times rather generous manner. A prime case in point was the long-established view of the supervisory bodies that the right to strike was an "intrinsic corollary" of freedom of association and thus protected by ILO Convention No 87, although it was not explicitly mentioned in the text of that convention.[143]

With the fall of the Berlin Wall, the tacit truce between workers and employers began to wither. Presumably reinforced by the decline of socialism and by the orthodox liberal *zeitgeist*, the employers began to bargain more assertively and to oppose tripartite compromises that had become established ILO practice during the Cold War.[144] In particular, the employers began to voice their unease with the perceived expansive interpretation of ILO conventions by the supervisory bodies.[145]

This unease fully discharged in June 2012. What happened, in essence, was that the employers' group announced during the 2012 International Labour Conference that they would refuse to further participate in the ILO's supervisory mechanism unless the interpretative competence of the CEACR was clarified by an explicit disclaimer in its annual report stating that the report and the interpretations therein were

> not an agreed or determinative text of the ILO tripartite constituents.[146]

The employers added that, should this clarification not be inserted, they would refuse to discuss cases involving 'problematic' interpretations in the CAS—as seen above, an essential element in the ILO's supervisory procedure.[147]

---

[142] Francis Maupain, 'The ILO Regular Supervisory System: A Model in Crisis?' (2013) 10 International Organizations Law Review 117, 123 et seq. This is in line with one of the main reasons that stood for the ILO's initial conception in 1919 – the threat of Bolshevism after the Russian Revolution in 1917, Servais (n 11) 21.

[143] Tonia Novitz, *International and European Protection of the Right to Strike* (Oxford University Press 2003) 192 et seqq.

[144] La Hovary, 'The ILO's Mandate and Capacity: Creating, Proliferating and Supervising Labour Standards for a Globalized Economy' (n 26) 45.

[145] Alfred Wisskirchen, 'The Standard-Setting and Monitoring Activity of the ILO: Legal Questions and Practical Experience' (2005) 144 International Labour Review 253, 273 et seqq.

[146] ILO, 'Report of the Committee on the Application of Standards Part One: General Report' (International Labour Conference, 101st Session May-June 2012) Provisional Record 19(Rev.) Part I, para 150.

[147] ibid.

The employers' request resembled a major escalation, mainly because it was not provoked by any immediate incident inside the ILO and it was backed by the threat to paralyze the tripartite functioning of the CAS, and, in consequence, of the ILO's entire regular supervisory procedure.[148] The ramifications of the employers' conduct can safely be described as existential for the ILO: The employers' threat concerned the organization's tripartite structure and working method, and it was understood as such by the other constituents and by commentators.[149] Furthermore, the threat of paralyzing tripartite procedures as a means to coerce concessions could easily be transferred to other activities than supervision, given that tripartism permeates the entire organization.[150] Therefore, it is not surprising that the request sparked a veritable constitutional crisis within the ILO.

2. The Employers' Claim Regarding 'Tripartite Ownership'

The employers' main argument was that the CEACR (and also the Office) had adopted and maintained interpretations of ILO instruments which exceeded these bodies' functions and mandate, and which were given undue argumentative weight outside the ILO. The prime case of concern was the CEACR's well-established view that the right to strike forms an intrinsic corollary of freedom association.[151]

The employers' statements of 2012 have as a general theme the issue of "ownership" of the interpretation of ILO instruments. In this vein, they complained that

> tripartite ownership of ILO standards supervision had been lost sight of, since the role of ILO tripartite constituents had been reduced to providing information and giving more visibility to the supervisory activities of the Committee of Experts and the Office.[152]

In the employers' view,

---

[148] The employers "indicated that, to maintain the credibility and coherence of the Employers' group, their views and actions in all areas of ILO action relating to the Convention and the right to strike would be materially influenced", ibid 82; La Hovary, 'The ILO and the Interpretation of Fundamental Rights at Work: A Closer Look at Establishing a Tribunal under Article 37(2)' (n 109) 49 et seqq.

[149] La Hovary, 'The ILO's Mandate and Capacity: Creating, Proliferating and Supervising Labour Standards for a Globalized Economy' (n 26) 46 et seqq.

[150] La Hovary, 'The ILO and the Interpretation of Fundamental Rights at Work: A Closer Look at Establishing a Tribunal under Article 37(2)' (n 109) 58.

[151] The employers' immediate reference point was the CEACR's General Survey, which, for the first time, covered all eight fundamental ILO conventions. In particular, the employers were concerned that the Survey contained the CEACR's view on the right to strike, which the employers objected to, and that the General Survey contained a significant number of observations on ILO Convention No 87, most of which concerned the right to strike. Besides, they extended their argument to interpretations rendered by the International Labour Office.

[152] ILO, 'Report of the Committee on the Application of Standards Part One: General Report' (n 146), para 48. Rather, in the employers' view, the CEACR "should do its work within an agreed tripartite framework", ibid 51.

> [t]he Employer members believed that ILO standards supervision, like any other ILO activity, should be at the service of ILO's tripartite constituents, and that the outcome of ILO standards supervision should reflect their needs.[153]

Based on this view, they sought to strengthen the role of tripartite bodies vis-à-vis the non-tripartite CEACR and Office. They argued that

> ILO standards were politically negotiated texts and, in case of problems of application or ratification, the body that had created those standards [i.e. the Conference - hg] should be able to review those matters and take a decision. It was not the role of the Committee of Experts to determine the development of standards application.[154]

The employers' argument was not confined to the ILO's internal distribution of competences. Importantly for the present study, it had an 'outward looking' dimension. The employers were particularly troubled by the reception of the CEACR's interpretations outside the ILO. They stated that

> the critical issue was that its observations were being viewed by the outside world as a form of soft law labour standards jurisprudence. Moreover, the ILO fundamental Conventions were embedded in several instruments outside the ILO, including the UN Global Compact, the OECD Guidelines, the UN Human Rights Council's "Protect, Respect and Remedy" Framework, the ISO 26000, etc.[155]

The employers' main concern was that the "outside world" would not sufficiently appreciate the fundamental role of tripartism for the ILO supervisory system:

> [The CAS] is the apex of the supervisory system and this must be respected. Outside of the ILO, this important distinction is either misunderstood or forgotten, and [the CEACR's] General Surveys are seen as being the position of the Organization which they are not. It would be damaging if the experts' views were taken as the views of the Organization in other United Nations or international forums. It undermines tripartite relationships and weakens the ILO supervisory machinery.[156]

They took a similar view regarding the International Labour Office's interpretations, stressing that

---

[153]ILO, 'Report of the Committee on the Application of Standards Part One: General Report' (n 146), para 48.

[154]ibid 49. As to the right to strike the employers argued that "[f]or instance, the following issues concerning the right to strike should be discussed on a tripartite basis, rather than left to the experts to develop on their own: lawful strikes, including sympathy strikes and political strikes; essential services, especially if on a narrow basis; legality of workplace occupations during strikes; legality of picketing; dissuasive sanctions for illegal strikes." ILO, 'Report of the Committee on the Application of Standards: Submission, Discussion, and Approval, Record of Proceedings' (International Labour Conference, 101st Session, May-June 2012) No 27 4. Tonia Novitz, 'The Restricted Right to Strike: "Far-Reaching" ILO Jurisprudence on the Public Sector and Essential Services' (2017) 38 Comparative Labor Law and Policy Journal 353, 359.

[155]ILO, 'Report of the Committee on the Application of Standards Part One: General Report' (n 146), paras 49 and 82.

[156]ILO, 'Report of the Committee on the Application of Standards: Submission, Discussion, and Approval, Record of Proceedings' (n 154) 3.

> the Office was not the ILO and that the ILO was the governments, workers and employers. The Office should therefore exercise restraint when referring to or promoting the views of the Committee of Experts, as they could be deemed to be the views of the ILO in other UN or international forums, which would undermine tripartite relationships and weaken the ILO supervisory machinery.[157]

The workers, largely taken by surprise, refused to continue work in the CAS at gunpoint. After the employers insisted on the requested clarification of the CEACR's interpretative competences, the 2012 International Labour Conference did not adopt a CAS report at all. For the first time ever, the ILO's supervisory procedure had reached an impasse.[158]

3. Subsequent Developments

In the following years, the CEACR successively 'clarified' its mandate in limiting language. In 2013, the CEACR issued a general statement in its report, in which it stated that its interpretations are non-binding both inside and outside the ILO unless another instrument of international law or domestic law explicitly recognized them as such.[159] It also argued that it needed to establish the meaning and legal scope of ILO conventions to perform its duties, and that, for the sake of legality and legal certainty, such interpretations should be considered valid and recognized unless contradicted by the ICJ.[160] This did not satisfy the employers, who pushed for further concessions. In its 2014 report, the CEACR rephrased its 2013 explanation, this time highlighting that it conducted "impartial and technical analysis", that its "non-binding" opinions and recommendations "derive their persuasive value from the legitimacy and rationality of the Committee's work" and that the international recognition of the Committee's conclusions and reports are based on the CEACR's "technical role and moral authority".[161] This decisively limiting interpretation of the CEACR's mandate was recognized by workers and employers in a joint statement in 2015[162] and has appeared in subsequent CEACR reports.[163] However, immediately

---

[157] ILO, 'Report of the Committee on the Application of Standards Part One: General Report' (n 146) para 50.

[158] Maupain, 'The ILO Regular Supervisory System: A Model in Crisis?' (n 142) 122.

[159] ILO, 'Collective Bargaining in the Public Service: A Way Forward, General Survey of the Committee of Experts on the Application of Conventions and Recommendations Concerning Labour Relations and Collective Bargaining in the Public Service' (2013) ILC.102/III/1B para 6.

[160] ibid 8.

[161] All quotes taken from ILO, 'Report of the Committee of Experts on the Application of Conventions and Recommendations: General Report and Observations Concerning Particular Countries' (International Labour Conference, 104th Session, 2015) ILC.104/III(1A) para 29.

[162] ILO, 'The ILO Standards Initiative – Joint Statement of Workers' & Employers' Groups' (23 February 2015) TMFAPROC/2015/2 2.

[163] E.g. in ILO, 'Report of the Committee of Experts on the Application of Conventions and Recommendations: General Report and Observations Concerning Particular Countries' (International Labour Conference, 106th Session, 2017) ILC.106/III(1A) para 17.

after the joint statement was signed, the employers reiterated their position that the right to strike was not protected under ILO Convention No 87, and urged the CEACR to change its interpretation on this matter.[164] While the 2015 Conference adopted a CAS report, solving the imminent deadlock in the regular supervisory procedure, the employers insistence shows that the underlying crisis of tripartism persists.[165]

4. Assessment

While the worst symptoms of the crisis seem to have been glossed over by solving the deadlock in the CAS, the crisis of tripartism is far from solved. The 'compromise' of rephrasing the CEACR's mandate was forced upon the Committee by the employers. On a more fundamental level, the 2012 events substantially compromised the fragile trust between employers and workers within the ILO.

As to the immediate subject-matter—the question whether the right to strike was protected by ILO Convention No 87—the employers' case is markedly weak, as several studies have convincingly argued.[166] In addition, there was no real issue of disregard for tripartism to begin with, since it was the (tripartite) CFA which first accepted the right to strike as an intrinsic corollary of freedom of association in 1952.[167] However, given the high systemic relevance of the employers' conduct, the actual merits of their arguments appear almost secondary. The post-2012 crisis is a prime example of one group's power to obstruct the ILO's system if placing group interests over institutional interests. This puts the other constituents—especially the workers—in a precarious position, since there is a continuous latent threat that employers will resort to obstructive behaviour again whenever the workers demand 'too much'.

It is also worth noting that even in the wake of the crisis, the ILO's constituents could not agree on taking action under Art. 37 ILO Constitution, i.e. to refer the issue of the right to strike to the ICJ or to establish an inhouse tribunal to decide the matter. In 2014, the International Labour Office prepared a detailed report on possible action to be taken under that provision.[168] This report included detailed operational proposals: A draft letter submitting the current dispute to the ICJ,[169] which the workers

[164]Claire La Hovary, 'The 2015 ILC and the Right to Strike: Business as Usual?' (2015) 22 International Union Rights 16.

[165]ibid 17.

[166]Janice R Bellace, 'The ILO and the Right to Strike' (2015) 153 International Labour Review 29, 31 et seqq.

[167]ibid 47.

[168]ILO, 'The Standards Initiative: Follow-up to the 2012 ILC Committee on the Application of Standards' (2014) GB.322/INS/5.

[169]ibid Appendix II.

supported but the employers opposed, and a draft statute for an in-house tribunal.[170] However, both options were deferred (indefinitely) in subsequent Governing Body meetings.[171] It has been suggested that the employers seek to avoid a legal solution of the right to strike question in order to maintain a state of pressure and uncertainty, to be of use in ongoing discussions on the reform of the ILO's supervisory system.[172] Be that as it may, the previous 'internalization' of supervision on grounds of tripartite rationales seems to fire back at the ILO now that tripartite social dialogue seems unable to resolve a question of interpretation.

All in all, the post-2012 constitutional crisis exemplifies in all clarity that tripartite social dialogue is fragile. Even more importantly for this study, it is extremely sensitive to exogenous influences. This is of course true for major geopolitical or economic developments, such as the end of the Cold War or a massive surge in market liberalization and economic globalization. However, as the employers' 2012 statements illustrate, tripartism can already be shaken by events that are of a much smaller scale, such as the fact that ILO standards and the supervisory bodies' and the Office's accompanying interpretations are increasingly being referred to by other institutions. Notwithstanding the boldness of the employers' claim, they have raised a point of systemic interest when arguing that other institutions might not sufficiently take into account the tripartite underpinnings of ILO instruments and supervisory practice. The right to strike was a doubtful case to make this argument of principle, and it is highly questionable whether the employers acted in good faith when using it to obstruct the entire supervisory system, endanger the fragile trust between the social partners and take the entire organization into proverbial headlock. Be that as it may, the point is that a 'mishandling' of tripartism by other institutions can have severe repercussions on tripartite social dialogue within the ILO, as the example has aptly shown.

E. Conclusion

This chapter has expounded the ILO's model of labour governance. It has introduced the ILO's objectives, its organizational structure, its activities, instruments and some of its most relevant procedures. It has done so in the light of the two fundamental choices on which the ILO was built, namely the choice for universal tripartite social

---

[170] ibid.

[171] ILO, 'The Standards Initiative: Follow-up to the 2012 ILC Committee on the Application of Standards, Revised Draft Decision Following the Governing Body Debate Held on 11 November 2014' (2014) GB.322/INS/5(Add.2) para 1 and 6; ILO, 'The Standards Initiative' (2015) GB.323/INS/5 para 25 lit. b. The in-house tribunal option was only supported by a small minority, while others considered a long-term solution only or even openly rejected it. The option to refer the dispute to the ICJ found support by the workers. The employers, which initially had been open, objected to such a referral in 2014. Moreover, government support was weak.

[172] La Hovary, 'The 2015 ILC and the Right to Strike: Business as Usual?' (n 164) 17.

dialogue and the choice for persuasion as the means to give effect to its instruments and policies. As has been shown, these choices deeply permeate the ILO's organizational structure and activities. Tripartism, on which this chapter put emphasis, determines the composition of ILO organs and bodies, the creation of labour standards and their further life cycle post-ratification, including their supervision.

This chapter has also illustrated that the ILO's model is fragile and has been subject to constant challenges. While some challenges, like attaining universal membership, have effectively been overcome today, others have dramatically aggravated, such as the still unresolved crisis of tripartism that escalated in 2012. The ILO's model is vulnerable to external influences, including not only major political or economic changes, but also other, less exceptional events, such a perceived 'mishandling' of triparism's intrinsic connection to labour standards by other institutions.

3. The Phenomenon and the Concept of Inter-Organizational Interactions

The ILO is frequently described as 'the' IO in the field of labour governance.[1] Without a doubt, it is a central IO in this field, and in many ways the most 'important'. Nonetheless, it is not the *only* one. If the ILO has ever really possessed an island position at all, it has lost it long ago.[2] It nowadays finds itself among a broad variety of IOs which, in one or the other way, are dealing with labour issues. The existence of such other IOs engaging in multi-institutional labour governance has frequently been noticed and discussed both in academia and practice. What has attracted less attention is the fact that the ILO and those other IOs not merely coexist, but *interact*, and that this interaction is a ubiquitous phenomenon that has a significant impact on both the ILO and those other IOs.

Multi-institutional labour governance and inter-organizational interaction are complex phenomena. In order to fully grasp their relevance and implications, it is necessary to tentatively chart their various dimensions. This exercise entails a brief account of other IOs' engagement in labour issues and of these IOs' various interactions with the ILO (A.). Moreover, it is necessary to unfold the concept of inter-organizational interaction and its different facets (B.).

---

[1]This terminology, indicating exclusivity, also appears in its own instruments see e.g. preambular clause 6 of the 1998 Declaration, which stipulates that "the ILO is the constitutionally mandated international organization and the competent body to set and deal with international labour standards, and enjoys universal support and acknowledgement in promoting Fundamental Rights at Work as the expression of its constitutional principles".

[2]Indeed, it never really had it in the first place, see the early inter-organizational interactions referred to by Steve Charnovitz, 'The International Labour Organization in Its Second Century' (2000) 4 Max Planck Yearbook of United Nations Law 147, 178.

H. Gött, *The Law of Interactions Between International Organizations*, Beiträge zum ausländischen öffentlichen Recht und Völkerrecht 299, https://doi.org/10.1007/978-3-662-62389-3_3

A. Multi-Institutional Labour Governance and the Phenomenon of Inter-Organizational Interactions

Besides the ILO, there is a vast number of other IOs working, in one way or another, on labour-relevant issues (I.). The ILO and these other IOs do not merely coexist and work in parallel, but interact with each other (II.).

I. 'Parallel' Labour Governance by Other IOs

Notwithstanding the ILO's exposed position in labour governance, there are numerous other IOs that work on labour issues. These IOs' mandates, means and structures differ from the ILO's, and hardly any of them would consider itself a dedicated labour governance organization. Nevertheless, their respective constitutional configurations and actual activities touch on issues the ILO is dealing with as well. Such overlaps can be small and isolated, or comprehensive and far-reaching, as the case may be. Either way, these overlaps lead to a situation of multi-institutional labour governance by the ILO and other IOs.

The following paragraphs will, without any claim to exhaustiveness, provide a short overview on a number of other IOs dealing with labour issues. For the purposes of this survey, 'labour issue' means any subject-matter the regulation of which also falls within the scope of the ILO.[3] As indicated before, the ILO's ambit is markedly broad, which inevitably results in overlaps with a large number of other IOs' activities.

In theory, there can be a complete or a partial overlap between the ILO's and other IOs' activities. However, a complete overlap does not exist in practice. The only IO that has more or less the same mandate as the ILO is the Arab Labour Organization (ALO), which was established in 1965 as a regional specialized organization of the League of Arab States.[4] Like the ILO, the ALO is mandated to improve working conditions by creating and supervising (its own) labour conventions and recommendations, as well as further activities.[5] However, the ALO's activities have been rather limited, and its impact has been assessed as low.[6] Therefore, despite perhaps being the ILO's closest 'relative', the ALO will not be considered further here.

---

[3]This 'ILO-centric' understanding is appropriate for the purposes of this study, naturally without denying the possibility that a different understanding might be better-suited in other contexts.

[4]League of Arab States (Council) Res No 2102 d/43 (21 March 1965). The ALO obtained specialized agency status on 8 January 1970 at the fifth Conference of Arab Labour Ministers, UIA, 'Arab Labour Organization (ALO)' (*UIA Open Yearbook*, 2015).

[5]Franz Christian Ebert and Claire La Hovary, 'International Labour Law', *Max Planck Encyclopedia of Public International Law* (Oxford University Press 2013) para 15 et seq.

[6]Abdellah Boudahrain, *The Arab Labour Organization* (Kluwer Law International 1996) 117.

All other relevant IOs have mandates that overlap only partially with the ILO's, i.e. they deal with labour issues and additional other topics, they only deal with specific labour issues, or they deal with labour issues from a certain perspective. The IOs with partially overlapping mandates are numerous and can only be presented here in a sketchy manner.

Among the IOs with universal or quasi-universal membership, a first major actor is the UN.[7] The UN engages in aspects of labour governance both through its primary organs and through its subsidiary bodies and legally dependent programmes and funds. The UN's engagement in labour issues is based on the UN Charter, notably the latter's provisions on the protection and promotion of human rights (Arts. 1(3) and 55 lit. c UN Charter) and on economic and social cooperation, including regarding full employment and conditions of economic and social progress (Art. 1(3) UN Charter, Art. 55 lit. a and b UN Charter). Labour issues have—early on and repeatedly—appeared on the agenda of the UN's principal organs, especially ECOSOC and the UNGA, and have been dealt within instruments adopted by them.[8] They have likewise been addressed by various other UN entities and been included in instruments created under the auspices of the UN. Examples include the array of work-related rights laid down in UN human rights instruments[9] and dealt with by the OHCHR, the UN Human Rights Council, the HRC, the CESCR and further bodies.[10] The issues covered are core ILO topics, such as freedom of

[7]The ILO is itself a UN specialized agency and integrated into the UN System.

[8]E.g. ECOSOC, 'Creating an Environment at the National and International Levels Conducive to Generating Full and Productive Employment and Decent Work for All, and Its Impact on Sustainable Development' Ministerial Declaration (5 July 2006) UN Doc E/2006/L.8; UNGA Res 63/230 (19 December 2008) UN Doc A/RES/63/230.

[9]E.g. Arts. 4, 20, 22 – 25 Universal Declaration of Human Rights (UNGA Res 217 A (III) (10 December 1948) UN Doc A/RES/3/217 A) (UDHR), Arts. 8 and 22 International Covenant on Civil and Political Rights (adopted and opened for signature, ratification and accession by General Assembly resolution 2200A (XXI) of 16 December 1966, entered into force 23 March 1976) 999 UNTS 171 (ICCPR), Art. 8 International Covenant on Economic, Social and Cultural Rights (adopted and opened for signature, ratification and accession by General Assembly resolution 2200A (XXI) of 16 December 1966, entered into force 3 January 1976) 993 UNTS 3 (ICESCR), Art. 5 International Convention on the Elimination of All Forms of Racial Discrimination (adopted and opened for signature and ratification by General Assembly resolution 2106 (XX) of 21 December 1965, entered into force 4 January 1969) 660 UNTS 195 (CERD), Art. 11 Convention on the Elimination of All Forms of Discrimination against Women (adopted and opened for signature, ratification and accession by General Assembly resolution 34/180 of 18 December 1979, entered into force 3 September 1981) 1249 UNTS 13 (CEDAW), Art. 32 Convention on the Rights of the Child (adopted 20 November 1989, entered into force 2 September 1990) 1577 UNTS 3 (CRC); Jean-Michel Servais, *International Labour Law* (4th edn, Kluwer Law International 2014) 94 et seqq.: Peter-Tobias Stoll, 'International Economic and Social Dimensions: Divided or Connected?' in Henner Gött (ed), *Labour Standards in International Economic Law* (Springer 2018) 11, 17.

[10]Christine Kaufmann, *Globalisation and Labour Rights. The Conflict Between Core Labour Rights and International Economic Law* (Hart Publishing 2007) 29 et seqq.; Servais (n 9) 94.

association,[11] gender equality,[12] racial discrimination,[13] or child labour.[14] Moreover, the UN Migrant Worker Convention of 1990 is a UN-facilitated and administered human rights treaty with a dedicated focus on labour rights.[15] However, the UN's engagement on labour issues is not confined to its work on human rights, but also spreads to other areas of UN activities. For instance, labour issues are also

---

[11]See Arts. 22 ICCPR and 8 ICESCR.

[12]For instance, Art. 11(1) CEDAW requires the parties to take appropriate measures to eliminate discrimination against women in the field of employment in order to ensure a number of labour-related rights. Art. 11(2) CEDAW imposes further obligations aiming for preventing discrimination on the grounds of marriage or maternity, whereas Art. 14(d) and (e) CEDAW addresses labour-related rights of rural women. The UN Committee for the Elimination of All Forms of Discrimination against Women has adopted a number of labour-related general comments and has, inter alia, recommended the ratification of ILO conventions, see UN Committee for the Elimination of All Forms of Discrimination against Women, 'General Recommendation No 13, Equal Remuneration for Work of Equal Value' (Eighth session, 1989) UN Doc A/44/38 para 76.

[13]The preamble of CERD explicitly refers to ILO Convention No 158 (ILO Termination of Employment Convention, 1982 (No 158) (adopted 22 June 1982, entered into force 23 November 1985) 1412 UNTS 1; CERD, Preambular Clause 11). Art. 5 CERD obliges the parties to prohibit and eliminate racial discrimination to a plethora of rights, including the rights to work, to free choice of employment, to just and favourable conditions of work, to protection against unemployment, to equal pay for equal work, to just and favourable remuneration (Art. 5(e)(i) CERD) and the right to form and join trade unions (Art. 5(e)(ii) CERD).

[14]For example, Art. 32 CRC contains the right of children to be protected from economic exploitation and hazardous work (see also Principle 9 of the 1959 UN Declaration on the Rights of the Child (UNGA Res 1386(XIV) (20 November 1959) UN Doc A/RES/14/1386). The 2000 Optional Protocol to the Convention on the Rights of the Child on the sale of children, child prostitution and child pornography (adopted and opened for signature, ratification and accession by UNGA resolution A/RES/54/263 of 25 May 2000, entered into force 18 January 2002) 2171 UNTS 227, requires the parties to penalize the sale of children, child prostitution and child pornography (Art. 3). Moreover, the 2000 Optional Protocol to the Convention on the Rights of the Child on the involvement of children in armed conflict, (adopted and opened for signature, ratification and accession by UNGA resolution A/RES/54/263 of 25 May 2000, entry into force 12 February 2002) 2173 UNTS 222, requires its parties to ensure that children under the age of 18 are not compulsorily recruited into the armed forces (Art. 2). See furthermore UN Committee on the Rights of the Child, 'General Comment No. 16 on State Obligations Regarding the Impact of the Business Sector on Childrens' Rights' (17 April 2013) CRC/C/GC/16.

[15]International Convention on the Protection of the Rights of All Migrant Workers and Members of Their Families (adopted by General Assembly Resolution 45/158 of 18 December 1990, entered into force 1 July 2003) 2220 UNTS 3 (ICMW). Besides a comprehensive body of substantive standards, the ICMW foresees a dedicated role for the International Labour Office in its procedural provisions. In particular, pursuant to Art. 74(5) ICMW, the Committee on Migrant Workers shall invite representatives of the International Labour Office to participate in its meetings in a consultative capacity. Not surprisingly, the UN Committee on Migrant Workers has had ample recourse to ILO instruments in its practice, see e.g. UN Committee on Migrant Workers, 'General Comment No 1 on Migrant Domestic Workers' (23 February 2011) CMW/C/GC/1 paras 37, 39 and 56; UN Committee on Migrant Workers, 'General Comment No 2 on the Rights of Migrant Workers in an Irregular Situation and Members of Their Families' (28 August 2013) CMW/C/GC/2 para 12.

dealt with by UN funds and programmes, such as e.g. UNICEF,[16] UN Women[17] or UNDP.[18]

Regarding economic and financial IOs, the picture is mixed. As already mentioned, the WTO has explicitly refused to play a more active role in the promotion of labour standards.[19] On the other hand, both the IMF and the World Bank have successively developed approaches to labour issues. For instance, they have engaged in structural lending including labour market reform conditionality.[20] Besides, as will be discussed in detail in Chap. 4, the World Bank has also engaged in comparative labour market evaluations and rankings, on the basis of which it has advocated labour market deregulation.[21] While both the IMF and the World Bank have traditionally refused to engage in ostensibly 'political' activity and shown great reticence towards labour issues, at least some of the IMF's and World Bank's contemporary activities undeniably qualify as labour governance (this is of course to be distinguished from the further question whether they qualify as *good* labour governance).[22]

[16]On UNICEF's mandate on providing aid for children and promoting child welfare, which covers work-related aspects such as child labour, see for an overview UNICEF, 'Factsheet Child Labour' (*UNICEF Website*) <https://data.unicef.org/topic/child-protection/child-labour/> accessed 26 April 2020 2 et seq. See further Franziska Humbert, *The Challenge of Child Labour in International Law* (Cambridge University Press 2009) 35 et seqq.

[17]For UN Women's various initiatives on employment issues, see UN Women, 'Employment and migration' (*UN Women Website*) <http://www.unwomen.org/en/what-we-do/economic-empowerment/employment-and-migration> accessed 26 April 2020.

[18]See e.g. UNDP, *Human Development Report 2015 - Work for Human Development* (UNDP 2015) 170 et seqq. and the policy suggestions therein.

[19]See above Chap. 2 D. II.; Friedl Weiss 'Trade and Labor I' in Patrick FJ Macrory, Arthur E Appleton and Michael G Plummer (eds), *The World Trade Organization: Legal, Economic and Political Analysis Vol II* (Springer 2005) 574 et seqq. By contrast, the ill-fated International Trade Organization (ITO) would have featured fair labour standards as an issue in its constituent instrument (see Art. 7 Havana Charter), Stoll, 'International Economic and Social Dimensions: Divided or Connected?' (n 9) 18 et seqq.

[20]Suzan Kang, 'Labor and the Bank: Investigating the Politics of the World Bank's Employing Workers' Index' (2009) 14 Journal of Workplace Rights 481, 484. See generally on structural adjustment programmes Sabine Schlemmer-Schulte, 'International Monetary Fund, Structural Adjustment Programme (SAP)', *Max Planck Encyclopedia of Public International Law* (Oxford University Press 2014).

[21]See the discussion in Chap. 4 and Henner Gött, 'Interactions between International Organizations - Approaching a Neglected Governance Dimension' (2020) 17 International Organizations Law Review 75, 88 et seqq. See also Michael Riegner, *Informationsverwaltungsrecht Internationaler Organisationen. Dargestellt am Entwicklungsverwaltungsrecht der Weltbank und der Vereinten Nationen* (Mohr Siebeck 2018) 433.

[22]The IMF's and World Bank's approaches have repeatedly been subject to critique, particularly from trade unions, but also from the ILO. See the discussion in Chap. 4 below.

Outside the economic and financial arena, a broad number of further IOs engage in labour issues. These comprise e.g. the FAO,[23] the WHO,[24] the UNESCO[25] or the UNWTO.[26] A noteworthy example of a rather 'technical' IO dealing with labour issues is the IMO,[27] which has adopted its own conventions, codes and guidelines concerning issues of maritime labour.[28]

Apart from the aforementioned universal IOs, regional IOs have increased their efforts in labour governance in all regions of the world.[29] In Europe, the EU has extensively worked on labour issues and has developed an entire body of EU labour law.[30] Moreover, together with the ECB, the IMF and the ESM, the EU has promoted structural labour market reforms in some of its crisis-stricken member states.[31] Beyond the EU, the CoE, mandated inter alia to promote human rights and economic and social progress (Arts. 1 lit. a and 3 CoE-Statute), has engaged in labour-related social policy-making, included central labour-related rights into its human rights instruments, including the ECHR, the ESC and the European Code of Social Security, and has given effect to them in its practice.[32] Likewise, a number of regional IOs with a clearer economic focus have engaged in labour governance,

[23]E.g. regarding child labour in the agricultural sector, see the information provided on FAO, 'Child Labour in Agriculture' (*FAO Website*) <http://www.fao.org/childlabouragriculture/en/> accessed 26 April 2020.

[24]E.g. regarding occupational health, see WHO (World Health Assembly), 'Workers' Health: Global Plan of Action' (2007) WHA60.26.

[25]E.g. regarding vocational education, see UNESCO, *Strategy for Technical and Vocational Education and Training (TVET) (2016-2021)* (UNESCO 2016).

[26]UNWTO, *World Tourism Report 2017* (UNWTO 2018) 72 et seq.

[27]On the widespread – though rather coarse-grained – distinction between 'political' and 'technical' IOs see Jan Klabbers, *An Introduction to International Organizations Law* (3rd edn, Cambridge University Press 2015) 25.

[28]E.g. the 1978 International Convention on Standards of Training, Certification and Watchkeeping for Seafarers, 1978 (adopted 7 July 1978, entered into force on 28 April 1984) 1361 UNTS 2 (STCW Convention), Felice Morgenstern, *Legal Problems of International Organizations* (Grotius Publications 1986) 27.

[29]For an overview, see Bob Deacon and others, 'Globalisation and the Emerging Regional Governance of Labour Rights' (2011) 32 International Journal of Manpower 334.

[30]Roger Blanpain, *European Labour Law* (11th edn, Kluwer Law International 2008) 206 et seqq.; Stefano Giubbioni, 'The Rise and Fall of EU Labour Law' (2018) 24 European Law Journal 7, 10 et seqq.

[31]E.g. European Commission (Directorate-General for Economic and Financial Affairs), 'The Economic Adjustment Programme for Greece' Occasional Papers No. 61). Aristea Koukiadaki and Damian Grimshaw, *Evaluating the Effects of the Structural Labour Market Reforms on Collective Bargaining in Greece* (ILO 2016).

[32]See Chaps. 4 and 5.

e.g. the OECD,[33] MERCOSUR,[34] ASEAN[35] or SADC.[36] The same applies for regional financial organizations. For instance, the EBRD has developed and applied performance requirements on labour issues similar to those developed within the World Bank Group.[37]

II. Interactions Between the ILO and Other IOs Engaging in Labour Governance

The ILO and the other IOs interact with each other on a markedly frequent basis. Such interactions can take various forms and can have a substantial impact on the work of both the ILO and the other IOs.

The most visible examples are the numerous cooperative activities between the ILO and other IOs. To name but one example, the ILO and the IMO have engaged in a particularly long-lived and fruitful cooperation, which inter alia led to the adoption of the jointly prepared 2006 Maritime Labour Convention[38] and the drafting and

---

[33] See e.g. Chapter V of the 2011 OECD Guidelines for Multinational Enterprises, reprinted in OECD, *OECD Guidelines for Multinational Enterprises on Employment and Industrial Relations* (OECD Publishing 2011) 35 et seqq.

[34] See e.g. the MERCOSUR declarations of 1998 and 2015, MERCOSUR, 'Declaración Sociolaboral del MERCOSUR' (10 December 1998) and MERCOSUR, 'Declaración Sociolaboral del MERCOSUR 2015' (17 July 2015), María Belén Olmos Giupponi, 'Free Trade and Labour and Environmental Standards in MERCOSUR' (2014) 81 Colombia Internacional 67, 75.

[35] E.g. in the area of movement of so-called skilled labour within the envisaged ASEAN Economic Community, Sharina Farihah Hasan and others, 'ASEAN Economic Community: The Potential Impacts of Labour Mobility on the Economy and Construction Industry' (2016) 3 Journal of Scientific Research and Development 144; Flavia Jurje and Sandra Lavenex, 'ASEAN Economic Community: What Model for Labour Mobility?' (2015) NCCR Trade Working Paper No 2015/02 <http://www.nccr-trade.org/fileadmin/user_upload/nccr-trade.ch/wp4/NCCR_working_Paper_ASEAN_Jurje_Lavenex.pdf> accessed 26 April 2020.

[36] See e.g. SADC, 'Charter of the Fundamental Social Rights in SADC' (1 August 2003). Reprinted in SADC, Charter of Fundamental Social Rights in SADC (SADC 2003).

[37] Tonia Novitz, 'Core Labour Standards Conditionalities: A Means by Which to Achieve Sustainable Development?' in Julio Faundez and Celine Tan (eds), *International Economic Law, Globalization and Developing Countries* (Edward Elgar Publishing 2010) 246.

[38] Maritime Labour Convention (adopted by the International Labour Conference at its 94th (Maritime) Session (2006) entered into force 20 Aug 2013) 2951 UNTS 1. Anne Trebilcock, 'The Maritime Labour Convention 2006: Breathing Life into Art. 94 of UNCLOS' (2010) 1 LOS Reports 1, 4. Moira L McConnell, Dominick Devlin and Cleopatra Doumbia-Henry, *The Maritime Labour Convention 2006 - A Legal Primer in an Emerging Regime* (Martinus Nijhoff Publishers 2011) 37 et seqq. See further Paul J Bauer, 'The Maritime Labour Convention: An Adequate Guarantee of Seafarer Rights, or an Impediment to True Reforms?' (2008) 8 Chicago Journal of International Law 643, and the contributions in Jennifer Lavelle (ed), *The Maritime Labour Convention 2006: International Labour Law Redefined* (Routledge 2013).

adoption of further instruments and guidelines on maritime labour issues.[39] Another example is the cooperative working relationship between the ILO and the CoE, in particular regarding the ESC[40] and the European Code of Social Security.[41]

The ILO and other IOs influence each other through channels with varying degrees of formalization and institutionalization. Examples span from informal personal contacts between executive officers over exchanges of letters, memoranda of understanding and further 'intermediate' instruments to the conclusion of formally binding international agreements.[42] Examples for institutionalization comprise representation and participation in the bodies and procedures of the respective other IO as observers or otherwise,[43] or the conferral of jurisdiction over administrative disputes to the ILOAT by various other IOs.[44] Moreover, the ILO and other IOs have occasionally established joint bodies, such as the Joint ILO/UNESCO Committee of Experts on the Application of the Recommendations concerning Teaching Personnel[45] or several joint ILO-IMO ad hoc

[39]Including e.g. several guidelines, ILO, 'Monitoring and Implementation Tools for the Maritime Labour Convention, 2006' (*ILO Website*) <https://www.ilo.org/global/standards/maritime-labour-convention/monitoring-implementation-tools/lang%2D%2Den/index.htm> accessed 26 April 2020; Henner Gött, 'Interactions between International Organizations - Approaching a Neglected Governance Dimension' (n 21) 85 et seqq.

[40]European Social Charter (adopted 18 October 1961, entered into force 26 February 1965) CETS No. 35 (ESC) and European Social Charter (Revised) (adopted 3 May 1996, entered into force 1 July 1999) CETS No. 163 (RESC). The ILO-CoE cooperation is discussed in detail in Chap. 6.

[41]European Code of Social Security (adopted 16 April 1964, entered into force 17 March 1968) CETS No. 46 (ECSS) and European Code of Social Security (revised) (adopted 6 November 1990, not yet in force) CETS No. 139 (Revised ECSS). The ECSS was drawn up in collaboration of the International Labour Office, as is mentioned in the ECSS's preamble. See also Art 74(4) and (5) ECSS and Art. 79(10) Revised ECSS.

[42]For an overview on written (binding and non-binding) agreements see ILO, 'ILO Cooperation Agreements with Other International Organizations' (*ILO Website*) <https://www.ilo.org/global/about-the-ilo/how-the-ilo-works/departments-and-offices/jur/legal-instruments/WCMS_442247/lang%2D%2Den/index.htm> accessed 26 April 2020. See also the discussion in Chaps. 12 and 13 below.

[43]Such arrangements can be made in a general fashion (see e.g. Art. 1(5) Agreement between the International Labour Organisation and the Council of Europe (entered into force 23 November 1951) XXXV ILO Official Bulletin 380 (ILO-CoE) or in an ad hoc and less formalized manner, see Katherine A Hagen, 'Policy Dialogue between the International Labour Organization and the International Financial Institutions: The Search for Convergence' (2003) FES Occasional Papers No 9, 14.

[44]Art. II(5) Statute Of The Administrative Tribunal of the International Labour Organization, (adopted by the International Labour Conference on 9 October 1946), reprinted in ILO, *Statute and Rules of the Administrative Tribunal* (ILO 2019).

[45]ILO, 'Joint ILO/UNESCO Committee of Experts on the Application of the Recommendations Concerning Teaching Personnel (CEART)' (ILO Website) <https://www.ilo.org/global/industries-and-sectors/education/WCMS_364850/lang%2D%2Den/index.htm> accessed 26 April 2020.

working groups.[46] Furthermore, they have established joint programmes, such as UNAIDS.[47]

But interaction and mutual influence can also occur where there is no direct communication at all. For instance, international courts and tribunals have had recourse to ILO instruments and practice as interpretative guidance for developing, modifying or even reversing their own jurisprudence without any direct contact between them and the ILO.[48]

Furthermore, mutual influence is not limited to cooperative or otherwise 'harmonious' cases. It can also—and importantly—occur in cases of non-cooperation, incongruence and conflict. As mentioned before, the WTO's decision not to deal with labour standards[49] provided important momentum for the ILO to prepare and pronounce its 1998 Declaration on Fundamental Principles and Rights at Work.[50] For another example, an early jurisdictional challenge between the newly established UN and the ILO over the question of which would be the best forum to deal with trade union rights induced the ILO to swiftly create the CFA and its special supervisory procedure for freedom of association cases in order to 'secure' primary responsibility for trade union rights for itself.[51] The EU-IMF-induced labour market reforms in Greece, including changes in legislation on collective bargaining which severely weakened the position of trade unions, led the ILO's supervisory bodies to criticize Greece's neglecting of ILO conventions[52] and further induced the ILO to send an own high level mission to examine the situation.[53] In a similar manner, deregulatory labour market reforms, induced or requested by the World Bank either as conditionalities for financial support or as general policy advice, have had a traceable impact on ILO initiatives and activities in a range of states.[54]

---

[46]The Joint IMO/ILO Ad Hoc Expert Working Group on Liability and Compensation regarding Claims for Death, Personal Injury and Abandonment of Seafarers, the Joint IMO/ILO Ad Hoc Expert Working Group on the Fair Treatment of Seafarers in the Event of a Maritime Accident, and the Joint ILO/IMO Working Group on Medical Examinations of Seafarers and Ships' Medicine Chests, ILO, 'Joint IMO/ILO Activities on Seafarers' (*ILO Website*) <https://www.ilo.org/global/standards/maritime-labour-convention/text/WCMS_162318/lang%2D%2Den/index.htm> accessed 26 April 2020.

[47]See notably ECOSOC Res 1994/24 (26 July 1994) UN Doc E/RES/1994/24.

[48]See the detailed account on the ECtHR in Chap. 5.

[49]One catalyst was the WTO's Singapore Declaration, WTO Ministerial Conference, Singapore Ministerial Declaration (13 December 1996) WT/MIN(96)/DEC, para 4.

[50]See e.g. Virginia A Leary, 'The WTO and the Social Clause: Post-Singapore' (1997) 8 European Journal of International Law 118.

[51]Antony Evelyn Alcock, *History of the International Labour Organization* (Palgrave Macmillan 1971) 253 et seqq.

[52]See e.g. *Greece (Case No 2820)* (21 October 2010) Report of the Committee on Freedom of Association No 365 (2012) XCV ILO Official Bulletin Ser B 228 para 991.

[53]ILO, 'Report on the High Level Mission to Greece' (2011) https://www.ilo.org/wcmsp5/groups/public/@ed_norm/@normes/documents/missionreport/wcms_170433.pdf accessed 26 April 2020.

[54]See the detailed discussion in Chap. 4.

B. Conceptualizing Inter-Organizational Interactions

This study embraces the various described cases of interaction and influence between the ILO and other IOs engaged in labour governance under the generic heading of 'inter-organizational interaction'. As this term will be central for purposes of further analysis, it is convenient at this point to clarify the concept of inter-organizational interaction in general terms. This entails specifying its meaning (I.) and providing a tentative taxonomy of characteristics which inter-organizational interactions may have (II.).

I. The Concept of Inter-Organizational Interactions

As exemplified above, interactions between the ILO and other IOs are manifold in form and substance. In order to embrace the full spectrum of interrelations between IOs, some scholars have begun to use the generic term of 'interaction'.[55] The focus on interactions also seems appropriate to approach the many interrelations and the varying forms of influence between the ILO and other IOs involved in labour governance.[56]

The following paragraphs will first elaborate on the concept of interaction (1.). Subsequently, they will elaborate on the choice of this study to conceptualize these interactions as inter-organizational interactions (2.).

1. The Meanings of 'Interaction' and 'Inter-Organizational Interaction'

Interaction is not a technical legal term. In general linguistic usage, interaction may be understood as

[55]Which they mostly conceptualize as "regime interactions", see for instance Margaret A Young, *Trading Fish, Saving Fish: The Interaction Between Regimes in International Law* (Cambridge University Press 2011) 19; Sophia Kopela, 'Climate Change, Regime Interaction, and the Principle of Common but Differentiated Responsibility: The Experience of the International Maritime Organization' (2014) 24 Yearbook of International Environmental Law 70; Jeffrey L Dunoff, 'How to Avoid Regime Collisions' in Kerstin Blome and others (eds), *Contested Regime Collisions - Norm Fragmentation in World Society* (Cambridge University Press 2016) 52. Regime interaction is also the main theme of the contributions to Margaret A Young (ed), *Regime Interaction in International Law - Facing Fragmentation* (Cambridge University Press 2012). See further Siobhán McInerney-Lankford, 'Human Rights and Development: Regime Interaction and the Fragmentation of International Law' (2012) 3 World Bank Legal Review 123.

[56]The concept of 'interaction' has occasionally been used in this context, but more in a casual way, see e.g. Deirdre McCann, 'Labour Law on the Plateau: Towards Regulatory Policy for Endogenous Norms' in Alan Bogg and others (eds), *The Autonomy of Labour Law* (Hart Publishing 2015) 399.

> reciprocal action or influence.[57]

The usage in legal academic language is less clear. While interaction is increasingly gaining attention in international legal scholarship, the term itself has not yet received much attention. A number of contributions entirely refrain from elaborating on its meaning.[58] Other authors have made an effort to clarify or circumscribe the term. For instance, Dunoff describes interaction as

> the myriad ways that international actors and institutions engage with and react to one another.[59]

Pasquet, theorizing judicial dialogue, employs the term 'interaction' as an alternative to 'dialogue', in order to include "transnational legal communication"[60] that cannot be qualified as dialogue because it takes other forms.[61] Finally, some authors have endeavoured to define 'interaction', such as Nunner, who defines it as

> the syndetic and mutually influencing action between at least two actors.[62]

These circumscriptions and definitions lay the ground for the understanding of interaction relied on here. For the purposes of this study, 'interaction' describes influence of one actor on another, and may therefore be understood as

> an actor's conduct directed at having, or actually having, an effect on the conduct of another actor.

This study focuses on a particular kind of interactions, namely those between IOs. This inter-organizational interaction will be defined here as

> one IO's conduct directed at having, or actually having, an effect on the conduct of another IO.

This definition warrants some explanation:

---

[57] Oxford Living Dictionaries English (Oxford University Press 2018) entry 'interaction'.

[58] Margaret A Young, 'Introduction: The Productive Friction between Regimes' in Margaret A Young (ed), *Regime Interaction in International Law - Facing Fragmentation* (Cambridge University Press 2012); Amanda Tsangalis Rologas, 'Fisheries Subsidies under the Trans-Pacific Partnership: Towards Positive Outcomes for Global Fisheries Sustainability and Regime Interaction under International Law' (2016) 17 Melbourne Journal of International Law 445.

[59] Jeffrey L Dunoff, 'Mapping a Hidden World of International Regulatory Cooperation' (2015) 78 Law and Contemporary Problems 267, 268.

[60] Luca Pasquet, 'Dialogue or Interaction? A Non-Cosmopolitan Reading of Transjudicial Communication' in Amrei Müller and Hege Elisabeth Kjos (eds), *Judicial Dialogue and Human Rights* (Cambridge University Press 2017) 469.

[61] He associates 'dialogue' with liberal and cosmopolitan theories, while arguing that 'interaction' would also fit pluralistic theories, ibid 470 et seqq.

[62] German original: "das aufeinander bezogene und einander beeinflussende Handeln von mindestens zwei Akteuren" (translation by author), Michael Nunner, *Kooperationen internationaler Gerichte - Lösung zwischengerichtlicher Konflikte durch herrschaftsfreien Diskurs* (Mohr Siebeck 2009) 73.

Firstly, interaction is used here as a descriptive term relating to facts. It describes the interplay among IOs as it actually occurs in reality. This interplay consists of joint and separate conduct of those IOs participating in the interaction.[63]

Secondly, in order to fit under the definition, an IO's conduct must have an actual or intended effect on the conduct of another IO.[64] As such, interaction can take the form of either one IO's initializing conduct or the other IO's reactive conduct.[65] On the initializing side, conduct can be either intentionally directed at influencing others or accidentally having that effect.[66] On the reactive side, conduct can take a variety of forms. It can e.g. be embracing the external influence, it can attempt to divert the external impulse, or it can be defensive, trying to prevent external influence.

Thirdly, the term interaction is understood here to describe a single concrete act of an IO influencing another. In practice, IOs usually influence each other through a sequence of actions and reactions. These sequences are seen as a 'bundle' of several interactions.

2. Choosing an Inter-Organizational Focus

This study focuses on inter-organizational interactions. The focus on IOs is not self-evident, as there are several ways to conceptualize the protagonists of interactions. In international relations scholarship, the terms "institutional interaction"[67] and "regime interaction" have been used.[68] These conceptualizations of the protagonists mirror different terminological usages, specific research interests as well as different underlying theoretical premises.[69] As far as this study is concerned, it examines the

---

[63]The focus on conduct prepares the stage for subsequent legal analysis, because all legal norms, whether permissive, prohibitive, programmatic or other, govern (human) conduct. They all formulate deontic normative propositions – *Sollenssätze* – concerning how such conduct ought to be, see Hans Kelsen, *Reine Rechtslehre - Einleitung in die rechtswissenschaftliche Problematik (Studienausgabe der 1. Auflage 1934) Hrsg. u. Eingel. v. Matthias Jestaedt* (Mohr Siebeck 2008) 180.

[64]This part of the definition is intended to cover the whole range of possible mutual influence, including both direct and indirect interactions (on the meaning of 'indirect interactions' see below, B. II. 2.

[65]This is of course a model and therefore necessarily resembles a simplification of social reality. However, this modelling is helpful in carving out the different form of conduct in interactions.

[66]The first category could be called 'extroverted', the other 'introverted' conduct. Nunner calls these categories "monologue" and "dialogue", Nunner (n 62) 110 et seq.

[67]See e.g. Sebastian Oberthür and Thomas Gehring, 'Institutional Interaction in Global Environmental Governance: The Case of the Cartagena Protocol and the World Trade Organization' (2006) 6 Global Environmental Politics 1.

[68]'Regime interaction' being used by legal scholars as well. See the references in n 55 above.

[69]See Sebastian Oberthür and Thomas Gehring, 'Conceptual Foundations of Institutional Interaction' in Sebastian Oberthür and Thomas Gehring (eds), *Institutional Interaction in Global Environmental Governance. Synergy and Conflict among International and EU Policies* (MIT Press 2006) 26; Rafael Biermann and Joachim A Koops, 'Studying Relations Between International

factual phenomenon of interaction between the ILO and other IOs with a view to later examine the international legal framework that applies to them. Therefore, this study will regard interactions between actors—individuals or groups—who either act in the name or otherwise act in close factual connection or proximity of an IO.[70] Since this study will almost exclusively comprise examples of official activities, this exposition of the factual focus is sufficient.[71]

II. The Multidimensional Spectrum of Inter-Organizational Interactions

As becomes apparent from the overview of the ILO's interactions given above, there is not one type of inter-organizational interaction, but many. Hence, in this section, the phenomenon of inter-organizational interaction in labour governance will be further explored and structured.

It should be noted from the start that this exercise is not meant to produce clear-cut and mutually exclusive categories and distinctions. Over-emphasizing categorial distinctions would hardly be reconcilable with the complexities of each case and

---

Organizations in World Politics: Core Concepts and Challenges' in Rafael Biermann and Joachim A Koops (eds), *Palgrave Handbook on Inter-Organizational Relations in World Politics* (Palgrave Macmillan 2017). This is also one reason why they should not be transplanted into legal scholarship without reflection. For example, some political scientists who examine "institutional interaction" understand institutions in a way that significantly departs from the common usage of this term in international law. This concept of 'institution' is usually broader than 'IO' and relies on different criteria, see Oberthür and Gehring 23 et seq.; Christer Jönsson, 'IR Paradigms and Inter-Organizational Theory: Situating the Research Program Within the Discipline' in Rafael Biermann and Joachim A Koops (eds), *Palgrave Handbook on Inter-Organizational Relations in World Politics* (Palgrave Macmillan 2017) 54 et seq.

[70]The focus on IOs is, of course, a certain 'short cut', since the term 'International Organization' presupposes a certain conception of a group of natural persons in the physical sense that are deemed by the law to form a legal person. Eventually, any conduct to be considered as being conduct of an IO can be traced back to conduct of one or more individuals. For an example of such a deconstruction see Nunner (n 62) 110. It is, however, not the agenda of this study to repeat the deconstruction of the term 'International Organization' (or legal person in general) that has so ably been performed by others before, see e.g. the somewhat underappreciated work by Kelsen on legal personality, Kelsen (n 63) 62 et seqq. On IOs see Roland Portmann, *Legal Personality in International Law* (Cambridge University Press 2010) 278 et seqq.

[71]For clarity, it should be noted that the inter-organizational focus is not ignorant to the fact that conduct qualifying as inter-organizational interaction can simultaneously also be qualified as interactive conduct between other actors. For instance, one IO's conduct may at the same time influence another IO and a common member state of both IOs. Or, what will happen in many cases is that one IO's conduct is intentionally influencing a member state and at the same time accidentally influencing another IO of which that state is also a member. What is important at this stage is that the possible existence of such simultaneous interactions with other actors is fully acknowledged. However, this does not prejudice to look at IOs with a particular (and, until fairly recently, rather neglected) focus on their interactions with other IOs.

might even compromise the results of the analysis.[72] Rather, the idea is to provide a tentative taxonomy of interactions, which will further elucidate the notion of inter-organizational interaction and, at the same time, will provide a terminological reference frame for the remainder of the study.[73] In particular, the terminology introduced here will resurface during the legal analysis in Parts II and III, where it will be seen that the legal assessment of inter-organizational interactions significantly differ depending on the type of interaction.

The common denominator of this taxonomy is the definition of inter-organizational interaction provided in the previous section. From this common point of reference, inter-organizational interactions in labour governance can be ordered along four axes showing an interaction's character (1.), 'directness' (2.), formality (3.) and the stage on which it occurs (4.). These four axes will now be explained in turn.

1. The Character: A Continuum from Conflict to Integration

The first axis concerns the character of an interaction. Cases of multi-institutional labour governance and interaction between the respective IOs have received most attention in cases involving incongruences and conflict.[74] However, laying the

[72]This point was rightly made by Young, *Trading Fish, Saving Fish: The Interaction Between Regimes in International Law* (n 55) 86.

[73]Several authors have proposed taxonomies of inter-organizational interactions for different purposes. Political scientists have endeavoured to structure inter-organizational interactions along different categories to distil a research matrix. For instance, Stokke developed a taxonomy based on different kinds of 'interplay', Olav Schram Stokke, 'The Interplay of International Regimes: Putting Effectiveness Theory to Work' (2001) FNI Report 14/2001 8 et seqq. For a related account see Oberthür and Gehring 'Conceptual Foundations of Institutional Interaction' (n 69) 31 et seqq. Further distinctions have been made as to whether interactions occur between two IOs, between one IO and a member state, or between an IO and a non-member of an IO. For instance, Deshman categorizes them as "horizontal", "vertical" and diagonal" interactions, respectively, Abigail C Deshman, 'Horizontal Review Between International Organizations: A Rejoinder to Rosa Raffaelli' (2013) 24 European Journal of International Law 1201, 1201. Dunoff has proposed an elaborate research matrix of regime interactions. By way of typologizing these interactions, he outlines a 3 x 3 matrix, consisting of three different "forms" (operational, regulatory and conceptual) and three different "natures" (rationalization, expansions of jurisdiction and conflicts) of interaction, see Blome et al., 'Contested Collisions: An Introduction', in K. Blome et al. (eds.), *Contested Regime Collisions - Norm Fragmentation in World Society* (Cambridge University Press 2016) 1, at 9; Dunoff, 'How to Avoid Regime Collisions' (n 55) 58 and 74. Although Dunoff himself does not highlight the distinction between the factual and the normative, it may be added that his matrix is descriptive and refers – similar to this study – to interactions as a factual phenomenon.

[74]Outstanding examples are the WTO's outright refusal to include a 'social clause' into its own law (see above Chap. 2 D. II), labour market deregulation requested by IMF and World Bank Structural Adjustment Programmes or induced by Business Climate Indexes (see below, Chap. 4), or the significant erosion of the right to strike in the CJEU's notorious *Viking* and *Laval* decisions, Case C-438/05, *International Transport Workers Federation, Finnish Seamens Union v. Viking Line ABP and OÜ Viking Line Eesti* (ECLI:EU:C:2007:772) [2007] ECR I-10779, Case C-341/05, *Laval Un*

analytical focus on conflicts does not cover the whole array of issues in multi-institutional labour governance. To begin with, defining the meaning of 'conflict' can in itself prove a complex undertaking.[75] More fundamentally, interrelations between ILO-created labour law and the law of other IOs involved in labour governance are by far not always conflictual. There are important interrelations of a non-conflictual nature which can vastly exceed the effects of a conflict. For instance, the interrelations between ILO instruments and practice and European human rights treaties comprise, aside from occasional elements of diversion and latent conflict, powerful elements of mutual reinforcement and alignment.[76] Similarly, the relations between international labour law and international financial law comprise other aspects than just conflicts. These non-conflictual aspects would be marginalized when focusing only on conflictual cases.

This study builds on the understanding that conflictual interactions only mark one end of a whole continuum of interactions of different characters. This continuum also includes coexistence, coordination, cooperation and—in some instances—mutual reinforcement and quasi-alignment between IOs.[77]

2. Direct and Indirect Interaction

As to the second axis, interactions differ as to the 'immediateness' of conduct and effect. Some interactions are direct, whereas others are of a more indirect nature.

At first glance, the notion of 'interaction' semantically implies direct, 'physical' and presumably intentional contact between actors. Indeed, those legal scholars who have analysed inter-organizational interactions often rely on instances of direct and purposeful interaction between IOs. They refer to instances where interaction occurred 'in person', i.e. through direct dialogue purposefully initiated and maintained by the interacting participants.[78]

By contrast, various branches of social and political sciences have moved beyond such a narrow understanding and include other, indirect forms of interaction into

---

Partneri Ltd v. Svenska Byggnadsarbetareförbundet, Svenska Byggnadsarbetareförbundets Avdelning 1, Byggettan and Svenska Elektrikerförbundet (ECLI:EU:C:2007:809) [2007] I-11767. The cases have sparked a massive and overwhelmingly critical response; see Catherine Barnard, 'Viking and Laval: An Introduction' (2008) 10 Cambridge Yearbook of European Legal Studies 463. See further the contributions in Mark R Freedland and Jeremias Prassl (eds), *Viking, Laval and Beyond* (Hart Publishing 2016).

[75]See the taxonomy provided by Nele Matz, *Wege zur Koordinierung völkerrechtlicher Verträge* (Springer 2005) 6 et seqq.

[76]See Chaps. 4 and 5.

[77]Similar Mario Savino, 'Linkages Between Global Regimes and Interactions with Civil Society' in Sabino Cassese (ed), *Research Handbook on Global Administrative Law* (Edward Elgar Publishing 2016) 131 et seq.

[78]See e.g. the examples used by Dunoff, 'How to Avoid Regime Collisions' (n 55) and Dunoff, 'Mapping a Hidden World of International Regulatory Cooperation' (n 59).

their analysis.[79] 'Interaction' in this sense is not understood as only comprising intentional or directed behaviour. Even less is it to be understood as 'dialogue'.[80] Rather, the respective authors acknowledge that interaction also occurs if the conduct of one actor affects another actor indirectly or by coincidence, but nevertheless causes an effect and possibly a reaction.[81] For instance, Oberthür and Gehring include interactions that do not directly affect another IO but instead affect the conduct of the other IO's addressees (mostly their member states) and thereby indirectly influence the other IO itself, e.g. by forcing the latter to adapt its own policies towards these states.[82] Such indirect interactions can occur in various ways, e.g. in the form of unilateral 'domain expansion' by one IO affecting another, by way of mutually reinforcing activities or by sheer coexistence in the same "organizational environment".[83]

For purposes of the present study, it is appropriate to adopt a similarly broad approach to interaction. Direct interaction is not always taking place in labour governance and is at times even avoided by actors. At the same time, even in the absence of direct and purposeful communication, one can observe steady and significant mutual influence between the ILO and other IOs. For example, as will be discussed further in Chap. 5, ILO conventions and their interpretation by ILO bodies have attained a significant role in the interpretation of certain fundamental rights by the ECtHR. This happened although there are no reports of any direct and purposeful communication between the ILO and the ECtHR on these issues.[84] Then again, in the context of the current constitutional crisis within the ILO, the employers justified their challenge of the CEACR's interpretative competence as a reaction to the reception and 'enforcement' of ILO soft law jurisprudence by "other (...) international forums".[85] These incidents illustrate mutual influence between the

---

[79]Steve Cropper and others, 'Introducing Inter-Organizational Relations' in Steve Cropper and others (eds), *Oxford Handbook on Inter-Organizational Relations* (Oxford University Press 2009) 11; Biermann and Koops (n 69) 8. Those who do not engage in the study of actors, but of 'regimes', tend to employ a broad and rather vague concept of interaction, reaching beyond common-sense physical interaction and encompassing 'intangible' forms of interplay which may be purely ideational. By contrast, those who adopt a narrower research focus on interactions between formal IOs tend to adopt a narrower concept of interaction, in order to maintain the focus on the IO as an actor, ibid 7.

[80]Pasquet (n 60) 469.

[81]In the context of side-effects of judicial decisions, Pasquet calls these "peripheral interactions", in reminiscence of systems theory, ibid 490 et seq.

[82]Outlining a theoretical conception of causal mechanisms driving instances of institutional interaction, they distinguish between cognitive interaction, interaction through commitment, behavioural interaction and interaction affecting the impact level, Oberthür and Gehring 'Conceptual Foundations of Institutional Interaction' (n 69) 31 et seqq.

[83]Biermann and Koops (n 69) 8.

[84]Instead, the Court, arguably following the pleadings of the parties appearing before it or drawing on expertise of some of its members, approached the ILO instruments 'on its own' (in some cases, this expertise may be provided by judges who have it, e.g. because of prior occupation).

[85]See Chap. 2 D. III. 2. and Chap. 5 D. III.

ILO and the ECtHR, in parts facilitated by third actors; in the example, the parties before the ECtHR and the employers group in the ILO, respectively. One could consider these instances examples of *indirect* interaction, or interaction *in absentia*.

Empirically, these instances are harder to trace than direct interactions.[86] Yet, whatever the exact fact pattern in every case may be, the widespread reaction to the ECtHR's jurisprudence and the veritable and still unsolved constitutional crisis within the ILO illustrate that instances of indirect interaction can attain significant importance.[87]

3. Formal and Informal Interaction

As to the third axis, interactions vary in terms of their 'formality'.[88] Some interactions involve formal conduct, i.e. conduct adhering to a specified order or procedure, such as e.g. official meetings or binding decisions. Other interactions remain informal, or 'semi-formal', such as the official publication of the Doing Business reports by the World Bank discussed further in Chap. 4, prompting the publication of studies and reports by the International Labour Office formulating criticisms.

[86]What is more, it is similarly difficult to determine whether the facilitation by third actors that led to the indirect interaction between the ILO and the human rights bodies amounted to a chain of direct interactions between these third actors. As to the level of empirical certainty to be demanded, Oberthür and Gehring argue that proving causality in the context of institutional interaction "(merely) requires proving that the observed changes within the target institution or the issue area governed by it could not be expected to have occurred in the absence of the source institution or its relevant parts (...)", Oberthür and Gehring 'Conceptual Foundations of Institutional Interaction' (n 69) 28. They further observe that "[s]erious causal analysis of institutional interaction requires disaggregation of a complex situation into an appropriate number of cases of interaction.", ibid 29.

[87]There is a related, but separate, further reason why the notion of interaction should not be limited to specific kinds, such as a 'dialogue'. Notions such as 'dialogue', while ostensibly only describing a fact pattern, may entail implicit normative assumptions or aspirations which predetermine the analytical focus and increase the risk of yielding results that conform with these assumptions or aspirations simply as a result of 'confirmation bias'. For example, the metaphorical notion of 'judicial dialogue' focuses analysis ab initio on a) interaction that qualifies as dialogue and b) occurs between judges (example taken from Pasquet (n 60) 467 et seqq. However, "[m]etaphors are desires of the mind, and judicial dialogue is no exception", ibid 500. One way to mitigate such effects is to deliberately employ broad and encompassing definitions. What is more, there is no need for reducing the analytical scope to those fact patterns that meet a certain type of stereotype. After all, the law formulates normative expectations to human conduct as it actually appears, in all its richness and diversity, not to some sort of idealized components of such conduct.

[88]Biermann and Koops (n 69) 9; Young, *Trading Fish, Saving Fish: The Interaction Between Regimes in International Law* (n 55) 93 et seqq.; Savino (n 77) 150.

4. Interaction Across Stages

Finally, inter-organizational interactions occur on (and across) different stages of IOs' activities. Dunoff has identified three such stages: A conceptual stage,[89] a regulatory stage[90] and an operational stage.[91] Young distinguishes between interaction during the making, the implementation and the adjudication of law.[92]

Building on these proposals, it may be constated that interactions can appear during the three stages of policy making, law-making and implementation.

The policy-making stage comprises interactions that influence an IO's policy agenda, broadly speaking. Included are interactions on a programmatic, political, conceptual and ideational level. It also comprises the creation of non-legal instruments, such as reports, studies and policy statements. Of the case studies discussed in this study, the drafting and publication of the World Bank's Doing Business reports would fall into this category.[93]

The law-making stage comprises interactions at the level of norm creation. This can comprise the setting of secondary law or the drafting of legal instruments under the auspices of an IO. An example would be the creation and adoption of the ESC within the CoE, discussed in Chap. 6. The law-making stage also comprises the joint setting of norms by IOs, e.g. the joint drafting of a treaty.

The implementation stage concerns interactions in the application, the implementation and the adjudication of law. An example is the reliance on ILO

---

[89]By "conceptual", Dunoff understands the social knowledge that is created in the course of the operation of a regime, especially during its regulatory or operational activities. He relies on the legal-sociologic works of Andrew Lang (Andrew TF Lang, 'Legal Regimes and Regimes of Knowledge: Governing Global Services Trade' (2009) LSE Law, Society and Economy Research Papers 15/2009 2): "Specifically, the activities of international legal regimes constitute part of the processes by which we collectively come to know, describe, and imagine the world in which we live'", Dunoff, 'How to Avoid Regime Collisions' (n 55) 70. Dunoff claims that knowledge production through interaction of regimes has been underresearched by legal scholarship so far, ibid. As an example for conceptual interaction in the field of social justice, he cites the joint WTO-ILO report on trade and employment (ibid 71).

[90]Interactions on this stage can result in, or be directed at, creating international legal standards through regulatory cooperation.

[91]Interactions in the operational stage aim at jointly implementing regulations and policies, with each participant contributing specific expertise or resources. Dunoff identifies five characteristics of the operational form. Firstly, they are showcases of "organisational creativity and dynamism" of the participating actors. Secondly, they tend to evolve and expand over time. Thirdly, there are of varying success. Fourthly, the actors initiating operational interactions vary significantly. Fifthly, operational activities regularly generate normative standards, Dunoff, 'How to Avoid Regime Collisions' (n 55) 61 et seqq.

[92]Young, *Trading Fish, Saving Fish: The Interaction Between Regimes in International Law* (n 55) 85. Savino further distinguishes between types of activities conducted on different stages, Savino (n 77) 132.

[93]See Chap. 4 below.

instruments and practice by international bodies, such as the ECtHR and the ECSR.[94]

One pattern of interactions can concern several stages at once. Moreover, the affected stages can differ with regard to each participating IO.[95] Therefore, with regard to the described stages, it is particularly important to understand them not as clinically clear-cut distinctions, but as reference points for orientation when examining complex fact patterns.

C. Conclusion

This chapter has made two points. The first one is that the ILO is not the only IO engaged in labour governance. Instead, there is a plethora of other IOs working on labour issues. These comprise a wide range of universal and regional IOs, with both general and specific responsibilities in a wide array of fields. The co-existence of the ILO and these other IOs results in multi-institutional labour governance.

The second point is that this parallelism does not mean that the ILO and other IOs are isolated and disconnected from each other. Rather, there is a significant degree of interaction among them, which influences how the respective IOs engage in labour governance. This chapter understands the term 'inter-organizational interaction' as referring to

> one IO's conduct directed at having, or actually having, an effect on the conduct of another IO.

In order to create a tentative taxonomy and terminological framework of reference for this study, it has further been suggested to order inter-organizational interactions along four axes. These axes indicate if, and to what extent, interactions are

- conflictual, synergetic, or located in between those two poles,
- direct or indirect,
- formal or informal, and
- occurring at one or more of the three stages of policy-making, law-making or implementation

[94] On inter-organizational influence caused by one IO's interpretation of the other's law Ruffert, 'Zuständigkeitsgrenzen Internationaler Organisationen im institutionellen Rahmen der internationalen Gemeinschaft', 38 *Archiv des Völkerrechts* (2000) 129, 160 et seqq.

[95] For example, for the ILO, its participation in the drafting of the ESC was largely a matter of implementing the ILO-CoE, whereas for the CoE, it was also a matter concerning its own law-making, see below, Chap. 6.

4. The ILO's Model Under Pressure: The World Bank's Employing Workers Indicator

To fully grasp the scope and nature of inter-organizational interactions and their implications for the ILO, it is useful to consider in detail how these interactions take place in practice. Accordingly, this chapter addresses a series of interactions between the ILO and the World Bank.

As mentioned in the previous chapter, the World Bank belongs to the IOs engaging in multi-institutional labour governance besides the ILO. It has engaged in numerous labour-related activities and, not least due to its financial leverage, has attained an important role in labour governance. Among other activities, the Bank has between 2004 and 2011 published rankings of the 'business-friendliness' of member states' labour regulations in its Doing Business Reports. To create the rankings, it used its self-created Employing Workers Indicator (EWI). As will be seen, the rankings, and the leverage they wielded, conflicted with ILO policies and ongoing initiatives in a number of countries. In response, the ILO lobbied for the EWI's modification or removal, eventually resulting in the Bank ceasing to rank states' labour regulations on the basis of the EWI.

A. The World Bank as an Actor in Labour Governance

In order to contextualize the case study presented here, some preliminary remarks about the World Bank as an actor in labour governance are warranted.

'World Bank' (or simply the 'Bank') is a commonly used generic term to describe two separate but closely interlinked IOs, the International Bank for Reconstruction and Development (IBRD) and the International Development Association (IDA).[1]

[1]See on the nomenclature Maurizio Ragazzi, 'World Bank Group', *Max Planck Encyclopedia of Public International Law* (Oxford University Press 2014) para 1. Deplorably, this terminology is

H. Gött, *The Law of Interactions Between International Organizations*, Beiträge zum ausländischen öffentlichen Recht und Völkerrecht 299,
https://doi.org/10.1007/978-3-662-62389-3_4

Together with three other IOs, the International Finance Corporation (IFC),[2] the Multilateral Investment Guarantee Agency (MIGA)[3] and the International Centre for the Settlement of Investment Disputes (ICSID),[4] the IBRD and IDA form the so-called World Bank Group (WBG).[5]

The World Bank is a leading provider of public-sector development financing and of economic expertise. Its main objective is to foster the economic development of its client states, notably insofar as they are developing countries.[6] The IBRD offers a wide array of financial products to middle-income and selected low-income

---

not always used in a consistent manner. Hence, in different contributions, 'World Bank' or 'Bank' may either refer to both IBRD and IDA or to the IBRD alone, as the case may be.

[2]The IFC provides and leverages investments, expertise and asset management to private sector clients in developing countries, Sheetal Asrani-Dann and Philipp Dann, 'International Finance Corporation (IFC)', *Max Planck Encyclopedia of Public International Law* (Oxford University Press 2014) para 1.

[3]MIGA provides investment guarantees, Stephan W Schill, 'Multilateral Investment Guarantee Agency (MIGA)', *Max Planck Encyclopedia of Public International Law* (Oxford University Press 2014) para 1.

[4]ICSID facilitates investor-state dispute settlement, Christoph Schreuer, 'International Centre for Settlement of Investment Disputes (ICSID)', *Max Planck Encyclopedia of Public International Law* (Oxford University Press 2013) para 1.

[5]Daniel L Bradlow, 'Developing Countries Debt Crises, International Financial Institutions and International Law: Some Preliminary Thoughts' (2009) Washington College of Law Research Paper No. 2009/01 3. The WBG is not itself an IO. Rather, it comprises five legally separate but institutionally closely interlinked IOs. The WGB member IOs are separate international legal subjects, are based on separate constituent instruments and have their own membership, organs and mandates. However, as a consequence of pertinent constitutional provisions and of institutional practice, they are closely intertwined. The IBRD, the IDA and the IFC each have three main organs: A Board of Governors as a plenary organ of all shareholders (as their member states are called), a Board of Executive Directors and a President. If a state is a member to more than one of the aforesaid three IOs (which most states are), this state's Governors and its Executive Directors are ex officio the governors and directors in all of them, Ibrahim FI Shihata, 'The Creative Role of the Lawyer – Example: The Office of the World Bank's General Counsel' (1999) 48 Catholic University Law Review 1041, 1045. The IBRD's President is ex officio also the president of the IDA, the IFC and the whole WBG. Moreover, IBRD and IDA share the same staff, ibid; Leonie Guder, 'International Development Association (IDA)', *Max Planck Encyclopedia of Public International Law* (Oxford University Press 2011) para 1. Besides their headquarters, the World Bank and IFC each operate through many country offices around the world.

[6]The particular interpretation and implementation of this overall objective has changed over time, not least because the concept of development itself has developed. Today, the WBG's two overarching goals are to effectively eradicate extreme forms of poverty and to promote sustainable development and shared prosperity in all countries, World Bank Group, 'Who we are' (*World Bank Website*) <https://www.worldbank.org/en/who-we-are> accessed 26 April 2020. Facing changing circumstances and new developments, the Bank's operations have significantly expanded since its inception, which has aptly been deemed "a story of an incremental, measured opening of space for the Bank to intervene", Hassane Cissé, 'Should the Political Prohibition in Charters of International Financial Institutions Be Revisited? The Case of the World Bank' (2012) 3 World Bank Legal Review 59, 63; Sabine Schlemmer-Schulte, 'International Bank for Reconstruction and Development (IBRD)', *Max Planck Encyclopedia of Public International Law* (Oxford University Press 2014) para 51.

countries, including public sector loans, guarantees, products for risk management, and expertise.[7] The IDA, for its part, provides concessional low- or zero-interest loans and grants with long repayment periods that are specifically offered to the poorest countries.[8]

Since its inception, and increasingly thereafter, the World Bank has been an important actor in labour governance.[9] The Bank's relevance reflects in its different activities. Firstly, the World Bank offers a range of financial products to support concrete projects in member states.[10] It provides so-called investment project financing for projects in all sectors, with a focus on infrastructure, human development, agriculture, and public administration sectors.[11] Funded projects can have labour-relevant ramifications, e.g. regarding the rights of involved trade unions or regarding labour conditions in the projects.[12]

Secondly, the Bank offers non-project-specific assistance, notably its so-called development policy financing (previously known as structural adjustment financing).[13] In essence, development policy financing supports a borrowing state on a macroeconomic scale by providing financing for a series of institutional and policy

---

[7]The IBRD provides funding on more favourable terms than commercial providers, Daniel D Bradlow, 'International Law and the Operations of the International Financial Institutions' in Daniel D Bradlow and David Hunter (eds), *International Financial Institutions and International Law* (Kluwer Law International 2010) 10.

[8]Guder (n 5) para 2 et seq.

[9]Its Articles of Agreement require the Bank to promote the balanced growth of international trade and the maintenance of equilibrium in balances of payments by encouraging international investment, "thereby assisting in raising productivity, the standard of living and conditions of labour" in the member states, Art. I(iii) Articles of Agreement of the International Bank for Reconstruction and Development (adopted at the UN Monetary and Financial Conference, Bretton Woods, New Hampshire, 22 July 1944, entered into force 27 December 1945) 2 UNTS 134 (IBRD-AoA).

[10]Historically, project financing resembled their main activity, leaving aside the IBRD's pre-Marshall Plan inception phase, in which the Bank engaged in more general activities, Schlemmer-Schulte (n 6) para 5. A classic example for project lending would be large infrastructure projects. The sectors in which the Bank operated gradually expanded, notably encompassing social sectors such as health, nutrition, population and education, ibid.

[11]The IFC, for its part, provides a range of financial products for specific business projects Asrani-Dann and Dann (n 2) para 14.

[12]For that reason, from 2006 onwards, the IFC has employed so-called performance standards, which inter alia seek to ensure that their clients and own staff comply with fundamental labour standards. Already from 1998, the IFC had employed internal guidelines intended to prevent support for projects involving child labour and forced labour. On this and on comparable MIGA standards Franz Christian Ebert, 'Labour Standards and the World Bank. Analysing the Potential of Safeguard Policies for Protecting Workers' in Henner Gött (ed), *Labour Standards in International Economic Law* (Springer 2018) 273, 280. In 2016, the World Bank followed suit by adopting comparable safeguard policies, see the evaluation of the World Bank's 2016 Environmental and Social Standards, ibid 281 et seqq.

[13]See Jane D Weaver and Ann Wilcox-Staats, 'The World Bank Group' (1986) 1 American University International Law Review 391, 403. A similar development was the one towards sectoral adjustment lending, Schlemmer-Schulte (n 6) para 15.

actions.[14] This type of financing is usually connected to so-called conditionalities, i.e. conditions that certain specified structural reforms be accomplished by the recipient state.[15] Development policy lending conditionalities have time and again demanded labour market and social security reforms.[16] Insofar as they do, they resemble a macro-level instrument of labour governance. Several authors observed that the overall direction of these conditionalities has been towards increased labour market flexibility and deregulation, while labour-related safeguards in the Bank's policies leave room for improvement.[17]

Finally, over the last decades, the Bank has increasingly become a "knowledge institution".[18] For one part, it renders specific advice as demanded by its member states. Moreover, it has undertaken to collect, evaluate and publish information on a broad range of development topics, including on various labour issues.[19] The Bank's

---

[14]Development policy lending is again determined by the Bank's Country Partnership Frameworks, which by themselves can touch on labour issues, see e.g. Christine Kaufmann *Globalisation and Labour Rights. The Conflict Between Core Labour Rights and International Economic Law* (Hart Publishing 2007) 122.

[15]Development policy lending has steadily gained importance and now comprises a significant portion of the Bank's financial engagements, Roberto Dañino, 'The Legal Aspects of the World Bank's Work on Human Rights' (2007) 41 The International Lawyer 21, 24; World Bank, '2015 Development Policy Financing Retrospective: Results and Sustainability' (2015) <http://pubdocs.worldbank.org/en/420441457100264616/DevelopmentPolicyRetrospective2015.pdf> accessed 26 April 2020. The conditionalities aim to reform a plethora of sectors and institutions in borrowing countries and have repeatedly aimed at enhancing these states' competitiveness through market liberalization, privatization and deregulation, Schlemmer-Schulte (n 6) para 6. Since the 1990s, the Bank has moreover employed 'good governance' conditionalities, requiring structural reforms of the public sector and public institutions, Bradlow, 'International Law and the Operations of the International Financial Institutions' (n 7) 14; Edith Brown Weiss and Ahila Sornarajah, 'Good Governance', *Max Planck Encyclopedia of Public International Law* (Oxford University Press 2013) para 6.

[16]Suzan Kang, 'Labor and the Bank: Investigating the Politics of the World Bank's Employing Workers' Index' (2009) 14 Journal of Workplace Rights 481, 484.

[17]Kang (n 16); Mark Anner and Teri Caraway, 'International Institutions and Workers' Rights: Between Labor Standards and Market Flexibility' (2010) 45 Studies in Comparative International Development 151, 161. For other examples, see Schlemmer-Schulte (n 6) para 6; Franz Christian Ebert and Anne Posthuma, 'Labour Standards and Development Finance Institutions: A Review of Current Policies and Activities' (2010) IILS Discussion Paper No 204 <http://www.oit.org/wcmsp5/groups/public/%2D%2D-dgreports/%2D%2D-inst/documents/publication/wcms_192837.pdf> accessed 26 April 2020; Franz Christian Ebert, 'Kohärenz der Politik der Weltbank mit den arbeitsrechtlichen Mindeststandards der Internationalen Arbeitsorganisation' in Wolfgang Däubler and Reingard Zimmer (eds), *Arbeitsvölkerrecht - Festschrift für Klaus Lörcher* (Nomos 2013) 72.

[18]Cissé (n 6) 91; Jean-Jacques Dethier, 'Producing Knowledge for Development: Research at the World Bank' (2007) 13 Global Governance 469.

[19]This form of knowledge production and dissemination is among the least 'legalized' fields of Bank activities, i.e. it operates largely without explicit basis in the constituent instruments, Michael Riegner, *Informationsverwaltungsrecht Internationaler Organisationen. Dargestellt am Entwicklungsverwaltungsrecht der Weltbank und der Vereinten Nationen* (Mohr Siebeck 2018) 434.

expertise is reinforced by its authority and its reputation as a multilateral development finance institution.[20] Such 'authoritative' knowledge dissemination and policy advice is another way the Bank engages in labour governance.[21] The Doing Business reports and their Employing Workers' indicator discussed in this chapter are a particularly exposed example in this regard.

B. The Doing Business Reports and Their Employing Workers' Indicator

I. Objectives, Method and Reformist Approach of the Doing Business Reports

Now in their 17th year of publication, the Doing Business reports have become a flagship publication of the World Bank.[22] They aim at providing guidance to investors by comparing regulation of economic activities in different economies.

To this end, the World Bank, the IFC and affiliated researchers gather and analyse comprehensive quantitative data on the regulations of business activity, at present covering 190 economies.[23] Data gathering is based on a questionnaire developed by the Bank's Doing Business team on applicable domestic regulations, using the example of a fictitious simple business case. Based on the questionnaire, data is gathered from four principal sources: States' laws and regulations, governments, World Bank Group regional offices, and collaboration with a vast number (more than 15.000 in 2019[24]) of "expert respondents" who encounter business regulations

---

[20]Cissé (n 6) 91.

[21]Kang (n 16) 495.

[22]The exact ownership and attribution of the reports is somewhat ambiguous: The reports are published using the logo of the WBG, whereas the copyright belongs to the World Bank (i.e. IBRD and IDA), see e.g. the front matter of Doing Business 2018. On the internal rules concerning official Bank publications see Ibrahim FI Shihata, *The World Bank Legal Papers* (Springer 2000) 236 et seq. The reports are officially prepared by World Bank staff, but there are reports of IFC staff taking a leading role in their preparation, Ralf Michaels, 'Comparative Law by Numbers? Legal Origins Thesis, Doing Business Reports, and the Silence of Traditional Comparative Law' (2009) 57 American Journal of Comparative Law 765, 771. For convenience of reading, and because of its copyright, the reports will be treated as an IBRD and IDA publication, while keeping sight of the IFC involvement.

[23]Information obtained from the project website, World Bank, 'Doing Business' (*World Bank Website*) <http://www.doingbusiness.org> accessed 26 April 2020. The number has steadily increased. For instance, in 2008, the reports covered 178 economies, Sangheon Lee, Deirdre McCann and Nina Torm, 'The World Bank's "Employing Workers" Index: Findings and Critiques – A Review of Recent Evidence' (2008) 147 International Labour Review 416, 416.

[24]World Bank, *Doing Business 2020* (World Bank 2019) 23 et seq.

in their daily practice, such as government officials, lawyers, accountants and other professionals.[25] The collected data is subject to internal verification processes prior to publication of the final report.[26]

Based on the gathered data, the Doing Business reports establish a benchmarking system that evaluates states' regulations as to their impact on business activities, particularly as to their 'rigidity'.[27] The reports build on a number of indicators covering important aspects of business activities. For each of these aspects, regulations are assessed as to how much they are conducive or obstructive to business activity. The initial report, issued in late 2003, contained indicators on the following topics: starting a business, hiring and firing workers (the EWI, discussed below), enforcing contracts, getting credit and closing a business.[28] Later reports renamed, added, changed and removed indicators.[29]

Regarding their approach, the Doing Business reports

> [take] the perspective of domestic, primarily smaller companies and [measure] the regulations applying to them through their life cycle.[30]

As is clarified in later reports, a Doing Business report does not

> attempt to measure all costs and benefits of a particular law or regulation to society as a whole. Nor does it measure all aspects of the business environment that matter to firms and investors or affect the competitiveness of an economy. Its aim is simply to supply business leaders and policy makers with a fact base for informing policy making and to provide open data for research on how business regulations and institutions affect such economic outcomes as productivity, investment, informality, corruption, unemployment and poverty.[31]

However, the reports themselves do not confine themselves to mere observation and data gathering. Instead, they also draw normative consequences. They explicitly build on the premise that business needs "good rules",[32] understood as

> rules that establish and clarify property rights and reduce the cost of resolving disputes; rules that increase the predictability of economic interactions and provide contractual partners with certainty and protection against abuse. The objective is regulations designed to be efficient, accessible to all and simple in their implementation. In some areas Doing Business gives higher scores for regulation providing stronger protection of investor rights (...).[33]

---

[25]ibid.

[26]ibid.

[27]The Doing Business reports' rankings were inspired by earlier rankings created by private institutions, e.g. the Heritage Foundation's 'Index of Economic Freedom' index, published since 1994, Peter Bakvis, 'The World Bank's Doing Business Report: A Last Fling for the Washington Consensus?' (2009) 15 Transfer: European Review of Labour and Research 419, 424.

[28]World Bank, *Doing Business in 2004 - Understanding Regulation* (World Bank 2003).

[29]Relevant for present purposes are subsequent changes to the Employing Workers Indicator and the introduction of the Paying Taxes Indicator in 2006.

[30]World Bank, *Doing Business 2012 - Doing Business in a More Transparent World* (World Bank 2011) v.

[31]ibid.

[32]ibid.

[33]ibid.

The reports' "fundamental premise",[34] the ideal of 'good' regulation, is a normative one. From this assumption, the reports have actively sought to induce reforms and to contribute its indicators as a benchmark for such reforms. The first Doing Business report stated that the reports sought to achieve the following objectives:

- motivating reforms through country benchmarking,
- informing the design of reforms,
- enriching international initiatives on development effectiveness, and
- informing theory of regulatory economics.[35]

In the same report, the World Bank claimed that

> the data analyzed in Doing Business highlight specifically what needs to be changed when reforms are designed.[36]

The reformist orientation was prominently maintained in subsequent reports.[37] For instance, later reports comprised exemplary economy case studies on reforms in particular countries[38] and summaries of "Doing Business reforms" in the respective reporting period.[39]

II. The Employing Workers Indicator

Of the indicators used in the reports, the already-mentioned Employing Workers Indicator (EWI) is of prime importance for this study.[40]

---

[34]ibid.

[35]World Bank, *Doing Business in 2004 - Understanding Regulation* (n 28) x.

[36]ibid 9 et seq; Bakvis, 'The World Bank's Doing Business Report: A Last Fling for the Washington Consensus?' (n 27) 425.

[37]Some were even given corresponding subtitles, e.g. Doing Business 2007 ("How to reform"), Doing Business 2010 ("Reforming through difficult times") or Doing Business 2018 ("Reforming to create jobs").

[38]World Bank, *Doing Business 2012 - Doing Business in a More Transparent* World (n 30) 26 et seqq.

[39]ibid 65 et seqq.; World Bank, *Doing Business 2018 - Reforming to Create Jobs* (World Bank 2017) 126 et seqq.

[40]A further indicator that has gained some relevance in labour governance, the Paying Taxes Indicator, is of no further relevance for this study and will therefore not be discussed. In brief, the Paying Taxes Indicator (PTI), introduced into the reports in 2006, is relevant from a labour perspective insofar as it concerns labour-related costs of employers. In Doing Business 2007, all nonwage labour costs to be paid by the employer, i.e. costs which are not wages and salaries, were included in the total tax rate (World Bank, *Doing Business 2007 - How to Reform* (World Bank 2006) preface). These include, inter alia, social security contributions and labour taxes paid by the employer (ibid 70). States received higher PTI scores the fewer taxes had to be paid by a business. This also counted for nonwage payments: States that required employers to make higher contributions to social security schemes received lower PTI scores than those requiring lower contributions, Bakvis, 'The World Bank's Doing Business Report: A Last Fling for the Washington Consensus?' (n 27) 425.

The EWI was used from the first Doing Business report, issued in late 2003, and was removed from the reports from 2011. It consisted of three sub-indicators, concerning the difficulty to hire and fire workers and the rigidity of working hours. Each of the sub-indicators used different components.[41] A state's EWI score was the average of the scores it obtained in each of the three sub-indicators.

In the initial Doing Business report, the EWI worked on the basis of a fictitious benchmark of 'ideal' employment regulation.[42] The highest score was awarded to those states that came closest to this benchmark. By opposite, any state that had more 'rigid' (i.e. less flexible) regulations in place received a lower score.[43] Since the fictitious benchmark envisaged regulations which were particularly flexible, the result was that many of the states with lowest standards of employment regulation ranked highest in the EWI ranking.[44]

The methodology employed in the EWI was subject to some changes over time. For instance, in the Doing Business 2007 report, nonwage costs for labour were excluded from the EWI (however, at the same time, they were added to the Paying Taxes Indicator).[45] In the Doing Business 2010 report, further methodological changes to the EWI were made. For example, the minimum wage parameter was

---

[41]The Doing Business Report 2008 described the components as follows: The difficulty of hiring workers sub-indicator was based on an evaluation of i) whether fixed-term contracts are prohibited for permanent tasks, ii) the maximum duration of fixed-term contracts, and iii) the ratio of the minimum wage for a trainee or first year employee to the average added value per worker. The difficulty of firing workers sub-indicator assessed (i) whether redundancy is disallowed as a basis for terminating workers, (ii) whether the employer needs to notify a third party, notably the government, to terminate one redundant worker, (iii) whether the employer needs to notify a third party to terminate a group of 25 redundant workers, (iv) whether the employer needs approval from a third party to terminate one redundant worker, (v) whether the employer needs approval from a third party to terminate a group of 25 redundant workers, (vi) whether the law requires the employer to consider reassignment or retraining options before redundancy termination, (vii) whether priority rules apply for redundancies, and (viii) whether priority rules apply for reemployment. The rigidity of hours index considered (i) whether night work is unrestricted; (ii) whether weekend work is unrestricted, (iii) whether the workweek can consist of 5.5 days, (iv) whether the workweek can extend to 50 hours or more (including overtime) for 2 months a year to respond to a seasonal increase in production, and (v) whether paid annual vacation is 21 working days or fewer, World Bank, *Doing Business 2008* (World Bank 2007) 72.

[42]Bakvis reports that in the 2003 Doing Business report, "[c]ountries that provided for a working week of any less than 66 hours, a weekly day of rest, a minimum wage exceeding 25% of average value added per worker, any recourse for appeal or severance pay in case of dismissal, or any limit on the use of term contracts, were considered to have excessive labour market rigidity. DB rated countries for difficulty of 'Hiring and Firing Workers' according to the degree to which labour regulations exceeded any of the minimal standards it considered acceptable and ranked countries accordingly", Bakvis, 'The World Bank's Doing Business Report: A Last Fling for the Washington Consensus?' (n 27) 424.

[43]ibid.

[44]ibid 429.

[45]World Bank, *Doing Business 2007 - How to Reform* (n 40) preface.

adjusted to avoid creating incentives for countries to decrease the minimum wage below the absolute poverty line of then 1,25 $ per day.[46]

Irrespective of the subsequent changes to its methodology, the EWI has always only measured selected aspects of a country's labour regulations, namely rules on hiring and firing workers and on working hours. This also means that the EWI does not assess regulation concerning other important aspects of such regulations.[47]

III. Dissemination and Use by the Bank

Almost immediately after their launch, the Doing Business reports gained significant importance. They advanced to the World Bank publication with the highest rate of circulation.[48] Moreover, they have also obtained a high reputational value and have been referred to as authoritative advice by policy makers.

The reports and their rankings have frequently been used as benchmarks, both inside and outside the World Bank.[49] In the World Bank, the reports and their

---

[46]World Bank, *Doing Business 2010 - Reforming Through Difficult Times* (World Bank 2009) 78.

[47]See for instance World Bank, 'Doing Business Employing Workers Consultative Group Final Report' (25 April 2011) <https://www.doingbusiness.org/content/dam/doingBusiness/media/Miscellaneous/Final-EWI-CG-report-2011.pdf> accessed 26 April 2020 4. It has been argued that, given that the EWI only targets issues which are not covered by ILO fundamental conventions, the Doing Business reports would base their deregulatory agenda on the ILO's very own dichotomy of fundamental and non-fundamental standards as laid down in the 1998 Declaration on Fundamental Principles and Rights at Work, Deirdre McCann, 'Labour Law on the Plateau: Towards Regulatory Policy for Endogenous Norms' in Alan Bogg and others (eds), *The Autonomy of Labour Law* (Hart Publishing 2015) 399, 400, referring to Alston's critique of the 1998 Declaration (Philip Alston, '"Core Labour Standards" and the Transformation of the International Labour Rights Regime' (2004) 15 European Journal of International Law 457). The non-core focus was also mentioned by the Bank itself, see World Bank, *Doing Business 2014 - Understanding Regulations for Small and Medium-Size Enterprises* (World Bank 2013) 122, fn 2. While it is true that the EWI does not directly address fundamental labour standards, it neither evaluates a broad range of other non-fundamental issues.

[48]Bakvis, 'The World Bank's Doing Business Report: A Last Fling for the Washington Consensus?' (n 27) 424; Michaels (n 22) 772.

[49]For instance, the IMF referred to Doing Business scores when recommending labour market deregulation in the context of the review of loans it had previously given, Yaraslau Kryvoi, 'The World Bank and the ILO: Two Visions of Employment Regulation' in Roger Blanpain and Claire Grant (eds), *Fixed-Term Employment Contracts - A Comparative Study* (Vanden Broele Publishers 2009) 49. What is more, the EWI has been used in international databases developed by private institutions that compare and rank labour market efficiency, regulation and competitiveness, e.g. the World Economic Forum's Labour Market Efficiency Index), the International Institute for Management Development's Government Efficiency Index and the Fraser Institute's Labor Market Regulations Index, see Mariya Aleksynska and Sandrine Cazes, 'Comparing Indicators of Labour Market Regulations Across Databases: A Post Scriptum to the Employing Workers Debate' (ILO 2014) 50 1.

indicators have been used in the Bank's overall labour market strategy[50] and on all levels of activities. For instance, they were used in the World Bank's Country Assistance Strategies, which inter alia determine development policy financing for borrowing countries.[51] In Country Assistance Strategies, the World Bank recommended labour market reforms based on the Doing Business rankings.[52]

Moreover, the EWI was used in practice to assess the quality of a country's labour law in the World Bank's Country Policy and Institutional Assessment (CPIA).[53] The CPIA is an annual assessment of all borrowing states and evaluates the quality of these states' institutions and policies as to their supportiveness of sustainable growth and poverty reduction.[54] In essence, higher scores in the CPIA correlate to a more advantageous allocation of the IDA's concessionary financing products.[55] Finally, the World Bank used the indicators as a basis to formulate conditions for specific loans.[56]

Since the Doing Business reports were presented—and are actually widely regarded—as a key source of knowledge and indicator of sound economic policy, the invocation of indicators such as the EWI is a powerful tool to influence the reputation of a state in the eyes of investors, enterprises and everyone else who relies on their authority.[57] The widespread dissemination and their use in several critical contexts, like development assistance policies and loan modalities, has made them an important catalyst for policy reform.

Besides its inclusion into financing products and other instruments, the World Bank also relied on the EWI as a basis for publicly assess countries' labour market

[50]Kryvoi (n 49) 49.

[51]The World Bank has also used the EWI in its Country Partnership Strategies, ibid 48.

[52]In a similar manner, they were used in the Bank's new Country Partnership Frameworks, which were launched post-2014 and replace the older Country Assistance Strategies, e.g. with respect to Belarus, WBG, 'Country Partnership Framework for the Republic of Belarus for the Period FY 18-22' (2018) Report No 123321-BY para 32.

[53]Bakvis, 'The World Bank's Doing Business Report: A Last Fling for the Washington Consensus?' (n 27) 427; Michael Riegner, 'Measuring the Good Governance State: A Legal Reconstruction of the World Bank's "Country Policy and Institutional Assessment"' (2016) 19 Journal of International Economic Law 1, 6.

[54]Using criteria of the four categories economic management; structural policies; policies for social inclusion and equity; and public sector management and institutions, Riegner, 'Measuring the Good Governance State: A Legal Reconstruction of the World Bank's "Country Policy and Institutional Assessment"' (n 53) 14.

[55]The overall CPIA country score is referred to as the IDA Resource Allocation Index and is the main element of the IDA's Country Performance Ranking, a benchmark index by which a significant share of the IDA's resources are allocated, ibid 15. For an evaluation see Elisa van Waeyenberge, 'Selectivity at Work: Country Policy and Institutional Assessments at the World Bank' (2009) 21 European Journal of Development Research 792.

[56]Bakvis, 'The World Bank's Doing Business Report: A Last Fling for the Washington Consensus?' (n 27) 427.

[57]Catherine Weaver, 'The World's Bank and the Bank's World' (2007) 13 Global Governance 492, 501.

regulations and to advocate in favour of reform. On the one hand, states were commended for their efforts if they reformed their labour market regulations according to the EWI. On the other hand, both the World Bank and the IMF exerted pressure on states with low EWI rankings to reform their labour market regulations. This happened in varying intensity and has led to a series of controversial cases of labour market reforms.[58] Some states openly strived for higher scores to build or increase an investor-friendly reputation.[59]

C. EWI-Induced Labour Market Reforms: Back and Forth Between the World Bank and the ILO

The publication, dissemination and use of the Doing Business reports and their EWI provide a telling example of "the quiet power of indicators"[60] in labour governance and of inter-organizational interaction between the ILO and the World Bank. In a number of cases, the Bank's use of the EWI to promote labour market deregulation undermined ongoing ILO activities (I.). This provoked criticisms by the ILO and the trade union movement (II.), which eventually resulted in the Bank removing the EWI from its Doing Business rankings (III.).

I. The Bank's Undermining of ILO Activities Through Its Use of the EWI

In a range of cases, the Bank relied on the EWI to promote labour market reforms that were at odds with ILO instruments or initiatives in the reforming countries. In some instances, the World Bank used the EWI as a reference point to demand certain labour market reforms from borrowing countries, for example in Nepal (1.). In other cases, the reports publicly lauded states with a record of persistent and egregious violations of fundamental labour standards, for instance in Georgia.[61]

[58] For an overview see Bakvis, 'The World Bank's Doing Business Report: A Last Fling for the Washington Consensus?' (n 27) 427 et seqq. See further the cases reported in ITUC/Global Unions, 'The IFIs' Use of Doing Business to Eliminate Workers' Protection: Analysis of Doing Business 2008 and New Country Evidence' (2007) <https://www.ituc-csi.org/IMG/pdf/doing_business.pdf> accessed 26 April 2020 18 et seqq.

[59] E.g. Belarus, Kryvoi (n 49) 49.

[60] Sally Engle Merry, Kevin E Davis and Benedict Kingsbury (eds), *The Quiet Power of Indicators: Measuring Governance, Corruption, and Rule of Law* (Cambridge University Press 2015).

[61] Further examples comprise Colombia and Belarus. Colombia achieved better Doing Business rankings than most Western European countries. The 2005 Doing Business report positively mentioned the creation of more flexible labour markets in Colombia, lauded Colombia as one of the top-10 reformers towards an investor-friendly climate, and argued that there was a causal link

1. Undermining ILO-Facilitated Labour Law Reforms: The Example of Nepal (2005–2007)

In Nepal, trade unions, employers' associations and the government had in early 2005 agreed on a labour market reform process. The envisaged reforms resembled a compromise made up of two parts: On the one hand, it was agreed to increase labour market flexibility by relaxing rules on job termination. On the other hand, the agreement also foresaw the creation of basic social protection schemes, to improve standards on occupational safety at the workplace and to ratify the ILO's fundamental conventions.[62] The ILO, which had provided technical assistance and advice to Nepal for a long time, supported this reform process, e.g. by promoting trade union involvement and by facilitating tripartite consultations and negotiations.[63]

However, the reform process came to a halt when the Nepalese king assumed direct and absolute power in February 2005.[64] Joined by a series of repressive action

---

between these reforms and the creation of a significant number of new jobs, World Bank, 'Doing Business 2005: Poor Nations Struggle to Reduce Red Tape for Business, Miss Large Growth Opportunities' *World Bank News Release No 2005/69/S* (Washington, DC, 8 September 2005). In the report itself, it was reported that "the government broadened the definition of just causes for dismissal. It cut the severance payment of a worker with 20 years of experience from 26 months to 11—and the mandated notice period from 8 weeks to 2" and concluded that this had led to the creation of 300.000 jobs, World Bank, *Doing Business 2005 - Removing Obstacles to Growth* (World Bank 2004) 29. Colombia, however, has been a repeatedly indicted perpetrator of trade union rights violations, Bakvis, 'The World Bank's Doing Business Report: A Last Fling for the Washington Consensus?' (n 27) 426 et seq.; Katrin Merhof, *Der internationale und innerstaatliche Schutz von Arbeitnehmerrechten in der kolumbianischen Blumenindustrie* (Mohr Siebeck 2014) 193 et seqq. In the case of Belarus, the ILO Governing Body in 2003 had appointed a Commission of Inquiry pursuant to Art. 26 ILO Constitution upon a complaint of various ILO member states. The appointment of a Commission of Inquiry marks an advanced step in the ILO's supervisory procedure that has only occurred a handful of times during the ILO's entire history and is usually taken in cases of particularly flagrant and persistent violations of ILO Conventions. Subsequent follow-up reports of ILO supervisory bodies repeatedly indicate severe deficits, e.g. as to trade union rights, see *Measures taken by the Government of the Republic of Belarus to implement the recommendations of the Commission of Inquiry,* Report of the Committee on Freedom of Association No 345 (2007) LC ILO Official Bulletin Ser B/2 353 paras 90 et seqq. This in turn had led other actors to take action, such as the EU's withdrawal of GSP preferences previously granted to Belarus, see e.g. Clara Portela and Jan Orbie, 'Sanctions under the EU Generalised System of Preferences and Foreign Policy: Coherence by Accident?' in Maurizio Carbone and Jan Orbie (eds), *The Trade-Development Nexus in the European Union: Differentiation, Coherence and Norms* (Routledge 2016) 68. By contrast, the World Bank's 2008 Country Assistance Strategy for Belarus commended Belarus's positive (i.e. business friendly) EWI ranking.

[62]Bakvis, 'The World Bank's Doing Business Report: A Last Fling for the Washington Consensus?' (n 27) 428.

[63]Robert Kyloh, 'Kyloh, Poverty and Reform in the Magical Kingdom: Nepal's PRSP' in International Labour Office (ed), *Trade Unions and Poverty Reduction Strategies* (ILO 2004) 33.

[64]Joanna Pfaff-Czarnecka, 'No End to Nepal's Maoist Rebellion' (2005) 46 Focaal, European Journal of Anthropology 158, 166.

against trade unions, the king suspended the reform process.[65] In response to this halt, the World Bank urged the king to increase labour market flexibility by cutting back the regulation of job termination, however without mentioning the other components of the previously agreed reform process the ILO had facilitated.[66] As reasons, the Bank invoked Nepal's low EWI score, especially the bad score in the firing workers sub-indicator. The Bank informed the Nepalese government and the ILO that continued World Bank financial support to Nepal depended on the swift implementation of reforms that would improve Nepal's EWI ranking.[67] In a letter to the ILO, the World Bank's Country Director for Nepal said he did

> not recall saying that we felt 'agreement' among tripartite constituents was essential to ensure effective implementation of reforms.[68]

The Nepalese king accordingly enacted a labour ordinance deregulating termination rules without enacting the other parts of the tripartite agreement in March 2006.[69] The period of absolute rule, however, was short-lived and ended soon after. After the king's government had been overthrown, his ordinance was repealed in May 2006 and the new government implemented the original reforms agreed in a tripartite setting in October 2007.[70] Shortly thereafter, the World Bank again publicly urged to deregulate the labour market as a condition for further assistance, but this time, the Nepalese government did not follow suit.[71]

---

[65]Peter Bakvis, 'How the World Bank & the IMF Use the Doing Business Report to Promote Labour Market Deregulation in Developing Countries' (2006) https://library.fes.de/pdf-files/gurn/00171.pdf accessed 26 April 2020 10.

[66]Bakvis, 'The World Bank's Doing Business Report: A Last Fling for the Washington Consensus?' (n 27) 428; ITUC/Global Unions (n 58) 5.

[67]Bakvis, 'The World Bank's Doing Business Report: A Last Fling for the Washington Consensus?' (n 27) 428. See also Robert Kyloh, *From Conflict to Cooperation: Labour Market Reforms That Can Work in Nepal* (ILO/Academic Foundation India 2008).

[68]Letter from Kenichi Ohashi, World Bank Country Director for Nepal, to the International Labour Organization, 12 January 2006, cited after Bakvis, 'How the World Bank & the IMF Use the Doing Business Report to Promote Labour Market Deregulation in Developing Countries' (n 65) 10.

[69]Lauded by a Bank as a "much-improved" ordinance, World Bank, 'Nepal - First Poverty Reduction Support Credit Project' (Implementation Completion Report, 28 March 2006) Rep No 35462 (IDA-38300) 18; Bakvis, 'The World Bank's Doing Business Report: A Last Fling for the Washington Consensus?' (n 27) 428.

[70]Bakvis, 'How the World Bank & the IMF Use the Doing Business Report to Promote Labour Market Deregulation in Developing Countries' (n 65) 11.

[71]Bakvis, 'The World Bank's Doing Business Report: A Last Fling for the Washington Consensus?' (n 27) 428. On the – somewhat more coherent and cooperative – work of UN System IOs in Nepal post-2006 see Gabriele Köhler, 'The Challenges of Delivering as One: Overcoming Fragmentation and Moving Towards Policy Coherence' (2011) ILO Policy Integration Department Working Paper No 100 https://www.ilo.org/wcmsp5/groups/public/%2D%2D-dgreports/%2D%2D-integration/documents/publication/wcms_153043.pdf accessed 26 April 2020, 5 et seqq.

2. Undermining the ILO Supervisory System's 'Naming and Shaming': The Example of Georgia (2006–2008)

In 2006, Georgia enacted major labour market reforms. The new legislation severely curtailed worker protection in several areas. For example, it allowed dismissals without reason, curtailed collective bargaining by expanding the scope of issues the employer could decide unilaterally, outlawed all strikes that lasted longer than 90 calendar days and created the possibility to prohibit trade unions which were considered to incite "social conflict".[72]

The reform catapulted Georgia, a long-time IDA borrowing country,[73] into the top ranks in the 2007 Doing Business report, which mentioned the country a "top reformer".[74] In the EWI, the country climbed from position 79 in the previous year to position six,[75] and in the overall score from position 112 to 37.[76] The World Bank and the US Agency for International Development (USAID) publicly honoured the Georgian Prime Minister as "top business environment reformer of the year" and inaugurated him and others into a newly created "reformers' club".[77] In the 2008 Doing Business report, Georgia's EWI position was even higher.[78] The report observed that more flexible labour market regulation

> [does not] mean giving up protections. Georgia has some of the most flexible labor regulations in the world and it has ratified all the core labor standards of the International Labour Organization.

---

[72]The issues the employer could decide on unilaterally were observed by the CEACR to include "the duration of a business week, the daily schedule, shifts, the duration of breaks, the time and place of remuneration payment, the duration of and the procedure for granting a leave and unpaid leave, the rules for complying with labour conditions, the type and the procedure for work-related incentives and responsibilities, the procedures for consideration of complaints/applications and other special rules subject to the specifics of the business of the organization", *Observation (CEACR) Right to Organise and Collective Bargaining Convention, 1949 (No 98) - Georgia (Ratification: 1993)* Report of the Committee of Experts on the Application of Conventions and Recommendations (2008) ILC.97/III(1A) 130. See also ITUC, '2007 Annual Survey of Violation of Trade Union Rights' (2007) https://www.ituc-csi.org/annual-survey-of-violations-of?lang=en accessed 26 April 2020 313; Bakvis, 'The World Bank's Doing Business Report: A Last Fling for the Washington Consensus?' (n 27) 430.

[73]Riegner, 'Measuring the Good Governance State: A Legal Reconstruction of the World Bank's "Country Policy and Institutional Assessment"' (n 53) 5.

[74]World Bank, *Doing Business 2007 - How to Reform* (n 40) 1.

[75]ibid 16.

[76]ibid 19.

[77]IFC, 'World Bank and USAID Honor Reformers of Business Environment: Zurab Nogaideli, Prime Minister of Georgia, Recognized as Top Reformer of the Year' *IFC Press Release, 13 April 2007* <https://ifcextapps.ifc.org/ifcext/pressroom/ifcpressroom.nsf/1f70cd9a07d692d685256ee1001cdd37/57dc18e02affaecb852572bc004fb5f7> accessed 26 April 2020.

[78]World Bank, *Doing Business 2008* (n 41) 19; Sam Schueth, 'Assembling International Competitiveness: The Republic of Georgia, USAID, and the Doing Business Project' (2011) 87 Economic Geography 51, 52.

In blatant contrast thereto, the CEACR found that several components of the new legislation were incompatible with some of the fundamental ILO conventions. Inter alia, the limitations placed on the right to strike were found to be incompatible with Conventions No. 87.[79] Moreover, Georgia was among the two-dozen shortlisted cases of serious violations in the 2008 CAS discussions on the CEACR's report, the ILO's 'naming and shaming' procedure.[80]

II. The ILO's (and Other Actors') Critical Response

Provoked by cases like the abovementioned, the Doing Business reports and their impact on labour regulations became the target of criticisms by the ILO, some governments and (especially) trade unions, including the International Confederation of Free Trade Unions (ICFTU)/International Trade Union Confederation (ITUC).[81] The latter responded within weeks of the first report being published in late 2003, undertook own research and attempted to engage in a dialogue with World Bank officials.[82] The ILO took part in Bank-union meetings and soon began to voice critique itself.[83] Concerns were most strongly voiced around the International Labour Office,[84] whereas the picture in the tripartite organs was more diverse, with particularly the employers' groups showing general support for the Doing Business reports.[85] The critique of both ILO and unions centred on methodological aspects (1.), on unbalanced policy suggestions and inferences made by the reports

[79] *Direct Request (CEACR) Freedom of Association and Protection of the Right to Organise Convention, 1948 (No 87) - Georgia (Ratification: 1999)* https://www.ilo.org/dyn/normlex/en/f?p=1000:13100:0::NO:13100:P13100_COMMENT_ID:2277861 accessed 26 April 2020; *Observation (CEACR) Right to Organise and Collective Bargaining Convention, 1949 (No 98) - Georgia (Ratification: 1993)* Report of the Committee of Experts on the Application of Conventions and Recommendations (2008) ILC.97/III(1A) 130; Riegner, 'Measuring the Good Governance State: A Legal Reconstruction of the World Bank's "Country Policy and Institutional Assessment"' (n 53) 5.

[80] ILO, *International Labour Conference, 97th Session, June 2008, Conference Committee on the Application of Standards, Extracts from the Record of Proceedings* (ILO 2008) 19 Part II/67. The opinions within the CAS diverged: While the workers and some governments found Georgia to be in violation of Convention No 87, the employers did not, ibid 19 Part II/70 et seq.

[81] In 2006, the ICFTU was dissolved and merged into the ITUC.

[82] See e.g. the research presented in ITUC/Global Unions (n 58).

[83] Kang (n 16) 488.

[84] See e.g. ILO, 'World Bank Doing Business Report: The Employing Workers Indicator' (2007) GB.300/4/1; ILO, 'The ILO and the Multilateral System' (Governing Body, 303rd Session, 2008) GB.303/6, para 42.

[85] See the various statements made in the Governing Body when it discussed the matter, ILO, 'Minutes of the 300th Session of the Governing Body of the International Labour Office' (2007) GB.300/PV 22 et seqq.

(2.), and the non-conformity of the Doing Business indicators with ILO conventions and other instruments (3.).[86]

1. The Methodological Critique

As to the EWI's methodology, the ILO identified shortcomings in the calculations and procedures underlying the ranking.[87] The International Labour Office argued that the World Bank had in some cases even abandoned the methodological assumptions of those models it had itself used to develop the Doing Business methodology.[88] Moreover, several commentators observed that observations and claims made in the reports lacked a sufficient empirical basis. In particular, this referred to straightforward claims made in the reports that labour market deregulation was a cause for job creation in ranked countries. These claims were found to be unsubstantiated, or without any scientific justification.[89] In some cases, the Bank later made less confident statements in other (albeit not as widely circulated) publications, thereby tacitly revising what it had claimed in the reports.[90]

---

[86]A further point of critique, not discussed here, was that the EWI stood at odds with the World Bank's own approach to labour issues in other policy areas. For example, Bakvis notes that the initialization of the Doing Business project happened at the same time when the Bank, after years of hesitation, finally announced its full support to all four ILO core labour standards contained in the 1998 Declaration on Fundamental Principles and Rights at Work, Bakvis, 'The World Bank's Doing Business Report: A Last Fling for the Washington Consensus?' (n 27) 432. The Bank itself took a positive stance on all four fundamental labour standards, including trade union rights, see 'Economies Perform Better In Coordinated Labor Markets' *World Bank Press Release No. 2003/211/S* http://web.worldbank.org/WBSITE/EXTERNAL/NEWS/0,,contentMDK:20091655~menuPK:34463~pagePK:34370~piPK:34424~theSitePK:4607,00.html accessed 26 April 2020.

[87]ILO, 'World Bank Doing Business Report: The Employing Workers Indicator' (n 84) para 28. Janine Berg and Sandrine Cazes, *The Doing Business Indicators: Measurement Issues and Political Implications* (ILO 2007). Janine Berg and Sandrine Cazes, 'Policymaking Gone Awry: The Labor Market Regulations of the Doing Business Indicators' (2008) 29 Comparative Labour Law and Policy Journal 349.

[88]The Bank had largely relied on a model developed by Botero and others, see Juan C Botero and others, 'The Regulation of Labor' (2004) 119 Quarterly Journal of Economics 1339. Critics argued that the Botero article does not support the methodological approach taken by the Bank regarding the EWI, Bakvis, 'The World Bank's Doing Business Report: A Last Fling for the Washington Consensus?' (n 27) 425 et seq.

[89]Bakvis, 'The World Bank's Doing Business Report: A Last Fling for the Washington Consensus?' (n 27) 425 et seq.

[90]For example, the claim made in Doing Business 2005 that Colombia's reforms had resulted in the creation of 300,000 jobs (World Bank, *Doing Business 2005 - Removing Obstacles to Growth* (n 61) 29) was later implicitly relativized in World Bank, 'Colombia Labor Market Adjustment, Reform and Productivity: What Are the Factors That Matter? (In Two Volumes), Volume I: Issues and Policy Brief November 2005' (2005) Report No. 32068-CO 33 et seqq.

2. The Critique Concerning Unbalanced Policy Suggestions

The International Labour Office also criticized that the EWI was insufficient to make sound indications on how labour market regulation created an investment climate that was conducive to the promotion of employment and decent work, many important factors were left out of account.[91] The reason for this was the selective treatment of only some aspects of labour regulation by the EWI's sub-indicators. Moreover, since the latter primarily focused on costs for enterprises, and not on benefits of worker protection, the EWI was perceived as unbalanced and biased in favour of excessive deregulation.[92] The Office emphasized the comparative advantage of the International Labour Conference's 2007 Tripartite Resolution on the Promotion of Sustainable Enterprises as a "more constructive and balanced" policy framework to achieve MDGs.[93] A related critique, mostly expressed by lawyers, was that the Doing Business indicators were based on an insufficient understanding of law and regulation in general.[94]

3. The Claimed Incompatibility with ILO Conventions

Critique was also voiced as to the compatibility with the EWI and its policy implications with ILO conventions and further instruments.[95] As a reaction, the World Bank stated in its 2008 Doing Business report that its methodology had been improved and that it was

> now possible for an economy to receive the highest score on the ease of employing workers – indicating the most flexible labor regulations – and comply with all 187 ILO conventions.[96]

---

[91]ILO, 'World Bank Doing Business Report: The Employing Workers Indicator' (n 84) para 10. See also Kryvoi (n 49) 57.

[92]Supiot evocatively speaks of "regulatory Darwinism", Alain Supiot, 'A Legal Perspective on the Economic Crisis of 2008' (2010) 149 International Labour Review 151, 155.

[93]ILO, 'World Bank Doing Business Report: The Employing Workers Indicator' (n 84) para 33.

[94]Michaels (n 22) 774; Alvaro Santos, 'Labor Flexibility, Legal Reform and Economic Development' (2009) 50 Virginia Journal of International Law 43, 56 et seqq.; Christoph A Kern, 'Die Doing-Business-Reports der Weltbank - Fragwürdige Quantifizierung rechtlicher Qualität?' (2009) 64 Juristenzeitung 498, para 503; Anne-Julie Kerhuel and Bénédicte Fauvarque-Cosson, 'Is Law an Economic Contest? French Reactions to the Doing Business World Bank Reports and Economic Analysis of the Law' (2009) 57 American Journal of Comparative Law 811, 820 et seqq.

[95]A specific case in point was the compatibility with Art. 2 of the ILO Termination of Employment Convention No 158, Kryvoi (n 49) 48 et seq.

[96]World Bank, *Doing Business 2008* (n 41) 68. The Bank repeated this assertion in more modest terms one year later, World Bank, *Doing Business 2009* (2008) 19.

This claim was, however, readily and forcefully rejected by ILO officials, who pointed at the fact that a large portion of EWI top scorers had not ratified any of the fundamental ILO conventions.[97]

III. The Eventual 'Un-Ranking' of Labour Regulation Data and Inconclusive Attempts to Reform the EWI

From 2007 onwards, pressure on the World Bank to change the EWI increased from several sides. Together with the onset of the global financial crisis, this ultimately led to the removal of the EWI from the Doing Business rankings and from the guide-posts for the World Bank's CPIAs.

In 2007, influential governments joined the critics and increased pressure on the World Bank to respond to the critique and to improve the EWI.[98] In 2008, the World Bank's own Independent Evaluation Group (IEG) issued an independent review of the Doing Business indicators. In the final report,[99] the IEG concurred in many of the criticisms that had been voiced before. It found that the EWI was unbalanced and biased, partially working with exaggerations and failing to establish a meaningful correlation between the EWI rankings and the actual employment situation.[100] The report concluded that the EWI was consistent

> with the letter of relevant [ILO conventions], but not always their spirit.[101]

Trade unions followed up on the IEG report to once again lobby for the abandonment of the EWI.[102]

In 2009, the World Bank finally agreed to discontinue the use of the EWI in its Doing Business rankings and its CPIAs. Since the Doing Business 2011 report, the

---

[97]One official reportedly said that '[i]n the view of the ILO, the statement that the Doing Business indicator is consistent with all 188 ILO labour standards is nonsense, misleading and wrong", Comments by José Manuel Salazar, Executive Director, Employment Sector, ILO at the launch of the 2009 Doing Business Report in Geneva, Monday 22 September 2008, cited after Bakvis, 'The World Bank's Doing Business Report: A Last Fling for the Washington Consensus?' (n 27) 432. See also ILO, 'World Bank Doing Business Report: The Employing Workers Indicator' (n 84) 10.

[98]Notably, the US House of Representatives, after conducting hearings on the Doing Business reports, discussed a bill making World Bank replenishments and funding conditional on the Bank refraining from using the EWI until it had been redesigned so as to give due regard to core labour standards and internationally recognized workers' rights, US House of Represenatives, Amendment in the Nature of a Substitute to HR 6306 (2008) 7; Kang (n 16).

[99]WBG Independent Evaluation Group, 'Doing Business: An Independent Evaluation - Taking the Measure of the World Bank-IFC Doing Business Indicators' (2008) Report No 44995.

[100]ibid xvi, 6 and 32.

[101]ibid xvi.

[102]Moreover, by the time the IEG report was published, the IMF had already instructed its staff to refrain from using the EWI due to similar concerns, Bakvis, 'The World Bank's Doing Business Report: A Last Fling for the Washington Consensus?' (n 27) 433.

Doing Business reports have left the EWI out of their country rankings.[103] However, data on employment regulation was not entirely removed from the reports. Instead, the Bank decided to include it in an annex as non-ranked data on labour markets and worker protection.[104]

As a further concession, the World Bank agreed to consult with the ILO and the social partners to create a new labour protection indicator.[105] To this end, the World Bank Group convened the Doing Business Employing Workers Consultative Group, composed of members of IOs, including the ILO, social partner organizations, NGOs, academia and related professions, acting in their individual capacity.[106] In 2011, the Consultative Group made some proposals for modifying the EWI methodology, but failed to reach consensus on several other important aspects and could not agree on a way forward.[107] The World Bank has since refrained from further work on improving the indicator, and consultations with the ILO on this matter were discontinued in the light of the upcoming World Bank-internal review of the Doing Business reports.[108] An Independent Review Panel, conducting this review in 2013, concurred in the World Bank's decision to suspend the use of the EWI.[109] It furthermore agreed with most of the aforesaid criticisms brought forward against the EWI.[110] The Panel recommended that the World Bank continued to develop better indicators and, for this purpose, suggested consultations with the ILO.[111] Interestingly, the Panel went as far as to question the necessity of the World Bank to focus on labour market regulations to respond to needs of enterprises at all,[112] albeit without bringing this practice to an end.

Data collection on job quality continued and, in 2015, was expanded to include the gender dimension. The Doing Business 2018 report includes a total of eight job quality sub-indicators, mostly covering gender-related questions such as equal

---

[103]World Bank, 'Guidance Note for World Bank Group Staff on the Use of the Doing Business Employing Workers Indicator for Policy Advice' (2009); McCann (n 47) 404.

[104]World Bank, 'Independent Panel Review of the Doing Business Report' (2013) http://pubdocs.worldbank.org/en/237121516384849082/doing-business-review-panel-report-June-2013.pdf accessed 26 April 2020 24.

[105]And to revise the Paying Taxes Indicator with regard to nonwage costs, Bakvis, 'The World Bank's Doing Business Report: A Last Fling for the Washington Consensus?' (n 27) 433.

[106]World Bank, 'Doing Business Employing Workers Consultative Group Final Report' (n 47) 2; Kang (n 16).

[107]World Bank, 'Doing Business Employing Workers Consultative Group Final Report' (n 47) 10, 12 and 13.

[108]World Bank, 'Independent Panel Review of the Doing Business Report' (n 104) 34.

[109]ibid.

[110]ibid 35.

[111]ibid 24 et seq. and 36.

[112]"Claims that the World Bank needs to focus on labour market regulations because enterprises in the Bank's client countries tend to consider these major obstacles to investment and job creation are not borne out by evidence. The IFC Jobs Study, which surveyed 45000 firms in 106 developing countries in early 2013, revealed that only 3 percent of firms surveyed regarded labour market regulations as obstacles to job creation", ibid 35 et seq.

remuneration or maternity leave, and unemployment protection.[113] These newer developments may well have been influenced by the World Bank's timid and cautious change of attitude towards labour regulation more generally, as heralded inter alia by its 2013 World Development Report.[114] Be that as it may, the sustained critique and the EWI's removal from the rankings have also been trailblazers for an overall decline of importance of the Doing Business project in general.[115]

Despite the World Bank now acknowledging the EWI's shortcomings, and despite the reduced relevance of the Doing Business reports in general, the continued inclusion of data on labour markets and worker protection in the reports has noteworthy side-effects. The data presented in newer Doing Business reports, even though unranked and only displayed in its 'raw data' form, is used by private or semi-private institutions as a basis for their own databases and rankings on labour market performance, regulation and competitiveness.[116] Furthermore, the IMF has occasionally referred to EWI rankings after the Bank's decision to discontinue their use.[117] Thus, while not being part of the aggregate Doing Business rankings anymore, the reports' labour-relevant data may still influence such other rankings, some of which tend to have an equally unbalanced perspective on labour market regulation as the initial EWI.[118]

D. The Observed Inter-Organizational Interactions and Their Relevance for the ILO's Model

The EWI episode provides a first lucid example of how inter-organizational interactions occur in practice and how they are relevant for the ILO's model of labour governance. The example comprised—in the terms of the taxonomy developed in Chap. 3—mostly interactions of an indirect and conflictual type (I.). A major underlying cause for this conflict was the EWI's alternative approach on labour (de)regulation (II.). The ensuing conflictual interactions with the World Bank posed a challenge to the ILO's model of labour governance on several levels (III.). That being said, at the same time, the ILO also showed noticeable resilience and managed, at least to a small extent, to even use the challenge in its favour (IV.).

---

[113]Information obtained from World Bank, 'Changes to the Methodology, 2005 - 2017' (Doing Business Website) <http://www.doingbusiness.org/en/methodology/changes-to-the-methodology> accessed 26 April 2020.

[114]World Bank, *World Development Report 2013: Jobs* (2012) 256; McCann (n 47) 406.

[115]McCann (n 47) 405.

[116]Like the World Economic Forum, the International Institute for Management and Development or the Fraser Institute, Aleksynska and Cazes (n 49) 2.

[117]Franz Christian Ebert, 'International Financial Institutions' Approaches to Labour Law: The Case of the International Monetary Fund' in Adelle Blackett and Anne Trebilcock (eds), *Research Handbook on Transnational Labour Law* (Edward Elgar Publishing 2015) 136.

[118]Aleksynska and Cazes (n 49) 2.

I. A Sequence of Mostly Indirect and Conflictual Inter-Organizational Interactions

1. Identifying the Relevant Interactive Conduct

The case study, though narrowed down to a relatively confined subject-matter, has revealed a complex pattern of inter-organizational interactions between the World Bank and the ILO.[119] To structure this complexity, the relevant interactive conduct shall be identified at the outset. To recall, this study defines 'inter-organizational interaction' as one IO's conduct directed at having, or actually having, an effect on the conduct of another IO.[120]

On the side of the Bank, relevant actions are notably the conceptualization and design of the EWI, the promotion of the Doing Business reports as flagship knowledge and their dissemination, their use as reference points in loan schemes and other activity to push for EWI-compatible labour market reforms, the 'authoritative lauding' of reforming states in spite of their records of labour standards violations, and finally the consultations with the ILO on reforming the EWI. On the side of the ILO, the relevant conduct comprises, on the one hand, supporting 'alternative' (i.e. its own) labour market reforms (like in Nepal) and condemning EWI-compatible reforms (like in Georgia), and, on the other hand, criticisms expressed by the International Labour Office, the official publication of research exposing the EWI's methodological weaknesses, lobbying activities and finally the participation in consultations aimed at reforming the EWI.[121]

2. The Predominance of Indirect Interactions

The interactions observed above were mostly indirect and only occasionally direct. In this respect, it is convenient to recall the understanding of inter-organizational

[119]The fact sample also included a variety of other actors, including the Bank's and ILO's respective member states, social partner organizations and their federations, NGOs, and researchers. As has been seen, some of these other actors have had a key influence, for example the trade unions and the ICFTU/ITUC. The latter's actions might have been more conducive to achieve the final outcome than the influence of the involved IOs. Possibly, the ILO and World Bank would have never managed reach the 'resolution' of the conflict (viz. the current situation) without the momentum generated by third actors. It becomes even clearer against this background that inter-organizational interaction can be closely interwoven with interactions between other actors and might be legitimately also categorized and analysed in this other way. For the purposes for this study, however, it is sufficient to conclude that the observed interaction *also* occurred between the World Bank and the ILO, notwithstanding other actors involved. It is therefore appropriate to regard it as qualifying as inter-organizational interaction.

[120]See above, Chap. 3 B. I.

[121]It would require meticulous empirical research to exactly isolate, quantify and measure the effect the Bank's and the ILO's aforesaid actions had on the respective other. However, taken as a whole, it is sufficiently likely that mutual influence occurred.

interaction employed in this study, which is not limited to direct communication, but also includes forms of indirect influence.[122]

As shown in the previous chapter, indirect interactions inter alia comprise instances where one IO influences the output of another by influencing the other's target actors. This is what happened here: The World Bank, using the EWI, inspired, requested or lauded labour market reforms in states in which the ILO was active and was pursuing its own agenda. In some cases, like Nepal, the Bank's influence was large enough to thwart the ILO-facilitated tripartite reform process altogether. In other cases, such as Georgia, the Bank's 'authoritative lauding' of labour market reforms contravened the ILO's public 'naming and shaming' of these reforms.

Apart from these instances of indirect interaction, there has also been occasional direct interaction, notably the ILO's participation in informal meetings with the Bank and trade unions, its public critique of the EWI and its participation in the process to reform the EWI.

3. The Largely Conflictual Character of the Observed Interactions

Moreover, the observed interactions were of a largely conflictual character. Especially from the publication of the first Doing Business report until 2009, there occurred manifest disagreement, open contradiction and opposing actions between the World Bank and the ILO. Conflict occurred both on the conceptual level, centring on the EWI's design and method, and on the implementation level, leading to policy clashes in Nepal, Georgia and further countries in which both the Bank and the ILO were active.

II. The Source of Inter-Organizational Conflict: The EWI's Alternative Approach to Labour Regulation

A major source of conflict was the fact that the EWI used an alternative approach of labour regulation as compared to the ILO's. Framed by the World Bank's different model of labour governance (1.), it embodied an alternative normative vision of 'good' labour regulation (2.) and used institutional authority and financial pressure as alternative methods for that vision's implementation (3.).

1. The Conflict's Backdrop: A Different Model of Labour Governance

The conflict between the ILO and the Bank did not appear in a vacuum. Rather, it must be regarded against the backdrop of the Bank's different model of labour

[122] See Chap. 3 B. II. 2.

governance, which inevitably resulted in a different 'institutional perspective', framed by its mandate, the political, professional and ideational background of its staff and, not least, the positions taken by its member states. As World Bank President Wolfensohn epitomized it in his address to the 1997 International Labour Conference:

> In our work in the Bank we extend to many areas in which you here, in the ILO, are involved, but we work somewhat differently. We start from an economic and development point of view, that is our mandate. When it comes to something like labour standards, we cannot make decisions as an institution of the Bank without the approval and support of our governments. Those of you who represent governments here can appear in another guise on my Board. (...) [Y]ou should understand that the Bank is really involved in so many of the dimensions that you here in the ILO are engaged in, but we are involved in a peripheral way to many of the central thrusts that you have.[123]

Distinct institutional features also played a role in prolonging the conflict. The World Bank's comparatively slow learning process concerning the EWI's methodological and conceptual shortcomings has been explained by the decentralized structure of the World Bank and the World Bank Group as a whole.[124] In a similar manner, the fact that the trade unions, including the ICFTU/ITUC, were quicker and more assertive in criticizing the EWI than the ILO can arguably be explained by the latter's tripartite structure, which needed to accommodate the more EWI-friendly stance of the employers.[125]

2. The EWI's Alternative Normative Vision of 'Good' Labour Regulation

In creating and disseminating the Doing Business reports and their EWI, the World Bank presented its own normative vision of how labour should be regulated. The Doing Business reports prominently claimed that the advocated indicator-based reforms would lead to 'good' regulation. Thus, the World Bank produced, at least regarding those aspects evaluated by the reports, an own benchmark of how 'good' labour regulation should look like. This vision was largely built from a perspective of economic orthodoxy, the primary concern of which was the effective functioning of an (idealized) business-friendly labour market, undisturbed by 'rigid' regulation.[126] From this perspective, it may have been plausible to consider regulation

---

[123]ILO, 'International Labour Conference, Address by Mr. James D. Wolfensohn, President of the World Bank, 13 June 1997' (*ILO Website*) <https://www.ilo.org/public/english/standards/relm/ilc/ilc85/wolf.htm> accessed 26 April 2020.

[124]Hannah Murphy, 'The World Bank and Core Labour Standards: Between Flexibility and Regulation' (2014) 21 Review of International Political Economy 399, 416.

[125]Conor Cradden, 'The True Cost of Doing Business' [2011] *Global Labour Column* 1, 2.

[126]Kryvoi (n 49) 49. The EWI's pledge to labour market efficiency is highly contingent on the underlying understanding of 'efficiency', which is again contingent on underlying economic premises about the functioning of labour markets and the role of their regulation. The Doing Business project has been regarded as being firmly rooted in orthodox liberal economic thought, see

primarily as a cost-driver for businesses and as an exogenous interference with the 'natural' free functioning of labour markets.

However, in doing so, the Bank inevitably relativized and competed with the ILO's normative vision of 'good' labour regulation, which is primarily concerned with promoting social justice and decent work and is based on universal tripartite social dialogue.[127] The ILO's vision rests on a quite different understanding of 'good' labour regulation. From this perspective, labour regulation is the 'better' the more it promotes the organization's decent work agenda, which was discussed and agreed on in universal tripartite social dialogue and has become manifest in the normative instruments the ILO has adopted. This understanding inevitably emphasizes other and more qualitative factors than the EWI and its sub-indicators.[128]

The conceptual discrepancies were finally recognized by both IOs when the World Bank discontinued the use of the EWI in 2009. Yet, they continue to linger, as consultations to reform the EWI have remained inconclusive.

3. The Bank's Alternative Modus of Implementing That Vision

Secondly, the Bank not only formulated an alternative normative vision of labour regulation, but also used its own modus for the latter's implementation.[129] As seen, the Bank used the EWI to develop country specific implementation schemes, to formulate loan conditionalities and to render tailor-cut policy advice to individual states.[130] Hence, the Bank used the EWI to translate its abstract normative vision of regulatory flexibility into concrete policy objectives.[131] What is more, the Bank went on to enforce its regulatory vision by wielding financial pressure, as the given example of Nepal illustrates. This alternative modus of enforcement stands in stark contrast to the ILO's constitutional choice for implementation through persuasion.[132]

---

e.g. Kang (n 16) 484; Sarah Babb and Alexander Kentikelenis, 'International Financial Institutions as Agents of Neoliberalism' in Damien Cahill and others (eds), *The SAGE Handbook of Neoliberalism* (SAGE Publishing 2018) 22.

[127]Kryvoi (n 49) 55 et seq.

[128]In its critique of the EWI, the International Labour Office made the underlying variance of policies visible by explicitly juxtaposing the EWI and the International Labour Conference's 2007 Tripartite Resolution on the Promotion of Sustainable Enterprises, finding that the latter was a "more constructive and balanced" policy framework, ILO, 'World Bank Doing Business Report: The Employing Workers Indicator' (n 84) para 33.

[129]The World Bank's implicit claim to examine labour market policies in the Doing Business reports comes close to a negation of the ILO's proclaimed competence to evaluate and consider economic and financial policies in the Philadelphia Declaration, Supiot (n 92) 156. On the ILO's competence see Chap. 8 B. IV.

[130]McCann (n 47) 401.

[131]ibid.

[132]See Chap. 2 B. II.

III. The World Bank's Interactive Conduct as a Multilevel Challenge to the ILO's Model of Labour Governance

The World Bank's development of the EWI and its forceful promotion of EWI-inspired reforms posed a challenge to the ILO's model of labour governance on several levels.

1. Thwarting ILO Efforts at Country Level

The most visible consequence of the Bank's activities appeared at country level. As the given examples of Nepal and Georgia illustrate, the Bank's conduct at times severely compromised and even thwarted the ILO's efforts to implement its own normative vision in these countries. In Nepal, the Bank bluntly wielded financial threats to pressure the king to deregulate job termination laws without implementing the other agreed-on components of the ILO-facilitated reform process. Regarding Georgia, the Bank directly contradicted the ILO's 'naming and shaming' of the country's labour market reforms by publicly lauding Georgia's leadership as 'top reformers' for implementing these very reforms. In both instances, the Bank's statements were not only backed by its considerable financial leverage, which outweighed the ILO's limited capacity for providing technical assistance. Rather, the weight of the Bank's invocation of EWI rankings was also reinforced by its reputation and authority as a 'knowledge institution' for economic and development questions. These interventions challenged the ILO's model of labour governance at country level.

2. Challenge on a Normative Level: Reaching Out for the 'Spirit' of ILO Instruments

Moreover, the Bank's promotion of EWI-inspired reforms stood at odds with ILO instruments and thus challenged the ILO's model on a normative level.

a) The EWI's Inconsistence with the 'Spirit' of ILO Conventions

As the ILO and other critics have pointed out, the EWI and the reforms it inspired stood at odds with ILO conventions.[133]

At the outset, it deserves mention that, legally speaking, the Bank can hardly be held in violation of ILO conventions. To begin with, such a violation presupposes the applicability of ILO instruments. However, the Bank itself has not ratified (nor

[133] See above, C. II. 3.

could it ratify) the ILO Constitution or ILO conventions and thus is not formally bound to observe them (a point further explored in Chap. 9). What is more, a number of states that scored high on the EWI had not ratified the relevant ILO conventions either.[134] But even insofar as ILO instruments were applicable, their clash with the EWI would hardly ever resemble a norm conflict in a strict, norm-logical sense, i.e. that observance of one norm necessarily entails the violation of the other.[135] This is because the EWI is not a legally binding benchmark to begin with. While the Bank can wield considerable financial pressure to implement EWI-inspired reforms, there is no legal obligation of states to follow suit.[136]

However, as the World Bank's IEG pointed out in 2008, the EWI did not conform to the "spirit" of ILO conventions.[137] This "spirit" is the manifestation of the ILO's underlying normative vision of 'good' labour market regulation, which again is the product of universal tripartite social dialogue within the ILO. The 'spirit' largely emanates from the application and (formally non-binding) interpretation of ILO conventions by the ILO supervisory bodies, shows itself in non-binding instruments, such as ILO recommendations, or underlies the ILO's technical assistance programmes.

---

[134]In some cases, the EWI top-listed states which had not ratified a single ILO convention. For instance, Palau and Marshall Islands received high scores on the EWI in 2006 and 2007 (World Bank, *Doing Business 2006 - Creating Jobs* (2005) 100 and 144; World Bank, *Doing Business 2007 - How to Reform* (n 40) 19). Palau only joined the ILO in 2012 and has ratified only the Maritime Labour Convention. The Marshall Islands only became an ILO member in 2007 and merely ratified two ILO conventions since.

[135]On the different types of norm conflicts see Clarence Wilfred Jenks, 'The Conflict of Law-Making Treaties' (1953) 30 British Yearbook of International Law 401, 425 et seqq.; Nele Matz, *Wege zur Koordinierung völkerrechtlicher Verträge* (Springer 2005) 9 et seqq.; Joost Pauwelyn, *Conflict of Norms in Public International Law: How WTO Law Relates to Other Rules of International Law* (Cambridge University Press 2003) 164 et seqq.; ILC, 'Fragmentation of International Law: Difficulties Arising from the Diversification and Expansion of International Law, Report of the Study Group of the International Law Commission, Finalized by Martti Koskenniemi' (2006) UN Doc A/CN.4/L.682 para 21 et seqq.

[136]Santos (n 94) 55; Kryvoi (n 49) 48. Moreover, the EWI's sub-indicators had a limited ambit (which, for example, did not evaluate the situation concerning trade union rights to begin with). However, sight should not be lost of the fact that there are cross-connections between the factors the EWI evaluates and the aforesaid violations. For example, Belarus reportedly used its employer-friendly legislation on fixed-term contracts aa means to combat independent trade unions, see ibid 54; Yaraslau Kryvoi, 'Discrimination and Security of Employment in a Post-Soviet Context' (2006) 22 The International Journal of Comparative Labour Law and Industrial Relations 5, 14.

[137]WBG Independent Evaluation Group (n 99) xvi. For a case of incompatibility with the 'letter' of ILO conventions see Art. 2 ILO Convention No 158 (Termination of Employment Convention, 1982 (No 158) (adopted 22 June 1982, entered into force 23 November 1985) 1412 UNTS 1), Kryvoi (n 49) 51 et seq.

b) The Bank's Subliminal Second-Guessing of Tripartite Social Dialogue

As seen, the Bank responded comparatively early, at least on paper, to the critique that the EWI was irreconcilable with ILO conventions. However, by claiming that a country could score high on the EWI and still "comply with all 187 ILO conventions",[138] the World Bank at the same time subliminally second-guessed what the normative content of ILO conventions and their 'spirit' actually was. To be able to argue that the EWI was consistent with ILO conventions, the World Bank necessarily had to verify the scope and content of the relevant ILO instruments in the first place. The Bank did not make its interpretation of ILO conventions explicit. Nevertheless, the Bank advanced a view on the EWI's consistence with ILO conventions that was clearly deviating from the ILO's (and was immediately rejected by ILO officials). In doing so, the Bank—arguably accidentally—also relativized the ILO's role as the interpreter of its own instruments. As McCann put it, this rang

> the death-knell of the ILO's unchallenged pre-eminence in the international labour law arena. The outcome is that the Organization no longer assuredly governs its own discourses on legal regulation, including as they relate to ILO norms.[139]

3. Accentuating Differences Between the ILO's Tripartite Constituents

Thirdly, the EWI and its use by the Bank also had implications for the functioning of the ILO's model, notably the fragile balance of power between the ILO's tripartite constituents.

Inside the ILO's tripartite organs and bodies, the EWI has sparked different reactions, with employers showing general sympathy for the Doing Business project and workers being decidedly against it.[140] It is likely that this is the reason why the tripartite Governing Body and CAS, respectively, treated the EWI rather hesitantly. Both bodies published their respective discussions but did not adopt clear positions. By contrast, the ILO's non-tripartite bodies, notably the International Labour Office, could take stronger positions against the EWI (as could the CEACR with respect to the Bank-lauded reforms in Georgia).

The EWI's actual repercussions on the functioning of tripartism inside the ILO seem to have remained neglectable. However, the EWI's argumentative reinforcement of one of the tripartite constituents' interests is a point of systemic interest for the ILO, especially since the EWI called into question the ILO's tripartite-backed own normative ideal of labour regulation. By advancing an alternative vision of 'good' labour regulation, articulated by a reputable organization like the Bank, the EWI could have contributed to dividing the ILO's constituents, and thus could have

---

[138] World Bank, *Doing Business 2008* (n 41) 68.

[139] McCann (n 47) 401.

[140] See above, C. II.

reached the ILO at its most vulnerable spot, namely its existential dependence on tripartite dialogue, consensus and trust.

IV. Small Opportunities for the ILO Resulting from the Bank's Conduct

Despite this large-scale multilevel challenge to the ILO's model, the EWI episode also provided small opportunities for the ILO's model that deserve to be mentioned. Firstly, the Bank's challenge induced a number of actors to gather behind the ILO's model of labour governance (1.). The second is that the observed interactions provided an opportunity for the ILO to get another 'foot in the door' with the Bank (2.).

1. Reaffirming Support from Actors

The significant challenge to the ILO's model posed by the Bank's powerful pursuit of the EWI-based reform agenda remains the most dominant aspect of the EWI episode. However, it should not be overlooked that, reversely, the ILO posed a challenge to the World Bank's model of labour governance, too.

For instance, as the debate on the EWI gained momentum, ILO conventions and their interpretation by ILO bodies quickly became a central reference point for critics. The conventions could be relied on by the International Labour Office and by 'labour-friendly' Bank officials and member states, but also by trade unions and other third actors. All these actors could refer to them as authoritative instruments that represented an alternative model of labour regulation compared to the one favoured by the EWI. In the same way, they could rely on the conventions' "spirit"—the tripartite consensus they embody, and their interpretation and application by established supervisory practice. The ILO and its instruments and practice provided a crystallization point for contestation.[141] The ILO had the 'soft' advantage of representing a model of labour governance based on universal tripartite social dialogue coupled with persuasion, rather than partisan 'business-friendliness' coupled with financial pressure. As the onset of the financial crisis called orthodox economic policies into question and reinforced demands for a more socially just globalization, the ILO's authority and persuasive power gained weight. It is remarkable that, although the ILO never posed an existential challenge to the Bank's model of labour governance, the Bank ultimately yielded to the criticisms voiced against the EWI. This is, of course, not the achievement of the ILO alone, but it may be doubted if the same result would have been occurred without it.

[141] On the ILO's own role as a provider of regulatory narratives Kerry Rittich, 'The ILO: Challenges in Times of Crisis' (2015) 154 International Labour Review 85, 87.

In sum, the EWI episode offered a chance for discursive reaffirmation of the ILO's model of labour governance. The EWI's weak spots—its methodological and conceptual weaknesses and its business-friendly bias—provided a chance to corrobate and publicly advocate the strengths of the ILO's approach. While hard to ascertain empirically, it might be that the EWI episode has even resulted in a comparative 'net gain' for the ILO in the long run.

2. The EWI Episode as a Potential Opportunity for the ILO

Moreover, the EWI episode provided the ILO with an additional possibility to expand its outreach to the Bank. The relevance of this point becomes clearer if one considers that the Bank has traditionally been rather reticent to cooperate with the ILO.[142] Therefore, the ILO was well-advised not just to fundamentally oppose the EWI, but to seek dialogue and to take part in discussions and consultations when offered by the Bank. In this way, the ILO could play out its persuasive capacity. Thus, even if conflict-ridden, the struggle over the EWI opened another door for the ILO to engage with the Bank.

E. Conclusion

This chapter has examined inter-organizational interactions between the ILO and the World Bank, centring on the World Bank's creation, dissemination and use of the EWI in its annual Doing Business reports, and the impact this had on the ILO and its work. It illustrated how the Bank created and the EWI to request deregulatory labour law reforms, which it backed with financial pressure. Moreover, it traced how the ILO reacted to these activities, coalescing with other actors and eventually pressuring the World Bank to discontinue the EWI's use in its Doing Business rankings.

The analysis revealed a complex pattern of mostly indirect and conflictual interactions. The conflict was rooted in the ILO's and World Bank's different models of labour governance. Both IOs advocated for differing visions of 'good' labour regulation. The World Bank's enforcement of its declaredly business-friendly approach through financial pressure posed a challenge to the ILO's approach on multiple levels. On the other hand, the observed interactions also resembled subtle challenges of the World Bank's approach by the ILO and provided the latter with certain limited opportunities to even strengthen its own model of labour governance in the long run.

[142] Katherine A Hagen, 'Policy Dialogue between the International Labour Organization and the International Financial Institutions: The Search for Convergence' (2003) FES Occasional Papers No 9 <http://library.fes.de/pdf-files/bueros/genf/50035.pdf> accessed 26 April 2020, 9; Francis Maupain, *The Future of the International Labour Organization in the Global Economy* (Hart Publishing 2013) 72 et seqq.; McCann (n 47) 412.

5. The ILO's Model and 'Benevolent Unilateralism': The ECtHR's Reception of ILO Instruments and Practice

Not all of the ILO's interactions with other IOs have been as openly conflict-ridden as those with the World Bank. For instance, interactions between the ILO and the Council of Europe (CoE), more particularly the European Court of Human Rights (ECtHR), have been of a quite different type. To a significant part, these interactions are characterized by the Court trying to align its jurisprudence to the ILO and its work. The Court has increasingly taken into account the ILO's work when interpreting the European Convention of Human Rights (ECHR),[1] up to the point where it modified and even reversed its own prior jurisprudence in the light of ILO instruments and practice.[2] On the other hand, the Court has asserted the sole competence to decide whether and to what extent to do so, and has on several occasions chosen not to give regard to, or to deviate from, the ILO and its positions.

---

[1]Convention for the Protection of Human Rights and Fundamental Freedoms (adopted 4 November 1950, entered into force 3 September 1953) CETS No 5 (ECHR).

[2]On systemic integration see ILC, 'Fragmentation of International Law: Difficulties Arising from the Diversification and Expansion of International Law, Report of the Study Group of the International Law Commission, Finalized by Martti Koskenniemi' (2006) UN Doc A/CN.4/L.682; Campbell McLachlan, 'The Principle of Systemic Integration and Article 31(3)(c) of the Vienna Convention' (2005) 54 International and Comparative Law Quarterly 279; Benn McGrady, 'Fragmentation of International Law or "Systemic Integration" of Treaty Regimes: EC-Biotech Products and the Proper Interpretation of Article 31(3)(c) of the Vienna Convention on the Law of Treaties' (2008) 42 Journal of World Trade 589; Bruno Simma and Theodore Kill, 'Harmonising Investment Protection and International Human Rights: First Steps towards A Methodology' in Christina Binder and others (eds), *International Investment Law for the 21st Century* (Oxford University Press 2009). Indeed, some of the cases discussed in this chapter have repeatedly been discussed under this heading, see Adamantia Rachovitsa, 'The Principle of Systematic Integration in Human Rights Law' (2017) 66 International and Comparative Law Quarterly 557.

H. Gött, *The Law of Interactions Between International Organizations*, Beiträge zum ausländischen öffentlichen Recht und Völkerrecht 299,
https://doi.org/10.1007/978-3-662-62389-3_5

A. The CoE and the ECtHR as Actors in Labour Governance

At the outset, it is convenient to contextualize the interactions discussed in this chapter by giving a brief overview on the CoE and the ECtHR as actors in labour governance.

The CoE, founded in 1949, is a European regional IO with currently 47 member states. Its aims are to "achieve a greater unity between its members for the purpose of safeguarding and realising the ideals and principles which are their common heritage and facilitating their economic and social progress" (Art. 1 lit. a CoE Statute[3]). Thematically, the CoE has an c almost unlimited purview (Art. 1 lit. b CoE Statute),[4] including inter alia an overall competence to promote human rights and to facilitate the economic and social progress of its member states. To pursue its aims, the CoE can engage in political activity and can adopt instruments, notably treaties and recommendations.[5]

The CoE has a decentralized organizational structure. Its only two statutory organs are the Committee of Ministers (CM)[6] and the Parliamentary Assembly (PACE).[7] Besides, there are numerous further institutions and bodies, like the ECtHR,[8] that are affiliated to the CoE and do a significant amount of the

[3]Statute of the Council of Europe (adopted 5 May 1949, entered into force 3 August 1949) CETS No. 1 (CoE Statute).

[4]Jörg Polakiewicz, 'Council of Europe (COE)', *Max Planck Encyclopedia of Public International Law* (Oxford University Press 2013) para 10. The only explicit exception are questions of national defence (Art. 1 lit. d CoE Statute). Its activities have centred on human rights, parliamentary democracy and the rule of law, Jörg Polakiewicz, 'Alternatives to Treaty-Making and Law-Making by Treaty and Expert Bodies in the Council of Europe' in Rüdiger Wolfrum and Volker Röben (eds), *Developments of International Law in Treaty Making* (Springer 2005) 245.

[5]Treaties are prepared within the CoE and are adopted by a decision of the CM. They become binding upon ratification by the member states, see Jörg Polakiewicz, *Treaty-Making in the Council of Europe* (Council of Europe Publishing 1999).

[6]Art. 10(i) CoE Statute. The intergovernmental CM is the CoE's principal decision-making body. It chooses and prioritizes the CoE's policies, adopts the latter's instruments, such as conventions and recommendations, adopts the CoE's budget and supervises a range of bodies, Polakiewicz, 'Council of Europe (COE)' (n 4) para 17. Notably, the CM supervises the execution of the ECtHR's judgments (Art. 46(2) – (4) ECHR).

[7]Art. 10(ii) CoE Statute.

[8]On the relations between the ECtHR and the PACE and the CM see Elisabeth Lambert-Abdelgawad, 'The Court as a Part of the Council of Europe: The Parliamentary Assembly and the Committee of Ministers' in Andreas Føllesdal, Birgit Peters and Geir Ulfstein (eds), *Constituting Europe. The European Court of Human Rights in a National, European and Global Context* (Cambridge University Press 2013).

organization's work.[9] Often, such bodies are erected by separate instruments, especially treaties adopted within the CoE, such as the ECHR.[10]

---

[9]The legal relations between the Court and the CoE as a whole is not self-evident, see the discussions by Georg Ress, 'Die Organisationsstruktur internationaler Gerichte, insbesondere des neuen Europäischen Gerichtshofs für Menschenrechte' in Alfred Rest and others (eds), *Liber Amicorum Professor Ignaz Seidl-Hohenveldern* (Brill 1998) 552 et seq. and Wittinger, *Der Europarat: Die Entwicklung seines Rechts und der 'Europäischen Verfassungswerte'* (Nomos 2005) 507 et seqq. Neither the CoE Statute nor the ECHR confer organ status on the ECtHR. Early commentators argued that the Court and the CoE were legally separate institutions. For instance, Carstens argued in 1956 that the ECHR established a separate community of states (*Staatengemeinschaft*), which was legally distinct from the CoE, and of which the ECtHR was an organ, Karl Carstens, *Das Recht des Europarats* (Duncker & Humblot 1956) 196; Heribert Golsong, *Das Rechtsschutzsystem der Europäischen Menschenrechtskonvention* (1958) 30. This idea was later picked up and discussed by Georg Ress, ibid 545 ("*Staatengemeinschaftsorgan*"). By contrast, more recent commentators have qualified the ECtHR as an organ (Fabian Wittreck, *Die Verwaltung der Dritten Gewalt* (Mohr Siebeck 2006) 232), a "de facto organ" (Marten Breuer, 'The Council of Europe and International Institutional Law – An Appraisal' in Stefanie Schmahl and Marten Breuer (eds), *The Council of Europe: Its Laws and Policies* (Oxford University Press 2017) para 38.37) or as belonging "to the institutional structure of the CoE" (Polakiewicz, 'Council of Europe (COE)' (n 4) para 28). Others have proposed a situation of *Organleihe* (Heinrich Klebes, 'Die Rechtsstruktur des Europarats und insbesondere der Parlamentarischen Versammlung' (Europa-Institut 1996) 340 11) or have confined themselves to describing the situation as unclear and calling for legislative clarification (Ress, ibid 574; Wittinger, ibid 519). To appraise these positions, it is important to recall that for present purposes, it is not necessary to determine whether the ECtHR is an organ. It suffices if its activities are attributable to the CoE. Against this backdrop, the arguments in favour of attributing the ECtHR to the CoE prevail. Membership to the CoE and ratification of the ECHR are nowadays mutually conditional, Arts. 58(3) and 59(1) ECHR. In addition, it is established CoE practice that membership is conditional on ratifying the ECHR, ibid 513. Submission to ECtHR jurisdiction is obligatory (Art. 32 ECHR). The Court's expenditure is borne by the CoE (Art. 50 ECHR). Moreover, there are numerous institutional, procedural and financial interlinkages between the Court and the CoE, discussed e.g. by Norbert Paul Engel, 'Status, Ausstattung und Personalhoheit des Inter-Amerikanischen und des Europäischen Gerichtshofs für Menschenrechte' (2003) 30 Europäische Grundrechte-Zeitschrift 122, 123 et seqq. To give but one example, the CM supervises the execution of the Court's judgments (Art. 46(2) – (4) ECHR). Insofar as the Court retains autonomy from CM supervision, this is often a necessary corollary of its judicial independence. Even if one rejects the idea of the Court a 'quasi-organ", the numerous interconnections and interdependencies between the Court and the CoE would allow attribution in two ways: One way would be to consider the Court the CoE's 'agent', as defined in Art. 2 lit. d DARIO, as the Court is an entity charged by the CoE to discharge the latter's constitutional task of promoting human rights. Alternatively, Art. 9 DARIO would apply, as the CoE has at numerous times acknowledged and adopted the Court's activities. This has occurred not only in countless statements of CoE organs, but also in the establishment of the aforesaid close institutional and procedural links, notably the supervision of the implementation of ECtHR judgments by the CM, which even has established a special procedure to this effect, see Council of Europe, *The Implementation of Judgments of the European Court of Human Rights* (Council of Europe Publishing 2018). Last not least, the Court's judgments nowadays bear the name and emblem of the CoE.

[10]Separate treaties with an institutional integration into the CoE can also be concluded as so-called partial agreements by only some the CoE's member states, CM, Statutory Resolution (93) 28 on Partial and Enlarged Agreements (92nd session, 14 May 1993) <https://search.coe.int/cm/Pages/result_details.aspx?ObjectID=0900001680534828> accessed 26 April 2020.

The CoE has early on engaged in labour governance. Already in the early 1950s, the CoE set up an own comprehensive social programme, involving substantive policies and the creation of the CM's Social Committee as an institutional forum.[11] The CoE has engaged in political activities in labour issues ever since.[12] Furthermore, it has created international legal norms on social questions, many of which concerning labour issues.[13] A prime case in point is the ESC, discussed further in Chap. 6, which contains a wide array of labour-related rights.[14]

Just as the CoE as a whole, the ECtHR has become an important actor of labour governance. While the regulation of work-related rights in the ECHR is piecemeal, the Convention prohibits forced and compulsory labour (Art. 4 ECHR) and guarantees freedom of association (Art. 11 ECHR). The ECtHR has built a considerably body of case-law on them.[15] This case-law has been influential for the development of domestic labour law in the CoE member states. Moreover, it has also had an important impact on other international organizations and non-CoE member states' domestic courts.[16]

---

[11]Which later drafted the ESC. The CoE worked on social question in parallel to, but also in cooperation with, the ILO and the WHO, Arthur Henry Robertson, *The Council of Europe: Its Structure, Functions and Achievements* (Stevens & Sons 1956) 132. See also the commitments in the 2005 Warsaw Action Plan, CoE, 'Warsaw Action Plan' (2005) CM(2005)80.

[12]See already the entire chapter on "social questions" in CoE, 'Programme of Work of the Council of Europe (Communication of the CM, Doc. 238, 20 May 1954)' <http://assembly.coe.int/nw/xml/XRef/Xref-XML2HTML-en.asp?fileid=560&lang=en>. See further Arthur Henry Robertson, *The Relations Between the Council of Europe and the United Nations* (UNITAR 1972). See as a further example PACE, Res 1442 (2005) The Right to Strike in Essential Services: Economic Implications (6 June 2005).

[13]By 1971, the CoE had already adopted 16 separate conventions and four protocols regarding social questions, many of which regarding labour issues in the narrower sense, see Robertson, *The Relations Between the Council of Europe and the United Nations* (n 12) 40.

[14]The ESC will be dealt with in more detail in Chap. 6.

[15]ECtHR cases with a labour law component have been comparatively rare, but include a line of important landmark decisions, Angelika Nußberger, 'Auswirkungen der Rechtsprechung des Europäischen Gerichtshofs für Menschenrechte auf das deutsche Arbeitsrecht' [2012] Recht der Arbeit 270, 276 and the cases discussed therein.

[16]See below, B. IV. 2.

B. Reception of ILO Instruments and Practice: The ECtHR's Evolving Stance on Collective Bargaining and the Right to Strike

Over time, the Court has, besides other international instruments,[17] increasingly taken ILO instruments and practice into account.[18] The ECtHR has referred to ILO instruments and practice in several ways. For one part, it has repeatedly included ILO conventions, recommendations, reports and practice of the supervisory bodies in the "Relevant Law" section of its judgments,[19] which serves to provide an overview over the pertinent domestic and international norms and practice on the subject-matter of the case.[20] In addition, the Court has repeatedly relied on ILO instruments and practice in its legal assessment (the "The Law" section of judgments).[21]

---

[17] *Veniamin Tymoshenko and Others v. Ukraine* App No 48408/12 (ECtHR, 2 October 2014), paras 23 et seqq.; *Trade Union of the Police in the Slovak Republic and Others v. Slovakia* App No 11828/08 (ECtHR, 25 September 2012), paras 35 et seqq. The Court virtually never referred *only* to ILO instruments and practice. Instead, it referred to them together with other international instruments and practice. This is particularly true for the ESC and the ECSR's practice, but also for other instruments of the CoE or of other origin.

[18] This by and large coincided with the incremental development of the Court's general interpretative approach, see below, C. II. In its early case law, the Court was markedly more reluctant. It would, if making references to other treaties at all, much rather refer to the ESC. The Court laid ground for this in its famous dictum in *Airey v. Ireland*, Judgment (1979) Series A No 32, para 26 that "[w]hilst the Convention sets forth what are essentially civil and political rights, many of them have implications of a social or economic nature. The Court therefore considers, like the Commission, that the mere fact that an interpretation of the Convention may extend into the sphere of social and economic rights should not be a decisive factor against such an interpretation; there is no water-tight division separating that sphere from the field covered by the Convention", Nußberger (n 15) 271.

[19] *Sindicatul "Păstorul Cel Bun" v. Romania* ECHR 2013–V 41, paras 56 et seqq.; *Vörður Ólafsson v. Iceland* ECHR 2010–III 281, para 23 et seqq.; *Danilenkov and Others v. Russian Federation* ECHR 2009–III 365, paras 105 et seqq.; *Manole and "Romanian Farmers Direct" v. Romania* App No 46551/06 (ECtHR, 16 June 2015), paras 22 et seqq.; *Trade Union of the Police in the Slovak Republic and Others v. Slovakia* (n 17), paras 33 et seqq.

[20] Even if those norms do not appear in the Court's legal analysis, Angelika Nußberger, 'The ECtHR' Use of Decisions of International Courts and Quasi-Judicial Bodies' in Amrei Müller and Hege Elisabeth Kjos (eds), *Judicial Dialogue and Human Rights* (Cambridge University Press 2017) 420.

[21] *Sindicatul "Păstorul Cel Bun" v. Romania* (n 19) para 142; *Vörður Ólafsson v. Iceland* (n 19) para 53; *ECtHR, Danilenkov and Others v. Russian Federation* (n 19) para 130; *Trade Union of the Police in the Slovak Republic and Others v. Slovakia* (n 17) para 67. Finally, ILO instruments and practice have not only informed the judgments themselves but have also been relied on to support the legal argument in concurring and dissenting opinions, *Sindicatul "Păstorul Cel Bun" v. Romania* (n 19) Joint partly dissenting opinion of Judges Spielmann, Villiger, López Guerra, Bianku, Møse and Jäderblom, para 3; *Hrvatski Liječnički Sindikat v. Croatia* App No 36701/09 (ECtHR, 27 November 2014) Concurring Opinion of Judge Pinto de Albuquerque, paras 3 and 6.

The ECtHR's recourse to ILO instruments and practice, and the wider impact it had, is lucidly illustrated by the development of the Court's jurisprudence on the scope of Art. 11 ECHR, guaranteeing freedom of association. The particular aspect examined here is the Court's evolving stance on whether that provision includes the rights to bargain collectively and to strike. While the ILO had early on engaged in the protection and promotion of both rights, they were not included in the ECHR's text (I.). Based on the latter, the ECtHR's earlier case-law took a restrictive view on them being included in Art. 11 ECHR (II.). However, as the Court gradually gave increasing weight to ILO instruments and practice when interpreting Art. 11 ECHR, this position changed. Eventually, the Court fundamentally reversed its earlier position and included the right to collective bargaining and the right to strike into the scope of freedom of association (III.). This reversal had repercussions reaching beyond the ECHR (IV.).

I. Background: The Rights to Bargain Collectively and to Strike in the ILO and in the ECHR

The ILO has early on promoted collective bargaining. Its own tripartite structure and working method itself embodies the idea of collective bargaining at international level. After initial steps had already been taken in the interwar period, the ILO adopted the Freedom of Association and Protection of the Right to Organise Convention (ILO Convention No 87) in 1948 and the Right to Organize and Collective Bargaining Convention (ILO Convention No 98) in 1949 as general instruments for the promotion of freedom of association and collective bargaining with a view to regulating terms and conditions of employment by collective agreements. As mentioned in Chap. 2, both ILO Convention No 87 and ILO Convention No 98 nowadays rank as two of the ILO's eight fundamental labour conventions. Further relevant conventions were adopted in the 1970s and 1980s.

The right to strike has always remained more controversial within the ILO. It is not explicitly protected by ILO conventions, but inter alia affirmed in the 1957 Resolution concerning the Abolition of Anti-Trade Union Legislation in the States Members of the International Labour Organisation,[22] the 1970 Resolution concerning Trade Union Rights and Their Relation to Civil Liberties,[23] and further

[22]International Labour Conference (40th session) Resolution concerning the Abolition of Anti-Trade Union Legislation in the States Members of the International Labour Organisation (26 June 1957) XL ILO Official Bulletin No 1 30.

[23]International Labour Conference (54th session) Resolution Concerning Trade Union Rights And Their Relation To Civil Liberties (25 June 1970) LIII ILO Official Bulletin No 3 287, para 15.

non-binding instruments. Moreover, the CFA affirmed as early as 1952 that the right to strike formed an "intrinsic corollary" of freedom of association.[24] The CEACR followed suit in 1959.[25] Accordingly, the right to strike was understood to be implied in Arts. 3, 8 and 10 ILO Convention No 87.[26] Since then, the ILO supervisory bodies have developed an elaborate body of 'soft law jurisprudence' on a broad array of aspects of the right to strike.

Notwithstanding this early and rich practice, the ILO's instruments and practice did not leave their mark on the text of the ECHR or its additional protocols.[27] On the contrary, the drafters of the ECHR deliberately abstained from mentioning the rights to bargain collectively and to strike.[28] One reason for this was that they pragmatically intended to quickly come up with a regional human rights instrument containing rights that were protected in the CoE member states' domestic legal orders and on which these states could agree.[29] As a result, Art. 11(1) ECHR merely provides that

> [e]veryone has the right to freedom of peaceful assembly and to freedom of association with others, including the right to form and to join trade unions for the protection of his interests.

---

[24]ILO, *Digest of Decisions and Principles of the Freedom of Association Committee of the Governing Body of the ILO* (5th edn, ILO 2006) para 523.

[25]ILO, 'Report of the Committee of Experts on the Application of Conventions and Recommendations' (International Labour Conference, 43rd Session, 1959) Part I, Report III 114 et seq.

[26]ILO, 'Report of the Committee of Experts on the Application of Conventions and Recommendations, General Survey on Freedom of Association and Collective Bargaining' (International Labour Conference, 81st Session, 1994), Report III (Part 4B) para 149.

[27]Neither was there any institutional collaboration between the ILO and the CoE. Unlike in the UN Human Rights Commission and its working committees, there was no ILO representative present in the ECHR drafting committees, see the list of members of the Committee of Experts, CoE, 'Report of the Committee of Experts' (16 March 1950) CM/WP 1 (50) 15; A 924, IV TP 2–55 4 et seq. Whether this was because there was no inter-organizational agreement in place that would regulate such an observer status (the ILO-CoE only came into force in 1952 when the ECHR had already been adopted) is hard to ascertain but seems possible. The ECHR drafting committees were instead focusing on the UN's Universal Declaration of Human Rights and the ongoing work on the UN Human Rights Covenants.

[28]Tonia Novitz, *International and European Protection of the Right to Strike* (Oxford University Press 2003) 133 et seq. Indeed, the final text of the ECHR does not contain any reference to ILO instruments. This is a noteworthy difference to other human rights treaties, in the preparation of which the ILO had participated, such as the ESC, which will be discussed in Chap. 6. Moreover, both UN Human Rights Covenants contain explicit references to ILO Convention No 87, one of the two fundamental conventions on freedom of association, in Art. 22(3) ICCPR and Art. 8 (3) ICESCR, due to the ILO's involvement and influence, see on the latter Philip Alston, 'The United Nations' Specialized Agencies and Implementation of the International Covenant on Economic, Social and Cultural Rights' (1979) 18 Columbia Journal of Transnational Law 79, 84.

[29]Novitz *International and European Protection of the Right to Strike* (n 28) 134.

II. Earlier Case-Law: 'Safe Distance' From ILO Instruments and Practice

The early jurisprudence of the ECtHR focused on this rudimentary wording of Art. 11(1) ECHR. In three leading decisions from the mid-1970s, *National Union of Belgian Police v. Belgium*,[30] *Swedish Engine Drivers' Union v. Sweden*[31] and *Schmidt and Dahlström v. Sweden*,[32] the ECtHR rejected claims that the right to collective bargaining and the right to strike were protected under the ECHR.[33] Thenceforth, it was established case law for 30 years that Art. 11(1) ECHR does not guarantee a right to pursue occupational interests by specific means, neither the conclusion of collective agreements nor strikes. At most, the ECtHR during this period would concede that strikes represented "without any doubt one of the most important of these means".[34]

In this early phase, the ECtHR remained in safe distance to developments in international labour law. By the time the ECtHR issued its three leading judgments, it had already been established ILO practice that the rights to collective bargaining and to strike were protected aspects of freedom of association as laid down in ILO Convention No 87 and other ILO instruments.[35] Nonetheless, in none of the three aforementioned trade union cases, the ECtHR referenced pertinent ILO instruments or practice.[36] In *National Union of Belgian Police*, the ECtHR noted that Belgium

[30] *National Union of Belgian Police v. Belgium* (1975) Series A No 19.

[31] *Swedish Engine Drivers' Union v. Sweden* (1976) Series A No 20.

[32] *Schmidt and Dahlström v. Sweden* (1976) Series A No 21.

[33] ibid para 36; *Swedish Engine Drivers' Union v. Sweden* (n 31) para 40. The European Commission of Human Rights had opined before that states "should recognise, as a matter of principle, the legal capacity of trade unions to conclude collective agreements in the interest of their members", but eventually reached the same conclusion, *Svenska Lokmannaförbundet v. Sweden* (1974) Series B No 18 (Commission Report), paras 69 et seqq. and 77 et seqq.

[34] *Schmidt and Dahlström v. Sweden* (n 32) para 36. See also *Unison v. United Kingdom* ECHR 2002–I 491. The Court held that Art. 11(1) ECHR did not provide a right for specific treatment that is not indispensable for trade union freedom, such as the retroactivity of benefits, *Schmidt and Dahlström v. Sweden* (n 32) para 34.

[35] Lee Swepston, 'Human Rights Law and Freedom of Association: Development Through ILO Supervision' [1998] International Labour Review para 187. What is more, outside the ILO, both rights had explicitly been included into treaties on economic, social and cultural rights, like Art. 6 ESC (in 1961) and Art. 8 ICESCR (in 1966).

[36] The only international instrument the ECtHR occasionally referred to in the context of the right to bargain collectively and the right to strike was the ESC. However, the Court made these references primarily to underline differences between the ESC and the ECHR. For example, in *Swedish Engine Drivers' Union*, the Court held that Art. 11 ECHR did not implicitly include a right to conclude a collective agreement with a public employer. For one part, it pointed out that Art. 6(2) ESC required the parties to promote voluntary – and not compulsory – collective bargaining machinery. For another part, the Court drew on the ESC's so-called 'à la carte approach' Art. 20 ESC, which leaves it to the state parties' to decide whether to accept the obligation enshrined in Art. 6(2) ESC or not. The ECtHR concluded that reading a right to the conclusion of a collective agreement into Art. 11 ECHR would render the parties' choice whether to accept obligations under Art. 6(2) ESC

had ratified ILO Convention No 87 and No 98 but did not draw further inferences from this circumstance.[37] The Court neither took into account the ILO's view of collective bargaining and strike were 'intrinsic corollaries' of freedom of association (even despite the applicants' hinting submission in *Schmidt and Dahlström* that the right to strike was an "organic right included in [Art. 11 ECHR]").[38]

Until well into the 2000s, the Court stood firmly by the principles developed in its three leading judgments from the 1970s. For instance, in 2002, it struck out two complaints, one against lack of statutory protection of industrial action and one against an outright prohibition of a strike by an act of government, as manifestly ill-founded and inadmissible, reasoning that Art. 11 ECHR did not include a right to strike.[39]

That being said, from the late 1990s onwards, the Court's jurisprudence incrementally began to undergo subtle but important changes. The ECtHR began to refer to ILO instruments and practice in the "Relevant Law" section of its judgments[40] and also cautiously began to note ILO supervisory practice in its actual legal assessment.[41] For instance, the 2002 decision in *Wilson and Palmer v. United Kingdom*, while again reaffirming earlier jurisprudence on collective bargaining and strikes, in some points paved the way for future developments.[42]

pointless, *Swedish Engine Drivers' Union v. Sweden* (n 31) para 37. The Court further observed that the Art. 6(4) ESC guarantees the right to strike only subject to domestic regulation and the requirements set forth in Art. 31 ESC and concluded that Art. 11(1) ECHR likewise left it open to the parties how to ensure that workers' and employers' associations could pursue their interests, ibid para 36. Thus, the Court used the ESC to restrain, rather than to thicken, the scope of Art. 11 ECHR, Keith D Ewing, 'The Implications of Wilson and Palmer' (2003) 32 Industrial Law Journal 1, 3. See also Franz Christian Ebert and Martin Oelz, 'Bridging the Gap Between Labour Rights and Human Rights: The Role of ILO Law in Regional Human Rights Courts' (2012) IILS Discussion Paper 212/2012 10. On the respective obligations under Art. 6 ESC see Henner Gött, 'Art. 6 RESC' in Eduardo Ales and others (eds), *International and European Labour Law - Article by Article Commentary* (Nomos 2018). The Court's silence on ILO instruments is all the more remarkable because the European Commission of Human Rights, for its part, had discussed the relevance of ILO instruments and practice in the very same cases and had even suggested to interpret Art. 11 ECHR in the light of these instruments and practice, *Svenska Lokmannaförbundet v. Sweden* (n 33) para 69 et seqq. and 78 et seqq.

[37] *National Union of Belgian Police v. Belgium* (n 30) para 16.

[38] *Schmidt and Dahlström v. Sweden* (n 32) para 36.

[39] *Unison v. United Kingdom* (n 34); *ECtHR, Federation of Offshore Workers' Trade Unions and Others v.* Norway ECHR 2002–VI 301, para 15. The latter case concerned the Norwegian practice of compulsory arbitration, discussed in Chap. 6. See also *Gustafsson v. Sweden (Revision)* ECHR 1998–V 483, para 45.

[40] *Wilson, National Union of Journalists and others v. United Kingdom* ECHR 2002–V 49, paras 34 et seqq.

[41] ibid 48.

[42] Ewing (n 36) 16 et seqq.

III. The Reversal in Demir and Baykara *and* Enerji Yapi-Yol Sen

But *Wilson and Palmer* was just a premonition of much more fundamental changes to come. In its unanimous 2008 Grand Chamber judgment in *Demir and Baykara v. Turkey* and its 2009 decision in *Enerji Yapi-Yol Sen v. Turkey*, the ECtHR dramatically reversed its earlier jurisprudence. It now accepted the rights to collective bargaining and to strike as elements of freedom of association guaranteed by Art. 11 ECHR. Both cases are landmark decisions for the development of Art. 11 ECHR's guarantee of freedom of association. They also provide elucidating insights on the Court's understanding of the position and function of the Convention vis-à-vis related norms of other areas of national and international law and its methodological approach.

In *Demir and Baykara*, the ECtHR was called to decide the question whether the right to bargain collectively was protected by Art. 11 ECHR, and whether civil servants could rely on it. The Court began the relevant part of its legal analysis by elaborating at considerable length on the interpretation of the ECHR in the light of other instruments. It reiterated its dynamic and evolutive approach to interpretation[43] and its readiness to take into account the "international law background" of the questions before it:[44]

> Being made up of a set of rules and principles that are accepted by the vast majority of States, the common international or domestic law standards of European States reflect a reality that the Court cannot disregard when it is called upon to clarify the scope of a Convention provision that more conventional means of interpretation have not enabled it to establish with a sufficient degree of certainty.[45]

The ECHR concluded that,

> in defining the meaning of terms and notions in the text of the Convention, [the Court] can and must take into account elements of international law other than the Convention, the interpretation of such elements by competent organs, and the practice of European States reflecting their common values. The consensus emerging from specialised international instruments and from the practice of Contracting States may constitute a relevant consideration for the Court when it interprets the provision of the Convention in specific cases.[46]

The ECtHR extensively put these principles to practice throughout its reasoning. In analysing whether there was a breach of Art. 11(1) ECHR, the ECtHR heavily relied on international and national developments to support that the right to collective bargaining had become an element of freedom of association. In doing

---

[43] *Demir and Baykara v. Turkey* ECHR 2008–V 395, paras 65–68, 146.

[44] ibid 76.

[45] ibid.

[46] ibid 85.

so, it prominently (albeit not exclusively[47]) relied on ILO instruments and practice. The Court first drew on ILO Convention No 98 ("one of the fundamental instruments concerning international labour standards") and followed the interpretation the CEACR had given to that Convention.[48] The ECtHR also took into account the provisions of ILO Convention No 151 concerning Protection of the Right to Organise and Procedures for Determining Conditions of Employment in the Public Service.[49] The Court's conclusion brought about an explicit reversal of its prior jurisprudence:

> 153. In the light of these developments, the Court considers that its case-law to the effect that the right to bargain collectively and to enter into collective agreements does not constitute an inherent element of Article 11 (...) should be reconsidered, so as to take account of the perceptible evolution in such matters, in both international law and domestic legal systems. While it is in the interests of legal certainty, foreseeability and equality before the law that the court should not depart, without good reason, from precedents established in previous cases, failure by the court to maintain a dynamic and evolutive approach would risk rendering it a bar to reform or improvement (...).
>
> 154. Consequently, the Court considers that having regard to the developments in labour law, both international and national, and to the practice of Contracting States in such matters, the right to bargain collectively with the employer has, in principle, become one of the essential elements of the 'right to form and to join trade unions for the protection of [one's] interests' set forth in Article 11 of the Convention (...).

The Court applied the same methodology of taking into account international instruments and developments to arrive at the conclusion that the breach of Art. 11 (1) ECHR was unjustifiable.

The ECtHR first disposed of Turkey's argument that the applicants fell within the restriction clause in Art. 11(2) ECHR of "members of the armed forces, of the police or of the administration of the State." The Court reasoned that there was "support of the majority of the relevant international instruments (...)"[50] for a narrow interpretation of the restriction clause.[51] To prove this point, the Court inter alia invoked ILO Convention No 87, which it identified as a "fundamental text" and the "principal instrument guaranteeing, internationally, the right of public officials to form trade unions".[52] It reasoned further that the CEACR and the CFA had interpreted comparable restriction clauses in ILO Convention No 87 narrowly.[53] Eventually, the Court

---

[47]Besides ILO conventions, it referenced the ESC and the ECSR's jurisprudence, the EU Charter of Fundamental Rights and state practice of European states, including Turkey itself, ibid 149–152.

[48]ibid 147.

[49]ibid 148.

[50]ibid 98.

[51]To the effect that it only covered civil servants engaged in administration of the state "as such", whereas, in principle, civil servants should enjoy the same rights as private employees, ibid 97.

[52]ibid 100, 123.

[53]Again, the Court also referenced other international instruments, including the ICCPR and the ICESCR, the ESC, a recommendation of the CM, and the EU Charter of Fundamental Rights, ibid 99–105. It also added that in all ECHR member states, the right of public officials to join trade

found a violation of Art. 11(2) ECHR and awarded just satisfaction pursuant to Art. 41 ECHR.[54]

The ECtHR confirmed its new jurisprudence in a line of cases against Turkey. Notably, in its chamber judgment in *Enerji Yapi-Yol Sen v. Turkey*,[55] delivered shortly after *Demir and Baykara*, the ECtHR extended the protection provided by Art. 11(1) ECHR to the right to strike. Compared to *Demir and Baykara*, the Court's judgment in *Enerji* is remarkably succinct. Applying the methodology expounded in *Demir and Baykara*, it adopted the ILO's approach to treat the right to strike as an intrinsic corollary of freedom of association in essentially one paragraph.[56] That being said, the Court put the right to strike on a lower footing. It maintained a distinction between collective bargaining (which it considered to have become an "essential element" of Art. 11 ECHR in *Demir and Baykara*) and the right to strike, which it considered protected by Art. 11 ECHR, but not an "essential element" thereof.[57]

Ever since, the Court has held that the rights to collective bargaining and to strike are protected by Art. 11 ECHR.[58]

---

unions was recognized and emphasized that the general rate of unionization was even higher in the public sector than the private sector in these countries, ibid 106.

[54]Ibid. 174–181.

[55]*Enerji Yapi-Yol Sen v. Turkey* App No 68959/01 (ECtHR, 21 April 2009) paras 6–9.

[56]*Enerji Yapi-Yol Sen v. Turkey* (n 55) para 24. The relevant passage reads: "(...) La Cour note également que le droit de grève est reconnu par les organes de contrôle de l'Organisation internationale du travail (OIT) comme le corollaire indissociable du droit d'association syndicale protégé par la Convention C87 de l'OIT sur la liberté syndicale et la protection du droit syndical (pour la prise en compte par la Cour des éléments de droit international autres que la Convention, voir Demir et Baykara, précité). Elle rappelle que la Charte sociale européenne reconnaît aussi le droit de grève comme un moyen d'assurer l'exercice effectif du droit de négociation collective. Partant, la Cour rejette l'exception du Gouvernement."

[57]See *National Union of Rail, Maritime and Transport Workers v. United Kingdom* ECHR 2014–II 1, para 84, with further references. There, the applicant attempted in vain to persuade the Court to consider the right to strike an "essential element".

[58]In *Özcan* and in *Kaya and Seyhan*, each concerning governmental sanctions for the participation of civil servants in strikes, the ECtHR followed the path chosen in *Demir and Baykara* and *Enerji*, albeit not referencing these cases and with an even more succinct reasoning, *Özcan v. Turkey* App No 22943/04 (ECtHR, 15 September 2009); *Kaya and Seyhan v. Turkey* App No 30946/04 (ECtHR, 15 September 2009). See also *Hrvatski Liječnički Sindikat v. Croatia* App No 36701/09 (ECtHR, 27 November 2014), para 50. Pursuant to a quantitative analysis, references to Demir and Baykara have remained the exception. Taking into account of international instruments has likewise remained on a low rate, see Klaus Lörcher, 'The New Social Dimension in the Jurisprudence of the European Court of Human Rights (ECtHR): The Demir and Baykara Judgment, Its Methodology and Follow-Up' in Filip Dorssemont, Klaus Lörcher and Isabelle Schömann (eds), *The European Convention on Human Rights and Employment Relation* (Hart Publishing 2013) 21 et seqq.

IV. The Wider Repercussions of the Reversal

From the ILO's perspective, the described change in the ECtHR's jurisprudence was of significant importance. It implied a boost to the ILO supervisory bodies' established position that the right to strike was an intrinsic corollary to freedom of association. The reasons for this are twofold. First, the ECtHR's judicial procedure is—and is being perceived as being—a much stronger enforcement mechanism than the ILO's own supervisory procedure. Second, the ECtHR and its jurisprudence are highly influential for domestic and international courts, both within and beyond Europe.

1. Creating an External 'Enforcement Mechanism'

As to the first point, compared to the ILO, the ECHR offers a much more powerful enforcement procedure for human rights at work. In particular, ECtHR judgments are binding judgments and must be executed by the respondent (Art. 46 ECHR), which renders them more attractive to applicants than ILO procedures. That this is not just a theoretical consideration is illustrated by the case of *RMT v. United Kingdom*, decided by the ECtHR in 2014. In this case, the applicant trade union, after filing the case with the ECtHR, had submitted a complaint in the same matter to the CFA, but had eventually withdrawn that complaint.[59] As the Court determined, the applicant

> had given clear priority to the [ECtHR] proceedings. This was because the United Kingdom had simply ignored the criticism voiced by the relevant ILO bodies, whereas it would be bound to execute a judgment in the applicant union's favour.[60]

2. The ECtHR's Influence on Domestic and International Law and Jurisprudence

What is more, the ECtHR's jurisprudence has attained great influence on other bodies of law.

A prime case in point is EU law. Pursuant to Art. 6(3) TEU, the ECHR, in its interpretation by the ECtHR,[61] informs those fundamental rights that constitute general principles of EU law. What is more, the rights enshrined in the Charter of

---

[59] *United Kingdom (Case No 2806)* (19 July 2010) National Union of Rail, Maritime & Transport Workers (RMT) <https://www.ilo.org/dyn/normlex/en/f?p=1000:50001:0::NO:50001:P50001_COMPLAINT_FILE_ID:2897817> accessed 26 April 2020.

[60] *National Union of Rail, Maritime and Transport Workers v. United Kingdom* (n 57) para 47.

[61] Case 4/73 *J. Nold, Kohlen- und Baustoffgroßhandlung v. Commission* (ECLI:EU:C:1974:51) [1974] ECR 00491, paras 12–14.

Fundamental Rights of the European Union (EUChFR) includes the prohibition of forced labour, freedom of association and the rights to collective bargaining and to strike (Arts. 5, 12 and 28 EUChFR). The interpretation of the EUChFR's guarantees is closely linked to the ECHR and the ECtHR's jurisprudence (Arts. 52(3) and 53 EUChFR). Accordingly, changes in the ECtHR's jurisprudence have the potential to spill over to EU law. A potential field of application for such spill-overs has already been identified. Only two years before *Demir and Baykara* and *Enerji Yapi-Yol Sen*, the CJEU had adopted an utterly rigid stance on the right to collective bargaining and the right to strike in its notorious *Viking* and *Laval* decisions.[62] In 2010, the CEACR criticized the CJEU's approach as overly restrictive and likely to restrain the right to strike in contravention of ILO standards.[63] The ILO's critique itself has not induced the CJEU to reconsider its stance. However, after *Demir and Baykara* and *Enerji Yapi-Yol Sen*, there have been speculations that the CJEU might revisit its *Viking* and *Laval* judgments in the light of the ECtHR's new approach to collective bargaining and the right to strike.[64]

What is more, the ECtHR's post-*Demir and Baykara* case-law has sparked a wealth of cases before domestic courts and tribunals. In some cases, the ECtHR's interpretative approach and its stance on collective bargaining and the right to strike being protected as parts of freedom of association has resulted in remarkable changes of domestic jurisprudence. A particularly interesting example is the Supreme Court of Canada. Canada is not a party to the ECHR, nor could it become one, given that the ECHR is only open for accession by European states and the EU (Art. 59(1) and (2) ECHR). Nevertheless, the Supreme Court of Canada, having recourse inter alia to the ECtHR's case-law, has reversed its prior jurisprudence on freedom of association as enshrined in section 2(d) of the Canadian Charter of Rights and Freedoms.[65] The

[62]*Case C-438/05 International Transport Workers Federation, Finnish Seamens Union v. Viking Line ABP and OÜ Viking Line Eesti* (ECLI:EU:C:2007:772) [2007] ECR I-10779; Case C-341/05 *Laval Un Partneri Ltd v. Svenska Byggnadsarbetareförbundet, Svenska Byggnadsarbetareförbundets Avdelning 1, Byggettan and Svenska Elektrikerförbundet* (ECLI: EU:C:2007:809) [2007] ECR I-11767.

[63]"(...) The doctrine that is being articulated in these ECJ judgements is likely to have a significant restrictive effect on the exercise of the right to strike in practice in a manner contrary to the Convention", *Observation (CEACR) Freedom of Association and Protection of the Right to Organise Convention, 1948 (No 87) - United Kingdom (Ratification: 1949)* Report of the Committee of Experts on the Application of Conventions and Recommendations (2010) ILC.99/III (1A) 210; Albertine Veldman, 'The Protection of the Fundamental Right to Strike within the Context of the European Internal Market: Implications of the Forthcoming Accession of the EU to the ECHR' (2013) 9 Utrecht Law Review 104, 115.

[64]Filip Dorssemont, 'The Right to Take Collective Action: The Prospects of the Accession to the European Convention on Human Rights. How the European Court on Human Rights Gave Us Enerji to Cope with Laval and Viking' in Marie-Ange Moreau (ed), *Before And After The Economic Crisis* (Edward Elgar Publishing 2011), which, however, the CJEU has not done to date.

[65]Part I of the Constitution Act, 1982, being Schedule B to the Canada Act 1982 (UK), 1982, c 11. In earlier cases, it had held that the right to strike was not protected under that section. In a line of judgments culminating in *Saskatchewan Federation of Labour v. Saskatchewan* [2015] 1 SCR 245, 2015 SCC 4, the Court reversed this position, to the effect that the right to strike was thenceforth protected.

Supreme Court employed an interpretative approach to the Canadian Charter of Fundamental Rights and Freedoms that was 'friendly' towards influences by international instruments and their interpretation by competent bodies.[66] The Court explicitly stated that these include the ECHR and the ECtHR's case-law.[67]

C. Reception as the Court's Unilateral Choice

It is important to recall that the reversal in *Demir and Baykara* was not the consequence of any sort of bilateral cooperation between the Court and the ILO. Neither was it a necessary consequence of anything the ILO had done, nor the inevitable consequence of coherent interpretation. Rather, it was the Court's deliberate choice (I.), which it made in accordance with its general approach—developed by itself over time—to interpret the ECHR in the light of other rules of international law (II.). The Court has consistently asserted full control over if and to what extent to apply this interpretative approach to take into account ILO instruments and practice (III.).

I. The Reversal in Demir and Baykara as a Deliberate Interpretative Choice

Firstly, the Court's reversal of jurisprudence was a deliberate choice. Considering the described developments of the ECtHR's case-law, it is striking that both the Court's initial and its reversed stance on collective bargaining and the right to strike

[66]Under Canadian law, international norms are non-binding by themselves, in the sense that they require legislative incorporation. However, international norms are considered an important interpretive tool. In this vein, the Court held that "[the Canadian Charter of Rights and Freedoms] should generally be presumed to provide protection at least as great as that afforded by the similar provisions in the international human rights documents which Canada has ratified", *Reference Re Public Service Employee Relations Act (Alta)* [1987] 1 SCR 313 para 59 [Alberta Reference]. See also *Saskatchewan Federation of Labour v. Saskatchewan* (n 65) para 64. Remarkably, as Langille observes, "[i]n applying this maxim of interpretation, the SCC has in fact looked at a wide variety of international human rights documents, including many that Canada has not and could not ratify", Brian A Langille, 'Consistency, Consensus, or Coherence? Legal Interpretation of Fundamental Labor Rights' in Social Justice Expertise Center (ed), *Ensuring Coherence in Fundamental Labor Rights Case Law: Challenges and Opportunities* (SJEC 2016) 63, fn. 8.

[67]*Supreme Court of Canada, Saskatchewan Federation of Labour v. Saskatchewan,* (n 65) para 71, cited along numerous other international and national authorities in order to establish an "international consensus", Langille (n 66).

resemble *prima facie* methodologically sound interpretations of Art. 11(1) ECHR.[68] Thus. the Court, in reversing its jurisprudence, did not merely react to international developments, nor was it 'compelled' in any way to adopt either of the interpretations. Rather, it made a proactive interpretative choice. This was pointed out by Judge Zagrebelsky in his separate opinion in *Demir and Baykara*: Highlighting that the Court had reaffirmed its previous jurisprudence up until 2002, he asked what the new developments in international and national labour law had been that the Court had based its evolutive interpretation on. Zagrebelsky considered that the only international development had been the proclamation of the EUChFR in 2000[69] (which already seems strangely delayed, as it could have already been taken into account in the 2002 decision in *Wilson and Palmer).* Against this background, Zagrebelsky persuasively concluded that the Court's departure from precedent was more a deliberate 'correction' of its own prior jurisprudence than a reaction to external developments in the law or the social ethos.[70]

II. Reversal Rooted in the Court's Evolved General Interpretative Approach

Secondly, at the heart of the Court's reversal was a change of attitude towards other international treaties, from regarding them primarily as means to negatively delimit the scope of Art. 11 ECHR (as in *Swedish Engine Drivers' Union*) to considering

[68]In *Demir and Baykara*, the ECtHR rightly pointed to the similarities in the wording of Art. 11 ECHR and Art. 22 ICCPR and Art. 8 ICESCR, respectively. As the Court itself acknowledged, however, there are also differences, which could have led to a different conclusion as to the grammatical argument. Furthermore, the Court considered it enough to point to the similarities, without expounding any further why comparable wording in two different treaties, albeit on the same subject-matter, but concluded between (partially) different parties necessarily indicates a similar understanding. Indeed, synchronisation is only one possible inference to draw from the occurrence of similar provisions in two separate treaties. A 'fragmentationist' (or indeed a regionalist) observer could as well infer that the regulation of an issue in two separate instruments indicates differences as to the intended scope and content of their respective provisions, or different understandings as to which substantive right should be enforceable through which particular system of implementation (i.e., in this case, the ECtHR or rather another forum, such as the ECSR, the ILO supervisory bodies or the Covenant bodies).

[69]*Demir and Baykara v Turkey* (n 43) Separate Opinion of Judge Zagrebelsky, para 2. Arguably, one could add the restatement of and emphasis on the right to bargain collectively in No. 2 lit. a of the 1998 ILO Declaration, bearing in mind that the Court emphasised that ILO Convention No 98 belong to "fundamental" labour standards (*Demir and Baykara v. Turkey* (n 43) para 147) Further developments, albeit not mentioned by the Court, include the progressing mainstreaming of the ILO's Decent Work Agenda within the UN System and beyond, discussed in Chap. 14.

[70]*Demir and Baykara v Turkey* (n 43) Separate Opinion of Judge Zagrebelsky, para 2.

them means to 'thicken' the ECHR guarantee (as in *Demir and Baykara*).[71] The ECtHR's reversal was arguably made possible by its own evolved general interpretative methodology. Perhaps most importantly, the ECtHR had adopted a dynamic and evolutive approach to interpretation. It has consistently held, from its 1978 landmark decision in *Tyrer v. United Kingdom* onwards, that

> the [ECHR] is a living instrument which must be interpreted in the light of present-day conditions.[72]

Following this now-classic 'living instrument'-approach, the Court has interpreted the ECHR in the light of subsequent developments, including subsequent state and social practice[73] and relevant international instruments and developments.[74] The Court has, on several occasions, modified and sometimes even reversed its prior jurisprudence in the light of international developments.[75] By applying its dynamic and evolutive 'living instrument' approach to international legal developments, the Court opened ECHR interpretation to influence from other areas of international law.[76]

---

[71]Mantouvalou has called this a change from an exclusionary to an integrated approach, Virginia Mantouvalou, 'Labour Rights in the European Convention on Human Rights: An Intellectual Justification for an Integrated Approach to Interpretation' (2013) 13 Human Rights Law Review 1.

[72]*Tyrer v. the United Kingdom* (1978) Series A No 26, para 31; *ECtHR, Loizidou v. Turkey (Preliminary Objections)* (1995) Series A No 310, para 71. Whether the living instrument approach is supposed to be a variation of object and purpose-interpretation as required under Art. 31(1) VCLT or instead must be seen as a separate approach to interpretation cannot be determined with sufficient certainty. At least, it adds a specific intertemporal dimension to interpretation, Georg Nolte, 'Jurisprudence Under Special Regimes Relating to Subsequent Agreements and Subsequent Practice' in Georg Nolte (ed), *Treaties and Subsequent Practice* (Oxford University Press 2013) 253 et seqq.

[73]Nolte (n 72) 256.

[74]ibid. The Court has repeatedly emphasized that the ECHR has to be interpreted in the light of pertinent international instruments, Lörcher (n 58) 6. In this vein, it held in *Al-Adsani v. United Kingdom* that "[t]he Convention [. . .] cannot be interpreted in a vacuum. The Court must be mindful of the Convention's special character as a human rights treaty, and it must also take the relevant rules of international law into account [. . .]. The Convention should so far as possible be interpreted in harmony with other rules of international law of which it forms part", *Al-Adsani v. United Kingdom* ECHR 2001–XI 79, para 55; *ECtHR, Saadi v. United Kingdom* ECHR 2008–I 31, para 62; *Mamatkulov and Askarov v. Turkey* ECHR 2005–I 293, para 112. The ECHR's dynamic and evolutive interpretation, as epitomized in the 'living instrument' approach, has become deeply engrained in the ECHR's system and has even been deemed a source of the Court's authority, Kanstantsin Dzehtsiarou, 'European Consensus and the Evolutive Interpretation of the European Convention on Human Rights' (2011) 12 German Law Journal 1730, 1732.

[75]*Mamatkulov and Askarov v. Turkey* (n 74) paras 109–113, 121–125; *Scoppola v. Italy (No. 2)*, App No 10249/03 (ECtHR, 17 September 2009) paras 96–110; *Sergey Zolotukhin v. Russian Federation* ECHR 2009–I 291, paras 78–83; Rachovitsa (n 2) 563.

[76]*Lithgow and Others v. United Kingdom* (1986) Series A No 23, para 118; *Al-Adsani v. The United Kingdom* (n 74) paras 61 et seqq.; *Chapman v. United Kingdom* ECHR 2001–I 41, para 93; *Christine Goodwin v. United Kingdom* ECHR 2002–VI 1, para 85.

The development of the Court's interpretative approach was not labour- or ILO-specific, but general. However, it paved the way for the increasing influence of ILO instruments and practice in the Court's case law on labour rights. The Grand Chamber in *Demir and Baykara* did not have to 'invent' its interpretative approach but could conveniently confine itself to consolidating a wealth of existing precedents, on which it relied as supporting authority.[77]

III. Assertion of Control Over the Interpretative Approach

Thirdly, the ECtHR has always asserted the prerogative to decide whether and to what extent it will use its interpretative approach to take into account the ILO's (or, for that matter, any other international) instruments and practice.

In *Demir and Baykara*, the Court's interpretative approach, and therefore also its stance regarding interpreting the ECHR in the light of ILO instruments and practice, remained somewhat ambiguous. As described above, the Court held that it "can and must take into account" relevant international instruments and their interpretation by competent organs, only to state in the next sentence in much weaker language that the consensus emerging therefrom "may constitute a relevant consideration".[78]

The Grand Chamber in *Tănase v. Moldova* specified this 'duty to take into account'. It succinctly asserted that

> [i]t is for the Court to decide which international instruments and reports it considers relevant and how much weight to attribute to them.[79]

The *Tănase* clarification is a straightforward reassertion of interpretative control. Given that the ECtHR is an independent judicial body and not under the control of the ILO, this is not surprising. However, it still means that the Court alone decides on the ILO's relevance in its jurisprudence. That also means that, regardless of whether the ILO welcomes the Court's reception, the ILO does not have any further say in the Court's use of its output.

All in all, as much as the change of jurisprudence enhanced the ILO's role and influence in the ECHR, the ECtHR has made sure that it still retains full control over this role and influence, and that it can, at any time, alter, divert or diminish it.

---

[77] Lörcher (n 58) 9 et seq.

[78] *Demir and Baykara v. Turkey* (n 43) para 85.

[79] *Tănase v. Moldova* ECHR 2010–III 361, para 176.

D. Choosing 'Against' the ILO

It is not merely a theoretical consideration that the Court may assert its interpretative autonomy in a way that will diminish the ILO's relevance for its jurisprudence. Despite what the reasoning in *Demir and Baykara* might suggest, the ECtHR has not aligned its case law to ILO instruments and practice in a consistent manner. Rather, even in cases in which the ECtHR has considered ILO instruments and their interpretation by the ILO supervisory bodies, it has repeatedly deviated from them and found alternative solutions. In some cases, it justified such deviations with the specific functions of the Court (I.). In other cases, it chose to deviate out of sheer preference (II.). What is more, even where the Court had previously aligned its case-law with ILO instruments and practice, it 'detached' this case-law from subsequent developments inside the ILO (III.).

I. Functional Deviations: The Example of Sympathy Strikes

Firstly, the ECtHR has more than once deviated from ILO practice arguing that its function was different from those of the ILO's supervisory bodies.[80]

One recent example concerns a legislative ban of so-called sympathy strikes in the United Kingdom.[81] Both the ILO and the ECSR had criticized that ban, arguing that it could lead to undue limitations of the right to strike and to abuse in certain constellations.[82] In the 2014 case of *RMT v. United Kingdom*, the applicant trade union urged the ECtHR to adopt the same position. However, the Court refused, finding that the ban on sympathy strikes would not disproportionately interfere with Art. 11 ECHR in the specific case at hand. In its reasoning, the ECtHR found the ILO bodies' to be not of sufficient persuasive weight.[83] It distinguished between its own function and that of the CEACR, highlighting the

[80] A case at hand is *ECtHR, Federation of Offshore Workers' Trade Unions and Others v. Norway* (n 39), in which both the ILO and the ECSR had criticized the Norwegian system of ending strikes and submitting them to compulsory arbitration for unduly restricting the right to strike (see p. 6 et seq., with references). The Court, by contrast, considered the complaint manifestly ill-founded and inadmissible, arguing that in the "specific and exceptional circumstances" existed in the case at hand and emphasizing "that its decision in the present case should not be taken as meaning that a system of compulsory arbitration for bringing lawful strikes to an end would be considered proportionate in all cases in which economic pressure is being exerted", ibid 18.

[81] Sympathy strikes, or secondary strike action, are cases in which workers engage in strike action not to exert pressure on their own employer, but to show solidarity with other ongoing strikes.

[82] *United Kingdom (Case No 2473)* (16 December 2005) Report of the Committee on Freedom of Association No 346 (2007) XC ILO Official Bulletin Ser B 395, para 1543.; ECSR Conclusions XIV-1 (1998), *United Kingdom, Article 6-4*.

[83] *National Union of Rail, Maritime and Transport Workers v. United Kingdom* (n 57) para 98.

> distinct character of the Court's review compared with that of the supervisory procedures of the ILO (...). The specialised international monitoring bodies operating under those procedures have a different standpoint, shown in the more general terms used to analyse the ban on secondary action (...). In contrast, it is not the Court's task to review the relevant domestic law in the abstract, but to determine whether the manner in which it actually affected the applicant infringed the latter's rights under [Art. 11 ECHR]. (...) The Court's review is bounded by the facts submitted for examination in the case.[84]

This type of deviation is a consequence of the inherent differences between the objectives, competences and procedures between the ECtHR on the one hand and the ILO on the other. Whether or not the Court's reasoning was convincing in the particular case before it, it certainly was as to the underlying principle. The ECtHR, unlike the CEACR, is not competent to review domestic labour regulation in the abstract. One could therefore say that deviations arising as a consequence of this different purview are prudent and, at least to some extent, unavoidable.

II. Discretionary Deviations: The Example of the Definition of Forced or Compulsory Labour

By contrast, the ECtHR made other deviations from the ILO out of sheer preference. An example for such 'discretionary deviations' is the Court's interpretation of prohibition of forced or compulsory labour as provided for in Art. 4(2) ECHR. The ECtHR has adopted a definition of the term 'forced or compulsory labour' that purposefully deviates from the definition of the same term contained in Art. 2(1) ILO Convention No 29 of 1930.[85]

The leading case for this interpretation is *van der Mussele v. Belgium*, in which the ECtHR added additional requirements to the ILO definition. Art. 2(1) ILO Convention No 29 requires that, in order to qualify as forced or compulsory labour, work was "exacted from any person under the menace of any penalty and for which the said person has not offered himself voluntarily". The ECtHR acknowledged the close proximity between Art. 4(2) ECHR and ILO Convention No 29 but found the ILO Convention's definition to be insufficient. It therefore refused to simply adopt the ILO criteria for Art. 4(2) ECHR.[86]

---

[84]ibid.

[85]The definition of forced or compulsory labour in Art. 2 ILO Convention No 29 reads: "1. For the purposes of this Convention the term **forced or compulsory labour** shall mean all work or service which is exacted from any person under the menace of any penalty and for which the said person has not offered himself voluntarily" (emphasis in original).

[86]On the one hand, *van der Mussele* made an early attempt to align ECHR guarantees with ILO instruments: The Court held that it was "evident" that the drafters of Art. 4 ECHR relied on the older ILO Convention No 29 and that there was "a striking similarity, which is not accidental, between [Art. 4(3) ECHR and Art. 2(2) ILO Convention No 29]", *van der Mussele v. Belgium* (1983) Series A No 70, para 32. The Court further took note of ILO Convention No 105 of 1957, requiring immediate abolition of forced labour in certain cases. Thus, the Court reasoned, the definition of

Instead, the Court created the additional requirement that either the obligation to work must have been "unjust" or "oppressive" or that its performance must have been an "avoidable hardship".[87] Since these additional requirements had not been met, the Court dismissed the case. These requirements, as the Court explicitly acknowledged, are not part of the ILO definition.[88] Yet, as it put it rather straightforwardly,

> [b]e that as it may, the Court prefer[red] to adopt a different approach.[89]

As the only argument for this deviation, the Court invoked Art. 4(3) ECHR. Art. 4 (3) ECHR sets forth four exceptions to the definition, enouncing specific types of work which shall not be considered forced or compulsory labour. These exceptions, the Court reasoned, were

> grounded on the governing ideas of the general interest, social solidarity and what is in the normal or ordinary course of affairs.[90]

Reading Art. 4(3) in context with Art. 4(2) ECHR, the ECtHR concluded that the aforesaid additional criteria were implicitly included in the ECHR's definition of forced labour.[91]

This reasoning is surprising, for the simple reason that Art. 2(2) ILO Convention No 29 contains—in slightly different order—the very same exceptions as Art. 4 (3) ECHR.[92] In other words, there is no relevant textual difference between Art. 4

---

forced or compulsory labour contained in Art. 2(1) ILO Convention No 29 "can provide a starting-point for interpretation" of Art. 4(2) ECHR, ibid. In the further course of its analysis, the ECtHR used the ILO conventions and corresponding observations and jurisprudence of ILO bodies as guidance in specifying elements of the ILO's definition of forced labour and applying it to the facts of the case (see especially ibid 35). However, the ECtHR refused to adopt an all too lenient approach to aligning ECHR guarantees with ILO Convention No 29. It held that "sight should not be lost of the Convention's special features or of the fact that it is a living instrument to be read 'in the light of the notions currently prevailing in democratic States' (. . .)", ibid 32.

[87] *Van der Mussele v. Belgium* (n 86) para 37. The common rationale behind these additional criteria was to exclude work that was considered 'normal' in a society, ibid 37–41.

[88] ibid para 37; Ebert and Oelz (n 36) 9.

[89] *Van der Mussele v. Belgium* (n 86) para 37.

[90] ibid 38.

[91] ibid 38 et seqq.

[92] The only exception contained in the ILO Convention that does not appear in Art. 4(3) ECHR – regarding so-called minor communal services – was deliberately not transposed to the ECHR by its drafters. This can be traced back to the ECHR drafters' use of the UN Commission on Human Rights' preparatory work for the UN Covenants, and indirectly even to the ILO itself. During the drafting on what was to become Art. 8 ICCPR on the prohibition of slavery and forced or compulsory labour, considerable discussions arose as to whether there should be an exception of the prohibition for "minor communal services". Reference was made to the definition of forced labour contained in Art. 2 ILO Convention No 29, which includes both an exception for 'normal civic obligations", applicable to sovereign states, and for "minor communal services", applicable to non-self-governing territories. The UN Human Rights Commission submitted a draft text to the ILO for comments, which the latter provided. In reaching its decision not to perpetuate the aforesaid distinction in the Covenant, the Commission inter alia relied on the ILO communication, which

(3) ECHR and ILO Convention No 29. Therefore, it is not persuasive of the Court to base its deviation from the ILO definition on the exception contained in Art. 4 (3) ECHR.[93]

The ECtHR provided no other reasoning on this matter. It therefore appears that the described deviation was entirely discretional, i.e. the Court has made use of its judicial independence to simply select an interpretation it preferred over another.

In later cases, the Court continued to use the additional criteria developed in *van der Mussele*, until well after *Demir and Baykara*.[94] Whether the ECtHR's deviation from the ILO Convention's definition of forced labour has led to different results in practice is secondary for present purposes. What matters is that the Court has purposefully created and maintained a difference, and it has done so essentially out of sheer preference. It has thereby proven its willingness and ability to assert its autonomy in practice.

III. 'Detachment' of Aligned Jurisprudence from Subsequent Developments in the ILO

Finally, the ECtHR's full assertion of control over the question of alignment or deviation can even become relevant in cases in which the Court had aligned its case-law but refuses to reconsider or adjust this alignment in the light of subsequent developments within the ILO.

---

suggested to abolish the term 'minor communal services' "in the shortest time possible", ILO communication CN.4/158, cited after: CoE, 'Preparatory Work on Article 4 of the Convention' (1962) DH (62) 10, 19. The ECHR drafters used the UN Human Rights Commission's drafting materials as guidance for the ECHR draft.

[93]It is worth noting that the IACtHR, albeit essentially following the ECtHR's living instrument approach, adopted a more lenient approach towards the definition of forced labour. Unlike the ECtHR in *van der Mussele*, the IACtHR did not modify the prerequisites of the prohibition of forced labour in the ACHR but straightforwardly adopted those of Art. 2(1) ILO Convention No 29, *Case of the Ituango Massacres v Colombia* (2006) IACtHR Series C No 148, paras 158–165. The case illustrates that, even though virtually the same interpretative approach concerning recourse to ILO instruments and practice is employed, this does not prevent two different bodies to deviate from these instruments and practice and from each other's jurisprudence. Whether the definition of forced labour is modified (as in *van de Mussele*) or not (as in *Ituango Massacres*) seems largely unpredictable.

[94]Likewise, it has reiterated that it regarded the definition of forced labour in Art. 2(1) ILO Convention No 29 "a starting point for interpretation", but not more, *Karlheinz Schmidt v. Germany* (1994) Series A No 291-B, para 22; *Stummer v. Austria* ECHR 2011–V 1, para 118; *CN and V v. France* App No 67724/09 (ECtHR, 11 October 2012), para 74., while at the same time considering the 2009 Cost of Coercion report of the ILO Director-General to the International Labour Conference (ILO, 'The Cost of Coercion, Global Report Under the Follow-up to the ILO Declaration on Fundamental Principles and Rights at Work' (International Labour Conference, 98th Session 2009) Report I(B)), which contains the unchanged ILO definition, paras 52 and 77. See also *Graziani-Weiss v. Austria* App No 31950/06 (ECtHR, 18 October 2011), paras 36–38.

1. The ECtHR's Jurisprudence as a Factor in the ILO's Post-2012 Constitutional Crisis

In this context, it becomes relevant that the Court's alignment to ILO instruments and practice is capable of fuelling disruptions within the ILO. As described in Chap. 1, the ILO's model of labour governance is fragile. Since the employers' intervention in the June 2012 International Labour Conference, tripartism has been in crisis. As mentioned above, one of the employers' main arguments for obstructing the work of the CAS was that the ILO bodies' interpretations of ILO instruments were regarded as a form of soft law jurisprudence and consented tripartite position outside the ILO. While the employers did not explicitly refer to the ECtHR (but only to "international forums"[95]), it is obvious that the Court's alignment to ILO instruments and practice was a prime case in point.[96] *Demir and Baykara* and *Enerji Yapi-Yol Sen* had only been decided a few years before, and their impact at domestic and international level was still unfolding. Further cases, like *RMT v. United Kingdom* (on the question whether sympathy strikes were protected under Art. 11 ECHR) were pending. In any case, given the abovementioned large impact of the ECtHR on other areas of law, it is hardly conceivable that the evolving ECtHR's jurisprudence on collective bargaining and the right to strike had not been a major concern for employers and at the same time a vivid example to supplement their argument.

2. 'Detaching' the ECtHR's Jurisprudence from the ILO

Against this background, the ECtHR's reaction to the post-2012 crisis is particularly interesting. In essence, the ECtHR chose not to concern itself with the post-2012 events in the ILO, even when it was explicitly brought to its attention by the parties to a case before it. In *RMT v. United Kingdom*, the applicants had invoked the practice of the CEACR, pursuant to which the British ban on sympathy strikes was irreconcilable with ILO instruments. The respondent government had presented a counterargument that was similar to the employers' statements during the 2012 International Labour Conference. The government had argued that the CEACR

> was not a judicial or quasi-judicial body (. . .), and its interpretation of ILO Conventions was not definitive. Rather, its role was to provide impartial and technical evaluation of the state of application of international labour standards. In fact, the question of a right to strike was currently the cause of sharp controversy within the ILO, as part of which the status of the interpretations given by the Committee of Experts had been called into question.[97]

---

[95]ILO, 'Report of the Committee on the Application of Standards Part One: General Report' (International Labour Conference, 101st Session May-June 2012) Provisional Record 19(Rev.) Part I, para 50.

[96]Francis Maupain, 'A Second Century for What? The ILO at a Regulatory Crossroad' (2019) 16 International Organizations Law Review 1, 20.

[97]*National Union of Rail, Maritime and Transport Workers v. United Kingdom* (n 57) para 69. The government made a similar argument with regard to the ECSR, ibid.

In this context, the government had also referred to the clarification of the CEACR's mandate, which, as mentioned in Chap. 1, was adopted by the CEACR in 2013 under the severe pressure exerted by the employers.[98]

However, the ECtHR rejected the government's argument. The Court reiterated its methodological approach taken in *Demir and Baykara*, implying that it considered the CEACR and the CFA sufficiently competent bodies to provide relevant interpretations of ILO conventions.[99] As to the 2013 clarification of the CEACR's mandate, the ECtHR did not consider

> that this clarification requires it to reconsider this body's role as a point of reference and guidance for the interpretation of certain provisions of the [ECHR] (. . .).

The ECtHR confined itself to observe that the 2012 incidents had been sponsored by the employers, while government representatives had reaffirmed that the right to strike was a well-established fundamental right.[100] Somewhat surprisingly, the Court further reasoned that, in any event, the United Kingdom had accepted before the Court that the ECHR in principle protected the right to strike[101] (while this was correct, the government had of course also argued that this right did not prevent it from banning sympathy strikes[102]).

Thus, in essence, the Court reduced the issue to whether the respondent government had itself submitted to the CEACR's view, while refraining from commenting any further on the CEACR's interpretative mandate. Nor did it seem to have given much weight to the implications for the ILO's ongoing constitutional crisis and the possibilities of its solution. Quite the contrary, the Court made it clear that ILO-internal struggles over the CEACR's interpretative competence would not affect the Court's reception of the latter's practice. In this way, the ECtHR 'detached' its own jurisprudence from subsequent developments within the ILO. What is more, the Court also reaffirmed the Grand Chamber's position in *Tănase v. Moldova*[103] that it considered it to be its own prerogative to determine the relevance of the CEACR's work for the interpretation of the ECHR. It thereby also implied a 'prerogative to disregard' the view of one of the ILO's constituents.

The Court made use of this prerogative in other cases.[104] For instance, in the 2014 case of *Veniamin Tymoshenko v. Ukraine*, the ECtHR referred to the CEACR's 2012

---

[98]ibid para 96. Furthermore, the government argued that the CEACR and the CFA had adopted diverging views on the issue and that the ILO Governing Body had refrained from taking a position, ibid 69.

[99]*National Union of Rail, Maritime and Transport Workers v. United Kingdom* (n 57) para 76.

[100]ibid 97.

[101]ibid.

[102]ibid 62.

[103]See above, C. III.

[104]The ECSR seems to have taken a similar stance. While the Committee never explicitly discussed the matter, it continued to refer to the CEACR's interpretations after the ILO's constitutional crisis had broken out, see e.g. ECSR, *Conclusions 2014 - Russian Federation - Article 6-4*, referring to the CEACR's conclusions on Russia on the right to strike (*Observation (CEACR) of Association and*

General Survey on the fundamental ILO conventions as relevant law.[105] In this General Survey, the CEACR had inter alia reaffirmed its view that the right to strike was implicit in ILO Convention No 87 on freedom of association.[106] The classification of the General Survey as "relevant law" is remarkable, because the CEACR's General Survey, and the recognition of the right to strike therein, was a central example invoked by the employers in the June 2012 International Labour Conference to argue that the CEACR was overstepping its mandate. The Court's reference to the General Survey was cursory and perhaps without further intentions. Nevertheless, including a directly contested document into a—selective—list of "relevant law" is capable of reinforcing the employers' argument and thus to further fuel the ILO-internal crisis of tripartism.

E. The Observed Inter-Organizational Interactions and Their Relevance for the ILO's Model

The ECtHR's evolving jurisprudence on the rights to bargain collectively and to strike provides a second example on how inter-organizational interactions occur in practice and how they are relevant for the ILO's model of labour governance.

I. A Sequence of Exclusively Indirect and Non-conflictual Interactions

1. Identifying the Relevant Interactive Conduct

At the outset, it is helpful to first identify the relevant interactive conduct. On the part of the ILO, there is the drafting, adoption and promotion of labour conventions, particularly ILO Convention No 87. Perhaps more importantly, there is the continuous and consistent interpretation by the ILO's supervisory bodies, to the effect that Convention No 87 implicitly includes the rights to bargain collectively to strike as an intrinsic corollary to freedom of association. This should be seen in context with the promotion of labour standards and the publication of reports on the subject.

Protection of the Right to Organise Convention, 1948 (No. 87) – Russian Federation (Ratification: 1956) Report of the Committee of Experts on the Application of Conventions and Recommendations (2013) ILC.102/III(1A) 156), without mentioning the ILO's constitutional crisis.

105 *Veniamin Tymoshenko and Others v. Ukraine* (n 17) para 34.

106 ILO, 'Giving Globalization a Human Face, General Survey on the Fundamental Conventions Concerning Rights at Work in Light of the ILO Declaration on Social Justice for a Fair Globalization', Report of the Committee of Experts on the Application of Conventions and Recommendations (International Labour Conference, 101st Session, 2012) ILC.101/III/1B, para 119.

On the side of the ECtHR, there is notably the rendition and publication of judgments taking into account ILO instruments and their interpretation by the ILO's supervisory bodies. This includes in particular the reversal of prior jurisprudence, accompanied with an elaborate pronunciation of the underlying interpretative method.

2. Indirect and Largely Non-Conflictual Interactions

As to the types of observed interactions, the case study revealed interaction without institutional or procedural links and even without any direct communication between the ILO and the ECtHR. The records do not imply that the observed influence was in any way directed by the ILO at the Court or vice versa. Rather, it was accidental, a kind of 'by-product', as it were, of the ECtHR's and the ILO's exercise of their respective functions.

Still, the described interplay between the ECtHR and the ILO meets the definition of inter-organizational interaction as set forth in Chap. 3, namely conduct of an IO directed at having, or actually having, an effect on the conduct of another IO.[107] Both the ILO's norm creating activity—the adoption and promotion of labour conventions—and its supervisory bodies' interpretations have had an impact on the ECtHR's case-law. The same is true for the repercussions the ECtHR's developing jurisprudence had on the emergence of the recent crisis within the ILO.

As mentioned in general in Chap. 3, indirect interactions are usually not included in legal studies addressing inter-organizational interactions. This is remarkable, because the ECtHR's approach to other areas of international law is in itself a relatively familiar topic of international legal scholarship and has received wide attention.[108] Moreover, the Court itself frequently pointed to the ILO and its bodies as the most eminent bodies in labour issues and has emphasized their functions and expertise. In fact, it was precisely for the ILO's eminent role as an institution that the Court took its conventions and practice into account, and it was the institutional standing and power of the ECtHR and further international and national bodies that reinvigorated the employers to escalate the dispute over the CEACR's interpretative competence within the ILO.

[107] See Chap. 3 B. I.

[108] See e.g. Luzius Wildhaber, 'The European Convention on Human Rights and International Law' (2007) 56 International and Comparative Law Quarterly 217; Geir Ulfstein, 'Evolutive Interpretation in the Light of Other International Instruments: Law and Legitimacy' in Anne van Aaken and Iulia Motoc (eds), *The European Convention on Human Rights and General International Law* (Oxford University Press 2018) 83.

II. The Court's 'Benevolent Unilateralism' and Its Implications for the ILO

The interactions with the ECtHR are of significant relevance for the ILO and its model of labour governance. On the one hand, the Court created an opportunity for the ILO to expand its outreach into other areas of international law (1.). On the other hand, whether or not this opportunity is given is not something the ILO has a say in, because it is dependent on the ECtHR's unilateral 'benevolence' (2.)

1. Expanding the ILO's Outreach and Validation of Its Work

The case study has shown how the ECtHR has used ILO instruments and practice in its case-law to develop and ultimately reverse its prior jurisprudence on the rights to bargain collectively and to strike. It has also elaborated on the relevance of these developments for the ECHR and beyond.

Obviously, the adoption of ILO positions by other, more powerful institutions offers significant opportunities to the ILO to increase its impact. In an 'ideal' case, so one could argue, the ECtHR's aligning to the ILO would help to overcome the latter's limited possibilities to implement and enforce the results of its work. While the ILO's only way to effectuate its work is via persuasion, the ECtHR can decide with binding force. The Court does of course not directly enforce ILO conventions. However, by interpreting the ECHR in the light of ILO instruments and practice, the Court transposes the gist of ILO decisions on policy and interpretation, reached in the special setting of universal tripartite social dialogue, from the ILO to the European human rights system.

What is more, one could consider the ECtHR's recourse to the ILO a success for the latter's efforts of persuasion, and a great validation and recognition of the ILO's standing and authority as a central institution in labour governance by the perhaps most important international human rights court. This persuasion succeeded without any formal ties between the ILO and the Court, which underlines the ILO's persuasive weight.

2. The Ambivalent Dependence on a Unilateral Choice

On the other hand, this opportunity comes with a downside. The Court's alignment to the ILO did not entirely prevent conflicts, but merely shifted them to another context. The described interaction between the ECtHR and the ILO illustrates how coherence at inter-organizational level can come at the price of providing the ground for new conflict within one of the interacting IOs. The ILO's constitutional crisis makes this apparent. The employers made it clear that their prior toleration of the CEACR's interpretation depended on this interpretation being 'enforced' exclusively through the ILO's own supervisory mechanisms. When the ECtHR accepted the right to strike to be a part of freedom of association under the ECHR as well, this provided fuel for conflict at ILO level.[109]

It is worth noting that the challenge revealed in this case study is of a different nature than the one in the EWI example presented in Chap. 4. The ECtHR's engagement in labour governance is not based on a different normative vision. On the contrary, the Court's alignment with the ILO's instruments and practice was rather an endorsement of the latter's model of labour governance. Rather, the challenge in the second case study centres on an issue that was only a minor point in the first case study: The issue of 'ownership' over interpretation. The ECtHR, while having recourse to ILO instruments and practice, acted as a gatekeeper when it asserted the prerogative to take into account ILO standards essentially as it deemed wise and expedient. It took the liberty to disregard or to depart from ILO instruments and practice. The ILO, for its part, was left with the fact that its soft law jurisprudence had been 'removed' from its tripartite embedment and had been transposed to another context, from where it now worked against the very tripartite compromise on which it had been built in the first place. In this respect, it does not matter whether the employers' claim during the 2012 International Labour Conference was justified or not. Either way, the ECtHR's claim to interpretative autonomy—straightforwardly epitomized in *Tănase v. Moldova*[110]—collides with the ILO's interpretative 'ownership' over its own instruments. In other words, the ILO's opportunity—the ECtHR's participation in the enforcement of its soft law jurisprudence—came at the expense of an indirect but traceable backlash against the underlying discourse which formed the basis of this jurisprudence.

F. Conclusion

This chapter has presented a second case study regarding the ILO's inter-organizational interaction with other IOs involved in labour governance. It traced the way the ECtHR had recourse to ILO instruments and practice, and the repercussions this had on the ILO.

Using the example of the Court's evolving case-law on the rights to bargain collectively and the right to strike, it was shown that the Court was increasingly willing to align its own jurisprudence to the ILO's instruments and practice, up to the point where it even reversed its earlier case-law to better accommodate ILO practice. By adopting the ILO's approach into its judgments, the ECtHR indirectly amplified the ILO's outreach and impact.

On the other hand, it was also shown that the ECtHR consistently asserted its unilateral prerogative over whether and to what extent it would align its case-law

---

[109] What is more, the ECtHR's approach to international instruments and practice has in itself been the subject of critique (see the sources cited by Lörcher (n 58) 11 et seq.

[110] See above, C. III.

with the ILO. In some cases, it chose not to align its case-law with the ILO's stance, even if only out of sheer preference. Moreover, even in cases in which the Court aligned its case-law, it maintained this aligned position even though this alignment fuelled disruptions within the ILO and led one of the ILO's constituents to question the legitimacy of the very ILO practice the Court had relied on in the first place. While the ECtHR's position towards ILO instruments and practice has in general been increasingly open, the Court's selective alignment and its forceful insistence on its prerogatives may best be described as 'benevolent unilateralism'. Notwithstanding the prospect of an expanded outreach, this 'benevolent unilateralism' ultimately remains structurally ambivalent from the perspective of the ILO.

6. The ILO's Model's Cooperative Promotion: The ILO's Influence on the European Social Charter

An examination of inter-organizational interactions in labour governance would not be complete without a look at a case of 'working' inter-organizational cooperation. The interactions between the ILO and the CoE regarding the drafting, reform and implementation of the European Social Charter (ESC) is a showcase in this regard.

The ESC and its primary supervisory body, the European Committee of Social Rights (ECSR) have become important elements of labour governance in Europe (A.). From the start, the ILO has had significant influence on the ESC and the ECSR. For one part, it left an important mark on the drafting of the ESC and subsequent textual reforms and revisions (B.) Moreover, it also had a continuous influence on the ESC's implementation, notably through a special institutional link created between the ECSR and the International Labour Office (C.). The interactions examined in this Chapter are again of noticeable importance for the ILO, this time primarily because they increased the outreach of its model of governance (D.).

A. The ESC and the ECSR in Labour Governance

The ESC is a regional European human rights treaty adopted by the CoE in 1961. It is the ECHR's 'sister treaty' and was created to complement the latter in the area of social rights.[1] The ESC has since undergone several reforms, which resulted in three

[1]It is a product of the Cold War era distinction between civil and political rights on the one hand and economic, social and cultural rights on the other, and their codification in separate treaties, Ulrich Becker, 'European Social Charter', *Max Planck Encyclopedia of Public International Law* (Oxford University Press 2007) para 2; Jordi Bonet Pérez, 'The European Social Charter' in Felipe Gómez

H. Gött, *The Law of Interactions Between International Organizations*, Beiträge zum ausländischen öffentlichen Recht und Völkerrecht 299, https://doi.org/10.1007/978-3-662-62389-3_6

protocols[2] and, in 1996, in the adoption of the revised ESC (RESC).[3] The (R)ESC allows the parties to accept only a certain number of its provisions (so-called 'à la carte approach'). Together with the protocols and revisions, this results in a rather complex patchwork of binding obligations in place, which can be different for every party.[4]

The (R)ESC contains a range of labour-related substantive provisions. Those include the prohibition of forced labour (Art. 1(2) (R)ESC) and freedom of association (Art. 5 (R)ESC), which are also protected under the ECHR. However, the ESC goes much further, setting forth e.g. a right to work (Art. 1 (R)ESC), the right to just conditions of work (Art. 2 (R)ESC), the right to safe and healthy working conditions (Art. 3 (R)ESC), the right to a fair remuneration (Art. 4 (R)ESC), an explicit right to bargain collectively and to take collective action (Art. 6 (R)ESC) or the right to social security (Art. 12 (R)ESC). Further rights were added by subsequent protocols and the RESC.

Supervision of the ESC takes place through a reporting system which bears close semblance to the ILO's regular supervisory procedure. The reporting procedure has been amended and refined on several occasions, notably by the 1991 Amending Protocol to the ESC, which has not yet entered into force but is applied based on a CM decision.[5] The parties have to submit reports on the implementation in two-year intervals (Art. 21 ESC), on which their domestic social partner organizations may comment (Art. 23 ESC). As in the ILO, the examination of the reports takes place in two stages.

On a first stage, the reports are examined by the European Committee of Social Rights (ECSR), formerly named Committee of Independent Experts,[6] composed of

---

Isa and Koen de Feyter (eds), *International Human Rights Law in a Global Context* (University of Deusto 2009) 692.

[2]The Additional Protocol to the European Social Charter (adopted 5 May 1988, entered into force 3 September 1992) CETS No 128, the Protocol amending the European Social Charter (adopted 21 October 1991) CETS No 142, and the Additional Protocol to the European Social Charter Providing for a System of Collective Complaints (adopted 9 November 1995, entered into force 1 July 1997) CETS No 158.

[3]The scope of the (R)ESC's substantive obligations can only be sketched here as far as they are relevant for this study, for an overview, see Becker (n 1) para 12 et seqq.

[4]In essence, parties do not have to ratify the whole Charter, but may choose which of the substantive obligations they accept, provided that they accept at least a defined minimum number of obligations (Art. A(1) lit. c RESC). To ensure a common minimum standard, the ESC further requires all parties to accept a set of 'core' obligations (Art. A(1) lit. b RESC). Furthermore, parties are free to ratify any the ESC's protocols and the RESC, which has to date been ratified by 34 states. Another eleven states have signed but not ratified the RESC, see CoE, 'Chart of Signatures and Ratifications of Treaty 163 - European Social Charter (Revised)' (*CoE Website*) <https://www.coe.int/en/web/conventions/full-list/-/conventions/treaty/163/signatures> accessed 26 April 2020.

[5]CM, Decision Relating to the Application of the 1991 Amending Protocol (467th Meeting of the Ministers' Deputies, 11 December 1991) CM/Del/Dec(1991)467. Furthermore, the reporting system was restructured in 2007 to cope with the workload and to focus on thematic reports.

[6]For the purposes of this study, both are referred to as ECSR.

15 independent experts with recognized competence in international social questions" (Art. 25(1) ESC).[7] The ECSR examines the reports and other information to assess whether a party has acted in compliance with its obligations under the ESC. The conclusions of the ECSR are declaratory as to the law, but not enforceable.

On the second stage, the ESC parties' reports and the ECSR's conclusions are examined from a social, economic and policy perspective by the Governmental Committee of the European Social Charter and European Code of Social Security (Art. 27(1) and (3) ESC), in which international trade union and employers' associations participate as observers (Art. 27(2) ESC).[8] Over time, this second stage has gradually moved to the background, while the ECSR has gained in relevance.

As a complement to supervision through reports, the 1995 Additional Protocol introduces a collective complaints procedure for international trade unions and employers' organizations, representative domestic social partner organizations and certain other associations (Art. 1 1995 Additional Protocol). This procedure, which has been accepted by 15 states to date,[9] introduces a quasi-judicial review mechanism into ESC supervision.[10]

B. The ILO's Influence on the ESC's Text

The ILO had a decisive influence on the ESC's text, both regarding its initial wording and subsequent protocols and revisions. The drafting, subsequent amendment and revision of the ESC provide an example of inter-organizational interaction in the area of institutionalized treaty making. As will be seen, the ILO's influence has been virtually omnipresent.

I. The ILO's Role in the Drafting of the ESC

In the early 1950s, the newly established CoE faced demands from trade unions and from within the PACE to engage in a European social policy and to create a European instrument on social issues.[11] This put the CoE in an intricate position.

[7]Which are appointed by the CM from a list of nominations by ESC parties (Art. 25(1) ESC).

[8]The Governmental Committee's reports are examined by the CM, which may make recommendations to a party (Art. 27(3), 28(1) ESC).

[9]CoE, 'Chart of Signatures and Ratifications of Treaty 158 - Additional Protocol to the European Social Charter Providing for a System of Collective Complaints' (*CoE Website*) <https://www.coe.int/en/web/conventions/full-list/-/conventions/treaty/158/signatures?p_auth=fCQiWTQl> accessed 26 April 2020.

[10]Becker (n 1) para 50. The ECSR takes a (declaratory) decision on the admissibility and the merits of each case and reports to the CM, which adopts a resolution and, in case of a violation, a recommendation (Arts. 8 and 9 ESC 1995 Additional Protocol).

[11]In addition, there was a CoE-internal institutional struggle between the CM and the PACE as to the legal character the instrument should have, see on both Tonia Novitz, *International and European Protection of the Right to Strike* (Oxford University Press 2003) 136 et seq.

On the one hand, it had been itself endowed with a competence to promote economic and social progress. On the other hand, the ILO had already acquired more than 30 years of institutional experience and reputation in this field and had been a prolific actor in norm-setting and implementation. The ILO was, therefore, both a natural role model and a factor to be taken into account during the discussions on the form and content of the CoE's social policy and especially of the envisioned social charter. From the outset, the CoE was eager to avoid unnecessary duplication of other IOs' work. As a general principle, the ESC was intended to set a level of protection which was at least equivalent to the one set by pertinent ILO conventions.[12]

In consequence, the CoE sought cooperation with the ILO early on. The further the drafting proceeded, the more the ILO played a role in it. ILO representatives and staff supported the CoE on several stages of the drafting process, which coincided with an increasing influence of existing ILO instruments and practice on the draft itself.[13] For instance, the express recognition of the right to strike in the Charter drafts (now covered by Art. 6(4) ESC) was inspired by, inter alia, the early recognition of the right to strike as an intrinsic corollary of freedom of association by the ILO supervisory bodies.[14] The ILO also served as inspiration when possible options for an ESC supervisory mechanism were contemplated. One proposal even suggested to vest supervision in the ILO's CEACR.[15] While the ESC eventually obtained its own, separate mechanism, there are striking similarities between the ESC's reporting procedure and the ILO's regular supervisory procedure.[16]

In December 1958, after a draft had been completed by the CoE, the ILO organized a consultative tripartite regional conference in Strasbourg, at which the social partners had an opportunity to comment on the draft.[17] Similar to the composition of the International Labour Conference, each participating state's delegation was composed of two government officials and one representative each for the workers' and employers' organizations.[18] The Strasbourg tripartite conference could provide some important suggestions which eventually found their way into

[12]Stein Evju, 'The European Social Charter and the International Labour Organisation – Interlinks Past and Present' in Wolfgang Däubler and Reingard Zimmer (eds), *Arbeitsvölkerrecht - Festschrift für Klaus Lörcher* (Nomos 2013) 148.

[13]ibid 147.

[14]Clarence Wilfred Jenks, *The International Protection of Trade Union Freedom* (Stevens and Sons 1957) 334; Novitz (n 11) 140.

[15]Evju, 'The European Social Charter and the International Labour Organisation – Interlinks Past and Present' (n 12) 150.

[16]ibid 151.

[17]Based on Art. 3 ILO-CoE, see Birte Wassenberg, *History of the Council of Europe* (Council of Europe Publishing 2013). See also David John Harris, *The European Social Charter* (Transnational Publishers 1984) 7 et seqq.

[18]ILO, *Tripartite Conference Convened by the International Labour Organization at the Request of the Council of Europe, Strasbourg 1-12 December 1958, Record of Proceedings* (ILO 1959) 3.

the Charter.[19] For instance, when the scope of ESC obligations became an issue, the ILO suggested, and the conference eventually proposed, that the ESC should contain a common core of obligations which all states were required to adopt, while placing the acceptance of other provisions at their disposition. This proposal was inspired by a number of ILO conventions that employ a similar approach.[20] Via the conference proposal, this structural feature of certain ILO conventions (the above mentioned 'à la carte approach') was introduced into the final ESC text.[21]

II. The Institutional Link with the ILO in the ESC and the ECSR's Rules

The ESC's final text itself includes several links to the ILO.

For one part, the right to social security (Art. 12(2) ESC explicitly references ILO Convention No 102.[22] Moreover, the ESC creates an institutional link between its own institutions and the ILO. Firstly, it obliges the CoE Secretary General to notify or inform the ILO, e.g. on new ratifications of the ESC.[23] Secondly, and perhaps most importantly for present purposes, Art. 26 ESC provides that:

> [t]he International Labour Organisation shall be invited to nominate a representative to participate in a consultative capacity in the deliberations of the [ECSR].

---

[19]Evju, 'The European Social Charter and the International Labour Organisation – Interlinks Past and Present' (n 12) 147. The conference, however, did not reach consensus on *all* points. For a detailed account, see ILO, 'Report of the International Organizations Committee of the Governing Body' (Governing Body, 141st Session, 10-13 March 1959) G.B.L41/Ll/22, 1 et seqq.

[20]Evju, 'The European Social Charter and the International Labour Organisation – Interlinks Past and Present' (n 12) 150.

[21]Albeit the exact scope of the 'core' was only determined after the conference, ibid. As a further contribution, the conference further moulded the express recognition of the right to strike, Novitz (n 11) 142.

[22]Pursuant to which the parties undertake "[...] to maintain the social security system at a satisfactory level at least equal to that required for ratification of International Labour Convention (No. 102) Concerning Minimum Standards of Social Security."

[23]Art. 20(4) ESC provides that notifications made under Part III of the 1961 Charter – i.e. notifications indicating the particular obligations a party accepted under the ESC's 'à la carte approach' – have to be communicated to the ILO Director-General. Furthermore, pursuant to Art. 30(3) ESC, the CoE Secretary-General shall not only inform the other ESC parties, but also the ILO Director-General, of all emergency derogations from the ESC declared by a party under that Article. As to the territorial scope, Art. 34(5) ESC contains a similar information requirement concerning subsequent notifications by which a party accepts an extension of the Charter's application to any of its non-metropolitan territories. As to the ESC's temporal scope of application, the CoE Secretary-General must inform the ILO Director-General of the Charter's entry into force (Art. 35(4) ESC), the entry into force of any amendments (Art. 36 ESC) and any denunciation by a party of the Charter or of any of its previously accepted facultative obligations (Art. 37(1) ESC). Similar information requirements can be found in Art. 12 of the Additional Protocol of 1988 and in Art. O RESC.

This institutional link is further specified in Rule 12(1) of the ECSR Rules of Procedure, which stipulates that the ECSR shall hold an annual exchange of views with a senior official of the ILO's International Labour Office.

Finally, the ESC secretariat maintains close working relations with the International Labour Office, from which it may obtain information for the preparation of ECSR meetings.[24] The underlying provision is Rule 12(2) of the ECSR Rules of Procedure, which provides:

> The Secretariat exchanges information with the International Labour Office and keeps the Committee informed of developments within the International Labour Organisation.

It is worth noting that the aforesaid provisions confer a special status onto the ILO. ILO Convention No 102 is the only non-CoE international instrument that is expressly being referred to in the original ESC.[25] Likewise, apart from the other ESC parties, the ILO Director-General is the only mandatory recipient of information to be transmitted by the CoE Secretary-General, despite that information being no less relevant for other institutions. Finally, the ILO is the only organization to be invited to participate in the work of the ECSR—unlike even the ECtHR.

III. The ILO's Role in Reforming the ESC

The ILO also inspired subsequent reforms of the ESC. A 1978 report of the CoE Parliamentary Assembly suggested inter alia to enhance cooperation between the ILO and the CoE with regard to state reports on the ESC and on ILO conventions.[26] In preparation of the Protocols of 1988, 1991 and 1995 and the ESC's revision of 1996, the CoE Committee of Ministers convened an ad hoc committee (the so-called Charte-Rel) to make proposals on appropriate reforms to enhance the effectiveness of the ESC and its supervisory system. The Charte-Rel comprised representatives of the social partners and—again as the only IO—the ILO, in a consultative capacity.[27]

The involvement of the ILO had a traceable impact on the 1988 Protocol. As to the substantive Charter provisions, there is a pattern of ILO-inspired changes and

[24] Evju, 'The European Social Charter and the International Labour Organisation – Interlinks Past and Present' (n 12) 153.

[25] Only in 1996, Art. 12(2) RESC replaced that reference in favour of a reference to the European Code of Social Security, a CoE treaty which sets a higher standard that ILO Convention No 102.

[26] PACE, Recommendation 839 (1978) on the Revision of the European Social Charter (adopted at its 30th session on 28 September 1978) 4.

[27] CoE, 'Explanatory Reports to the Revised European Social Charter' in CoE (ed), *European Social Charter - Collected Texts* (7th edn, Council of Europe Publishing 2015) 153.

amendments.[28] A similar influence can be observed regarding the ESC revision of 1996, leading to the adoption of the RESC. For example, Art. 8(4) RESC, a provision concerning the protection of maternity during night work, was informed by the then-recently adopted ILO Convention No 171 of 1990.[29] Likewise, Art. 24 RESC, on the right to protection in cases of termination of employment, has been inspired by Art. 8 ILO Convention No 158.[30] The same applies to the rights enshrined in Art. 25 RESC (influenced by ILO Convention No 173 of 1992),[31] Art. 27 RESC (inspired by ILO Convention No 156 and ILO Recommendation No 156),[32] Art. 28 RESC (inspired by ILO Convention No 135)[33] and Art. 29 (inspired by ILO Convention No 158).[34]

ILO influence is further discernible as to reforms of the ESC's supervisory system. The Charte-Rel, among other points, reflected on the institutional link with the ILO, and at some point even discussed granting the ILO the right to appoint a full member to the ECSR.[35] Perhaps most importantly, the collective complaints procedure, introduced by the Additional Protocol of 1995 and introducing the right of associations to file collective complaints with the ECSR, was designed after the equivalent ILO procedures.[36]

[28]To name one example, the definition of the term 'workers' representatives' contained in the Appendix to the Additional Protocol of 1988 (and used in Arts. 2 and 3 of that Protocol) is taken from Art. 3 of the ILO Workers' Representatives Convention, 1971 (No 135) (adopted 23 June 1971, entered into force 30 June 1973) 883 UNTS 111. According to the Explanatory Report to the 1988 Protocol, this definition was used to harmonise the definitions in both instruments, CoE, 'Explanatory Reports to the Additional Protocol of 1988' in CoE (ed), *European Social Charter - Collected Texts* (7th edn, Council of Europe Publishing 2015) 133.

[29]CoE, 'Explanatory Reports to the Revised European Social Charter' (n 27) 158 8 ILO Night Work Convention, 1990 (No. 171) (adopted on 26 June 1990, entered into force on 4 January 1995), 1846 UNTS 418).

[30]ibid 162 ((ILO Termination of Employment Convention, 1982 (No 158) (adopted 22 June 1982, entered into force 23 November 1985) 1412 UNTS 1).

[31]ibid 163 (ILO Protection of Workers' Claims (Employer's Insolvency) Convention, 1992 (No. 173) (adopted on 23 June 1992, entered into force on 8 June 1995), 1886 UNTS 1).

[32]ibid 164 (ILO Workers with Family Responsibilities Convention, 1981 (No 156) (adopted 23 June 1981, entered into force 11 August 1983) 2029 UNTS 297; ILO Working Environment (Air Pollution, Noise and Vibration) Recommendation, 1977 (No 156) (1977) LX ILO Official Bulletin Ser A Vol 3 146).

[33]ibid 165 (ILO Workers' Representatives Convention, 1971 (No 135) (adopted 23 June 1971, entered into force 30 June 1973) 883 UNTS 111).

[34]ibid.

[35]Manfred Mohr, 'The Turin Protocol of 22 October 1991: A Major Contribution to Revitalizing the European Social Charter' (1992) 3 European Journal of International Law 362, 363, fn. 9.

[36]CoE, 'Explanatory Reports to the 1995 Protocol' in CoE (ed), *European Social Charter - Collected Texts* (7th edn, Council of Europe Publishing 2015) 145.

C. ILO Instruments and Practice in the ECSR's Supervisory Practice

Besides the ESC's text, ILO instruments and practice have also played a distinct role in the ECSR's supervisory practice, reinforced by the institutional link in the ESC and the Rules of Procedure mentioned above.[37] The ECSR has continuously used ILO instruments and practice in its work (I.). The institutional link between the ECSR and the ILO has been of considerable practical importance, because it has created synergies in the majority of instances (II.). Nevertheless, even the exceptional interconnection between the ILO and the ECSR did not prevent the latter to deviate from ILO instruments and practice in some instances, limiting the ILO's influence (III.).

I. The Use of ILO Instruments and Practice in the ECSR's Work

The ECSR has used ILO instruments and practice for two main purposes. First, as a source of factual information when examining states' reports, and second, in its legal argumentation.

Firstly, the ECSR referred to the ILO committees' examinations of state reports[38] as well as to other ILO publications[39] as a source of information, for instance when

---

[37]It does not come as a surprise that the ECSR first referred to ILO jurisprudence in the context of Art. 12(2) ESC, the provision explicitly referencing ILO Convention No 102. In its conclusions on Denmark, Italy, Norway and Sweden, made in 1969, the ECSR noted the CEACR's observations on the four countries under scrutiny, which indicated compliance issues under ILO Convention No 102: "In this regard, the Committee did not lose sight of the fact that the implementation of one or other of the provisions of Convention No 102 might present some problems, but it considered that, even if the Committee of Experts on the Application of Conventions and Recommendations of the International Labour Organisation were to conclude that, on these points, Convention No 102 was not being observed, the four governments in question would still be fulfilling the minimal condition laid down for the ratification of the said Convention, since they had accepted a greater number of parts than the minimum required", ECSR, *Conclusions I (1969) Norway, Article 12-2.*

[38]ECSR, *Conclusions IX-2 (1985-86), Italy, Article 1-2*; ECSR, *Conclusions 2014, Lithuania, Article 4-1*; *European Trade Union Confederation (ETUC) Centrale Générale Des Syndicats Libéraux de Belgique (CGSLB) and Others v. Belgium* Collective Complaint No. 59/2009 (ECSR, 13 September 2011), para 19; *General Federation of Employees of the National Electric Power Corporation (GENOP-DEI) / Confederation of Greek Civil Servants Trade Unions (ADEDY) v. Greece* Collective Complaint No 65/2011 (ECSR, 23 May 2012), para 39. Sometimes, the ECSR has also had recourse to the states' reports themselves. For example, it examined the Italian report to the ILO on ILO Convention No 29 and ILO Convention No 105, ECSR, *Conclusions IX-2 (1985-86) Italy, Article 1-2.*

[39]For example, statistical data published by the ILO, ECSR, *Conclusions X-2 (1987-90) Ireland, Article 4-1.*

the ESC parties' reports to the ECSR fell short of providing sufficient information by themselves.[40] The ECSR has also used the ILO supervisory bodies' observations as a peg for own requests for information. For example, in its 2014 Conclusions on Serbia and Ukraine, the ECSR requested the two states to comment on observations the CEACR had previously made on them regarding the right to organise and the rights to collective bargaining and collective action.[41] Furthermore, as a noteworthy result of the institutionalized contacts between the ECSR and the ILO, it has further happened that the International Labour Office has furnished the ECSR with information on its own initiative. Based on this information, the latter has conducted a re-examination—and, as will be explained further in the next section, also to a legal re-evaluation—of its prior opinion on situations in certain ESC member states.[42]

Secondly, the ECSR has continuously had recourse to ILO instruments and practice in its legal reasoning, which has created considerable synergies and spill-over effects. In some cases, the ECSR simply stated ILO instruments as "relevant international materials", without coming back to them in its legal assessment.[43] However, in other cases, the Committee used ILO references to foster its legal analysis. In some of these instances, this happened to make a point of principle.[44] On other occasions, the ECSR interpreted ESC provisions in the light of ILO instruments in a detailed fashion.[45] In most of these cases, the ECSR's practice is marked by attempts to align its jurisprudence with ILO instruments and practice.

[40] E.g. ECSR, *Conclusions 2014, Serbia, Article 6-4*. In other cases, the ESCR used ILO documents to obtain special information, e.g. from the ILO High Level Mission to Greece with regard to certain implications of the post-2007 global financial crisis, *General Federation of Employees of the National Electric Power Corporation (GENOP-DEI) / Confederation of Greek Civil Servants Trade Unions (ADEDY) v.* Greece Collective Complaint No. 66/2011 (ECSR, 23 May 2012), para 61.

[41] ECSR, *Conclusions 2014, Serbia, Article 5* (on the formation of trade unions); ECSR, *Conclusions 2014, Serbia, Article 6-2* (on the representativeness of unions); ECSR, *Conclusions 2014, Ukraine, Article 6-4* (on the entitlement to call for collective action). In the case of Ukraine, the ECSR requested information from Ukraine on the status of certain amendments to domestic labour law which the CEACR had requested Ukraine to enact.

[42] Evju, 'The European Social Charter and the International Labour Organisation – Interlinks Past and Present' (n 12) para 153.

[43] *Finnish Society of Social Rights v. Finland* Collective Complaint No 107/2014 (ECSR, 6 September 2016), para 25.

[44] For instance, in *LO and TCO v. Sweden*, the Committee noted "that the right to collective bargaining and action receives constitutional recognition at national level in the vast majority of the Council of Europe's member States, as well as in a significant number of binding legal instruments at the United Nations and EU level", referring inter alia to ILO Conventions No 87, No 98 and No 151 (ILO Labour Relations (Public Service) Convention, 1978 (No 151) (adopted 27 June 1978, entered into force 25 February 1981) 1218 UNTS 87), *Swedish Trade Union Confederation (LO) and Swedish Confederation of Professional Employees (TCO) v. Sweden* Collective Complaint No 85/2012 (ECSR, 3 July 2013), para 110.

[45] For example, the right of the worker to earn his living in an occupation freely entered upon (Art. 1 (2) ESC) was interpreted to prohibit all kinds of forced and compulsory labour. To this end, the Committee had recourse to the definition of forced labour contained in Art. 2(1) of the pertinent ILO

II. The Relevance of the Institutional Link Between the ILO and the ECSR

A distinct feature of the ESC is its abovementioned institutionalized link with the ILO, which resembles a showcase for direct inter-organizational interaction at the stage of interpretation and implementation. In practice, the institutionalized link has provided a basis for a thriving working relationship between the ECSR Secretariat and the International Labour Office.

1. The Working Relationship at Secretariat Level

As mentioned earlier, Art. 26 ESC and Art. 12(1) ECSR Rules of Procedure envisage the participation of an ILO representative in the ECSR's meetings. In practice, such participation in the Committee's sessions themselves is the exception.[46]

Instead, the cooperation largely occurs at secretariat level, between the ECSR Secretariat and the International Labour Office, as envisaged in Art. 12(2) ECSR Rules of Procedure. The ECSR Secretariat's function is to support the Committee in its tasks. One important task in this regard is the preparation of the ECSR's conclusions on the parties' reports. Apart from collecting information from the ESC parties,[47] the Secretariat gathers information from European and international

Convention No 29, CoE, 'Form for the Reports Submitted in Pursuance of the European Social Charter (1961) and the Additional Protocol of 1988' in CoE (ed), *European Social Charter - Collected Texts* (7th edn, Council of Europe Publishing 2015) 219. As another example, in its 2016 conclusions on Ukraine, the ECSR concluded that the situation in Ukraine was in conformity with the requirement of Art. 24 ESC to appropriately adjust the burden of proof between employers and employee in dismissal proceedings. The ECSR reached that conclusion inter alia because Ukraine had ratified ILO Convention No 158, Art. 9 of which imposed the burden of proof on the employer. The ILO Convention was applicable in domestic law and took precedence over other provisions of Ukrainian procedural law, ECSR, *Conclusions 2016, Ukraine, Article 24.*

[46]In practice, ILO representatives attend ECSR sessions whenever matters of general principle or issues specifically relating to ILO instruments are on the agenda, Evju, 'The European Social Charter and the International Labour Organisation – Interlinks Past and Present' (n 12) 152. While no statistics on the frequency of these meetings exist, anecdotal reports suggest that ILO representatives only participate in a relatively small number of sessions.

[47]To this end, the Secretariat sends report forms – essentially questionnaires – to the ESC parties, in which the latter provide information on their implementation of Charter obligations. See e.g. CoE, 'Form for the Reports Submitted in Pursuance of the European Social Charter (1961) and the Additional Protocol of 1988' (n 45). The reports are adopted by the CM, not the ECSR itself, Renate Kicker and Markus Möstl, *Standard-Setting Through Monitoring? The Role of Council of Europe Expert Bodies in the Development of Human Rights* (Council of Europe Publishing 2013) 96. As guidance to the states on how to understand the report forms, the report forms have always prominently referred to ILO conventions, both in the questionnaire itself (CoE, 'Form for the Reports to Be Submitted in Pursuance of the European Social Charter (1961) and the Additional Protocol of 1988' (n 45) 6 (on the definition of forced labour) and in an Appendix enlisting relevant international instruments for each (R)ESC article, ibid 45 et seqq. and CoE, 'Form for the Reports to

sources, including the ILO.[48] It appears that the cooperation between the ECSR Secretariat and the International Labour Office has gradually developed a fruitful routine over time. During the discussions in the Charte-Rel in 1990, some members still deplored an "uneven use" of the ILO's cooperation by the ECSR.[49] By contrast, in its 2012 General Survey, the CEACR expressed the view that the cooperation between the ILO and the ECSR

> should be mentioned as a particularly effective example with a view to developing greater coherence in the supervision of the international and regional obligations of States in relation to fundamental principles and rights at work.[50]

2. An Example: The ECSR's Examination of Compulsory Arbitration in Norway

An intriguing example of how the ECSR and the ILO put their working relationship to use is their coordinated action against the Norwegian practice of submitting disputes between trade unions and employers to compulsory arbitration (*Tvungen lønnsnemnd*) by way of a legislative act of parliament. According to this practice, which had been established since the 1950s, the Norwegian parliament could intervene in ongoing industrial disputes. For certain concrete disputes, it could prohibit recourse to strike action and require the parties to submit their dispute to compulsory arbitration.[51] The parliament passed such case-specific ad hoc legislative acts when it considered that there was a special public interest to prevent disruptions by strike action.

In its early practice, the ECSR had not addressed the question whether this practice was in conformity with Norway's obligations under the ESC. However, Norwegian trade unions began to submit complaints against this practice to the ILO supervisory bodies, especially the CFA.[52] As a result, from 1982 onwards, the CFA consistently decided that the practice of compulsory arbitration was incompatible

---

Be Submitted in Pursuance of the European Social Charter (Revised) Adopted by the Committee of Ministers on 26 March 2008' in CoE (ed), *European Social Charter - Collected Texts* (7th edn, Council of Europe Publishing 2015) 268.

[48]Moreover, Art. 27 ESC confers a right on trade unions and employers' organizations to comment on the reports, Kicker and Möstl (n 47) 97.

[49]Mohr (n 35) 363.

[50]ILO, 'Giving Globalization a Human Face, General Survey on the Fundamental Conventions Concerning Rights at Work in Light of the ILO Declaration on Social Justice for a Fair Globalization', Report of the Committee of Experts on the Application of Conventions and Recommendations (International Labour Conference, 101st Session, 2012) ILC.101/III/1B, 15.

[51]Stein Evju, 'The Right to Collective Action under the European Social Charter' (2011) 2 European Labour Law Journal 196, 222 et seq.

[52]The 'precursor' was a case lodged in 1963. The topic had repeatedly brought to the attention of ILO bodies from 1981 onwards, Evju, 'The Right to Collective Action under the European Social Charter' (n 51) 222.

with the principles of freedom of association.[53] This has essentially remained the CFA's stance ever since.[54]

Norway itself did not report the developments in the CFA to the ECSR. However, the ILO itself proactively informed the ECSR of the matter.[55] In reaction thereto, in 1985, the ECSR began to examine the practice of compulsory arbitration itself.[56] The ECSR subsequently found on several occasions that the Norwegian practice constituted an unjustifiable infringement on the right to take collective action enshrined in Art. 6(4) ESC.[57] In this example, the ILO had used existing communication channels to spread controversial issues which had come up in its own practice. It thereby induced the ECSR to take up the same matter the ILO had itself been dealing with and taken a position on. What is more, the ILO continued to inform and update the ECSR on later occasions on its supervisory practice on compulsory arbitration and on further developments in Norway.[58] The collaboration between ILO and ECSR, and the influence the former has on the latter, is a striking example of how the institutionalized link was used in practice.

The impact of the link can be illustrated when looking at coinciding events in the ECtHR. In the late 1990s, Norwegian trade unions brought measures imposing compulsory arbitration before the ECtHR. At the time, the CFA had already found that the Norwegian practice was inconsistent with principles of freedom of association. Drawing on these findings, the ECSR had already found that the very same measures brought before the ECtHR were inconsistent with the ESC.[59] The ECtHR took note of these developments in its 2002 decision in *Federation of Offshore Workers' Unions v. Norway*.[60] Nevertheless, it struck out the application as

---

[53]*Norway (Case No 1099) (8 December 1981) The Norwegian Society of Engineers* <https://www.ilo.org/dyn/normlex/en/f?p=1000:50001:0::NO:50001:P50001_COMPLAINT_FILE_ID:2896698> accessed 26 April 2020. This first case was followed by at least nine others, Evju, 'The Right to Collective Action under the European Social Charter' (n 51) 222.

[54]*Norway (Case No 3147)* Report of the Committee on Freedom of Association No 378 (2016) XCIX ILO Official Bulletin Ser B/1 146, 569 et seqq., with further references to previous reports.

[55]In ECSR, *Conclusions IX-1 (1987-90) Norway, Article 6-4*, "[t]he Committee noted, as regards Norway, that this State's report mentioned no new developments in the field covered by this provision of the Charter. However, it was informed by ILO that instances of compulsory arbitration had been noted in the recent past. It hoped that the next Norwegian report would provide detailed particulars on this point. Pending receipt of this information, it confirmed its previous positive conclusion, reserving its right to re-examine the position in the light of the details to be provided."

[56]ibid.

[57]E.g. ECSR, *Conclusions XII-1 (1991-92) Norway, Article 6-4*; ECSR, *Conclusions XIII-1 (1993-97) Norway, Article 6-4*; ECSR, *Conclusions XIII-3 (1993-97), Norway, Article 6-4*; ECSR, *Conclusions XIV-1 (1998) Norway, Article 6-4.*

[58]ECSR, *Conclusions XIII-1 (1993-97) Norway, Article 6-4*: "It also learned from ILO information that the Government had started to review possible modifications to the arbitration system and asked to be informed of any developments in the matter, with regard to this provision also."

[59]ECSR, *Conclusions XIV-1, Volume 2 (1998-2000) Norway, Article 6-4.*

[60]*Federation of Offshore Workers' Trade Unions and Others v. Norwa*y ECHR 2002–VI 301, 7 et seqq.

manifestly ill-founded, invoking its (pre-*Demir and Baykara*) case-law that the right to strike was not protected under the ECHR.[61] One might wonder if the case had been decided differently if an institutional link between the ILO and the ECtHR had been in place.

III. Limits of ILO Influence

Notwithstanding the described impact of the institutional link, it must be noted that the latter did not lead to a complete harmonization between the ECSR's and the ILO's practices.

1. Deviations Due to Pressure from Member States

In the Norwegian compulsory arbitration episode discussed in the previous section, the ECSR did not blindly adopt the ILO's position. Instead, the Committee gradually developed its stance into a case-by-case examination of whether the Norwegian compulsory arbitration was compliant with Art. 6(4) ESC. In particular, it examined if the requirements for restricting Charter rights (Art. 31 ESC/Art. G RESC) were met, i.e. if the restrictions were "provided for by law" and were "necessary in a democratic society". Moreover, as a form of compromise to address strong criticisms from Norway,[62] the ECSR decided

> to no longer consider as part of the reporting procedure the situations in which arbitration has been imposed by Parliament to end a strike in the sectors which are prima facie covered by [Art. 31 ESC/Art. G RESC].[63]

The CFA, by contrast, did not exercise such self-restraint. Instead, it stood by its established practice, whereby prohibitions of strikes are only permissible either with regard to the public service or with regard to essential services in the strict sense of the term, i.e. "those services whose interruption would endanger the life, personal safety or health of the whole or part of the population" or "vital public interests".[64]

Hence, the established, close and mutually satisfactory cooperation between the ECSR and the ILO, while significantly enhancing convergence and coherence, did not prevent the ECSR from maintaining or developing particular stances, based on the peculiarities of its law and prior practice.

---

[61] ibid 15.

[62] The ECSR had been criticized for having misunderstood the Norwegian practice, see Evju, 'The Right to Collective Action under the European Social Charter' (n 51) 222.

[63] ECSR, *Conclusions 2014, Norway, Article 6-4.*

[64] ILO, *Digest of Decisions and Principles of the Freedom of Association Committee of the Governing Body of the ILO* (5th edn, ILO 2006) para 564 et seqq.; *Norway (Case No 3147)* (n 54).

2. Jointly Deviating from ILO Instruments and Practice with the ECtHR: The Example of Closed Shop Arrangements

What is more, the institutional link has not prevented the ECSR to deviate from ILO instruments and practice and to give preference to another international body's position instead. A case in point where such a deviation occurred was the question whether the rights to organize and to collective bargaining (Arts. 5 and 6 ESC) prohibited so-called closed shop practices. As will be explained in the following, there has been a sequence of 'back and forth' between the ECtHR and the ECSR, in the course of which both bodies mutually reinforced their rejection of closed shop practices and jointly deviated from the ILO's position.

The term "closed shop" refers to a collective agreement that all employees of a certain employer have to be unionized or have to join a certain trade union within a certain period of time or at least have to pay the union's membership fees.[65] Closed shop arrangements usually play in favour of trade unions, which benefit from the mandatory membership of workers.[66]

ILO instruments and practice have always taken a differentiated stance on closed shop agreements.[67] They distinguish between closed shops imposed by law and those agreed upon through collective bargaining. The CFA has deemed union monopolies created by law (which have the same effect as a closed shop) to be incompatible with ILO Conventions No 87 and No 98.[68] By contrast, as to closed shop arrangements contained in collective agreements, the ILO supervisory bodies neither prohibit nor specifically allow such arrangements and deliberately leave the issue to domestic regulation.[69]

---

[65]The ECtHR itself gave a concise explanation of the phenomenon: "In essence, a closed shop is an undertaking or workplace in which, as a result of an agreement or arrangement between one or more trade unions and one or more employers or employers' associations, employees of a certain class are in practice required to be or become members of a specified union", *Young, James and Webster v. United Kingdom* (1981) Series A No 55, para 13.

[66]Closed shops raise the issue whether there is a negative dimension of freedom of association, i.e. whether one has a right not to join an association, in this case a trade union. If that right exists, closed shop arrangements, forcing a worker to be or become a trade union member when taking up an occupation, will be illegal.

[67]Generally speaking, international law remains ambiguous as to such a negative dimension of freedom of association, Art. 20(2) UDHR expressly recognizes it, albeit in general and vague terms and after lengthy discussion in the Human Rights Commission. The Commission, following ILO recommendations, debated extensively precisely on the question of closed or open shops, Johannes Morsink, *The Universal Declaration of Human Rights: Origins, Drafting, and Intent* (University of Pennsylvania Press 1999) paras 174 et seqq. Art. 22(1) ICCPR does not expressly stipulate a negative right, neither does Art. 8 ICESCR.

[68]ILO, *Digest of Decisions and Principles of the Freedom of Association Committee of the Governing Body of the ILO* (n 64) para 324.

[69]ibid 363 et seqq. *France (Case No 120)* Report of the Committee on Freedom of Association No 17, 1956, XXXIX ILO Official Bulletin Ser B 17, para 95 et seq.; Nivedita M Hosanee, 'A Critical Analysis of Flag State Duties As Laid Down Under Article 94 of the 1982 United Nations Convention on the Law of the Sea' (UN 2009) 30; Franz Christian Ebert and Martin Oelz, 'Bridging

In its first supervision cycle (concluded in 1969), the ECSR had essentially adopted the ILO's differentiated view on closed shops that closed shops imposed by law were impermissible, but closed shop arrangements in collective agreements were not.[70] The ECSR's position was in conformity with the varying domestic rules on closed shops in the CoE member states at the time.[71]

The ECSR's ILO-aligned initial position rapidly changed after the ECtHR had begun to develop its jurisprudence on closed shop arrangements. Given the varying legal traditions in CoE member states, the ECHR drafters had left the question of closed shops deliberately open.[72] However, in *Young, James and Webster v. United Kingdom*, the ECtHR held that a British closed shop arrangement contained in a collective agreement was incompatible with Art. 11 ECHR.[73] It reasoned that the

---

the Gap Between Labour Rights and Human Rights: The Role of ILO Law in Regional Human Rights Courts' (2012) IILS Discussion Paper 212/2012) 9 et seq.

[70] In its statement of interpretation on Art. 5 ESC, the ECSR expressed the view that "in accordance with the Appendix to the Charter, Article 5 does not rule on the admissibility of union security clauses or practices. The Committee considered, however, that any form of compulsory unionism imposed by law must be considered incompatible with the obligation arising under this article of the Charter", ECSR, *Conclusions I (1969) Statement of interpretation, Article 5*. It neither had taken umbrage at closed shop practices in the United Kingdom. In its 1969 Conclusions, the Committee had taken the view that the United Kingdom was "essentially" in conformity with Art. 5 ESC. It did so "on the basis of the information supplied by the United Kingdom to the ILO on the application of Convention 87 (to which reference is made)", ECSR, *Conclusions I (1969) United Kingdom, Article 5*. In its 1981 Conclusions on the United Kingdom, the ECSR explicitly reversed its prior stance, ECSR, *Conclusions VII (1981) United Kingdom, Article 5*.

[71] Pertinent arrangements have had a long tradition in certain countries and in particular in certain sectors. In other countries, they have been prohibited.

[72] Because of this variety, the Conference of Senior Officials, when drafting the ECHR, considered a prohibition "undesirable" and deliberately left out any explicit reference to negative freedom of association, which was invoked by the respondent in *Young, James and Webster v. United Kingdom* (n 65) para 51.

[73] Ever since, the ECtHR has reiterated its prohibitive stance on closed shops. In the relevant later decisions, it – not surprisingly – touched on ILO instruments only cursorily. Rather, it focused on developments at European level instead. In *Sørensen and Rasmussen v. Denmark*, the ECtHR was confronted with the question whether a pre-entry closed shop arrangement in a collective agreement was compatible with Art. 11 ECHR, *Sørensen and Rasmussen v. Denmark* ECHR 2016–I 24, paras 56–58. The Court noted as 'relevant international law' that ILO Convention Nos. 87 and 98 leave the matter of closed shops for domestic regulation, but made this observation rather as an 'also-ran', presumably without putting much weight on this, ibid 38. In its legal assessment, the ECtHR based its conclusion – that the pre-entry closed shop arrangements at hand were incompatible with the ECHR – on its own margin of appreciation doctrine. In determining the scope of the margin, it had recourse to the ongoing discussions and the rendered conclusions and decisions under the ESC, as well as to EU instruments, ibid 72 et seqq. The pertinent ILO instruments and practice apparently did not play a role in the reasoning. ILO instruments and practice played a slightly more prominent role in *Sigurður A. Sigurjónsson v. Iceland*, a case concerning a closed shop arrangement for taxi drivers imposed by public regulation. Here, the ECtHR referred to the ILO CFA's stance in its legal analysis, more precisely as evidence for a growing consensus on the international level to the effect that such closed shop arrangements are incompatible with freedom of association, to which it applied its living instrument-approach, *Sigurður A Sigurjónsson v. Iceland* (1993) Series A No

closed shop practices at hand struck "at the very substance" of freedom of association.[74] The ECtHR based its findings solely on the ECHR itself, neither discussing ILO nor other international instruments.[75] However, various references to the ILO were made in the parties' submissions to the European Commission of Human Rights[76] and in the Commission's dissenting opinions.[77] It is, therefore, safe to assume that the majorities in the Court was aware it was deviating from the ILO's stance on this point, but did not consider this aspect decisive.

After the ECtHR had set the precedent, the ECSR followed suit the same year, holding that

> [i]n accordance with the statement of the European Court of Human Rights in [*Young, James and Webster v. United Kingdom*] concerning [Art. 11 ECHR], it should be underlined that also as regards Article 5 of the Charter, to interpret this provision 'as permitting every kind of compulsion in the field of trade union membership would strike at the very substance of the freedom it is designed to guarantee'.[78]

This change of the ECSR's view is remarkable. It did not give further reasons for its reorientation and alignment with ECtHR jurisprudence but has nevertheless continuously reaffirmed its new position that closed shop practices are prohibited under Art. 5 ESC.[79] Whatever the actual reasons may have been, the records show that the ECSR was aware that its new stance was a deviation from ILO practice,

---

264, para 35. This is hardly surprising, given that the ILO has always considered closed shops imposed by law impermissible. Still, as in *Sørensen and Rasmussen*, the reference to the ILO was rather superficial. The Court clearly put more emphasis on the developments at European level.

[74]*Young, James and Webster v. United Kingdom* (n 65) para 55.

[75]The Court relied on its approach to interpreting the ECHR in a practically effective way, see *Case Relating to Certain Aspects of the Law on the Use of Languages in Education in* Belgium (1967) Series A No 5, para 5; *Golder v. United Kingdom* (1975) Series A No 18, para 38; *Winterwerp v. Netherlands* (1979) Series A No 47, para 6.

[76]In support of their arguments, both the applicants and the United Kingdom pointed to ILO Conventions Nos. 87 and 98 and to ILO practice, *James and Webster v. United Kingdom* (1979) Series B No 39 (Commission Report), paras 95 and 115.

[77]*James and Webster v. United Kingdom* (n 76) Dissenting Opinion by Mr Fawcett, para 6. Commission member Kellberg included ILO instruments in a survey of pertinent international legal instruments in order to support his conclusion that closed shops were compatible with the ECHR, *James and Webster v. United Kingdom* (n 76) Dissenting Opinion by Mr. Kellberg, Joined by Mr. Nørgaard, para 2.1. Making a similar argument, Judge Sørensen relied on the ECHR's *travaux*, arguing that the Conference of Senior Officials had left it to national legislation whether to permit or prohibit closed shop practices. This, he further reasoned, had been "entirely consistent with the attitude previously adopted within the framework of the International Labour Organisation" and its supervisory bodies, *Young, James and Webster v United Kingdom* (n 65) Dissenting Opinion by Judge Sørensen, joined by judges Thór Vilhjálmsson and Lagergren, para 3.

[78]ECSR, *Conclusions VII (1981), United Kingdom, Article 5.*

[79]E.g. ECSR, *Conclusions XIII-3 - France - Article 5*; ECSR, *Conclusions 2006 - Sweden - Article 5.*

which was discussed controversially and sparked a rare dissenting opinion to its 1981 Conclusions.[80]

The change of the ECSR's view is also remarkable because it led to a generalization of the prohibition. The ECtHR in *Young, James and Webster* had explicitly abstained from taking a general position on the permissibility of closed shop arrangements under the ECHR. Rather, the Court had highlighted that its judgment was specific to the particular circumstances of the case before it.[81] By contrast, the ECSR made a *general* conclusion on the permissibility of closed shop arrangements in the United Kingdom. The ECSR thus significantly abstracted the ECtHR's position. This abstraction was no isolated incident, Rather, the Committee subsequently issued a whole range of conclusions as to the inconformity of closed shop clauses in other states.[82]

The ECSR's instant abstraction of the *Young, James and Webster* decision and the line of further conclusions by the Committee had again implications on the ECtHR's further jurisprudence. The ECSR's position now encouraged the ECtHR to solidify its position.[83] In the Court's 1993 judgment in *Sibson v. United Kingdom*, the dissenting judges referred to the then newly published ECSR conclusions which supported a prohibition of closed shop arrangements.[84] Only two months later, the minority at the ECtHR had turned to a majority. In *Sigurdur A. Sigurjónsson v. Iceland*, this majority stated that

> [e]ven in the absence of an express provision, the [ECSR] (...) has in several instances disapproved of closed-shop practices found in certain States Parties.[85]

Judge Thór Vilhjálmsson, who argued in vain that *Young, James and Webster* was a case-specific decision of limited precedential value, was the only dissenter.[86]

In sum, it appears that the Court and the ECSR have, to a considerable extent,[87] mutually reinforced each other's practice in establishing a ban on closed

---

[80]ECSR, *Conclusions VIII (1984) "Dissenting Opinion" by Prof. Zanetti Concerning the Application of Article 5 by the United Kingdom*, referring to ILO instruments and practice and explicitly acknowledging that ILO conventions served as a model for the ESC on the question of closed shops.

[81]*Young, James and Webster v. United Kingdom* (n 65) para 53.

[82]E.g. ECSR, *Conclusions XIII-3 - France - Article 5*; ECSR, *Conclusions XIV-1 - Iceland - Article 5*; ECSR, *Conclusions 2006 - Sweden - Article 5*; ECSR, *Conclusions 2006 - Ireland - Article 5*.

[83]Which had been controversial, George Letsas, *A Theory of Interpretation of the European Convention of Human Rights* (Oxford University Press 2007) 65 et seqq.

[84]The ECSR's case-law was invoked by the minority in *Sibson v. United Kingdom* favour of a prohibition of closed shop arrangements in the case, *Sibson v. United Kingdom* (1993) Series A No 258-A, Dissenting Opinion of Judge Morenilla, joined by Judge Russo, para 2.

[85]*Sigurður A Sigurjónsson v. Iceland* (n 73) para 35.

[86]*Sigurður A Sigurjónsson v Iceland* (n 73) Dissenting Opinion of Judge Thór Vilhjálmsson.

[87]However, the mutual reinforcement did not result in a total alignment, which can be seen in more recent ECSR practice. Both in the 14th and 15th supervision circles, Denmark asserted that its legislation allowing closed shop practices was in conformity with the ECHR. In its Conclusions on Denmark in both circles, the ECSR rejected that argument, reiterating the separate character of the ECHR and the ESC: "The Committee wishes to underline that the European Convention on Human

shop arrangements, thereby jointly deviating from ILO instruments and practice.[88]

D. The Observed Interactions' Relevance for the ILO's Model

The interactions examined in this Chapter are again of noticeable importance for the ILO's model of labour governance.

I. The Nature of the Observed Interactions

The inter-organizational interactions observed in this Chapter are of a different character than those examined in the previous chapters. In the terminology set forth in Chap. 3, the interactions involve exclusively direct interactions that are non-conflictual, even more, are mutually reinforcing and creating synergies. Moreover, the interactions examined in this chapter appear on the stages of norm creation and norm interpretation and implementation, and take place within the context of formal instruments, notably provisions on cooperation in the ILO-CoE agreement and in the ESC and the ECSR's Rules of Procedure, but nevertheless are conducted mostly by informal means.

II. Decisive and Continuous Expansion of the ILO's Outreach

For one part, it hardly needs mention that through the observed inter-organizational interactions, the ILO seized the rare opportunity to graft considerable elements of its model of labour governance onto a newly established IO, founded by like-minded states and in search for an own social policy. As seen, the ILO could not only 'export' many of its substantive standards and essential elements of its own supervisory system to the ESC but could also maintain its influence on the latter's implementation. In consequence, the ILO's model of labour governance has been engrained in the ESC from the start and through its subsequent development. The

Rights and the Social Charter are two separate instruments; according to Article 5 of the Charter there can be no sort of obligation to become or remain a member of a trade union", ECSR, *Conclusions XIV-1 (1998), Denmark, Article 5.*

[88] See, as to the expansion of the prohibition to so-called pre-entry closed shops *Sørensen and Rasmussen v. Denmark* (n 73) para 72.

inter-organizational interactions between the ILO and the CoE/ECSR thus essentially provided the ILO with an 'extension' and a reinforcement of its own model.

III. Dormant Challenges

Despite the apparent success story of cooperation and alignment, there remain challenges for the ILO's model, which the most part lie dormant at present, but nevertheless are of systemic interest.[89]

1. The Persisting Potential for Deviations

For one part, the ILO's extensive involvement in the ESC did not prevent the ECSR from deviating from ILO positions, either in nuances (e.g. when exercising self-restraint as to the review of compulsory arbitration in Norway) or more systemically (when considering closed shop arrangements to be prohibited under the ESC). The given examples are rare, but nevertheless should not be considered to be single and isolated cases. Both the ECSR and other bodies involved in the ESC supervision have reiterated the ESC's distinct and in principle separate character as compared to the ILO.[90] What is more, in its recent practice, the ECSR has made general statements emphasizing the ESC's distinctiveness vis-à-vis other treaties and IOs.[91] Thus, there is no 'automatic' alignment with ILO instruments and practice, and the potential for future deviations remains.

---

[89]There are also interesting implications for the ECSR's model, which are, however, outside this study's purview, e.g. that the institutionalized link has largely proven to be a 'one-way street' in favour of the ILO, while ECSR practice does not seem to have any relevant impact on the ILO.

[90]For an early example, the PACE, in its 1971 opinion on the ECSR's first supervision cycle, showed itself "[p]ersuaded that the provisions of the Charter should not, save where specifically stated in the Charter itself, and in conformity with the general principles of public international law, be regarded as a mere reiteration of undertakings contained in other legal instruments of a treaty nature which are not only applied in a different context and subscribed to by a group of States other than those of the Council of Europe, as for example International Labour Convention No 100 concerning equal remunerations for men and women workers for work of equal value, but which also occur in political contexts other than that constituted by the States contracting to the Charter", PACE, 'Opinion No. 57 (1971) on the Application of the European Social Charter' in CoE (ed), *European Social Charter - Collected Texts* (7th edn, Council of Europe Publishing 2015) 338, para 10. While the alignment with the ILO in many decisions rendered in the meantime may have alleviated the practical relevance of this opinion, it has arguably not entirely lost its point of principle.

[91]In *LO and TCO v. Sweden*, the ECSR noted that "the different – and less favourable – treatment concerning posted workers has been provided for, by the Swedish normative acts in question, in order to facilitate free cross border movement of services and guarantee freedom to provide services abroad, in conformity with EU law. In this respect, the Committee recalls that, from the point of view of the system of values, principles and rights embodied in the Charter, the facilitation of free

This point might not be surprising as such. However, given the ILO's extensive involvement in the ESC, it still needs mention. The ILO's extensive influence both on the ESC's text and its implementation is clearly exceptional. It seems fair to assume that there are not many other inter-organizational constellations in which the ILO would be able to exert a comparable degree of influence. The underlying conclusion to be drawn from this is that, even if the ILO interacts in most favourable conditions and exerts significant influence over decades, it cannot entirely secure the other IO's alignment to its instruments and practice. Notably, the given examples of Norwegian compulsory arbitration and closed shop arrangements suggest that third actors can have a diverting influence.

2. Repercussions of the ILO's Interactional 'Forum-Shopping' on Tripartism?

A second dormant issue is whether the International Labour Office's influence exercised through the institutional link with the ECSR can have adverse repercussions on the (now more than ever) fragile tripartite dialogue between its constituents.

The question has not arisen in ILO practice so far, presumably because the ESC does not have a particularly 'strong' enforcement mechanism. This is, however, not to say that it might not arise in the future, along the lines of the post-2012 constitutional crisis of tripartism.[92] To recall, when launching their intervention in 2012, the employers invoked their unease about the International Labour Office's and CEACR's interpretations of ILO instruments being 'misunderstood' by external actors as being agreed on by the tripartite constituents, whereas in the view of the employers, they were not. Given the employers' readiness to launch a major

---

cross-border movement of services and the promotion of the freedom of an employer or undertaking to provide services in the territory of other States – which constitute important and valuable economic freedoms within the framework of EU law – cannot be treated as having a greater a priori value than labour rights . . .), including the right for posted workers to receive from the host State treatment not less favourable than that of other workers, in respect of the enjoyment of the benefits of collective bargaining, as well as in respect of remuneration and other employment conditions. In this regard, the Committee recalls that applying the principle of non-discrimination, as set out in Art. 19(4) b of the Charter to the context of collective bargaining, requires that State parties have to take action to ensure that migrant workers enjoy equal treatment when it comes to benefiting from collective agreements aimed at implementing the principle of equal pay for equal work for all workers in the workplace, or from legitimate collective action in support of such an agreement, in accordance with national laws or practice." The ECSR even went so far as to hold that there was no presumption of conformity of measures, *Swedish Trade Union Confederation (LO) and Swedish Confederation of Professional Employees (TCO) v. Sweden* (n 44) para 140. Similar language can be found in the ECSR's many decisions relating to the Greek debt crisis. In these cases, the respondent Greek government argued – eventually unsuccessfully – that the massive infringements on social rights had been the consequence of Greece's obligations to the so-called Troika of EU, ECB and IMF, *Pensioners Union of the Athens-Piraeus Electric Railways (ISAP) v. Greece* Collective Complaint No. 78/2012 (ECSR, 7 December 2012), paras 46 et seqq.

[92]See Chap. 2 D. III.

escalation for this reason alone, it does not take much fantasy to imagine what could happen if the International Labour Office used its working relationship with the ECSR Secretariat to even *actively promote* such 'contested' interpretations in external fora.[93]

What is more, an underlying structural issue remains: Here as there, the transposition of the ILO's output into other fora decontextualizes these outputs from the (ongoing) ILO-internal tripartite dialogue. Once an ILO position has successfully been grafted onto the ECSR, there is no certainty it can be 'taken back' at any later stage, e.g. if the ongoing tripartite social dialogue within the ILO leads to a different result. Should this happen, the ILO will have to work the ECSR towards a change of opinion anew. For the achievement of such a change, the institutional link provides an opportunity, but not a guarantee.

E. Conclusion

This chapter has focused on the ILO's influence on the drafting and subsequent development of the ESC, as well as on the supervisory practice of the ECSR. The analysis has revealed a pattern of cooperative direct interactions at the stages of norm creation and norm implementation. Through these interactions, the ILO has seized plenty of opportunities to shape the ESC and the ECSR's practice in a way that is compatible with, and reinforces, its own model of labour governance. The analysis has also revealed persistent challenges, which, despite their potentially systemic relevance, lie dormant at present.

The chapter has presented the last out of three case studies on the ILO's inter-organizational interactions with other IOs. Despite their diversity and disparity, all case studies have revealed an underlying duality of opportunity and challenge for the ILO's model of labour governance. In the following chapter, which will conclude Part I of this study, this duality will move centre-stage.

[93] Moreover, opposition could not only come from the employers (or the workers, for that matter), but also from governments. For example, in the Norwegian compulsory arbitration example, the ILO-induced change of opinion within the ECSR has urged Norway to defend its position in two fora. It takes not much to imagine how, depending on the subject-matter, the ILO's use of the institutionalized link may lead governments to contemplate counter-initiatives.

7. The Impact of Inter-Organizational Interactions on the ILO's Model of Labour Governance

The three case studies presented in the preceding chapters provide a solid factual basis for drawing more general inferences as to the relevance of inter-organizational interactions for the ILO and its model of labour governance.

A. The Ambivalence of Inter-Organizational Interactions and Its Impact on the ILO

At the outset, the three case studies presented in the preceding chapters illustrate that inter-organizational interactions cannot easily be qualified as beneficial or detrimental for the ILO. Rather, inter-organizational interactions are ambivalent, because they bring about challenges and opportunities at the same time (I.). This ambivalence has considerable implications for the ILO's model of labour governance (II.).

I. Opportunities and Challenges: The Ambivalence of Inter-Organizational Interactions

The extent to which interactions result in challenges or opportunities varies from case to case. That being said, the fundamental dichotomy between the two can be found in each of the case studies presented in the preceding chapters.

As to the first case study, the World Bank's creation and use of the EWI predominantly resembled a challenge for the ILO. As seen, the World Bank's

H. Gött, *The Law of Interactions Between International Organizations*, Beiträge zum ausländischen öffentlichen Recht und Völkerrecht 299, https://doi.org/10.1007/978-3-662-62389-3_7

alternative normative vision of 'good' labour market regulation and its swift implementation through the publishing of rankings, combined with financial pressure, put the ILO's model in competition and on the proverbial defensive, with detrimental consequences. The Bank compromised ILO initiatives at domestic level and blatantly contradicted the ILO's supervisory bodies and their public 'naming and shaming' of non-compliant member states. What is more, as seen, the challenge extended to the ILO's 'ownership' over its own normative discourses.

On the other hand, the Bank's forceful and at times outright reckless infringement on ILO initiatives, and the outcry this provoked among trade unions, NGOs and some governments, also presented an opportunity for the ILO to play out one of its 'comparative advantages' over the Bank: Its tripartite expertise and legitimation. The ILO could use the EWI to publicly advocate its own tripartism-backed normative vision of labour market regulation as a (more balanced and legitimate) alternative to the EWI's decidedly business-partisan approach. In doing so, the ILO was able to lever moral pressure against the Bank. Eventually, despite the Bank's forceful infringements, it is remarkable that the ILO and like-minded other actors managed to convince the Bank to discontinue the use of the EWI in the Doing Business rankings. While this does not mean that the Bank has abandoned its alternative vision of labour market (de)regulation altogether, and while it still publishes the EWI raw data, the ILO nevertheless obtained and seized a rare opportunity to be heard (and to be taken seriously) with labour-related concerns by the traditionally very reserved and reticent World Bank.

The second case study, the ECtHR's reception of ILO instruments and practice, presented a mixed picture. On the one hand, it entailed a much subtler challenge, which lies, firstly, in the Court's insistence on referencing the ILO only on its own terms, i.e. to decide which aspects of the ILO's work to take into account, and where to disregard or deviate from the ILO, even if only as a matter of pure discretion. Secondly, the Court has, for better or worse, chosen not to give relevance to the fact that the ILO instruments and practice it was relying on were contested within the ILO, and that its own jurisprudence was again fuelling this contestation.

On the other hand, the ECtHR's reception of ILO instruments and practice also presented an opportunity for the ILO to increase its impact in Europe and beyond, to have its output transposed to a human rights context, and to obtain recognition and validation by another institution with a high international reputation. This opportunity, however, is tarnished by the fact that the ILO essentially remains in a passive role, benefitting from the Court's 'benevolent' jurisprudence, but hardly having any chance to participate proactively and directly in the latter's development.

Finally, the third case study on the drafting and implementation of the ESC portrayed a major opportunity for the ILO to continuously influence one of the CoE's central social policy instruments. The scope and duration of the ILO's opportunity to exert influence is exceptional. By contrast, the potential challenges of interaction have remained dormant. Nevertheless, it deserves mention that they exist on a structural level. For one part, as seen, there persists a certain possibility that the ECSR would deviate from the ILO (as it occasionally did), despite their exceptionally close relationship. Moreover, the mutually lauded cooperation via the institutionalized link can give rise to challenges from the CoE's and ILO's member states, which—as the Norwegian compulsory arbitration example shows—may find themselves under the joint purview of two IOs joining forces. Finally, on a systemic level, it is worth noting how the CoE set the scene for interacting differently with the ILO through different bodies (ECtHR and ECSR) by creating two different instruments (ECHR and ESC) with diverging institutional mechanisms, and differing involvement of the ILO in their drafting and application.

In sum, all three case studies presented in this study showcase the ambivalence of inter-organizational interactions.

II. The Impact on the ILO's Model of Labour Governance

This ambivalence affects central aspects of the ILO's model of labour governance.

1. Adding Complexity to Tripartite Decision-Making

Firstly, interactions may have a chilling effect on the ILO's process of decision-making. As seen in Chap. 1, the ILO crucially depends on tripartite consensus, or at least stable support from a majority of its tripartite constituents. It hardly needs to be mentioned that reaching such consensus or majorities is an intricate task in itself.

The ambivalence of inter-organizational interactions adds another layer of complexity to the ILO's decision-making process. Even insofar as internal consensus can be reached, the implementation of any such consensus is still subject to influence from other IOs. In a similar vein, if the ILO's tripartite constituents decide that the ILO should influence other IOs, there are still many ways in which the other IO will react (if at all).

The influence/reaction by other IOs is a factor that needs to be considered by the ILO's tripartite constituents already at the stage of decision-making inside the ILO. The reason for this is that the more effort is put into adopting a tripartite-consented strategy that later fails because another IO rejects or dilutes it, the more this effort will appear in vain, and the more the ILO's credibility to be a suitable and capable organization to achieve its targets may be called into question.[1]

[1]This risk is, for instance, one reason why the 2008 Declaration's provisions on inter-organizational interaction do not explicitly refer to the WTO, although it was obvious that the latter could be a key collaborator. The WTO had shown great reticence to cooperate with the ILO, and any too explicit offer of cooperation by the ILO that would have been straightforwardly rejected by the WTO would have appeared as a defeat for the ILO and the 2008 Declaration, Francis Maupain, *The Future of the International Labour Organization in the Global Economy* (Hart Publishing 2013) 113.

2. The Impact on the ILO's Effectivity

The case studies have also shown that inter-organizational interactions can have an impact on the ILO's effectivity.

On the one hand, the ILO's effective pursuit of its objectives can be substantially compromised by interaction, e.g. if the implementation of its initiatives is contradicted by another IO, as happened in the EWI example. This can not only result in a frustration of efforts and resources, but also in a loss of confidence in the ILO as an organization capable of effectively pursuing its objectives.

On the other hand, the ILO's output can be significantly enhanced through interaction, e.g. if the ILO manages to influence another IO to adopt the ILO's positions and to cooperate closely with the ILO as has happened with the CoE in the case of the ESC. Interaction can also expand the ILO's room for manoeuvre. Considerable restraints on the ILO's resources and budget have repeatedly spawned proposals and actual efforts to increase its access to outside resources, including through arrangements with other IOs.[2]

Often, gains and losses of effectivity will be closely interconnected. For example, this can be the case if positions reached by the ILO backed by tripartite consensus (e.g. on the right to strike being an element of freedom of association) are adopted and 'enforced' by the ECtHR by judicial means in a more effective way than the ILO could have done by itself, while at the same time such enhanced effectiveness leads ILO constituents to call into question the very tripartite consensus the ECtHR drew on in the first place.

3. The Impact on Accountability

Inter-organizational interactions can further affect the ILO's and the other IO's accountability to their constituents and to further stakeholders.[3]

In particular, interactions can mitigate the accountability of interacting IOs, because they can blur patterns of political, legal or ethical attribution and responsibility for governance. For instance, as seen in Chap. 4, the difficulties accompanying labour market reforms in Nepal and Georgia were not due to lacking commitment on the ILO's side, but were the result of contradicting World Bank interventions in these countries. However, while it seems difficult to hold the ILO accountable for these events, it does not automatically follow that the World Bank can be held accountable instead, given that the Bank is not bound by ILO conventions and had arguably operated within the confines of its own governance model when promoting

[2] E.g. the support sought from UNDP for large-scale research during the World Employment Programme, ibid 120.

[3] Following Freeman's seminal definition, a stakeholder is understood here as any group or individual who can affect or is affected by the achievement of the IO's objectives, see R Edward Freeman, *Strategic Management: A Stakeholder's Approach* (Pitman 1984) 46.

business-friendly deregulation. Furthermore, even if the ILO is not accountable for the actual World Bank interventions, some actors might hold it accountable for not sufficiently anticipating them and adjusting its activities accordingly. Irrespective of whether such accountability claims are actually justified, the ILO faces them, for better or worse.

For another example, as to the interactions between the ILO and the ECtHR discussed in Chap. 5, the Court could argumentatively shift responsibility for a contentious decision (that freedom of association comprises the rights to bargain collectively and to strike) to the ILO, because this view was not its own judicial-activist 'invention' but was established practice within the ILO. Conversely, the ILO can credibly deny responsibility vis-à-vis the employers' group for the consequences arising from the ECtHR's alleged 'misinterpretation' of the view of the ILO's tripartite constituents on this matter.

Finally, even in the ESC example, accountability can become an issue. Given that the interaction between the ILO and the CoE/ECSR 'worked' in a mutually satisfactory way, which IO is responsible for this positive outcome? In a world where IOs compete for scarce resources, reputation and support, and constantly have to prove their continued relevance to their constituents, the proper attribution of positive outcomes can become as relevant as allocating responsibility for negative ones.

4. The Impact on the ILO's Model's Legitimacy

Finally, inter-organizational interactions raise issues regarding the ILO's model's legitimacy.

As to the 'input' side of legitimacy,[4] interaction can become relevant if other IOs directly or indirectly influence the ILO's internal decision-making procedures. Direct influence can e.g. occur if other IOs take part in sessions of ILO bodies. The case studies presented in the previous chapters entail examples of more subtle, indirect influence on the ILO's procedures, e.g. when the World Bank 'second-guesses' the ILO's interpretation of labour standards by rendering its own opinion on whether the EWI is compatible with them, or when the ECtHR's reception of ILO practice fuels intra-ILO disputes.

The impact of inter-organizational interactions and their ambivalence is even more visible on the 'output' side of legitimacy, i.e. legitimacy that flows from the ILO's effective discharge of its functions and from its success in catering to its constituents' needs.[5] On the one hand, expanding its reach through interaction can

---

[4]On the distinction between input and output legitimacy see Fritz Wilhelm Scharpf, 'Economic Integration, Democracy and the Welfare State' (1997) 4 Journal of European Public Policy 18, 19. See also Fritz Wilhelm Scharpf, *Governing in Europe: Effective and Democratic?* (Oxford University Press 1999).

[5]Whether output legitimacy is tantamount to an IO's effectiveness or entails a distinct democratic dimension is subject to debate, see Jens Steffek, 'The Output Legitimacy of International Organizations and the Global Public Interest' (2015) 7 International Theory 263.

help the ILO prove its continued capability to achieve its objectives. Such proof has been necessary on more than one occasion: There have been repeated claims that the ILO was a rather 'toothless' organization which is ill-equipped to face the challenges of twenty-first century globalization.[6] The ILO has been under constant pressure to prove its capability of achieving its objectives and, ultimately, its relevance. As seen, inter-organizational interactions are one way to enhance the ILO's output and impact by transposing the ILO's positions and work results on the agenda of other IOs and, in a manner of speaking, 'recruiting' them for the ILO's cause. As is laid down in the 2008 Declaration on Social Justice for a Fair Globalization:

> Other international and regional organizations with mandates in closely related fields can have an important contribution to make to the implementation of the integrated approach. The ILO should invite them to promote decent work (…).[7]

Successful interactions, proving the ILO's capability and relevance, can thus help to enhance its (output) legitimacy.[8]

On the other hand, there is an inherent risk of losing legitimacy if interaction 'fails', i.e. if the result of it is not conducive or even detrimental to the ILO's goals. Failure can occur for many reasons, for instance because the other IO rejects and fends off the ILO's interactive conduct (e.g. by rejecting collaborations), or because the aspired gains of interaction do not materialize. As Dunoff observed,

> (…) interactions can challenge or undermine the legitimacy of claims to authority in particular domains. For example, unsuccessful efforts to collaborate, or exclusion of a particular body from an international partnership, can signal substantial concerns over whether the agency is a legitimate participant in a particular policy domain.[9]

Finally, a further degree of complexity is added by the fact that legitimacy is often assessed differently by different actors. While the ILO may appear the more legitimate to its own constituents the more it manages to place labour issues on the agenda of other IOs, such other IOs' constituents may question the ILO's legitimacy to influence IOs beyond a certain limit.

---

[6]Criticisms have been epitomized e.g. in the emblematic dictum, ascribed to Jessica Tuchman Matthews, that the ILO "has indeed been around forever, but it has also done nothing forever, so it is not terribly interesting", cited after Steve Charnovitz, 'The International Labour Organization in Its Second Century' in Jochen Abraham Frowein and Rüdiger Wolfrum (eds), *Max Planck Yearbook of United Nations Law* (2000) 148. For an overview see e.g. Stephen Hughes and Nigel Haworth, *The International Labour Organization: Coming in from the Cold* (Routledge 2011) 2 et seqq.; Guy Standing, 'The ILO: An Agency for Globalization?' (2008) 39 Development and Change 355.

[7]2008 Declaration Part II C.

[8]In Dunoff's words, "[w]hen two international bodies collaborate on issues of mutual concern, their interactions effectively reaffirm the stature and legitimacy of each agency to operate in the area under consideration", Jeffrey L Dunoff, 'Mapping a Hidden World of International Regulatory Cooperation' (2015) 78 Law and Contemporary Problems 267, 296.

[9]Dunoff (n 8) 296, using inter alia the example of ILO-IMO collaboration on maritime safety issues.

B. The ILO's Dilemma

The described ambivalence of inter-organizational interactions and its impact on the ILO's model of labour governance results in an unavoidable dilemma for the ILO. On the one hand, seizing the opportunities of inter-organizational interaction is in the ILO's own interest. Given the limits of its own model of labour governance, the ILO needs to seize the opportunities arising from interaction with others. While there is no 'hard' legal obligation to seize every opportunity that presents itself,[10] there are several compelling arguments for the ILO to be aware of the potentials of inter-organizational interactions. As seen, such interactions can increase the ILO's out-reach, lead to access to other IOs' resources and support, thereby increasing the ILO's effectivity and, ultimately, its legitimacy.

On the other hand, interactions with other IOs almost inevitably come with the risk of being exposed to challenges and, from the perspective of the ILO's model, potentially adverse influence. In the words of Francis Maupain:

> It is impossible to commit to the ideal of coherence without accepting exposure to the influence of others while optimizing one's capacity to influence them.[11]

There is no way to escape this dilemma once and for all. The ILO is clearly not in a position of inter-organizational hegemony from which it could unilaterally determine the course that inter-organizational interactions take.[12] Neither would it be possible for the ILO to simply avoid inter-organizational interactions altogether. Even if, hypothetically, the ILO decided to refrain from proactively engaging in any and all inter-organizational interactions, other IOs could and would still influence the ILO.[13] The EWI episode provides a good example. In these instances, the ILO is forced to either (re)act to external influence or accept the detrimental effects to its own work. As a practical matter, the ILO cannot 'not interact'.[14] Finally, no external relief for the dilemma seems to be on the way. Hopes that the interacting IOs'

---

[10]As will be discussed more closely in Chap. 8, the ILO has an – albeit general and vague – constitutional obligation to cooperate with other IOs involved in labour governance (Art. 12(1) ILO Constitution). This obligation, as will be seen, does not entail that the ILO has to seize each and every opportunity, but nevertheless it underlines that the ILO Constitution deems inter-organizational cooperation, which is one form of inter-organizational interaction, desirable.

[11]Maupain, *The Future of the International Labour Organization in the Global Economy* (n 1) 111.

[12]Ibid 114. Half-hearted attempts to achieve a central position in international economic and social cooperation have failed long ago. On the ILO's attempt to install itself within the UN System as the economic and social 'master agency' through the Philadelphia Declaration see Henner Gött, 'Interactions between International Organizations - Approaching a Neglected Governance Dimension' (2020) 17 International Organizations Law Review 75, 81 et seqq.

[13]Involvement in inter-organizational interaction does not necessarily require a conscious and proactive decision to do so. Rather, interaction can also be 'forced on' the ILO by another IO, as the ILO can become intentionally or accidentally influenced by another IO's activities.

[14]To variegate Watzlawick's famous dictum, Paul Watzlawick, Janet H Beavin and Don D Jackson, *Menschliche Kommunikation. Formen, Störungen, Paradoxien* (11th edn, Huber 2007) 53 et seqq.

member states may come together and solve the situation through the establishment of a more coherent and hierarchical international framework for decision-making remain illusory.

Thus, the pivotal question is not how to avoid the dilemma, but how to put up with its existence.

C. The Potential of International Law as an Existing Normative Framework

Given the ambivalence and the impact of inter-organizational interactions, it is in the ILO's best interest that they do not occur and affect the ILO randomly. One means that could help preventing this is a normative framework providing guidance for the ILO and the IOs it interacts with.

There is certainly no lack of proposals and initiatives to create normative parameters for the ILO's inter-organizational interactions. The ILO itself, wary to reap the benefits of such interactions while minimizing their adverse repercussions, has early on proactively addressed the issue in several ways, as have scholars, policy advisers and other commentators.[15] However, efforts to implement such proposals have often

[15]Some contributions suggest initiatives for pursuing inter-organizational coherence within already existing structures. The ILO itself has actively reached out by convening high-level conferences and meetings with other IOs, e.g. in the field of employment (such as the 1976 Global Employment Conference and the 1987 high level tripartite meeting with economic organizations, or by promoting the generation and proliferation of knowledge and policy advice, directed also to other IOs, which some see as a means to create an 'epistemic community', Maupain, *The Future of the International Labour Organization in the Global Economy* (n 1) 115 et seq.; M Peter Haas, 'Epistemic Communities and International Policy Coordination' 46 International Organization 1. The World Commission on the Social Dimension of Globalization, convened by the ILO in 2002, is one visible example in this regard. In a similar vein, the 2008 Declaration envisages that other IOs will be invited to participate in ILO bodies' sessions and to take part in the evaluation of the Declaration, see Part III A and Annex III C of the 2008 Declaration. In a similar manner, the 2019 Report of the Global Commission on the Future of Work called for a strengthening of coherence and coordination between the ILO and other IOs, Global Commission for the Future of Work, *Work for a Brighter Future* (ILO 2019) 55 et seq. The 2019 Centenary Declaration calls for reinforced cooperation within the multilateral system (Part F of the Centenary Declaration) Another strand points at the ILO member states and argues that they should promote the ILO's model in other IOs to which they are members. Part B iv of the 2008 Declaration stipulates that members may consider "the taking of appropriate steps for an adequate coordination between positions taken on behalf of the member State concerned in relevant international forums and any steps they may take under the present Declaration", Maupain, *The Future of the International Labour Organization in the Global Economy* (n 1) 105. Charnovitz has proposed to employ a World Bank/IMF-type conditionality in technical assistance programmes, Charnovitz 'The International Labour Organization in Its Second Century' (n 6) 177. Some authors go further and propose that the existing structures should be amended, or new structures be built. For instance, there are proposals that the ILO should make formal arrangements with other IOs or invite them to participate in its work, with the goal of creating deliberative spaces in which the ILO can use its

been strained by limited resources and a lack of political will and consensus, both among the ILO's tripartite constituents and between the ILO and other IOs.

The difficulties in *establishing* a framework for inter-organizational interactions raise the question whether and to what extent such a framework *already exists*. Such a framework could exist in norms of positive international law. Indeed, one of the most basic functions of international law (and law more generally) is to reduce uncertainty and unpredictability by structuring and ordering conduct.[16] It provides a normative framework that extends across political camps, power structures and ideational divides. Moreover, it is meant to enhance the predictability and reliability of conduct in international relations.[17]

In this vein, international law can formulate normative expectations that are transcending the respective institutional setting of the ILO and the IOs it interacts with, as well as the political ideational, professional or other positions of their constituents and other stakeholders.[18] Insofar as it does, international law may

---

persuasive capacity to influence these other IOs. The idea behind the latter is that the ILO brings to the fore its comparative advantage, i.e. its tripartite structure and the character of the International Labour Conference as a "universal and tripartite parliament", Maupain, *The Future of the International Labour Organization in the Global Economy* (n 1) 102 et seq. Advocating an institutional interface: ILO, 'Working Party on the Social Dimensions of the Liberalization of International Trade, Future of the Working Party' (1999) GB.276/ WP/SDL/1 para 15. Furthermore, there are proposals calling for the conclusions of inter-organizational agreements on the delimitation of competences, the establishment of joint bodies or mechanisms or on cooperation on substantive matters like child labour or trade-related aspects of labour, see e.g. the examples given by Charnovitz 'The International Labour Organization in Its Second Century' (n 6) 160 et seq., further Franziska Humbert, *The Challenge of Child Labour in International Law* (Cambridge University Press 2009) 376 et seqq. and Kofi Addo, *Core Labour Standards and International Trade* (Springer 2015) 320 et seqq.

[16]Andreas von Arnauld, *Völkerrecht* (3rd edn, C F Müller 2016) 1, para 2; Malcolm N Shaw, *International Law* (8th edn, Cambridge University Press 2017) 1; Wolfgang Graf Vitzthum, 'Begriff, Geschichte und Rechtsquellen des Völkerrechts' in Wolfgang Graf Vitzthum and Alexander Proelß (eds), *Völkerrecht* (8th edn, de Gruyter 2019) 7. Regarding law in general Bernd Rüthers, *Rechtstheorie* (10th edn, C H Beck 2018) 47 et seqq. specifically for inter-organizational interactions Luca Pasquet, 'Dialogue or Interaction? A Non-Cosmopolitan Reading of Transjudicial Communication' in Amrei Müller and Hege Elisabeth Kjos (eds), *Judicial Dialogue and Human Rights* (Cambridge University Press 2017) 467.

[17]Traditionally, international law was primarily concerned with fulfilling these functions among states. But, as international legal subjects (and international legal relationships between them) proliferate (Christian Walter, 'Subjects of International Law', *Max Planck Encyclopedia of Public International Law* (Oxford University Press 2007) para 29 et seqq.; Christian Walter, 'International Law in a Process of Constitutionalization' in Janne E Nijman and André Nollkaemper (eds), *New Perspectives on the Divide Between National and International Law* (Oxford University Press 2007) 207), international law may likewise fulfil these functions with regard to other international legal subjects, including among IOs.

[18]By contrast, unclear (or unexplored) legal obligations can have a chilling effect on the exercise of the mandate and hence on the achievement of constitutional objectives. This concern has been voiced by IOs themselves. See e.g. the comments of the IMF on the ILC's work on what would later become the DARIO ("Unless clear definitions and precise criteria are set forth in the articles, the international organizations would confront such an uncertain and potentially destructive legal

provide standards for IOs' interactive conduct, on the observance of which the ILO can reasonably rely to mitigate adverse impact on its model while maintaining the promotional opportunities of inter-organizational interaction. In this way, international law may help the ILO to put up with the dilemma that the ambivalence of inter-organizational interactions puts it in.

In particular, an international legal framework for inter-organizational interactions could facilitate tripartite consensus by diminishing the unpredictability of external factors. Moreover, it could positively affect the ILO's effectivity. The more there are reliable international legal rules for inter-organizational interactions, the better the ILO can plan if and how to take measures that may influence other IOs, and how to anticipate how other IOs will influence its own work.[19] Such rules could also provide guidance on how to reconcile two IOs' differing understandings of what constitutes effective governance.[20] In addition, international legal norms on how inter-organizational interactions ought to take place would provide a reference point for assessing the ILO's and other IOs' accountability and legitimacy.[21] While legality does not necessarily imply sufficient accountability or legitimacy, international law will indicate some conditions under which the ILO can be held accountable for achieving or not achieving certain purposes. By the same token, conformity with international law can at least indicate if it was legitimate that the ILO and other IOs engaged in inter-organizational interactions and, accidentally or intentionally, influenced each other in a certain manner, whether it was legitimate to ignore another IO and its governance model, to defy another IO's influence or to yield to it, and so forth.

In the light of the above, Parts II and III of this study will strive to identify and examine existing norms of international law that apply to the ILO's inter-organizational interactions. The main goal of this analysis is to discern whether and to what extent there is an existing legal-normative framework on which the ILO can rely to protect or to promote its model of labour governance when engaging in inter-organizational interaction with other IOs.

---

environment that, out of concern that their activities could subject them to endless claims and litigation, they could become substantially inhibited in carrying out their mandates."), UN, 'Responsibility of International Organizations, Comments and Observations Received from International Organizations' (2004) UN Doc A/CN.4/545 7.

[19]This in turn enables it to allocate its resources more economically, which may again have an impact on how the ILO is perceived by its constituents.

[20]Measuring effectivity requires a benchmark of an 'ideal performance' against which specific activities of an IO can be assessed. In the case of inter-organizational interactions, there are more than one effectivity benchmark at play. Every interacting IO follows its own concept of what is effective in a given situation. As the EWI episode illustrates, these different concepts can compete, and in the worst case even mutually contradict each other.

[21]Claims about (sufficient or insufficient) accountability and legitimacy always entail an explicit or implicit normative premise of how the ILO (or for that matter, other IOs) ought to act. Such a normative premise can, for example, be derived from what is considered politically desirable, ethically important, or legally required.

D. Conclusion

This chapter has extrapolated more general conclusions from the case studies presented in the preceding chapters. It has been seen that, structurally, inter-organizational interactions are an ambivalent matter for the ILO. This ambivalence has a significant impact on the ILO's model of labour governance, affecting tripartite decision-making, the ILO's effectiveness, its accountability and its legitimacy. These repercussions put the ILO in a dilemma: While it has a genuine interest to engage in inter-organizational interactions (and while it hardly can avoid being drawn into them anyway), actually interacting with other IOs exposes the ILO's model of labour governance to potentially adverse influence. Against this background, the ILO has a genuine interest that inter-organizational interactions do not occur in an erratic and random manner but are guided by a normative framework. As the creation of new normative frameworks faces severe practical difficulties, this study will focus on the question whether and to what extent there is already a normative framework in place, centring on whether such a framework exists under positive international law. This question lies at the heart of the analysis to be conducted in Part II and Part III of this study.

Part II
'Egocentric' Institutional Laws and the ILO's Relativization

The ILO and the IOs it interacts with are each involved in a range of different legal relationships.[1] In practice, the perhaps most important of these relationships is the one between the respective IO and its members, as laid down in the IO's constituent instrument and as established in organizational practice. This legal relationship is governed by a body of norms that will be referred to as the IO's institutional law.[2] It sets forth the IO's objectives, institutional features, competences and obligations, and thus largely predetermines how the IO may or may not interact with others. Thus, when looking for a normative framework governing inter-organizational interactions, the interacting IOs' institutional laws are an appropriate starting point.

---

[1]In general, several legal relationships can be distinguished:

1) The 'internal' legal relationship between the IO and its members acting as parts of the IO's organs,
2) The 'external' legal relationship between the IO and its members acting as such,
3) The legal relationships between the IO's organs and between the components of one organ among each other (the IO's *Innenrecht*),
4) The legal relationships between the IO and its officers and staff, and
5) The legal relationships between the IO and non-members, including non-member states, other IOs, individuals and other international legal subjects,
6) The legal relationships between the IO and states, individuals or other subjects under domestic (public or private) law.

[2]As already mentioned in the introduction to this study (Chap. 1 C.), the term 'institutional law' is understood here to refer to the IOs' constituent instruments and the relevant further sources of positive law as presented in the following chapters.

8. Inter-Organizational Interactions in the ILO's Institutional Law: A 'Carte Blanche' for the ILO

Whether, how and to what extent the ILO, the Bank and the CoE may engage in interactions with one another under their respective institutional laws crucially depends on which constitutional competences and obligations they possess. There are two principal legal bases for such competences and obligations. They can either be explicitly attributed, typically in the IO's constituent instrument,[1] or they can be derived by implication, applying the implied powers doctrine.[2] Both attributed and

[1]The underlying so-called attributed powers doctrine essentially seeks to limit IOs' competences to those explicitly conferred upon it by its member states. The underlying so-called attributed powers doctrine essentially seeks to limit IOs' competences to those explicitly conferred upon it by its member states, Jan Klabbers, *An Introduction to International Organizations Law* (3rd edn, Cambridge University Press 2015) 53 et seqq. Under the attributed powers doctrine, the principal basis for IOs' competences is the IO's constituent instrument, to which the member states voluntarily agreed. Locus classicus: *Jurisdiction of the European Commission of the Danube* (Advisory Opinion) (1927) PCIJ Rep Series B No 14, 64.

[2]René-Jean Dupuy, 'Le Droit Des Relations Entre Les Organisations Internationales' (1960) 100 Recueil des Cours de l'Académie de Droit International 461, 536. Constituent instruments do not regulate IOs' competences and obligations comprehensively. Where there are no explicit provisions, such competences may and must be assumed under the so-called implied powers doctrine. The implied powers doctrine is an adjunct to a functionalist approach to IOs. According to the doctrine, an IO does not only possess those competences which have been explicitly conferred on it, but also possesses such competences which are necessary to enable it to pursue its functions and achieve its objectives and which, therefore, may be implied to have been granted by its founders, ibid 533. There are different readings of the implied powers doctrine. A narrower reading bases the implication of powers on a generous interpretation of explicit provisions in the IO's constituent instrument, *Interpretation of the Greco-Turkish Agreement of 1 December 1926 (Final Protocol, Article IV)* (Advisory Opinion) PCIJ Rep Series B No 16; *Case 8/55 Case 8/55 Fédération Charbonnière de Belgique* (ECLI:EU:C:1956:11) [1956] ECR 00292; *Joined Cases 281, 283, 284, 285 and 287/85, Federal Republic of Germany and others v. Commission* (ECLI:EU:C:1987:351) [1987] ECR 03203; *Reperation for Injuries Suffered in the Service of the United*

H. Gött, *The Law of Interactions Between International Organizations*, Beiträge zum ausländischen öffentlichen Recht und Völkerrecht 299, https://doi.org/10.1007/978-3-662-62389-3_8

implied powers are relevant when it comes to identifying IOs' competences and obligations to interact with other IOs. As to attributed powers, a large number of IOs' constitutional instruments and internal rules, including the ILO's, World Bank's and CoE's, contain at least some express provisions on these IOs' competences in external relations[3] with other IOs.[4] As to implied powers, they become relevant because explicit provisions on inter-organizational interactions typically remain vague and piecemeal. Furthermore, as will be seen, such explicit provisions typically only address certain types of interactions.[5]

It is convenient to first consider the ILO's own institutional law. The different sources of ILO institutional law (Sect. A.) contain a range of legal norms that are relevant for the ILO's interactions with other IOs. These norms endow the ILO with

---

Nations, Dissenting Opinion by Judge Hackworth [1949] ICJ Reports 196, 28; Klabbers, *An Introduction to International Organizations Law* (n 1) 57 et seqq.; Andrzej Gadkowski, 'The Doctrine of Implied Powers of International Organizations in the Case Law of International Tribunals' (2016) 6 Adam Mickiewicz University Law Review 45, 51 et seq., with further references. By contrast, a broader reading merely requires, as the ICJ put it in *Reparation for Injuries*, that the implied competence is "essential to the performance" of the IO's duties, *Reparation for Injuries Suffered in the Service of the United Nations* (Advisory Opinion) [1949] ICJ Reports 174, 182. In *Effect of Awards*, the ICJ went even further and required merely that the power was necessary to ensure the proper functioning of one of the UN's organs, the Secretariat, *Effect of Awards of Compensation Made by the United Nations Administrative Tribunal* (Advisory Opinion) [1954] ICJ Reports 47, 57. Arguably stretching the doctrine to its breaking point, the ICJ in *Certain Expenses* even promulgated a presumption in favour of the UN's action being *intra vires* if it "takes action which warrants the assertion that it was appropriate for the fulfilment of one of the stated purposes of the United Nations", *Certain Expenses of the United Nations (Article 17, Paragraph 2 of the Charter)* (Advisory Opinion) [1962] ICJ Reports 151, 168. The concept of 'inherent powers' derived from 'organizationhood', developed as an alternative approach to the attributed and implied powers doctrines, will not be discussed at this point, because it does not exclude that each IO has its own specific set of competences and obligations regarding inter-organizational interaction (see Chap. 15 A. II. 2. c)).

[3]These provisions differ from IO to IO and can cover a broad array of subject-matters. from an express conferral of international legal personality over responsibilities regarding non-members (e.g. Art. 2(6) UN Charter), relations with the IO's host state (e.g. Art. 40 CoE Statute), privileges and immunities (e.g. Art. 40 ILO Constitution), or, in some instances, genuine and exclusive foreign policy competences for certain fields (e.g. the EU's Common Commercial Policy Art. 207 Treaty on the Functioning of the European Union (Consolidated Version) [2016] OJ C202/47 (TFEU)).

[4]See Art. 12(1) ILO Constitution, Art. V(8) lit. a IBRD-AoA and Art. 1 lit. c CoE Statute, but also e.g. Arts. 57, 62 et seqq. UN Charter, Arts. 59 et seqq. Convention on the International Maritime Organization (adopted 6 March 1948, entered into force 17 March 1958) 289 UNTS 3 (IMO Convention), Arts. X and XI Constitution of the United Nations Educational, Scientific and Cultural Organization (adopted 16 November 1945, entered into force 4 November 1946) 4 UNTS 275 (UNESCO Constitution) or Art. 34 Treaty on European Union (Consolidated Version) [2016] OJ C202/01 (TEU) and Art. 220 TFEU.

[5]Namely direct and intentional ones. By contrast, indirect or accidental interaction are usually not explicitly regulated. Instead, competences to engage in such types of interactions will often have to be implied. For instance, they can be implied to be a part of internal competences, which do not explicitly address relations with other IOs. For an example, as will be seen in Chap. 8, the ILO's competence to draft and adopt labour conventions implicitly entails the competence to do so in a way that would have repercussions on other IOs working on the topic governed by the prospective labour convention (Chap. 8 B. V. 2.).

fairly comprehensive competences to engage in inter-organizational interactions (Sect. B.). Nevertheless, these competences are limited, because they are embedded in the ILO's wider institutional legal framework (Sect. C.).

A. Overview on the Relevant Sources of the ILO's Institutional Law

In order to set the scene, and to recall and supplement what has already been expounded in Chap. 2, a brief overview on the relevant sources of ILO institutional law is warranted. As already mentioned above, the primary source of the ILO's institutional law is the ILO Constitution, which is a multilateral treaty and the organization's constituent instrument. It was adopted in 1919 as Part XIII of the Treaty of Versailles and thus formed a part of the peace settlement after the First World War. The ILO Constitution was subsequently severed from the Treaty of Versailles and adopted as a separate treaty. It was formally amended on several occasions. The most profound changes were made after the Second World War with the constitutional amendments of 1946.[6] The ILO Constitution consists of 40 Articles, grouped in four chapters (Organs, Procedure, General Provisions and Miscellaneous Provisions). Its Annex comprises the 1944 Philadelphia Declaration, which forms an integral part of the ILO Constitution (Art. 1(1) ILO Constitution).

Besides the Constitution and the Declaration of Philadelphia, three further Declaration deserve mention. Firstly, the 1998 ILO Declaration on Fundamental Principles and Rights at Work focuses on the promotion of fundamental labour standards as universal 'rules of the game'. It solidified the concept of core labour standards and readjusted the ILO's mandate and resources to prioritize their promotion. Secondly, the 2008 Declaration on Social Justice for a Fair Globalization resembles the most comprehensive reformulation and interpretation of the ILO's mandate since the Philadelphia Declaration.[7] The 2008 Declaration can be used as an 'authoritative' interpretation, in the sense that it has received support of all of the ILO's constituents and has remained uncontested.[8] Thirdly, the 2019 Centenary Declaration for the Future of Work seeks to further adjust the ILO's mandate and define priorities according to current transformative changes in the world of work. Although fairly new, concise and arguably not as comprehensively adjusting the ILO's mandate nature as the 2008 Declaration, the 2019 Declaration may be seen as a contemporary

---

[6]ILO, Instrument for the Amendment of the Constitution of the International Labour Organisation (1946) XXIX ILO Official Bulletin 203.

[7]In the words of then-ILO Director-General Juan Somavia, the 2008 Declaration "marks the most important renewal of the Organization since the Declaration of Philadelphia.", ILO, *ILO Declaration on Social Justice for a Fair Globalization* (ILO 2008) 4.

[8]Formally binding interpretations of the ILO Constitution can only be rendered by the ICJ, Art. 37 (1) ILO Constitution.

understanding of the ILO's mandate and inform the interpretation of ILO institutional law.

B. The ILO's Competences and Obligations to Engage in Inter-Organizational Interaction

As is the case with many other IOs' constituent instruments, the ILO Constitution's express provisions on relations and interactions with other IOs are scant and piecemeal. They concern the ILO's integration into the UN System (Sect. I.), the cooperation with other IOs (Sect. II.), the invitation of other IOs to participate as observers (Sect. III.), and the ILO's role in reviewing the policies of other IOs (Sect. IV.). Further competences to interact can be assumed under the implied powers doctrine (Sect. V.).

I. The ILO Constitution's Decision for Integration into the UN System

The ILO Constitution's provisions on the ILO's relations with other IOs are essentially the result of the constitutional amendments prepared between 1944 and 1946 and adopted in 1946. Before, the ILO had been integrated into, and had in many ways been dependent on, the League of Nations, which performed important functions of supervision.[9] The 1946 amendments primarily sought to integrate the ILO into the newly created UN System. They endowed the ILO with greater autonomy vis-à-vis the UN, along the lines of the general approach of 'functional decentralization' of the UN System,[10] but also provided machinery for cooperation between the two IOs. Until today, most of the ILO Constitution's provisions concerning inter-organizational interactions contain specific competences or obligations to interact with the UN. For instance, pursuant to Art. 13(1) ILO Constitution, the ILO is competent (but not obliged) to conclude financial or budgetary agreements with the UN. Other provisions impose certain competences or obligations that presuppose, envisage or explicitly require cooperation with the UN.[11] Not least, as

[9] E.g. regarding the ILO's budget and requests for advisory opinions form the PCIJ, see Art. 24 Covenant of the League of Nations (signed 28 June, entered into force 10 January 1920) 225 CTS 195 (LoN Covenant), Art. 12 ILO Constitution in the pre-1946 version and further John HE Fried, 'Relations Between the United Nations and the International Labor Organization' (1947) 41 The American Political Science Review 963, 965 et seqq.

[10] Fried (n 9) 963. See also Chap. 14.

[11] Pursuant to Arts. 20 and 21(2) ILO Constitution, labour conventions adopted by the International Labour Conference or agreed upon between some of the ILO member states must be registered with the UN in accordance with Art. 102 UN Charter. An authenticated copy of adopted labour

mentioned in Chap. 2, the ILO Constitution endows the ICJ, the principal judicial organ of the UN, with certain judicial functions, including the competence to render binding interpretations of the ILO Constitution and ILO conventions.[12]

II. The General Competence (and Obligation) to Cooperate with Other IOs

Beyond those provisions specifically tailored to interactions with the UN, Art. 12 (1) ILO Constitution[13] sets forth in general terms both a competence and an obligation to cooperate with other IOs. The provision reads:

> The International Labour Organization shall cooperate within the terms of this Constitution with any general international organization entrusted with the coordination of the activities of public international organizations having specialized responsibilities and with public international organizations having specialized responsibilities in related fields.

By virtue of this provision, the ILO, vis-à-vis its members, is obliged to cooperate ("shall") with other IOs. This necessarily entails the competence to do so. It is convenient at this point to analyse the elements of this competence and obligation in turn.

1. The Meaning of 'Cooperation'

The content of the obligation to cooperate is, on its face, fairly vague. "Cooperate" can mean virtually anything from occasional and informal contacts on specific matters to permanent, in-depth and resource-intensive cooperation on a broad range of topics. The drafting history confirms that such flexibility was intended in order to enable the ILO to establish "effective working relationships" with other

---

conventions must be deposited with the UN Secretary-General (Art. 19(4) ILO Constitution). Moreover, according to Art. 35(5) lit. b ILO Constitution, an international authority administering a non-self-governing territory – the practically most relevant example being the UN – may declare its acceptance of obligations under any ILO labour convention in respect of that territory to the ILO Director-General.

[12]For one part, the ICJ is the final instance against findings and recommendations made by a Commission of Inquiry established under Arts. 26 ILO Constitution (Art. 29(2), 31 and 32 ILO Constitution). For another part, the ICJ is the (only) competent body to render binding interpretations of the ILO Constitution and ILO conventions, Art. 37(1) ILO Constitution.

[13]ILO, Instrument for the Amendment of the Constitution of the International Labour Organisation (1946) XXIX ILO Official Bulletin 203, 216.

IOs.[14] In subsequent practice, virtually the whole array of possible forms has been employed.[15]

The choice of language indicates that the ILO must make a certain minimum effort to engage in constructive interaction with other IOs. Otherwise, the provision could have used 'exchange', 'interact', 'communicate' or similar terms instead. Thus, making no attempts to cooperate at all, or making so little effort that no other IO could reasonably be expected to join in, would not suffice. Furthermore, the choice of words also indicates that Art. 12(1) ILO Constitution envisages direct interactions rather than indirect ones. One example of what the ILO has to do is expressly mentioned in Art. 14(1) ILO Constitution, which provides that when preparing the agenda for the International Labour Conference, the Governing Body has to consider any suggestion made by another IO.

That being said, Art. 12(1) ILO Constitution only speaks of cooperation in general terms, not with regard to specific common topics, initiatives or goals. Therefore, from a legal point of view, limited cooperative activities and even outright refusals to cooperate with another IO on a specific issue (or under specific conditions) would be in conformity with Art. 12(1) ILO Constitution, as long as the ILO remains by and large cooperative towards that other IO.

---

[14]The Committee on Constitutional Questions observed that "[t]he manner in which effective working relationships between the International Labour Organisation and the specialised agencies can most appropriately be organised will require fuller consideration in the near future. These relationships may be expected to be of varied types. In some cases, there will be extensive frontiers of common interest which will make comprehensive arrangements for the exchange of documents and representatives and the creation of joint committees desirable. In other cases, the interest of the International Labour Organisation will be limited to a particular sector of the work of another body or the other body will be interested in a particular branch of the work of the International Labour Organisation. In some cases, collaboration will be desirable to secure results which can only be achieved by the combined efforts of a number of international organisations; in other cases, its main object will be to eliminate overlapping and unnecessary duplication of work; in still others the main interest of the International Labour Organisation will be in the social results and adequacy of the policies followed by other bodies in fields for which they have full executive responsibility. The detailed arrangements appropriate in these different types of case will have to be worked out progressively", ILO, 'Report of the Committee on Constitutional Questions to the 27th Session of the International Labour Conference' (1945) XXXVIII ILO Official Bulletin 64, para 12.

[15]On informal contacts with the World Bank and IMF see e.g. Katherine A Hagen, 'Policy Dialogue between the International Labour Organization and the International Financial Institutions: The Search for Convergence' (2003) FES Occasional Papers No 9 <http://library.fes.de/pdf-files/bueros/genf/50035.pdf> accessed 26 April 2020, 13 et seqq. and Francis Maupain, *The Future of the International Labour Organization in the Global Economy* (Hart Publishing 2013) 72 et seqq. On consultations in the drafting of labour conventions see Clarence Wilfred Jenks, 'The Conflict of Law-Making Treaties' (1953) 30 British Yearbook of International Law 401, 430, see also Felice Morgenstern *Legal Problems of International Organizations* (Grotius Publications 1986) 26 et seqq.

2. The Subject-Matters of Cooperation

As to the subject-matters of cooperation, Art. 12(1) ILO Constitution remains silent. In other instruments, the ILO has envisaged cooperation with other IOs as a means to further its own objectives.[16] In the Philadelphia Declaration (Part IV), the International Labour Conference,

> [c]onfident that the fuller and broader utilization of the world's productive resources necessary for the achievement of the objectives set forth in this Declaration can be secured by effective international and national action (. . .), pledges the full cooperation of the International Labour Organization with such international bodies as may be entrusted with a share of the responsibility for this great task and for the promotion of the health, education and well-being of all peoples.

The 1998 Declaration, after stipulating that all members, by virtue of their membership, have the obligation to respect, to promote and to realize fundamental principles and rights at work,[17] recognized

> the obligation on the Organization to assist its Members (. . .) in order to attain these objectives by making full use of its constitutional, operational and budgetary resources, including (. . .) by encouraging other international organizations with which the ILO has established relations, pursuant to article 12 of its Constitution, to support these efforts (. . .).[18]

The 2008 Declaration stipulates that the ILO "should invite" other IOs to promote decent work.[19] The International Labour Conference's 2016 Resolution on Advancing Social Justice through Decent Work identifies "partnership and policy coherence" as one priority area of action. It calls upon the ILO

> to make the best use of its means of action to
>
> (. . .)
>
> [d]evelop a strategy for promoting decent work through partnerships and policy coherence with relevant international, regional and national organizations which have mandates in closely related fields. In all such partnerships the ILO should promote understanding and recognition of its values, mandate and standards.[20]

Finally, the 2019 Centenary Declaration requests in its Part F that

> [o]n the basis of its constitutional mandate, the ILO must take an important role in the multilateral system, by reinforcing its cooperation and developing institutional arrangements with other organizations to promote policy coherence in pursuit of its human-centred

---

[16]Besides specific objectives of the ILO, the Philadelphia Declaration also proclaims that certain objectives are common aims of all national and international policy. While the ILO thus stipulated common objectives, this stipulation is nevertheless contained in a document belonging to the ILO's institutional law, which, as will be seen in Chap. 9, is not binding on other IOs.

[17]No 2 1998 Declaration.

[18]No 3 1998 Declaration.

[19]Part II C 2008 Declaration.

[20]International Labour Conference (105th session) Resolution on Advancing Social Justice through Decent Work (9 June 2016) XCIX ILO Official Bulletin Ser A No 2 30, para 15.6 lit. a.

approach to the future of work, recognizing the strong, complex and crucial links between social, trade, financial, economic and environmental policies.

Thus, regarding the subject-matter of cooperation, the ILO's institutional law envisages that the ILO promotes *its own* objectives vis-à-vis other IOs. Under the 1998 Declaration, the ILO has a legal obligation to promote fundamental principles and rights at work at least vis-à-vis those other IOs with which it has an established relationship.[21] Whether this is also true for the promotional and cooperative activities mentioned in the 2008 Declaration and the 2016 Resolution remains somewhat ambiguous.[22] The language employed in these instruments ("should") does not indicate a 'hard' obligation. Yet, it still implies that promotion of its values, mandate and standards is desired. Consequently, at the very least, the ILO cannot entirely refrain from promotional activities. In practice, a precise delimitation has not become virulent, because the ILO would promote its model of labour governance vis-à-vis other IOs anyway, whether or not there are established relations with them. The 2019 Centenary Declaration mentions "institutional arrangements" as one means to cooperate. This term, albeit vague, seems to express a preference for more formalized and permanent inter-organizational cooperation.

3. The Potential Partners for Cooperation

Art. 12(1) ILO Constitution qualifies the obligation to cooperate by defining the potential partners for cooperation. These are, on the one hand, "any general" IO "entrusted with the coordination of the activities of public international organizations having specialized responsibilities" and, on the other hand, IOs "having specialized responsibilities in related fields."

---

[21]The World Bank initially denied support to the 1998 ILO Declaration. The World Bank's reticence, which the drafters of the 1998 Declaration anticipated, was one reason to confine the ILO's obligation, set forth in the 1998 Declaration, to encourage other IOs to those "with which the ILO has established relations" (No. 3 1998 Declaration), Maupain, *The Future of the International Labour Organization in the Global Economy* (n 15) 77.

[22]Whereas the 1998 Declaration explicitly speaks of an obligation to assist members by encouraging other IOs to promote fundamental principles and rights and work, the 2008 Declaration formulates that the ILO "should invite to encourage" other IOs to promote decent work, and the 2016 Resolution provides that the ILO "should" promote recognition and understanding of its values, mandate and standards. However, whether these formulations were intended to express a legally relevant difference remains unclear. On the one hand, one could argue that, following the wording, encouraging other IOs to promote fundamental principles and rights at work is required, while the ILO's promotion of decent work with other IOs is only legally desired. Yet, on the other hand, the 1998 Declaration only considers encouraging other IOs as one option to fulfil the obligation to assist the ILO member states. It could thus likewise be argued that both the 1998 and 2008 Declarations and the 2016 Resolution merely sought to secure the necessary flexibility to decide in each concrete case whether encouraging other IOs is a suitable means. Moreover, care must be taken not to overstretch the interpretation of the wording.

The first alternative refers exclusively to the UN.[23] The second alternative, by contrast, is fairly broad. It is not restricted to certain kinds of IOs, say, the UN specialized agencies, or all IOs with universal membership. On the contrary, the cooperating IO must only have responsibilities in "related fields". Given that the ILO itself is broadly mandated to improve labour conditions and to promote social justice, it will be difficult to identify any IOs that would clearly fall outside the second group of cooperating IOs contemplated by Art. 12(1) ILO Constitution. One brief glance at the impressive range of topics covered by the ILO's 190 conventions, 205 recommendations, its 7 declarations and numerous further instruments and documents suffices to illustrate that virtually every major IO is a potential candidate for cooperation in one or the other way.

4. Conclusion

In sum, the ILO Constitution sets forth a general obligation to cooperate with other IOs. In particular, the ILO must promote its own values, mandate and standards in appropriate cases. Apart from these specifications, the general obligation to cooperate is hardly defined further. It extends to virtually every topic within the ILO's mandate, virtually every activity and to cooperation with the vast majority of IOs.

Therefore, the ILO retains a broad margin of discretion as to how to fulfil its obligation to cooperate. In essence, as long as it remains 'generally cooperative' towards other IOs, the obligation could arguably be fulfilled by almost any plausible means, as long as the ILO does not outright antagonize other IOs or refuses to cooperate as a matter of principle (it should be recalled that the ILO has never been anywhere near that line throughout a whole century of existence).

The combination of a general obligation to cooperate and very few more concrete provisions specifying the content of this obligation effectively results in the ILO having, from a legal point of view, a broad margin of discretion of how to cooperate. Thus, what is phrased in Art. 12(1) ILO Constitution as an obligation to cooperate is, in essence, a comprehensive entitlement to engage in cooperative interactions with other IOs in order to promote its own values, mandate and standards.

[23]Technically, there are other IOs entrusted with coordinative tasks. However, both the requirement that the IO be "general" and the circumstances at the time of the adoption of the ILO Constitution strongly suggest that the phrase is referring to the UN.

III. The Competence to Invite Other IOs as Observers

Pursuant to Art. 12(2) ILO Constitution, the ILO may invite other IOs' representatives to attend the ILO's meetings and deliberations without vote, i.e. as observers.[24] Such invitations are more closely regulated by the International Labour Conference's and Governing Body's Standing Orders.[25] Unlike Art. 12(1) ILO Constitution, the provision uses permissive language. Hence, the ILO is not obliged to invite other IOs (even if they work on related topics) but retains discretion as to whom to invite and as to the appropriate arrangements.

As mentioned in Chap. 7, inviting observers to its own meetings is seen as a means for the ILO to promote its model. First of all, the participation of other observers opens space for direct and formalized communication. Secondly, by providing a 'showroom' for universal tripartite social dialogue, observers might get a better understanding (and greater respect) for the ILO's model.[26] Art. 12 (2) ILO Constitution has been applied, in different ways, to many IOs, including both the World Bank and the CoE.[27]

IV. The Competence to Review Other IOs' Economic and Financial Policies

The Philadelphia Declaration enables the ILO to evaluate the policies of states and other IOs. It declares the ILO "responsible" for examining other IOs' economic and financial policies in the light of its own objectives and to act accordingly, which implies the conferral of a competence to do so.[28]

---

[24]Ebere Osieke, *Constitutional Law and Practice in the International Labour Organization* (Martinus Nijhoff Publishers 1985) 73 et seq. The 2008 Declaration reaffirms the possibility of other IOs to take part in the work of ILO organs and bodies, Part III A 2008 Declaration.

[25]Art. 17bis(1) International Labour Conference Standing Orders prescribes consultations with attending representatives of other IOs. The International Labour Conference Standing Orders lay down the rights of IO observers in more detail, including for instance the right of admission to sittings (Art. 2(3) lit. b), the right to address the Conference (Art. 14(6)), the right to participate in the discussions (Art. 14(9)) and the right to be present and participate in discussions in the Conference's committees (Art. 56(7)). Likewise, the ILO Governing Body's Standing Orders foresee that representatives of IOs which have been invited to participate in the Governing Body's sessions may be present and participate in the discussions (No. 1.9.1 GB Standing Orders).

[26]On the different functions of observers see Erik Suy, 'The Status of Observers in International Organizations' (1978) 160 Recueil des Cours de l'Académie de Droit International 75; Mario Savino, 'Linkages Between Global Regimes and Interactions with Civil Society' in Sabino Cassese (ed), *Research Handbook on Global Administrative Law* (Edward Elgar Publishing 2016) 131, 134.

[27]Hagen (n 15) 13 et seqq. See also arrangements in relationship agreements, e.g. Art. 1 (2) ILO-CoE, and Part II C of the 2008 Declaration.

[28]The wording "responsibility" does not in itself imply that the ILO is obliged to evaluate other IOs' policies. The wording in the 2008 Declaration (speaking of the ILO's "role", see below, 215 et seq.)

While such a 'review' can of course take place in a cooperative and consensual fashion, it is nevertheless conceptually distinct from the cooperation envisaged in Art. 12(1) ILO Constitution. After all, an examination and consideration of policies can also take place if the other IO is not willing or able to cooperate, and it could in theory even take place without any direct communication with other IOs whatsoever. Either way, the envisaged 'review' almost inevitably includes inter-organizational interaction. If conducted cooperatively, such interaction will likely be direct. If conducted otherwise, it could still amount to indirect interaction.

The scope and content of the review competence was initially conceived in an assertive fashion (Sect. 1.). However, the interpretation of the competence subsequently aligned with realities (Sect. 2.).

1. The Initial Idea: Installing the ILO as a "Master Agency" Within the UN System

The review competence was created as part of the 1944 Philadelphia Declaration's overall attempt to affirm the ILO's objectives, reformulate its mandate in the light of the interwar experiences, and to define its status in the then emerging post-war world order.[29] The Philadelphia Declaration promulgates the right of "all human beings, irrespective of race, creed or sex, (...) to pursue both their material well-being and their spiritual development in conditions of freedom and dignity, of economic security and equal opportunity" and identifies it as "the central aim of all national and international policy", which "should be judged in this light and accepted only in so far as they may be held to promote and not to hinder the achievement of this fundamental objective".[30] As a corollary, Part II lit. d and e Philadelphia Declaration stipulate that

> (d) it is a responsibility of the International Labour Organization to examine and consider all international economic and financial policies and measures in the light of this fundamental objective;
>
> (e) in discharging the tasks entrusted to it the International Labour Organization, having considered all relevant economic and financial factors, may include in its decisions and recommendations any provisions which it considers appropriate.

This language is remarkable, because it defines policy objectives not only for the ILO itself, but for "all national and international policy", and thus also for other IOs.

---

neither implies more than a competence. Commentators have likewise treated the "responsibility" like a competence, see e.g. Steve Charnovitz, 'The International Labour Organization in Its Second Century' (2000) 4 Max Planck Yearbook of United Nations Law 147, 179.

[29]A detailed description is provided by Ernst B Haas, *Beyond the Nation State: Functionalism and International Organization* (Stanford University Press 1964) 155 et seqq. See further Antony Evelyn Alcock, *History of the International Labour Organization* (Palgrave Macmillan 1971) 171 et seqq.

[30]Part II lit. a–c Philadelphia Declaration.

What is more, it assumes for the ILO the central task of watching over these policies and deciding whether they should be "accepted" (Part II lit. c).

The breadth of this language is no coincidence. It emanates from the historical context that this passage sought to install the ILO as a "master agency"[31] in economic and social matters. Its main objective was to obtain a position within the emerging UN framework from which the ILO could review the policies of other agencies. This especially targeted the Bretton Woods organizations, the founding of which was well underway when the Philadelphia Declaration was adopted.[32] The responsibility to "examine and consider" (lit. d), combined with the competence to include any provisions deemed appropriate (lit. e), witness this attempt. While the Philadelphia Declaration also pledged "full cooperation" to other IOs (Part VI), the ILO asserted a right to examination and, therefore, a 'last word'. These provisions have never been fully applied in practice. If they had been taken literally, the ILO would have been in a position to second-guess any policy of economic and financial IOs as to their soundness regarding the ILO's enhanced and enlarged social objectives. It would have been the central global economic and social agency.[33]

The said provisions of the Philadelphia Declaration have never been formally revoked or amended. On the contrary, at least on paper, they have been prominently reaffirmed on various occasions.[34] Therefore, technically speaking, the ILO still retains its constitutional review competence today. However, as is well known, the ILO has never succeeded in attaining the envisaged status (and in fact, it has been observed that it never seriously attempted to do so). The UN founding members swiftly vested the relevant oversight functions in the ECOSOC. Thus, while the ILO retains this competence, the legal relationship vis-à-vis the UN and all other relevant IOs is such that this competence could not be exercised to its full envisaged extent today, not least because this would potentially conflict with the respective relationship agreements the ILO has concluded with the UN and other IOs in the meantime.[35] Even if that was not the case, the ILO is hardly in a political position to unilaterally assert the status contemplated in the Philadelphia Declaration in full.[36]

---

[31] As Ernst Haas pointed out: "If the Philadelphia Declaration had been taken literally by those who voted for it, the ILO would have developed into the master agency among the emerging family of functional international bodies; it would have taken the place intended for the United Nations Economic and Social Council – though not in fact attained – by some of the drafters of the Charter", Haas (n 29) 156.

[32] Maupain, *The Future of the International Labour Organization in the Global Economy* (n 15) 67 et seqq.

[33] Haas (n 29) 156; Henner Gött, 'Interactions between International Organizations - Approaching a Neglected Governance Dimension' (2020) 17 International Organizations Law Review 75, 81.

[34] E.g. in the 2008 Declaration, preambular clause 3.

[35] On these agreements see Chaps. 13 and 14.

[36] Earlier attempts of the ILO to exercise its review competence failed already at the stage of obtaining intra-organizational consensus among its tripartite constituents, Charnovitz 'The International Labour Organization in Its Second Century' (n 28) 179 et seq.

2. The More Modest Reading in the 2008 Declaration on Social Justice for a Fair Globalization

The 2008 Declaration on Social Justice for a Fair Globalization provides a different and more modest reading of the ILO's review competence.

The Declaration's preamble reaffirms the ILO's "responsibility to examine and consider all international economic and financial policies in the light of the fundamental objective of social justice" as laid down in the Philadelphia Declaration.[37] However, the 2008 Declaration uses a quite different tone. Part II C of the 2008 Declaration reads:

> Other international and regional organizations with mandates in closely related fields can have an important contribution to make to the implementation of the integrated approach. The ILO should invite them to promote decent work, bearing in mind that each agency will have full control of its mandate. As trade and financial market policy both affect employment, it is the ILO's role to evaluate those employment effects to achieve its aim of placing employment at the heart of economic policies.

The clause strikes a much more modest note. It still contemplates an evaluation of other IOs' activities by the ILO but does not connect this with any assertion of oversight. No mention is made of Part II lit. e Philadelphia Declaration, the audacious clause on "making any provisions deemed appropriate" after examining other IOs' economic and financial policies. Instead, the cited clause in the 2008 Declaration highlights that other IOs' retain "full control" over their mandates and should be invited to promote decent work. In a similar vein, an accompanying resolution, adopted by the International Labour Conference on the same day as the 2008 Declaration, calls on the ILO Director-General to make proposals on "partnerships", specified as cooperation with other IOs.[38] Finally, Part III C of the 2008 Declaration's Follow-up even envisages that interested other IOs could take part, at a later stage, in the evaluation of the 2008 Declaration itself.

All in all, the 2008 Declaration makes explicit what had been the reality since 1945, and what had not been in dispute when the 2008 Declaration was adopted: that the ILO does not aspire the status of an economic and social 'master agency', but rather seeks consensual cooperation to further its objectives.

What remains is the ILO's proclaimed responsibility to 'evaluate' other IOs' policies. A certain caution is warranted to extrapolate legal conclusions from a non-binding document like the 2008 Declaration. Still, there is no indication in the 2008 Declaration that the constituents intended to transform the ILO's responsibility to review into a mere political proclamation. It may thus be concluded that the ILO still has a legal competence to review other IOs' policies.

---

[37] 2008 Declaration, preambular clause 3.

[38] International Labour Conference (97th session) Resolution on Strengthening the ILO's Capacity to Assist Its Members' Efforts to Reach Its Objectives in the Context of Globalization (10 June 2008) XCI ILO Official Bulletin Ser A No 2 66, para 2 lit. b III.

V. Supplementary Implied Competences for Other Types of Indirect Interactions

Besides the aforesaid explicitly attributed competences, further competences to interact can be derived by implication.

1. Room for Implied Competences

At the outset, the fairly broad scope of the ILO's attributed competences to interact with other IOs leaves little room for any additional implied competences. The competence to cooperate essentially governs most, if not all, cases of direct interaction. As to indirect interaction, the competence to evaluate other IOs' policies steps in even if no cooperation with these other IOs can be achieved.

Yet, the competence to evaluate is by its very nature a reactive one. Neither the ILO Constitution nor the Philadelphia Declaration say anything about proactively engaging in indirect interaction. For proactive indirect interaction, there is room for implied competences. For instance, the ILO may, on its own initiative, seek to adopt its own policies, instruments or practice that influence other IOs, viz. that constitute indirect interaction. Whether this is politically advisable is one thing—in most cases, cooperation will be the preferable means of choice. However, cooperation may not always be achievable, be it because the other IO is unable or unwilling to cooperate, be it because such cooperation is not living up to the ILO's expectations.

The implication of competences to interact with other IOs will in many cases not require a particularly extensive handling of the implied powers doctrine. Implied competences will in many cases by derivable by way of teleological interpretation of explicit competencial provisions.[39]

---

[39]Eventually, whether there is an implicit competence to proactively engage in indirect interaction depends on the interpretation of the ILO's mandate and the degree of effectiveness one considers appropriate. In two of its rare authoritative opinions on the ILO Constitution, the PCIJ has early on taken a firm stance as to the effective execution of the ILO's mandate. In the 1922 *Agricultural Production* Opinion, the Court was asked to examine whether the ILO had the competence to regulate the means and methods of agricultural production. The Court answered this question in the negative. However, it accepted that, while the ILO did not have a principal competence, it could nevertheless regulate other matters which fell in its competence and had, incidentally, an effect on agricultural production. The PCIJ held that "it is evident that the Organisation cannot be excluded from dealing with the matters specifically committed to it by the Treaty on the ground that this may involve in some aspects the consideration of the means or methods of production, or of the effects which the proposed measures would have upon production", *Competence of the ILO to Examine Proposal for the Organization and Development of the Methods of Agricultural Production* (Advisory Opinion) PCIJ Rep Series B No 3, 59. In the 1926 *Competence to Regulate the Work of the Employer* Opinion, the PCIJ affirmed this view and extended it to incidental regulation: "It is true that Opinion No. 3 deals with incidental effects on production whilst the question now pending before the Court concerns incidental regulation of the persona l work of the employer. No sharp line can, however, in practice be drawn between incidental effect and incidental regulation, and the

2. Example: An Implied Competence to Influence Other IOs Through the Adoption of Labour Conventions and Recommendations

As an example for an implied competence to interact, one might resort to the ILO's competence to adopt labour conventions and recommendations. This competence includes the adoption of such instruments that regulate matters falling within the ambit of other IOs. Such standards can lead to indirect interaction, as they may influence the conduct of other IOs. The cases of the World Bank feeling the urgency to justify its EWI against the benchmark of ILO conventions,[40] the ECtHR adjusting its jurisprudence to ILO conventions,[41] or the ESC being drafted and revised under the impression of ILO conventions[42] are pertinent examples.

There is no explicit provision in the ILO Constitution prohibiting such indirect influence when adopting labour instruments. The obligation to cooperate in Art. 12 (1) ILO Constitution does not go as far as requiring the ILO to avoid such influence on other IOs.

On the contrary, there is overwhelming evidence that the ILO has an implicit 'competence to affect' other IOs when adopting labour standards. One argument is the ILO's established practice of norm-setting. As mentioned above, the ILO's body of labour standards extensively covers topics that clearly fall within the ambit of other IOs,[43] and still the respective instruments have been adopted. A second argument can be inferred from the International Labour Conference's and Governing Body's respective Standing Orders,[44] the adoption of which can be taken to reflect an underlying consensus among the ILO's tripartite constituents. The Standing Orders do not prohibit influence of labour standards on other IOs. Rather, they merely require that other IOs be consulted during the drafting process, and that the

---

question whether the effect or the regulation is primary or only incidental cannot depend upon the mere circumstance that the employer is or is not mentioned in the proposed legislation. It follows, therefore, from the reasoning cited from Opinion No. 3 that, if it is assumed for the purpose of the argument that the competence of the International Labour Organization is limited to the work of the wage-earner, the Organization is not excluded from proposing regulations for the protection of wage-earners because such regulation may have the effect of regulating at the same time and incidentally the work of the employer", *Competence of the International Labour Organization to Regulate, Incidentally, the Personal Work of the Employer* (Advisory Opinion) (1926) PCIJ Rep Series B No 13, 21. In sum, the Court thus established that the ILO may use its competences even if this incidentally affects, or even incidentally regulates, topics for which the ILO has no competence. It is perhaps no coincidence that the ICJ referred to the PCIJ's *Employer* opinion as establishing the implied powers doctrine, *Reparation for Injuries Suffered in the Service of the United Nations* (n 2) 182 et seq. In the light of the Court's findings, it seems safe to assume that the ILO may incidentally address labour issues even if they also fall within the ambit of another IO.

[40]Chapter 4 C. II. 3.

[41]Chapter 5 B. III.

[42]Chapter 6 B.

[43]E.g. the IMO, see Chap. 3 A. and Gött (n 32), 85 et seqq.

[44]These regulate the legal relationships within each of the ILO's organs (*Innenrecht*) and, strictly speaking, do not belong to the legal relationship between the ILO and its members examined here.

results of such consultations be taken into consideration.[45] For one part, these procedural requirements serve the ILO's own interest in benefitting from expertise and input by other IOs. Besides, however, they also acknowledge that (a) influence on other IOs can occur, and (b) that such influence does not resemble an insurmountable bar to the adoption of a new ILO convention.

VI. Conclusion

With regard to inter-organizational interactions, the ILO possesses a competence and an obligation to cooperate with the UN and other IOs working in related fields, requiring best efforts to promote its values, mandate and standards in appropriate cases. The ILO further has a competence to invite other IOs as observers, and a competence to evaluate and consider other IOs economic and financial policies. These attributed competences are formulated in broad and encompassing language. They remain at a general level, leaving enough latitude to cover a wide range of activities. Besides, inter-organizational interactions which are not covered by an explicit competence, such as notably certain indirect interactions, can be based on

[45] Art. 17bis International Labour Conference Standing Orders, entitled „Prior consultation in respect of proposals for new activities relating to matters of direct concern to the United Nations or other specialised agencies", reads:

> 1. Where a proposal submitted to the Conference involves new activities to be undertaken by the International Labour Organisation relating to matters which are of direct concern to the United Nations or one or more specialised agencies other than the International Labour Organisation, the Director-General shall enter into consultation with the organisations concerned and report to the Conference on the means of achieving coordinated use of the resources of the respective organisations. Where a proposal put forward in the course of a meeting for new activities to be undertaken by the International Labour Organisation relates to matters which are of direct concern to the United Nations or one or more specialised agencies other than the International Labour Organisation, the Director-General shall, after such consultation with the representatives of the other organisation or organisations concerned attending the meeting as may be possible, draw the attention of the meeting to these implications of the proposal.
>
> 2. Before deciding on proposals referred to in the preceding paragraph, the Conference shall satisfy itself that adequate consultations have taken place with the organisations concerned.

With special regard to the drafting of labour standards, Art. 39bis International Labour Conference Standing Orders provides:

> Where items are placed on the agenda of the Conference with a view to the adoption of a Convention or a Recommendation, the International Labour Office shall, at the same time as it is requesting governments for their comments on the proposed Convention or Recommendation, consult the United Nations and other specialised agencies in respect of any provision of the proposed Convention or Recommendation which affects the activities of such organisation or organisations, and the comments of such organisation or organisations shall be brought before the Conference, together with the comments received from governments.

implied competences. In sum, the ILO's competences to engage in inter-organizational interactions are fairly comprehensive.

C. The Constitutional Embeddedness of the ILO's Competences to Interact

Although being of considerable latitude, the ILO's competences to interact are nevertheless limited, because they are embedded into the ILO's wider institutional legal framework.

I. The ILO's Obligation to Comply with Its Institutional Law During Interactions

The ILO's wider institutional legal framework influences the ILO's competences to interact and determines how they may be exercised.[46]

For cooperative interactions, this is explicitly spelled out in Art. 12(1) ILO Constitution, which specifies that cooperation shall take place "within the terms of this Constitution". As seen, some provisions of the ILO Constitution specifically regulate situations in which the ILO cooperates with other IOs and, therefore, qualify as "terms" in the sense of Art. 12(1) ILO Constitution.[47] However, the general and open wording does not only comprise constitutional provisions that explicitly address cooperation with other IOs. Rather, it speaks, without differentiation or limitation, of "this Constitution". This must be understood as referring to the entirety of the ILO Constitution, including all of its provisions. It purports to ensure that cooperation does not lead to transgressions of the ILO Constitution or any of its provisions. In other words, the clause formulates a general condition of compliance with the ILO Constitution. In consequence, inconformity with any norm of ILO institutional law will render interactive conduct unlawful under ILO institutional law.

Other provisions are less explicit, but nevertheless envisage that the ILO interacts with other IOs in the light of its institutional law's legal principles. For instance, regarding the ILO's competence to review the economic and financial policies of other IOs, the 2008 Declaration provides that the envisaged review will be

---

[46]On the influence of the respective normative context see e.g. *MOX Plant Case (Ireland v. United Kingdom)* (Provisional Measures, Order of 3 December 2001) ITLOS Reports 2001, 95, paras 50 et seq.

[47]The constitutional provisions concerning the ILO's integration into the UN System, for instance, have already been mentioned. These provisions all qualify as "terms" capable of concretizing the ILO's duty to cooperate.

conducted "in the light of the fundamental objective of social justice",[48] i.e. in the light of the ILO's foremost objective.

But even if not explicitly spelled out, the ILO's wider institutional legal framework predetermines the ILO's interactive competences. This is particularly true for its implied competences to indirectly interact with other IOs. Under the implied powers doctrine, competences can only be implied if and insofar such an implication is necessary to effectively pursue the respective IO's objectives, which again are specified in its institutional law. Implied competences that would allow an IO to disregard its own institutional law, especially its objectives, would not meet this criterion, and therefore could hardly be justified under the implied powers doctrine in the first place.[49]

In sum, when engaging in inter-organizational interactions, the ILO is required to comply with its institutional law. In principle, this refers to the institutional law in its entirety, including all of its provisions and norms.[50] Of particular relevance are the rules on competence allocations between organs, on tripartism and its central role in governing the ILO, and on the ILO's objectives and the obligation laid down in Art. 1(1) ILO Constitution to pursue them.

II. The Extent of the Predetermination

The ILO's obligation to comply with its institutional law moulds the exercise of its competences to interact with other IOs. That being said, to what extent this is the case depends on the respective norm of institutional law in question.

Rules on organs, bodies and their respective purviews, or procedural rules, will usually pose a stricter framework. For an example, interactions with other IOs conducted by the International Labour Office in a manner contrary to the Governing Body's explicit directions (Art. 8(1) ILO Constitution) would be unlawful. Similarly, the adoption of an instrument, for instance a labour convention, that will influence the work of another IO (and therefore would qualify as indirect interactive conduct) will only be permissible insofar as the procedure prescribed in the ILO Constitution for drafting and adopting labour conventions is observed.

By contrast, constitutional provisions on the ILO's objectives will usually be less specific. While the ILO Constitution, the Philadelphia Declaration and the 1998,

[48] 2008 Declaration, preambular clause 3.

[49] Moreover, the mere fact that the ILO is competent to indirectly interact with other IOs during its activities cannot possibly mean that the ILO is also authorized to disregard its own constitutional rules governing such activities.

[50] As discussed in Chap. 2, the ILO Constitution and the relevant ILO Declarations pronounce the ILO's objectives, establish its organs and their respective remits, regulate the ILO's procedures, e.g. regarding policy making, norm setting, or implementing and supervisory activities, and even set forth some basic substantive obligations, e.g. to promote fundamental principles and rights at work, full and productive employment, social protection and social dialogue.

2008 and 2019 Declarations set forth a broad array of objectives, they are less specific as to the means to achieve them.

However, despite the ILO's objectives being spelled out in this more lenient way, they are capable of moulding the ILO's competences to interact with other IOs. As an outer limit, the ILO is not competent to engage in interactions that would severely hamper or thwart the pursuit of its objectives, e.g. through collusion with another IO. For example, it is doubtful whether the ILO would have been competent to actively support the World Bank's EWI-inspired labour market deregulation agenda in Nepal or Georgia described in Chap. 4, given this agenda's detrimental effects on the ILO's own work. But even beyond this outer limit, the ILO's obligation to pursue its constitutional objectives (Art. 1(1) ILO Constitution) moulds its competences to interact with other IOs. While it will usually not be possible to derive from Art. 1 (1) ILO Constitution an obligation to adopt *specific* measures influencing another IO, any interactive conduct must be designed and exercised in the light of its constitutional objectives, with a view of their effective promotion. Moreover, should there be, in an exceptional case, no other way to promote one of its objectives except by interacting with another IO in a specific manner, the ILO would arguably even be obliged to act in this specific manner to the extent possible.

In sum, the ILO's wider institutional legal framework does not necessarily pose a strict corset definitively prescribing how the ILO may or not interact in a concrete case, but it normatively guides and informs how the ILO may or may not use of its competences, by indicating and limiting the objectives that may be pursued, prescribing the procedures to be followed, and defining the measures that each ILO organ or body may take.

III. The Prioritization of the ILO's Agenda and the Relativization of Other IOs' Governance Models, Needs and Demands

At the same time, the ILO's institutional law does not accord particular relevance to the governance models, needs and demands of the IOs the ILO is interacting with.

To be sure, the obligation to adhere to the ILO's wider institutional legal framework does not require the ILO to entirely ignore other IOs. Neither does it prevent the ILO from giving regard to the interacting IOs or to compromise with them. In fact, the obligation to cooperate in Art. 12(1) ILO Constitution and the pledge to "full cooperation" in the Philadelphia Declaration indicate that the ILO retains some flexibility to adapt its conduct in order to meet the needs or demands of other IOs.

However, the ILO's institutional law consistently prioritizes its own agenda over other IOs. As seen above, while Art. 12(1) ILO Constitution requires the ILO to cooperate with other IOs, the ILO must only do so "within the terms" of its Constitution. The Philadelphia Declaration pledges full cooperation but envisages it as a means to secure the resources necessary to achieve the ILO's *own* objectives (Part IV Philadelphia Declaration). The 1998 and 2008 Declarations foresee inter-organizational cooperation but envisage other IOs primarily as contributors to the ILO's own agenda, namely as potential promoters of fundamental principles and rights at work (No 3 1998 Declaration) and collaborators to realize the ILO's Decent Work Agenda (Part II C 2008 Declaration). The Centenary Declaration requests the ILO to reinforce inter-organizational cooperation "to promote policy coherence in pursuit of its human-centred approach to the future of work" (Part F Centenary Declaration). There is nothing in the ILO Constitution or in the Declarations obliging the ILO to unconditionally alter, downsize, adapt or abandon its efforts for the purpose of giving deference to another IO.

Thus, while the ILO retains discretion to interact with other IOs and to find mutually satisfactory solutions for issues, the ILO's institutional law nevertheless considers other IOs' governance models, needs and demands to be of secondary relevance as compared to the principal aim of fulfilling its own constitutional mandate.

D. Consequence: The ILO's Constitutional Carte Blanche for Protecting and Promoting Its Model

How, then, do the provisions discussed in the previous sections protect or promote the ILO's model of labour governance during interactions with other IOs?

The ILO's encompassing competences to interact with other IOs endow the ILO with broad discretion to take measures protecting or promoting its model of labour governance in inter-organizational interactions.

In particular, the obligation to adhere to the wider institutional legal framework does not pose a significant limit to such protection or promotion. The reason for this is that the pertinent constitutional norms are the very same ones that also shape the ILO's model of labour governance in the first place, because they determine the specific way in which the ILO deals with labour issues. They define the ILO's objectives, they embody and operationalize the fundamental choices for universal tripartite social dialogue and persuasion, and they provide important rules on the organization's output. Hence, the ILO may interact with other IOs within the same constitutional framework that defines its model, including through the same organs and procedures, with the same arsenal of instruments and other means, decided on (or backed) by tripartite social dialogue, effectuated by means of persuasion, and in pursuit of the same objectives of social justice and decent work for all. One could even go as far as to conclude that, from the perspective of the ILO's institutional law, interaction with other IOs is part and parcel of the ILO's model of labour governance, i.e. it is an element of the specific way in which the ILO engages in labour governance.

With regard to the ILO's interactive conduct observed in the three case studies presented in Chaps. 3, 4 and 5, this wide legal discretion has a simple but noteworthy consequence: None of the ILO's aforesaid activities seem to violate the provisions on inter-organizational interactions in the ILO's institutional law.

Against this background, despite the ILO's competences being embedded in its wider institutional legal framework, the ILO is by and large free under its institutional law to promote its model of labour governance and, at the same time, to avert adverse influences from other IOs on that model. Figuratively speaking, it has been given a constitutional 'carte blanche' to bring its model of labour governance to bear vis-à-vis other IOs.

E. Conclusion

The analysis of the ILO's institutional law in this chapter has revealed that it endows the organization with broad discretion as to whether and by what means it may protect or promote its model of labour governance in inter-organizational interactions.

The ILO has comprehensive competences to engage in inter-organizational interactions. First, it has an attributed competence and obligation to cooperate with IOs working in related fields. Second, the ILO has an attributed competence to evaluate and review the economic and financial policies of other IOs. Finally, besides these attributed competences, there is room to imply further competences, notably a competence to proactively engage in unilateral and indirect inter-organizational interaction, e.g. by adopting labour standards that have an influence on other IOs.

The analysis has also shown that the ILO's competences to interact are embedded in its wider institutional legal framework. This framework predetermines and moulds the way the ILO may exercise its competences. While using its competences to interact with other IOs, the ILO must observe its own institutional law in its entirety. In essence, the ILO's institutional law prioritizes the ILO's own constitutional imperatives (i.e. the pursuit of its own objectives, and the abidance by its institutional, procedural and substantive provisions) and relativizes the role and relevance of other IOs. Since the pertinent norms of the ILO's institutional law are the same that define and shape the ILO's model of labour governance, the overall effect of these norms is that the ILO is given a 'carte blanche' to make full use of its competences to protect and promote its model of labour governance vis-à-vis other IOs.

9. The ILO's Relativization in the Institutional Laws of the World Bank and the CoE

The observed situation under the ILO's institutional law is, of course, only one part of the picture. Every IO the ILO interacts with has its own institutional law, which takes its own perspective on labour governance. These other institutional laws contain their own distinct rules on how the respective IO may and must interact with the ILO.

Therefore, this chapter will broaden the perspective to include the World Bank's and CoE's institutional laws. The Bank and the CoE are not legally bound to observe the ILO's institutional law and its provisions on inter-organizational interactions (A.). Therefore, this chapter will examine the relevant norms on inter-organizational interactions in the institutional laws of the World Bank (B.) and the CoE (C.). It will carve out the two IOs' respective competences to engage in inter-organizational interactions and will examine how these coimpetences are embedded in the respective wider institutional legal framework. It will also examine if and to what extent the Bank's and CoE's institutional laws contain norms protecting or promoting the ILO's model of labour governance in inter-organizational interactions. The analysis will reveal that the Bank's and the CoE's institutional laws prioritize their respective own objectives, institutional structure, procedures and results, and relativize the ILO and its model of labour governance. In essence, this mirrors the prioritization of the own and relativization of other IOs observed in ILO institutional law in the preceding Chapter. As a result, none of the examined institutional laws mitigates the ambivalence of inter-organizational interactions (D.).

H. Gött, *The Law of Interactions Between International Organizations*, Beiträge zum ausländischen öffentlichen Recht und Völkerrecht 299, https://doi.org/10.1007/978-3-662-62389-3_9

A. The World Bank's and CoE's Legal Independence from ILO Institutional Law

Before the World Bank's and CoE's institutional laws can be examined in detail, it needs to be recapitulated that neither the ILO Constitution nor any of the other relevant sources of ILO institutional law impose binding international legal obligations on either the World Bank or the CoE. This includes the ILO's institutional law's conferral of a carte blanche on the ILO to protect or promote its model of labour governance.

It hardly needs mention that the World Bank and the CoE are not bound to observe ILO institutional law by virtue of membership, as neither the World Bank IOs nor the CoE have attained ILO membership (nor could they, as membership is only open to states, Art. 1 ILO Constitution). Rather, the question is whether they are bound to observe ILO institutional law for other reasons. As will be shown in the following, this is not the case.

I. No Binding Effect Via Acceptance in Treaties

A subjugation to ILO law does not emanate from international treaties the Bank or the CoE are parties to. Neither the Bank nor the CoE have ratified (nor could they ratify) ILO conventions.[1] Moreover, while the CoE has entered into a cooperation agreement with the ILO (the ILO-CoE, discussed in Chap. 13), this agreement does not oblige the CoE to observe ILO institutional law. To begin with, the agreement does not contain provisions to that effect. Furthermore, even assumed it did, the source of the CoE's obligation would still not be the ILO Constitution itself, but the ILO-CoE, i.e. a separate agreement (which could of course also limit or alter any such obligation to observe ILO law).

II. No Binding Effect Via Customary Law

Moreover, neither the World Bank nor the CoE are bound to observe ILO institutional law by virtue of customary international law. There has been a protracted debate whether IOs are bound by customary international law, inter alia on the question whether IOs like the World Bank were bound by customary guarantees of

[1]Which would e.g. lead to reporting obligations under Arts. 19(5) and 22 ILO Constitution. The issue of IOs not being able to ratify ILO conventions arose in practice e.g. with regard to the EU, see Opinion 2/91 *Convention No 170 of the International Labour Organization concerning Safety in the Use of Chemicals at Work* (ECLI:EU:C:1993:106) [1993] ECR I-01061.

human rights.[2] Following this discussion, one could be tempted to argue that the Bank and the CoE were bound to observe those substantive ILO labour standards that also form part of customary international law.[3] However, regardless of whether these IOs are bound by customary law in the first place, the overwhelming part of ILO institutional law does not reflect customary law, including many of the ILO's objectives as well as all its institutional and procedural provisions laying the basis for tripartite social dialogue. These provisions, however, are constitutive for the ILO's model of labour governance. Therefore, there is, at this stage of the analysis, no need to dive deeper into the question to what extent IOs are bound by customary law (the issue will be revisited in a more comprehensive manner in Chap. 15).[4]

III. No Relaxation of the pacta tertiis *Rule*

In addition, the World Bank and the CoE are not bound to observe ILO institutional law as 'third IOs'. To begin with, ILO law does not envisage this to be the case. But even if it did, the World Bank and CoE would only be bound by ILO law if they had consented to it, which is not the case either. Without such consent, ILO law cannot impose rights or obligations on non-parties (*pacta tertiis nec nocent nec prosunt*).

According to Art. 34 VCLT, treaties do not impose rights or obligations on third states without their consent. Pursuant to Art. 5 VCLT, the *pacta tertiis* rule also applies to constituent instruments of an IO and treaties adopted within an IO. Art. 34 VCLT itself only applies regarding third states, not to IOs and other non-state actors.[5] However, the same principle applies, as a norm of customary international law, to non-member IOs, including the IOs examined in this study.

[2]See e.g. Daniel D Bradlow, 'The World Bank, the IMF, and Human Rights' (1996) 6 Transnational Law & Contemporary Problems 47; Sigrun Skogly, *The Human Rights Obligations of the World Bank and the IMF* (Cavendish Publishing 2001); Bahram Ghazi, *The IMF, The World Bank Group and the Question of Human Rights* (Transnational Publishers 2005) 99 et seqq.; Willem van Genugten, *The World Bank Group, the IMF and Human Rights - A Contextualised Way Forward* (Intersentia 2015) 9 et seqq. The argument of human rights obligations of the Bank has also been made with reference to the UN Charter, see Mac Darrow, *Between Light and Shadow - The World Bank, The International Monetary Fund and International Human Rights Law* (Hart Publishing 2003) 124 et seqq. For a more general focus Cornelia Janik, *Die Bindung Internationaler Organisationen an Internationale Menschenrechtsstandards* (Mohr Siebeck 2012) passim.

[3]Furthermore, the source of any customary obligation would in any event not be ILO institutional law but customary law with partially similar content. There is a significant difference between the two, since any customary labour rights would not be embedded in the ILO's particular governance structure in the same way as ILO instruments are, and therefore not be as influenced by its governance model.

[4]Chapter 15 B.

[5]Alexander Proelß, 'Art 34 VCLT' in Oliver Dörr and Kirsten Schmalenbach (eds), *Vienna Convention on the Law of Treaties - A Commentary* (2nd edn, Springer 2018) para 12.

The VCLT embodies the *pacta tertiis* rule in a straightforward and rather rigid way. Before and after its adoption, there have been repeated discussions about whether there are treaties to which the *pacta tertiis* rule does not apply, or only applies in a relaxed manner.

Notably, it has repeatedly been argued that Art. 34 VCLT did not apply to certain categories of treaties establishing so-called objective regimes. However, the very existence of such regimes as an exception to the *pacta tertiis* rule has constantly been disputed and is widely rejected.[6] In any event, the overwhelming part of the debate on objective regimes focuses on other treaties than constituent instruments of IOs.[7] The only recognized case of a constituent instrument having external effect on third parties is the UN Charter. As the ICJ held in *Reparation for Injuries Suffered in the Service of the United Nations*, the UN has objective legal personality and is capable to bring international claims vis-à-vis non-member states.[8] The notion of objective personality and its relevance for present purposes will be examined further in Chap. 15.[9] Suffice it to say here that, even if one applied the ICJ's reasoning in *Reparation* to the ILO, this alone would not bind the World Bank and the CoE to the ILO's institutional law.

Besides the debate on objective regimes, some authors have suggested that the customary *pacta tertiis* rule was less rigid than Art. 34 VCLT and did not automatically apply to obligations of non-state third parties.[10] This would be of interest in the present context, because it could mean that ILO law could indeed impose obligations on the World Bank and the CoE. However, it is doubtful if this is the case. At the outset, part of the discussion focused on other non-state actors than IOs, notably individuals and armed groups, which are not relevant here and which might indeed not benefit from the *pacta tertiis* rule.[11] Insofar as IOs are concerned, the debate centres on the UN[12] or on cases of uncertain precedential value.[13] What is more, Art. 34 VCLT-IO embodies the pacta tertiis rule with the same rigidity as its counterpart

[6]ibid para. 32 et seqq.; Mark Eugen Villiger, 'Art. 34' in Mark Eugen Villiger (ed), Commentary on the 1969 Vienna Convention on the Law of Treaties (Kluwer Law International 2009) para 11. See also Theodor Schweisfurth, 'International Treaties and Third States' (1985) 45 Zeitschrift für ausländisches öffentliches Recht und Völkerrecht 653, 665 et seqq.

[7]Proelß (n 5) Art 34, paras 39 et seqq.

[8]*Reparation for Injuries Suffered in the Service of the United Nations* (Advisory Opinion) [1949] ICJ Reports 174, 179 and 185.

[9]Chapter 15 A.

[10]Proelß (n 5) Art 34, para 12, with further references.

[11]ibid.

[12]ibid.

[13]For example, reference is sometimes made to the International Criminal Tribunal for the Former Yugoslavia, which held in a line of decisions that it was empowered to order other IOs to provide judicial assistance under its Statute, see e.g. *Prosecutor v. Simić et al* (Decision on Motion for Judicial Assistance) ICTY-IT-95-9-PT (18 October 2000) para 48. Yet, first of all, the Tribunal was also a UN body. Second of all, in the cases at hand, the ordered IOs actually consented in providing assistance, ibid para 43. In any event, it is doubtful if the Tribunal's teleological reasoning can be generalized.

in the VCLT.[14] The VCLT-IO applies to treaties concluded between states and IOs or between IOs and explicitly protects "third organizations" (Art. 34 VCLT-IO). It would be inconsistent to protect IOs regarding these treaties but not regarding treaties exclusively concluded between states.

For present purposes, it therefore seems preferable to proceed on the understanding that the customary *pacta tertiis* rule applies without relaxation to IOs' constituent instruments and to the benefit of 'third IOs'.

IV. No 'Inherited' Obligations

Finally, neither the World Bank nor the CoE have 'inherited' obligations under ILO law from their member states. The mere fact that virtually all CoE and World Bank member states are also ILO members does not subjugate the Bank and the CoE themselves to the ILO Constitution and other ILO instruments.[15]

As to IOs in general, some authors have argued that IOs can be bound by treaties they have not actively acceded to. They argue that, upon their erection, new IOs 'inherit' their member states' pre-existing legal obligations under the law of existing IOs. The rationale behind these proposals is to prevent states from circumventing their pre-existing obligations by creating a legally unrestrained IO acting in their place. Accordingly, in the present context, one could argue that the World Bank and the CoE were bound by the ILO Constitution or other ILO instruments, regardless of their consent, because they 'inherited' the respective obligations from their member states that are also ILO members.

Two bases are presented in support of 'inherited' obligations: the principle of *nemo plus juris transferre potest quam ipse habet* (1.) and functional succession (2.).[16] However, there are pervading counterarguments against the World Bank and CoE 'inheriting' their member states' obligations under either of them.

---

[14]On the eventually abandoned idea of relaxing the *pacta tertiis* rule during the ILC's work on the VCLT-IO see Fernando Lusa Bordin, *The Analogy Between States and International Organizations* (Cambridge University Press 2019) 169 et seq.

[15]See *mutatis mutandis Case C-308/06 International Association of Independent Tanker Owners (Intertanko) et al v. Secretary of State for* Transport (ECLI:EU:C:2008:312) [2008] ECR I-04057 para 49. The role of common member states will be examined in Chap. 12.

[16]August Reinisch, 'Securing the Accountability of International Organizations' (2001) 7 Global Governance 131, 136 et seq.; Frédéric Mégret and Florian Hoffmann, 'The UN as Human Rights Violator? Some Reflections on the United Nations Changing Human Rights Responsibilities' (2003) 25 Human Rights Quarterly 314, 318; Daniel Halberstam and Eric Stein, 'The United Nations, the EU, and the King of Sweden: Economic Sanctions and Individual Rights in a Plural World Order' (2009) 46 Common Market Law Review 13, 22 et seq.; Henry G Schermers, 'The Legal Bases of International Organization Action', in: René-Jean Dupuy, *A Handbook on International Organizations* (Martinus Nijhoff Publishers 1998) 402; Henry G Schermers and Niels M Blokker, *International Institutional Law* (6th edn, Brill 2018) para 1574. For a succession in

1. *Nemo plus juris transferre potest quam ipse habet*

The principle of *nemo plus juris transferre potest quam ipse habet* (or *nemo dat quod non habet)*—no one can transfer more rights than he possesses—originates from Roman law. In international law, it has primarily become relevant in the context of cessation of territory. As mentioned before, certain international obligations are considered to be connected to territory. If territory is ceded by one state to another, the obligations connected to that territory may 'move' with it and become obligations of the new state. Therefore, the ceding state cannot transfer territory without transferring the connected obligations.[17] The underlying rationale is to maintain rights and obligations of third states connected to that territory. Applying the principle to the present context, it would mean that ILO member states could not have endowed the World Bank and the CoE with any competences that would contravene these states' obligations under ILO law.

However, it cannot simply be assumed that the principle also applies to the establishment of IOs.[18] It relies on the questionable conceptualization of IOs' competences as solely delegated powers that moreover are perfectly symmetrical to those of their member states.[19]

Moreover, it is questionable if the scenarios of cession of territory and establishing an IO are comparable. The ceding state loses its territory and will no longer be in a position to fulfil the obligations connected to it without infringing on the territorial sovereignty of the acquiring state. In this situation, 'moving' its obligations to the acquiring state serves an imminent need to protect the rights of third states. By contrast, IO member states do not lose control of the IO. They remain, at least to a certain extent, in a position to exercise control and influence and, thus, to fulfil their obligations owed to third parties, including their membership obligations in other IOs.

However, even in the context of territory, the principle's relevance is reduced by third states acquiescing or recognizing the loss of rights.[20] The same mitigation could become relevant in the present context. While the ILO has certainly not agreed to relieving its member states from their obligations under ILO law, it has acquiesced the formation of both the World Bank and the CoE, and has recognized their existence.

---

exceptional cases Kristina Daugirdas, 'How and Why International Law Binds International Organizations' (2016) 57 Harvard International Law Journal 325, para 335 et seq. and 368 et seqq.

[17] *Island of Palmas (Netherlands v. USA)* (1928) 2 RIAA 829, 842; James Crawford, *Brownlie's Principles of Public International Law* (8th edn, Oxford University Press 2012) 213 et seq.

[18] Robert Cryer, 'Immunities and International Criminal Tribunals' in Alexander Orakhelashvili (ed) *Research Handbook on Jurisdiction and Immunities in International* Law (Edward Elgar Publishing 2015) 468, 492.

[19] See e.g. Carsten Stahn, 'The ICC, Pre-Existing Jurisdictional Treaty Regimes, and the Limits of the Nemo Dat Quod Non Habet Doctrine - A Reply to Michael Newton' (2016) 49 Vanderbilt Journal of Transnational Law 443, 446 et seqq.

[20] Crawford, *Brownlie's Principles of Public International Law* (n 17) 213.

2. Functional Succession

Some authors have proposed that IOs 'inherited' their member states' obligations by virtue of functional succession. Proponents of this approach rely on the seminal example of the European Economic Community's succession in its member states' obligations under the General Agreement on Tariffs and Trade (GATT) before the creation of the WTO. In this context, the European Court of Justice held in *International Fruit Company v. Produktschap voor Groenten en Fruit* that the EEC had succeded in these obligations and was therefore bound to observe them.[21]

However, it is questionable if the EEC/GATT example supports the general suggestion that all IOs succede in their member states' obligations arising from the institutional laws of other IOs. To begin with, it is questionable if the EEC's functional succession can actually be considered 'automatic'. In fact, all relevant actors—the Community, the member states and the GATT's other contracting parties—consented to this succession, a fact explicitly relied on by the Court in *International Fruit Company.*[22] Moreover, the Court also relied on the fact that EEC Treaty conferred an exclusive competence for the subject-matters in question on the EEC.[23] By contrast, neither the World Bank nor the CoE have been accorded an exclusive competence over labour-related matters. Finally, the EU is also the best example of alternatives to functional succession: instead of succeeding into all relevant obligations of its member states under the laws of other IOs, the EU has adopted different approaches for different IOs. For example, it has attained full membership in the WTO and FAO, while coordinating its member states in the ILO without itself becoming an ILO member or succeeding into its members' obligations under ILO law.[24]

3. Arguments Against Both Bases

In addition, a range of arguments militate against both the principle of *nemo plus juris transferre potest quam ipse habet* and functional succession as bases for 'inherited' obligations.

To begin with, the idea that states would somehow be prevented by law from establishing a new IO which is competent to disregard its member states' obligations

---

[21] *Joined Cases 21-24/72 International Fruit Company NV and Others v. Produktschap Voor Groenten En Fruit* (ECLI:EU:C:1972:115) [1972] ECR 01219 paras 11–18.

[22] ibid para 16.

[23] ibid para 15.

[24] See e.g. Marco Ferri, 'Coordination between the EU and its Member States', in Christina Kaddous (ed), *The European Union in International Organisations and Global Governance* (Hart Publishing 2017) 77; Geneviève Pons-Deladrière, 'European Union Participation and Cooperation in ILO Institutions and Activities: An ILO Perspective', in: Christina Kaddous (ed), *The European Union in International Organisations and Global Governance* (Hart Publishing 2017) 93.

under the law of pre-existing IOs is, except for specific constellations, difficult to sustain. ILO member states erecting another IO in violation of any of their obligations under ILO law may commit an internationally wrongful act.[25] However, even if ILO member states had erected the World Bank, the CoE or any other IO as a mere vehicle to circumvent their obligations under ILO law, and even if that amounted to a violation of ILO law, this erection would still have been legally valid and therefore 'possible'. There is a distinction between a) an IO member state's violation of that IO's law by erecting another IO and b) the legal validity of the treaty establishing that other IO. The grounds for invalidity are exhaustively enumerated in the VCLT. They comprise reasons invalidating consent, such as error, fraud or coercion, as well as violations of substantive international legal norms having the status of jus cogens. Thus, in essence, the only case in which any newly established IO's constituent instrument could at all be invalid because of a violation of ILO law would be if that constituent instrument violated a norm of jus cogens.[26] It is already rather uncertain if any norm of ILO institutional law has even attained this status.[27] In any event, the constituent instruments of the World Bank and the CoE would not violate it.

By contrast, a 'simple' violation of states' other obligations by establishing an IO is not a ground for invalidity under the VCLT. Therefore, such a violation does not lead to the invalidity of that IO's constituent instrument or parts thereof. Thus, even if the erection of the World Bank and the CoE violated ILO law (which is improbable in itself), this would not affect the validity of the Bank's or CoE's constituent instruments. It would therefore neither affect the conferral of competences by ILO member states onto these IOs.[28]

Besides these legal considerations, the idea of an 'automatic' conferral of obligations raises significant practical difficulties. It might be feasible insofar as all member states have assumed the same international obligations.[29] However, it will frequently be the case that not all members of an IO are also members of another IO in question, or that not all members of one IO have ratified the same treaty which had been adopted within the context of another IO. The latter will frequently be the case with regard to the ILO, given that the number of ratified ILO conventions vary significantly between the member states. For instance, whereas Palau has only

[25]See Chap. 12 B. I. See also Committee on the Accountability of International Organizations 'Final Report of the Committee on the Accountability of International Organizations' in International Law Association Report of the Seventy-First Conference (Berlin 2004) (International Law Association 2004) 4, 18; Schweisfurth (n 6) 661. See also Arts. 58 et seqq. DARIO.

[26]Daugirdas 'How and Why International Law Binds International Organizations' (n 16) 329.

[27]It has occasionally been argued that certain fundamental worker rights, such as the prohibition of child labour, had attained the status of jus cogens, see Franziska Humbert *The Challenge of Child Labour in International Law* (Cambridge University Press 2009) 114 et seqq.

[28]Whether the newly established IO's law would have to be interpreted in the light of the law of ILO law will be discussed in Chap. 11.

[29]This was e.g. the case in *Kadi*: all EU member states had either been UN members as of 1 January 1958 or had otherwise accepted to observe UNSC resolutions, *Case T-315/01 Yassin Abdullah Kadi v. Council and Commission* (ECLI:EU:T:2005:332) [2005] ECR II-03649 para 187.

ratified two ILO conventions (the Maritime Labour Convention, 2006 and the Worst Forms of Child Labour Convention, 1999 (No 182)),[30] Poland has ratified a total of 92 conventions and one protocol, out of which 66 are currently in force.[31] Given these divergences, which ILO obligations should be deemed conferred by its member states on, say, the World Bank? Only those obligations which all the members had assumed?[32] If that was the case, the Bank would arguably not have inherited any obligations at all, since two of its members are not ILO members[33] and could therefore not have 'bequeathed' any rights or obligations to the Bank.

A further practical difficulty is to determine which precise rights and obligations an IO would inherit. Taking the idea of inherited obligations seriously, potentially all rights and obligations incumbent on the member states could be inherited by newly established IOs. In the case of ILO law, this would mean that other IOs could not only inherit obligations under substantive labour standards, but also institutional or procedural obligations, such as the obligation to contribute to the ILO's budget and resources, to present adopted ILO conventions to its internal organs, to submit reports to the ILO's supervisory bodies etc. As the idea to focus on functional (rather than complete) succession already indicated that this is not what is intended even by proponents of inherited obligations. Still, these ideas say little about why the inherited obligations do (not) include certain specific obligations.

Furthermore, there is a temporal dimension: The idea of a new IO inheriting its members' obligations under the law of a pre-existing IO only works out if all relevant member states first became members of the older IO and then of the new IO. However, while many states first joined the ILO and the World Bank, there are

---

[30]ILO, 'Ratifications for Palau' (*ILO Website*) <https://www.ilo.org/dyn/normlex/en/f?p=1000:11200:0::NO:11200:P11200_COUNTRY_ID:2466492> accessed 26 April 2020.

[31]ILO, 'Ratifications for Poland' (*ILO Website*) <https://www.ilo.org/dyn/normlex/en/f?p=NORMLEXPUB:11200:0::NO::P11200_COUNTRY_ID:102809> accessed 26 April 2020.

[32]Contemplated e.g. by Lusa Bordin (n 14) 170. By contrast, the CJEU considered the EU not be bound by the International Convention on Civil Liability for Oil Pollution Damage and the The International Convention on the Establishment of an International Fund for Compensation for Oil Pollution Damage via functional succession because not all EU member states were parties to them, *Case C-188/07 Commune de Mesquer v. Total France SA and Total International Ltd* (ECLI:EU:C:2011:864) [2008] ECR I-4501, para 85. Generally speaking, there would also be the further question what should be the solution if one or more members have assumed a different scope of obligations, e.g. have made reservations. Should these reservations be conferred onto the IO or should the IO be bound without them, which would not only preserve, but even expand the rights of third actors? This question, however, is not significant in the ILO context, as ILO law prohibits reservations to ILO conventions, see Chap. 2 C. II. 2.

[33]Bhutan, Kosovo and the Federated States of Micronesia are members of both the IBRD and the IDA, but not of the ILO. Nauru is another IBRD member that is not a member of the ILO. See World Bank, 'Member Countries' (*World Bank Website*) <https://www.worldbank.org/en/about/leadership/members#1> accessed 26 April 2020 and ILO, 'Member States' (*ILO Website*) https://www.ilo.org/global/about-the-ilo/how-the-ilo-works/member-states/lang%2D%2Den/index.htm accessed 26 April 2020.

states that joined these IOs in reverse order.[34] Given this mixed sequence of 'inheritance', which IO is supposed to inherit membership obligations from which other IO?

Finally, it is questionable if the idea of 'inherited' obligations would be compatible with ILO law itself. Both ILO membership and ratification of ILO conventions are exclusively open to states. The World Bank, the CoE and other IOs could thus not actively attain rights or obligations under ILO law even if they intended to. Would that still matter if one accepted that these IOs 'inherited' their member states' obligations under ILO law instead?

There is no easy answer to these questions. What can be constated is that—in addition to the lack of a legal norm requiring it—the idea of automatically conferring member states' obligations onto newly created IOs seems unfeasible if really put to the test in practice.

V. Conclusion

In sum, taking IOs' separate legal personality and the distinction between their different legal relationships seriously, ILO institutional law is not binding on the World Bank and the CoE. For them, it qualifies as *res inter alios acta* properly speaking. This means in particular that ILO institutional law does not oblige the Bank or the CoE to pursue the ILO's objectives as laid down in the ILO Constitution and the several ILO declarations, nor to adhere to any substantive or procedural norms of ILO institutional law. Moreover, the Bank and the CoE are not bound under ILO institutional law to respect the ILO's competences to protect or promote its model of labour governance during inter-organizational interactions.

B. The ILO's Model in the World Bank's Institutional Law

Aside from this legal independence from ILO institutional law, the World Bank and the CoE have their own institutional laws. Each of them contains an own set of competences to interact with other IOs, again embedded in the respective wider institutional legal frameworks.

Therefore, the analysis will now turn to the World Bank's institutional law regarding inter-organizational interactions.[35] Given the abundant similarities

[34] E.g. Marshall Islands, which joined the IBRD on 21 May 1992, the IDA on 19 January 1993 and the ILO on 3 July 2007. Several other countries were members of the ILO, then withdrew from it, became members of the Bank and later rejoined the ILO, e.g. Honduras or El Salvador.

[35] Notably, the special competences regarding interactions with other members of the WBG, although explicitly regulated in the constituent instruments (Art. IV(6) Articles of Agreement of the International Finance Corporation (entered into force 20 July 1956) 264 UNTS 117 (IFC-AoA);

between the IBRD's and IDA's constituent instruments, the analysis will centre on the former, but will provide references to the latter where appropriate.[36]

I. Overview on the Relevant Sources of the World Bank's Institutional Law

At the outset, it is convenient to provide a brief overview over the relevant sources of the World Bank's institutional law. The central sources are the two constituent instruments of the IBRD and the IDA, the International Bank of Reconstruction and Development's Articles of Agreement (IBRD-AoA)[37] and the International Development Association's Articles of Agreement (IDA-AoA,[38] together simply referred to here as "AoA").[39]

The AoA's wording has, safe for minor amendments, essentially remained unchanged. That being said, the actual scope of the World Bank's constitutional mandate has significantly expanded.[40] This expansion occurred outside the AoA's

Art. VI(6) Articles of Agreement of the International Development Association (approved for submission to Governments by the Executive Directors of the International Bank for Reconstruction and Development on 26 January 1960, entered into force 24 September 1960) 439 UNTS 249 (IDA-AoA); Art. 35 Convention establishing the Multilateral Investment Guarantee Agency (adopted 11 October 1985, entered into force 12 April 1988) 1508 UNTS 99 (MIGA Convention)), will not be discussed.

[36]These references will be provided in footnotes as appropriate.

[37]Articles of Agreement of the International Bank for Reconstruction and Development (adopted at the UN Monetary and Financial Conference, Bretton Woods, New Hampshire, 22 July 1944, entered into force 27 December 1945) 2 UNTS 134 (IBRD-AoA).

[38]Articles of Agreement of the International Development Association (approved for submission to Governments by the Executive Directors of the International Bank for Reconstruction and Development on 26 January 1960, entered into force 24 September 1960) 439 UNTS 249 (IDA-AoA).

[39]The IBRD-AoA were adopted at the 1944 Bretton Woods Conference, alongside the constituent instrument of the IMF, the IDA-AoA were drafted under the auspices of the IBRD and adopted in 1960 in response to increasing demands for affordable funds by newly independent developing countries, Leonie Guder, 'International Development Association (IDA)', *Max Planck Encyclopedia of Public International Law* (Oxford University Press 2011) para 3. Furthermore, the World Bank's internal by-laws (By-laws of the International Bank for Reconstruction and Development, as amended by IBRD Board of Governors Res No 360 (26 September 1980) <https://www.worldbank.org/en/about/leadership/directors/by-laws> accessed 26 April 2020) and policies should be mentioned. They mostly regulate organizational and procedural questions and play an exorbitant role in the Bank's practice, Heribert Franz Köck and Peter Fischer, *Das Recht der Internationalen Organisationen* (3rd edn, Linde Verlag 1997) 442. The Bank has also established a vice presidency for external relations, World Bank, *A Guide to the World Bank* (3rd edn, World Bank 2011) 41.

[40]See Chap. 4 A.

formal amendment procedure[41] and was mostly based on an expansive interpretation of other AoA provisions.[42] In this regard, it is noteworthy that the World Bank is competent to render authoritative interpretations of its AoA (Art. IX IBRD-AoA). In the Bank's contemporary practice, the World Bank's Legal Counsel drafts a legal opinion on matters of interest, which is then endorsed or concurred in by the Executive Directors. In consequence, the Legal Counsel's legal opinions have become important points of reference for understanding the World Bank's institutional law.[43]

II. Competences and Obligations to Engage in Inter-Organizational Interaction

Regarding competences and obligations to engage in inter-organizational interactions, the World Bank's institutional law contains an attributed competence and obligation to cooperate (I.). Further competences to interact can be implied (II.).

1. The Competence (and Obligation) to Cooperate with Other IOs

First of all, the Bank has an attributed competence to cooperate with other IOs. Similar to the ILO Constitution, the IBRD-AoA entitle the IBRD to cooperate with other IOs. Art. V(8) lit. a IBRD-AoA, first sentence, reads:

> The Bank, within the terms of this Agreement, shall cooperate with any general international organization and with public international organizations having specialized responsibilities in related fields.[44]

---

[41]The IBRD-AoA have been formally amended only on very few occasions, the IDA-AoA not at all, Hassane Cissé, 'Should the Political Prohibition in Charters of International Financial Institutions Be Revisited? The Case of the World Bank' (2012) 3 World Bank Legal Review 59, 84.

[42]See Ibrahim FI Shihata, 'The Creative Role of the Lawyer – Example: The Office of the World Bank's General Counsel' (1999) 48 Catholic University Law Review 1041, 1048. As far as structural adjustment lending is concerned, a normative basis for this has been Art. III(4) (vii) IBRD-AoA, which enables the Bank to provide loans for other than the objectives laid down in Art I IBRD-AoA in case of "special circumstances", John D Ciorciari, 'The Lawful Scope of Human Rights Criteria in World Bank Credit Decisions: An Interpretive Analysis of the IBRD and IDA Articles of Agreement' (2000) 33 Cornell International Law Journal 331, 348; Sabine Schlemmer-Schulte, 'International Bank for Reconstruction and Development (IBRD)', *Max Planck Encyclopedia of Public International Law* (Oxford University Press 2014) para 55. On the pertinent provisions regarding authoritative interpretation see below, Chap. 10 B. I. 2.

[43]Shihata, *The World Bank Legal Papers* (Springer 2000) lix.

[44]Similar provisions are contained in Art. V(4) IDA-AoA and Art. 35 MIGA Convention. Moreover, Art. 19 MIGA Convention envisages cooperation with, inter alia, regional entities. Regarding cooperative arrangements, Art. VI(7) IDA-AoA differentiates between the UN, with which formal arrangements must be made, and other IOs, with which they may be made.

The wording is virtually identical to its counterpart in Art. 12(1) ILO Constitution. Thus, much of what has been said above applies *mutatis mutandis* to the case of the World Bank.

Like the ILO, the IBRD is not only competent, but also obliged, to cooperate with the UN and other IOs working in 'related' fields. Similar to the ILO Constitution, 'cooperation' is left undefined by the IBRD-AoA and appears to be a rather broad and encompassing term. Other provisions of the IBRD-AoA envisage certain modalities of cooperation, from which conclusions as to the Bank's competence to cooperate can be drawn.[45] Notably, Art. V(8) lit. a IBRD-AoA and Art. V(2) lit. b (v) IBRD-AoA contemplate the making of formal and informal arrangements.[46] These provisions underline that the IBRD has the competence to conclude treaties and arrangements, and to engage in other forms of direct interaction with other IOs. In its practice, the World Bank has relied on a wide understanding of the term 'cooperation'. It repeatedly cooperated with other IOs in a variety of contexts and formats. In principle, this also applies, although on markedly low level, to the ILO, which the Bank has e.g. invited to attend some of its meetings on an ad hoc basis.[47]

2. Implied Further Competences to Interact

As in the case of the ILO Constitution, the Bank's AoA only provide a piecemeal regulation of its competences to engage in inter-organizational interactions. In particular, the express provisions do not cover indirect interactions. Still, during the Bank's history, there have been prominent instances of indirect interactions.[48] What is more, the incremental expansion of the Bank's activities, in particular its turn to more macroeconomic policies, almost inevitably caused influence on the work of other IOs, as is not least exemplified by the example of the Doing Business reports and their EWI given in Chap. 4. It is nowadays established that this expansion of activities occurred in conformity with the Bank's AoA. Therefore, it may be concluded that the Bank also has implied competences to indirectly interact with other IOs when pursuing these activities.

---

[45]See e.g. Art. V(8) lit. b IBRD-AoA, which envisages the receipt of views and recommendations of other IOs.

[46]That this implies a treaty-making power of the IBRD is supported by Art. IV(7) IFC-AoA, which provides that "[the IFC], *acting through the Bank*, shall enter into formal arrangements with the United Nations and may enter into such arrangements with other public international organizations having specialized responsibilities in related fields" (emphasis added).

[47]Katherine A Hagen, 'Policy Dialogue between the International Labour Organization and the International Financial Institutions: The Search for Convergence' (2003) FES Occasional Papers No 9 <http://library.fes.de/pdf-files/bueros/genf/50035.pdf> accessed 26 April 2020, 13 et seq.; Francis Maupain, *The Future of the International Labour Organization in the Global Economy* (Hart Publishing 2013) 72 et seqq. On the long history of cooperation between the Bank and the IMF see Shihata, *The World Bank Legal Papers* (n 43) 773 et seqq.

[48]The most famous example involving both direct and indirect (conflictual) interactions is perhaps the cases of extending loans to apartheid South Africa and colonial Portugal, discussed in Chap. 14.

III. The Embeddedness of the World Bank's Competences to Interact

The World Bank's aforesaid competences to interact with other IOs are embedded in its wider institutional legal framework. As is the case with the ILO, this embeddedness moulds the Bank's competences to interact.

1. The World Bank's Obligation to Comply with Its Institutional Law During Interactions

The Bank's institutional law limits the Bank's competences to interact with other IOs in several ways. One major limitation it that. when engaging in inter-organizational interactions, the World Bank remains obliged to comply with its wider institutional legal framework.

The obligation to comply is explicitly spelled out in Art. V(8) lit. a IBRD-AoA, which requires that inter-organizational cooperation must occur "within the terms of" the IBRD-AoA. The wording and telos of this clause place inter-organizational cooperation within the IBRD's constitutional framework. Therefore, the clause can be seen as imposing a general condition of conformity with the (entirety of the) AoA.[49] Art. V(8) lit. a IBRD-AoA ties the Bank's inter-organizational interactions to norms in the AoA laying down the Bank's objectives, institutional structures and procedures.

It is striking that the wording of Art. V(8) lit. a IBRD-AoA is virtually identical to the 'within the terms' clause in Art. 12(1) ILO Constitution, examined in the previous chapter. Both clauses thus use the same formula to achieve an embedment into the respective own wider institutional legal framework.

2. The Obligation to Pursue the Bank's Objectives

A second important component of the Bank's wider institutional legal framework is its objectives. Art. I IBRD-AoA *in fine* explicitly requires that

> [t]he Bank shall be guided in all its decisions by the purposes set forth [in Art. I IBRD-AoA].[50]

Broadly speaking, the Bank's main objective has always been to promote the economic development of its member states. The particular interpretation and implementation of this overall objective has changed over time, not least because the concept of development itself has evolved. Today, the World Bank's two

[49] See *mutatis mutandis* Chap. 8 C. I.

[50] Similarly: Art. I IDA-AoA.

overarching goals are to effectively eradicate extreme forms of poverty and to promote sustainable development and shared prosperity in all countries.[51]

The Bank's obligation to pursue these objectives persists in the context of inter-organizational interactions.[52] As in the case of the ILO, the objectives usually leave a margin of discretion as to which measures the Bank may take. Still, they guide the Bank's interactive conduct.

3. Interaction-Specific Institutional and Procedural Rules

Moreover, the IBRD-AoA contain certain institutional and procedural rules specifically addressing aspects of inter-organizational interaction.[53]

As to the allocation of competences between the Bank's organs, Art. V(2) lit. b (v) IBRD-AoA provides that the power to "make arrangements to cooperate with other international organizations" is exclusively vested in the Bank's Board of Governors, which is its most senior organ. However, insofar as "informal arrangements of a temporary and administrative character" are concerned, the Board may delegate its power to the Executive Directors, the Bank's executive organ.

Regarding procedure, Art. V(8) lit. a IBRD-AoA provides that

> [a]ny arrangements for (...) cooperation which would involve a modification of any provision of this Agreement may be effected only after amendment to this Agreement under Article VIII.

---

[51] As formulated on the Bank's website: World Bank, 'Who we are' (*World Bank Website*) <https://www.worldbank.org/en/who-we-are> accessed 26 April 2020.

[52] Shihata, *The World Bank Legal Papers* (n 43) lviii.

[53] A clause which does not affects the IBRD's competences as an IO, but the allocation of competences to interact between its organs, is Art. V(2) lit. b (v) IBRD-AoA, according to which:

> [t]he Board of Governors may delegate to the Executive Directors authority to exercise any powers of the Board, except the power to: (...)
>
> (v) Make arrangements to cooperate with other international organizations (other than informal arrangements of a temporary and administrative character).

The clause reaffirms, and at the same time provides a limit to, the IBRD's internal organizational autonomy by reserving the competence to conclude formal inter-organizational agreements to the IBRD Board of Governors. This provision does not explicitly attribute competences on the IBRD or influences the scope of the IBRD's external competences. Instead, by allocating competences among its organs, it implicitly presupposes that the IBRD has the corresponding competence to conclude formal agreements. Similar provisions are Art. VI(2) lit c (v) IFC-AoA and Art. VI(2) lit c (v) IDA-AoA. Furthermore, an identical provision was made in the original 1944 Articles of Agreement of the International Monetary Fund (adopted at the UN Monetary and Financial Conference, Bretton Woods, New Hampshire, 22 July 1944, entered into force 27 December 1945) 2 UNTS 39 (IMF-AoA) (Art. XII(2) lit. b (iv)), but is not contained anymore in the present version of the IMF-AoA.

Art. VIII IBRD-AoA regulates the procedure for amendments of the IBRD-AoA.[54] According to this procedure, amendments require the acceptance by at least of three-fifths of the members holding 85 per cent of the voting power (Art. VIII lit. a IBRD-AoA). What is more, certain amendments in particularly sensitive matters require the acceptance of all members (Art. VIII lit. a IBRD-AoA). In the Bank's practice, it has proven extremely difficult to formally amend the AoA according to this procedure.[55] If taken literally, Art. V(8) lit. a IBRD-AoA would thus put a significant strain on the Bank's inter-organizational interactions, notably its competence to make arrangements for cooperation. However, as mentioned above, the AoA have almost never been formally amended, while at the same time, the Bank's purview has significantly expanded through interpretation. Against the backdrop of these developments, the practical relevance of Art. V(8) lit. a IBRD-AoA today is unclear.

Irrespective of their practical importance, both cited provisions indicate that the Bank's institutional law considers inter-organizational interactions that may result in legal obligations for the Bank or that are capable of influencing its constitutional framework a matter of fundamental importance and sensitivity. In line with this cautiousness, the Bank itself has (selectively) invoked Art. V(8) lit. a IBRD-AoA as justification to refuse to cooperate with other IOs.[56]

4. The Prohibition of 'Political' Activity

Perhaps the most impactful part of the Bank's wider institutional legal framework is its obligation to only be guided by economic considerations and to refrain from "political activity". This limitation is of central importance for inter-organizational interactions with the ILO, and indeed for labour governance writ large. Therefore, it deserves closer examination.

The prohibition to engage in political activity has played a prominent role throughout the World Bank's history.[57] One reason for this is that the prohibition puts the Bank in a dilemma: Many of its activities have, for better or worse, a

---

[54]René-Jean Dupuy, 'Le Droit Des Relations Entre Les Organisations Internationales' (1960) 100 Recueil des Cours de l'Académie de Droit International 461, 535.

[55]Shihata, *The World Bank Legal Papers* (n 43) 104; Daniel D Bradlow, 'Developing Countries Debt Crises, International Financial Institutions and International Law: Some Preliminary Thoughts' (2009) Washington College of Law Research Paper No. 2009/01, 9; Cissé (n 41) 83 et seq.

[56]For example with the UN and some of its specialized agencies regarding measures against Apartheid South Africa and colonial Portugal in the 1960s, Samuel A Bleicher, 'UN v. IBRD: A Dilemma of Funcationalism' (1970) 24 International Organisation 31, 40. While the Bank has been reluctant to cooperate with other IOs on other occasions, it appears that it has not publicly invoked Art. V(8) lit. a IBRD-AoA as justification since the 1960s.

[57]It has been repeatedly invoked by the Bank's Legal Counsel as being mandatory, Shihata, *The World Bank Legal Papers* (n 43) 805, with further references.

political dimension. This is especially true for macroeconomic activities like development policy lending, which are almost inevitably political in one or the other way. Moreover, other activities that explicitly or implicitly include the expression of preference for one or the other economic policy can easily be perceived as being 'political', including the Doing Business reports with their forthright support for reforms towards increased market liberalization and deregulation.[58] In such cases, the classification of an activity as 'political' becomes a decisive factor for assessing whether that activity is in conformity with the AoA.[59]

As the example of Doing Business illustrates, the prohibition of political activity can also become relevant with regard to inter-organizational interaction and influence. Direct and indirect interactions with other IOs can resemble political activity, and thus may exceed the World Bank's competence. Thus, the core question is whether, and to what extent, the prohibition moulds the World Bank's competence to engage in inter-organizational interaction.

a) The Clauses and Their Elements

The prohibition of political activity is not laid down in one central provision. Rather, it is included in several articles in different contexts, and in slightly varying language.

Art. IV(10) IBRD-AoA covers any and all activities of the Bank.[60] It provides that

> [t]he Bank and its officers shall not interfere in the political affairs of any member; nor shall they be influenced in their decisions by the political character of the member or members concerned. Only economic considerations shall be relevant to their decisions, and these considerations shall be weighed impartially in order to achieve the purposes stated in Article I.[61]

With special regard to loan conditionalities, Art. III(5) lit. b IBRD-AoA[62] provides that

> [t]he Bank shall make arrangements to ensure that the proceeds of any loan are used only for the purposes for which the loan was granted, with due attention to considerations of economy and efficiency and without regard to political or other non-economic influences or considerations.

---

[58] ibid 236.

[59] ibid 220.

[60] This textual interpretation is reinforced by the drafting history. A previous draft, which contained a narrower wording and only related to the granting of loans, was broadened up at the Bretton Woods Conference, United States Department of State, 'Proceedings and Documents of the United Nations Monetary and Financial Conference, Vol. I' (United States Government Printing Office 1948) 567 et seqq.; Shihata, *The World Bank Legal Papers* (n 43) 225.

[61] Similar prohibitions are laid down in Art. V(6) IDA-AoA, Art. III(9) IFC-AoA and Art. 34 MIGA Convention.

[62] Art. V(1) lit. g IDA-AoA provides similarly.

Finally, Art. V(5) lit. c IBRD-AoA[63] reads:

> The President, officers and staff of the Bank, in the discharge of their offices, owe their duty entirely to the Bank and to no other authority. Each member of the Bank shall respect the international character of this duty and shall refrain from all attempts to influence any of them in the discharge of their duties.[64]

From these three clauses, two principal elements can be distilled. Firstly, the Bank may base its decisions solely on economic considerations, thereby excluding non-economic considerations. Secondly, it may not engage in political activity, which is a particular kind of non-economic activity.[65] Though not being entirely congruent, both elements raise the question how to distinguish economic from non-economic, especially political, considerations.

aa) Wording, Context and Telos

The ostensibly clear-cut distinction in the wording of the respective provisions contrasts with significant difficulties to distinguish economic and political issues in practice.[66] Eventually, the wording remains rather inconclusive.[67] The interpretation of the context of the prohibition only provides minor insights. The IBRD-AoA anecdotally envisage activities which may fall in either of the 'economic' or 'non-economic' categories.[68] However, eventually, contextual interpretation does not provide a clear answer.[69]

---

[63]See also the similar provision of Art. VI(5) lit c IDA-AoA.

[64]This provision resembles a typical provision in IO constitutions regarding the international character of the IO's civil servants and their independence from member state influence. In the context of the World Bank Group, it reinforces the political independence of Bank staff, which in turn enables the latter to exercise their functions in a 'non-political' manner.

[65]As can be derived from the wording of Art. III(5) lit. b IBRD-AoA ("political or other non-economic influences or considerations").

[66]Ciorciari (n 42) 344.

[67]ibid 350. To approach the ordinary meaning of the cited clauses' wording, the World Bank's Legal Counsel has associated 'political' activities with political partisanship, whereas 'economic' activity concerned the "management" of a state's assets and resources, Shihata, cited in ibid 345. However, he himself recognizes that this distinction between 'partial' and 'objective' considerations alone will, however, hardly suffice to disentangle economic and 'other' considerations not least because it is contingent on the assumption that 'economic' considerations are always objective and non-partisan, which, especially in labour governance, can be questionable.

[68]For instance, Art. III(4)(v) IBRD-AoA implies that it is an economic consideration whether a borrower will be able to meet his obligations under a loan, Ciorciari (n 42) 346 et seq.

[69]To give but one example, Art. I(iii) IBRD-AoA enlists as activities "encouraging international investment" and "assisting in raising productivity, the standard of living and conditions of labor", both of which can have political ramifications, but are permissible, Shihata, *The World Bank Legal Papers* (n 43) 241.

The understanding of the object and purpose of the prohibition has undergone an interesting development.[70] During the Second World War, the prohibition of political activity was drafted and inserted into the IBRD-AoA with three particular reasons in mind. Firstly, the prohibition was supposed to ensure universal membership of the Bank and acceptability of the AoA for all states, regardless of their political and socio-economic character. This was particularly (though not only) relevant with regard to the USSR, which was then considered a potential Bank member.[71] Secondly, the prohibition was meant to safeguard economic sovereignty of the members.[72] Thirdly, the prohibition was intended to install the Bank as a technical, functional and neutral provider of guarantees for private investment, which was how the Bank was originally intended to function.[73]

However, the immediate post-war developments largely obsoleted these considerations. The first rationale of the prohibition faded as the USSR decided not to join the IBRD and it became apparent that the Bank would not attain universal membership.[74] Moreover, since private investors did not show interest in obtaining Bank guarantees, the IBRD could not function as a mere guarantor as originally envisaged. It had to engage in direct lending in order to fulfil its mandate. This also meant that the Bank had to obtain much larger amounts of liquid capital as it would have had to do as a mere guarantor for private investments.[75] This additional capital had to be borrowed from the capital markets, and, as Janse put it, "Wall Street did not trust an organization where political considerations played a role in decision-making."[76] Therefore, from 1947 onwards, the prohibition clause was employed to gain and maintain the trust of the capital markets. This has essentially remained its purpose and function until today.[77] Read in this light, 'political' in the sense of the prohibition means 'detrimental to trust in the Bank', a still rather vague interpretative result.

---

[70]See Eric Helleiner, 'Incremental Origins of Bretton Woods' in Orfeo Fioretos, Tulia G Falleti and Adam Sheingate (eds), *The Oxford Handbook of Historical Institutionalism* (Oxford University Press 2016) 617.

[71]Ronald Janse, '(Why) Was the World Bank Supposed to Be a Nonpolitical Organization? An Interpretation of the Original Meaning and Rationale of Article 4(10) of the Articles of Agreement of the International Bank for Reconstruction and Development, 1941–1948' (2014) 16 Journal of the History of International Law / Revue d'histoire du droit international 113, 155; Shihata, *The World Bank Legal Papers* (n 43) 226; Ciorciari (n 42) 365.

[72]Ciorciari (n 42) 368.

[73]Janse (n 71) 155; Shihata, *The World Bank Legal Papers* (n 43) 226; Cissé (n 41) 61.

[74]One could consider that, now that the Bank actually has attained quasi-universal membership, this first reason could be exhumed.

[75]The Bank had subscribed assets of 10 billion US$. However, 80 per cent thereof were not paid in, but resembled a guarantee fund subject to call only in case the Bank had to exercise its guarantor functions. Another 18 per cent were payable under certain conditions.

[76]Janse (n 71) 155; Cissé (n 41) 60.

[77]Albeit the importance of access particularly to the US financial markets has decreased, Kathryn C Lavelle, 'American Politics, the Presidency of the World Bank, and Development Policy' (2013) Policy Research Working Paper No. 6377 <https://elibrary.worldbank.org/doi/pdf/10.1596/1813-9450-6377> accessed 26 April 2020, 24.

In sum, the clauses make it difficult to distinguish 'economic' and 'political' considerations. The distinction seems to sever 'objective' considerations from 'partisan' views or interests. Permissible 'objective' considerations are meant to ensure the Bank's neutrality and impartiality, which serves to secure states' economic sovereignty, the Bank's creditworthiness in the eyes of its own creditors, and, last but not least, trust of those who rely on the Bank's authority as a provider of knowledge and advice.[78] With all necessary caution, 'political' considerations may thus be understood as all considerations which make the Bank appear 'biased' or 'partial' in the eyes of those who put trust in it.

bb) The Distinction of 'Political' and Other Activities in Subsequent Practice

The remaining unclarity has resulted in a rich and controversial subsequent practice. In the first decades of its existence, the World Bank essentially interpreted 'economic' as 'effective'.[79] The World Bank took on a decisively narrow economic approach, pointing to its limited competences. It hardly made 'political' conditionalities to loans.[80] Neither did it consider relevant glaring political grievances in borrowing countries, such as severe violations of human rights. The World Bank's philosophy led to an outright inter-organizational conflict within the UN System in the 1960s. when the UN General Assembly and several specialized agencies, including the ILO, condemned continuing apartheid in South Africa and Portugal's continuing colonial policy, and requested the Bank to cease financial support to these countries. The Bank, however, did not follow suit. Instead, it extended loans to both countries, invoking its 'non-political' mandate.[81]

The World Bank's rather strict interpretation of its AoA and its mandate prompted significant and persistent critique. The concerns were reinforced when the Bank turned to more macroeconomic policies, such as structural adjustment programmes, which sparked fears that the Bank will extend its competences, but not its responsibilities. Partially as a reaction thereto, the Bank gradually softened its stance on its interpretation of the prohibition clauses.[82]

---

[78] On the latter aspect Antony Angbie, 'International Financial Institutions' in Christian Reus-Smit (ed), *The Politics of International Law* (Cambridge University Press 2004) 223.

[79] Maupain, *The Future of the International Labour Organization in the Global Economy* (n 47) 73.

[80] Such as the extensive structural adjustment programmes of later decades, Sabine Schlemmer-Schulte, 'International Monetary Fund, Structural Adjustment Programme (SAP)', *Max Planck Encyclopedia of Public International Law* (Oxford University Press 2014) para 12 et seqq. (also elaborating on World Bank SAPs).

[81] Bleicher (n 56) 31; Maupain, *The Future of the International Labour Organization in the Global Economy* (n 47) 74.; Ciorciari (n 42) 351 et seqq. The case will be revisited in Chap. 14.

[82] One such case—compliance with measures the UN Security Council adopts under Arts. 41 and 42 UN Charter—is of no relevance for the present study, see Schlemmer-Schulte, 'International Bank for Reconstruction and Development (IBRD)' (n 42) para 107. The second exception refers to obvious internal political instability which could have a direct effect on the member's economic

From the 1990s onwards, the Bank has gradually developed a slightly less narrow stance on political issues.[83] Under the impression of pressure by human rights groups and upon a proposal by its General Counsel Ibrahim Shihata, the World Bank accepted that violations of human rights that could result in a loss of economic efficiency were 'economic' considerations that could lead to a termination or denial of projects.[84] In doing so, the Bank was relatively more open as to such rights it considered to be economic rights, whereas 'political' human rights were met with more scepticism.[85]

That being said, with regard to the 'political' traits of labour governance, the World Bank's stance has remained ambiguous and overall reserved. The Bank has actively engaged in issues of employment policy for decades. Moreover, as compared to its orthodox position in earlier decades, the Bank's general stance in recent years has opened a certain latitude for taking labour rights into account. Shihata's 'efficiency and economic growth-standard' has led the World Bank to focus on child labour, forced labour and discrimination, which were perceived as contributing to an efficiently functioning labour market.[86] In the late 1990s, the World Bank ceased activities in Myanmar, inter alia because of incidents of forced labour had occurred.[87] In 2014, the World Bank put on hold a loan to Uganda as a reaction of the country's adoption of a bill introducing life sentences for convictions of

---

development, which the Bank accepted as early as 1968, see Shihata, *The World Bank Legal Papers* (n 43) 228. In either case, the World Bank may take the respective conditions into account.

[83] As a kind of precursor to these developments, the General Counsel held in 1989, in the light of the Tiananmen square massacre, that political events in a member state can cause the President of the Board to postpone matters that are on the Board's agenda, Shihata, *The World Bank Legal Papers* (n 43) 199. See also Robert W Kneller, 'Human Rights, Politics, and the Multilateral Development Banks' (1980) 6 Yale Studies in World Public Order 361.

[84] Maupain, *The Future of the International Labour Organization in the Global Economy* (n 47) 74. Critical on Shihata's "direct and obvious" standard Ciorciari (n 42) 353. In 2006, General Counsel Roberto Daniño sought to further broaden Shihata's approach. Daniño's Legal Opinion on Human Rights and the Work of the World Bank stipulated, inter alia, that in cases of most serious human rights violations, the World Bank should withdraw its support regardless of whether these violations had an economic impact. The sole standard was that the World Bank could "no longer achieve its purposes." A summary of his stance is published in Roberto Dañino, 'The Legal Aspects of the World Bank's Work on Human Rights' (2007) 41 The International Lawyer 21. However, his proposal did not obtain the Executive Directors' approval and thus cannot be regarded an authoritative interpretation of the respective provision, Maupain, *The Future of the International Labour Organization in the Global Economy* (n 47) 75 et seq. Still, as per the 'Shihata doctrine', ubiquitous violations of human rights which can have an adverse effect on the economy of the country to which the Bank provides assistance do not fall under the prohibition and may therefore be taken into consideration, Schlemmer-Schulte, 'International Bank for Reconstruction and Development (IBRD)' (n 42) 107. See further The World Bank and OECD, *Integrating Human Right into Development* (2013).

[85] See Maupain, *The Future of the International Labour Organization in the Global Economy* (n 47) 74; Ciorciari (n 42) 356.

[86] Maupain, *The Future of the International Labour Organization in the Global Economy* (n 47) 75.

[87] ibid 77, fn. 42.

homosexuality.[88] Compared to its conduct in the cases of South Africa and Portugal in the 1960s, these developments show that the Bank has to some extent opened its policy for issues of forced labour and discrimination, which in the 1960s had been perceived as 'political'.

On the other hand, with regard to trade union rights, the World Bank has remained much more hesitant. In the long-held view of the Bank, trade union activity, while being capable of having positive effects,[89] can lever adverse effects on economic growth.[90] In this spirit of caution towards trade union rights, the World Bank initially denied support to the 1998 ILO Declaration on Fundamental Principles and Rights at Work.[91] In the following years, the Bank on several occasions stated its principal support for the declaration and the concept of fundamental principles and rights at work.[92] However, this principal support was not always followed through. The labour market reforms advocated for in the Doing Business reports indicate that the World Bank has retained an 'economized' stance on labour issues, with only a "limited accommodation" of labour standards and rights.[93]

In sum, subsequent practice has remained in flux and in dispute. The Bank has time and again strived to maintain the role of a technical, neutral and impartial institution. This, however, has repeatedly sparked critique and contestation. The mere fact that the Bank has been criticized for wrongly engaging in political

[88]Janse (n 71) 115. At the same time, WBG president Jim Jong Kim publicly stated that "Institutionalized discrimination is bad for people and for societies. Widespread discrimination is also bad for economies." He added that "[e]liminating discrimination is not only the right thing to do; it's also critical to ensure that we have sustained, balanced and inclusive economic growth in all societies", World Bank, 'World Bank Group President Jim Yong Kim: Discrimination by Law Carries a High Price' (*World Bank Website*) <http://www.worldbank.org/en/news/opinion/2014/02/28/world-bank-group-president-jim-yong-kim-discrimination-law-price> accessed 26 April 2020.

[89]World Bank, 'World Development Report 1995: Workers in an Integrating World' (1995) 80.

[90]For example, the World Bank's 1995 World Development Report names as a negative effect a "monopolistic behaviour" by unions: "Unions do often act as monopolists, improving wages and working conditions for their members at the expense of capital holders, consumers, and non-union (unorganized) labor. The higher wages unions win for their members either reduce business profits or get passed on to consumers in the form of higher prices. Either result leads unionized firms to hire fewer workers, increasing the supply of labor to the unorganized sector and depressing wages there", ibid 81. The policy recommendations made in that report, while emphasizing the importance of the individual right to join trade unions of one's choosing, include increasing domestic competition, promoting international liberalization, deregulation of the nonunionized labour market and decentralized collective bargaining at enterprise level in order to curtail unions' "monopoly power", i.e. to bargain for perceived unduly high wages, ibid 82 et seqq.

[91]Maupain, *The Future of the International Labour Organization in the Global Economy* (n 47) 77.

[92]Mark Anner and Teri Caraway, 'International Institutions and Workers' Rights: Between Labor Standards and Market Flexibility' (2010) 45 Studies in Comparative International Development 151, 156 et seqq.

[93]Franz Christian Ebert, 'Labour Standards and the World Bank. Analysing the Potential of Safeguard Policies for Protecting Workers' in Henner Gött (ed), *Labour Standards in International Economic Law* (Springer 2018) 277.

activities by some, while having been accused of ignoring political ramifications of its actions and 'not being political enough' by others, serves to illustrate the constant dilemma the prohibition clauses create.

b) The Prohibition as an Inherently Volatile Limit for Inter-Organizational Interactions

The prohibition of political activity limits the Bank's competence to engage in inter-organizational interactions.

At the outset, inter-organizational interactions do not per se amount to prohibited political activity. This can already be drawn from the aforesaid explicit obligation to cooperate with other IOs in the AoA. In addition, telling from the Bank's described subsequent practice, the mere fact that political questions are involved do not prevent the Bank from engaging in interactions. The Bank has on numerous occasions interacted with other IOs, including on a range of controversial and politically contentious matters.

However, the Bank has consistently attempted to maintain its neutral and impartial reputation during such interactions. In labour governance, this has at times led to a decidedly 'isolationist' practice, with the Bank refusing to cooperate altogether.[94] In a range of other cases, the World Bank has assumed only a limited role in an inter-organizational partnership or has only provided support for parts of the activities.[95] Again in other cases, the Bank has shown reticence in lending its support to other IOs, as the aforesaid examples of limited support for trade union rights or the contravention of ILO-supported processes (like those discussed in Chap. 4) show. All of these examples show the Bank's impetus, for better or worse, to stay out of politically contentious questions and leave them to other IOs.

That being said, the prohibition remains vague in concrete cases. One could ask, for instance, if the drafting and publication of the Doing Business reports and the promotion of the EWI as an authoritative benchmark for labour market regulation was compatible with the prohibition of political activity. As to the Bank's official publications, Legal Counsel Shihata held (before the Doing Business project was launched) that

> Bank research cannot serve its purposes if it is conducted according to a predetermined ideological or political orientation or subjected to revision based on such grounds (…). [Staff] should have freedom from political pressure and be subject only to the highest standards of excellence through review of their work by their peers and supervisors. Such review should also correct any ideological bias which may have influenced the research work, consciously or otherwise.[96]

---

[94] Cissé (n 41) 82.

[95] Examples provided by ibid 66 et seqq.

[96] Shihata, *The World Bank Legal Papers* (n 43) 236.

Given the deregulatory agenda of the Doing Business project, and given the Bank's hesitant reaction to methodological critiques, one might have serious questions if the Bank lived up to these standards. Assumed it did not, this would render the EWI and any emanating interaction to the detriment of the ILO a violation of the prohibition clause. However, it remains doubtful whether the Bank (which, as seen above, is competent to render authoritative interpretations of the prohibition) would concur in this view. Ironically, it would seem that the Doing Business reports' declaredly business-oriented approach was precisely aiming at producing 'non-political' rankings. Moreover, the IEG's 2008 report, which was a major step towards the EWI's eventual removal from the Doing Business ranking,[97] did not base its critique of the EWI on the latter being "political".

Either way, the discrepancy between Shihata's opinion and the early EWI practice illustrates how the delusive distinction between political and non-political issues even survives within the realm of competing normative visions and scientific methods.

c) Conclusion

In sum, the prohibition of political activity poses a highly relevant and yet inherently blurry legal limit on the Bank's exercise of its competences to interact with other IOs. Broadly speaking, 'political' considerations may thus be understood as all considerations which make the Bank appear 'biased' or 'partial' in those who put trust in it. However, the Bank's changeful practice has shown that, in the context of labour governance, the understanding of what is 'political' is subject to development and change. For the time being, one can thus only note that, for better or worse, the prohibition of political activity is an inherently volatile legal factor.

5. The Bank's Institutional Law's View on Other IOs' Governance Models, Needs and Demands

The Bank's institutional law does not only contain the aforesaid elements that mould and predetermine the Bank's competences to interact with other IOs. Rather, it also takes a reserved stance on these other IOs' governance models, needs and demands that might play a role during such interactions. At first glance, this reserved stance is less obvious than in the ILO's institutional law, because in comparison, the Bank's law contains more provisions requiring taking other IOs' positions and views into account. However, upon closer examination, these provisions are limited in scope and relevance (a). Moreover, beyond these clauses, the Bank's wider institutional legal framework does not accord particular importance to other IOs (b).

---

[97] See Chap. 4 C. III.

a) Obligation to Consider Views and Recommendations of Other IOs

As one relevant clause, the IBRD-AoA contain an explicit obligation to consider views and recommendations of other IOs regarding the granting of loans or financial guarantees. Art. V(8) lit. b IBRD-AoA provides:

> In making decisions on applications for loans or guarantees relating to matters directly within the competence of [any general IO or IOs having specialized responsibilities in related fields] and participated in primarily by members of the Bank, the Bank shall give consideration to the views and recommendations of such organization.

The provision aims at promoting inter-organizational coherence. However, the provision sets forth a number of important qualifications, some of which severely curtail the provision's scope and effect in practice.[98]

Firstly, Art. V(8) lit. b IBRD-AoA only refers to decisions on applications for loans and guarantees. *E contrario*, it does not apply to other activities.[99]

Secondly, the matter must fall "directly within" another IO's ambit. While the overall gist of Art. V(8) lit. b IBRD-AoA is to give deference to other IOs and draw on their expertise, the term 'directly' seeks to limit the scope of the provision.[100] However, this limitation is difficult to fill with meaning. "Directly within" semantically presupposes that a distinction between matters falling 'directly' and those falling 'indirectly' (or 'remotely') in another IO's competence is always possible and appropriate, which is a questionable premise to begin with.[101] Moreover, the determination of what is a 'direct' matter necessarily involves drawing distinctions within another IO's mandate that this other IO itself might draw differently, or not draw at all. Such 'second-guessing' of other IOs' mandates is prone to provoke dissonances with other IOs, which is the opposite of what the provision seeks to achieve. In sum, the 'directly within'-criterion adds to legal uncertainty concerning the Bank's competences to interact with other IOs.

Thirdly, if the aforementioned conditions are met, the legal consequence is that the Bank shall 'give consideration' to the other IO's views and recommendations.

---

[98] Other qualifications are less restricting. For instance, the loan or guarantee must relate to a matter that falls within the competence of another IO. The other IOs are those in the sense of Art. V(8) lit. b IBRD-AoA, which are the UN and all IOs working in "related fields". This is not qualification of great practical significance. The field of 'development finance' is broad enough to cover a wide range of IOs working in economic, social or other matters. Neither does the requirement that the other IOs' 'participants' must primarily be members of the IBRD result in much limitation, since the IBRD has 189 member states at the time of writing (April 2020).

[99] For example, it does not apply to views or recommendations of other IOs regarding the Bank's gathering or distribution of information, or the making of policy recommendations, like e.g. those based on the Doing Business reports.

[100] Somewhat alleviated by the fact that the loan or guarantee must only "relate" to the matter at issue.

[101] On its face, the "directly within"-criterion appeals to intuition, which indeed might help to come to plausible solutions in a number of cases, but eventually remains imprecise. How, for example, could one distinguish a matter falling directly in the ILO's competence from a matter which does not, given that the ILO's objectives are fairly broad and comprehensive themselves?

While in principle imposing an obligation, this obligation does not extend to actually adopting any considered view, or to follow any recommendation. The Bank has interpreted this obligation narrowly, both with reference to the wording of Art. V (8) lit. b IBRD-AoA and with the more teleological argument that the Bank needs to retain its independence from external influence.[102]

In sum, the obligation to give consideration specifies the Bank's general obligation to cooperate with other IOs when deciding on giving loans or guarantees. However, it embodies unclear prerequisites and does not impose any obligation to adjust the final decision according to the views and recommendations of other IOs.

b) The Abandoned IBRD Advisory Council

Interestingly, the drafters of the IBRD-AoA also contemplated an institutionalized form of inter-organizational cooperation. According to Art. V(6) lit. a IBRD-AoA,

> [t]here shall be an Advisory Council of not less than seven persons selected by the Board of Governors including representatives of banking, commercial, industrial, labor, and agricultural interests, and with as wide a national representation as possible. In those fields where specialized international organizations exist, the members of the Council representative of those fields shall be selected in agreement with such organizations. The Council shall advise the Bank on matters of general policy (...).

This provision, however, has quickly fallen into desuetude. The Advisory Council has not been convened since 1950.[103] In the subsequent practice of the Bank, other mechanisms have developed. Although sometimes labelled 'Advisory Council' too, they resemble topic-specific and more informal mechanisms.[104]

c) The 'Prioritization' Over Other IOs' Governance Models, Needs and Demands

In the remainder of the Bank's institutional law, other IOs' governance models, needs and demands do not play a particular role. The situation is comparable to the

[102]Bleicher (n 56) 36.

[103]Shihata, *The World Bank Legal Papers* (n 43) iv.

[104]Recent examples include the Advisory Council on Gender and Development (members of which comprise government officials, NGO representatives, academics and the Director of UN Women (World Bank, 'World Bank Advisory Council on Gender and Development' (*World Bank Website*) <http://www.worldbank.org/en/topic/gender/publication/world-bank-advisory-council-on-gender-and-development> accessed 26 April 2020), and the Advisory Council for the Strategic Framework for Mainstreaming Citizen Engagement in World Bank Group Operations (World Bank, 'Engaging with Citizens for Improved Development Results Strategic Framework for Mainstreaming Citizen Engagement in World Bank Group Operations, Expert Advisory Council, Terms of Reference' (2014) <https://consultations.worldbank.org/Data/hub/files/consultation-template/engaging-citizens-improved-resultsopenconsultationtemplate/materials/ce_advisory_group_tor_final_04072014.pdf> accessed 26 April 2020). Both of these mechanisms mostly comprise government officials, NGO representatives and academics. IOs are occasionally represented.

one under the ILO's institutional law: The Bank's institutional law does not prevent the Bank from giving regard to other IOs during interactions. However, aside from the aforementioned clauses, there is nothing in the IBRD-AoA *requiring* the Bank to do so.[105] While far from being outright 'hostile' to other IOs, the Bank's law nevertheless considers other IOs' governance models, needs and demands a matter of secondary importance, subjugated under the priority to fulfil the Bank's own objectives. By virtue of its institutional law, the Bank may choose to interact with other IOs in manifold ways, without giving regard to the implications its own conduct would have on the other IO's governance model, needs and demands.

IV. Consequence: The Relativization of the ILO's Model in the Law of the World Bank

The combination of the Bank's wide competences to interact, the guidance provided by its wider institutional legal framework, including the Bank's obligation to pursue its own objectives and the prohibition to engage in political activity, and the prioritization over other IOs' governance models, needs and demands is of high relevance for the role of the ILO and its model in the Bank's institutional law: As a consequence of these traits, the Bank's institutional law 'relativizes' the role and relevance of the ILO.

At the outset, none of the World Bank's constitutional provisions examined in the preceding sections mention the ILO. Those provisions that explicitly speak of other IOs address them globally as an undefined group, without particular mention of any specific IO. This is not too surprising, given the wealth and diversity of the international institutional landscape. Still, it also means that the Bank's institutional law does not put particular emphasis on the ILO and its model of labour governance. Rather, it treats the ILO as one out of many potential partners for inter-organizational interaction.[106]

What is more, the Bank's own institutional legal framework contains provisions that significantly predetermine the Bank's competences to interact with the ILO. The Bank's objectives—nowadays subsumed under the heading of eradicating poverty and promoting sustainable development—are at the same time sufficiently close to the ILO's to create major overlaps, and sufficiently different to give rise to the Bank having different priorities, agendas and policies.

---

[105]Notably, the obligation to cooperate with other IOs is, like in Art. 12(1) ILO Constitution, placed under the condition of such cooperation remaining "within the terms" of the IBRD-AoA, thus prioritizing the latter.

[106]This does not mean that the Bank's law is particularly hostile to the ILO. The ILO can play a role in the Bank's law, and so can its model of labour governance. Rather, one could say that the Bank's law is indifferent towards the ILO and its model.

A further case in point is the prohibition of political activity. To begin with, in labour governance, political impartiality is particularly hard to achieve, especially if understood as exclusively 'economic' considerations. Labour law and politics are dealing with inherent tensions and conflicting interests between workers, employers, governments and other stakeholders, which makes it particularly difficult to define and maintain a truly 'neutral' position. This difficulty persists when it comes to inter-organizational interactions. Just as the Bank struggles to cope with substantive 'political' issues, the Bank is bound to struggle with another IO's model of governance that is inherently 'political'. The ILO's model of labour governance is one such model. It is based on tripartite social dialogue, which is an institutionalized incarnation, as it were, of 'political' collective bargaining. Tripartite social dialogue does not always lead to solutions of pure economic reason, and, more importantly, it is not meant to do so. What is more, as mentioned in Chap. 2, the ILO's model is deeply engrained in its functioning and its output. Thus, the ILO's model cannot be reduced to its 'non-political' components. Neither can the Bank choose to focus on the ILO's output, e.g. by focusing solely on the text of ILO conventions, without considering their institutional contingency. Attempting to do so has led the Bank to assume that the EWI was compatible with all existing ILO conventions—a position the Bank itself later came to concede was erroneous.[107] Thus, the prohibition of political activity puts a major legal limit on the Bank's inter-organizational interactions with the ILO. Given the prohibition's inherently ambiguous and volatile character, it is at the same time a source of continuous legal uncertainty. Whether and to what extent the prohibition predetermines the Bank's interactions with the ILO significantly depends on how the pertinent clauses are interpreted and applied with regard to a certain subject-matter and at a given point in time.

In sum, the role of the ILO's model in the Bank's institutional law is relativized, in the sense that the Bank's institutional law gives precedence to other aspects, and widely allows the Bank to put the ILO on the backburner. Moreover, the prohibition of political activity requires the Bank, for better or worse, to 'filter' the ILO's work as to its 'political' or 'economic' character, because any engagement by the Bank in interactions with the ILO that can be qualified as non-economic or political would potentially be illegal under the Bank's institutional law.

V. Conclusion on the World Bank's Institutional Law

To conclude, the World Bank has broad competences to interact with other IOs. It has an attributed competence and obligation to cooperate, which bears close semblance to the ILO's. It has, moreover, an implied competence to interact with other IOs to pursue its objectives, which notably covers indirect interactions.

---

[107]See Chap. 4 C. III.

On the other hand, the Bank's competences are embedded in its wider institutional legal framework, which the Bank is bound to observe during inter-organizational interactions. In particular, the Bank is required to pursue its own objectives, to adhere to certain institutional and procedural provisions, and is prevented from engaging in 'political' activity. At the same time, the Bank's law is largely indifferent towards other IOs and—like the ILO's law—prioritizes the fulfilment of its own mandate over the concerns of other IOs.

These findings are of significant importance for inter-organizational interactions between the Bank and the ILO. The ILO does not play any particular role within the Bank's law. Rather, it is treated as one out of many IOs the Bank could potentially interact with. In addition, important AoA provisions, especially the prohibition of political activity, require the Bank to interact with the ILO only in a 'non-political' and 'economic' manner. Given that both the subject-matter the ILO is dealing with and its own institutional setup have inherently political traits, the prohibition, as it stands at present, may significantly reduce the scope of the Bank's competences to interact with the ILO and to give due regard to the ILO's model of labour governance.

C. The ILO's Model in the CoE's Institutional Law

The CoE's institutional law regulates how the CoE and its bodies may engage in inter-organizational interactions with other IOs. Insofar as relevant for interactions with the ILO, the pertinent provisions will be examined in the following.

I. Overview on the Sources of the CoE's Institutional Law

Again, it is convenient to start with a brief overview on the relevant sources of CoE institutional law. As mentioned in Chap. 5, the CoE has a decentralized institutional legal framework, i.e. its institutional law is spread across several instruments.

At the 'centre', there is the CoE Statute of 1949, a regional European treaty and the CoE's constituent instrument. It was adopted in 1949 with the intention of erecting a (western) European political IO that would promote European integration after the Second World War. Compared to other IOs, the CoE's constitutional framework is relatively open. The CoE Statute itself is rather sparse, both in terms of length and content.[108] Its provisions provide a 'platform', on the basis of which

[108] Christian Walter, 'Interpretation and Amendments of the Founding Treaty' in Stefanie Schmahl and Marten Breuer (eds), *The Council of Europe: Its Laws and Policies* (Oxford University Press 2017) para 2.12.

the CoE and its member states subsequently developed policies, instruments and 'constitutional dynamics'.[109]

Notwithstanding these developments and dynamics, the CoE Statute has almost never been formally amended.[110] Instead, the CoE has developed a practice of informal 'amendments' through so-called statutory resolutions. By their content and relevance, they have attained a constitutional character, and have had a significant part in developing the CoE's institutional legal framework. These statutory resolutions also deal with inter-organizational interactions. For present purposes, the most important ones are:

1) the Resolution adopted by the Committee of Ministers at its 8th Session, 3 May 1951, which was not yet officially called 'statutory' (hereinafter for reading convenience called "Statutory Resolution (51) 30"),[111] and
2) the (officially so called) 1993 Statutory Resolution (93) 26 on Observer Status.[112]

The legal character of statutory resolutions is not easy to ascertain.[113] For present purposes, it is not necessary to delve deeper into this question. As will be discussed below, the external competences laid down in Statutory Resolutions have never been called into question and are firmly established by consistent organizational practice. They are also necessary for an effective execution of the CoE's mandate. Thus, whatever their precise legal qualification, statutory resolutions will be included into this analysis as a basis for the CoE's competence to engage into inter-organizational interaction.

[109] ibid 2.20.

[110] Of the two formal amendment procedures foreseen in Art. 41 CoE Statute, one requires ratification by all CoE members and has never been successfully used, ibid 2.25. The other is thematically limited to issues concerning the PACE and financial matters, see Art. 41 lit. d CoE Statute and ibid 2.26.

[111] CM, Resolution (8th session, 3 May 1951) CETS No 8 (Statutory Resolution (51) 30).

[112] CM, Statutory Resolution (93) 26 on Observer Status (92nd session, 14 May 1993) <https://search.coe.int/cm/Pages/result_details.aspx?ObjectID=09000016804e42f6> accessed 26 April 2020.

[113] A specific category named 'statutory resolutions' is not foreseen in the CoE Statute. Technically, these resolutions, which are adopted by the CM, would count as CoE secondary law, Marten Breuer, 'The Council of Europe and International Institutional Law – An Appraisal' in Stefanie Schmahl and Marten Breuer (eds), *The Council of Europe: Its Laws and Policies* (Oxford University Press 2017) 946, para 38.13. However, they address constitutional issues and have explicitly been chosen to avoid a formal amendment procedure, Walter, 'Interpretation and Amendments of the Founding Treaty' (n 108) para 2.29). This 'intermediate' position has inspired various legal classifications by commentators. Statutory resolutions have been regarded as interpretations of the CoE Statute (see Michaela Wittinger, *Der Europarat: Die Entwicklung seines Rechts und der 'Europäischen Verfassungswerte'* (Nomos 2005) 114), internal customary law of the CoE (Karl Carstens, *Das Recht des Europarats* (Duncker & Humblot 1956) 219); Stefanie Schmahl, 'The Council of Europe Within the System of International Organizations' in Stefanie Schmahl and Marten Breuer (eds), *The Council of Europe: Its Laws and Policies* (Oxford University Press 2017) para 37.09), or a restatement of the CoE's implied powers, Wittinger (n 113) 114.

The substantive, institutional and procedural law of the CoE has evolved beyond the CoE Statute. Important matters are governed by separate treaties adopted within the CoE and separately ratified by the CoE members. As will be seen, many competences are tailored to certain specific of the CoE's organs or bodies. Other pertinent provisions are formulated more generally, but by their very nature only apply to some organs or bodies.[114] For present purposes, this normative decentralization is relevant, because the interactions between the ILO and the CoE examined in Part I largely occurred between the former and the ECtHR and the ECSR, both of which being bodies established by separate agreements.

II. Competences and Their Embeddedness

The CoE Statute is largely silent on inter-organizational interactions, leaving more room for implied competences than the laws of the ILO and the World Bank (1.). Explicit competences exist regarding inter-organizational agreements (2.).

1. The Basis: Implied Competences to Interact

The CoE Statute itself only contains few provisions on inter-organizational interactions. Virtually the only provision relevant in the present context is the subsidiarity clause of Art. 1 lit. c CoE, discussed below, which does not positively confer competences, but negatively limits the CoE's scope of action.[115] Therefore, the implied powers doctrine becomes relevant.

Pursuant to the implied powers doctrine, the CoE has implied competences to interact with other IOs. The main reason for this is the doctrine's objective of ensuring an effective performance of IOs' functions and achievement of objectives. The effective pursuit of most of the CoE's objectives will most likely require some kind of interaction with other IOs.

[114] However, conceptually, each body's competences discussed here should ultimately be conceived as those of the CoE.

[115] Art. 1 lit. d CoE Statute provides that the CoE shall not be competent to deal with maters of national defence. This provision is not relevant for present purposes and will thus not be discussed further here (on this provision and its application see Schmahl (n 113) para 37.06). Art. 32 CoE Statute, concerning the coordination of PACE and UNGA sessions, has fallen into desuetude (ibid 37.07). The CoE Statute does not contain any explicit provision on inter-organizational cooperation. Even more, except for Art. 40 CoE Statute, dealing with the seat agreement between the CoE and France, the CoE Statute does not contain any provision on the CoE's treaty-making power, Breuer (n 113) para 38.12.

In this regard, much comes down to the understanding of what is, in the sense of the implied powers doctrine, "essential, "necessary" or "appropriate".[116] Hypothetically, the CoE could perhaps manage to pursue its overall objective of European integration in complete isolation from any other IO. For instance, it could have drafted the ECHR without any recourse to the UN, the UDHR and the UN's preparatory work for the two UN human rights covenants, it could have drafted the ESC without any advice or assistance rendered by the ILO, and it could have promoted "greater unity between its members" (Art. 1 lit. a CoE Statute) without taking any notice of other IOs concerned with European integration. However, this would have hardly lived up to any reasonable standard of effectiveness. In all of the aforementioned examples, it arguably was "essential", necessary" or at least "appropriate" for the pursuit of the CoE's aims to interact with other IOs.

The subsequent practice of the CoE and its members have repeatedly confirmed this interpretation. The CoE's history includes a long and elaborate record of inter-organizational interaction of all kinds, e.g. including mutual consultations,[117] invitations to participate in CoE organs[118] and other bodies, or the conclusion of inter-organizational treaties.[119] The CoE Secretariat has an own Directorate of External Relations (DER), the mandate of which explicitly comprises inter-organizational relations.[120] In the Warsaw Declaration and Action Plan, adopted at the third CoE Summit of Heads of State and Government in 2005, the CoE member states reaffirmed their desire for complementarity and enhanced cooperation and interaction between the CoE and other IOs.[121]

Thus, the CoE must be deemed to have implied competences to interact with other IOs for the effective execution of its mandate.

---

[116]On the different strands of the implied powers doctrine see the references cited in the introduction to Part II.

[117]For early examples see e.g. Arthur Henry Robertson, *The Council of Europe: Its Structure, Functions and Achievements* (Stevens & Sons 1956) 133.

[118]See the extensive list of participating IOs and the respective bodies, CoE, 'Participation of International Organizations and Institutions in Council Of Europe Bodies' (2017) DER/INF(2017) 4.

[119]See CoE, 'Lists of Agreements Concluded by the Council of Europe with Other International Intergovernmental Organisations or Public International Institutions' (*CoE Website*) <https://www.coe.int/en/web/conventions/bi-or-multilateral-agreements> accessed 26 April 2020.

[120]CoE, 'Directorate of External Relations (DER)' (*CoE Website*) <https://rm.coe.int/16805970bf> accessed 26 April 2020.

[121]CoE, Warsaw Declaration, Adopted the Third Summit of Heads of State and Government of the Council of Europe (Warsaw, 16–17 May 2005) <https://www.coe.int/t/dcr/summit/20050517_decl_varsovie_EN.asp> accessed 26 April 2020 para 10; CoE, 'Warsaw Action Plan' (2005) CM (2005)80 para 8 et seqq., and Annexes 1 and 2.

2. Explicit Competence to Conclude Inter-Organizational Agreements

Contrary to the CoE Statute itself, Statutory Resolution (51) 30 contains a section entitled "Relations with intergovernmental and non-governmental international organisations" (fifth subheading of the Resolution). According to the provisions in this section, the CoE is competent to conclude inter-organizational agreements. It reads, in relevant parts:

> i. The Committee of Ministers may, on behalf of the Council of Europe, conclude with any intergovernmental organisation agreements on matters which are within the competence of the Council. These agreements shall, in particular, define the terms on which such an organisation shall be brought into relationship with the Council of Europe.

The CoE retains full discretion on whether or not to conclude such agreements. If it chooses to do so, the competence covers treaties with any IO on any matter falling within the CoE's ambit.[122] Within this outer boundary, the CoE is thus free to include any topic into an agreement.[123] The Resolution gives examples of topics to be included. It names the exchange of reports and information and the provision of services and giving of opinions by the CoE to other IOs.[124]

In practice, the CoE has entered into more than 30 working arrangements with other IOs, including some legally binding agreements, but also a broad spectrum of less formal arrangements, including so-called gentlemen's agreements, MoUs, exchanges of letters and others.[125]

Resolution (51) 30 only envisages agreements concluded by the CM. In practice, however, the PACE has developed parallel external relations.[126] These relations are

---

[122]Breuer argues that, since the CoE lacks the internal competence to legislate, the CoE was not competent to conclude law-making treaties containing substantive provisions (which he juxtaposes with treaties with other IOs, Breuer (n 113)) para 38.15. This is arguable for treaties which would necessarily require implementation via legislation by the CoE itself. Such treaties, however, will be the exception.

[123]The only 'mandatory' content required is that an agreement "define the terms on which such an organisation shall be brought into relationship with the Council of Europe" (para. i). This, however, virtually poses no limitations at all, as it essentially rephrases what a treaty would do anyway.

[124]The relevant passages read:

> iii. The agreement referred to in paragraph i may provide, in particular:
>
> a. that the Council shall take appropriate steps to obtain from, and furnish to, the organisations in question regular reports and information, either in writing or orally;
> b. that the Council shall give opinions and render such services as may be requested by these organisations.

[125]Schmahl (n 113) para 37.123.

[126]In the course of these parallel external relations, the PACE has entered into inter-organizational agreements, notably with other parliamentary assemblies, ibid 37.11. Furthermore, the PACE has developed a particular form of inter-organizational interaction, which could be called 'parliamentary review' of other IOs. Beginning with the OEEC in the 1950s, the PACE has made arrangements with other IOs to the effect that these other IOs inform the PACE about their activities by transmitting information and also by reporting in person to the assembly, Arthur Henry Robertson,

inter-parliamentary instead of intergovernmental in nature, reflecting the different nature of the CM and the PACE.[127] The PACE's bureau has issued guidelines for the Assembly's external action, which have been qualified as "internal soft law" of the CoE.[128] Whether and to what extent the PACE has the according organ competence to engage in inter-organizational interactions is unclear.[129] However, it has not been called into dispute that the CoE as a legal person has.

3. Specific Competences to Interact in the ECHR

The ECHR contains virtually no provision on direct inter-organizational interaction. The only exception is Art. 36(2) ECHR, pursuant to which the ECtHR's President may, "in the interest of the proper administration of justice", invite "any person concerned who is not the applicant" to make written submissions. Pursuant to this provision, other IOs have occasionally made submissions to the Court.[130] As to practice, the ECtHR's direct inter-organizational relations are sparse. The Court and individual judges maintain largely informal contacts with some other international judicial bodies, e.g. the CJEU or the IACtHR.[131] There is occasional hearsay evidence of (unpublished) presidential cooperation arrangements the ECtHR has made, e.g. with ITLOS.[132] Such agreements seem to be limited to matters concerning the Court's administration. Given the lack of practice, it remains unclear

Constitutional Developments in the Council of Europe (1964) 9. On the one hand, this enables the participating other IOs, which are mostly intergovernmental entities, to present their work to a parliamentary audience and to obtain parliamentary political support. On the other hand, this parliamentary interaction can also be seen as a nucleus for parliamentary political 'control' of those other IOs which do not have their own parliamentary body, Robertson, *The Council of Europe: Its Structure, Functions and Achievements* (n 117) 189 et seq.

[127]Schmahl (n 113) para 37.124.

[128]ibid 37.125.

[129]Similarly, it is unclear if the agreements thus concluded are binding on the CoE. Regarding both, see however the extensive rules on the PACE's external relations in Annex XII of the PACE's Rules of Procedure, PACE, Resolution 1202 (1999) 'Rules of Procedure of the Assembly (consolidated version of July 2019)' (4 November 1999).

[130]See e.g. *M.S.S. v. Belgium and Greece* ECHR 2011–I 255, para 7; William A Schabas, *The European Convention on Human Rights - A Commentary* (Oxford University Press 2015) 793. See also Rule 44(3) ECtHR Rules of Court (ECtHR, Rules of Court (2020) (adopted 4 November 2019, entered into force 1 January 2020 (ECtHR Rules of Court).

[131]Michael Nunner, *Kooperationen internationaler Gerichte - Lösung zwischengerichtlicher Konflikte durch herrschaftsfreien Diskurs* (Mohr Siebeck 2009) 174 et seqq.; Schmahl (n 113) para 37.117.

[132]Nunner (n 131) 173.

if and to what extent the ECtHR as a body has a competence to enter into such agreements.[133]

However, the Court is competent to engage in certain indirect inter-organizational interactions. First of all, regarding inter-state disputes, the ECHR explicitly concentrates jurisdiction in the Court. Pursuant to Art. 55 ECHR, the parties may not submit a dispute concerning the interpretation or application of the ECHR to any other dispute settlement mechanism than the one provided for in the ECHR.[134] In pending cases, the ECtHR has the competence to assume jurisdiction, even if the parties have brought the same matter before another body. This manifests a competence to interact indirectly with this other body, e.g. by deciding on the same subject-matter and thus influence the other body's further treatment of the case, should it not decline jurisdiction.

Furthermore, competences to interact indirectly can be implied, as they seem necessary for the exercise of its functions. Notably, according to Art. 31(1) lit. c VCLT, and as established in its jurisprudence, the Court has to take into account other rules of international law when interpreting and applying the ECHR. As was exemplified in Chap. 5, such recourse to other IOs' instruments and practice by the Court can have influence on those other IOs.

4. Specific Competences in the ESC

As already explained above, the relevant provisions in the ESC are themselves the result of inter-organizational interaction between the CoE and the ILO. The express provisions in the ESC concerning inter-organizational interaction fall into three categories: Obligations to inform or notify, an obligation to invite representatives and an obligation to establish a working relationship. The relevant provisions have already been dealt with in a sufficient manner in Chap. 6.[135]

III. The Embeddedness of the CoE's Competences to Interact

Similar to the ILO and the World Bank, the CoE is required to observe its own institutional law during inter-organizational interactions.

[133] The scarcity of practice which would support implied competences is hardly surprising, given that the ECtHR as an independent judicial body is not mandated to engage in direct interaction with other IOs on a significant scale. The Court as a judicial body primarily communicates though its decisions, which do not resemble direct communication with other IOs.

[134] The only exception foreseen in Art. 55 ECHR is a "special agreement".

[135] See Chap. 6 B. II.

1. The CoE's Objectives

Pursuant to Art. 1(1) CoE Statute, the CoE's aim is

> to achieve a greater unity between its members for the purpose of safeguarding and realising the ideals and principles which are their common heritage and facilitating their economic and social progress.

Building on this objective, both the ECHR and the ESC stipulate as their respective purposes the protection and realization of the rights each of them contains.[136]

In principle, the CoE and its organs and bodies have to observe and pursue these objectives during inter-organizational interactions. However, given the extraordinary breadth of these objectives, their moulding effect on the CoE's competences to interact will be modest at most.

2. Interaction-Specific Rules

Furthermore, there are certain provisions specifically addressing inter-organizational interactions.

a) The Subsidiarity Clause in Art. 1 lit. c CoE Statute

The only relevant explicit provision in the CoE Statute is Art. 1 lit. c CoE Statute. This provision contains a general subsidiarity clause, pursuant to which:

> [p]articipation in the Council of Europe shall not affect the collaboration of its members in the work of the United Nations and of other international organisations or unions to which they are parties.

The scope of this provision is fairly comprehensive. It covers all IOs, regardless of any qualifying criteria, such as subject-matter, functions and objectives, territorial scope of operation or scope of membership. Moreover, the clause applies irrespective of whether the other IO was established before or after the CoE or if all or just some CoE members are also members in the other IO.[137]

The legal consequence is, in principle, a general and unqualified subsidiarity of CoE activities. Taken literally, this would mean that the CoE has to refrain from any activities which would affect the collaboration of CoE members in other IOs. The French version (*ne doit pas altérer*) suggests that Art. 1 lit. c CoE Statute only refers to adverse effects. Still, the wording can be understood as being thoroughly strict,

---

[136] See ECHR, preambular clause 5; ESC, preambular clauses 3 and 4. The overall object and purpose of the ESC is to secure the enjoyment of social rights without discrimination, to improve the standard of living and to promote the social well-being of the parties' populations.

[137] With convincing arguments Carstens (n 113) 217.

and indeed was applied rather rigidly in the CoE's early days, especially by the CM.[138]

However, the subsidiarity clause appears less restrictive when seen in the systematic context of the whole CoE Statute. An example for such a less restrictive systemic perspective are provisions on the PACE's competences. As is apparent from Art. 23 lit. a CoE Statute, the PACE in any case retains its competence to discuss and make recommendations on any matter falling within the scope of the CoE. When drafting its agenda for doing so, the PACE shall merely have regard to the work of other (European) IOs (Art. 23 lit. b CoE Statute). It does not have to refrain from discussing issues dealt with by other IOs, even if doing so would have adverse effects.[139] On the contrary, such spill-over effects are intended, as they can also give new impulses to other IOs.[140]

Subsequent practice has confirmed a less restrictive reading of the subsidiarity clause. In particular, as illustrated in Chaps. 4 and 5, the subsidiarity clause has not prevented the CoE from extensively engaging in labour governance. Today, the subsidiarity clause is employed to the effect that the CoE "steers clear"[141] of issues concurrently dealt with by other IOs.

In sum, despite its broad wording, Art. 1 lit. c CoE Statute cannot be read as posing an overly strict limitation on the CoE's competence to interact with other IOs.

b) The Lis Alibi Pendens Rule in Art. 35(2) lit. b ECHR

An explicit provision governing the ECtHR's indirect interactions is Art. 35(2) lit. b ECHR. Pursuant to that provision's second alternative, the ECtHR shall not deal with any individual application that is substantially the same as a matter that has already been submitted to another international procedure for investigation or settlement and contains no relevant new information. The provision embodies the

---

[138] ibid. For example, precautions were taken to ensure that CoE meetings would not be scheduled for the same time as meetings of other IOs, Florence Benoît-Rohmer and Heinrich Klebes, *Council of Europe Law: Towards a Pan-European Legal Area* (Council of Europe Publishing 2005) 22. With regard to ongoing parallel work on social security within the CoE and the ILO in the early 1950s, the CM stalled its own efforts to enhance social security until the ILO had completed its work on what was to become ILO Convention No 102 (ILO Social Security (Minimum Standards) Convention, 1952 (No 102) (adopted 28 June 1952, entered into force 27 April 1955) 210 UNTS 131). After the ILO had completed its work, the CM resumed its own work with the aim of achieving higher levels of protection than those adopted by the ILO, Arthur Henry Robertson, *The Relations Between the Council of Europe and the United Nations* (UNITAR 1972) 132.

[139] Schmahl (n 113) para 37.08. Carstens' more general argument that political deliberations can never adversely affect other IOs' work (Carstens (n 113) 218) is too optimistic—and ultimately depends on whether one assesses an effect to be negative or positive.

[140] CM, 'Programme of Work of the Council of Europe' Communication of the CM (6th session (first part), 20 May 1954) Doc 238, para 16; Carstens (n 113) 218.

[141] Schmahl (n 113) para 37.06.

lis alibi pendens rule in favour of other bodies.[142] It seeks to avoid parallel proceedings in the same matter and, thus, a situation in which mutual influence could occur reading the same subject-matter.[143] The ECtHR has also applied this rule in favour of the ILO.[144]

3. Limitation Through Narrow Mandates and Formalized Procedures

Besides the aforementioned explicit provisions moulding the competences to interact, institutional and procedural constitutional rules gain particular relevance in the case of the ECtHR and the ECSR. As judicial or quasi-judicial bodies, the two bodies' activities are neatly regulated through the ECHR and ESC and their respective rules of procedure. Both bodies have comparatively narrow mandates of supervision and dispute settlement and operate though highly formalized procedures.

The high degree of formalization and 'legalization' has important implications for the ECtHR's and ECSR's competences to engage in inter-organizational interactions. The strict organizational and procedural rules serve as *a priori* limitations on any inter-organizational interaction the two bodies could legally engage in. No inter-organizational interactions may exceed either the ECtHR's and ECSR's institutional rules, including their composition, competences and independent functioning, or their procedural rules. Given the comparable density of institutional and procedural rules in the ECHR and the ESC, these rules predetermine the exercise of the Court's and the Committee's competences to interact with other IOs to a significant extent. This is particularly relevant for the ECtHR. The Court has only limited options for interaction with other IOs. For instance, in the absence of specific rules to this effect, the ECtHR cannot enter into consultations with the ILO, nor can it invite ILO representatives to participate in its deliberations in a consultative capacity (like the ECSR can, pursuant to Art. 26 ESC). Rather, it is confined to informal personal contacts or to indirect interaction.

---

[142] E.g. UN human rights bodies or investment tribunals, Jens Meyer-Ladewig and Birgit Peters, 'Art. 35' in Jens Meyer-Ladewig, Martin Nettesheim and Stefan von Raumer (eds), *Europäische Menschenrechtskonvention* (4th edn, Nomos 2017) para 32 et seqq.

[143] See *OAO Neftyanaya Kompaniya Yukos v. Russian Federation* App No 14902/04 (ECtHR, 20 September 2011), para 520.

[144] In *POA and others v. United Kingdom*, the ECtHR declared the complaint inadmissible because the matter was already pending before the CFA, *POA and Others v. United Kingdom* App No 59253/11 (ECtHR 21 May 2013); Angelika Nußberger, 'The ECtHR' Use of Decisions of International Courts and Quasi-Judicial Bodies' in Amrei Müller and Hege Elisabeth Kjos (eds), *Judicial Dialogue and Human Rights* (Cambridge University Press 2017) 419, 427. In *RMT v. United Kingdom*, the applicant trade union had submitted a parallel complaint to the CFA, which it had, however, "irrevocably withdrawn" at a later point. The ECtHR found that, since there was no risk of parallel decisions, the case was admissible, *ECtHR, National Union of Rail, Maritime and Transport Workers v. United Kingdom* ECHR 2014–II 1, paras 46 et seqq.

IV. Consequence: The ILO's Relativization in the Law of the CoE

What, then, is the role and relevance of the ILO in the CoE's institutional law? The only provisions in the examined parts of the CoE's institutional law that explicitly mention the ILO and create concrete competences and obligations regarding inter-organizational interactions with it are those in the ESC which have been examined in Chap. 6. These are the only provisions that, to a limited extent, contain rules aiming at the recognition and promotion of the ILO and its work. By contrast, in the other examined provisions, the ILO is not given any particular relevance. While the CoE's law is not treating the ILO 'worse' than other IOs, it does not accord particular importance to the latter. Leaving the aforementioned provisions aside, the CoE has rather large discretion under its institutional law to prioritize its own agenda over the ILO's, or simply to disregard the ILO altogether.

Again, given the number and the diversity of IOs, a 'special treatment' for the ILO in the CoE's law was not to be expected. Still, the ILO's limited role even in the ESC is remarkable: As seen, the relevant (R)ESC provisions are the result of a cooperation of exceptional character, based on the CoE's conscious decision to draft a treaty with a close thematic proximity to ILO instruments, the institutional and procedural mechanisms of which were inspired by and closely modelled after the ILO's, and the ILO's prolonged and extensive involvement in the ESC's drafting and reform. What is more, while the institutional link between the ECSR and the ILO exists and endows the ILO with a more 'favourable' position vis-à-vis the ECSR than other IOs, the link does not expand the ECSR's competences to interact with the ILO beyond establishing and maintaining a working relationship. The Committee's competences remain embedded in, and thus moulded by, the (R)ESC's wider constitutional framework, including notably the limitation arising from the latter's institutional and procedural rules mentioned above.

But also beyond the question of explicit mention and reference to the ILO, it appears that, like in the case of the World Bank, the CoE's institutional law relativizes the ILO's model. However, in the CoE's case, the relativization is of a different nature. Unlike in the case of the World Bank, there are no major substantive prohibitions, such as the prohibition to engage in political activity. Rather, the ILO's relativization in the CoE's institutional law mostly emanates from the institutional and procedural rules of the Court and the Committee. Both bodies can only have regard to the ILO insofar as their comparatively strict and formalized institutional and procedural rules allow. The relativizing effect of this is most visible in the case of the Court. The ECtHR can only have regard to the ILO in the context of a specific case in which usually only the individual applicant and the respondent state are parties. The Court can consider then ILO and its work either in the context of the facts presented to it by the parties or in the course of legal reasoning and interpretation of the ECHR. Moreover, since the Court is constituted as an independent judicial body, it must retain the 'last word' on whether and how to have recourse to the ILO. This institutional and procedural setting almost inevitably implies that the

ILO's model of governing through universal tripartite social dialogue and persuasion cannot fully resound in the ECtHR's activities. Given that the CoE's institutional law creates this situation, it relativizes the role and relevance of the ILO.

V. Conclusion on the CoE's Institutional Law

Determining the CoE's competences to interact with other IOs almost inevitably involves an element of uncertainty and approximation. This is due to the decentralized structure of the CoE and the scarcity of written provisions on inter-organizational interaction, which make it necessary to rely on the implied powers doctrine and on organizational practice. Nonetheless, the survey has revealed that the CoE as a whole has wide competences to interact with other IOs. Moreover, the only explicitly spelled-out limitation to these competences, the subsidiarity clause in Art. 1 lit. c CoE Statute, has not gained much relevance in organizational practice.

That being said, the analysis has also shown that the CoE's competences to interact are embedded within, and therefore limited by, its wider constitutional framework. Notably, the ECtHR's and ECSR's narrow mandates and highly formalized procedures limit these bodies' margin in which they can legally engage in inter-organizational interaction. The obligation to adhere to each and any provision of CoE institutional law, whether or not specifically regulating inter-organizational interaction, gains specific relevance here. As is the case with the World Bank, the CoE's institutional law relativizes the ILO and its model of labour governance.

D. The Implications of the ILO's Relativization in the Bank's and CoE's Institutional laws

As shown in Chap. 8 and in the course of this Chapter, the ILO's, World Bank's and CoE's institutional laws each prioritize their respective own objectives, institutional structure, procedures and results. While each of these institutional laws allows and sometimes even demands interaction with other IOs, each of them ultimately subjugates such interaction to the imperatives of its own legal framework.

For the ILO, this means that its institutional law allows it to protect and promote its own model of labour governance in inter-organizational interactions and prioritize it over the governance models, needs or demands of other IOs. However, at the same time, it also means that these other IOs may likewise prioritize their own governance models, irrespective of whether this has repercussions on the ILO or not. In sum, each of the interacting IOs finds legal justification for its activities, and for influencing the respective other, in its respective own institutional law.

The implications of this abstract finding can be illustrated by (tentatively) applying it to the instances of inter-organizational interactions presented in Chaps. 3–5. Judging by their respective institutional laws, there is a prima facie case that all observed activities of all examined IOs were legal. For instance, it would appear that the ILO was competent under its own institutional law to criticize the Bank's conception and use of the EWI, and to work actively against it, in order to promote its own initiatives, its labour conventions and its normative vision of 'good' labour regulation based on universal tripartite social dialogue and persuasion. However, at the same time, it seems that the World Bank, judging by *its* institutional law, was entitled to create, disseminate and use the EWI, to maintain it over years and to ignore the ILO's critique. Not being bound by ILO law, it appears further that the Bank may have also been entitled to render its own assessment on whether the EWI was in conformity with ILO standards, and to insist on EWI-induced labour law reforms regardless of the latter's conformity with ILO conventions.

In much the same way, it would appear that the ILO was competent to directly and indirectly influence the CoE and its bodies regarding the protection and promotion of labour-related human rights. At the same time, the CoE was, pursuant to *its* own law, competent to follow (and repeatedly ask for) the ILO's input in the case of the ESC, while also being competent to largely ignore the ILO when drafting the ECHR. The ECtHR, for its part, was competent to align its jurisprudence to ILO instruments and practice in some cases, while deviating from them in others as a matter of sheer discretion. The ECSR was competent to follow ILO practice in most of its work. Yet it would arguably also be competent not to do so in future cases, despite the existence of the institutional link between the ECSR and the ILO.

As can be seen from these examples, the fact that each IO's institutional law relativizes the role of the respective other is not negative per se. It does not automatically lead to inter-organizational incoherence and conflict. The ILO's influence on the drafting and the implementation of the ESC shows that interactions can still present themselves as harmonious and synergetic. However, the examined IOs' institutional laws provide a legal basis for inter-organizational interactions *regardless of* whether they have a conflictual character or not. Indeed, they provide a legal basis for a vast array of inter-organizational interactions of all different types and sorts. What is more, while each IO's institutional law values inter-organizational interaction with other IOs, it ultimately rates the potential impact of such interactions on other IOs lower than the observance and fulfilment of its respective own institutional imperatives. This means that in cases of doubt, the other IO has to stand back.

In sum, the ILO's, World Bank's and CoE's institutional laws do not mitigate the ambivalence of inter-organizational interactions described in Chap. 7. Given the prevailing structural relativization of the role and relevance of other IOs, one could even be inclined to claim that the institutional laws *reinforce* inter-organizational interactions' ambivalence (a point to be revisited in Chap. 17).

E. Conclusion

The chapter has scrutinized the legal framework that the respective institutional laws of the World Bank and the CoE set for inter-organizational interactions with the ILO.

On a general level, the analysis has revealed that both the World Bank and the CoE have wide and permissive competences to interact with other IOs. On the other hand, the analysis also revealed that these competences are embedded in the World Bank's and CoE's respective wider institutional legal framework, which include important limitations. In the case of the World Bank, the prohibition of political activity is such a limitation. In the case of the ECtHR and the ECSR, it is the body-specific tight regulation and formalization of their mandates and procedures. These limitations significantly mould the Bank's and CoE's competences to interact with the ILO.

What is more, it became apparent that, with the exception of the (R)ESC, the ILO and its model of labour governance are relativized in the institutional law of the World Bank or the CoE. There are neither explicit references, nor is there any indication that the organizational practice of the Bank or the CoE has developed the institutional legal framework of these IOs with a particular view to promote the ILO and its model. This does not mean that the ILO is entirely irrelevant for the Bank or the CoE, but it mostly takes the role of one out of many other IOs. This does not really come as a surprise. Considering the breadth of the Bank's and the CoE's respective mandates, there is no real reason why particularly the ILO should be mentioned. Broadly speaking, labour issues simply are not in the centre of attention for the Bank and the CoE.

However, it needs to be constated that the Bank's and CoE's institutional laws subjugate the ILO and its model to their own principles and normative priorities. While both the Bank and the CoE may widely use their competences to interact in a way that would give (more) deference to the ILO's model, the fact that these competences are embedded into (and must be exercised with regard to) the wider institutional legal framework critically mitigates the urgency to actually do so. The embeddedness reduces the relative importance the ILO and its work are given by the World Bank's and CoE's institutional laws.

All in all, given the structural prioritization of the respective own organization and the relativization of the ILO, the examined institutional laws hardly, if at all, mitigate the ambivalence of inter-organizational interactions described in Chap. 7.

10. The ILO's Relativization: Predetermination and Dynamic Evolution

The ILO's relativization in the institutional laws of the World Bank and CoE is, at least in parts, idiosyncratic in the text of the respective constituent instruments. Yet, as was seen, both the respective competences and the wider institutional legal framework they are embedded in have developed over time. Some of them have significantly expanded, as is illustrated by the ECtHR's living instrument approach. Some have gradually changed their meaning, like the prohibition of political activity in the World Bank's institutional law. And finally, the relevance of some written constitutional provisions has decreased, such as the subsidiarity clause in Art. 1 lit. c CoE Statute, or entirely fallen into desuetude, such as the Advisory Council foreseen in Art. V(6) lit. a IBRD-AoA.

These examples highlight an underlying dynamic: the institutional legal norms leading to the ILO's relativization are not entirely static—they can evolve. This implies that the ILO's relativization could evolve with them and become diminished (or aggravated) over time. It is therefore warranted to address in more detail the underlying legal mechanisms of this dynamic, which are, firstly, dynamic interpretation and, secondly, the 'specialization' of the applicable law of treaties. This chapter will elaborate on these mechanisms in abstracto, before Chap. 11 will discuss to what extent these mechanisms could mitigate the relativization of the ILO's model of labour governance in the institutional laws of the other IOs.

A. Predetermination in Constituent Instruments

At the outset, it needs to be mentioned that the relativization of other IOs is, at least to a certain extent, idiosyncratic in IOs' institutional laws. Pertinent examples are the aforementioned requirement to cooperate "within the terms" of the constituent

H. Gött, *The Law of Interactions Between International Organizations*, Beiträge zum ausländischen öffentlichen Recht und Völkerrecht 299, https://doi.org/10.1007/978-3-662-62389-3_10

instruments (Art. 12(1) ILO Constitution; Art. V(8) lit. a IBRD-AoA) or the obligation to pursue the respective own objectives (Art. 1(1) ILO Constitution; Art. I IBRD-AoA). In addition, implied powers to interact with other IOs tend to emphasize the respective own IO's objective, mandate and agenda.[1] The pertinent institutional legal provisions provide the normative framework within which each IO may deal with other IOs according to its administrative needs and policy choices.

B. The Malleability of Relativization Through Constitutional Dynamics

However, the stance that the ILO's, the Bank's and the CoE's institutional laws take on the respective other IOs is not static. Rather, the pertinent constitutional provisions defining how and to which extent other IOs are relativized are malleable and subject to development.

It has frequently been observed that IOs' institutional laws, notably their constituent instruments, are particularly prone to development and evolution. Two types of developments can be distinguished, namely developments via interpretation (I.) and a process of incremental 'specialization' of the law (II.). Both may lead to modifications of IOs' institutional laws' relativizing perspectives on the role and relevance of other IOs.[2] What is more, IOs themselves have considerable influence on whether and to what extent such developments happen. As the analysis in Chaps. 8 and 9 has shown, all examined IOs retain discretion to design their mutual interactions according to their political or administrative needs and preferences. Some of the choices thus made can become legally relevant, e.g. when particular interpretations of constitutional provisions are chosen over others, when amendments to the constituent instrument or other relevant instruments are made, or when a practice is deliberately repeated and 'hardens' into law.

[1] This is a consequence of the method of implying powers whenever this is 'necessary' for the effective attainment of an IO's objectives. Every IO has its specific objectives, which may overlap, but will virtually never be identical with those of other IOs. Thus, deriving competences and obligations from an IO's individual set of objectives will inevitably result in an individual set of implied powers suited to pursue them, whether or not this is reconcilable with other IOs.

[2] Changes can occur regarding the attributed or implied powers to interact with other IOs, or regarding the wider context of an IO's institutional law in which the IO's rules on inter-organizational interaction are embedded. See in general Christian Djeffal, *Static and Evolutive Treaty Interpretation - A Functional Reconstruction* (Cambridge University Press 2015).

I. Interpretative Dynamics

Interpretation of IOs' institutional laws, particularly their constituent instruments, can evolve in different directions. The constituent instruments of the IOs examined in this study are treaties, to which—at least in principle—the general law of treaties applies, including the general rules of interpretation laid down in Arts. 31–33 VCLT.[3] This is made explicit by the first part of Art. 5 VCLT. These rules leave ample leeway to choose different interpretative approaches or emphasize methods, thus developing the interpretation of IOs' institutional law in different directions (1.). The IOs examined in this study can take an active and important role in initiating or reinforcing such developments (2.).

1. Choosing Interpretative Approaches and Methods

Arts. 31-33 VCLT do not provide a strict normative corset for interpretation but leave leeway to adopt different interpretative approaches and to emphasize one or another of the enumerated interpretative methods.

Regarding the interpretation of IOs' constituent instruments, scholarly literature often distinguishes 'traditional' and 'constitutionalist' approaches.[4] Each approach emphasises different interpretative methods.[5] Essentially, traditionalist approaches

[3]The determination of competences and obligations of IOs depends on the interpretation of their constituent instruments, *Conditions of Admission of a State to Membership in the United Nations (Article 4 of the Charter)* (Advisory Opinion) [1948] ICJ Reports 57, 61.

[4]This distinction is based on two major conceptual approaches to understanding constituent instruments: the 'traditionalist' approach (emphasizing the treaty nature of most constituent instruments) and the 'constitutionalist' approach (highlighting the constitutive function of the constituent instrument). The terms are being used here following Shabtai Rosenne, *Developments in the Law of Treaties 1945–1986* (Cambridge University Press 1989) 191, with further references. The debate is related to earlier debates on typological distinctions between treaties, such as the distinction between *traités-contrats* and *traités-lois*, the origins of which date back over a century, See ibid 182 et seqq.; Arnold D McNair, 'The Functions and Differing Legal Character of Treaties' (1930) 11 British Yearbook of International Law 100, 105 et seqq and 117. It is often emphasized that IOs' constituent instruments have a dual function: They are, on the one hand, (usually) treaties concluded between member states. On the other hand, they are constituting the IO. In its *Use of Nuclear Weapons in Armed Conflict* opinion, the ICJ held that "[f]rom a formal standpoint, the constitutive instruments of international organizations are multilateral treaties, to which the well-established rules of treaty interpretation apply. [...] But the constitutive instruments of international organizations are also treaties of a particular type; their object is to create new subjects of law endowed with a certain autonomy, to which the parties entrust the task of realising common goals. Such treaties can raise specific problems of interpretation owing, inter alia, to their character which is conventional and at the same time institutional", *Legality of the Threat or Use of Nuclear Weapons* (Advisory Opinion) [1996] ICJ Reports 226, paras 74 et seq.

[5]José E Alvarez, 'Constitutional Interpretation in International Organizations' in Jean-Marc Coicaud and Veijo Heiskanen (eds), *Legitimacy of International Organizations* (United Nations University Press 2001) 136; Nigel D White, *The Law of International Organizations* (2nd edn, Juris

seek to fit IO's constituent instruments squarely into the general law of treaties. In consequence, their interpretation is considered essentially a matter of 'normal' treaty interpretation.[6] By contrast, constitutionalist approaches highlight the special character of constituent instruments, the need for uniform interpretation, flexibility and dynamics in order to achieve the organizational objectives.[7] Against this background, they tend to relativize 'traditional' elements of treaty law, such as the requirement of consent and unanimity in the implementation and further development of the treaty.[8] Constitutionalist writers also often highlight the evolutive interpretative practice to be observed in IOs and in adjudicatory proceedings dealing with such practice.[9]

Interpretative practice does not strictly follow these different approaches but is more nuanced.[10] That being said, constitutionalist interpretation has gained much relevance in the ILO, the World Bank and the CoE, significantly affecting these IOs' institutional laws' perspective on the role and relevance of other IOs. For instance, the World Bank's turn to engage in non-project-specific lending and in providing development policy expertise led it to define an own normative vision of labour regulation that conflicted with the ILO's. The ECtHR's development of its 'living instrument approach' enabled it to accord a more important role to the ILO and its work.

Publishing 2005) 26; Christopher Peters, *Praxis Internationaler Organisationen - Vertragswandel und völkerrechtlicher Ordnungsrahmen* (Springer 2016) 137 et seqq.; Christian Walter, 'Interpretation and Amendments of the Founding Treaty' in Stefanie Schmahl and Marten Breuer (eds), *The Council of Europe: Its Laws and Policies* (Oxford University Press 2017) 23; Ian Brownlie, 'Problems Concerning the Unity of International Law', *Le droit international à l'heure de sa codification. Études en l'honneur de Roberto Ago, vol I (Giuffrè 1987)* 160.

[6]Rosenne (n 4) 194.

[7]Saunders proposes to apply domestic legal principles of constitutional interpretation as general principles of law in the sense of Art. 38(1) lit. c ICJ Statute, Imogen Saunders, 'General Principles of Law and a Source-Based Approach to the Regulation of International Security Institutions' in Hitoshi Nasu and Kim Rubenstein (eds), *Legal Perspectives on Security Institutions* (Cambridge University Press 2015) 138 et seqq.

[8]Rosenne (n 4) 194 et seq.

[9]ibid 194.

[10]Catherine Brölmann, 'Specialized Rules of Treaty Interpretation: International Organizations' in Duncan B Hollis (ed), *The Oxford Guide to Treaties* (Oxford University Press 2012) 507; Rosenne (n 4) 183; Isabelle van Damme, 'Treaty Interpretation by the Appellate Body' (2010) 21 European Journal of International Law 605, 618. For instance, in its *Use of Nuclear Weapons in Armed Conflict* opinion, the ICJ did not satisfy itself with an abstract determination of the constitutional character of the WHO Constitution, but engaged in an extensive and detailed interpretation of the pertinent rules of the WHO Constitution, the UN Charter and the UN-WHO Agreement, as well as in a range of resolutions of the World Health Assembly *Legality of the Use By a State of Nuclear Weapons in Armed Conflict (Request of the World Health Organization)* (Advisory Opinion) [1996] ICJ Reports 66, paras 74 et seq., 77 and 80. Results may vary even with respect to individual provisions of one treaty, some of which (e.g. those using broader generic terms) will be more open for teleological reading than others with a more clear-cut wording.

2. Rendering Authoritative and 'Simple' Interpretations

Moreover, interpretative developments are not something that is merely imposed on IOs by their member states or other actors. Rather, IOs can play an active and important role in creating or reinforcing interpretative developments that affect their institutional laws' stance on other IOs.

For one part, IOs can cause or reinforce interpretative dynamics insofar as they possess the competence to interpret their own laws authoritatively. Generally speaking, authoritative interpretation of a treaty is the prerogative of its parties, i.e. the IO's member states.[11] That being said, in the ILO's[12] and the World Bank's[13] constituent instruments, as well as the ECHR and the ESC',[14] the competence for authoritative interpretation is partially vested into specific organs or bodies. Such authoritative interpretations can set important impulses for developing the

[11]The PCIJ stated in its *Jaworzina* opinion that "it is an established principle that the right of giving an authoritative interpretation of a legal rule belongs solely to the person or body who has power to modify or suppress it", *Delimitation of the Polish-Czechoslovakian Frontier (Question of Jaworzina)* (Advisory Opinion) PCIJ Rep Series B No 8, 37. See also *Territorial Dispute (Libyan Arab Jamahiriya/Chad)* [1994] ICJ Reports 6, 31 et seq.

[12]The ICJ's competence for authoritative interpretation of the ILO Constitution and ILO conventions has already been discussed above. The ICJ's opinions are binding by virtue of Art. 37 ILO Constitution. As explained, this competence was only used during the interwar period and has laid dormant since 1932, see Chap. 2 C. III. 3.

[13]In the World Bank, questions of interpretation are decided by the Executive Directors (Art. IX lit. a IBRD-AoA). If a member state objects to the interpretation, the Board of Governors takes the final decision (Art. IX lit. b IBRD-AoA). Hence authoritative interpretation is formally vested in the Board of Governors. In the Bank's early practice, the Executive Directors issued a number of formal interpretations. Subsequent practice, however, developed in a less formal direction. With one exception, it has been consistent practice since 1964 that the World Bank's Legal Counsel drafts a legal opinion on matters of interest, which is then endorsed or concurred in by the Executive Directors. In this vein, the development of the Bank's mandate is to a significant part the work of its Legal Counsel, Ibrahim FI Shihata, 'The Creative Role of the Lawyer – Example: The Office of the World Bank's General Counsel' (1999) 48 Catholic University Law Review 1041, 1048; 'International Law and the Operations of the International Financial Institutions' in Daniel D Bradlow and David Hunter (eds), *International Financial Institutions and International Law* (Kluwer Law International 2010) 1, 13. By now, this can be seen as a form of established practice to obtain 'authoritative' interpretations of the AoA.

[14]The CoE Statute does not provide rules on its authoritative interpretation. Yet, as to the ECHR, Arts. 32 and 55 ECHR vest interpretative competence in the ECtHR. The ECtHR's judgments are formally binding only inter partes (Art. 46(1) ECHR), but nevertheless may be regarded as authoritative interpretations of the ECHR at large. Regarding the ESC, the 1991 Amending Protocol vests competence in the ECSR to interpret the ESC from a legal point of view. This has been considered as conferring the competence of authoritative interpretation on the ECSR, Klaus Lörcher, 'Interpretation' in Niklas Bruun and others (eds), *The European Social Charter and the Employment Relation* (Hart Publishing 2017) 52. Moreover, both the 1961 original Charter and the RESC contain Annexes which set forth various agreed interpretations, which form integral parts of the respective treaties (Arts. 38 ESC and Art. N RESC).

interpretation of the IO's constituent instrument. Moreover, they tend to be resilient against subsequent reversal.[15]

An organ of an IO which is not competent to render authoritative interpretations will still almost inevitably render 'simple' interpretations. The reason for this is that as a very practical matter, IOs must at least incidentally interpret their own law in order to properly discharge their functions.[16] For present purposes, such non-authoritative interpretations are of great importance as well, because they can trigger interpretative dynamics by themselves.[17] Insofar as 'simple' interpretations are progressive and put emphasis on teleological or 'constitutional' considerations, they contribute to the dynamic development of an IO's institutional law. The relevance is even higher given that many mechanisms for authoritative interpretations that are built-in in IOs' constituent instruments are hardly ever being used.[18]

---

[15]In order to reverse or to adjust them, the member states would either have to formally amend the constituent instrument or to adopt a binding interpretation by themselves (insofar the law of the IO allows—as seen in Chap. 1, such interpretative declarations by member states alone are not permissible under ILO law).

[16]In order to assert whether a norm was properly applied or implemented, it can be necessary to incidentally verify what exactly it is that the norm requires the IO's organ or the member states to do—the answer to which is to be given by (incidental) interpretation. For example, with regard to the UN, the ICJ held in *Certain Expenses* that "each organ must, in the first place at least, determine its own jurisdiction", *Certain Expenses of the United Nations (Article 17, Paragraph 2 of the Charter) (Advisory Opinion)* [1962] ICJ Reports 151, 168; Chittharanjan Felix Amerasinghe, *Principles of the Institutional Law of International Organizations* (Cambridge University Press 2005) 25 et seq. As Hexner put it, "in this sense the application of the provisions of the basic instruments is co-extensive with their interpretation", Ervin P Hexner, 'Interpretation by Public International Organizations of Their Basic Instruments' (1959) 53 American Journal of International Law 341. Such interpretations might, depending on the procedural rules at play, result in granting organs, or certain constituents thereof, a wide margin to make interpretative choices, see critical Rosenne (n 4) 227 et seqq.; Henry G Schermers and Niels M Blokker, *International Institutional Law* (6th edn, Brill 2018) para 1344.

[17]For instance, they can resemble subsequent practice in the sense of Art. 31(3) lit. b VCLT, which is the case at least insofar as such interpretation can be understood as practice of the IO's member states, Oliver Dörr, 'Art. 31 VCLT' in Oliver Dörr and Kirsten Schmalenbach (eds), *Vienna Convention on the Law of Treaties - A Commentary* (2nd edn, Springer 2018) para 86.

[18]As seen in Chap. 1, in the ILO, this reluctant use of authoritative mechanisms is no coincidence, but part of an intentional choice of the IO to keep interpretations 'in the balance' between the tripartite constituents. It thus largely remains untested whether 'simple' interpretations rendered and acted upon by an IO resemble authoritative interpretations.

II. 'Specialization' of the Applicable Rules of General International Law

Besides interpretative dynamics, there is a second way how IOs' institutional laws' perspective on the role and relevance of other IOs can develop. This second type of dynamics can be described as a process of incremental 'specialization' of rules of general international law that apply to IO's institutional laws.

In principle, IOs' institutional laws are embedded in general international law, notably the general law of treaties. However, any special rule pertaining to either the constituent instrument or treaties adopted within the IO (such as e.g. ILO conventions, the ECHR or the ESC[19]) take precedence over these general rules as *leges speciales*.[20] This precedence of special rules is laid down in a range of international instruments.[21] For instance, Art. 5 VCLT reads:

> [The VCLT] applies to any treaty which is the constituent instrument of an international organization and to any treaty adopted within an international organization *without prejudice to any relevant rules of the organization.* (emphasis added)

Art. 5 VCLT determines not only the scope, but already the *applicability* of the VCLT. This is an important conceptual point.[22] It means that any existing "rules of the organization" take precedence, irrespective of how different they are from the VCLT's general provisions.[23] This is not to say that special rules on these topics

[19]As to the ECHR, the CoE's observer at the 1968 Vienna Conference voiced doubts if it would qualify as a constituent instrument, UN, Summary Records of the Plenary Meetings and of the Meetings of the Committee of the Whole, United Nations Conference on the Law of Treaties (1st session, Vienna, 26 March-24 May 1968) Official Records (1969) UN Doc A/CONF.39/11, 47, para 18. However, in any case, the ECHR qualifies as a treaty adopted within an IO, namely the CoE (Art. 15 CoE Statute). The same is true for the ESC.

[20]As can be drawn from both the wording ("without prejudice") and from the drafting history, the last part of Art. 5 VCLT confer on the "relevant rules of the organization" the status of *lex specialis* over the general rules laid down in the VCLT, Mark Eugen Villiger, 'Art. 5' in Mark Eugen Villiger (ed), *Commentary on the 1969 Vienna Convention on the Law of Treaties* (Brill 2009) para 7; Kirsten Schmalenbach, 'Art. 5 VCLT' in Oliver Dörr and Kirsten Schmalenbach (eds), *Vienna Convention on the Law of Treaties: A Commentary* (2nd edn, Springer 2018) para 15. This is also true for Art. 5 VCLT-IO, David Heywood Anderson, 'Art. 5 VCLT-IO' in Olivier Corten and Pierre Klein (eds), *The Vienna Conventions on the Law of Treaties - A Commentary, vol 1* (Oxford University Press 2011) para 17. The French version ("sous reserve") is even more emphatic, ibid 5.

[21]It is recognized that Art. 5 VCLT codifies customary international law, see Villiger (n 20) para 10, with further references. This was already stated at the Vienna Conference, UN, Summary Records of the Plenary Meetings and of the Meetings of the Committee of the Whole (n 19) 52, para 73.

[22]For this systemic relevance, Art. 5 VCLT was considered one of the most important provisions at the time of drafting the VCLT, see UN, Summary Records of the Plenary Meetings and of the Meetings of the Committee of the Whole (n 19) 44, para 31.

[23]Depending on their own scope and content, special "rules of the organization" can take precedence over any rule of the general law of treaties, including the rules on central issues such as conclusion, amendment, making of reservations, validity, interpretation, termination, or suspension.

exist in every IO.[24] However, Art. 5 VCLT opens the gate for creating a 'special law of treaties' that applies to an IO's constituent instrument and treaties adopted within it. Thus, IOs cannot only develop the *understanding of their constituent instrument* by dynamic interpretation, but also the *law of treaties* which applies to their constituent instrument.

Importantly, the term 'rules of the organization' is not limited to written rules laid down in the IO's constituent instrument or its secondary law. Rather, it is common ground that the rules also encompass unwritten rules that emerge from the established practice of IOs.[25] Hence, any unwritten rules emerging from established practice take precedence over the general VCLT rules.

For instance, Art. 5 VCLT can replace the interpretative rule contained in Art. 31(3) lit. b VCLT that "any subsequent practice in the application of the treaty which establishes the agreement of the parties regarding its interpretation" needs to be taken into account, by a rule merely requiring subsequent organ practice of an IO, regardless of whether all member states agreed to it, Christopher Peters, 'Subsequent Practice and Established Practice of International Organizations: Two Sides of the Same Coin?' (2011) 3 Goettingen Journal of International Law 617, 637. On the problems of meeting the evidentiary standard of Art. 31(3) lit. b VCLT Julian Arato, 'Subsequent Practice and Evolutive Interpretation: Techniques of Treaty Interpretation over Time and Their Diverse Consequences' (2011) 9 Law and Practice of International Courts and Tribunals 443, 455 et seq. Aust gives as examples rules on the adoption and amendment of treaties and on reservations, Anthony Aust, 'Vienna Convention on the Law of Treaties (1969)', *Max Planck Encyclopedia of Public International Law* (Oxford University Press 2008) para 10; Schmalenbach (n 20) para 16 highlights rules on interpretation and amendment.

[24]Nor does it mean that every kind of organizational practice surpasses the threshold of Art. 5 VCLT and elevates to become *lex specialis*. For a comprehensive study of the prerequisites of Art. 5 VCLT see Peters, *Praxis Internationaler Organisationen - Vertragswandel und völkerrechtlicher Ordnungsrahmen* (n 5).

[25]The VCLT does not define the term "rules of the organization" any further. The requirement of a "rule" merely implies that there must be some kind of normative proposition, the observance of which is mandatory. This view, with a tendency to assume that rules should have a legal character, was also prevailing at the 1968 Vienna Conference, UN, Summary Records of the Plenary Meetings and of the Meetings of the Committee of the Whole (n 19) 147, para 15. Moreover, Art. 5 VCLT simply speaks of "*any* relevant rules" (emphasis added), without imposing limits as to the form or the substance of these rules. Hence, the wording suggests that, as to substance, the provision covers all procedural, institutional, substantive and methodological rules. As to form, the wording does not impose any qualifying conditions. Similar Rudolf Bernhardt, 'Interpretation and Implied (Tacit) Modification of Treaties. Comments on Arts 27, 28, 29 and 38 of the ILC's 1966 Draft Articles on the Law of Treaties' (1967) 27 Zeitschrift für ausländisches öffentliches Recht und Völkerrecht 491, 494. Unlike the VCLT, Art. 2(1) lit. j VCLT-IO contains an explicit definition of the term 'rules of the organization', which "means, in particular, the constituent instruments, decisions and resolutions adopted in accordance with them, and established practice of the organization." This definition reappears in almost identical language in further instruments, such as in Art. 2 lit. b DARIO (which lists, next to decisions and resolutions, "other acts of the organization") and in Art. 1 (1) No 34 Vienna Convention on the Representation of States in their Relations with International Organizations of a Universal Character (adopted 14 March 1975, not yet in force) UN Doc A/CONF.67/16. Moreover, the ILC purposefully drafted the list as a non-exhaustive one, "since the rules of the organization may also include such instruments as agreements concluded by the organization with third parties and judicial or arbitral decisions binding the organization", ILC, 'Draft Articles on the Responsibility of International Organizations, with Commentaries' [2011]

The inclusion of 'established practice' increases the dynamics of the 'specialization' of IOs' institutional laws. Practices are, firstly, different in every IO, with the effect that 'established practice' can refer to different things in different IOs.[26] Secondly, established practice is particularly prone to changes and modifications over time. Indeed, these temporal dynamics were intended from the start. The ILC highlighted that it was

> not its wish to freeze practice at a particular moment in an organization's history.[27]

For the present study, this is of important systemic relevance. As indicated before, both the ILO and the other examined IOs have developed own rules for 'their' treaties. In particular, the ILO's manifold specific rules for ILO conventions, described in Chap. 2, must be mentioned here. The ILO had done so long before the VCLT was adopted, and it is no coincidence that it had a decisive influence on

---

YILC Vol II Part Two 46, Art. 2, para 16. A similar explanation was given as to the VCLT-IO, ILC, 'Draft Articles on the Law of Treaties between States and International Organizations or between International Organizations, with Commentaries' [1982] YILC Vol II Part Two 17, Art. 2, para 25. It seems to be common ground that the definitions in the VCLT-IO and further instruments are of indicatory relevance for the construction of Art. 5 VCLT, Schmalenbach (n 20) para 15. This view is also supported by the VCLT's drafting history. At the 1968 Vienna Conference, the UK delegation suggested to rewrite the phrase as "relevant rules *and established practices*" (emphasis added), UN, Summary Records of the Plenary Meetings and of the Meetings of the Committee of the Whole (n 19) 44, para 31. Special Rapporteur Waldock stated in response to the UK's proposal that the ILC had understood the term 'rules of the organization' to encompass established practice, ibid 57, para 40. In an interpretive statement, Mustafa Kamil Yasseen, the Chairman of the Drafting Committee (to which the UK's proposal had been referred), stated that the Drafting Committee "had taken the view that the term 'rules' in article 4 [now Art. 5 VCLT] applied both to written rules and to unwritten customary rules", ibid 147, para 15.

[26]As to the VCLT-IO, the ILC emphasized that the reference to established practice was "in no way intended to suggest that practice has the same standing in all organizations; on the contrary, each organization has its own characteristics in that respect", ILC, 'Draft Articles on the Law of Treaties between States and International Organizations or between International Organizations, with Commentaries' (n 25) 21, para 25.

[27]ibid. Furthermore, and perhaps most oddly, as far as the VCLT-IO is concerned, the definition of 'rules of the organization' contained in Art. 2(1) lit. j VCLT-IO, including 'established practice', is itself subject to deviating definitions which might be contained within the rules of an IO. This is the consequence of Art. 2(2) VCLT-IO, according to which the definitions in Art. 2(1) VCLT-IO are without prejudice to any deviating use of those terms or meanings set forth by the rules of any IO.

the drafting of Art. 5 VCLT,[28] to which some even refer to as the 'ILO clause'.[29] The relevance of Art. 5 VCLT will be exemplified in Chap. 11, with regard to unwritten special interpretative practices established in the IOs under consideration here.

C. Conclusion

The World Bank's and CoE's rules relativizing the ILO, i.e. their competences to interact and the wider institutional legal framework they are embedded in, are not static, but can develop dynamically and 'specialize'. This is due to both interpretative dynamics and the possibility for IOs to develop their special 'rules of the organization' which take precedence over otherwise applicable general rules of international law, notably the law of treaties. This chapter has elaborated on these mechanisms in abstracto.

In the light of these findings, it needs to be examined next what legal relevance these dynamics have for the ILO's role and relevance in the Bank's and CoE's institutional laws.

[28]In the 1960s, the ILO inter alia sent legal memoranda and letters to the UN; Trebilcock, 'The International Labour Organization' in Michael J Bowman and Dino Kritsiotis (eds), *Conceptual and Contextual Perspectives on the Modern Law of Treaties* (Cambridge University Press 2018) 854 et seq.; Ralf Günther Wetzel and Dietrich Rauschning, 'Waldock Report IV' in Ralf Günther Wetzel and Dietrich Rauschning (eds), *Commentary on the 1969 Vienna Convention on the Law of Treaties, Travaux préparatoires* (Metzner 1978) 90 et seq. At the Vienna Conference on the Law of Treaties in 1968, the ILO had observer status, which it allowed to take influence on the draft of what was to become Art. 5 VLT. The ILC had previously discussed how to reconcile the aspired general codification of the law of treaties with the fact that IOs had developed their own rules and practice. This in particular concerned the ILO, which then already was an elderly IO with almost 50 years of established practice concerning inter alia the drafting, adoption, interpretation and modification of treaties, namely international labour conventions. In his Fourth Report, Special Rapporteur Waldock had proposed to draft a general rule, ILC, 'Fourth Report on the Law of Treaties, by Sir Humphrey Waldock, Special Rapporteur' (1965) UN Doc A/CN.4/177, 18. However, at the seventh session of the Conference's Committee of the Whole in May 1968, a number of states proposed to deal with the issue in a selected number of provisions only. Against this proposal, the ILO's then Principal Deputy Director-General and Former Legal Adviser Clarence Wilfred Jenks, appearing as observer for the ILO in the Committee, presented a list of numerous instances in which established ILO rules and practice were at odds with the proposed draft VCLT. He argued that only a general provision—like the one ultimately agreed on in Art. 5 VCLT—would ensure the compatibility of ILO rules and the VCLT, UN, Summary Records of the Plenary Meetings and of the Meetings of the Committee of the Whole (n 19) 36 et seqq., para 2 et seqq. The Committee of the Whole, similar to the Conference later on, followed this proposal. Jenks' intervention has received widespread reception until today, with the effect of ILO practice still being cited as one prominent example of the scope of application of Art. 5 VCLT, e.g. Schmalenbach (n 20) para 4.

[29]Trebilcock, 'The International Labour Organization' (n 28) 855.

11. Mitigating Relativization via Coherent Interpretation?

If the ILO's relativization is subject to constitutional dynamics, such dynamics may enhance the ILO's role and relevance in the institutional laws of the World Bank and the CoE.

One way how this could happen is through coherent interpretation, i.e. through interpreting provisions in the World Bank's and CoE's institutional laws in a manner that gives deference to the ILO, its instruments and its activities. Indeed, coherent interpretation is one of the most frequently discussed means of enhancing the relevance of topics across different bodies of international law. The goal of such debates is to pursue what has been referred to as systemic integration of different bodies of international law, thereby enhancing the role and relevance of the respective other and eliminating conflicts.[1] The normative basis for coherent interpretation is Art. 31(3) lit. c VCLT, pursuant to which the interpreter shall take into account

> any relevant rules of international law applicable in the relations between the parties.

With its extensive study of Art. 31(3) lit. c VCLT, which formed a significant part of its 2006 report on the issue of fragmentation of international law, the ILC has

[1]ILC, 'Fragmentation of International Law: Difficulties Arising from the Diversification and Expansion of International Law, Report of the Study Group of the International Law Commission, Finalized by Martti Koskenniemi' (2006) A/CN.4/L.682 para 419. See also Campbell McLachlan, 'The Principle of Systemic Integration and Article 31(3)(c) of the Vienna Convention' (2005) 54 International and Comparative Law Quarterly 279, 311. On the desirability to avoid conflicts see Clarence Wilfred Jenks, 'The Conflict of Law-Making Treaties' (1953) 30 British Yearbook of International Law 401, 427 et seqq. A presumption against conflict has been accepted, inter alia, by the *Case concerning the Right of Passage over Indian Territory (Portugal v India)* (Preliminary Objections) [1957] ICJ Reports 125, 142.

H. Gött, *The Law of Interactions Between International Organizations*, Beiträge zum ausländischen öffentlichen Recht und Völkerrecht 299, https://doi.org/10.1007/978-3-662-62389-3_11

markedly reinforced the debate.[2] The ILC and several commentators have expressed optimism that systemic integration could help to avoid conflict and promote coherence.[3]

In the light of such optimism, it appears appropriate to enquire into the prospects of systemic integration through coherent interpretation to enhance the role of the ILO's model in the institutional laws of the World Bank and the CoE.[4]

A. Specifying the Question Pursued in This Chapter

At the outset, the question pursued in this chapter needs to be clarified. The bulk of the debate on systemic integration has centred on whether it is *possible* to reconcile different international legal norms via interpretation. For two reasons, this is not the question that will be pursued here.

First, the preceding chapters have already revealed that the ILO, the World Bank and the CoE each have substantial discretion to decide whether and how to design their mutual inter-organizational interactions. This includes the option to do so in a 'systemically integrated' way, i.e. to take the law of other IOs into account when interpreting the respective own law. Thus, discussing the *possibility* of systemic integration through interpretation, while of course not futile, would not lead much further than the result already arrived at in the preceding chapters.

Second, discussing only the possibility of systemic interpretation largely ignores the human (or in this context: organizational) factor: The mere fact that a certain interpretation is possible does not imply that an IO must actually avail itself of this possibility. As seen above, IOs have considerable leeway to influence the interpretation of their own laws, and they may choose not to adopt a 'systemically integrated' interpretation. In this light, it is important to know not only whether coherent interpretation is possible, but whether it is legally *required.*

Hence, this chapter will ask whether and to which extent the World Bank and the CoE are *obliged* to adopt an interpretation of their own laws that would enhance the role of the ILO's model of labour governance.

[2]ILC, 'Fragmentation of International Law: Difficulties Arising from the Diversification and Expansion of International Law, Report of the Study Group of the International Law Commission, Finalized by Martti Koskenniemi' (n 1) para 410 et seqq.

[3]ibid Conclusions 17-21; Oliver Dörr, 'Art. 31 VCLT' in Oliver Dörr and Kirsten Schmalenbach (eds), *Vienna Convention on the Law of Treaties - A Commentary* (2nd edn, Springer 2018) para 95.

[4]Some authors consider the question of the relation between two IOs' constituent instruments as a question of inter-organization relations, see e.g. Tobias Winkler, *Die Vereinten Nationen im Gefüge der internationalen Organisationen – Eine rechtsdogmatische Untersuchung* (Nomos 2019) 61. Coherent interpretation, however, is best understood as a question of every IO's respective institutional law, because it concerns the interpretation of one IO's particular constituent instrument, in which other IOs' constituent instruments are merely taken into account as part of the applicable rules of international law.

B. Fundamental Issues

Asking not for the potentials, but for the legal imperatives of interpretative rules leads to a range of fundamental questions. Two of these questions will be addressed: Whether interpretative rules resemble international legal obligations at all (Sect. I.) and whether the World Bank and the CoE are the legal addressees of any such obligations (Sect. II.).

I. Do Interpretative Rules Resemble Legal Obligations?

At the outset, it needs to be clarified if the VCLT's interpretative rules contain legal obligations at all.

When approaching this question, one first encounters the methodological dilemma that the obligatory character of interpretative rules again needs to be determined by norm interpretation, resulting in a potentially infinite regress of interpreting rules on interpretation. This methodological dilemma cannot be addressed in full here. Therefore, it shall be assumed here that the question whether the VCLT's rules on interpretation are obligatory is one that can be answered by interpretation of these rules.[5]

Secondly, one might ask if the process of interpretation can be regulated by international law at all. The ILC famously observed that the rules of interpretation

> are, for the most part, principles of logic and good sense valuable only as guides to assist in appreciating the meaning which the parties may have intended to attach to the expressions that they employed in a document.[6]

It further constated that

> recourse to many of these principles is discretionary rather than obligatory and the interpretation of documents is to some extent an art, not an exact science.[7]

However, the relevant question here is not whether the process of interpretation *can or should* be regulated by international law, because states *actually incorporated* "principles of logic or good sense" into the VCLT, a binding international treaty. Insofar as they did, these principles have attained, for better or worse, the status of

[5]On the question of applicability to the VCLT: Wolfram Karl, *Vertrag und spätere Praxis im Völkerrecht* (Springer 1983) 358 et seqq. Mark Eugen Villiger, 'Art. 31' in Mark Eugen Villiger (ed), *Commentary on the 1969 Vienna Convention on the Law of Treaties* (Kluwer Law International 2009) para 95. By contrast, Marek rejects the idea of applying the VCLT's rules on the VCLT itself, Krystyna Marek, 'Thoughts on Codification' (1971) 31 Zeitschrift für ausländisches öffentliches Recht und Völkerrecht 489, 510.

[6]ILC, 'Report of the International Law Commission to the General Assembly' (1966) 16 YILC Vol II 169, 218.

[7]ibid.

treaty provisions. This status cannot simply be ignored by reference to their subject-matter being a process resembling "art". On the contrary, the existence of the VCLT's provisions on interpretation implies that these provisions shall be a part of the *law* of treaties that the VCLT codifies.[8]

Focusing on the VCLT's rules *in concreto*, Arts. 31 and 33 VCLT provide further arguments in favour of a legal obligation. Both provisions employ obligatory language ("shall"). In a similar vein, the heading of Art. 31 VCLT refers to a general 'rule'—a word the VCLT uses for legal obligations in other contexts.[9] Furthermore, the fact that the VCLT's rules use broad and vague terms is not a sufficient argument against an obligatory character either. By itself, broad wording merely increases the threshold for findings of noncompliance. By contrast, vague terms do not necessarily imply that there was no legal obligation at all. Moreover, the ILC itself, while recognizing the difficulties of codifying interpretative rules, considered it compelling to do so, as is evidenced by the VCLT's *travaux préparatoires*.[10] Thus, in sum, the VCLT's interpretative rules, at least insofar as they employ obligatory language, resemble in principle legal obligations.

However, accepting this point in principle does not say much about these obligations' content. Indeed, the legal obligations arising from the rules of interpretation are so faint that they cannot resemble more than an outer limit. Arts. 31–33 VCLT offer a broad spectrum of approaches, each of which can legally be employed in interpretation. The only thing interpreters must not do is to disregard all of them. Failure to adopt any of the many tenable interpretations amounts to a violation of Arts. 31–33 VCLT. (Only) then, an interpretation is wrongful in a strict, legal sense. The VCLT's interpretative rules thus must be understood as merely obliging the interpreter to operate within a general framework within which questions of

[8]On the principle of *ut res magis valeat quam pereat* see *Asian Agricultural Products, LTD (AAPL) v. Sri Lanka* ICSID Case No ARB/87/3, para 40.

[9]For the same meaning of 'rule' in Art. 5 VCLT see Chap. 10 B II. and the sources cited there. A comparison with Art. 32 VCLT, which merely speaks of supplementary "means" that "may" be taken into account, implies that this terminology was chosen consciously.

[10]In its 1966 commentary on the draft, the ILC argued that "there were cogent reasons why it should be attempted. First, the interpretation of treaties in good faith and according to law is essential if the *pacta sunt servanda* rule is to have any real meaning. Secondly, having regard to the divergent opinions concerning methods of interpretation, it seemed desirable that the Commission should take a clear position in regard to the role of the text in treaty interpretation. Thirdly, a number of articles adopted by the Commission contain clauses which distinguish between matters expressly provided in the treaty and matters to be implied in it by reference to the intention of the parties; and clearly, the operation of such clauses can be fully appreciated and determined only in the light of the means of interpretation admissible for ascertaining the intention of the parties. In addition, the establishment of some measure of agreement in regard to the basic rules of interpretation is important not only for the application but also for the drafting of treaties", ILC, 'Report of the International Law Commission to the General Assembly' (n 6) 219.

interpretation are to be solved.[11] While these outer limits have occasionally become relevant in practice,[12] clear cases of violations are unlikely to occur.

II. Are the World Bank and the CoE Addressees of Interpretative Obligations?

The second question to be clarified when asking whether the Bank and the CoE have to interpret their laws in coherence with the ILO's is whether the World Bank and the CoE are the addressees of the legal obligations set forth by the VCLT's interpretative rules.

Arts. 31–33 VCLT are formulated in an impersonal manner. They merely state that treaties "shall be interpreted", but do not specify by whom. Given that interpretations can be made by virtually every natural or legal person, this could be read as simply obliging everybody who is interpreting a treaty. As a factual matter, the VCLT's rules will indeed form the common reference point for anybody engaging in interpretation, not least because there is often no real alternative at hand. However, on the other hand, it is hardly conceivable that Arts. 31–33 VCLT were intended to *legally oblige* literally 'everybody', which could lead to odd results e.g. in case of interpretations proposed in academic literature.

The scope of addressees does not need to be defined in an exhaustive manner here. Suffice it to say that, although no IO is (nor could become) a party to the VCLT,[13] the VCLT still applies to IOs' constituent instruments and to treaties

[11]Richard Gardiner, *Treaty Interpretation* (2nd edn, Oxford University Press 2017) 455. As Klabbers put it, "rules on interpretation can do little more than set the outward parameters: certain things are not acceptable to begin with", Jan Klabbers, 'Interpretation as the Continuation of Politics by Other Means' (*Opinio Juris*, 2 March 2009) <http://opiniojuris.org/2009/03/02/continuation/> accessed 26 April 2020. See also Anne Peters, 'Das Gründungsdokument Internationaler Organisationen als Verfassungsvertrag' (2013) 68 Zeitschrift für Öffentliches Recht 1, 29.

[12]An example is the Ad Hoc Committee's decision on annulment in the so-called *Lucchetti* case, in which it reasoned that "treaty interpretation is not an exact science, and it is frequently the case that there is more than one possible interpretation of a disputed provision, sometimes even several. It is no part of the Committee's function, as already indicated above, to purport to substitute its own view for that arrived at by the Tribunal (…). The Committee is not charged with the task of determining whether one interpretation is 'better' than another, or indeed which among several interpretations might be considered the 'best' one. The Committee is concerned solely with the process by which the Tribunal moved from its premise to its conclusion", *Industria Nacional de Alimentos, S.A. and Indalsa Perú, S.A. v. Peru* (Decision on Annulment) ICSID Case No ARB/03/4, para 112. Despite observing several flaws in the Tribunal's interpretation, the Ad Hoc Committee held that, "[a]lthough the Tribunal's interpretation (…) does not reflect all relevant aspects of treaty interpretation according to the Vienna Convention, the Committee has no basis for concluding that the Tribunal disregarded any significant element of the well-known and widely recognised international rules of treaty interpretation", ibid 113.

[13]What seems clear is that states that have ratified the VCLT must observe legal obligations emanating from its interpretative rules. The VCLT, however, is only open for ratification by states,

adopted within them (Art. 5 VCLT).[14] Pursuant to Art. 5 VCLT, IOs can deviate from the VCLT by developing their own rules of the organization, including their own rules on interpretation. This implies that if they do not, they need to observe the general rules. Furthermore, to argue otherwise would blatantly disregard the fact that IOs are in practice the most frequent interpreters of their own laws.

III. Conclusion

Interpretative rules enshrined in Arts. 31–33 VCLT can in principle impose legal obligations on interpreters, which are, however, not more than an outer normative parameter leaving ample discretion. The Bank and the CoE are addressees of these obligations and required to observe legal obligations emanating from interpretative rules when interpreting their own institutional law.

C. The Faint General Obligation to Coherent Interpretation (Art. 31(3) lit. c VCLT)

As mentioned above, the relevant interpretative rule requiring coherent interpretation is laid down in Art. 31(3) lit. c VCLT, pursuant to which any relevant rules of international law applicable between the parties must be taken into account when interpreting a treaty. When examining the obligatory content of Art. 31(3) lit. c VCLT, the provision raises three points which are of relevance in the context of this study. Firstly, it is worth noting that the 'rules' to be taken into account are to be seen in the light of institutional practice pertaining to them (Sect. I.). Secondly, there are persisting uncertainties regarding the phrase "relevant rules of international law applicable in the relations between the parties" (Sect. II.). Thirdly, the content of the obligation to "take into account" needs to be clarified (Sect. III.).

Arts. 81-83 VCLT. The fact that they could accede to the VCLT-IO (and the ILO has done so) does not help either, because the ILO's, the Bank's and the CoE's constituent instruments, as well as the ECHR, the ESC and all ILO conventions, are exclusively governed by the VCLT, not the VCLT-IO (Art. 5 VCLT and Art. 5 VCLT-IO).

[14]This comprises all examined IOs' constituent instruments, further the ECHR and ESC, and finally all ILO conventions.

I. Institutional Practice as Part of the "Relevant Rules"

At the outset, it is worth noting that the 'relevant rules' ought to be considered in the light of any existing institutional practice pertaining to them. While there are different views on the extent to which this should happen, it is, at least in principle, agreed that relevant rules of international law cannot be considered in clinical isolation from institutional practice applying and interpreting these rules.[15] Including such institutional practice in the 'relevant rules' under Art. 31(3) lit. c VCLT is of high importance for any attempt to systemically integrate the ILO's model with the other IOs' institutional laws. As seen in Chap. 1, the ILO has developed a rich body of practice, including not least its supervisory bodies' 'soft law jurisprudence'. This practice is part and parcel of the ILO's model of labour governance. Art. 31(3) lit. c VCLT provides a basis for this practice to be considered.

II. The Meaning of "Applicable in the Relations Between the Parties"

The second issue of particular importance with respect to inter-organizational interactions is the meaning of the phrase "[relevant rules of international law] applicable in the relations between the parties".

The VCLT leaves it open whether "parties" in Art. 31(3) lit. c VCLT refers to the parties to a particular dispute at hand or to all the parties to the treaty that is being interpreted. As is well-known, the latter view was adopted by the WTO Panel in *EC-Biotech Products*.[16] If one takes this view seriously, the relevance of Art. 31 (3) lit. c VCLT for the present study would be dramatically diminished. Despite the ILO's quasi-universal membership, the ILO Constitution could then only be 'systemically integrated' with another IO's constituent instrument if *all* of the other IO's members were also members of the ILO. This is neither true for the CoE[17] nor for the IBRD and IDA.[18] As to ILO conventions, the situation would be even more questionable, as systemic integration would be entirely dependent on the ratification record of each convention. The view expressed in *EC-Biotech* would, therefore,

---

[15]Dörr (n 3) para 101, with further references.

[16]WTO, *European Communities—Approval and Marketing of Biotech Products, Panel Report* (29 September 2006) WT/DS291-3/R, paras 7.68 et seqq.; Dörr (n 3) para 104. Similar Ulf Linderfalk, 'Who Are "The Parties"? Article 31, Paragraph 3 (c) of the 1969 Vienna Convention and the "Principle of Systemic Integration" Revisited' (2008) 55 Netherlands International Law Review 343. By contrast, the ICJ took into account a bilateral treaty when interpreting a multilateral convention, *Case Concerning Certain Questions of Mutual Assistance in Criminal Matters (Djibouti v. France)* [2008] ICJ Reports 177, para 112 et seqq.

[17]For instance, Liechtenstein is not an ILO member, but a member of the CoE and has ratified the ECHR.

[18]See Chap. 9 A. IV. 3.

severely hamper any attempt to systemically integrate ILO instruments and other IOs' constituent instruments through interpretation.

As has been frequently criticized, the *EC-Biotech* Panel's view conflicts with the telos of Art. 31(3) lit. c VCLT,[19] because it effectively obstructs the coherent interpretation of treaties. This is particularly true for treaties with a large number of parties, where it is unlikely that all parties to that treaty will be parties to other treaties.[20]

That being said, in the context of inter-organizational interactions, the view adopted in *EC-Biotech* should not too readily be brushed aside. In cases where treaty obligations are synallagmatic and based on reciprocity,[21] understanding "parties" as 'parties to the dispute' indeed produces more appropriate results than the *EC-Biotech* approach. However, as the ILC has indicated in its report on fragmentation, the case may be different with regard to treaties which are not "reciprocal" or "synallagmatic", but "integral" or "interdependent", i.e. those treaties which create obligations *erga omnes partes*.[22] Arguably, most constituent instruments of IOs and many treaties adopted within them are treaties of this latter category, including the ILO Constitution and ILO conventions. If one were to understand 'parties' as parties to the dispute, this would inevitably open the door for divergent interpretations among different parties of the same "integral" treaty. In the context of an IO, the impact of those divergences can be significantly higher than in cases where there is no institutional dimension involved. For example, an IO's mandate as laid down in its constituent instrument could be interpreted differently vis-à-vis different members, depending on which other treaties a particular member is bound by.[23] For instance, the interpretation of the World Bank's prohibition of

---

[19]The Panel's view is reconcilable with the wording and arguably also the systematic context of Art. 31(3) lit. c VCLT, McLachlan (n 1) 315.

[20]ILC, 'Fragmentation of International Law: Difficulties Arising from the Diversification and Expansion of International Law, Report of the Study Group of the International Law Commission, Finalized by Martti Koskenniemi' (n 1) 471. The "relevant rules" in the sense of Art. 31(3) lit. c VCLT also comprise customary rules and general principles. The *EC-Biotech* Panel did not oppose taking customary law into account. Aside from creating difficulties in general (McLachlan (n 1) 315; Diane A Desierto, *Public Policy in International Economic Law: The ICESCR in Trade, Finance, and Investment* (Oxford University Press 2015) 205), this would be of little help to the ILO, whose model of labour governance in its entirety does not resemble customary international law or general principles.

[21]On the different categories of treaty obligations Joost Pauwelyn, 'Typology of Multilateral Treaty Obligations: Are WTO Obligations Bilateral or Collective in Nature?' (2003) 14 European Journal of International Law 907, 909 et seqq.; Peter-Tobias Stoll, 'The World Trade Organization as a Club: Rethinking Reciprocity and Common Interest' in Ulrich Fastenrath and others (eds), *From Bilateralism to Community Interest: Essays in Honour of Bruno Simma* (Oxford University Press 2011) 173 et seq.

[22]ILC, 'Fragmentation of International Law: Difficulties Arising from the Diversification and Expansion of International Law, Report of the Study Group of the International Law Commission, Finalized by Martti Koskenniemi' (n 1) para 472.

[23]In an extreme case, and to the extent that the rules of the IO do not outrule such behaviour, some members could even actively modify the IO's competences, or the reach of instruments adopted

political activity in the context of trade union rights could be different with regard to each of its members, given that some World Bank member states have ratified all relevant ILO conventions and human rights treaties protecting trade union rights, whereas others have ratified only some, or none at all.

In order to avoid a 'special treatment' of some members, one could alternatively consider interpreting the IO's mandate *inter omnes partes* in the light of relevant other rules of international law even if only some of the IO's members are bound by these other rules. However, this would obviously put significant constraints on the IO's other members and limit their sovereign choice to accept or not to accept legal obligations.[24]

Eventually, no satisfactory solution to the problem is in sight.[25]

III. The Obligation to 'Take into Account'

The third issue to be mentioned is the meaning and content of the obligation to "take into account" relevant international rules. The ILC's fragmentation report touches briefly on this issue. It points out that the purpose of the obligation to take into account was to link specialized areas of international law to each other and to more general principles.[26] However, it added cautiously that:

> [n]one of this predetermines what it means to 'confront' a norm with another or how they might enter into 'concurrence'. These matters must be left to the interpreter to decide in view of the situation. The point is only - but it is a key point - that the normative environment cannot be ignored and that when interpreting the treaties, the principle of integration should

---

within one IO, by concluding respective treaties among themselves, in accordance with Art. 41 VCLT, see Christopher Peters, *Praxis Internationaler Organisationen - Vertragswandel und völkerrechtlicher Ordnungsrahmen* (Springer 2016) 190.

[24]In an extreme case, an IO's mandate would have to be interpreted in the light of another relevant treaty to which only two of the IO's members were a party. For example, the ILO Constitution, or a fundamental ILO Convention, would have to be interpreted in an 'investor-friendly' way if only two of the ILO's members (or two of the parties to the ILO Convention) would have concluded a bilateral investment treaty.

[25]When addressing the issue in *EC-Large Civil Aircraft*, the WTO Appellate Body (obiter) departed from the rigidity of *EC-Biotech*, *WTO, European Communities and Certain Member States—Measures Affecting Trade in Large Civil Aircraft, Report of the Appellate Body* (18 May 2011) WT/DS316/AB/R, para 845; Anne Peters, 'The Refinement of International Law: From Fragmentation to Regime Interaction and Politicization' (2017) 15 International Journal of Institutional law 671, 694. The Appellate Body's call for a "delicate balance" and for "due account", however, does in itself provide little guidance to a possible solution of the problem (Desierto (n 20) 206). Even more, it seems to depart from the – contestable, but at least clear-cut – position in *EC-Biotech*, while neither arriving at a comparatively clear-cut solution nor being really reconcilable with Art. 31 (3) lit. c VCLT.

[26]ILC, 'Fragmentation of International Law: Difficulties Arising from the Diversification and Expansion of International Law, Report of the Study Group of the International Law Commission, Finalized by Martti Koskenniemi' (n 1) para 474.

> be borne in mind. This points to the need to carry out the interpretation so as to see the rules in view of some comprehensible and coherent objective, to prioritize concerns that are more important at the cost of less important objectives. This is all that [Art 31(3) lit. c VCLT] requires; the integration into the process of legal reasoning - including reasoning by courts and tribunals - of a sense of coherence and meaningfulness. Success or failure here is measured by how the legal world will view the outcome.[27]

Some authors have attempted to develop the obligation further. For instance, van Aaken suggests that an interpreter should engage in rational balancing, using the principle of proportionality, to achieve practical concordance (*praktische Konkordanz*).[28] Whatever the merits of this proposal, it seems doubtful whether such balancing is actually *required* (as opposed to being permissible or desirable) under Art. 31(3) lit. c VCLT, not least because of the syntactic position of "take into account" within the provision.[29] In any event, requiring 'rational balancing' would not provide much more contours to the obligation.

Eventually, what can safely be salvaged from the wording of Art. 31(3) lit. c VCLT is that the obligation to take into account requires, as a minimum, that the interpreter does not entirely ignore or fail to give any reasonable consideration to a relevant other rule.[30] The obligation to take into account thus only provides minimum requirements, while remaining blurry and unspecified beyond that.

If one tentatively applies this standard to the instances of inter-organizational interactions presented in Chaps. 3–5, it will become apparent that both the World Bank and the CoE have met it. The World Bank has explicitly taken pertinent ILO conventions into account and even asserted that the EWI was compatible with them—it simply seemed to have not given decisive weight to them. The precise

---

[27]ibid 419. The "normative weight" of other relevant rules, so the ILC held, depended on a case-by-case basis, ibid 475.

[28]Anne van Aaken, 'Defragmentation of Public International Law through Interpretation: A Methodological Proposal' (2009) 16 Indiana Journal of Global Legal Studies 483, 502 et seqq. Similar Peters, 'The Refinement of International Law: From Fragmentation to Regime Interaction and Politicization' (n 25) 694.

[29]It should not be overlooked that the phrase "be taken into account", which specifies the obligation, appears in the chapeau of Art. 31(3) VCLT and refers, without any distinction, to all three subparagraphs (lits. a- c). This syntax suggests that the obligation must have a similar meaning with regard to all three subparagraphs. If this is correct, care must be taken not to overly narrow-lead the obligation under the impression of just one subparagraph, as this might prejudice the very same obligation under another. For example, an interpretation of 'take into account' as an obligation to engage in balancing treaty provisions and other elements makes sense in the context of other relevant rules of international law (lit. c) but would risk compromising the intended efficacy of subsequent interpretative agreements concluded between the parties (lit. a).

[30]What is more, the interpreter is required to take these other rules into account not as mere facts, but as an aspect of law. This follows from the aim of interpretation to precisely determine the scope and content of legal norms. The mere existence of other rules as social facts would not change the legal normative content of the norm which is to be interpreted. In order for this social fact to be of any relevance in the deontic realm of the legal-normative, there has to be another norm stipulating that the other rule ought to be of relevance for the interpreted norm's legal-normative scope and content.

reasons for doing so remain difficult to reconstruct. In any case, however, the obligation to take into account another rule in the interpretative process does not require to actually adhere to it in the end. As far as the ECtHR and ECSR are concerned, both bodies have not only taken ILO instruments and practice into account, but at times actually aligned their own practice accordingly—and thus have done more than legally required by Art. 31(3) lit. c VCLT.

IV. Conclusion

Art. 31(3) lit. c VCLT requires to take into account relevant rules of ILO law, in principle also including pertinent institutional practice, when interpreting the institutional law of the Bank and the CoE. However, the obligatory content of Art. 31 (3) lit. c VCLT remains faint. The obligation to "take into account" requires barely more than to consider a relevant other rule as a relevant legal consideration. Moreover, there is no satisfactory solution to the question whether the relevant rule must apply between all parties to the interpreted treaty or if it suffices if it applies between the parties to a dispute, since neither alternative produces compelling results in the inter-organizational context.

D. Systemic Integration and Special Interpretative 'Rules of the Organization'

Apart from the scope and content of Art. 31(3) lit. c VCLT, the inter-organizational constellation raises another issue regarding coherent interpretation: The rules of coherent interpretation can 'specialize', as IOs can develop their own special interpretative rules on coherent interpretation. As shown in Chap. 10, such special interpretative rules take precedence over the general rule of Art. 31(3) lit. c VCLT by virtue of Art. 5 VCLT (Sect. I.). The more an IO's special rules modify or entirely supersede Art. 31(3) lit. c VCLT, the less there is a common normative parameter for requiring coherent interpretation (Sect. II.). This 'specialization' of interpretative rules can have significant implications for attempts to mitigate the ILO's relativization in the laws of the World Bank and CoE by means of coherent interpretation (Sect. III.).

I. Deviating from Art. 31(3) lit. c VCLT by 'Specializing' Rules on Interpretation

It is part of the dynamics of IOs' institutional laws that IOs can develop their own special interpretative practices. Depending on how established such practices become, they can attain the status of 'rules of the organization' in the sense of Art. 5 VCLT and, as such, take precedence over the general rules of interpretation, including Art. 31(3) lit. c VCLT.

As explained in Chap. 10, pursuant to Art. 5 VCLT, the VCLT applies to IOs' laws "without prejudice to any relevant rules of the organization".[31] Art. 5 VCLT also applies to special interpretative rules of IOs.[32] This means that any special interpretative rules that may apply to IOs' constituent instruments or to treaties adopted within an IO take precedence over Arts. 31–33 VCLT. The only condition is that they qualify as 'rules of the organization' in the sense of Art. 5 VCLT. Given that this term comprises unwritten established practice, it suffices that an IO's approach to interpretation is established in the practice of its organs.[33] It is not required that the special rules entirely replace the general rules. Rather, it is sufficient that they modify them, e.g. by putting emphasis on a particular interpretative approach or method.[34]

[31]Chapter 10 B. II.

[32]Mark Eugen Villiger, 'Art. 5' in Mark Eugen Villiger (ed), *Commentary on the 1969 Vienna Convention on the Law of Treaties* (Brill 2009) para 8; Kirsten Schmalenbach 'Art. 5 VCLT' in Oliver Dörr and Kirsten Schmalenbach (eds), *Vienna Convention on the Law of Treaties: A Commentary* (2nd edn, Springer 2018) para 16; Christopher Peters, 'Subsequent Practice and Established Practice of International Organizations: Two Sides of the Same Coin?' (2011) 3 Goettingen Journal of International Law 617, 640.

[33]For a detailed analysis Peters, *Praxis Internationaler Organisationen - Vertragswandel und völkerrechtlicher Ordnungsrahmen* (n 23) passim. In the ILO's, Bank's and the CoE's law, written special interpretative rules are rare. Pursuant to Art. 19(8) ILO Constitution, ILO labour conventions and recommendations shall not be interpreted as to affect any law, award, custom or agreement according more favourable treatment to workers. Pursuant to Art. 53 ECHR, nothing in the ECHR shall be interpreted as to limiting of derogating from human rights enshrined in domestic law or other treaties. A similar clause is contained in Art. 32 ESC. These clauses limit the scope of interpretations the respective IO may arrive at. They are relevant for present purposes, because their application presupposes that other international instruments are taken into account in the first place, see, with regard to Art. 53 ECHR *National Union of Rail, Maritime and Transport Workers v. United Kingdom* ECHR 2014–II 1 Concurring Opinion of Judge Wojtyczek, para 3.

[34]Richard D Kearney and Robert E Dalton, 'The Treaty on Treaties' (1970) 64 American Journal of International Law 495, 505 et seq.; Villiger 'Art. 5' (n 32) para 7.; Peters, 'Subsequent Practice and Established Practice of International Organizations: Two Sides of the Same Coin?' (n 32) 636.

II. The Structural Issue: A Multiplication of Normative Parameters for Interpretation and the Gradual Erosion of the Common Standard

One could ask now what the practical consequences of these findings are. After all, the VCLT's general interpretative rules also leave ample room for each IO to choose between one or another interpretative stance on their laws. Accordingly, one could consider it irrelevant whether their stance formally attains the character of special 'rules of the organization' or not.

Indeed, the crucial point lies elsewhere. It is not the *lex specialis* character per se that is important, but the fact that each IO can refer to it to entrench its particular interpretative approach against contestation. If criticized for overstepping the boundaries of Art. 31(3) lit. c VCLT, an IO can counter the critique by arguing that its approach resembles its own established practice and that, therefore, the general rule of Art. 31(3) lit. c VCLT is not applicable to begin with. In this vein, each IO can develop its very own 'excuse' for deviating from the general rules when interpreting its own law, including its approach to taking into account (or not) the law of other IOs. At the same time, the possibility of 'specializing' the interpretative rules reduces the need to maintain a common standard for coherent interpretation. Figuratively, the normative parameters not only multiply, but drift apart.

III. Example: The ECtHR's Recourse to ILO Instruments and Practice Revisited

The foregoing structural point can be exemplified by revisiting the interactions between the ILO and the ECtHR examined in Chap. 5.

As will be argued in turn, the ECtHR's 'living instrument' and 'European consensus' approaches each qualify as special interpretative 'rules of the organization' in the sense of Art. 5 VCLT (Sect. 1.). As compared to Art. 31(3) lit. c VCLT, they enhance the role the ILO plays within the ECHR (Sect. 2.). However, the ILO has developed its own special interpretative rules for its instruments, which form an important part of its model of labour governance (Sect. 3.). Despite the ECtHR's relative openness to ILO instruments and practice, it remains unclear how to reconcile the respective special interpretative rules of two interacting IOs (Sect. 4.).

1. 'Living Instrument' and 'European Consensus' as Special Interpretative Rules

As already explained in Chap. 5, the ECtHR has developed special interpretative practices, including its long-established 'living instrument' and 'European consensus' approaches.[35] Both approaches modify or even completely transcend the general rule enshrined in Art. 31(3) lit. c VCLT with regard to the interpretation of the ECHR, a treaty adopted within the CoE. They therefore qualify as 'rules of the organization' in the sense of Art. 5 VCLT.

This might seem surprising at first, because the ECtHR has—if at all—mostly referred to Arts. 31–33 VCLT as the pertinent basis for coherent interpretation.[36] Yet, its 'living instrument' approach with its strong reliance on teleological considerations has pushed the general interpretative rules in one particular direction, often at the expense of the other interpretative methods laid down in Art. 31(1) VCLT. Seen in this light, it is perhaps no coincidence that one of the very few occasions in which the Court actually cited Art. 5 VCLT was *Golder v. United Kingdom*, still one of the leading cases on ECHR interpretation.[37] The speciality of the approach may also stand behind the Grand Chamber's statement in *Demir and Baykara* that its dynamic and evolutive interpretation of the ECHR would "mainly" be guided by the rules of interpretation laid down in the VCLT,[38] a statement that has caused irritation among commentators.[39] The 'living instrument' approach therefore modifies the general rule of Art. 31(3) lit. c VCLT.

Going even further, the Court's 'European consensus' approach has moved beyond Art. 31(3) lit. c VCLT altogether. Art. 31(3) lit. c VCLT requires to take into account any rule *applicable* between the parties. This is commonly understood to the effect that the rules must be binding upon the parties.[40] By contrast, the ECtHR takes international instruments into account even if the respondent is not bound by them, either because it has not consented to them, or because they are non-binding instruments to begin with.[41]

In sum, the Court's by-now long standing and consolidated interpretative approaches may be considered as established interpretative practice, and therefore as 'rules of the organization' in the sense of Art. 5 VCLT.[42]

---

[35]See above, Chap. 5 C. II.

[36]The Court's references to Arts. 31-33 VCLT have remained rather sparse, George Letsas, *A Theory of Interpretation of the European Convention of Human Rights* (Oxford University Press 2007) 59.

[37]*Golder v. United Kingdom* (1975) Series A No 18, para 29; Letsas (n 36) 61.

[38]*Demir and Baykara v. Turkey* ECHR 2008–V 395, para 65.

[39]E.g. Geir Ulfstein, 'Evolutive Interpretation in the Light of Other International Instruments: Law and Legitimacy' in Anne van Aaken and Iulia Motoc (eds), *The European Convention on Human Rights and General International Law* (Oxford University Press 2018) 85.

[40]Dörr (n 3) para 105.

[41]*Demir and Baykara v. Turkey* ECHR 2008–V 395 para 75.

[42]Similar Klaus Lörcher, 'The New Social Dimension in the Jurisprudence of the European Court of Human Rights (ECtHR): The Demir and Baykara Judgment, Its Methodology and Follow-Up' in Filip Dorssemont, Klaus Lörcher and Isabelle Schömann (eds), *The European Convention on Human Rights and Employment Relation* (Hart Publishing 2013) 13.

2. An Enhanced Role for the ILO Through Special Rules on Coherent Interpretation

Both the Court's 'living instrument' and European consensus' approaches enhance the ILO's relevance within the ECHR. As shown in Chap. 5, their development coincided with an increased reception of ILO instruments and practice in the ECtHR's jurisprudence. The living instrument approach, applied by the Court to international developments, paves the way for having recourse to ILO conventions and their interpretation in ILO practice. The 'European consensus' approach, for its part, helps to overcome the argument that a particular ILO instrument or practice was not binding on the respondent. It is true that the special interpretative rules do not prevent (and have not prevented) the ECtHR from deviating from ILO instruments and practice in certain cases. However, especially in comparison to other international bodies that apply the general rule in Art. 31(3) lit. c VCLT (e.g. the WTO Panel in *EC-Biotech*, discussed in the previous section), the Court's approach is markedly enhancing the ILO's relevance.

3. The ILO's Own Special Interpretative (and Other) Rules

However, as seen in Chap. 5, the ECtHR's reception of ILO instruments and practice, although firmly based on the Court's special interpretative approaches, 'backlashed' to the ILO by fuelling the latter's constitutional crisis. How is this reconcilable with the comparatively greater lenience of the ECtHR's interpretative approach towards the ILO that has just been described?

To answer this question, it is important to consider that, as already described in Chap. 1, the ILO has itself developed special approaches, both on interpretation and other aspects of treaty law. Most importantly for present purposes, the ILO has developed established practice regarding the rendition and the function of 'unofficial' interpretations by the International Labour Office and the ILO supervisory bodies. Further special aspects comprise the Office's greater emphasis on the ILO instruments' *travaux* (contrary to the supplementary character ascribed to them by Art. 32 VCLT) and the impermissibility of interpretative declarations by states (which, under the general rules of Art. 31(2) lits. a and b and (3) lit. a VCLT, are permissible and have to be taken into account).[43]

It is recognized that these established ILO practices resemble special 'rules of the organization' in the sense of Art. 5 VCLT. Indeed, as mentioned above, Art. 5 VCLT, the unofficially so-called 'ILO clause', was drafted and adopted under the imminent impression of this ILO practice.[44] As can be seen from the VCLT's

[43]This established interpretative practice does not entirely replace the general VCLT rules of interpretation. However, it embodies many nuanced deviations and differences.

[44]See Chap. 10 B. II.

travaux, the ILO's approach to interpretation was a prime case in point.[45] The ILO's special rules on interpretation, same as its other special rules, form part and parcel of the ILO's model of labour governance.

4. 'Relativization' Recurring: The Unresolved 'Art. 5 VCLT^2 Constellation'

In consequence, the ECtHR, when taking into account ILO instruments under its special interpretative 'rules of the organization', deals with instruments to which the 'rules of *another* organization' apply. This 'Art. 5 VCLT^2 constellation' has not been discussed as such in practice or academia. Nevertheless, it is inherent in cases such as *RMT v. United Kingdom*, discussed in Chap. 5, in which the Court took into account ILO instruments and the accompanying interpretation provided by the CEACR on the right to call sympathy strikes, without however considering (or better: while explicitly ignoring) that the CEACR's competence to render such interpretations was rooted in established practice borne by the ILO's tripartite constituents and had just been called into question by one of these constituents.[46]

The occurrence of two parallel sets of special 'rules of the organization' was not an issue of particular bearing in *RMT*. However, this may change in future cases, as the 'Art. 5 VCLT^2 constellation' raises structural questions: To what extent may the ECtHR take into account ILO instruments and practice on the basis of its own special interpretative rules and, if it deems fit, second-guess, deviate from, or entirely ignore these instruments and practice? To what extent (if at all) should the Court give deference to the ILO's special (interpretative and other) rules that apply to the ILO instruments the Court is taking into account? If the ECtHR was interpreting the ECHR on the basis of the general rules of Arts. 31–33 VCLT, it would be clear that, due to Art. 5 VCLT, the ILO's special rules would take precedence. But there is no solution at hand if both the Court and the ILO can refer to Art. 5 VCLT.

The issue does not need to be resolved here. The important point for present purposes is to show that even where the ECtHR has developed special interpretative rules that enhance the ILO's role and relevance, these special rules will still only protect and promote the ILO's model if they pay sufficient regard to the ILO's own special rules on the interpretation of ILO conventions and other aspects.

The underlying theme of this Part of this study, the ILO's relativization in the institutional laws of other IOs, resurfaces here, this time in the form of the

---

[45] Clarence Wilfred Jenks, then Deputy Director-General of the ILO and observer for the ILO at the Vienna Conference in 1968, explicitly mentioned the ILO's particular take on interpretation of ILO conventions as one example of ILO practice which would require the lex specialis rule which is now laid down in Art. 5 VCLT, UN, Summary Records of the Plenary Meetings and of the Meetings of the Committee of the Whole, United Nations Conference on the Law of Treaties (1st session, Vienna, 26 March-24 May 1968) Official Records (1969) UN Doc A/CONF.39/11, 37, para 12; Kearney and Dalton (n 34) 505 et seq.

[46] See the discussion of the ILO's post-2012 constitutional crisis in Chap. 2 D. III.

ECtHR potentially prioritizing its own 'specialized' interpretative rules over the ILO's.

IV. Conclusion

The existence of special interpretative rules as 'rules of the organization' has important conceptual implications. Special interpretative rules can influence the nature and the extent of these IOs' obligations to coherent interpretation. If special interpretative rules require a more extensive consideration of other international law instruments than Art. 31(3) lit. c VCLT does, they pave the way for increasing the relevance of ILO law in the law of the other IO. This, in turn, would provide more certainty and predictability for the ILO during its interactions with that other IO. However, they also give rise to hitherto unresolved disparities between special interpretative rules if, as in the case of the ILO and the ECtHR, both interacting sides have developed their own approaches.

E. Conclusion on Chap. 11

This chapter has examined whether the World Bank and the CoE are required, by virtue of the pertinent rules of interpretation, to enhance the role of the ILO's model in their institutional laws. It has found that, in principle, interpretative rules enshrined in Arts. 31–33 VCLT can impose legal obligations, in the form of an outer limit that must not be transgressed. The World Bank and the CoE are both required to observe these outer limits when interpreting their institutional laws.

That being said, there are significant uncertainties as to what the pertinent interpretative rules demand. Art. 31(3) lit. c VCLT, often referred to as an embodiment of the "principle of systemic integration", neither regulates with significant clarity which other rules should be taken into account nor what the obligation to take into account actually requires, apart from a minimum effort. To be sure, this is not to say that systemic integration is not possible or does not work. However, in the absence of clear and meaningful requirements, it will remain at the discretion of the interpreting IO whether and to what extent it adopts an integrating interpretation.

Moreover, the chapter has elucidated the relevance of special interpretative rules, including established interpretative practices, in the institutional law of the examined IOs. Established interpretative practices take precedence over the general rules of interpretation insofar as they contain modifications of or deviations from them. If, as in the case of the ECtHR, they take precedence over Art. 31(3) lit. c VCLT, they can substantially alter the trajectory of systemic integration, most likely with a bias in favour of the respective own organizational rules. While this may in principle enhance the ILO's relevance, there is the almost entirely unexplored question whether and how systemic integration should be conducted if two IOs' special interpretative rules collide, a situation which e.g. appears between the ILO and the ECtHR.

In sum, coherent interpretation is an option that the World Bank and CoE may have resort to enhance the ILO's role and relevance in their laws. However, they are hardly legally obliged to do so.

12. Mitigating Relativization via Member States' Loyalty and Sincere Cooperation?

The preceding chapters have shown that the Bank's and the CoE's institutional laws prioritize their own agendas over the ILO's governance model, needs and demands, and neither IO is under a tangible legal obligation to develop its law in a way that would give greater deference to the ILO. At this point, it is therefore appropriate to turn to the Bank's and CoE's member states. While IOs and their member states must be distinguished as a matter of law, the member states have a significant and often decisive influence on the World Bank's and the CoE's conduct. Hence, one could ask if and to what extent the World Bank's and CoE's member states must ensure that the Bank and the CoE have due regard of the ILO's governance model during inter-organizational interactions, thereby mitigating the ILO's relativization in the laws of these other IOs.

Coordination of IOs and their mutual influence is often considered a task of their respective member states.[1] Over time, various suggestions have been made, both in academia and practice, to enhance policy coherence through better coordination of a states' different IO memberships.[2] The common rationale behind these approaches is that member states are capable and—at least in a political sense—'responsible' for coordinating their memberships, given it was their sovereign choice to participate in several IOs to begin with.

Drawing on these considerations, it is to be examined whether and to what extent international law requires the Bank's and CoE's member states to steer the way in which other IOs interact with the ILO. As the ILO's and World Bank's memberships

[1]As to social rights, this has e.g. been the stance of the CESCR, see UN Committee on Economic, Social and Cultural Rights, 'General Comment No 18: The Right to Work (Art. 6 of the Covenant)' (6 February 2006) E/C.12/GC/18, para 30.

[2]Henry G Schermers and Niels M Blokker, *International Institutional Law* (6th edn, Brill 2018) para 1739 et seqq., with further references.

H. Gött, *The Law of Interactions Between International Organizations*, Beiträge zum ausländischen öffentlichen Recht und Völkerrecht 299,
https://doi.org/10.1007/978-3-662-62389-3_12

are virtually identical, and given that all CoE members are also ILO member states, it is appropriate to focus on the obligations of those Bank and CoE member states that are also ILO member states. Like in the previous chapter, the analysis will ask whether ILO member states are *legally obliged* to promote the ILO's model in the Bank and the CoE.[3]

A. The Principal Means of ILO Member States to Influence Other IOs

At the outset, a brief overview on the various means by which the ILO's, World Bank's and CoE's common member states can exert influence on the Bank or the CoE is warranted. In principle, these are the same means that member states have at their hands to control 'their' other IOs in general.

The most obvious way is to exert influence through their representatives in the Bank's and CoE's organs and bodies. States can launch initiatives, take positions and jointly make decisions. They can do so with regard to institutional, procedural and substantive questions.

Moreover, through their representatives, member states usually also have influence on appointing and supervising the IO's leading personnel.

Thirdly, since the member states are *Herren der Verträge*, they can induce systemic changes, e.g. by changing the interpretation of treaty provisions or by sponsoring constitutional amendments.

Fourthly, a significant avenue is controlling the IO's resources, namely its financing and its budget. At the outset, every IO has rules on member states' contributions. Moreover, all examined IOs foresee sanctions in case of defaults,

---

[3]It hardly needs mention that ILO member states with parallel memberships in other IOs are to a large extent free to decide to use their other memberships in the described way whenever they want to. Importantly, this chapter does not examine the seminal question whether member states are liable for fulfilling obligations the other IO might owe to the ILO. This form of accessory member state liability has taken most room in scholarly discussions and in practice, see on the seminal *Westland Helicopters* and *Tin Council* cases Marten C Zwanenburg, *Accountability Of Peace Support Operations* (Martinus Nijhoff Publishers 2005) 75 et seqq.; Ian Brownlie, 'The Responsibility of States for the Acts of International Organizations' in Maurizio Ragazzi (ed), *International Responsibility Today: Essays in Memory of Oscar Schachter* (Martinus Nijhoff Publishers 2005) 361. See also the discussions surrounding Draft Art. 36bis VCLT-IO, Catherine Brölmann, *The Institutional Veil in Public International Law: International Organisations and the Law of Treaties* (Hart Publishing 2007) 212 et seqq. However, to examine whether there was accessory liability of member states would require ascertaining whether the IO is liable towards the ILO in the first place. As will be seen in Part III, this is far from clear. Therefore, this chapter will not look for accessory liability, but will ask if there is genuine, non-accessory liability of ILO member states for the conduct of another IO, i.e. if there are obligations the ILO member states owe to the ILO regardless of whether the other IO itself owes any obligation to the ILO or not.

arrears or other failures to contribute.[4] However, despite legal rules, financial and budgetary questions are essentially questions of power. There are various legal, 'semi-legal' and illegal ways for member states to decisively influence an IO's conduct via the 'golden rein', i.e. the (threat of) making, altering or non-making of contributions. The experience of the IO's examined here is no exception in this regard.[5] Financial pressure can also be used by member states to induce an IO to change its behaviour in matters involving inter-organizational interaction. For instance, as mentioned in Chap. 4, the US House of Representatives in 2008 sought to change the design and methodology of the EWI to better protect core labour standards and internationally recognized workers' rights by making such changes a condition for providing further US replenishments to the Bank.[6]

Finally, as an ultima ratio, member states can threaten to withdraw from the Bank or the CoE. Withdrawal is clearly the 'nuclear option' and in any event a very blunt one-off tool to (attempt to) influence an IO's conduct in inter-organizational interactions.[7] However, threats to withdraw may lever severe pressure, because they are an immediate and visible sign of delegitimization. What is more, withdrawal can have substantial material effects on an IO, especially if the withdrawing state is a

[4]In the ILO, member states whose arrears sum up to two full years' contributions lose their voting rights (Art. 13(4) ILO Constitution). In the World Bank, membership may be suspended pursuant to Art. VI(2) IBRD-AoA if subscribed shares are not paid for in accordance with Art II IBRD-AoA. In the CoE, the right of representations may be suspended (Art. 9 CoE-Statute).

[5]In the ILO's history, budgetary pressure has time and again had significant influence on the organization's policy. Budgetary pressure by the USA, which then contributed around one quarter of the ILO's budget, even played a key role in the non-conventional approach taken by the 1998 Declaration on Fundamental Principles and Rights at Work, one of the most influential ILO instruments of all time, Philip Alston, '"Core Labour Standards" and the Transformation of the International Labour Rights Regime' (2004) 15 European Journal of International Law 457, 467. As is well-known, the 1998 Declaration, while mentioning the pertinent ILO Conventions, only expounds the ILO core labour standards in the form of principles. One reason for this non-convention-based approach was that the USA was among those ILO countries with a poor ratification record. By the time, it had only ratified one out of eight fundamental conventions, ibid 497.

[6]US House of Represenatives, Amendment in the Nature of a Substitute to HR 6306 (2008) 7.

[7]Moreover, even if one state was to withdraw from one IO or treaty, this would not put an end to the question of steering inter-organizational interaction. Withdrawal would eliminate the risk of conflicting rights and obligations, and thereby eliminate the risk of the withdrawing state to incur international responsibility by being unable to conform with the instruments and policies of two IOs. However, as long as the withdrawing state remains a member to at least one IO or relevant treaty, 'its' IO might still engage in direct or indirect inter-organizational interaction. At the very least, that IO will continue to be exposed to indirect influence by other IOs. For example, an ILO member would experience that ILO instruments and policies would remain subject to influence by, for instance, activities such as the World Bank's Doing Business reports or the ECtHR's evolutive jurisprudence. For this influence to occur, it is simply irrelevant of that ILO member has withdrawn from the World Bank or the ECHR – or has never been a member to either of them to begin with. Withdrawal, often hailed as a safeguard for sovereignty and independence, is thus not only a 'nuclear option', but might prove plain futile when it comes to steering inter-organizational interactions.

major contributor of resources.[8] The World Bank's[9] and the CoE's[10] constituent instruments, as well as the ECHR[11] and the ESC,[12] all contain provisions on withdrawal. Be that as it may, it is in any case not realistically conceivable that loyalty to the ILO would legally oblige an ILO member state to terminate its parallel

[8]For instance, the USA's withdrawal from the ILO in 1977 resulted in the latter losing around 25% of its budget, leading to reductions of staff, programmes and activities, Yves Beigbeder, 'The United States' Withdrawal from the International Labor Organization' (1979) 34 Relations industrielles / Industrial Relations 223, 236. A way larger impact could be expected from the USA's withdrawal from the World Bank. However, even for powerful states, the leverage created by threats to withdraw is not unlimited. This is exemplified by the run-up to the USA's 1977 withdrawal. In its notice of withdrawal transmitted to the ILO in 1975, the USA outlined four areas of fundamental concern and criticism of the ILO, all of which were based on a perception that the ILO had become too politicized. Although presented in a withdrawal notice, the US administration's initial strategy was to push the ILO towards reform, placing the ILO on 'probation' during the mandatory two years' notice period. During that period, however, the ILO did not submit to the USA's requests, ibid 229 et seq. Furthermore, in the aftermath of the USA's withdrawal, no structural reforms took place in response, ibid 237.

[9]The World Bank's constituent instruments allow for a swift withdrawal. Any member of the IBRD may withdraw with immediate effect at any point in time (Art. VI(1) IBRD-AoA), but remains liable for all its direct obligations towards the Bank (Art. VI(4) IBRD-AoA). The same applies in respect of the IDA (Art. VII(1) and (4) IDA-AoA), the IFC (Art. V(1) and (4) IFC-AoA) and, with some variations, the MIGA (Arts. 51 and 53 MIGA Convention). Art. VI(4) IBRD-AoA also contains detailed rules on the settlement of accounts of withdrawing members. Furthermore, there is the case of accessory withdrawals. States withdrawing from the IMF also cease to be members of the IBRD, unless the latter decides otherwise (Art. VI(3) IBRD-AoA). Similar accessory withdrawals, in case a member state withdraws from the IBRD, are foreseen in Art. VII(3) IDA-AoA and Art. V(3) IFC-AoA.

[10]Withdrawal from the CoE requires that a member notifies its intention to withdraw to the CoE Secretary-General. Withdrawal becomes effective at the end of the current fiscal year, or, if the notification occurs in the last three months of that year, at the end of the next fiscal year (Art. 7 CoE Statute). According to Art. 28 CM Rules of Procedure (CM, Rules of Procedure of the Committee of Ministers of the Council of Europe (9th session, August 1951)), the CM shall decide on the legal and financial consequences of the withdrawal. The decision will be notified to the withdrawing member.

[11]The ECHR may be denounced pursuant to Art. 58 ECHR. Under section 1 of that provision, denunciation is permissible after five years from the date of becoming a party and upon six months' notice to the CoE Secretary-General. As another avenue, a party that ceases to be a member of the CoE also ceases to be a party to the ECHR. Importantly, Art. 58(2) ECHR contains a 'survival clause', according to which the ECHR continues to apply to any conduct of a party prior to the date on which its withdrawal from the ECHR becomes effective. This clause applies to both possibilities of withdrawal, i.e. both to the denunciation of the ECHR under Art. 58(1) ECHR and the withdrawal from the CoE (Art. 58(3) CoE).

[12]The (R)ESC contains comparatively nuanced rules for denunciation. According to Art. 37(1) ESC / Art. M(1) RESC a party may denounce the whole charter within six months' notice after five years from the date of entering into force, or after any subsequent period of two years. Under the same conditions, a party may denounce single articles or paragraphs of Part II (R)ESC, provided that a minimum number of 16 articles or 63 paragraphs remain accepted (Art. 37(2) ESC / Art. M (2) RESC).

membership in the Bank or the CoE, or to denounce the ECHR or the ESC. Therefore, withdrawal will not be considered further here.

B. ILO Member States' Exceptional Obligation to Actively Promote the ILO's Model in Other IOs

While member states thus have a broad array of means at their disposal, it needs to be ascertained whether they are obliged to use them. In general, ILO law requires the member states to fulfil their membership obligations regardless of any membership in other IOs (Sect. I.). However, this does not automatically amount to an obligation to actively influence other IOs in the ILO's favour—such an obligation only arises in exceptional cases as a matter of loyalty and sincere cooperation (Sect. II.). Moreover, in fulfilling this obligation, states can encounter a range of limitations within the other IOs (Sect. III.).

I. The Duty to Fulfil ILO Membership Obligations Regardless of Parallel Membership Obligations

ILO law sets forth a range of membership obligations (Sect. 1.). The way these obligations are formulated and applied mirror ILO institutional law's relativization of other IOs: ILO member states have to fulfil their membership obligations regardless of whether they are also members in other IOs (Sect. 2.).

1. A Brief Outline of ILO Membership Obligations

ILO member states are required to fulfil all their membership obligations arising under the ILO Constitution, the Declarations and any further ILO instrument binding on them.

On a general note, all members are obliged to pursue the ILO's objectives. For instance, as formulated in the 1998 Declaration,

> in freely joining the ILO, all Members have endorsed the principles and rights set out in its Constitution and in the Declaration of Philadelphia and have undertaken to work towards attaining the overall objectives of the Organization to the best of their resources and fully in line with their specific circumstances.

On a substantive level, ILO membership entails the obligation to respect, promote and realize fundamental principles and rights at work.[13] Moreover, as to the ILO's objectives, the 2008 Declaration stipulates in Part II B that:

> Members have a key responsibility to contribute, through their social and economic policy, to the realization of a global and integrated strategy for the implementation of the strategic objectives, which encompass the Decent Work Agenda outlined in Part I of this Declaration.

Furthermore, there are a number of institutional and procedural obligations. They comprise obligations ensuring the ILO's functioning, e.g. by nominating non-governmental delegates to the Conference (Art. 3(5) ILO Constitution)[14] or by paying financial contributions (Art. 13(3) ILO Constitution).

Moreover, there are obligations to observe and implement the ILO's output, e.g. by requiring member states to submit adopted conventions and recommendations to their competent bodies (Art. 19(5) lit. b and c, (6) lit. b ILO Constitution), by submitting progress reports (Art. 19(5) lit. e, (6) lit. d and Art. 22 ILO Constitution) or by cooperating during inquiries (Art. 27 ILO Constitution). Additionally, member states are obliged to faithfully implement the accepted ILO conventions which they have ratified. This obligation is explicitly enshrined in Art. 19(5) lit. d ILO Constitution, but would also ensue from the general principle of *pacta sunt servanda*, enshrined in Art. 26 VCLT.

2. ILO Law's Indifference Regarding Parallel Membership Obligations

The ILO's institutional law requires the fulfilment of membership obligations regardless of whether an ILO member state is also a member of another IO. On the one hand, this means that ILO member states are free to participate in other IOs (Sect. a). However, on the other hand, such participation does not relieve them from fulfilling obligations as ILO members, which must strictly and fully be observed (Sect. b). As the law stands today, ILO member states cannot invoke competing parallel membership obligations under the law of another IO as justification for not observing ILO membership obligations (Sect. c).

a) ILO Member States' Freedom to Participate in Other IOs

ILO member states are free to establish and to join other IOs. It is nowadays established in international law that a state does not incur international responsibility for violations of its obligations solely because of its membership in an IO.[15]

---

[13] No 2 1998 ILO Declaration.

[14] On this obligation see *Designation of the Workers Delegate for the Netherlands at the Third Session of the International Labour* Conference (Advisory Opinion) PCIJ Rep Series B No 1.

[15] ILC, 'Draft Articles on the Responsibility of International Organizations, with Commentaries' [2011] YILC Vol II Part Two 46, Art. 62, para 5, each with further references.

Obligations arising from ILO membership are no exception in this regard. On the contrary, the ILO Constitution itself explicitly envisages the existence of other IOs. It even anticipates a particular mechanism—the UN System—to coordinate them.[16] Thus, the mere fact that an ILO member state is also a member of other IOs does not put that member at variance with its ILO membership obligations.

b) The Persisting Duty to Fulfil ILO Membership Obligations

That being said, membership in other IOs does not absolve ILO member states from fulfilling their ILO membership obligations. On the contrary, ILO members remain liable to fulfil their membership obligations regardless of any parallel membership in other IOs.[17]

This conclusion is firstly supported by the wording of the aforesaid constitutional provisions stipulating ILO membership obligations. These provisions are formulated in an unqualified and unconditional manner and do not mention parallel membership. This implies that parallel membership in other IOs is not deemed a relevant factor when it comes to the fulfilment of ILO membership obligations.

Secondly, the conclusion is reinforced by ILO supervisory practice. The ILO supervisory bodies, while not ignoring member states' other international commitments, have taken the position that such other obligations do not alter their scope of obligation under ILO instruments. On a general level, the CFA has consistently held that

> a State cannot use the argument that other commitments or agreements can justify the non-application of ratified ILO Conventions.[18]

---

[16]See Chap. 8 B. I. Not least because the ILO was erected with a view to attain universal membership, the existence of these provisions on other IOs necessarily implies that ILO members may erect and join such other IOs.

[17]Outside the ILO context, a number of domestic and international courts and bodies have held that a state cannot invoke its membership in an IO and ensuing obligations as grounds for noncompliance with its international obligations, including those assumed as members of other IOs. In other words, states must not evade their international obligations by erecting or joining an IO, see e.g. *Bosphorus Hava Yollari Turizm ve Ticaret Anonim Sirketi v. Ireland* ECHR 2005–VI 107, para 154; *Luke Munyandu Tembani and Benjamin John Freeth v. Angola and Thirteen Others* Communication 409/12 (African Commission on Human and Peoples' Rights, 30 April 2014), paras 132 et seqq. Art. 61(1) DARIO, which was drafted by the ILC in the light of ECtHR's jurisprudence (ILC, 'Draft Articles on the Responsibility of International Organizations, with Commentaries' (n 15) Art. 61 DARIO, 99), reads: "1. A State member of an international organization incurs international responsibility if, by taking advantage of the fact that the organization has competence in relation to the subject-matter of one of the State's international obligations, it circumvents that obligation by causing the organization to commit an act that, if committed by the State, would have constituted a breach of the obligation."

[18]*Guatemala (Case No 2194)* Report of the Committee on Freedom of Association No 330 (2003) LXXXVI ILO Official Bulletin Ser B/1 267, para 791; ILO, *Digest of Decisions and Principles of the Freedom of Association Committee of the Governing Body of the ILO* (5th edn, ILO 2006) para 21.

This also applies to other international commitments emanating from parallel membership in other IOs, even when such commitments have a decisive influence on the ILO member state's ability to fulfil ILO obligations. An example is the so-called *BALPA case* examined by the CEACR. In that case, the United Kingdom invoked the CJEU's notorious *Viking* and *Laval* judgments (setting forth an overly restrictive interpretation of the right to strike)[19] and the primacy of EU law to argue that it was prevented from giving full effect to ILO Convention No 87 on freedom of association.[20] In a line of observations on the matter, the CEACR inter alia observed that

> its task is not to judge the correctness of the [CJEU's] holdings in *Viking* and *Laval* as they set out an interpretation of the European Union law, based on varying and distinct rights in the Treaty of the European Community, but rather to examine whether the impact of these decisions at national level are such as to deny workers' freedom of association rights under Convention No 87 (emphasis in original).[21]

The Committee moved on to consider

> that the doctrine that is being articulated in these [CJEU] judgements is likely to have a significant restrictive effect on the exercise of the right to strike in practice in a manner contrary to the Convention.[22]

Following up on these observations, the CEACR repeatedly requested the government to review the incriminated legislation with a view of achieving compliance with ILO Convention No 87.[23] Remarkably, the CEACR did not reflect further on

---

[19]Case C-438/05 *International Transport Workers Federation, Finnish Seamens Union v. Viking Line ABP and OÜ Viking Line Eesti* (ECLI:EU:C:2007:772) [2007] ECR I-10779; Case C-341/05 *Laval Un Partneri Ltd v. Svenska Byggnadsarbetareförbundet, Svenska Byggnadsarbetareförbundets Avdelning 1, Byggettan and Svenska Elektrikerförbundet* (ECLI: EU:C:2007:809) [2007] ECR I-11767.

[20]*Observation (CEACR) Freedom of Association and Protection of the Right to Organise Convention, 1948 (No 87) - United Kingdom (Ratification: 1949)* Report of the Committee of Experts on the Application of Conventions and Recommendations (2010) ILC.99/III(1A) 208, 209; *Observation (CEACR) Freedom of Association and Protection of the Right to Organise Convention, 1948 (No 87) - United Kingdom (Ratification: 1949)* Report of the Committee of Experts on the Application of Conventions and Recommendations (2011) ILC.100/III(1A) 186, 187.

[21]*Observation (CEACR) Freedom of Association and Protection of the Right to Organise Convention, 1948 (No 87) - United Kingdom (Ratification: 1949)* (2010) (n 20) 209. Similarly, in *Case No 2820 (Greece)*, the CFA carefully abstained from assessing deregulatory labour law reforms adopted by the Greek government on the recommendation of the IMF as part of austerity measures, *Greece (Case No 2820)* (21 October 2010) Report of the Committee on Freedom of Association No 365 (2012) XCV ILO Official Bulletin Ser B 228, para 991.

[22]*Observation (CEACR) Freedom of Association and Protection of the Right to Organise Convention, 1948 (No 87) - United Kingdom (Ratification: 1949)* (2010) (n 20) 209.

[23]ibid. *Observation (CEACR) - adopted 2010, published 100th ILC session (2011), Freedom of Association and Protection of the Right to Organise Convention, 1948 (No 87) - United Kingdom (Ratification: 1949)* (2011) (n 20) 187. The CEACR took a similar stance in subsequent observations, see e.g. on the Swedish so-called Lex Laval of 2010, *Observation (CEACR) Freedom of Association and Protection of the Right to Organise Convention, 1948 (No 87) - Sweden (Ratification: 1949)* Report of the Committee of Experts on the Application of Conventions and Recommendations (2013) ILC.102/III(1A) 176 et seqq.

the United Kingdom's invocation of the primacy of EU law over domestic law. Neither did it reflect on it in other cases involving EU law, nor, for that matter, did any ILO supervisory body reflect in more depth on any other IO's law and ILO member states' obligations thereunder.

It emanates from the CFA's general stance and the CEACR's reasoning in the *BALPA case* that ILO member states must fulfil their obligations irrespective of membership in another IO, and any obligation this may encompass.

c) Can Adherence to Parallel Membership Obligations Justify Violating ILO Membership Obligations?

In the light of other international developments, one could consider that, under certain circumstances, giving effect to parallel membership obligations could serve as justification for disobeying ILO membership obligations. If that was the case, the strict 'blindness' of the ILO's law regarding parallel membership obligations would be mitigated.

Such justifications have been discussed in the area of human rights protection, with a view to reconcile member states' obligations under IOs' laws on the one hand, and the interest in avoiding circumvention of human rights obligations on the other. To achieve this result, several domestic and international human rights bodies have employed a standard of 'equivalent protection'.[24] For instance, the ECtHR held that if state parties to the ECHR encroach on ECHR guarantees in the course of fulfilling a membership obligation under the law of an IO they are members of, this encroachment is justified as long as that IO substantively and procedurally protects human rights on a level that is equivalent to the one provided by the ECHR.[25]

As far as is apparent, the ILO has so far not decided whether and to what extent it accepts such justifications. In any event, transposition of concepts from other areas of international law had to be handled with care. For instance, the equivalent protection test could be employed with regard to substantive levels of protection

[24] See e.g. *Solange II* (ECLI:DE:BVerfG:1986:rs19861022:2BvR19783) BVerfGE 73, 339, 374 et seqq.; *Bosphorus Hava Yollari Turizm ve Ticaret Anonim Sirketi v. Ireland* (n 17) para 154 et seq.; *Waite and Kennedy v. Germany* ECHR 1999–I 393, para 50 et seqq.

[25] As put by the ECtHR's Grand Chamber in *Bosphorus*, "[s]tate action taken in compliance with such legal obligations is justified as long as the relevant organisation is considered to protect fundamental rights, as regards both the substantive guarantees offered and the mechanisms controlling their observance, in a manner which can be considered at least equivalent to that for which the Convention provides (...). By 'equivalent' the Court means 'comparable'; any requirement that the organisation's protection be 'identical' could run counter to the interest of international cooperation pursued (...). However, any such finding of equivalence could not be final and would be susceptible to review in the light of any relevant change in fundamental rights protection", *Bosphorus Hava Yollari Turizm ve Ticaret Anonim Sirketi v Ireland* (n 17) para 155. See also *Waite and Kennedy v. Germany* (n 24) para 51 et seq.

of labour rights, but not necessarily with regard to the ILO's institutional and procedural peculiarities.[26]

For the time being, it must therefore be concluded that ILO member states remain fully liable for fulfilling obligations under ILO law, regardless of any parallel membership obligations under the law of another IO.

II. Loyalty and Sincere Cooperation as a Legal Basis for Obligations to Promote

The fact that ILO member states remain obliged to fulfil their membership obligations despite parallel membership in other IOs, however, does not automatically imply that the member states are also obliged to actively influence these other IOs' behaviour towards the ILO. As will be seen in this section, ILO law does not impose a general legal obligation of ILO member states to promote the ILO and its work in other IOs (Sect. 1.). However, it is possible that, depending on the particular case at hand, such an obligation can arise in the form of a legal obligation to loyalty and sincere cooperation (Sect. 2.). That being said, the threshold for such an obligation is high (Sect. 3.).

1. No General Obligation to Promote the ILO in Other IOs

There is no general obligation incumbent on the ILO member states to promote the ILO and its model in other IOs.

Firstly, there are no explicit duties of this kind. The 2008 Declaration on Social Justice for a Fair Globalization, designed as a contemporary reformulation and recalibration of the ILO's mandate and capacities, contains only aspirational language when addressing the implications of parallel membership. It contemplates in Part B (iv) that members

> *may consider*
>
> (...)

[26]In the context of ILO members' substantive obligations, e.g. the obligation to faithfully implement fundamental principles and rights at work or rights enshrined in ratified ILO conventions, it could be argued that a human rights instrument foresees an equivalent level of protection to the one of pertinent ILO conventions. However, as to procedural equivalence, it is already questionable whether, say, (quasi-)adjudicatory supervision by human rights bodies is equivalent to tripartite supervision in the ILO or if it is simply different. Moreover, as seen, ILO membership also comes with a range of procedural obligations intended to ensure the functioning of the ILO's model. As to these obligations, substantial modifications to the test would become necessary in order to be in a position to assess whether another IO provides equivalent protection.

> (iv) the taking of appropriate steps for an adequate coordination between positions taken on behalf of the member State concerned in relevant international forums and any steps they may take under the present Declaration (...).[27] (emphasis added)

The desire to enhance the ILO's relevance in other IOs is also mentioned in a range of other ILO documents.[28] Yet, there are no legally binding obligations to promote the ILO's model in other IOs laid down in ILO instruments.

Secondly, there is no implicit duty to promote the ILO's model in other IOs. In particular, such a duty is not an implicit corollary of ILO membership obligations, because promoting the ILO's model in other IOs is not necessary to fulfil these obligations. Rather, each ILO member state is in principle free to choose the means by which it fulfils its ILO membership obligations.[29] This is true whether or not that member state possesses legal obligations under the law of another IO, the fulfilment of which would lead to incoherence or even a conflict with its membership obligations under ILO instruments. Thus, an ILO member state is not necessarily required to strive to align 'its' other IOs' conduct to the ILO's agenda. It is true that influencing other IOs may be a viable option to fulfil certain ILO membership obligations effectively (e.g. the constitutional obligation to respect, promote and realize fundamental principles and rights at work). However, the mere existence of an effective option to fulfil obligation does not in itself imply that it has to be chosen over all other available options. An ILO member state can also choose other means, e.g. compensatory measures on the domestic level to account for incoherencies with other IOs' policies. The only conceivable situation in which influence on other IOs is legally required is if there is no other reasonable means to fulfil ILO membership obligations, or if another option would be substantially less effective—a case which is the exception.

In consequence, ILO member states are not generally obliged to promote the ILO's model in other IOs.

2. Obligation to Promote the ILO's Model in Other IOs as a Matter of Loyalty and Sincere Cooperation

That being said, an obligation to promote the ILO and its model can exist in certain situations. Such obligations can be based on considerations of loyalty and sincere cooperation between the ILO and its members. Legal obligations based on loyalty and sincere cooperation have been discussed with regard to the EU (Sect. a). They

---

[27] See further Francis Maupain, *The Future of the International Labour Organization in the Global Economy* (Hart Publishing 2013) 105.

[28] International Labour Conference (105th session) Resolution on Advancing Social Justice through Decent Work (9 June 2016) XCIX ILO Official Bulletin Ser A No 2 30, para 13 and 16.

[29] The 2008 Declaration stipulates that "implementation of the Decent Work Agenda at national level will depend on national needs and priorities and it will be for member States, in consultation with the representative organizations of workers and employers, to determine how to discharge that responsibility", 2008 Declaration, Part II B.

can in principle also exist in the law of other IOs than the EU (Sect. b). That being said, the EU's rules cannot simply be transposed to the ILO context, because obligations to loyalty and sincere cooperation are highly contingent on the respective particular institutional context (Sect. c).

On a terminological note, there are several synonyms in use.[30] For purposes of the present study, the terms 'loyalty' and 'sincere cooperation' will be employed.

a) The EU as a Leading Case for the Concept of Loyalty and Sincere Cooperation

Obligations to loyalty and sincere cooperation have been most elaborately pronounced in EU law.[31] Essentially, the principle of loyalty and sincere cooperation requires the EU and its members to cooperate in good faith, to provide each other mutual assistance in the fulfilment of their tasks, to respect the other's legitimate interests and not to counteract each other's actions.[32] Loyalty and sincere cooperation encompasses positive obligations to assist, inform and consult, and negative obligations to refrain from impairing the effective attainment of Union objectives.[33]

The principle of sincere cooperation is fully applicable to the EU's external relations. In this area, sincere cooperation promotes unity in the representation of the EU at international level.[34] It applies to the establishment and implementation of

[30]On the terminology Christian Calliess, Wolfgang Kahl and Adelheid Puttler, 'Art. 4 EUV' in Christian Calliess and Matthias Ruffert (eds), *EUV/AEUV - Das Verfassungsrecht der Europäischen Union mit Europäischer Grundrechtecharta, Kommentar* (5th edn, C H Beck 2016) para 29 et seqq.

[31]EU law contains several explicit provisions: Loyalty and sincere cooperation are the subject of Art. 4(3) TEU and numerous special provisions, for example in Art 24(3) TEU regarding the Common Foreign and Security Policy, see further Calliess, Kahl and Puttler (n 30) and Marcus Klamert, *The Principle of Loyalty in EU Law* (Oxford University Press 2016). In EU external relations law, sincere cooperation is supplemented by the principle of consistency, laid down in Art. 21(3) TEU, see Pieter Jan Kuijper and others, *The Law of EU External Relations - Cases, Materials, and Commentary on the EU as an International Legal Actor* (2nd edn, Oxford University Press 2015) 24.

[32]Henri de Waele, *Legal Dynamics of EU External Relations,* (2nd edn, Springer 2017) 179; Geert De Baere and Timothy Roes, 'EU Loyalty as Good Faith' (2015) 64 International and Comparative Law Quarterly 829.

[33]Eleftheria Neframi, 'The Duty of Loyalty: Rethinking Its Scope Through Its Application in the Field of EU External Relations' (2010) 47 Common Market Law Review 323, 359; Hermann-Josef Blanke, 'Art. 4' in Hermann-Josef Blanke and Stelio Mangiameli (eds), *The Treaty on European Union (TEU) - A Commentary* (Springer 2013) para 85.

[34]Ruling 1/78 *Draft Convention of the International Atomic Energy Agency on the Physical Protection of Nuclear Materials, Facilities and Transports* (ECLI:EU:C:1978:202) [1978] ECR 02151, paras 34 et seqq.; Opinion 2/91 *Convention No 170 of the International Labour Organization concerning Safety in the Use of Chemicals at Work* (ECLI:EU:C:1993:106) [1993] ECR I-01061 para 36; Opinion 1/94 *Competence of the Community to Conclude International Agreements concerning Services and the Protection of Intellectual Property* (ECLI:EU:C:1994:384)

contractual relations with third parties, including both treaties concluded by either the EU or the member states alone and mixed agreements.[35] This comprises establishing membership in other IOs, as the CJEU does not draw a distinction between constituent instruments of IOs and other treaties. In external relations, loyalty obliges member states to act in the Union interest.[36]

The EU treaties lay down comparatively detailed provisions on EU member states' obligations to sincere cooperation with the Union. Art. 4(3) TEU, EU law's central provision on loyalty and sincere cooperation, specifically provides that:

> (...)
>
> [t]he Member States shall take any appropriate measure, general or particular, to ensure fulfilment of the obligations arising out of the Treaties or resulting from the acts of the institutions of the Union.
>
> The Member States shall facilitate the achievement of the Union's tasks and refrain from any measure which could jeopardise the attainment of the Union's objectives.

Furthermore, EU law contains a number of more specific provisions on sincere cooperation in external relations,[37] including on EU member states' conduct in other IOs. For instance, Art. 34(1) TEU provides that:

> Member States shall coordinate their action in international organisations (...). They shall uphold the Union's positions in such forums. (...)
>
> In international organisations (...) where not all the Member States participate, those which do take part shall uphold the Union's positions.

The CJEU has repeatedly interpreted the obligations to loyalty and sincere cooperation to impose obligations of EU member states to respect and to promote EU positions in IOs and to avoid conduct in other IOs that would risk undermining the attainment of EU policy objectives.[38] In sum, in EU law, there are general and specific positive obligations incumbent upon the member states to promote and safeguard EU positions and interests in other IOs in which they are members.

[1994] ECR I-05267, para 108; Case C-25/94 *Commission v. Council* (ECLI:EU:C:1996:114) [1996] ECR I-01469, para 48; Case C-246/07 *Commission v. Sweden* (ECLI:EU:C:2010:203) [2010] ECR I-03317, para 73.

[35] Calliess, Kahl and Puttler (n 30).

[36] Marise Cremona, 'Member States as Trustees of the Union Interest: Participating in International Agreements on Behalf of the European Union' in Anthony Arnull and others (eds), *Constitutional Order of States: Essays in EU Law in Honour of Alan Dashwood* (Oxford University Press 2011) 435; Neframi (n 33) 359.

[37] For instance, regarding the EU's Common Foreign and Security Policy, Art, 24(3) TEU.

[38] E.g. Opinion 2/91 *Convention No 170 of the International Labour Organization concerning Safety in the Use of Chemicals at Work* (ECLI:EU:C:1993:106) [1993] ECR I-01061 para 5; Case C-45/07 *Commission v. Greece* (ECLI:EU:C:2009:81) [2009] ECR I-00701, paras 15 et seqq.; Case C 399/12 *Federal Republic of Germany v. Council* (ECLI:EU:C:2014:2258) para 52.

The aforesaid provisions and practice from EU law give an initial idea on how the general duty to loyalty and sincere cooperation owed by the ILO member states to the ILO could be understood.

b) Obligations to Loyalty and Sincere Cooperation Beyond EU Law

A number of commentators has argued that loyalty and sincere cooperation are not peculiar to EU law, but equally apply in the relations between other IOs and their respective member states.[39] Beyond EU law, established practice is sparser. However, in its *WHO/Egypt* opinion, the ICJ indicated that obligations to sincere cooperation also exist in other IOs. It held that

> [t]he very fact of Egypt's membership of the [WHO] entails certain mutual obligations of co-operation and good faith incumbent upon Egypt and upon the Organization.[40]

Given that loyalty and sincere cooperation are based on fulfilling membership obligations in good faith, accepting them in the context of other IOs seems consequent as a matter of principle. If, then, loyalty and sincere cooperation give rise to legal obligations in the laws of other IOs, there is in principle a good arguable case that they also apply regarding the ILO.

c) Loyalty and Sincere Cooperation in the ILO Context

In the light of the foregoing, loyalty and sincere cooperation may in principle also give rise to obligations of ILO member states to promote the ILO and its model within other IOs.

That being said, the general relevance of loyalty and sincere cooperation does not mean that the EU's comparatively developed case-law and institutional practice could simply be transposed to the ILO context. Loyalty means different things in different contexts, and every IO's institutional law creates its very own context in which loyalty is demanded and given. The context of the EU is peculiar in many ways. On a general note, the EU has extensive external competences, which in some policy areas are exclusive.[41] As far as the external relations to other IOs are

---

[39]Matthias Ruffert and Christian Walter, *Institutionalisiertes Völkerrecht* (2nd edn, C H Beck 2015) para 258; Henry G Schermers and Niels M Blokker, 'International Organizations or Institutions, Membership', *Max Planck Encyclopedia of Public International Law* (Oxford University Press 2008) para 12 et seqq. Limiting cooperation to a procedural principle Konrad Ginther, 'Mitgliedschaft in Internationalen Organisationen - Grundfragen' in Konrad Ginther and Thomas Oppermann (eds), *Grundfragen der Mitgliedschaft in Internationalen Organisationen - Referate und Diskussion der 14. Tagung der Deutschen Gesellschaft für Völkerrecht* (C F Müller 1978) 21.

[40]*Interpretation of the Agreement of 25 March 1951 between the WHO and Egypt* (Advisory Opinion) [1980] ICJ Reports 73, 93.

[41]E.g. the Common Commercial Policy, Art. 3(1) lit. e TFEU.

concerned, the EU has engaged in inter-organizational treaty-making on a large scale and has established direct relations and representations with other IOs, for which it has an own political and administrative framework, including the High Representative for Foreign Affairs and the European External Action Service.[42] Another special circumstance is that the EU has sought and attained membership in other IOs, mostly alongside its member states.[43] It is not by coincidence that a good portion of CJEU jurisprudence on sincere cooperation on external relations relate to cooperation between the EU and its members with or within other IOs.[44] The relatively elaborate provisions and practice obliging the EU member states to loyalty and sincere cooperation can be seen as a correlate to these peculiarities.[45]

By contrast, the situation in the ILO context is markedly different. While the ILO also interacts with other IOs on a large scale, it neither has exclusive external competences nor an administrative apparatus that is comparable to the EU's. Moreover, the ILO's tripartite structure places its external relations under the joint control of its tripartite constituents. The ILO's non-governmental constituents can be major drivers (or obstructors, as the case and the perspective may be) of the ILO's inter-organizational relations. All these factors may play out when assessing if and to what extent an ILO member state is obliged to promote the ILO in other IOs. The relevance of loyalty and sincere cooperation in the ILO context is contingent on the latter.

3. The High Threshold of Illoyalty

To assess the scope and extent of ILO members' loyalty obligations to protect or promote the ILO's model in other IOs, it is necessary to ascertain under which circumstances refraining from protecting or promoting it would be 'illoyal'.

a) The Case-Dependence of the Threshold

At the outset, it needs to be recalled that, since loyalty and sincere cooperation are case-dependent, it is hardly possible to define more than outer limits in abstract terms.

---

[42]Arts. 18 and 27 TEU; Council Decision 2010/427/EU of 26 July 2010 Establishing the Organisation and Functioning of the European External Action Service [2010] OJ L201/30.

[43]E.g. the WTO and the FAO, Piet Eeckhout, *EU External Relations Law* (2nd edn, Oxford University Press 2011) 228 et seq.

[44]Opinion 1/94 *Competence of the Community to Conclude International Agreements concerning Services and the Protection of Intellectual Property* (n 34) para 106 et seqq.; Case C-25/94, *Commission v. Council* (n 34) para 40 et seqq.; Kuijper and others (n 31) 190 et seqq.

[45]As to the Common Foreign and Security Policy, the elaborate provisions on loyalty and sincere cooperation are to be seen in the context of limited judicial review and enforcement of the respective obligations, de Waele (n 32) 54.

On the one hand, it is safe to say that member states may not intentionally thwart the ILO's objectives and agenda through their participation in other IOs. This would violate their duty to fulfil their ILO membership obligations in good faith, as enshrined in Art. 26 VCLT. Despite many unclarities in the field, it may be regarded relatively settled customary international law that ILO member states incur international responsibility if they circumvent their international obligations by intentionally inducing another IO to take measures that would violate their obligation if the member state had taken the measure itself.[46]

On the other hand, it seems equally clear that the mere fact that an ILO member state participates in another IO that adversely influences the ILO does not amount to illoyal behaviour. As seen above, ILO law explicitly envisages that member states participate in other IOs and still does not contain a general obligation to promote the ILO in such other IOs.[47] Thus, while the ILO can demand a faithful fulfilment of ILO membership obligations, it seems questionable if the ILO could also legally demand its members to take concrete measures in the other IO by which that member state would violate the other IO's law or severely compromise its position there.

Between these two poles, however, the threshold inevitably remains blurry and dependent on the case at hand. This point becomes even clearer when tentatively looking for illoyal behaviour of ILO member states in the case studies presented in Part I. What exactly, for example, would have been a bona fide approach to the publication and dissemination of the Doing Business reports and their EWI, and why? Did the ILO member states owe to ensure that a World Bank flagship publication did not advocate, or be used to support, labour market deregulation that would be at variance with ILO initiatives and the "spirit" of ILO conventions and recommendations? What exactly would such a duty entail? To be transparent about the fact that the reports purposefully took a business-friendly perspective (which the Bank had already mentioned itself in the reports)? To somehow ensure that the EWI would not be mistaken as indicating overall decent working conditions? To induce the Bank to consult with the ILO on the topic of EWI improvement? Or to require the Bank to discontinue the use of the EWI? Even more pointedly, were the ILO member states obliged to induce the Bank to abandon orthodox liberal conceptions of competitiveness and growth through liberalization, privatization and deregulation? To be sure, asking these questions here is not meant to completely deny the

---

[46]The responsibility for circumvention finds expression in. Art. 61(1) DARIO. In its commentary, the ILC suggested a narrow reading of Art. 61 DARIO, according to which a circumvention requires that the state avoids its responsibility intentionally, explicitly excluding unintended circumventions, ILC, 'Draft Articles on the Responsibility of International Organizations, with Commentaries' (n 15) Art. 61 DARIO, 99, para 2. Moreover, Art. 61(1) DARIO requires that the state has caused the IO's conduct, which the ILC reads as requiring a "significant link" between the state's and the IO's conduct, ibid 99, para 7; Mirka Möldner, 'Responsibility of International Organizations – Introducing the ILC's DARIO' (2012) 16 Max Planck Yearbook of United Nations Law, Volume 281, 320 et seq.

[47]Moreover, loyalty is reciprocal, which means that the ILO itself needs to have regard to the interests of its member states.

possibility that any of them could be answered in the affirmative under certain circumstances. However, raising these issues illustrates that it is everything but clear what the threshold for illoyal behaviour actually is.

b) Loyalty and Concrete Action

Moreover, it needs to be emphasized that the obligation to loyal behaviour and to cooperate sincerely usually does not predefine concrete steps to be taken. In principle, ILO member states remain free to take whichever action fulfils the standard of loyalty and sincere cooperation. This may, but need not, entail the promotion of the ILO and its model in other IOs. Only in cases in which such promotion is the only available means of sincere cooperation, the ILO could actually demand it.[48] For purposes of this study, this further diminishes the relevance of loyalty obligations.

4. Conclusion

In sum, it appears that, in principle, loyalty and sincere cooperation form a basis for an obligation incumbent on ILO member states to influence other IOs in a manner that is conducive to the ILO's model of labour governance. This obligation, however, is likely to be limited to a minimum standard, arguably entitling the ILO to claim specific acts of influence only in rare cases.

III. Excursus: ILO Member States' Means of Promotion and Their Constraints

Having established that loyalty and sincere cooperation may—even if only in rare constellations—require ILO member states to promote the ILO's model in other IOs, it is appropriate to have a closer look at the means they have at their disposal to do so. The several ways in which ILO member states with parallel membership can influence the Bank or the CoE have already been outlined at the beginning of this chapter. What needs to be added here is that there are important limitations in place that may curtail their ability to influence inter-organizational interaction between the ILO and the Bank and CoE.[49]

---

[48] Armin von Bogdandy, 'General Principles of International Public Authority: Sketching a Research Field' (2008) 9 German Law Journal 1909, 1932.

[49] Guglielmo Verdirame, *The UN and Human Rights: Who Guards the Guardians?* (Cambridge University Press 2011) 33; Michael Barnett and Martha Finnemore, 'The Power of Liberal International Organisations' in Michael Barnett and Raymond Duvall (eds), *Power in Global Governance* (Cambridge University Press 2005) 169.

To be sure, conceptually, any claim to loyalty and sincere cooperation the ILO may have against its member states in principle exists whether or not the member states have the legal or factual means to actually fulfil this obligation. Still, having a closer look at these legal and factual means is worthwhile. For one part, examining what an ILO member state could actually do allows inferences as to whether that member acted in good or bad faith. For another part, examining the means and their limits elucidates the actual relevance that loyalty obligations can have.[50]

1. Organizational and Procedural Independence of Bodies

First of all, there are organizational and procedural limitations.[51] Some of the CoE's and Bank's organs and bodies have an institutionalized degree of independence from such influence. Usually, such independence is provided for in the bodies' respective legal bases and connected to the bodies' respective functions. Such independence exists, firstly regarding the Bank's and CoE's Secretariat and staff, and, secondly, regarding their judicial and quasi-judicial bodies, notably the ECtHR and the ECSR.[52]

As to secretariats and staff, there are three principal ways in which member states can exert influence.[53] Firstly, states can exercise influence by creating or amending

[50]To be sure, it is not submitted here that, because of these limitations, ILO member states were not able at all to significantly influence the Bank's or the CoE's conduct in a manner conducive to the ILO's model of labour governance. Obviously, whether and to what extent they can do so heavily depends on the particular constellation at hand. Moreover, much depends on whether one state acts alone or more member states act jointly, whether these states are politically powerful and, finally, how ambitious they are, e.g. whether they are willing to induce systemic changes. Still, the discussed limitations indicate that it is not self-evident that member states can always control 'their' IOs at will.

[51]A somewhat 'atypical' further limitation exists in the World Bank. According to Art. III(2) IBRD-AoA, "[e]ach member shall deal with the Bank only through its Treasury, central bank, stabilization fund or other similar fiscal agency, and the Bank shall deal with members only by or through the same agencies." This does not include the member states' representatives in the Bank's organs, e.g. the Board of Governors, which are usually Finance Ministers or persons of comparable rank. The clause rather refers to the "external" relations with members. Still, it obviously resembles a limitation, which excludes the more political branches of governments. This narrowed channel for interaction becomes even more relevant if seen in connection with the fact that the domestic counterpart, e.g. a member's central bank, can itself be structurally independent from the government. This is e.g. the case in Germany, see Art. 88 German Basic Law (Grundgesetz für die Bundesrepublik Deutschland, BGBl 1949, 1).

[52]The World Bank Inspection Panel will be left aside, for the sole reason that it played no role in the case studies underlying this study.

[53]Formally, secretariats and staff have a 'serving' function. However, as a factual matter, they possess significant leverage to set agenda or influence the activities of their IO, including its inter-organizational interactions, Ruffert and Walter (n 39) para 386; Verdirame (n 49) 33. Art. V(5) lit. c IBRD-AoA and Art. 36 lit. d – f CoE Statute endow the Bank's and CoE's secretariats, their principal executive officers and their staff with independence and autonomy from member state influence (see also Art. 9(4) ILO Constitution and Art. 1.1 ILO Staff Regulations 2019).

the IO's administrative law or by adopting policies or instruments that must be applied by the Secretariats and staff members.[54] Secondly, state-driven organs usually retain a right of oversight and direction over the IO's staff.[55] Thirdly,

[54]The status and employment relations of staff members is governed by a distinct set of norms. In principle, every IO has its own rules on the status of and the employment relations with its staff. A unified international civil service law does not exist, although several attempts have been made at approximating or harmonizing the rules for international civil service among certain IOs, Yves Beigbeder, 'Civil Service, International', *Max Planck Encyclopedia of Public International Law* (Oxford University Press 2007) para 3. It comprises norms e.g. on posts and their classification, recruitment, legal status, salaries and allowances, training and evaluation, social security, leave, retirement and pensions and termination of service, ibid 28 et seqq. Furthermore, it also includes the basic duties of staff, such as the duty to loyalty towards the IO, and rules on discipline, unsatisfactory execution of service and misconduct, ibid 41. The long-debated question whether these rules governing the relations between an IO and its staff constitute law and form part of international law shall not be revisited here, see Chittharanjan Felix Amerasinghe, *The Law of the International Civil Service: (as Applied by International Administrative Tribunals), vol I* (Clarendon Press 1994) 274 et seqq. Today, it is established that the relations between an IO and its staff is governed by that IO's internal administrative law. The sources of this law have not been comprehensively and authoritatively determined. However, in their practice, international administrative tribunals have had recourse to a variety of sources, including employment contracts and instruments of appointment, the IO's constituent instrument, staff regulations, staff rules, manuals and circulars, contracts, further general principles of law and the practice of the IO. Remarkably, international administrative tribunals have shown great reluctance to apply international law, unless it has been incorporated into the respective IO's internal law, ibid 293 et seq. Employment disputes are decided on by the World Bank Administrative Tribunal and the Administrative Tribunal of the Council of Europe, both of which are special and separate international administrative tribunals. As a corollary thereto, IO staff members enjoy functional immunity in the member and seat states, which provides additional shielding against influence by member states, Ruffert and Walter (n 39) para 392. In consequence, the law governing the status and employment of staff is independent from domestic law and, therefore, out of reach of the IO's member states. Jurisprudence of several administrative tribunals has confirmed this independence. For example, in a line of cases starting with *Duberg v. UNESCO*, the ILOAT held that in the event of a conflict between UNESCO administrative law and the law of a staff member's state of nationality, the former prevails, Judgment No 17 *Duberg v.* UNESCO (ILO Administrative Tribunal, 5th session, 26 April 1955); Amerasinghe (n 54) 278.

[55]For instance, the ILO Governing Body may instruct the ILO Director-General (Art. 8(1) ILO Constitution). The World Bank's Board of Governors and the Bank's Executive Directors may specify the responsibility of the Bank's President, inter alia by giving directives and instructions, see World Bank, Terms of Appointment of David R Malpass as President of the International Bank for Reconstruction and Development (2019) <http://documents.worldbank.org/curated/en/665771554752513452/Terms-of-Appointment-of-David-R-Malpass-as-President-of-the-International-Bank-for-Reconstruction-and-Development> accessed 26 April 2020. The CoE Secretary-General is responsible to the CM for the CoE Secretariat's activities (Art. 37(2) CoE Statute). That being said, as to the World Bank, the Board of Governors and the Executive Directors are themselves organs of the Bank, and as such restrained by the prohibition of political activity, which is a fact repeatedly highlighted by the Bank's Legal Counsel, see Bartram Stewart Brown, *The United States and the Politicization of the World Bank: Issues of International Law and Policy* (Kegan Paul International 1992) 106.

state-driven organs can influence the appointment of chief officers.[56] It should be noted, however, that all three ways of influence require joint action by at least a majority of members.[57] Moreover, all three principal ways to influence are of an abstract and general nature.[58] Thus, they do not lend themselves to target specific instances of inter-organizational interaction within a reasonable period of time.

Judicial and quasi-judicial bodies likewise possess significant substantive and personal independence from the member states.[59] There are only limited possibilities to exert influence on these bodies.

Firstly, as has occasionally happened in other contexts, states could attempt to play one body off against another, threatening to litigate a case elsewhere unless the body approached concedes to certain demands.[60] This, however, will not be possible

[56]The ILO Director-General is appointed by the ILO Governing Body, Art. 8(1) ILO Constitution. The CoE Secretary-General and Deputy Secretary-General are proposed by the government-driven CM; however, they are appointed by the PACE, Art. 36 lit. b CoE Statute.

[57]What is more, constitutional rules on majority come to bear here. For instance, the USA have always been the World Bank's largest shareholder. Moreover, by virtue of an informal 'gentlemen agreement' between the USA and European Members of the Bank and the IMF, the World Bank's President has always been a US national. Notably, the former fact prepares the ground for enhanced influence of the USA, Kathryn C Lavelle, 'American Politics, the Presidency of the World Bank, and Development Policy' (2013) Policy Research Working Paper No. 6377 https://elibrary.worldbank.org/doi/pdf/10.1596/1813-9450-6377 accessed 26 April 2020, 4. The same increased influence exists for other major shareholders, such as Japan or Germany.

[58]For example, state-driven organs' competence to appoint staff usually only refers to leading personnel, whereas other staff are appointed by the leading officers. See Art. 9(1) ILO Constitution and Art. 36 lit. c CoE Statute. In the IBRD, the Executive Directors only exercise "general control" over the President in this regard, Art. V(5) lit. b IBRD-AoA.

[59]See in general John Merills, 'International Adjudication and Autonomy' in Richard Collins and Nigel D White (eds), *International Organizations and the Idea of Autonomy - Institutional Independence in the International Legal Order* (Routledge 2011) 166 et seqq. In addition to what has been said in this respect in Part I, there are further aspects to be mentioned. For instance, ECtHR judges serve in their individual capacity and must not engage in any activity that would compromise their independence or impartiality. As to the ECtHR, see Art. 21(2) and (3) ECHR. This includes in particular political or administrative activity (Rule 4 ECtHR Rules of Court). See also the corresponding oath or solemn declaration each judge has to take or make before taking up office, Rule 3(1) ECtHR Rules of Court. According to Rule 13 ECtHR Rules of Court, a judge may not preside over a case where the state of his nationality or that proposed him for office is a party. The judges enjoy the same privileges and immunities as employees of the CoE (Art. 51 ECHR, referencing Art. 40 CoE Statute and the agreements made pursuant to that provision). A judge's dismissal without consent is conditional on a two-thirds majority of the Court's judges deciding that this judge does no longer fulfil the conditions of service (Art. 23(4) ECHR, Rule 7 ECtHR Rules of Court). Likewise, the ECSR members are required to perform their duty independently and impartially (Rule 3(1) ECSR Rules). Rule 5 ECSR Rules contains a comprehensive incompatibility rule prohibiting any function incompatible with their independence, impartiality and availability.

[60]For example, in the *Gulf of Maine* Case, the parties pushed to be involved in the composition of the ICJ chamber, threatening that they could otherwise withdraw the case from the Court and refer it to arbitration, *Delimitation of the Maritime Boundary in the Gulf of Maine Area (Canada v. United States)* (Constitution of Chamber, Order) [1982] ICJ Reports 3; Merills (n 59) 162.

with regard to the bodies in question here, either because there are *lis alibi pendens* rules in place,[61] or because another body simply does not exist.[62]

Secondly, states could simply refrain from bringing cases to a specific dispute settlement body.[63] However, given that the bodies in questions here can also be approaches by individuals or associations, states' leverage is again limited.[64]

A third option could be to withdraw consent to a body's jurisdiction, which can pose a serious challenge to that body's reputation and relevance. That being said, withdrawal of consent may come at a high price. For example, as to the ECtHR, the jurisdiction of which is compulsory, withdrawing consent would require denouncing the ECHR, which again would call into question membership in the CoE (and perhaps other organizations, such as the EU).

Lastly, states could attempt to use channels of influence that some bodies in question here foresee. For instance, the involvement of the Governmental Committee on the second stage of the (R)ESC supervisory procedure opens an avenue for the (R)ESC parties to exert influence. In the early decades of ESC supervision, states' influence has resulted in the Governmental Committee occasionally 'reviewing' the ECSR and expounding its own legal interpretations of the Charter, particularly in politically sensitive areas like the right to strike.[65] However, according to the 1991 Amending Protocol's clarification of functions, the Governmental Committee is confined to making political and other non-legal considerations. This clarification has resulted in a loss of influence of the parties over the ECSR's legal interpretations,[66] including its interactions with the ILO described in Chap. 6.

2. Limitations Within State-Driven Organs

Furthermore, ILO member states' influence can also be reduced in those organs which are primarily state-driven.

---

[61] Art. 55 ECHR expressly prohibits to submit inter-state disputes concerning the ECHR to other fora.

[62] As to disputes between states and individuals (as under the ECHR and the (R)ESC's collective complaint procedure), other dispute settlement mechanisms that the *member state* can initiate are not available.

[63] The underlying leverage would be that "courts cannot choose their cases" (Merills (n 59) 163), i.e. they cannot proactively decide to examine cases in the absence of any complaint.

[64] Cases can be brought by individuals or associations, as is the case under the ECHR or the (R)ESC's collective complaint procedure. In the case of the mandatory (R)ESC reporting system, supervision does not depend on the submission of certain cases. It is true that states could also stop submitting reports. However, contrary to the non-submission of a case to a dispute settlement body, the non-submission of a report amounts to a violation of the respective reporting obligations.

[65] Manfred Mohr, 'The Turin Protocol of 22 October 1991: A Major Contribution to Revitalizing the European Social Charter' (1992) 3 European Journal of International Law 362, 364; Klaus Lörcher, 'Interpretation' in Niklas Bruun and others (eds), *The European Social Charter and the Employment Relation* (Hart Publishing 2017) 52.

[66] Lörcher (n 65) 53.

Firstly, in some organs, decisions are not taken unanimously, but by either a simple[67] or qualified[68] majority. While the members as a whole retain control, a single member or a minority can be outvoted.

Secondly, the rules of the World Bank establish inequalities between the member states. They lead to a comparatively higher influence of some members and a corresponding diminished influence of others. According to the Bank's law, member states have a composite set of votes, consisting of basic votes allocated to each member on an equal basis, and further votes which are weighed according to their contribution. The higher one state's contribution, the more voting power it possesses. Thus, pursuant to Art. V(3) lit. a IBRD-AoA, the amount of votes a member has depends on the amount of shares it holds.[69] In the IDA, voting power is contingent on the rules set forth in replenishment resolutions by the Board of Governors (Art. VI(3) lit. a IDA-AoA).[70]

Finally, influence can also be unequal as to the very composition of organs, notably executive organs. For instance, five of the World Bank's Executive Directors are elected by the five members holding the largest number of shares (Art. V(4) lit. b (i) IBRD-AoA), whereas the others are appointed by all the Governors appointed by the other members (Art. V(4) lit. b (ii) IBRD-AoA).

3. Limited Capacity to Induce Systemic Changes

The limitations discussed so far all relate to the internal organization of certain organs or to questions of procedure. While of significant practical importance for the question of controlling inter-organizational interactions, these aforementioned limitations are somewhat expectable. After all, the facilitation, acceleration and rationalization of work is one fundamental incentive to establish an IO, and sometimes a limitation of member states' influence is a necessary corollary thereto.

Against this background, it is important to address ILO member states' systemic influence on the Bank's and CoE's conduct. One could be tempted to think that the ILO member states, being '*Herren der Verträge*', could at least steer the Bank's and CoE's conduct vis-à-vis the ILO on a larger scale, e.g. by changing the interpretation of relevant provisions of the constituent instruments, or by amending them. As a matter of principle, this is of course the case. Yet, there are important limitations.

---

[67] Simple majority is the default rule in the IDA (Art. VI(3) lit. b IDA-AoA). Likewise, as to the International Labour Conference, the default rule is that decisions are taken by a simple majority of the members present (Art. 17(2) and (3) ILO Constitution).

[68] For instance, under Art. 29 ESC, the CM may, by a two-thirds majority, make recommendations on the basis of the Governmental Committee's report.

[69] This sum is added to number of basic votes which are the same for each member. counted together, these figures make up a member's voting power.

[70] In the MIGA, voting power is allocated according to a member's shares of stock and to its categorization of one of two categories in Schedule A to the MIGA Convention and the overall parity between these two categories (Art. 39 MIGA Convention).

For one part, as seen above, the examined IO's have mechanisms for authoritative interpretation. These mechanisms make definitive interpretations. Member states have an opportunity to present their views and thus take influence.[71] Still, eventually, none of the mechanisms needs to decide unanimously, which means that single member states or the respective minority can be outvoted. Once in place, authoritative interpretations can only be altered through the same procedure or the amendment of the interpreted provision. Both are comparably slow and politically 'costly' avenues. For another part, as has been seen in Part I, inter-organizational interaction can also be triggered through 'simple', i.e. non-authoritative, interpretation. As to these interpretations, it might be even more difficult for member states to exert influence, particularly when they are rendered by bodies with a high degree of independence and autonomy.

In a similar manner, there are significant constraints for conducting formal constitutional amendments. Both the Bank's and the CoE's pertinent procedures pose high thresholds and have proven highly burdensome in practice.[72] In both cases, alternative ways of developing the constituent instruments have evolved. In the World Bank, the formal amendment procedure has largely been substituted by evolutive authoritative interpretations of the AoA rendered by the Executive Directors, with wide opportunities for the Bank's Legal Counsel (instead of the member states) to pre-shape the Directors' interpretation. As to the CoE, the ECHR and ESC have each been amended via separate protocols,[73] the adoption of which essentially follows the procedure for adopting new treaties within the CoE.[74] Apart from these

[71] Art. 36(1) ECHR; Art. IX lit. a IBRD-AoA.

[72] Under Art. VIII lit. a IBRD-AoA, amendments can be proposed by a member state, a Governor or the Executive Directors. Amendments must first be approved by the Board of Governors and then be accepted by three-fifths of the members, holding 85 per cent of the total voting power. Certain amendments require acceptance by all members (see Art. VIII lit. b BRD-AoA). Virtually identical language can be found in Art. IX IDA-AoA, Art. VII IFC-AoA and, with minor deviations, Arts. 59 and 60 MIGA Convention. Single provisions of the IBRD-AoA have been amended as of 1965, 1989 and 2012, mainly to adjust the Bank's authorized capital stock or to implement adjustments resulting from increased membership. As to the CoE, Art. 41 CoE Statute envisages two ways of amending the statute. The first option is an amendment protocol, proposed in the CM or the PACE (Art. 41(1) – (3) CoE Statute). It has never been used in practice. The second is an accelerated amendment procedure for certain provisions on financial matters and the functioning of the PACE, which merely requires approval of amendments by the CM and the PACE.

[73] The ECHR does not explicitly regulate its amendment. In practice the parties have significantly developed the Convention by concluding 16 additional protocols. The (R)ESC explicitly contemplates amendments. Pursuant to Art. 36 ESC / Art. J RESC, every party may propose, and the CM may adopt, amendments to the (R)ESC. Regarding the original ESC, such amendments enter into force immediately upon their adoption by the CM. Amendments to the RESC additionally require the acceptance of the parties (Art. J(1) and (2) RESC). With regard to the entry into force of such amendments, Art. J(3) and (4) RESC differentiate depending on which of the RESC's Parts are amended. In practice, however, important amendments have been effectuated via separate protocols.

[74] Jörg Polakiewicz, *Treaty-Making in the Council of Europe* (Council of Europe Publishing 1999) 161 et seqq.

difficulties, it needs mention that amendments are typically responses to systemic issues. Given that they typically require time, resources and a large level of political consensus, they hardly ever lend themselves to steer inter-organizational interaction at operational level in the first place.

IV. Conclusion on Section B

In sum, the analysis has shown that, depending on the particular case at hand, ILO member states can be obliged to promote the ILO and its model in other IOs as a matter of loyalty and sincere cooperation. While the exact contours of such an obligation can only be determined on a case-by-case basis, it is safe to say that the threshold for a concrete obligation to promote the ILO's model in another IO is high. It is likely that loyalty and sincere cooperation only resemble an outer limit, triggering concrete results only in manifest cases.[75] Insofar as an obligation exists, member states have a broad array of means at their disposal. However, there are also limitations that constrain the deployment of these means.

C. Conclusion on Chap. 12

This chapter has examined whether the ILO's, World Bank's and CoE's common member states are legally obliged to use their parallel membership to steer inter-organizational interactions in a way that is conducive to the ILO's model of labour governance. It has shown that ILO member states remain responsible for faithfully fulfilling their ILO membership obligations, regardless of whether they are also members in other IOs and incur obligations under these other IOs' laws. However, this does not per se put ILO member states under an obligation to exert influence on other IOs. While the law on these questions cannot be regarded settled, it appears that there is no general obligation to actively promote the ILO's model in other IOs. Rather, an obligation to influence other IOs will only arise in certain situations as an element of loyalty and sincere cooperation owed by the ILO member states to the ILO. Insofar as such an obligation exists at all, member states have a broad array of means at their disposal to promote the ILO's model in the other IOs. However, there are also important limitations to the deployment of these means. Not all of these limitations are insurmountable, but they will require increased or concerted efforts, e.g. a certain number of like-minded other member states, or the will to implement not only operational, but systemic changes.

---

[75] von Bogdandy (n 48) 1932.

D. Conclusion on Part II

Overall, the analysis conducted in Part II has revealed that all examined IOs have wide competences to engage in interactions with one another under their respective institutional laws. However, for each IO, these competences are embedded in the IO's wider institutional legal framework. They are thus to be read in conjunction with other provisions of the respective IO's institutional law, such as those setting forth the IO's objectives, as well as the respective institutional, procedural and substantive provisions. As these other provisions must be observed, they predetermine and mould the way in which that IO may use its competences to interact with other IOs.

The effect of this moulding of competences is that the respective 'own' IO is prioritized, while the role and relevance of other IOs is relativized. For one part, each IO is obliged to observe its own institutional law when interacting with other IOs. At the same time, neither IO's institutional law defines and ensures that other IOs' governance models, needs and demands ought to have a particular role or relevance. In consequence, as long as an IO faithfully abides by its own institutional law, it is entitled under this law to influence other IOs, regardless of what the nature of this inter-organizational interaction may be.

For the ILO and its model of labour governance, this has important structural implications. On the one hand, the ILO's own institutional law relativizes the role and relevance of other IOs, which enables the ILO to take measures protecting or promoting its model regardless of whether and to what extent these measures influence the World Bank or the CoE. However, on the other hand, this is hardly relevant for other IOs. Neither the World Bank nor the CoE are legally bound to observe the ILO's law. Moreover, the Bank's and the CoE's own institutional laws prioritize their respective own IOs and relativize the role and relevance of the ILO. Accordingly, the Bank and the CoE can likewise adopt any measure consistent with their relevant institutional laws, irrespective of any consequences for the ILO.

It has further been shown that each IO's competences to interact, as well as its institutional legal framework embedding them, are subject to legally relevant dynamic evolution. This opens avenues for the World Bank and the CoE to develop their own laws' stances on the ILO. However, such efforts, while legally permissible, are essentially never legally required. Notably, the World Bank and the CoE may enhance the ILO's role and relevance in their laws by way of coherent interpretation, but they are hardly (if at all) obliged to do so.

Finally, the ILO's member states do not have an obligation to exert influence on the World Bank or the CoE with a view to enhancing the ILO's role and relevance within these IO's institutional laws. While it is conceivable that such an obligation may exist on the basis of loyalty and sincere cooperation, it can only be assumed on a case-by-case basis and under rather strict conditions.

All in all, the ILO's, World Bank's and CoE's institutional laws each provide a normative framework for inter-organizational interactions. However, each of them approaches inter-organizational interaction under the premise that the own objectives and governance models are pivotal and surpass the importance of other IOs' governance models, needs and demands. Thus, the examined institutional laws each approach inter-organizational interaction in an introverted—if not to say 'egocentric'—way. This does not necessarily manifest itself in ruptures and open conflict between the interacting IOs and their respective institutional laws. Notably, it remains possible that they interact in a way that is permissible under both IOs' institutional laws and that both consider fruitful. Nevertheless, from the perspective of the ILO, the ILO's relativization significantly decreases the capability of the World Bank's and CoE's institutional laws to structure inter-organizational interactions in a way that protects or promotes the ILO's model of labour governance.

Part III
The Silence of Inter-Organizational Law

In the light of the preceding part's findings, it is necessary to have a closer look at the inter-organizational legal relationships between the ILO and other IOs. Unlike IOs' institutional laws, inter-organizational law is equally binding on both interacting IOs. It thus has the potential to orchestrate IOs' institutional laws' prioritizations and relativizations by providing a common standard for inter-organizational interactions between the ILO and other IOs. Ideally, this common standard would define, or allow to determine, to what extent other IOs must have regard to the ILO and its governance model, and whether and to what extent the ILO can promote its model and demand that it be taken into account by other IOs. The prospect of a common inter-organizational legal standard makes inter-organizational law a worthwhile field for analysis.

13. Bilateral Inter-Organizational Treaties Between the ILO, the World Bank and the CoE

The legal bases, scope and content of inter-organizational legal norms have so far attracted only little scholarly attention—both in general and regarding the ILO in particular.[1] In principle, the sources of inter-organizational law are the same as those of other fields of public international law. Following the canon of Art. 38(1) ICJ Statute, they notably comprise treaties, customary law and general principles of

[1]Inter-organizational law has time and again flared up on the agenda of international lawyers. In the past, there have been discussions on whether public international law can extend to inter-organizational relations at all (for the early view of Soviet writers that international organizations are not subjects of international law, see Serge M Krylov, 'Les Notions Principales Du Droit Des Gens: La Doctrine Soviétique Du Droit International' (1947) 70 Recueil des Cours de l'Académie de Droit International 407, 448; Kirsten Schmalenbach, 'Art. 6' in Oliver Dörr and Kirsten Schmalenbach (eds), *Vienna Convention on the Law of Treaties - A Commentary* (2nd edn, Springer 2018) para 26. This question has in principle been settled in the affirmative, see *Interpretation of the Agreement of 25 March 1951 between the WHO and Egypt* (Advisory Opinion) [1980] ICJ Reports 73, 89 et seq.; Kristina Daugirdas, 'How and Why International Law Binds International Organizations' (2016) 57 Harvard International Law Journal 325, 326.

H. Gött, *The Law of Interactions Between International Organizations*, Beiträge zum ausländischen öffentlichen Recht und Völkerrecht 299, https://doi.org/10.1007/978-3-662-62389-3_13

law.[2] Other sources, like e.g. binding unilateral declarations,[3] will not be examined further here, due to their utter rarity in inter-organizational relations.[4]

Inter-organizational treaties are the most visible and most accessible source of inter-organizational rights and obligations. Therefore, inter-organizational treaties between the ILO and the World Bank and the CoE, respectively, are appropriate starting points for examining these IOs' mutual inter-organizational legal rights and obligations regarding interactions.[5]

Just as inter-state treaties, inter-organizational treaties create international rights and obligations between the IOs that conclude them and must be performed in good

[2]Moreover, certain further bases for international rights and obligations have been recognized. On the non-exhaustiveness of the enumeration in Art. 38(1) ICJ Statute see Rüdiger Wolfrum, 'Sources of International Law', *Max Planck Encyclopedia of Public International Law* (Oxford University Press 2011) para 10.

[3]As was highlighted in the ICJ's *Nuclear Tests case* (*Nuclear Tests (Australia v. France)* [1974] ICJ Reports 253), unilateral conduct can create binding obligations. In principle, this is true for states and IOs alike. Such conduct can have the effect that the other IO has a corresponding right to request fulfilment. One general difficulty is the determination of the IO's intent to be legally bound, and—no less important—to be legally bound vis-à-vis a certain other subject, e.g. another IO, or even to be bound *erga omnes*. Some IOs have used an "avoidance strategy" by voluntarily complying with international norms without taking a stand as to whether they consider themselves legally bound to do so, see Kristina Daugirdas, 'Reputation and the Responsibility of International Organizations' (2014) 25 European Journal of International Law 991, 1012 et seqq.; José E Álvarez, *International Organizations as Law-Makers* (Oxford University Press 2006) 179. Even if it can be established that IOs intended a legally binding effect, they might only be addressed to the IO's staff, organs or member states. Arguably, most unilateral declarations by IOs will fall into either of these categories. A second difficulty is IO-specific: Even if an IO intends to unilaterally accept an obligation vis-à-vis another, it remains to be ascertained whether and to what extent that IO can legally do so, especially whether it has the constitutional competences to assume the respective obligations.

[4]While practice is scarce, this scenario is not entirely theoretical. Occasionally, IOs have unilaterally declared that they will apply certain international legal norms by which they are not otherwise bound. For an example, UNMIK has unilaterally declared that it will apply, albeit in a qualified manner, the 1954 Hague Convention for the Protection of Cultural Heritage in the Event of Armed Conflict, to which neither UNMIK nor the UN were parties, UN Secretary-General, 'Note to the Assistant Secretary-General for Peacekeeping Operations Regarding the United Nations Mission in Kosovo and the Protection of Cultural Heritage' [2004] United Nations Juridical Yearbook 350, 350 et seq. It is conceivable that this also entails certain legal rights and duties with regard to UNESCO, which has a role in the Convention's implementation.

[5]For reading convenience, the VCLT-IO will be cited hereinafter when referring to the applicable customary international legal norms, see Chap. 1 D. As a preliminary issue, it should be noted that the research interest of this chapter is solely to identify legal rights and obligations, not to determine the actual scope and content of consensual inter-organizational interactions between the ILO and the other IOs in general. It should be recalled that the existence or non-existence of treaty relations does not necessarily indicate the actual amount of cooperation taking place between two IOs. As mentioned before, a significant amount of inter-organizational interaction is informal, or, for that matter, non-consensual, and thus neither based on nor envisaged in inter-organizational treaties. That being said, the lack of treaties between the ILO and the Bank coincides with a still somewhat inhibited cooperation between them, whereas the existence of a relationship agreement between the ILO the CoE coincides with a comparatively larger degree of cooperation between the two IOs.

faith.[6] They are governed by the inter-organizational law of treaties, which itself is part of customary inter-organizational law and has emerged from a decades-long inter-organizational practice. These customary rules are adequately depicted in the substantive parts of the VCLT-IO, which was adopted in early 1986 but has not yet entered into force.[7]

A. The ILO and Inter-Organizational Treaties

The ILO has a long-standing and comparatively rich practice of concluding inter-organizational agreements. The ILO website lists more than 70 different agreements with other IOs or legally dependent branches thereof.[8] Not all of these agreements are binding international treaties.[9] As is the case with other IOs, the ILO has entered into a number of arrangements that cannot be interpreted as creating legal rights and obligations.[10] That being said, the ILO's portfolio of agreements includes a range of binding international treaties.

---

[6]It is by now settled that IOs can conclude treaties with each other, Nicolas Levrat, 'Art. 6 VCLT-IO' in Olivier Corten and Pierre Klein (eds), *The Vienna Conventions on the Law of Treaties - A Commentary, vol 1* (Oxford University Press 2011) para 7 et seq.; René-Jean Dupuy, 'Le Droit Des Relations Entre Les Organisations Internationales' (1960) 100 Recueil des Cours de l'Académie de Droit International 461, 536. See further Karl Zemanek, *Das Vertragsrecht der Internationalen Organisationen* (Springer 1959) 43 et seqq.; Hungdah Chiu, *The Capacity of International Organizations to Conclude Treaties, and the Special Legal Aspects of the Treaties so Concluded* (Martinus Nijhoff 1966) 19 et seqq.

[7]Karl Zemanek, 'Vienna Convention on the Law of Treaties between States and International Organizations or between International Organizations - Introductory Note' (2009) United Nations Audiovisual Library of International Law <https://legal.un.org/avl/ha/vcltsio/vcltsio.html> accessed 26 April 2020. James Crawford, *Brownlie's Principles of Public International Law* (8th edn, Oxford University Press 2012) 179 et seq. Inter alia, the UN, the ILO and the CoE have acceded to it.

[8]ILO, 'ILO Cooperation Agreements with Other International Organizations' (*ILO Website*) <https://www.ilo.org/global/about-the-ilo/how-the-ilo-works/departments-and-offices/jur/legal-instruments/WCMS_442247/lang%2D%2Den/index.htm> accessed 26 April 2020.

[9]Occasionally, binding force is even explicitly excluded, see e.g. Para. 6.1 of the 2015 EIB-ILO Memorandum of Understanding, which stipulates that "[t]his Memorandum of Understanding constitutes a good faith commitment and is not intended to create legal relations between the two organizations or to impose formal obligations on them", Memorandum of Understanding between the European Investment Bank and the International Labour Organization (16 July 2015) <https://www.ilo.org/global/about-the-ilo/how-the-ilo-works/departments-and-offices/jur/legal-instruments/WCMS_442247/lang%2D%2Den/index.htm> accessed 26 April 2020.

[10]In general, not every consensus reached among two IOs amounts to an inter-organizational treaty. For instance, joint political declarations and so-called 'gentlemen's agreements' do not qualify as treaties. Still, as they are resembling (politically) normative propositions, such statements and declarations can become relevant in other contexts, e.g. when examining the 'soft law' applying between IOs, see in a general context Andreas von Arnauld, *Völkerrecht* (3rd edn, C F Müller 2016) para 185. However, the form is usually not decisive, *Maritime Delimitation and Territorial*

Moreover, the ILO has served as a pioneer in the field of inter-organizational agreements. In 1946, the ILO was the first IO to conclude a relationship agreement with the UN (the UN-ILO). The UN-ILO quickly became a model for subsequent relationship agreements between the UN and other specialized agencies, as well as for inter-organizational agreements in general.[11]

The ILO's inter-organizational agreements vary in scope and content.[12] Many of them resemble general relationship agreements, like the UN-ILO, discussed in Chap. 14, and the ILO-CoE, discussed further below in this Chapter. Other agreements concern specific topics or arrangements.[13] There is also a distinction between 'main' agreements, usually concluded upon approval by the Governing Body or the

---

Questions between Qatar and Bahrain (Qatar v. Bahrain) (Jurisdiction und Admissibility) [1994] ICJ Reports 112, para 23. The VCLT-IO only applies to agreements in writing. Whether an agreement is a legally binding treaty is determined objectively, having regard to the agreement's actual terms and the particular circumstances surrounding its conclusion, *Aegean Sea Continental Shelf (Greece v Turkey)* [1978] ICJ Reports 3, 96; *Maritime Delimitation and Territorial Questions between Qatar and Bahrain (Qatar v. Bahrain)* (Jurisdiction und Admissibility) [1994] ICJ Reports 112, para 24 et seqq.; PK Menon, *The Law of Treaties Between States and International Organizations* (Edwin Mellen 1992) 10.

[11]This is particularly apparent in the case of other early cooperation agreements, see e.g. the Agreement between the International Labour Organization and the Food and Agriculture Organization of the United Nations (entered into force 11 September 1947, 18 UNTS 335 (ILO-FAO), the Agreement between the International Labour Organisation and the United Nations Educational, Scientific and Cultural Organization (entered into force 15 December 1947) 18 UNTS 346 (ILO-UNESCO) or the Agreement between the International Labour Organisation and the Intergovernmental Maritime Consultative Organisation (entered into force 16 January 1959) XLII ILO Official Bulletin 261 (ILO-IMO), Francis Maupain, *The Future of the International Labour Organization in the Global Economy* (Hart Publishing 2013) 111. See also Clarence Wilfred Jenks, 'Coordination: A New Problem of International Organization' 77 Recueil des Cours, Collected Courses of the Hague Academy of International Law 151, 205 et seqq.

[12]For instance, the Agreement between the International Labour Office and the United International Bureaux for the Protection of Intellectual Property (entered into force 9 June 1969) LII ILO Official Bulletin No 1 331 (ILO-WIPO) is only a short exchange of letters, whereas the 'standard' relationship agreements are comparatively more elaborate.

[13]See e.g. the Memorandum of Understanding between the Director-General of the International Labour Office and the President of the Council of the International Civil Aviation Organisation (Proposed Joint Civil Aviation Commission) (1954) XXXVII ILO Bulletin 402, the Executing Agency Agreement between the United Nations Development Programme (UNDP) and the International Labour Organization (ILO) (entered into force 8 July 1993) LXXVI ILO Official Bulletin Ser A 218, or the 1960 Arrangement between the International Labour Organisation and the Council of Europe on the Creation and Activities of the International Vocational Training Information and Research Centre (adopted and entered into force 8 December 1960) 398 UNTS 291.

International Labour Conference,[14] and supplementary or implementing agreements, concluded by the ILO Director-General.[15]

B. The Absence of Relevant Binding Treaties Between the ILO and the World Bank

Despite both IOs sharing a long common history, contractual relations between the ILO and the World Bank are still a rarity. Although repeatedly suggested,[16] there exists no general relationship agreement between ILO and any of the WBG's member IOs.[17] Instead, insofar as they have cooperated at all, they have chosen to do so in an issue-specific—and usually less formal—manner. This is remarkable, given the substantial thematic overlap between the ILO's and the World Bank's work.

Three major forms of ILO-World Bank cooperation can be distinguished. First, ILO and World Bank have invited each other to attend meetings as observers (I.). Second, they have launched joint projects and initiatives at country level (II.). Third, they have cooperated in plurilateral contexts, involving other IOs (III.). The bases for these cooperative activities will be discussed in turn. As will be seen, while some are based on agreements that can be regarded as legally binding, they are all case-specific and do not allow general inferences beyond the particular case at hand.

---

[14]E.g. the UN-ILO, which was approved by the International Labour Conference, see ILO, 'Protocol Concerning the Entry into Force of the Agreement between the United Nations and the International Labour Organization' (1946) XXIX ILO Official Bulletin 383, 384.

[15]E.g. the 2004 ILO-FAO Memorandum of Understanding (ILO and FAO, Memorandum of Understanding between the International Labour Organization (ILO) and the Food and Agriculture Organization of the United Nations (FAO) (2004) <https://www.ilo.org/wcmsp5/groups/public/%2D%2D-dgreports/%2D%2D-jur/documents/genericdocument/wcms_434511.pdf> accessed 26 April 2020), which was concluded as a supplementary agreement pursuant to Art. 8 of the 1947 ILO-FAO by the ILO Director-General and the FAO Director-General.

[16]See e.g. Willem van Genugten, 'Tilburg-GLOTHRO Guiding Principles on the World Bank Group, the International Monetary Fund and Human Rights', *The World Bank Group, the IMF and Human Rights: A Contextualised Way Forward* (Intersentia 2015) Annex I, Guiding Principle 8; Maupain, *The Future of the International Labour Organization in the Global Economy* (n 11) 111.

[17]The same is true for the IMF, Lorenza Mola, 'Governance of Financial Crises: A Role for the International Protection of Economic and Social Rights?' in Photini Pazartzis and Maria Gavouneli (eds), *Reconceptualizing the Rule of Law in Global Governnce, Resources, Investment and Trade* (Hart Publishing 2016) 113.

I. Agreements Regarding Consultation, Representation and Observer Status

At several occasions, the ILO and the World Bank have conducted consultations, sent representatives to meetings and events of the respective other, and have granted each other observer status. In a number of cases, this happened on an informal basis, e.g. through the attendance of meetings and discussions by staff members.[18] Over time, however, some of these interactions took a more formal shape. In 1995, in the run-up to the Copenhagen Social Summit, the ILO was for the first time ever invited to attend the World Bank's annual meeting (Art. V(2) lit. c IBRD-AoA) as an observer.[19] In 1997, the World Bank President addressed the International Labour Conference.[20] From 1999, the ILO was invited to participate as an observer in the joint IMF-World Bank Development Committee.[21] The ILO, for its part, has

---

[18]ILO staff repeatedly participated in World Bank committees and meetings working on Comprehensive Development Framework (CDF) and Poverty Reduction Strategy Paper (PRSP) processes, ILO, 'ILO Relations with the Bretton Woods Institutions' (Governing Body, 279th session, November 2000) GB.279/ESP/1, para 10.

[19]Katherine A Hagen, 'Policy Dialogue between the International Labour Organization and the International Financial Institutions: The Search for Convergence' (2003) FES Occasional Papers No 9 <http://library.fes.de/pdf-files/bueros/genf/50035.pdf> accessed 26 April 2020, 9. The ILO has participated in subsequent annual meetings as an observer, see e.g. World Bank, List of Observers - 2018 Annual Meetings (2018) <http://www.worldbank.org/content/dam/meetings/external/annualmeeting/2018-AMs-Observers-Final.pdf> accessed 26 April 2020, 2. The ILO Governing Body has positively evaluated the existing formal and informal working contacts, ILO, 'ILO Relations with the Bretton Woods Institutions' (n 18) para 1.

[20]ILO, Provisional Record (International Labour Conference, 85th session, 13 June 1997) <https://www.ilo.org/public/english/standards/relm/ilc/ilc85/wolf.htm> accessed 26 April 2020.

[21]This invitation, it should be noted though, was mainly the result of preceding informal contacts between the ILO and the IMF, which also extended the invitation to the IMF Board of Governors' Interim Committee, Hagen (n 19) 14. In the aftermath of the 1995 Copenhagen Summit, relations between the ILO and the IMF had intensified, albeit mostly in the form of a policy dialogue in fields such as employment and core labour standards. This dialogue had yielded some tangible manifestations during the post-1997 Asian Financial Crisis. What is more, it arguably had led to the IMF's principal acceptance and support of the ILO core labour standards. As a kind of 'modus vivendi', the IMF had aimed at allocating spheres of expertise and deference for each IO. As then-ILO Deputy Director-General for External Affairs Katherine Hagen reports, "the Fund established, early on in the policy dialogue, an approach aimed at distinct institutional integrity, which meant in effect that the ILO had its domain (including core labour standards) and the Fund had its domain (financial and macroeconomic policy). The Fund expected the ILO to defer to its expertise on financial and macroeconomic policy, and the Fund's staff was prepared, at least officially, to defer to the ILO on its expertise on labour standards" (ibid). That being said, IMF-ILO relations had remained virtually completely informal. Two very preliminary and diffident steps towards institutionalizing the mutual relations can be identified. For one part, in 1995, the Interim Committee of the IMF Board of Governors issued a communiqué, in which it called for strengthened cooperation, in particular for an exchange of views and information during the preparation of the IMF's World Economic Outlook and the ILO's World Employment Outlook, IMF, 'Communiqué of the Interim Committee of the Board of Governors of the International Monetary Fund' *IMF Press Release No 95/51, 8 October 1995* <www.imf.org/external/np/sec/pr/1995/pr9551.htm> accessed 26 April 2020,

regularly extended invitations to the World Bank to attend meetings and the World Bank has, albeit more hesitantly, accepted some of these invitations.[22]

The aforesaid participations are necessarily consensual. Importantly, however, not every such participation is based on a legally relevant agreement. At the outset, it needs to be recalled that there is no legal instrument that regulates consultations, participation, or observer status between the ILO and the World Bank in general terms. The institutional law of each IO allows the invitation of observers.[23] At the inter-organizational level, however, these provisions do not in themselves provide an obligation on behalf of the Bank towards the ILO to admit the ILO as an observer. Neither do they confer on the ILO a corresponding general right to participation. Notably, the ILO and World Bank have never regulated these matters in a relationship agreement, as both the ILO and the Bank have done with a number of other IOs.[24]

In the absence of any such agreement between the ILO and the Bank, any legal basis must be created ad hoc with every invitation to participate. In this respect, invitation and acceptance can be conceptualized in two ways: Either as the conclusion of a case-specific (written or oral) inter-organizational agreement[25] or as the creation of a right of the invited IO as a third party under the constituent instrument of the host IO (Art. 36(2) VCLT-IO). In practice, the legal effects of both constructions would arguably be similar.[26]

Caution is warranted, however, to interpret invitations to participate in such a legally relevant way. Whether the parties actually intended to conclude a

para 12. The other step is the 1999 invitation to the joint IMF-World Bank Development Committee.

[22]For instance, a World Bank observer participated in the 2017 International Labour Conference, ILO, 'Final List of Delegations, Supplement to the Provisional Record' (International Labour Conference, 106th session, June 2017) <https://www.ilo.org/ilc/ILCSessions/previous-sessions/106/lang%2D%2Den/index.htm> accessed 26 April 2020, 121.

[23]In the ILO, this is explicitly spelled out in Art. 12(2) ILO Constitution. As to the World Bank, while no explicit constitutional provision exists, Section 4 lit. b IBRD By-Laws provides that the Chairman of the Board of Governors is entitled, after consultation with the Executive Directors, to invite observers to attend meetings of the Board of Governors. Whether this comprises other IOs is not specified but is covered by the wording. For an early example of agreement-based staff exchanges of economists, see Devesh Kapur, John P Lewis and Richard C Webb, *The World Bank: Its First Half Century, vol 1* (Brookings Institution Press 1997) 255.

[24]Erik Suy, 'The Status of Observers in International Organizations' (1978) 160 Recueil des Cours de l'Académie de Droit International 75, 97 et seq.; Henry G Schermers and Niels M Blokker, *International Institutional Law* (6 edn, Brill 2018) para 185.

[25]In principle, binding agreements can be concluded orally, *The Mavrommatis Palestine Concessions (Greece v. United Kingdom)* PCIJ Rep Series A No 2, 37; *Legal Status of Eastern Greenland (Denmark v. Norway)* PCIJ Rep Series A/B No 53, 91 et seq.; Menon (n 10) 11. Yet, since invitation and acceptance will usually be issued in writing, this would fulfil the prerequisites of a conclusion by exchange of instruments.

[26]In particular, Art. 36(1) VCLT and Art. 36(2) VCLT-IO require the assent of the beneficiary IO.

case-specific binding agreement (or grant a third party right granted under the respective constituent instrument) depends on the circumstances of the case. Unless there are any specific circumstances indicating otherwise, it appears reasonable to assume the ILO and the Bank were willing to be legally bound only if the participation is connected with conferring on the participant a certain status and certain participatory rights in the host IO's bodies, or if the invitation is extended for a longer period.[27]

Yet, even if one construed the basis of consultation, reciprocal representation and observer status as a binding agreement, such an agreement will usually reserve for the inviting IO important unilaterally exercisable rights, such as to alter the procedural rules that apply to the observer, and even to revoke the invitation.[28] The legal relevance of the agreement would then lie in the fact that, while it lasts, it has to be fulfilled in good faith (Art. 26 VCLT-IO), which means that both parties have to treat each other accordingly, including taking due regard of legitimate interests of the respective other. Good faith would also have to be exercised when the host IO chooses to revoke observer status and rights, which might e.g. require it to adhere to a certain revocation procedure that is provided for in the host IO's own rules.[29]

That being said, in the absence of a general agreement with a standing invitation to participate, such case-specific agreements on consultation or participation, if construable at all, would be tailored to the specific instance. Therefore, they would be of no relevance when it comes to governing inter-organizational interactions between the ILO and the Bank on a more general level. What is more, there are ways to further reduce their relevance. For instance, when the World Bank convened the Doing Business Employing Workers Consultative Group to explore ways reform the EWI, it invited ILO officials (and the other members of the group) not in an official, but in their individual capacity.[30] Questions of the legal character (if any) of this participation left aside, in any event, this would have not amounted to a legally relevant agreement with the ILO.

---

[27]That at least some invitations of participants are seen as legally relevant can be seen by existing provisions as those mentioned before, but also by practices of the Chief Executive Officer seeking permission of the competent organ to invite certain IOs. Sending special observer missions to other IOs can also have legal implications for the individual members of such a mission, e.g. concerning their status and rights in the host IO's host state, see Schermers and Blokker, *International Institutional Law* (n 24) para 1840.

[28]Which could be conceptualized as an implied right to termination.

[29]An example is CoE Statutory Resolution (93) 26, which provides that the CM must consult with PACE before withdrawing observer status, CM, Statutory Resolution (93) 26 on Observer Status (92nd session, 14 May 1993) <https://search.coe.int/cm/Pages/result_details.aspx?ObjectID=09000016804e42f6> accessed 26 April 2020 (Statutory Resolution (93) 26), para VIII.

[30]See Chap. 4 C. III.

II. Agreements on Technical and Country-Level Cooperation

Secondly, the ILO and the WBG IOs have established numerous technical cooperation programmes at country level, involving the respective governments and sometimes further domestic public and private actors. A prominent example is the joint IFC-ILO Better Work programme on improving working standards and competitiveness in global supply chains in the garment sector in selected countries.[31] Better Work is based on an agreement between the ILO and the IFC, which has however not been published[32] and, therefore, cannot be examined here.

In other contexts, cooperation was limited to providing specific support or services. For example, the World Bank and ILO cooperated in the context of a follow-up to complaints brought before the World Bank Inspection Panel concerning organized child labour and forced labour in certain World Bank-funded projects in the Uzbek cotton production.[33] Cooperation concerned the four aspects of capacity building, awareness-raising, facilitation of a "Feedback Mechanism" and so-called Third Party Monitoring, i.e. an independent monitoring and evaluation by the ILO.[34] The basis of this cooperation was a Memorandum of Understanding the World Bank

[31]Daniel Berliner and others, *Labor Standards in International Supply Chains: Aligning Rights and Incentives* (Edward Elgar Publishing 2015) 54 et seq.; Janelle M Diller, 'Pluralism and Privatization in Transnational Labour Regulation: Experience of the International Labour Organization' in Adelle Blackett and Anne Trebilcock (eds), *Research Handbook on Transnational Labour Law* (Edward Elgar Publishing 2015) 335; Paul Alois, 'Lessons for Effective Governance: An Examination of the Better Work Program' (2018) 24 Global Governance 139.

[32]Diller (n 31) 341, fn 53.

[33]ILO, 'Third-Party Monitoring of Measures against Child Labour and Forced Labour during the 2017 Cotton Harvest in Uzbekistan - A Report Submitted to the World Bank by the International Labour Office' (2018) <https://www.ilo.org/wcmsp5/groups/public/%2D%2D-ed_norm/%2D%2D-ipec/documents/publication/wcms_617830.pdf> accessed 26 April 2020, 9.

[34]ILO, 'Third-Party Monitoring of Measures against Child Labour and Forced Labour during the 2016 Cotton Harvest in Uzbekistan - A Report Submitted to the World Bank by the International Labour Office' (2017) <https://www.ilo.org/wcmsp5/groups/public/%2D%2D-ed_norm/%2D%2D-ipec/documents/publication/wcms_543130.pdf> accessed 26 April 2020, 3. Reactions to the impact of the cooperation vary. While the ILO's monitoring report was positive, NGOs evaluated the situation more skeptically, see Kristian Lasslett and Vanessa Gstrein, 'Measuring Forced Labour in an Authoritarian Context: An Evaluation of ILO Third Party Monitoring in Uzbekistan' (The Corruption and Human Rights Initiative 2018) <https://pure.ulster.ac.uk/ws/files/77749500/isci_ilo_tpm_report_2018.pdf> accessed 26 April 2020. See also the CEACR's observations (*Observation (CEACR) Abolition of Forced Labour Convention, 1957 (No 105) - Uzbekistan (Ratification: 1997)* Report of the Committee of Experts on the Application of Conventions and Recommendations (2013) ILC.105/III(1A) 216*)*) and the Human Rights Committee's observations (UN Human Rights Committee, 'Concluding Observations on Uzbekistan' (114th Session, 29 June–24 July 2015) UN Doc CCPR/C/UZB/CO/4, para 19).

and the ILO signed in October 2014.[35] For another example, in November 2016, the ILO and the World Bank signed a non-country-specific Memorandum of Understanding, in which the Bank and the ILO approved a standard form for technical assistance agreements between the ILO and governments concerning projects financed by the Bank.[36] The 2016 Memorandum of Understanding provides that the approved standard form "shall be used and should not be amended except by agreement in writing".[37]

While these cooperative activities are partly based on binding agreements, these agreements are country- or topic-specific. They do not lend themselves to infer more general rules from them. Thus, they are of no legal relevance for other inter-organizational interactions between the ILO and the World Bank. In particular, they do not regulate in any general way if and how the World Bank should have regard to the ILO's model of labour governance.

III. Agreements on Cooperation in Pluri-Organizational Contexts and the UN System

Thirdly, the ILO and the World Bank have cooperated in pluri-organizational settings. Examples include the Inter-Organizational Task Force on Employment and Sustainable Livelihoods, created to pursue the 1995 Copenhagen Social Summit's goal of full employment and sustainable livelihoods,[38] further the Joint United Nations Programme on HIV/AIDS (UNAIDS), the Inter-Organization Coordinating Committee (IOCC) in the area of chemical safety[39] or the Global Partnership for Universal Social Protection.[40]

---

[35]ILO, 'Third-Party Monitoring of Measures against Child Labour and Forced Labour during the 2017 Cotton Harvest in Uzbekistan - A Report Submitted to the World Bank by the International Labour Office' (n 33) 9.

[36]Memorandum of Understanding Between the World Bank and the International Labour Organization of 17 November 2016 (text and further related documents available on the World Bank's website, <http://www.worldbank.org/en/projects-operations/products-and-services/brief/procurement-new-framework#un> accessed 26 April 2020).

[37]ibid.

[38]Copenhagen Declaration on Social Development and Programme of Action of the World Summit for Social Development, Commitment 3, UN, 'Report of the World Summit for Social Development' (6–12 March 1995) UN Doc A/CONF.166/9, 4.

[39]Mario Savino, 'Linkages Between Global Regimes and Interactions with Civil Society' in Sabino Cassese (ed), *Research Handbook on Global Administrative Law* (Edward Elgar Publishing 2016) 140 et seq.

[40]A further example concerns a number of so-called Standard Agreements on Operational Assistance, concluded in the early 1970s between developing countries or on behalf of non-self-governing territories on the one hand and various UN specialized agencies on the other, see e.g. the Standard Agreement on Operational Assistance (with Annex) between the United Nations (including the United Nations Industrial Development Organization and the United Nations

These cooperative activities involve other UN specialized agencies and have been interlinked to the wider UN System, which will be addressed in further detail in Chap. 14. At this point, it sufficient to enquire into the legal bases (if any) of these pluri-organizational cooperations.

The Global Partnership for Universal Social Protection does not have a published legally relevant contractual basis at all. Instead, it is based on a range of public declarations and a Concept Note, which are formulated as policy statements.[41]

The Task Force was not erected by a formal inter-organizational agreement, but on reciprocal statements, the legal relevance of which remains unclear. When difficulties between the World Bank and the ILO in the implementation of the Task Force's agenda occurred, no legal consequences ensued.[42]

UNAIDS was prepared by a line of ECOSOC resolutions and separate decisions of the original cosponsoring IOs, which included the World Bank.[43] In 1996, UNAIDS was formally established by the signing of a Memorandum of Understanding (UNAIDS-MoU) by the six founding cosponsors,[44] which was open to adhesion by further IOs.[45] The ILO, not among the original cosponsors but engaged in other

Conference on Trade and Development), International Labour Organisation, Food and Agriculture Organization of the United Nations, United Nations Educational, Scientific and Cultural Organization, International Civil Aviation Organization, World Health Organization, International Telecommunication Union, World Meteorological Organization, International Atomic Energy Agency, Universal Postal Union, Inter-Governmental Maritime Consultative Organization and International Bank for Reconstruction and Development, and Central African Republic (signed 13 January 1972) 807 UNTS 284.

[41]The Partnership envisages that the Bank and the ILO support developing countries to use existing and create new opportunities to create and improve social protection. The Partnership's Concept Note sets forth objectives and contains declarations of commitment. However, they are formulated as mere political statements. Neither by their form nor by their content can they be understood as legally binding declarations. See ILO and World Bank, 'A Shared Mission for Universal Social Protection - Concept Note' (2015) <https://www.ilo.org/wcmsp5/groups/public/%2D%2D-dgreports/%2D%2D-dcomm/documents/genericdocument/wcms_378996.pdf> accessed 26 April 2020.

[42]Hagen (n 19) 15.

[43]See in particular ECOSOC, 'Joint and Co-Sponsored United Nations Programme on Human Immunodeficiency Virus/Acquired Immunodeficiency Syndrome, Resolution 1994/24 of 26 July 1994'.

[44]UNAIDS, Memorandum of Understanding on a Joint and Cosponsored United Nations Programme on HIV/AIDS (1996), reproduced in ILO, 'Instrument of the Adhesion of the International Labour Organization to the Memorandum of Understanding on a Joint and Cosponsored United Nations Programme on HIV/AIDS' (2001) LXXXIV ILO Official Bulletin Ser A No 3 153, Annex I (UNAIDS-MoU).

[45]Para 12.2 UNAIDS-MoU.

activities concerning HIV/AIDS, first signed a Cooperation Framework Agreement in 2000.[46] In 2001, the ILO formally acceded to UNAIDS as a cosponsor.[47]

The Memorandum of Understanding, the Cooperation Framework and the ILO's accession instrument can be interpreted as legally binding instruments.[48] The UNAIDS MoU contains, inter alia, commitments to cooperate and to contribute to achieve common objectives in combating HIV/AIDS, inter alia by developing worldwide and national plans of action, and to implement the jointly developed policies, strategies and technical guidelines into each IO's policy and strategy mainstream, "subject to their governance processes and reflected in the activities specific to their own mandates."[49] This clause illustrates that the cooperating IOs were mindful of their internal procedures and constitutional peculiarities. Arguably, no cooperating IO could demand from the ILO to implement UNAIDS outputs in a manner contrary to its model of labour governance.[50] However, the clause provides this safeguard only for the specific case of UNAIDS. It is not possible to generalize its output in the absence of a more allowing normative basis.

IV. Conclusion

As the foregoing survey of the contractual practice between the ILO and the World Bank has shown, legally binding agreements often do not exist at all. Insofar as they do, they are case-specific, with a focus on specific topics, issues or countries. In the absence of a general relationship agreement, it seems difficult to derive any general conclusions as to the protection or promotion of the ILO's model in interactions with

---

[46]UNAIDS and ILO, Cooperation framework between the Joint United Nations Programme on HIV/AIDS (UNAIDS) and the International Labour Organization (ILO), reproduced in ILO, 'Instrument of the Adhesion of the International Labour Organization to the Memorandum of Understanding on a Joint and Cosponsored United Nations Programme on HIV/AIDS' (2001) LXXXIV ILO Official Bulletin Ser A No 3 153, Annex II.

[47]ILO, 'Instrument of the Adhesion of the International Labour Organization to the Memorandum of Understanding on a Joint and Cosponsored United Nations Programme on HIV/AIDS' (2001) LXXXIV ILO Official Bulletin Ser A No 3 153.

[48]The title of a "Memorandum of Understanding" speaks against this conclusion. However, the UNAIDS-MoU contains detailed institutional and procedural rules. What is more, para. 12.1 UNAIDS-MoU envisages the "entry into force".

[49]Paras. 4 and 9 UNAIDS-MoU. See also Laurence Boisson De Chazournes, 'Relations with Other International Organizations' in Jacob Katz Cogan, Ian Hurd and Ian Johnstone (eds), *The Oxford Handbook of International Organizations* (Oxford University Press 2016) 697.

[50]The clause is reminiscent of a ratification requirement for results of intergovernmental cooperation as existent in a range of international contexts., e.g. in free trade agreements for decisions of intergovernmental committees, see e.g. Art. 30.2 Comprehensive Economic and Trade Agreement between Canada, of the one part, and the European Union and its Member States, of the other part (adopted 28 October 2016) [2017] OJ L11/23 (CETA).

the World Bank. Such a general agreement appears, however, out of reach for the foreseeable future.[51]

C. The Modest Regulation of Direct and Cooperative Interactions in the ILO-CoE

While ILO and CoE share a long history of various interactions, their record of formal agreements is short. Judging from the published agreements of both IOs, the ILO and the CoE have almost completely abstained from concluding formal agreements. There are only two reported bilateral agreements, the 1951 Agreement Between the ILO and the CoE (ILO-CoE) and the 1960 Arrangement Between the International Labour Organisation and the Council of Europe on the Creation and Activities of the International Vocational Training Information and Research Centre.[52] The following analysis will focus on the ILO-CoE, since the 1960 Arrangement is of no further relevance for the present study.[53]

This section will first outline the content of the ILO-CoE (I.). Subsequently, it will evaluate the ILO-CoE's relevance for protecting or promoting the ILO's model during interactions involving the ECtHR and the ECSR (II.).

---

[51] Such a general relationship agreement, 'rightly' negotiated and drafted, would have notable potential, given the substantial overlap between the ILO's and the Bank's mandates and activities, Maupain, *The Future of the International Labour Organization in the Global Economy* (n 11) 111. See also Global Commission for the Future of Work, 'Work for a Brighter Future' (ILO 2019) 55 et seq.

[52] Arrangement between the International Labour Organisation and the Council of Europe on the Creation and Activities of the International Vocational Training Information and Research Centre (adopted and entered into force 8 December 1960) 398 UNTS 291 (ILO-CoE 1960 Arrangement). Furthermore, both the ILO and the CoE have consented to be bound by the VCLT-IO, which is the only reported multilateral treaty, albeit not yet in force, to which both IOs are parties.

[53] The ILO-CoE 1960 Arrangement is an administrative agreement concluded on the basis of Arts. 5 (2) and 11 ILO-CoE (see preambular clause 3 of the ILO-CoE 1960 Arrangement). It provides for the creation and operation of the International Training Centre of the ILO, located in Turin, by the ILO, with contributions and support by the CoE. The 1960 Arrangement is of no further relevance for the present study, except that it evidences, besides the 1958 Regional Tripartite Conference on the ESC draft, another instance in which the ILO-CoE has provided the basis for formalized ILO-CoE interaction.

I. The ILO-CoE: A Legal Framework for 'Cooperation for Coordination'

The ILO-CoE is a general relationship agreement, which defines a framework for future cooperation.

1. The ILO-CoE's Two Objectives

The ILO-CoE's preamble expounds the two principal purposes of the agreement. Firstly, the parties seek

> to co-ordinate their efforts to give effect, within the terms of the Charter of the United Nations, the Constitution of the International Labour Organisation, the Statute of the Council of Europe and other applicable instruments, to their respective principles and objectives

Secondly, they purport to secure

> the most effective use of the resources available to all international and regional organisations [to be achieved by] avoiding unnecessary duplication and overlapping and [by] facilitating concentration of efforts.

These two purposes—the pursuit of the two IOs' respective objectives and the effective use of resources—are repeatedly mentioned throughout the agreement.

As to the first objective, it is worth noting that the desire to give effect is limited to the "respective" principles and objectives of both IOs. Other than the second objective (the effective use of resources), there is no definition of any sort of *common* principle or objective. Instead, the parties chose to refer only to the respective principles and objectives of each organization. The definition, development, implementation and interpretation of these principles is not regulated and thus left to the respective IOs and their constituents, subject only to limits emanating from their respective constituent instruments.

One reason for this might be the early date of the agreement—at the time of its conclusion, the CoE had only existed for two years, and the entire post-war order had only been in place for six years. The new variety of IOs had just unfolded and cooperation between them was yet to be tested. Still, even then, the definition of some common principles or objectives would have been possible, given that both the CoE Statute (with its objective of economic and social progress) and the newly adopted ECHR (with its prohibition of forced labour and its guarantee of freedom of association) offered at least some commonalities with the ILO's mandate and would have been suitable points of reference. Another reason could be that both IOs sought to preserve their independence from each other. This would correspond to the fact that the ILO-CoE is a framework agreement and envisages closer and more concrete cooperation in selected matters. Either way, the ILO-CoE leaves the definition of common objectives to the parties' discretion.

The ILO-CoE's second objective aims at maximizing mutual benefits in a situation of scarce resources. For both IOs, this responds to reality, within which the scarcity of resources is one of the biggest obstacles for the effective achievement of objectives. The ILO-CoE does not provide a normative yardstick to measure effectiveness. Given the syntactical and semantical connection to the two IOs' resources, the notion refers to some kind of economical deployment of the latter. Still, whether resources are used in an economically effective way also depends on the purpose for which they are meant to be used.[54] Given the absence of a definition of "effective" (or of a common objective), it is, again, on the parties to decide what is an effective use of resources in a given situation.

2. The Operative Provisions' Focus on Procedural Matters and the Provision of Services

The ILO-CoE's operative provisions address a variety of issues, including

- regular consultations on matters of mutual interest (Art. 1(1), (3) and (6) ILO-CoE);
- mutual information about planned activities (Art. 1(2) and (4) ILO-CoE);
- mutual representation of representatives as observers in each other's organs (Art. 1(5) ILO-CoE).[55] On this basis, the ILO has invited the CM to be represented at the ILO Governing Body and the International Labour Conference;[56]
- a right to propose items to be placed on each other's agenda (Art. 2 ILO-CoE);
- a procedure to convene regional tripartite meetings in Europe, which the CM may propose to the ILO Governing Body, and which the latter may convene (Art. 3 ILO-CoE). On this basis, the 1958 tripartite conference on the draft ESC, mentioned in Chap. 6,[57] was convened;
- the coordination and possible joint organization of regional technical experts' meetings (Art. 4 ILO-CoE);
- the rendition of technical assistance by the ILO to the CoE (Art. 5 ILO-CoE);
- combining efforts to obtain, assemble, analyse, publish and disseminate statistical and legislative information, in order to enhance efficient use of resources and alleviate the burden of governments and other entities from which information is collected (Art. 6 ILO-CoE);
- exchange of information and documents (Art. 7 ILO-CoE);

[54]To use a simplified example, funding extensive research on unemployment benefits can be effective if the goal is to enhance social protection, but not so effective if the goal is to promote non-discrimination at the workplace.

[55]See also the corresponding provision in Statutory Resolution (93) 26, para VII. For an enumerative list of CoE bodies in which the ILO participates see CoE, 'Participation of International Organizations and Institutions in Council Of Europe Bodies' (2017) DER/INF(2017)4.

[56]ILO, 'Letter of the Director-General of the International Labour Office to the Secretary-General of the Council of Europe of 19 March 1952' (1952) XXXV ILO Official Bulletin 384.

[57]Chapter 6 B. I.

- facilitation of cooperation between the ILO and European specialized authorities working on matters of interest to the former and operating under the auspices of the CoE (Art. 8 ILO-CoE);[58]
- the conclusion of administrative agreements between the ILO Director-General and the CoE Secretary-General to facilitate cooperation and liaison between staff (Art. 9 ILO-CoE);
- consultations to achieve an equitable distribution of expenses in case of mutual assistance (Art. 10 ILO-CoE);
- the implementation of the agreement, including consultations, arrangements on technical issues and the conclusion of supplementary agreements by the ILO Director-General and the CoE Secretary-General (Art. 11 ILO-CoE).

As can be seen from this list, the agreement almost exclusively contains procedural provisions or, exceptionally, provisions on the rendition of certain services. Consistent with the ILO-CoE's preamble, their overall goal is to promote dialogue, exchange and complementarity. On the other hand, the agreement's operative provisions do not go beyond that goal. They do not formulate any substantive objective, mutually shared values or common ground. While it may be assumed that both IOs factually shared a common understanding of at least some matters, they did not include this understanding in the relationship agreement. There is no commitment to pursue complementary policies, or even a common policy, in a specified field, e.g. work-related human rights protection.

On a further note, the ILO-CoE does not contain any delimitation of competences or jurisdictional spheres. While it mentions each IO's "respective principles and objectives in the preamble", it does not say that these principles and objectives must not overlap. Indeed, the agreement's overall thrust, namely to "co-ordinate (...) efforts to give effect" to these principles and objectives and to avoid "*unnecessary* duplication and overlapping" (emphasis added), suggests that the ILO-CoE presupposes that both IOs at least partially work on the same topics.[59]

[58]The term "European specialized authorities" refers to the nowadays-so-called Conferences of Specialized Ministers of the CoE, Klaus Brummer, *Der Europarat: Eine Einführung* (Springer VS 2008) 55.

[59]Furthermore, one could be inclined to think that both IOs committed themselves to observe each other's constituent instruments, because the ILO-CoE's preamble envisages that both IOs combine their efforts "*within the terms* of the Charter of the United Nations, the Constitution of the International Labour Organisation, the Statute of the Council of Europe and other applicable instruments". However, it cannot readily be assumed that this reference was meant to legally bind one IO to observe all these instruments. First of all, this would effectively sidestep each IO's constitutional rules on membership (which are open to states only) and their procedures for admitting new members. Second of all, the wording speaks of "other *applicable* instruments" (emphasis added), which indicates that each of the enumerated instruments is only to be observed insofar as it applies—i.e. creates rights or obligations—which neither does for the respective other IO.

3. The Commitments' Reticent Character

In addition, hardly any of the ILO-CoE's provisions contains 'automatisms', in the sense that one of the parties has a right or obligation towards the other aiming at an immediate result. Rather, the ILO-CoE largely employs permissive language with ample margins for discretion. The provisions typically phrase the envisaged activities in vague or hortatory language. For example, "appropriate arrangements" for reciprocal representation "shall be made by agreement from time to time" (At. 1 (5) ILO-CoE), the placing of items on each other's agenda pursuant to Art. 2 ILO-CoE is "[s]ubject to such preliminary consultation as may be necessary". Regional tripartite meetings, envisaged in Art. 3 ILO-CoE, must be "deem [ed] necessary" by the CM and can only be "propose[d]" to, not requested from, the ILO. Arrangements for cooperation with European specialized authorities must only be "discuss[ed]" (Art. 8 ILO-CoE). Regarding the equitable distribution of expenses for mutual assistance, Art. 10 ILO-CoE merely provides that "consultations shall take place". Administrative and implementing supplementary agreements must be "appropriate" or "necessary" (Art. 9 and Art. 11 ILO-CoE).

More assertive language is only used exceptionally, namely regarding obligations to inform, e.g. about future plans (Art. 1(2) ("will inform"), Art. 6 and Art. 7(2) and (3) ILO-CoE), and to consult (e.g. Art. 1(1) and Art. 4 ILO-CoE).[60]

4. Conclusion

All in all, the ILO-CoE provides a legal-normative framework for mutual interaction, but one that almost exclusively contains procedural provisions on cooperation, largely phrased in hortatory language. Much depends on the parties' readiness to make use of the ILO-CoE's provisions and on their 'good will' to cooperate. By opposite, the ILO-CoE does not define substantive goals or common understandings on subject matters of joint interest.

This situation leaves ample discretion for the parties to shape their interactions. In essence, the ILO-CoE expands the 'playground' of both IOs by defining jointly accepted procedural rules, but without requiring their use. By contrast, administrative or policy decisions are left within the respective IOs' internal sphere. Undoubtedly, the ILO-CoE is a cooperation agreement. Yet, it facilitates 'cooperation for coordination', rather than cooperation to pursue a joint endeavour.

[60]And—to a limited extent—technical assistance, Art. 5 ILO-CoE, according to which the ILO "will make every effort" to render assistance.

II. The ILO-CoE's Limited Relevance as a Common Legal Framework for Interactions

To assess the ILO-CoE's relevance in the present context, it will now be examined whether and to what extent the agreement provides normative guidance for interactions between the ILO and CoE.

1. The ILO-CoE's Focus on Direct and Cooperative Inter-Organizational Interactions

The ILO-CoE only governs certain types of inter-organizational interactions, namely direct and cooperative ones. First of all, the agreement seeks to open and maintain channels for direct interaction, e.g. by agreeing on regular consultations, by envisaging the invitation of the respective other IO to meetings, by providing for the convention of joint meetings and conferences or by foreseeing an exchange of information. It further provides a certain degree of formalization by envisaging formal forms of interaction, such as consultations, formal representation or the conclusion of supplementary agreements.

Second of all, as discussed in the previous section, most of the ILO-CoE's provisions contain hortatory language without entitling either side to demand an immediate result from the other. The respective provisions thus envisage and presuppose a certain willingness on both sides to cooperate and to comply with requests from the respective other. The only exceptions are the aforementioned rights to consultations and to the exchange of information, which are formulated in a way that does not leave it to the discretion of the respective other IO whether to consult or provide information if requested to. Only in these exceptional cases, the ILO-CoE governs non-cooperative interactions, in the sense that it provides unilateral rights to demand a certain behaviour even if the other side is not willing to act accordingly.

The interactions between the ILO and the ECSR described in Chap. 6 provide a lucid example for how the ILO-CoE can shape direct and cooperative interactions. As shown there, the ILO was involved in the ESC's drafting process. For this involvement, the ILO-CoE with its manifold provisions on consultation, information exchange, mutual representation etc. provided a normative basis. Perhaps most prominently, the 1958 Regional Tripartite Conference that the ILO organized at the CoE's request to discuss the draft was convened pursuant to Art. 3 ILO-CoE.[61] What is more, the provisions in the ESC and the ECSR Rules of Procedure establishing the institutional link between the ECSR and the ILO, as well as the ILO's subsequent formal representation in the ECSR and the informal working

[61] See the discussion in Chap. 6 above.

relationship with the ECSR Secretariat arguably resemble an "arrangement" in the sense of Art. 1(4) and (5) ILO-CoE.

2. No Obligation to Enhance the ILO's Role and Relevance

While providing a legal framework for direct and cooperative interactions between the ILO and the CoE, the ILO-CoE does not require the CoE to enhance the ILO's role and relevance in its law or practice.

First of all, where the CoE has discretion whether and to what extent to take the ILO into account in its work, the ILO-CoE does not limit this discretion. To stay with the ESC example, the ILO-CoE did not predetermine the ILO's influence on the text and implementation of the (R)ESC. Rather, it was the CoE's free choice to avail itself of the ILO's assistance in drafting the ESC, as the ILO-CoE merely provides that such assistance should be an option, but not that it is mandatory. Moreover, it was a policy decision to establish an institutional link between the ECSR and the ILO. The same is true for the decision to design and effectuate it the way it was actually designed and effectuated in practice. Arguably, it would have been equally consistent with the ILO-CoE if the CoE had not taken any assistance from the ILO and had not included any link, or a differently designed link, into the ESC.[62]

Second of all, where the CoE's competences to interact with the ILO are limited or moulded by other provisions of its institutional law, the ILO-CoE does not oblige the CoE to disregard such other provisions. For example, as seen in Chap. 9, the ECtHR's competences to interact are significantly moulded by the fact that the ECHR incepts the Court as an independent judicial body that follows a formalized procedure. The ILO-CoE does not oblige the CoE/ECtHR to disregard the pertinent ECHR provisions to give greater deference to the ILO.[63] Neither does the ILO-CoE

---

[62]On that note, as far as the ECHR and its Additional Protocols are concerned, the CoE indeed *did refrain* from involving the ILO in the drafting of the texts. Neither did it establish an institutional, procedural or substantive link between the ECtHR and the ILO, which would have been conceivable in cases of work-related ECHR guarantees. By way of comparison, Arts. 22(3) ICCPR and Art. 8(3) ICESCR each make explicit reference to ILO Convention No 87, thereby creating a substantive link. Furthermore, these treaties' supervisory bodies' reports may be transmitted to the ILO and other specialized agencies, see Art. 40 (3) ICCPR and Arts. 16–21 ICESCR, thereby creating a procedural link. See also the safeguard clauses for the specialized agencies' constitutional mandates and procedures, Arts. 44, 46 ICCPR, Art. 24 ICESCR.

[63]That being said, a cooperation agreement involving a body organized as a court is not impossible—indeed, there are concrete examples of such agreements, such as the agreements between the UN and the International Criminal Court (ICC) and the International Tribunal for the Law of the Sea (ITLOS), respectively. Most of the provisions in these agreements resemble those in the ILO-CoE, which can be explained by the fact that the ITLOS and the ICC are organized as independent IOs. Moreover, it has also occurred that international courts were bound, by virtue of provisions in treaties, to observe the case law of another court, see e.g. Art. 6 Agreement on the European Economic Area (signed 2 May 1992, entered into force 1 January 1994) [1994] OJ L1/3, Art. 3 Agreement between the EFTA States on the Establishment of a Surveillance Authority and a Court of Justice (signed 2 May 1992, entered into force 1 January 1994) [1994] OJ L 344/3, Till

contain clauses that would further define or demarcate the Court's jurisdiction or independence vis-à-vis the ILO.[64]

III. Conclusion

The ILO-CoE provides a normative framework for direct and cooperative interactions. However, it does not take on the issue of relativization. The ILO-CoE does not define by itself how and to what extent either IO's governance model ought to play a role in the activities of the other. Instead, it seems to 'trust' in the ILO's and CoE's will and ability to reconcile their activities in a way that sufficiently takes into account both their governance models. It provides procedural and other machinery intended to enable both IOs to do so through dialogue, exchange, reciprocal representation, mutual supply of certain services and so forth.

This strategy mostly paid off in the case of the (R)ESC. Yet, it would hardly protect the ILO's model in case the CoE or the ECSR suddenly decided to diminish the ILO's influence and relevance on the ESC's text or implementation. Moreover, the ILO-CoE's strategy reaches its limits when one IO sets up a body—like the ECtHR—that is vitally dependent on maintaining its independence and on closely adhering to its own procedure, and that has, by virtue to its internal constitution, only very limited means to use the machinery provided by the ILO-CoE.

Patrik Holterhus, 'EWR' in Horst-Günther Krenzler, Christoph Herrmann and Marian Niestedt (eds), *EU-Außenwirtschafts- und Zollrecht Vol II* (14th edn, C H Beck 2019) 1, para 155.

[64]Such clauses can occasionally be found in other agreements. For instance, Art. 1 Agreement on Cooperation and Relationship between the United Nations and the International Tribunal for the Law of the Sea ((signed 18 December 1997, entered into force 8 September 1998) 2000 UNTS 467 (UN-ITLOS)), contains a mutual recognition and 'respect' clause. Art. 1(1) and (2) UN-ITLOS provides:

1. The United Nations recognizes the International Tribunal for the Law of the Sea as an autonomous international judicial body with jurisdiction as provided for in the relevant provisions of the Convention and the statute of the International Tribunal annexed thereto.
2. The International Tribunal recognizes the responsibilities of the United Nations under the Charter, in particular in the fields of international peace and security, economic, social, cultural and humanitarian development and the peaceful settlement of international disputes.

Art. 1(3) UN-ITLOS sets forth an explicit undertaking of the parties to

respect the status and mandate of the other (...).

D. Conclusion on Chap. 13

This chapter has examined whether there are provisions in bilateral inter-organizational treaties concluded between the ILO and the World Bank and the CoE, respectively, protecting or promoting the ILO's model of labour governance.

With regard to the World Bank, the chapter has found that there are hardly any binding agreements in place. Insofar as they exist, they are case- or topic-specific and do not allow general inferences as to the legal relationship between the ILO and the Bank.

As to the CoE, the only relevant agreement is the ILO-CoE, which sets forth a legal framework of mostly procedural provisions designed to facilitate cooperation between the ILO and the CoE. However, the ILO-CoE essentially limits itself to regulating direct and cooperative interactions, which makes it largely irrelevant for other forms of interaction.

As the ESC's drafting illustrates, the ILO's inter-organizational agreements can provide a basis for fruitful cooperation and for the promotion of its model during such cooperation if both parties are willing.[65] However, in sum, it must be concluded that they hardly contain legal rules that would protect or promote the ILO's model of labour governance during non-cooperative inter-organizational interactions, in the sense that they would require the other IO to have due regard even if it refused to do so voluntarily.

[65]For example, the ILO and the UNESCO managed to resolve potential conflicts between some of their instruments regarding migration through negotiation, see Clarence Wilfred Jenks, 'The Conflict of Law-Making Treaties' (1953) 30 British Yearbook of International Law 401, 417. For further examples see Felice Morgenstern *Legal Problems of International Organizations* (Grotius Publications 1986) 27.

14. The ILO and the World Bank Within the UN System's Legal Framework

Besides stand-alone inter-organizational treaties, the UN System provides treaty-based machinery for coordination and cooperation among the IOs and other entities belonging to it,[1] including the ILO and the World Bank.[2] Given the lack of bilateral

[1]For a taxonomy of the different types of legally independent and dependent entities of the UN System see Paul C Szasz, 'The Complexification of the United Nations System' (1999) 3 Max Planck Yearbook of United Nations Law 1.

[2]The analysis of this chapter is not relevant for interactions between the ILO and the CoE, as the latter is not a specialized agency of the UN and not a member of the UN System. It deserves mention, however, that the UN and CoE have established and maintained close relations and the latter was, at least in its initial phase, considered a European pillar of the organization of the world as embodied in the UN. Robertson, writing in the mid-1950s, reports on early informal meetings between the UN Secretary-General and the CoE Secretary-General aiming at avoiding duplication of work and to further develop cooperation in fields of common interest, Arthur Henry Robertson *The Relations Between the Council of Europe and the United Nations* (UNITAR 1972) 201. The UN and CoE perpetuated their relations early on, through the 1951 Agreement between the Secretariat General of the Council of Europe and the Secretariat of the United Nations (exchange of letters of 15 December 1951) UN Doc SG 324/080 <https://rm.coe.int/CoERMPublicCommonSearchServices/DisplayDCTMContent?documentId=090000168059acd8> accessed 26 April 2020, which was supplemented and updated by the 1971 Arrangement on Co-operation and Liaison between the Secretariats of the United Nations and the Council of Europe (exchange of letters of 19 November 1971) <https://rm.coe.int/CoERMPublicCommonSearchServices/DisplayDCTMContent?documentId=090000168059acd9> accessed 26 April 2020. These agreements are no relationship agreements in the sense of Arts. 57 and 63(1) UN Charter and it has been doubted whether they are legally binding, see Tobias Winkler, *Die Vereinten Nationen im Gefüge der internationalen Organisationen – Eine rechtsdogmatische Untersuchung* (Nomos 2019) 147 with further references. Still, their content, regulating exchange of information, mutual consultation, reciprocal representation and technical cooperation, mirrors essential components of relationship agreements. What is more, on the initiative of CoE member states, the CoE became an observer at the UN and has established a permanent mission to the UN, CoE, 'The Council of Europe's Relations with the

H. Gött, *The Law of Interactions Between International Organizations*, Beiträge zum ausländischen öffentlichen Recht und Völkerrecht 299, https://doi.org/10.1007/978-3-662-62389-3_14

inter-organizational treaties between the ILO and the World Bank observed in the previous chapter, the UN System could serve as an alternative legal framework for interactions between them. It is therefore appropriate to examine whether the UN System's legal framework provides a common normative framework protecting and promoting the ILO's model of labour governance during interactions with the World Bank.

At the outset, it is worth noting that the UN System is more than a mere legal framework for IO policy coordination in labour (and other fields of) governance. Rather, it establishes a 'triangular' constellation: Coordination must not only be achieved between the different specialized agencies—for present purposes the ILO and the World Bank—but also between the agencies and the UN. In this regard, it deserves mention that the UN plays a double role: On the one hand, it serves as the 'umbrella IO' intended to coordinate the UN System's component entities, including the ILO and the Bank. On the other hand, as mentioned in Chap. 3, the UN itself actively engages in labour governance, and it has interacted with the ILO on numerous occasions.[3] Although having been of considerable relevance throughout the ILO's history,[4] the analysis presented here will leave out UN-ILO interactions and focus on the UN System's coordinative role regarding interactions between the ILO and the World Bank.

For present purposes, the UN System's legal framework (A.) can potentially become relevant in two ways: Firstly, as an instrument to avert World Bank influence on the ILO's model of labour governance (B.), and secondly, as a framework for promoting this model (C.).

A. Overview on the UN System's Legal Framework

The founders of the UN endeavoured to create a central structure for the maintenance of peace and security while at the same time providing sufficient flexibility for states to cooperate in some areas without having to cooperate in others.[5] Thus, while creating the UN as a central universal organization, they left important fields of

United Nations' (*CoE Website*) <https://www.coe.int/en/web/der/united-nations> accessed 26 April 2020. Biennially since 2000, the UNGA has adopted a resolution concerning the cooperation with the CoE. Formal and informal cooperation on all levels between the two IOs has extended over a vast range of topics, including some with a labour aspect, such as the protection of social rights, discrimination or the fight against trafficking in human beings.

[3]See the examples given in Chap. 3 above.

[4]See e.g. Antony Evelyn Alcock, *History of the International Labour Organization* (Palgrave Macmillan 1971) 188 et seqq.; Henner Gött, 'Interactions between International Organizations - Approaching a Neglected Governance Dimension' (2020) 17 International Organizations Law Review 75, 81 et seqq.

[5]*Legality of the Use by a State of Nuclear Weapons in Armed Conflict (Request of the World Health Organization)* (Advisory Opinion) [1996] ICJ Reports 66, para 26.

international cooperation to the purview of largely autonomous and legally separate IOs, the specialized agencies, which, together with the UN, should form a coherent system. Accordingly, the UN Charter establishes the UN System as a system of 'functional decentralization'.[6] It thereby departs from the more centralistic model of the League of Nations.[7]

At the same time, the founders of the UN anticipated that this model would require coordination among the UN System's component entities. As a result, the UN Charter foresees a legal framework for coordination, vesting coordinative functions in the UN, distributing tasks among UN organs (I.) and providing instruments for coordination (II.). This legal framework provides a range of potential legal bases of the UN System's component entities' rights and obligations in the context of coordination (III.).

I. Coordinating Bodies

According to Arts. 60, 63(2) UN Charter, coordination within the UN System is the responsibility of the ECOSOC, under the authority of the UNGA. In practice, after an initial period of self-restraint, the UNGA has broadly assumed the authority to coordinate, constantly diminishing the ECOSOC's role.[8] Whereas in more recent years, several review initiatives have sought to strengthen ECOSOC, there is still a noticeable predominance of the UNGA.[9] The ongoing UN reform process has

---

[6]Clarence Wilfred Jenks, 'Coordination: A New Problem of International Organization' 77 Recueil des Cours de l'Académie de Droit International 151, 172 et seq.; Douglas Williams, *The Specialized Agencies and the United Nations – A System in Crisis* (Hurst 1987) 14 et seq.; Christian Tietje, 'Global Governance and Inter-Agency Co-Operation in International Economic Law' (2002) 36 Journal of World Trade 501, 510; Laurence Boisson De Chazournes, 'Relations with Other International Organizations' in Jacob Katz Cogan, Ian Hurd and Ian Johnstone (eds), *The Oxford Handbook of International Organizations* (Oxford University Press 2016) 693.

[7]See e.g. Art. 24(1) LoN Covenant and Art. 399 Treaty of Peace between the British Empire, France, Italy, Japan and the United States (the Principal Allied and Associated Powers), and Belgium, Bolivia, Brazil, China, Cuba, Czechoslovakia, Ecuador, Greece, Guatemala, Haiti, the Hedjaz, Honduras, Liberia, Nicaragua, Panama, Peru, Poland, Portugal, Roumania, the Serb-Croat-Slovene State, Siam, and Uruguay, and Germany (signed 28 June, entered into force 10 January 1920) 225 CTS 195 (Treaty of Versailles). The UN founders sought to create a more effective successor for the ill-fated League of Nations, Klaus Dicke, *Effizienz und Effektivität Internationaler Organisationen* (Duncker & Humblot 1994) 72 et seqq.; Williams (n 6) 15; Boisson De Chazournes (n 6) 692.

[8]Werner Meng, 'Art. 63' in Bruno Simma and others (eds), *The Charter of the United Nations - A Commentary, vol II* (3rd edn, Oxford University Press 2013) para 39 et seqq. and 48 et seqq. The UNGA even created new bodies entrusted with coordination issues, such as UNDP, UNCTAD or UNIDO, the latter later being transformed into a separate IO, Werner Meng, 'Art. 60' in Bruno Simma and others (eds), *The Charter of the United Nations - A Commentary, vol II* (3rd edn, Oxford University Press 2013) para 7.

[9]Meng, 'Art. 63' (n 8) para 42; Rosalyn Higgins and others, *Oppenheim's International Law - United Nations* (Oxford University Press 2017) para 5.29.

yielded some ambitions reform proposals that could significantly upgrade the role of ECOSOC.[10]

In practice, programming, planning and coordination is mainly dealt with in the Committee for Programme and Coordination (CPC) and the Chief Executives Board for Coordination (CEB). Both the CPC and the CEB are common subsidiary bodies of the UNGA and the ECOSOC.[11]

The CPC is currently composed of 34 ECOSOC member states on the basis of equitable geographic distribution.[12] One of the CPC's most important tasks is to review and evaluate the programmes and the functioning of the UN System and its programmes, and to make recommendations as to their enhancement.[13] With regard to the specialized agencies, the CPC reviews the effectiveness of coordination with other UN System entities and assists the ECOSOC in the exercise of its coordinating functions.[14] To this end, the CPC considers the programmes and activities of the specialized agencies, with a view to their mutual compatibility and complementarity.[15] The CPC may also make recommendations to the specialized agencies containing guidelines on their programmes and activities.[16] Further, the CPC reviews and assesses, upon recommendation of the UNGA or the ECOSOC, the implementation and impact within the UN System of important legislative decisions.[17] Finally, it studies reports, among others the annual reports of the CEB and the specialized agencies.[18]

[10]See Independent Team of Advisors to the ECOSOC Bureau, 'The Future We Want, the UN System We Need - Papers by the Independent Team of Advisors to the ECOSOC Bureau' (2016) <https://www.un.org/ecosoc/sites/www.un.org.ecosoc/files/files/en/qcpr/ecosoc-dialogue-publication.pdf> accessed 26 April 2020; UN Secretary-General, 'Repositioning the United Nations Development System to Deliver on the 2030 Agenda: Our Promise for Dignity, Prosperity and Peace on a Healthy Planet, Report of the Secretary-General' (2017) UN Doc A/72/684.

[11]For the CPC see ECOSOC Res 2008 (LX) (14 May 1976) UN Doc E/RES/2008(LX), para 1; Higgins and others (n 9) para 6.39. For the CEB see Meng, 'Art. 63' (n 8) para 45.

[12]UNGA Dec 42/450 (17 December 1987) UN Doc A/DEC/42/450. Previously, the CPC consisted of 21 members, which again had increased the number from formerly eleven members, see ECOSOC Res 2008 (LX) (14 May 1976) UN Doc E/RES/2008(LX), para 7; ECOSOC Res 920 (XXIV) (3 August 1962) UN Doc E/RES/920(XXIV), para 1.

[13]According to UNGA Res 72/266, adopting an annual instead of a biennial budget period on a trial basis, the CPC contributes Part I (the plan outline, which endorses the long-term priorities and the objectives of the Organization) and Part II (the programme plan for programmes and subprogrammes and programme performance information), UNGA Res 72/266 (24 December 2017) UN Doc A/RES/72/266, para 10 et seq.

[14]ECOSOC, Committee for Programme and Coordination, Terms of Reference, ECOSOC Res 2008 (LX) (14 May 1976) UN Doc E/RES/2008(LX), Annex (CPC Terms of Reference), Nos. 2 lit. a (iii) and lit. b.

[15]CPC Terms of Reference, No 3 lit. a.

[16]CPC Terms of Reference, No 3 lit. b.

[17]CPC Terms of Reference, No 3 lit. c.

[18]CPC Terms of Reference, No 3 lit. d.

The CEB is composed of 31 chief executive officers of UN programmes and funds, of specialized agencies, including the ILO Director-General and the President of the World Bank Group, and of three further IOs.[19] Its biannual sessions are chaired by the UN Secretary-General.[20] The CEB's main task is to effectively coordinate the UN System's practical work through consultations and exchange of information, making use of the practical administrative and financial knowledge its members have about their respective institutions.[21]

Apart from the CPC and the CEB, further UN organs' subsidiary bodies that have not been specifically created for coordination purposes play a role, notably the Advisory Committee on Administrative and Budgetary Questions (ACABQ),[22] a subcommittee of the UNGA.[23] With regard to the specialized agencies, the ACABQ examines the administrative budgets of the specialized agencies and proposals for financial arrangements with such agencies; and considers and reports to the UNGA on auditors' reports on the UN and the Agencies.[24] The ACABQ surveys the specialized agencies' budgets, but, due to time and resource constraints, does not conduct a full examination.[25]

---

[19]UN, 'United Nations Chief Executives Board for Coordination' (*UN Website*) <https://www.unsystem.org/content/who-we-are> accessed 26 April 2020.

[20]The CEB's predecessor, the Administrative Committee on Coordination (ACC) was founded in 1946 and has since remained the most senior inter-agency coordinating body within the UN System. In the course of a review of its activities in 2000/2001, the ECOSOC decided to rename the ACC into Chief Executives Board for Coordination, without, however, changing the body's mandate, ECOSOC Dec 2001/321 (24 October 2001) UN Doc E/DEC/2001/321, para a).

[21]Meng, 'Art. 60' (n 8) para 13. The CEB also considers the many mechanisms for inter-agency coordination which have developed over time within the UN System. For a list of these mechanisms see UN, 'Inter-Agency Coordination Mechanisms' (*UN Website*) <https://www.unsystem.org/iacms> accessed 26 April 2020. The CEB carries out its functions through three pillars. Firstly, the High-Level Committee on Programmes (HLCP), which was created to promote system-wide cooperation, coordination a knowledge-sharing. Secondly, the High-Level Committee on Management (HLCM), which aims to improve the UN System's efficiency and business practices by identifying and analysing possible reforms of system-wide administrative management issues, UN, 'Article 63' in Repertory of Practice of United Nations Organs Vol IV (Supplement No 10, 2000–2009) para 19. In addition, in 2008, the pre-existing UN Development Group was integrated as a third pillar into the CEB structure. The three pillars are supported by the CEB Secretariat, which supports the HLCP and the HLCM, and the UN Development Operations Coordination Office as administrative support for the UN Development Group, UN, 'United Nations Chief Executives Board for Coordination' (n 19).

[22]The UN Statistical Commission, an ECOSOC subsidiary organ tasked with coordination in statistical matters (Meng, 'Art. 63' (n 8) para 47), will not be discussed here, neither will the Joint Inspection Unit and others (see Meng, 'Art. 60' (n 8) para 5).

[23]It is composed of currently 16 independent members elected by the UNGA and serving in their individual capacity, Rule 155 Rules of Procedure of the General Assembly (September 2016) UN Doc A/520/Rev.18 (UNGA Rules of Procedure).

[24]Rule 157 UNGA Rules of Procedure.

[25]Peter Woeste and Thomas Thomma, 'Art. 17' in Bruno Simma and others (eds), *The Charter of the United Nations - A Commentary, vol I* (3rd edn, Oxford University Press 2012) para 158.

II. Instruments of Coordination

Coordination within the UN System is conducted through a variety of instruments and their interplay.

The UN Charter explicitly mentions two kinds of formal instruments for coordination. Firstly, it provides that the UN, through ECOSOC, shall enter into relationship agreements with the specialized agencies (Arts. 57 and 63(1) UN Charter). The UN Charter does not prescribe that such agreements shall be legally binding international treaties, albeit many binding relationship agreements have in fact been concluded.[26] Binding or not, most relationship agreements have a comparable structure and similar contents.[27] They set forth institutional and procedural rules concerning the envisaged coordination and cooperation between the UN and the respective specialized agency. In this vein, they usually entail provisions on consultations, recommendations, proposals of issues to be placed on each other's agendas, reciprocal representation in the respective other's organs and bodies, exchanges of information and documents, statistical services, personal arrangements, and budgetary and financial issues.[28] Many relationship agreements also regulate the agencies' relations with specific UN organs.[29] Depending on the IO in question, a relationship agreement may be of varying regulatory intensity.[30] For example, as discussed further below, the agreement with the World Bank particularly emphasizes the latter's autonomy from the UN.

Furthermore, Art. 63(2) UN Charter provides that the ECOSOC may co-ordinate the activities of the specialized agencies through consultation with and recommendations to them, as well as through recommendations to the UNGA and to the UN Member States. Neither the ECOSOC nor the UN as a whole can make decisions that are legally binding for the specialized agencies.[31]

[26]Neither does the UN Charter define or restrict the matters to be covered by relationship agreements, John HE Fried, 'Relations Between the United Nations and the International Labor Organization' (1947) 41 The American Political Science Review 963. That being said, the Charter contains other provisions regarding specialized agencies which are arguably best implemented by agreement, see the examples given by Meng, 'Art. 63' (n 8) para 2, who considers these issues as mandatory content of relationship agreements.

[27]Eckart Klein, 'United Nations, Specialized Agencies', *Max Planck Encyclopedia of Public International Law* (Oxford University Press 2006) para 19; Higgins and others (n 9) para 7.35.

[28]Moreover, a number of relationship agreements envisage subsequent implementation agreements, to be concluded by the UN Secretary-General and the specialized agency's chief executive officer, e.g. the ILO Director-General (Art. XVIII UN-ILO), and the amendment of the relationship agreement itself, e.g. Art. XIX UN-ILO.

[29]Such as the ECOSOC, the UNSC or the ICJ, including the latter's jurisdiction on rendering advisory opinions at the specialized agency's request (Art. 96(2) UN Charter), Klein (n 27) para 19.

[30]Meng, 'Art. 63' (n 8) para 4.

[31]ibid 37.

Beyond instruments explicitly mentioned in the UN Charter, further instruments and practice have developed over time, which partially supplement, and sometimes even factually replace, the formal instruments of coordination. For instance, the UN Secretary-General has promulgated the Regulations and Rules Governing Programme Planning, the Programme Aspects of the Budget, the Monitoring of Implementation and the Methods of Evaluation.[32]

Apart from normative instruments, coordination also occurs through other means, e.g. fact-finding initiatives, studies and analyses.[33] Finally, time and again, UN activities occurring outside the immediate context of coordination have had a traceable impact on the UN System, e.g. the series of high-level summits in the 1990s and 2000s.[34]

III. Legal Bases for Specialized Agencies' Rights and Obligations

As this brief survey shows, coordination within the UN System is not primarily a matter of 'hard law' and its enforcement. Yet, for present purposes, it is nonetheless necessary to isolate the potential legal bases of the UN System's component entities' rights and obligations in the context of coordination.

The UN's coordinative function and a significant part of its coordinative machinery is laid down in the UN Charter and other instruments of UN institutional law. It goes without saying that these provisions of UN institutional law are legally binding on UN member states and those UN System entities without a separate legal personality from the UN's. However, it is far less certain that the said provisions are also binding on legally separate specialized agencies. If they are, they directly create rights and obligations for the specialized agencies. If not, specialized

[32]UN, 'Regulations and Rules Governing Programme Planning, the Programme Aspects of the Budget, the Monitoring of Implementation and the Methods of Evaluation' (2018) UN Doc ST/SGB/2018/3, 1. The Regulations and Rules are a set of provisions providing guidance to the UN System's constituents in the four steps of planning, budgeting, implementing and reviewing policies and activities within the UN System. The Regulations and Rules conceive these four steps as successive phases of one integrated management process, programme-planning cycle. For each phase, the Regulations and Rules foresee one corresponding instrument: The Strategic Framework, Programme budgets, Reports on Programme Performance and, lastly, Evaluation reports. The Strategic Framework is the UN's principal policy directive and serves as the basis for programme planning, budgeting, monitoring and evaluation, UNGA Res 58/587 (23 December 2003) UN Doc A/RES/58/587, para 7. It is prepared by the CPC, which makes according conclusions and recommendations, and decided on by the UNGA. The two-year UN Strategic Framework replaces the previous four-year medium-term plans.

[33]Werner Meng, 'Art. 58' in Bruno Simma and others (eds), *The Charter of the United Nations - A Commentary, vol II* (3rd edn, Oxford University Press 2012) para 1.

[34]Werner Meng, 'Art. 62' in Bruno Simma and others (eds), *The Charter of the United Nations - A Commentary, vol II* (3rd edn, Oxford University Press 2012) para 46.

agencies' rights and obligations will have to be derived from other bases, notably from pertinent relationship agreements. This distinction is structurally relevant: if specialized agencies' rights and obligations emanate solely from relationship agreements and not the UN Charter itself, this means that (a) they are in a position to negotiate these rights and obligations and (b) agencies' legal independence vis-à-vis the UN may be greater or smaller, depending on the agency. This again has an impact on the UN's legal coordinative powers.

At the outset, the *pacta tertiis* rule protects specialized agencies from being bound by UN institutional law without their consent.[35] However, despite that rule, some authors have suggested that the UN Charter nonetheless created rights and obligations for non-members. The underlying idea of these proposals is that the UN Charter resembles a 'constitution' not only for the organization itself, but for the international community as a whole.[36] Supporters of this idea refer to a range of Charter provisions and other developments.[37]

Whether and in what sense these arguments hold merit and the UN Charter qualifies as a constitution of the international community has been debated extensively and does not need to be revisited here in detail.[38] Irrespective of how justified such a qualification might be in terms of categorization and conceptualization, it is in any event highly doubtful that it provides a legal basis for specialized agencies to be directly bound by UN institutional law. It may be the case that certain provisions—notably Art. 103 UN Charter—have an indirect legal effect on the ILO or the World Bank. Similarly, it may be the case that the integration of IOs into the UN System leads to certain loyalty obligations vis-à-vis that system and its other component entities. Both aspects will be discussed in context below. Still, it must be concluded at this point that UN institutional law is not in itself binding on specialized agencies.

---

[35] See above, Chap. 9 A. III.

[36] See e.g. Alfred Verdross and Bruno Simma, *Universelles Völkerrecht* (3rd edn, Duncker & Humblot 1984) 221; Bardo Fassbender, 'The United Nations Charter as Constitution of the International Community' (1998) 36 Columbia Journal of Transnational Law 529. See also the discussion in Andreas L Paulus, *Die internationale Gemeinschaft im Völkerrecht* (C H Beck 2001) 293 et seqq., with further references.

[37] E.g. including the fact that the UN enjoys universal membership or a constitutional resemblance of certain Charter provisions. These include e.g. Arts. 1 and 2 UN Charter with their catalogues of purposes and principles, the UN's responsibility vis-à-vis non-member states (Art. 2(6) UN Charter), the supremacy of Charter obligations over members' conflicting obligations (Art. 103 UN Charter) and the amendment provisions in Chapter XVIII UN Charter; Bruno Simma, 'From Bilateralism to Community Interest in International Law' (1994) 250 Recueil des Cours de l'Académie de Droit International 217, 261; Paulus, *Die internationale Gemeinschaft im Völkerrecht* (n 36) 307; Matthias Ruffert and Christian Walter, *Institutionalisiertes Völkerrecht* (2nd edn, C H Beck 2015) 23 et seqq.

[38] Andreas L Paulus, *Die internationale Gemeinschaft im Völkerrecht* (n 36) 293 et seqq.; Winkler (n 2) 118 et seqq., with further references.

This has an important consequence: insofar as the UN's coordinative machinery is based in UN institutional law, this machinery is *res inter alios acta* for the ILO and the World Bank unless and to the extent the latter consent to it or there is an inter-organizational norm pursuant to which they are bound by the UN Charter regardless of consent.[39] It is therefore necessary to examine pertinent inter-organizational norms in closer detail, notably the respective relationship agreements. This will be the main focus in the two following sections.

B. Can the ILO Rely on 'Protection' Through UN Coordination?

As mentioned initially, the UN System's legal framework is of relevance for present purposes in two ways: Firstly, it could provide a normative framework to coordinate the conduct of other specialized agencies, including the World Bank, in a manner 'protecting' the ILO's model of labour governance by averting adverse influence. Secondly, it could serve as legal machinery to disseminate and mainstream the ILO's model, especially its agenda and outputs, to the Bank.

This section will address the former aspect. In doing so, two separate questions have to be distinguished: Firstly, if the UN is obliged vis-à-vis the ILO to coordinate the conduct of other specialized agencies (I.), and, secondly, whether and to what extent the World Bank has to follow the UN's coordinative measures (II.).

I. Is the UN Obliged to Coordinate the Conduct of Other Agencies to Protect the ILO?

The ILO's rights and obligations vis-à-vis the UN are governed by a series of agreements with the UN and its funds and programmes. The principal agreement between the UN and the ILO is the 1946 UN-ILO Relationship Agreement (UN-ILO) (1.). Besides, the ILO has also entered into agreements with various of the UN's not legally independent Funds and Programmes (2). Finally, rights could emerge under an unwritten duty to 'system loyalty' owed by the UN to the ILO (3.).

[39] Similar Winkler (n 2) 120.

1. The 1946 UN-ILO Relationship Agreement

The 1946 UN-ILO agreement was the first relationship agreement ever to be concluded between the UN and a specialized agency.[40] The overall purpose of the UN-ILO is to establish an "effective liaison" between both IOs.[41] This includes coordination and cooperation, the efficient use of resources and avoidance of unnecessary duplications of work.[42] There is no need to consider all of the structural components in detail here. Rather, the analysis will focus on selected features.

a) Recognition of the ILO's Status

As a first feature to be mentioned, the UN-ILO contains a number of mutual recognitions. Interestingly for present purposes, one such recognition concerns the ILO's status.[43] Art. I UN-ILO reads:

> The United Nations recognises the International Labour Organisation as a specialised agency responsible for taking such action as may be appropriate under its basic instrument for the accomplishment of the purposes set forth therein.

The agreement leaves it open what the exact legal consequence of the recognition as a specialized agency is. In terms of the scope of this 'speciality', Art. 1 UN-ILO essentially refers the question to the ILO's "basic instrument", i.e. the ILO Constitution.

In terms of the content of the recognition, one could ask if the recognition clause gives the ILO a contractual right to exclusively exercise its responsibility, i.e. without (or at least with only limited) interference by the UN. Such an exclusive right would have potentially far-reaching consequences. Firstly, it would grant the ILO a protected sphere, regarding which any UN interference would be in need of justification. Secondly, it would also be conceivable that the UN could be required to

[40] Meng, 'Art. 63' (n 8) para 5.

[41] According to Art. XVII UN-ILO, both IOs "agree to the [provisions of the UN-ILO] in the belief that they will contribute to the maintenance of effective liaison between the two organizations."

[42] The purpose of this liaison is the furtherance of the objectives of the UN. However, it is noteworthy that the UN-ILO does not go so far as to make these objectives a common goal of both contracting IOs. Art. IV(1) UN-ILO even explicitly designates the promotion of the objectives enshrined in Art. 55 UN Charter as an "obligation of the United Nations". The ILO does not commit to the same objectives but is put in the role of the cooperating partner.

[43] As a second recognition, on a much more practical level, both IOs mutually recognize each other's competences for specific statistical services. The ILO recognizes the UN as the "central agency" for the collection, analysis, publication, standardization and improvement of statistics "serving the general purposes of international organizations", whereas the UN recognizes the ILO as the "appropriate agency" for the same tasks "within its special sphere, without prejudice to the right of United Nations to concern itself with such statistics so far as they may be essential for its own purposes or for the improvement of statistics throughout the world."

use its coordinating powers to safeguard this exclusivity against other component entities of the UN System, including the World Bank.

However, it is questionable if Art. I UN-ILO establishes any such degree of jurisdictional exclusivity in favour of the ILO. The ILO Governing Body has early on emphasized that it understood the clause in Art. 1 UN-ILO as a promise by the UN not to assume direct responsibility over maters falling within the ILO's scope of action.[44] However, this assertion is based on weak ground. While the UN-ILO[45] speaks of "a" specialized agency, some other relationship agreements between the UN and other specialized agencies speak of "the" specialized agency.[46] Given that relationship agreements are typically quite similar, if not to say 'standardized', and modelled precisely after the UN-ILO Agreement, deviations must at least be considered.

Moreover, an interpretation as suggested by the ILO Governing Body, taken together with the ILO's considerably broad mandate to promote social justice and decent work, would practically install the ILO as the only competent agency for most economic and social concerns, including many human rights and development issues. There is nothing in the practice of the ILO, the UN or any other specialized agency suggesting that this was the intended allocation of competences.[47] On the contrary, the UN—and other specialized agencies—have repeatedly assumed primary responsibility for many matters that arguably belong to the ILO's sphere of action.[48]

Hence, the preferable interpretation of Art. I UN-ILO is that it does not confer an exclusive jurisdictional sphere on the ILO that the UN would have to respect or even to protect.

b) Obligations Regarding Coordinating Measures by the UN

Further, the UN-ILO contains a range of provisions regarding coordinative action taken by the UN. However, virtually all these provisions impose obligations on the ILO and not the UN. Apart from a range of more specific obligations,[49] the ILO

[44] Jenks, 'Coordination: A New Problem of International Organization' (n 6) 208.

[45] A similar wording exists in some other relationship agreements with specialized agencies, like Art. I UN-UNESCO.

[46] Jenks, 'Coordination: A New Problem of International Organization' (n 6) 207 et seq.

[47] Although the ILO did pursue such a strategy in its Philadelphia Declaration passed only two years earlier, see Chap. 8 B. IV. 1. and Gött, 'Interactions between International Organizations - Approaching a Neglected Governance Dimension' (n 4) 81 et seqq.

[48] See the examples given in Chap. 3 A. I.

[49] Notably, regarding the treatment of formal UN recommendations issued under Art. 63 UN Charter, the ILO commits to transmit them to its competent organs, to enter into consultations with the UN on such recommendations if so requested, and to report on the result of its consideration of the recommendations and on any action taken (Art. IV(1) and (2) UN-ILO). Moreover, under Art. V(2) UN-ILO, the ILO also commits to transmit reports and studies to the UN. Further

"affirms its intention" of co-operating in any necessary measures to make co-ordination fully effective (Art. IV(3) UN-ILO).

2. Other UN-ILO Agreements

In addition to the UN-ILO, the ILO has made various agreements with other component entities of the UN System. Some, but not all of them, are legally binding.[50] This section will only address those agreements with legally non-independent bodies of the UN, which technically bind the ILO and the UN as international legal subjects and form part of the legal framework of their overall relations. The main purpose is to point to some noteworthy differences between these agreements and the UN-ILO.

One such difference is that, unlike the UN-ILO, some of the agreements name common objectives.[51] Additionally, some agreements contain a certain degree of institutionalization by establishing common bodies.[52] Moreover, some agreements prescribe a concrete division of tasks and responsibilities.[53] Further, as a rare sight among IOs, UNOPS explicitly commits to observe parts of substantive ILO law,

---

the ILO pledges cooperation with, and assistance to, the UN Security Council, the UN Trusteeship Council and with the ICJ (Arts. VI, VII, VIII and IX(1) UN-ILO). In case the ILO concludes agreements with other specialized agencies, the ILO commits to inform the ECOSOC (Art. XVI UN-ILO).

[50]Some agreements contain language that suggests they are non-binding, see e.g. No 10 of the Memorandum of Understanding between the International Labour Organization and the United Nations Conference on Trade and Development (signed 4 December 2014) <https://www.ilo.org/wcmsp5/groups/public/%2D%2D-dgreports/%2D%2D-jur/documents/genericdocument/wcms_433858.pdf> accessed 26 April 2020. On the other hand, notably, some of the agreements contain, for their respective provisions, inter-organizational dispute settlement mechanisms, which indicates a degree of legal commitment, e.g. Art. 5.1 Memorandum of Understanding between the International Labour Organization and the United Nations Office for Project Services (signed 10 December 2015) <https://www.ilo.org/wcmsp5/groups/public/%2D%2D-dgreports/%2D%2D-jur/documents/genericdocument/wcms_458165.pdf> accessed 26 April 2020.

[51]For instance, Art. 1 of the Memorandum of Understanding Concerning Co-operation between the International Labour Organisation and the United Nations Centre for Human Settlements (HABITAT) (1984) LXVII ILO Official Bulletin Ser A 74 (ILO-UN HABITAT-MoU) defines it as a common objective to "promote sustainable satisfaction of basic human needs in urban and rural settlements." The Preamble of the 2014 ILO-UNCTAD-MoU refers to cooperation as a means to achieving "the shared objective of enhancing sustainable development through their respective mandates".

[52]No 3 ILO-UNCTAD-MoU foresees a Joint Steering Committee to make recommendations.

[53]The preamble of the ILO-UNDCP-MoU (Memorandum of Understanding for cooperation between the United Nations International Drug Control Programme and the International Labour Organization (signed 15 August 1994) <https://www.ilo.org/wcmsp5/groups/public/%2D%2D-dgreports/%2D%2D-jur/documents/genericdocument/wcms_433887.pdf> accessed 26 April 2020) contains a reciprocal recognition of exclusive responsibilities and leading agencies. No 1.2 and No 1.3 ILO-UN HABITAT-MoU contain a recognition of coordinating roles, of mandates and special competences.

namely certain principles relating to ILO labour standards (Art. 2.2 ILO-UNOPS-MoU).

The number and variety of these other agreements indicate that the ILO and the UN programmes and funds are willing and able to intensify the formalization, and at least in parts the 'legalization', of their relations in certain areas. That being said, these other agreements are too specific to be of relevance in the present context. Due to their speciality and their diversity, they do not provide general guidance to the ILO's rights and obligation in the UN System as a whole.

3. A Duty to 'System Loyalty' and Sincere Cooperation?

Some commentators have suggested that there was an unwritten duty to 'system loyalty' and sincere cooperation between the component IOs of the UN System. Some draw an analogy to obligations between IOs and their members (as discussed above) or loyalty between the constituent entities of federal states and the federation, like the concept of *Bundestreue* in German constitutional law.[54] The aim is to secure at least a minimum level of cooperation and coherence. Such a duty to 'system loyalty' would, firstly, set limits to activities of other agencies, such as the World Bank. Secondly, it could require the UN to use its coordinative machinery to protect the ILO's model from adverse influence by other agencies, and it could confer on the ILO a corresponding right to demand such coordination. Indeed, the ILO itself has in the past attempted to promote the idea that all UN System member IOs should at least be obliged not to weaken or thwart their member states' obligations under the law of other UN System IOs.[55]

However, as far as a specific obligation to 'system loyalty' in the UN System is concerned, the prospects are rather meagre.[56] It needs to be recalled that loyalty can mean different things in different contexts.[57] There are important structural differences between the UN System's legal framework on the one hand and the institutional law of IOs or a constitution of a federal state on the other. In a federal state, the relations between the states and the federation are exhaustively governed by the federal constitution. The legal relations between the member states of an IO are governed by the IO's constituent instrument, which is a treaty between *all* of them. By contrast, the UN System does not oblige the specialized agencies to enter into binding contractual relations among each other.[58] Moreover, the level of integration within the UN System is lower than within one IO or even in a federal state. It is true

[54]Francis Maupain, *The Future of the International Labour Organization in the Global Economy* (Hart Publishing 2013) 112, fn. 26.

[55]ibid.

[56]The prospects and limits of a general obligation among IOs to treat each other in good faith will be discussed further in Chap. 15.

[57]See *mutatis mutandis* Chap. 12 B. II. 3.

[58]Neither does it oblige other IOs to become specialized agencies in the first place.

that all specialized agencies have made agreements with the UN, integrating them into the UN System as foreseen in the UN Charter. These agreements must be fulfilled in good faith (Art. 26 VCLT-IO). However, the UN and the agencies have only committed to the relatively weak coordination machinery that the Charter and the relationship agreements envisage, and some have only done so in a very limited manner.[59] This greater emphasis on autonomy of the specialized agencies was a conscious decision. Therefore, the leniency of relationship agreements, or the absence of a right of an agency to demand positive action by the UN, must not too readily be glossed over by assuming an unwritten duty to loyalty.

To be sure, this is not to say that loyalty and good faith have no room in the relations between UN specialized agencies. Such a duty could well be deemed to exist as a matter of principle. Moreover, in extreme situations, e.g. if the influence of another specialized agency was so predominant that it would threaten to compromise the attainment of the UN-ILO's object and purpose, such a duty might require the UN to step in and use its coordinative machinery, and it might require the other agency to follow the coordinative measures. However, at present, it seems difficult to argue that this duty is substantially more developed than the general principle of good faith.

It would therefore be premature to speak of a special unwritten duty of 'system loyalty' among the ILO and the UN as a basis for distinct rights for the ILO against the UN.

4. Conclusion

The UN has no contractual obligation, and the ILO has no contractual right to demand from the UN, coordinative action to protect the ILO's model of labour governance from adverse influence by other agencies. Such a right is only conceivable on the basis of a good faith execution of the UN-ILO in a (hypothetical) case of extremely far-reaching influence by another agency on the ILO. The ILO can of course try to persuade the UN to become active. However, the UN-ILO's machinery presupposes that the UN is willing to coordinate the agencies' activities in the ILO's favour.

II. Coordination Without the Consent of the World Bank? The UN's Coordination Constraints

What is more, even if the UN was willing to use its coordinating machinery, such coordination would not necessarily result in enhancing the ILO's role and relevance

[59] See the discussion of UN-World Bank relations in the next section.

in World Bank activities. Rather, whether the UN can coordinate the ILO's and the World Bank's interactions crucially depends on the means the UN has at its disposal. The relevant relationship agreement between the UN and the Bank puts a significant strain on the UN's capability to coordinate (1.). which in practice has enabled the World Bank to essentially evade coordinative measures with which it did not agree (2.). The World Bank's large degree of independence from UN coordinative measures is not diminished by the primacy of UN Charter obligations as laid down in Art. 103 UN Charter (3.).

1. Coordination Constraints Under the UN-IBRD Relationship Agreement

Like the ILO, the WBG IOs are specialized agencies of the UN. The present analysis will, again, focus on the IBRD. The IBRD has made arrangements for cooperation with the UN and its funds and programmes.[60] For the purposes of this study, the most relevant is the 1947 UN-IBRD relationship agreement (UN-IBRD).[61]

a) Stronger Emphasis on Institutional Independence

The UN-IBRD is similar, and in several parts virtually identical, to the UN-ILO. Much of what has been said about the UN-ILO thus applies to the UN-IBRD *mutatis mutandis*. That being said, there are some important differences. More than the UN-ILO or other relationship agreements, the UN-IBRD contains strong language emphasizing the independence of the Bank. Art. I(2) UN-IBRD stipulates that:

> [b]y reason of the nature of its international responsibilities and the terms of its Articles of Agreement, the Bank is, and is required to function as, an independent international organization.

---

[60]Such cooperation actually takes place in a range of contexts. For instance, the UN and the Bank are high level observers in the respective other's meetings. The World Bank is an observer to the UNGA, the UNSC and ECOSOC. Since 2012, the UN Secretary-General has participated in the World Bank/IMF Spring and Annual Meetings, World Bank, *A Guide to the World Bank* (3rd edn, World Bank 2011) 49.

[61]Agreement between the United Nations and the International Bank for Reconstruction and Development (adopted 15 November 1947, entered into force 13 April 1948) 16 UNTS 341 (UN-IBRD). The Bank has made further arrangements with the UN, its funds and its programmes. Some of them take the form of inter-organizational agreements, such as the 2017 United Nations-World Bank Partnership Framework for Crisis-Affected Situations ((signed 22 April 2017) <https://www.un.org/peacebuilding/sites/www.un.org.peacebuilding/files/documents/un-wb_partnership_framework_for_crisis-affected_situations_signed_april_22_2017.pdf> accessed 26 April 2020.

This emphasis on independence results in weaker ties to the UN System in a number of respects.[62] Importantly for the present analysis, according to Art. IV (3) UN-IBRD, the UN recognizes that

> [t]he action to be taken by the Bank on any loan is a matter to be determined by the independent exercise of the Bank's own judgment in accordance with the Bank's Articles of Agreement (...).

As has often been observed, the main reason behind this stronger emphasis of institutional independence is to enable the Bank to execute its non-political mandate and facilitate decision-making solely on economic considerations, as provided for in its AoA.[63]

b) Relaxed Obligations Regarding Coordinating Measures

The preservation of independence as a rationale resurfaces in other provisions of the UN-IBRD. With regard to coordination within the UN System, the Bank's obligations are relaxed. Art. X(2) UN-IBRD makes the Bank's participation in the CEB conditional "to the extent consistent with the provisions of this agreement". With regard to formal recommendations, Art. IV(2) UN-IBRD provides that

> [n]either organization, nor any of their subsidiary bodies, will present any formal recommendations to the other without reasonable prior consultation with regard thereto. Any formal recommendations made by either organization after such consultation will be considered as soon as possible by the appropriate organ of the other.

Furthermore, pursuant to Art IV(3) UN-IBRD,

> (...) the United Nations recognizes (...), that it would be sound policy to refrain from making recommendations to the Bank with respect to particular loans or with respect to terms or conditions of financing by the Bank.

[62]The UN-IBRD does not, like other relationship agreements, envisage a harmonization or standardization of administrative or employment rules, with the result that the Bank's administration is detached from any such efforts within the UN System, Szasz (n 1) 37 et seq. See also UN Joint Inspection Unit, 'Relationship Agreements Between the UN and the Specialized Agencies: Review and Strengthening of Sections Pertaining to the Common System of Salaries, Allowances and Conditions of Service' (1993) UN Doc JIU/REP/93/3, para 45 et seq. Furthermore, the Bank does not have to submit its annual budget to the UNGA for scrutiny by the ACABQ, Szasz (n 1) 36.

[63]Ronald Janse, '(Why) Was the World Bank Supposed to Be a Nonpolitical Organization? An Interpretation of the Original Meaning and Rationale of Article 4(10) of the Articles of Agreement of the International Bank for Reconstruction and Development, 1941–1948' (2014) 16 Journal of the History of International Law / Revue d'histoire du droit international 113, 155; Hassane Cissé, 'Should the Political Prohibition in Charters of International Financial Institutions Be Revisited? The Case of the World Bank' (2012) 3 World Bank Legal Review 59, 60; Cornelia Janik, *Die Bindung Internationaler Organisationen an internationale Menschenrechtsstandards* (Mohr Siebeck 2012) 341.

In return,

> [t]he Bank recognizes that the United Nations and its organs may appropriately make recommendations with respect to the technical aspects of reconstruction or development plans, programmes and projects.

2. Coordination Constraints in Practice: Continued World Bank Support for South Africa and Portugal

The strong emphasis on independence has allowed the World Bank to remain reserved towards UN coordination. This is impressively illustrated by the World Bank's financial support to South Africa during the apartheid era and to colonial Portugal, which has become a classic example for the UN System's limited capacity to coordinate.[64] Because of its general implications for the functioning of the UN System's legal framework, the case, briefly mentioned in Chap. 9 above, is of continued relevance today. What is more, even though it is mostly portrayed as a clash between the UN and the IBRD alone, it also resembles an instance of blatant disharmony between the Bank and the ILO.

a) Background: The UN's and ILO's Policies Against Racial Discrimination and Colonialism

The case must be seen in the context of the ongoing decolonization and increased efforts to combat racism and racial discrimination by the UN, several other IOs and large parts of the international community.[65]

Already during the 1950s and early 1960s, the UNGA had adopted a series of resolutions condemning both racial discrimination in general and the apartheid regime in South Africa in particular, and had called on states and specialized agencies to cooperate to overcome policies of racial discrimination.[66] In 1963, the

[64]Furthermore, it has also become an example for the Bank's interpretation of the prohibition of political activity clause in its AoA. A very similar situation arose in the early 1980s, when South Africa filed a loan application with the IMF, Henry G Schermers and Niels M Blokker, *International Institutional Law* (6th edn, Brill 2018) para 1720.

[65]On 14 December 1960, the UNGA adopted the Declaration on the Granting of Independence to Colonial Countries and Peoples, UNGA Res 1514 (XV) (14 December 1960) UN Doc A/RES/1514 (XV). The following year, the UNGA established a Special Committee tasked with supervising the implementation of the Declaration and adopting appropriate recommendations, UNGA Res 1654 (XVI) (27 November 1961) UN Doc A/RES/1654(XVI), para 3. The UNGA further requested all specialized agencies to assist the Special Committee within their respective spheres of work, ibid para 8.

[66]UNGA Res 1510 (XV) (12 December 1960) UN Doc A/RES/1510(XV); UNGA Res 1597 (XV) (13 April 1961) UN Doc A/RES/1597(XV); UNGA Res 1598 (XV) (13 April 1961) UN Doc A/RES/1598(XV) and the prior resolutions cited therein. Further see UNGA Res 1779 (XVII) (7 December 1962) UN Doc A/RES/1779(XVII).

UNSC unanimously considered the apartheid regime to be "seriously disturbing international peace and security."[67]

The ILO for its part, had already taken position against racial discrimination in the Philadelphia Declaration and had in 1947 adopted a series of conventions specifically designed for non-metropolitan (i.e. colonized) territories.[68] Moreover, during the 1950s, the ILO had adopted two general non-discrimination conventions (No 100 and No 111), which nowadays rank among the eight fundamental labour conventions. ILO Convention No 111 obliges all parties to promote equality by adoption of a national policy, with a view to eliminating any discrimination on grounds of race, colour, sex, religion, political opinion, national extraction or social origin in respect of employment and occupation, including access to vocational training, access to employment and to particular occupations, and terms and conditions of employment (Arts. 1 and 2 ILO Convention No 111).

With particular regard to South Africa, the CFA, the CEACR and an ad hoc UN-ILO Committee on Forced Labour all found that the apartheid regime violated ILO instruments. As South Africa refused to implement changes, the conflict escalated. In its 1961 session, the International Labour Conference called upon South Africa to withdraw from the ILO until its apartheid regime was abolished. South Africa followed suit and notified its intent to withdraw in early 1964.[69] In its 1964 session, the International Labour Conference adopted the ILO Declaration Concerning the Policy of Apartheid of the Republic of South Africa, in which it emphatically condemned apartheid, proclaimed an ILO programme for the elimination of apartheid in labour matters and pledged cooperation with the UN.[70]

Concerning Portugal, the ILO had repeatedly dealt with the latter's refusal to renounce its colonial policy and to terminate the accompanying labour standards

[67]UNSC Res 181 (1963) (7 August 1963) UN Doc S/RES/181(1963) preamble. Later in 1963, the UNGA requested the ECOSOC to draft a declaration and a convention against racial discrimination, UNGA Res 1780 (XVII) (7 December 1962) UN Doc A/RES/1780(XVII). These efforts culminated in the adoption of the International Convention on the Elimination of All Forms of Racial Discrimination (adopted and opened for signature and ratification by General Assembly resolution 2106 (XX) of 21 December 1965, entered into force 4 January 1969) 660 UNTS 195 (CERD).

[68]The Social Policy (Non-Metropolitan Territories) Convention, 1947 (No 82) (adopted 11 July 1947, entered into force 19 June 1955) 218 UNTS 345, the Labour Standards (Non-Metropolitan Territories) Convention, 1947 (No 83) (adopted 11 July 1947, entered into force 15 June 1974) 943 UNTS 104, the Right of Association (Non-Metropolitan Territories) Convention, 1947 (No 84) (adopted 11 July 1947, entered into force 1 July 1953) 171 UNTS 329, the ILO Labour Inspectorates (Non-Metropolitan Territories) Convention, 1947 (No 85) (adopted 11 July 1947, entered into force 26 July 1955) 214 UNTS 33 and the ILO Contracts of Employment (Indigenous Workers) Convention, 1947 (No 86) (adopted 11 July 1947, entered into force 13 February 1953, abrogated by decision of the International Labour Conference at its 107th Session (2018)) 161 UNTS 113.

[69]For a detailed account of the dramatic events at the 1963 International Labour Conference, where the issue of apartheid almost led to a paralyzation of the ILO as a whole, see Alcock (n 4) 318 et seqq.

[70]ILO, Declaration Concerning the Policy of "Apartheid" of the Republic of South Africa (International Labour Conference, 48th session) (1964) XLVII ILO Official Bulletin Ser A 1 (Apartheid Declaration).

violations, notably concerning forced labour. Upon a Ghanaian formal representation concerning Portugal's non-implementation of the 1957 Abolition of Forced Labour Convention (ILO Convention No 105), the ILO Governing Body took the rare step of appointing a Commission of Inquiry pursuant to Art. 26 ILO Constitution to investigate the matter.[71]

b) The Inter-Organizational Dispute Concerning the Bank's Loans to South Africa and Portugal

The UN's and ILO's policies clashed with continuing World Bank financial support to the two states. The chronology of events has been exhaustively reported elsewhere,[72] hence a brief summary will suffice here. In 1964, the UNGA's Special Committee on the Implementation of the Declaration on the Granting of Independence to Colonial Countries and Peoples asked the IBRD to provide information and to appear before it to clarify its loan practices regarding Portugal.[73] The Bank provided information but did not send a representative.[74] When South Africa and Portugal applied for the continuation of World Bank loans, both the UNGA's Special Committee and the UNGA itself intervened. Both bodies requested the Bank not to grant financial assistance to Portugal because of its colonial policy.[75] Furthermore, both bodies reiterated their request to the specialized agencies, "in particular the International Bank for Reconstruction and Development and the International Monetary Fund",[76] to fully cooperate to oppose the South African apartheid regime[77] and to withhold any financial, economic or technical assistance to Portugal and South Africa until they abandon their policy of colonial domination and racial discrimination.[78]

Despite these requests, the IBRD granted new loans to Portuguese companies and to the South African Electricity Supply Commission in 1966.[79] In consequence, a legal argument ensued between the Legal Advisers of the Bank and the UN on the

[71] ILO, 'Report of the Commission Appointed under Article 26 of the Constitution of the ILO to Examine the Complaint Filed by the Government of Ghana Concerning the Observance by the Government of Portugal of the Abolition of Forced Labour Convention, 1957' (1962) XLV ILO Official Bulletin 1.

[72] See Samuel A Bleicher, 'UN v. IBRD: A Dilemma of Funcationalism' (1970) 24 International Organisation 3131; Schermers and Blokker, *International Institutional Law* (n 64) para 1720.

[73] Bleicher (n 72) 32.

[74] ibid.

[75] UNGA Res 2107 (XX) (21 December 1965) UN Doc A/RES/2107(XX), para 9.

[76] ibid.

[77] UNGA Res 2054 (XX) (15 December 1965) UN Doc A/RES/2054(XX), section A, para 11.

[78] UNGA Res 2105 (XX) (20 December 1965) UN Doc A/RES/2105(XX), para 11.

[79] Bleicher (n 72) 33.

legality of the Bank's conduct.[80] The Bank's legal adviser essentially gave two reasons for not following the UNGA's recommendations: Firstly, he argued that the UN-IBRD agreement required formal consultations before the UN could make recommendations. In the view of the Bank, such formal consultations had not taken place. Secondly, in any event, due to the prohibition of political activity enshrined in Art. 4(10) IBRD-AoA, the Bank was not competent to include political factors into its considerations and had to grant loans solely according to economic considerations. Hence, in the Bank's view, it would in any event have been unable to follow any recommendations to cease support for South Africa and Portugal.[81]

In December 1966, the UNGA repeated its request that the IBRD and the IMF refrained from further assisting Portugal and requested the UN Secretary-General to commence consultations with the IBRD in order to secure compliance with the UNGA's prior resolutions,[82] which took place in writing in early 1967 but ended without agreement.[83] In this situation, the IBRD expressed its

> earnest desire (. . .) to co-operate with the United Nations by all legitimate means and, to the extent consistent with its Articles of Agreement, to avoid any action that might run counter to the fulfilment of the great purposes of the United Nations.[84]

In a subsequent resolution on South Africa, the UNGA

> expressed the hope that the Bank will stand by its assurance that it will avoid any action that might run counter to the fulfilment of the great purposes of the United Nations.[85]

In further resolutions, the UNGA essentially repeated its requests to the IBRD. In 1968, the UNGA recommended that the Bank withdrew previously given loans,[86] which the Bank rejected, invoking lack of competence.[87]

Eventually, the dispute ended in a tacit truce. The UNGA did not call upon the UN Secretary-General to take any further action against the Bank.[88] The Bank, on its part, voluntarily refrained from granting new loans to South Africa and Portugal at a later point in time.[89]

The case casts a spotlight on the limits of the UN-IBRD. The agreement was created as a framework agreement for policy coordination within a newly created

---

[80]Schermers and Blokker, *International Institutional Law* (n 64) para 1720; Ibrahim FI Shihata, *The World Bank in a Changing World* (Springer 1991) 99 et seqq.

[81]Bleicher (n 72) 33 et seq.

[82]UNGA Res 2184 (XXI) (12 December 1966) UN Doc A/RES/2184(XXI), para 9 und 10; UNGA Res 2202 (XXI) (16 December 1966) UN Doc A/RES/2202(XXI), para 6 lit. d.

[83]In July 1967, the UN legal counsel concluded that there was a persisting disagreement and no further approximation by legal argument was possible, Bleicher (n 72) 34.

[84]Cited after Bleicher (n 72).

[85]UNGA Res 2307 (XXII) (13 December 1967) UN Doc A/RES/2307(XXII), para 7.

[86]UNGA Res 2426 (XXIII) (18 December 1968) UN Doc A/RES/2426(XXIII), para 5.

[87]Schermers and Blokker, *International Institutional Law* (n 64) para 1720.

[88]Bleicher (n 72) 34 et seq.

[89]Schermers and Blokker, *International Institutional Law* (n 64) para 1720.

system. The Bank took advantage of that and used the limited legal obligations to excuse itself from submitting to UN coordination. The Bank was under no contractual duty to follow the UN's requests and withdraw its support to South Africa and Portugal. Therefore, the UN, and with it the ILO and the remaining UN System, were confined to political appeals.

3. The Limited Role of Art. 103 UN Charter

Given the considerable degree of independence granted to the Bank in the UN-IBRD, some authors have argued that the UN-IBRD might not be compatible with the UN Charter, in particular Arts. 17, 57, 58, 60 and 62 UN Charter.[90] Indeed, the UN has contracted away a good portion of its coordinative potential. On the other hand, deriving legal consequences from this critique is difficult.

To begin with, under the customary inter-organizational law of treaties, incompatibilities between the UN-IBRD and the UN Charter are secondary, if not entirely irrelevant. Even insofar as such incompatibilities existed, they would not affect the UN-IBRD's validity and the UN's obligation to honour its terms: the UN Charter resembles the institutional law, the 'rules of the organization', of one party to the relationship agreement. According to Art. 27(2) VCLT-IO, an IO treaty may not invoke its 'rules of the organization' as justification for its failure to perform the treaty. The only exception to this rule is Art. 46(2) VCLT-IO, which, however, only concerns violations of rules of the organization regarding competence to conclude treaties. In addition, Art. 46(2) and (3) VCLT-IO require that the violation concerns a "rule of fundamental importance", and is "manifest", i.e. it would be "objectively evident to any State or any [IO] conducting itself in the matter in accordance with the normal practice of States and, where appropriate, of [IOs] and in good faith." Therefore, colliding provisions of the UN Charter are mostly irrelevant for the validity of the relationship agreement and the UN's and IBRD's duty to fulfil it.

Against this background, some authors have invoked Art. 103 UN Charter as a basis for expanding the World Bank's obligations to adhere to UN coordinative measures. In particular, it has been argued that, by virtue of Art. 103 UN Charter, UN Charter provisions prevailed over the limitations imposed on UN coordination in the UN-IBRD.[91]

What, then, is the effect of Art. 103 UN Charter on the World Bank's obligations? In order to answer this question, it has to be recalled that Art. 103 UN Charter functions as a collision rule in the event of a conflict between obligations under the

[90] See René-Jean Dupuy, 'Le Droit Des Relations Entre Les Organisations Internationales' (1960) 100 Recueil des Cours de l'Académie de Droit International 461, 541.

[91] Fergus Mackay, 'Universal Rights or a Universe Unto Itself? Indigenous Peoples' Human Rights and the World Bank's Draft Operational Policy 4.10 on Indigenous Peoples' (2002) 17 American University International Law Review 527, 547; Manisuli Ssenyonjo, 'The Applicability of International Human Rights Law to Non-State Actors: What Relevance to Economic, Social and Cultural Rights?' (2008) 12 The International Journal of Human Rights 725, 741.

UN Charter and other international obligations (a). On the one hand, this could have an effect on the World Bank's inter-organizational obligations vis-à-vis the UN to comply with the latter's coordinative measures (b). On the other hand, Art. 103 UN Charter could have an effect on the Bank's institutional law and thus indirectly influence the Bank's obligations vis-à-vis the UN (c).

a) The Scope and Function of Art. 103 UN Charter

According to Art. 103 UN Charter, the obligations of UN members under the UN Charter shall prevail over their obligations under any other international agreement in the event of a conflict between the two.

It is broadly accepted that the terms "obligations under the Charter" and "conflict" in Art. 103 UN Charter should not be construed too narrowly. Aside from obligations under the UN Charter, the provision also applies in case of binding UN secondary law. Moreover, it applies to permissions granted pursuant to the UN Charter, e.g. in a UN Security Council resolution. Thus, a conflict exists if fulfilling an obligation imposed by the Charter or UN secondary law, or exercising a right granted pursuant to the Charter, would require violating or otherwise not fulfilling an obligation under another agreement.[92] However, insofar as a conflict can be solved by other means, e.g. through coherent interpretation of the other agreement, Art. 103 UN Charter does not apply.[93]

As to the legal consequence, it has occasionally been suggested that Art. 103 UN Charter voids other treaties or limits the capacity of UN member states to conclude other treaties, in the sense that they are prevented from concluding any agreement that collided with their Charter obligations.[94] This view, however, is inconsistent with the VCLT. Art. 6 VCLT provides in unconditional terms that any state has the capacity to conclude treaties. Moreover, there is no provision indicating that a treaty obligation conflicting with Charter obligations is void or voidable. Rather, the VCLT addresses Art. 103 UN Charter in the context of the application of successive treaties relating to the same subject-matter (Art. 30(1) VCLT). In conformity with this, the predominant view is that Art. 103 UN Charter supersedes the conflicting obligation but does not affect the latter's legal validity.[95]

---

[92] Andreas L Paulus and Johann Ruben Leiß, 'Art. 103' in Bruno Simma and others (eds), *The Charter of the United Nations - A Commentary, vol II* (3rd edn, Oxford University Press 2013) para 30 et seqq.

[93] Paulus and Leiß (n 92) para 36.

[94] Henri Rolin, 'Les principes de droit international public' (1950-II) 77 Recueil des Cours de l'Académie de Droit International 305434; Arnold D McNair, *The Law of Treaties* (Clarendon Press 1961) 217 et seqq.; Wolfram Karl, *Vertrag und spätere Praxis im Völkerrecht* (Springer 1983) 70.

[95] ILC, 'Fragmentation of International Law: Difficulties Arising from the Diversification and Expansion of International Law, Report of the Study Group of the International Law Commission, Finalized by Martti Koskenniemi' (2006) A/CN.4/L.682, paras 331 et seqq.; Paulus and Leiß (n 92) para 77; Thomas Kleinlein, *Konstitutionalisierung im Völkerrecht* (Springer 2012) 417 et seq.; Rain

b) Effects on the World Bank's Obligations to Comply with UN Coordinative Measures Under Inter-Organizational Law

What effects does Art. 103 UN Charter have on the World Bank's obligations to comply with UN coordinative measures under inter-organizational law? As mentioned before, Art. 103 UN Charter, is not directly binding on specialized agencies.[96] Thus, on the inter-organizational plane, the Bank only needs to accept the primacy of obligations under the UN Charter if it has consented to that primacy or if the latter is also part of customary inter-organizational law.

As to the former alternative, the Bank has not accepted the primacy of UN obligations. The UN-IBRD does not contain any provision in this regard. Furthermore, it is difficult to argue that the Bank implicitly accepted the primacy of UN Charter obligations when concluding the UN-IBRD. Some authors have suggested that all IOs entering into an agreement with the UN automatically accept the primacy of UN Charter obligations pursuant to Art. 103 UN Charter.[97] In this generality, however, this suggestion is highly doubtful. There is, of course, nothing that prevents an IO from accepting the primacy of UN Charter obligations in a relationship agreement. It is also true that specialized agencies have agreed to cooperate with the UN, particularly with the Security Council, in their relationship agreements.[98] Such commitments, however, do not resemble acceptances of the primacy of UN law, but contractual promises to cooperate. Their scope and content are defined solely by the relationship agreement. As far as the UN-IBRD is concerned, assuming an implied acceptance of the primacy of UN Charter obligations could hardly be reconciled with the aforementioned UN-IBRD's provisions meticulously preserving the Bank's independence from the UN.

As to the second alternative, it is already doubtful whether the primacy of UN law has attained the status of customary international law.[99] It is even more doubtful if it reflects customary *inter-organizational* law. The issue whether the primacy of UN Charter obligations was part of customary inter-organizational law came up on several occasions. For example, the UN Security Council has repeatedly addressed

---

Liivoja, 'The Scope of the Supremacy Clause of the United Nations Charter' (2008) 57 International and Comparative Law Quarterly 583, 596 et seq.; Winkler (n 2) 118; all with further references.

[96]See above A. III. ILC, 'Fragmentation of International Law: Difficulties Arising from the Diversification and Expansion of International Law, Report of the Study Group of the International Law Commission, Finalized by Martti Koskenniemi' (n 95) para 343; Kleinlein (n 95) 414 et seq.; Joost Pauwelyn, *Conflict of Norms in Public International Law: How WTO Law Relates to Other Rules of International Law* (Cambridge University Press 2003) 338.

[97]Paulus and Leiß (n 92) para 60.

[98]The World Bank has done so in Art. VI UN-IBRD, according to which it "will, in the conduct of its activities, have due regard for decisions of the Security Council under [Arts. 41 and 42 UN Charter]."

[99]Kleinlein (n 95) 415.

binding resolutions to IOs, which do not seem to have protested against this practice.[100] However, it is not clear whether IOs complied because of a perceived primacy of obligations or for other reasons: after all, they could have done so voluntarily, on the basis of a relationship agreement with the UN, or the question of primacy was simply irrelevant to them because there was no conflict of obligations in the first place.

The issue also came up when drafting the VCLT-IO's provisions on collisions between successive treaties on the same subject matter. While it was uncontentious that Art. 103 UN Charter applied to states, it was debated whether it was also binding on IOs. The debate ended without a common position. Thus, Art. 30(6) VCLT-IO contains a provision that deliberately leaves the question open.[101] When the same question came up during the drafting of the DARIO, the ILC chose a similar solution (see Art. 67 DARIO).[102]

In sum, the World Bank has neither accepted the primacy of UN Charter obligations, nor does this primacy form part of customary inter-organizational law. Therefore, Art. 103 UN Charter does not alter the World Bank's obligations to comply with UN coordinative measures under inter-organizational law.

In any event, Art. 103 UN Charter does not extend the scope and content of any obligations under the UN Charter. As noted above, all instruments of coordination provided for in the UN Charter are non-binding. Neither the ECOSOC nor the UN as a whole can legally bind the specialized agencies through their decisions.[103] Even if inter-organizational law embodied the primacy of UN law, no conflict would arise, because there would be no 'obligations under the UN Charter' in the sense of Art. 103 UN Charter.

c) Effects on the World Bank's Institutional Law

What effects does Art. 103 UN Charter have on the Bank's institutional law?

At the outset, the World Bank member states are bound by Art. 103 UN Charter. In case of a conflict, their Charter obligations prevail over their obligations under any other agreement, including constituent instruments of IOs like the IBRD-AoA.[104]

[100]UNSC Res 748 (1992) (31 March 1992) UN Doc S/RES/748(1992), para 7; UNSC Res 1132 (1997) (8 October 1997) UN Doc S/RES/1132(1997) para 11; Alexander Orakhelashvili, 'Art. 30 VCLT-IO' in Olivier Corten and Pierre Klein (eds), *The Vienna Conventions on the Law of Treaties - A Commentary, vol 1* (Oxford University Press 2011) para 5.

[101]Liivoja (n 95) 592; Kerstin von der Decken, 'Art 30 VCLT' in Oliver Dörr and Kirsten Schmalenbach (eds), *Vienna Convention on the Law of Treaties - A Commentary* (2nd edn, Springer 2018) para 37.

[102]ILC, 'Draft Articles on the Responsibility of International Organizations, with Commentaries' [2011] YILC Vol II Part Two 46, Art. 67, para. 2

[103]Meng, 'Art. 63' (n 8) para 4.

[104]See *Military and Paramilitary Activities in and against Nicaragua (Nicaragua v. United States of America)* (Jurisdiction and Admissibility) [1984] ICJ Reports 392, 440.

This has two consequences: Firstly, member states continue to be fully obliged to fulfil obligations under the UN Charter when participating in the Bank.[105] Secondly, to the extent that there is a conflict, the member states are absolved from fulfilling their obligations under World Bank law (Art. 30(1) VCLT).

Notwithstanding these consequences, member states still retain considerable leeway. As Art. 103 UN Charter does not affect the validity of the other treaty, UN member states are not prevented from erecting the World Bank and endowing it with a wide array of competences. Moreover, they are free to act as they prefer within World Bank organs. Arguably, their representatives may even vote in favour of decisions that might collide with UN law as long as there remains at least one way to implement that decision in a way that is compatible with member states' UN obligations. Therefore, the World Bank member states' votes supporting the Board of Governors' decision to approve the UN-IBRD[106] are arguably not affected by Art. 103 UN Charter.[107]

What effects does Art. 103 UN Charter have on the Bank's own position under its institutional law? Unlike the constituent instruments of some other IOs,[108] no constituent instrument of any of the five World Bank Group IOs incorporates obligations under the UN Charter or recognizes their primacy. Unlike its members, the Bank itself is therefore not obliged under its institutional law to give preference to UN obligations. In principle, this has the following consequences:

1) World Bank primary and secondary institutional law exclusively concerning the Bank itself (e.g. rules concerning its internal organization and procedures) remains unaffected by Art. 103 UN Charter.
2) Member states' obligations under World Bank primary or secondary law remain in principle unaffected by Art. 103 UN Charter, but member states must only fulfil them insofar as this is compatible with their obligations under UN law.
3) Norms of World Bank primary or secondary law containing member state obligations are only set aside by Art. 103 UN Charter if such obligations cannot be implemented by the member states without violating their Charter obligations.

Besides, the World Bank may be required to have due regard to its members' obligations under the UN Charter. As discussed in Chap. 12, IOs' institutional laws contain duties to loyalty and sincere cooperation between the IO and its member

---

[105] Winkler (n 2) 207, with further references.

[106] IBRD Board of Governors Res No 24 (16 September 1947) <http://documents.worldbank.org/curated/en/532521468149674407/International-Bank-for-Reconstruction-and-Development-IBRD-Board-of-Governors-resolution-no-24-agreement-between-the-United-Nations-and-the-Bank> accessed 26 April 2020.

[107] Some authors have contemplated that Art. 103 UN Charter set aside UN member states' conduct in other IOs directed at the adoption of a relationship agreement which is incompatible with the UN Charter, Dupuy (n 90) 541.

[108] Art. 131 Charter of the Organization of American States (signed 30 April 1948, entered into force 13 December 1951) 119 UNTS 3.

states. That being said, the precise content of such obligations again remains diffuse.[109] On the one hand, it seems prudent that the Bank must not hinder its member states to fulfil their obligations under the UN Charter. On the other hand, the Bank's duty to loyalty must not be used to circumvent the *pacta tertiis* rule and render it a 'de facto member' of the UN.

Moreover, even insofar as one accepts a loyalty obligation of the Bank, it is unclear if this obligation would be relevant in the present context. Pursuant to Arts. 55 and 56 UN Charter, the UN member states are obliged to cooperate to achieve the goals of economic and social cooperation laid down in Art. 55 UN Charter. However, UN member states are not obliged under the UN Charter to engage with one specialized agency in order to protect the governance model of another. Neither are UN member states required to follow coordinative measures by the UN. Pursuant to Art. 62(2) UN Charter, the ECOSOC may again only make recommendations to the UN member states when it comes to coordinating the specialized agencies.

Thus, in sum, Art. 103 UN Charter may become relevant in the context of the Bank's obligation to loyalty and sincere cooperation vis-à-vis its member states. However, for present purposes, this is unlikely to be of practical significance.

4. Inferences for the UN's Capacity to Coordinate Without the Consent of the Bank

In sum, the UN System's legal framework does not force the World Bank to comply with coordinative measures against its will. Hence, the UN cannot prevent the Bank from adversely influencing the ILO and its model of labour governance without the Bank's consent. As illustrated by the South Africa/Portugal example, the World Bank can subject the role and relevance of the ILO's (and, indeed, the UN's) work on these countries to its own institutional legal imperatives, as interpreted and applied by itself. By pointing to its prohibition to engage in political activity and the obligation to base its decisions solely on economic considerations, the Bank was able to maintain support for South Africa, even though the latter had just been urged to withdraw from the ILO for grave violations of fundamental labour standards on discrimination. In much the same way, it was able to continue supporting Portugal, a persistent perpetrator of forced labour. There is nothing in the UN-IBRD obliging it to do otherwise, even less to change its handling of the political activities prohibition, or to disregard it in favour of aligning with the other UN System entities.

The ILO's relativization in the Bank's law only loses its effect insofar as both the Bank and the UN agree on a consensual position that benefits the ILO, with or without the means provided by the UN-IBRD to reach such a consensus.

---

[109] See above, Chap. 12 B. II.

III. Conclusion

The UN System's legal framework hardly provides a normative framework protecting the ILO's model by averting adverse influence.

First of all, it has been shown that the ILO does not have any practically relevant rights to demand coordination from the UN. The ILO's agreements with the UN and its subdivisions either remain on a very general level (the UN-ILO) or are so case-specific that they do not lend themselves for generalizing inferences. As to their content, they reserve considerable discretion for the UN and containing comparatively reticent obligations.[110]

Second of all, the UN does not have any noteworthy legal rights to demand cooperation from the Bank. The UN-IBRD goes far in preserving the Bank's autonomy. No coordinating instrument can produce binding effect without the Bank's consent. As the given example illustrates, the UN cannot avert adverse influence on the ILO against the Bank's will.[111]

To be sure, this does not necessarily mean that the UN System's legal framework is unsuitable to fulfil its intended purposes of coordination and direction. However, aversion of influence on the ILO's model by other specialized agencies is essentially a matter of political will, persuasion and compromise.

C. The UN System as a Legal Framework for Promoting the ILO's Model?

The UN System can also become relevant in a second manner, namely as a legal framework to promote the ILO's model of labour governance. In this constellation, the ILO does not rely on 'protection' by the UN, but actively reaches out to mainstream its model throughout the UN System and its component agencies, including the World Bank.[112]

---

[110]Moreover, like the ILO-CoE, the UN-ILO maintains in principle a separation of agendas. This is hardly surprising, given that any commitment to the full bandwidth of UN objectives would arguably have conflicted with Art. 12(1) ILO Constitution and its abovementioned obligation to cooperate "within the terms" of the ILO Constitution—and the more limited objectives set forth therein.

[111]While the UN-IBRD puts particular emphasis on the Bank's independence, the case is also a showcase for the weaknesses of the UN System's legal framework to enforce coordination more generally. As seen, similarly open language is used in other relationship agreements, including the UN-ILO. Were the UN to request a certain conduct from the ILO, the ILO would likewise have considerable options to argumentatively 'downsize' its obligations under the UN-ILO.

[112]The ILO has also engaged in 'bilateral' interaction with other specialized agencies and has promoted its Decent Work Agenda through them. Some of these interactions had groundbreaking success, such as the long-standing cooperation with the IMO, which inter alia resulted in the drafting and adoption of the 2006 Maritime Labour Convention, Henner Gött, 'Interactions between

I. Promotion in Practice: Mainstreaming the ILO's Decent Work Agenda Within the UN System

As a factual matter, the ILO has consistently promoted its agenda in the UN and in other specialized agencies. One major recent example is the active promotion and the mainstreaming of the concept of decent work throughout the UN System. Over the last two decades, decent work diffused into the successive UN development agendas (1.). To some extent, it 'trickled down' from there to the World Bank and became a factor in its policies, and operations (2.).

1. Including Decent Work into the UN Development Agendas

As mentioned in Chap. 1, the ILO launched its Decent Work Agenda in 1999. From the beginning, one goal of the Decent Work Agenda was to infuse social objectives into the multilateral system.[113] Early attempts of the International Labour Office to operationalize the concept were of limited success.[114] However, the World Commission on the Social Dimension of Globalization, a group of experts and high-level political leaders established in 2001 and sponsored by the ILO, provided new momentum. The Commission's 2004 final report, which received wide attention within and beyond the ILO, recommended inter alia that

> [d]ecent work for all should be made a global goal and pursued through more coherent policies within the multilateral system. All organizations in the multilateral system should deal with international economic and labour policies in a more integrated and consistent way.[115]

The World Commission's final report was published at a point in time where the UN was about to review its 2000 Millennium Declaration, which set the UN's development agenda until 2015. The Millennium Declaration had proclaimed that globalization should become a "positive force for the people of the entire world".[116] Recalling this goal, the UNGA in 2004 included the World Commission's report and

---

International Organizations - Approaching a Neglected Governance Dimension' (n 4) 85 et seqq. Such 'bilateral' cooperation with other UN specialized agencies will not be addressed here.

[113]Maupain Francis, 'A Second Century for What? The ILO at a Regulatory Crossroad' (2019) 16 International Organizations Law Review 1, 30.

[114]Maupain, *The Future of the International Labour Organization in the Global Economy* (n 54) 54.

[115]World Commission on the Social Dimension of Globalization, *A Fair Globalization - Creating Opportunities for All, Final Report* (ILO 2004) 145 (Recommendation No 10), see also paras 502 et seqq.

[116]United Nations Millennium Declaration, UNGA Res 55/2 (8 September 2000) UN Doc A/RES/55/2, para 5.

its findings into the ongoing MDG review process.[117] In 2005, the CEB's High-Level Committee on Programmes selected employment as one of the prioritization areas for the inter-agency agenda.[118] As a result, the UNGA included central aspects of the ILO's Decent Work Agenda in its 2005 World Summit Outcome resolution[119] and designated them as central objectives of domestic and international policies.[120] In the aftermath of the World Summit, a new target to achieve full and productive employment and decent work for all was introduced into MDG No 1.[121] The ILO's Decent Work Agenda had thus arrived at the apex of the UN development agenda.[122]

In 2006, the ECOSOC followed up with a ministerial declaration, in which it recognized the fundamental importance of full and productive employment and decent work for all and recognized then ILO's Decent Work Agenda as an "important instrument" for achieving this objective.[123] The Ministers resolved to promote fundamental principles and rights at work, "recognizing the central role of the International Labour Organization in this regard."[124] In 2007, the ECOSOC requested

> the funds, programmes and agencies of the United Nations system to continue their efforts to mainstream the goals of full and productive employment and decent work for all in their policies, programmes and activities with a view to sustained and well-coordinated follow-up of the ministerial declaration (. . .).[125]

---

[117]UNGA Res 59/57 (2 December 2004) UN Doc A/RES/59/57, para 2; Hamish Jenkins, Eddy Lee and Gerry Rodgers, *The Quest for a Fair Globalization Three Years On - Assessing the Impact of the World Commission on the Social Dimension of Globalization* (ILO 2007) para 21.

[118]UN, 'Article 63' (n 21) para 32.

[119]Which was later followed up by a number of international and regional organizations and bodies, UN, 'Promoting the MDGs: The Role of Employment and Decent Work', XLIV UN Chronicle No 4 (December 2007) <https://unchronicle.un.org/article/promoting-mdgs-role-employment-and-decent-work> accessed 26 April 2020.

[120]Notably, para 47 of the Outcome reads: "We strongly support fair globalization and resolve to make the goals of full and productive employment and decent work for all, including for women and young people, a central objective of our relevant national and international policies (. . .) as part of our efforts to achieve the Millennium Development Goals. (. . .) We also resolve to ensure full respect for the fundamental principles and rights at work", UNGA Res 60/1 (16 September 2005) UN Doc A/RES/60/1, para 47. At the same time, the World Summit Outcome called to strengthen the ECOSOC as the principal coordinating body, ibid 155.

[121]As Target 1B, ILO, 'Millennium Development Goals (MDGs) Employment Indicators' (*ILO Website*) <https://www.ilo.org/empelm/what/WCMS_114244/lang%2D%2Den/index.htm added in 2005> accessed 26 April 2020.

[122]As a kind of 'precursor', decent work had already been mentioned on the 2000 Millennium Declaration, however only in the context of youth employment, UNGA Res 55/2 (8 September 2000) UN Doc A/RES/55/2, para 20.

[123]ECOSOC, Ministerial Declaration 'Creating an Environment at the National and International Levels Conducive to Generating Full and Productive Employment and Decent Work for All, and Its Impact on Sustainable Development' (5 July 2006) UN Doc E/2006/L.8, para 2 et seq.

[124]ibid 5 lit. a.

[125]ECOSOC Res 2007/2 (17 July 2007) UN Doc E/RES/2007/2, para 1.

In 2008, the UNGA endorsed the ILO Declaration on Social Justice for a Fair Globalization, which, as explained in Chap. 1, resembles a major reformulation of the ILO's mandate and at the same time institutionalizes the Decent Work Agenda. Later in 2008, the UNGA chose "full employment and decent work for all" as the theme for the Second UN Decade for the Eradication of Poverty (2008–2017)[126] and further promoted decent work in a line of further resolutions.[127] In a 2012 Ministerial Declaration,[128] the ECOSOC inter alia called for

> strengthened policy coherence and partnerships across the United Nations system, including the international financial institutions, as appropriate, while recognizing the respective mandates and governance structures of the constituent parts of the system, with a view to promoting the creation of decent work (. . .).[129]

As the design of the post-2015 development agenda gained pace, the ILO sought to enhance the status of decent work in the emerging Sustainable Development Goals (SDGs). It issued a concept note proposing to 'upgrade' full and productive employment and decent work into a fully-fledged and stand-alone development goal, and to support it through the implementation of social protection floors.[130] Interestingly, the World Bank, among others, proposed to integrate employment and decent work as one of several targets which, together with other targets, promotes the goal

---

[126]UNGA Res 63/230 (19 December 2008) UN Doc A/RES/63/230, para 14. See also ECOSOC Res 2008/18 (24 July 2008) UN Doc E/RES/2008/18.

[127]UNGA Res 64/135 (18 December 2009) UN Doc A/RES/64/135; UNGA Res 65/185 (21 December 2010) UN Doc A/RES/65/185; UNGA Res 66/125 (19 December 2011) UN Doc A/RES/66/125.

[128]ECOSOC, Ministerial Declaration 'Promoting Productive Capacity, Employment and Decent Work to Eradicate Poverty in the Context of Inclusive, Sustainable and Equitable Economic Growth at All Levels for Achieving the Millennium Development Goals' (9 July 2012) UN Doc E/2012/L.10. The declaration was prepared by a UN Secretary-General report which had been jointly prepared with the ILO, UN Secretary-General, 'Promoting Productive Capacity, Employment and Decent Work to Eradicate Poverty in the Context of Inclusive, Sustainable and Equitable Economic Growth at All Levels for Achieving the Millennium Development Goals, Report of the Secretary-General' (2012) UN Doc E/2012/63.

[129]ECOSOC, Ministerial Declaration 'Promoting Productive Capacity, Employment and Decent Work to Eradicate Poverty in the Context of Inclusive, Sustainable and Equitable Economic Growth at All Levels for Achieving the Millennium Development Goals' (n 128) para 43. The ECOSOC went on to "invite and encourage donors and international organizations, including the United Nations system, as well as the international financial institutions, the regional development banks, major groups and the private sector, to support the implementation of global strategies on employment", ibid 45.

[130]ILO, 'Jobs and Livelihoods at the Heart of the Post-2015 Development Agenda - ILO Concept Note on the Post-2015 Development Agenda' (2013) <https://www.ilo.org/global/about-the-ilo/newsroom/statements-and-speeches/WCMS_193483/lang%2D%2Den/index.htm> accessed 26 April 2020, 2; UN Department of Economic and Social Affairs and UNDP, 'Employment and Decent Work' TST Issues Brief (4 June 2013) <https://sustainabledevelopment.un.org/content/documents/18331106tstissuesemploywork.pdf> accessed 26 April 2020, 4. See further ILO, 'Keynote Address by Greg Vines, ILO Deputy Director-General, at the Fourth Session of the Open Working Group on Sustainable Development Goals' (17 June 2013) https://www.ilo.org/newyork/speeches-and-statements/WCMS_216335/lang%2D%2Den/index.htm accessed 26 April 2020.

of poverty eradication.[131] The fact that the World Bank suggested to 'subjugate' decent work to the 'higher' goal of poverty eradication, while the ILO proposed it to be a goal on its own, mirrors the varying main organizational objectives of the ILO (decent work as an aim in itself) and the Bank (striving for poverty eradication and sustainable growth).

Eventually, the Decent Work Agenda and its four strategic objectives were mainstreamed across the SDGs. Nearly all of the 17 SDGs and 169 associated targets connect to elements of the Decent Work Agenda. Notably, SDG 8 calls to

> promote sustained, inclusive and sustainable economic growth, full and productive employment and decent work for all.[132]

The UN has since promoted the ILO's Decent Work Agenda as a component of the SDGs. For example, in September 2019, the UNGA endorsed the ILO's Centenary Declaration and reaffirmed the key importance of the goal of full employment and decent work.[133] In the relevant resolution, the UNGA:

> requests the United Nations funds, programmes, specialized agencies and financial institutions to continue to mainstream the goals of full and productive employment and decent work for all in their policies, as well as to consider the integration of the policy contents of the International Labour Organization Centenary Declaration for the Future of Work, as part of the United Nations Sustainable Development Cooperation Framework, in order to inform the work of the United Nations country teams, as appropriate, and in line with national priorities.[134]

While neither the ILO nor the UN promoted decent work with a particular focus on the World Bank, the gradual inclusion of decent work into the UN development agendas slowly modified the very paradigm the Bank is operating on: The concept of development. If decent work is part of the UN's development agenda, then so are its four strategic objectives, i.e. fundamental principles and rights at work, decent employment and income, universal social protection and social dialogue, as well as the cross-cutting objective of promoting gender equality and non-discrimination. Thus, figuratively speaking, the UN System served as an 'amplifier' for the ILO's agenda to create a system-wide policy consensus. For the very reason that it was consented within and also beyond the UN System, this consensus is less 'political' (viz. partisan) and thus is harder for the Bank to ignore.

---

[131] UN Department of Economic and Social Affairs and UNDP, 'Employment and Decent Work' (4 June 2013) TST Issues Brief <https://sustainabledevelopment.un.org/content/documents/18331106tstissuesemploywork.pdf> accessed 26 April 2020, 4.

[132] Goal 8 is highly integrated into the sustainable development agenda and has links to a total of 10 other goals, David Le Blanc, 'Towards Integration at Last? The Sustainable Development Goals as a Network of Targets' (2015) 23 Sustainable Development 176, 180.

[133] UNGA Res 73/342 (16 September 2019) UN Doc A/RES/73/342, para 4.

[134] ibid para 5.

2. The Modest Success of Institutionalizing and Operationalizing Decent Work in the World Bank

The ILO, with the support of the UN System's coordinating bodies, continuously sought to operationalize and to institutionalize the Decent Work Agenda, or certain elements thereof, within the UN System and the work of other specialized agencies. Of central interest here is whether the ILO, through the UN System, managed to actually 'implant' decent work in the Bank's agenda.

In 2006, the CEB's HLCP invited the ILO to take the lead in developing what was to become the Toolkit for Mainstreaming Employment and Decent Work. For the ILO, this provided an opportunity to further mainstream its Decent Work Agenda into the UN System.[135] The Toolkit provides a reference point for decent work against which IOs can evaluate and enhance their policies, to promote knowledge management and sharing of tools, to raise awareness and build capacity, and to promote and mainstream decent work at country level.[136] In 2007, the ECOSOC endorsed its use by the UN System's entities.[137] As part of its participation in the CEB, the World Bank agreed to implement the Toolkit in a number of countries to be determined jointly with the ILO.[138]

The ILO has, moreover, used existing and joined new inter-agency groups or processes (like the G20[139]) to promote its Decent Work Agenda vis-à-vis other UN System entities, including the World Bank.[140] For instance, in the area of social protection, the ECOSOC invited the ILO and the international financial institutions

[135]See UN, *Independent Evaluation of "Delivering as One" - Main Report* (UN 2012) para 102. Accordingly, the ILO developed the Toolkit through a CEB-coordinated inter-agency process and an ECOSOC-coordinated intergovernmental process, including other interested specialized agencies and governments. In its 2006 Ministerial Declaration, the ECOSOC encouraged all relevant organizations to collaborate actively in the development, ECOSOC, Ministerial Declaration 'Creating an Environment at the National and International Levels Conducive to Generating Full and Productive Employment and Decent Work for All, and Its Impact on Sustainable Development' (n 123) para 36.

[136]ILO, *Toolkit for Mainstreaming Employment and Decent Work - Country Level Application* (2008) viii et seq. The Toolkit provides three main tools: 1) a self-diagnostic tool in the form of a self-assessment checklist to raise awareness and to review and optimize the impact of an IO's policies, instruments and practice regarding decent work; 2) knowledge management and dissemination elements, intended to share experiences and best practices; 3) the Toolkit includes advocacy and training materials, ibid ix.

[137]ECOSOC Res 2007/2 (17 July 2007) UN Doc E/RES/2007/2, para 3. See also ECOSOC Res 2008/18 (24 July 2008) UN Doc E/RES/2008/18, para 35.

[138]ILO, 'World Bank Doing Business Report: The Employing Workers Indicator' (2007) GB.300/4/1, para 2.

[139]The ILO has also promoted decent work in the context of the G20, ILO, *Independent Evaluation of the ILO's Strategy for Coherent Decent Work Policies* (ILO 2014), 31.

[140]The ILO has participated in inter-agency groups before the Decent Work Agenda was developed. Examples are UNAIDS or the Inter-Agency Task Force on Sustained Livelihoods, discussed above in Chap. 13 B.

to collaborate in providing assistance to developing countries.[141] As one out of nine initiatives adopted in response to the global financial crisis, the CEB in 2009 adopted the Social Protection Floor Initiative.[142] As a complement thereto, the ILO and the World Bank launched in 2013 the Social Protection Inter-Agency Cooperation Board (SPIAC-B),[143] which inter alia conducted the Inter-Agency Social Protection Assessment (ISPA) together with other development partners.[144]

Together with further bodies, the ILO and the World Bank in 2016[145] launched the Global Partnership for Universal Social Protection. The initiative aims at increasing the number of states with universal and sustainable social protection schemes through either immediate or progressive measures and through the prevention of retrogression.[146] The Partnership was designed to serve objectives of both the World Bank and the ILO.[147] As mentioned before, the World Bank pursues the objective to eradicate poverty and boost shared prosperity and has developed several policy instruments to this end. The ILO's goal to achieve and improve social protection is one of the strategic objectives of its Decent Work Agenda and has been the subject of various labour conventions and recommendations, including the

[141] ECOSOC, Ministerial Declaration 'Creating an Environment at the National and International Levels Conducive to Generating Full and Productive Employment and Decent Work for All, and Its Impact on Sustainable Development' (n 123) para 19. Remarkably, this happened when the struggle over the Nepalese labour market reform and its social protection element (Chap. 4 C I. 1.) was ongoing. See also ECOSOC, Ministerial Declaration 'Promoting Productive Capacity, Employment and Decent Work to Eradicate Poverty in the Context of Inclusive, Sustainable and Equitable Economic Growth at All Levels for Achieving the Millennium Development Goals' (n 128) paras 10, 27 and 46.

[142] In 2009, the CEB issued a communiqué on the impact of the financial crisis on the work of the UN System, in which it endorsed nine joint initiatives of its member organizations, CEB, 'The Global Financial Crisis and Its Impact on the Work of the UN System' (1 April 2009) <http://www.unsystem.org/content/ceb-issue-paper-global-financial-crisis-and-its-impact-work-un-system> accessed 26 April 2020, 29 et seq. As to employment, it endorsed the ILO's Global Jobs Pact, ibid 14 and 30. Under the co-leadership of ILO and the WHO, a range of entities cooperate in the initiative, among others the World Bank.

[143] See Social Protection Interagency Cooperation Board, '1st Social Protection Inter-Agency Cooperation Board Meeting' (2–3 July 2012) Report <https://www.ilo.org/wcmsp5/groups/public/%2D%2D-dgreports/%2D%2D-nylo/documents/genericdocument/wcms_226913.pdf> accessed 26 April 2020.

[144] The initiative aims at developing tools to build and strengthen Social Protection systems at the country level by providing an integrated assessment framework. Inter-agency collaboration to pilot-test the ISPA tools at the country level started in 2013 with the Public Works Tool.

[145] World Bank, 'Joint Statement by World Bank Group President Jim Yong Kim and ILO Director General Guy Ryder' (World Bank Website) <http://www.worldbank.org/en/news/press-release/2015/06/30/joint-statement-world-bank-group-president-ilo-director-general-guy-ryder> accessed 26 April 2020.

[146] ILO and World Bank, 'A Shared Mission for Universal Social Protection - Concept Note' (2015) <https://www.ilo.org/wcmsp5/groups/public/%2D%2D-dgreports/%2D%2D-dcomm/documents/genericdocument/wcms_378996.pdf> accessed 26 April 2020, 3.

[147] The Concept Note speaks of a "shared" and a "common vision", ibid.

Social Protection Floors Recommendation, 2012 (No 202).[148] In addition to the ILO's and World Bank's respective own goals, the Partnership is explicitly presented as a means to achieve UN SDGs.[149] The explicit recognition of social protection as a primary development goal has been considered a major policy shift by the World Bank.[150] Moreover, the ILO and the Bank have commissioned joint research projects on specific topics or regions.[151]

While the Decent Work Agenda found support throughout the UN System in terms of statements of principle, the picture is mixed when it comes to using decent work as a theme for programming and operational practice.[152] The implementation of the Toolkit for Mainstreaming Employment and Decent Work remained below expectations. In 2014, an ILO independent evaluation found the implementation to be "somewhat satisfactory".[153] A 2015 evaluation by the UN Joint Inspection Unit, while constating an overall "moderate success",[154] found significant shortcomings: none of the UN System entities had fully implemented the Toolkit, only a handful reflected decent work in their strategic policies and documents, and awareness of the

---

[148] ILO, Social Protection Floors Recommendation, 2012 (No 202) (adopted 14 June 2012) XCV ILO Official Bulletin Ser A No 2 64. The Recommendation envisages that states may receive funding and technical assistance form the ILO and other IOs. Para. 12. reads: "National social protection floors should be financed by national resources. Members whose economic and fiscal capacities are insufficient to implement the guarantees may seek international cooperation and support that complement their own efforts." Para. 24(2) reads: "In implementing this Recommendation, Members may seek technical assistance from the International Labour Organization and other relevant international organizations in accordance with their respective mandates." Earlier ILO instruments include the Social Security (Minimum Standards) Convention, 1952 (No 102) (adopted 28 June 1952, entered into force 27 April 1955) 210 UNTS 131, the Income Security Recommendation, 1944 (No 67) (adopted 12 May 1944) XXVI ILO Official Bulletin 4, and the ILO, Medical Care Recommendation, 1944 (No 69) (adopted 12 May 1944) XXVI ILO Official Bulletin 29.

[149] Namely Goal 1.3 ("Implement nationally appropriate social protection systems and measure for all, including floors, and by 2030 achieve substantial coverage of the poor and vulnerable"), ILO and World Bank, 'A Shared Mission for Universal Social Protection - Concept Note' (n 146) 4.

[150] Sergei Zelenev, 'Universal Social Protection: The World Bank Group and ILO Join Forces in Launching the Universal Social Protection Initiative' (2015) 58 International Social Work 840.

[151] See e.g. ILO, UNICEF and World Bank, 'Understanding Trends in Child Labour' (2017) <https://cocoainitiative.org/wp-content/uploads/2019/04/Understanding-Child-Labour-Trends-2017.pdf> accessed 26 April 2020; ILO and World Bank, *Export to Jobs - Boosting the Gains from Trade in South Asia* (ILO and World Bank 2019).

[152] Stuart Bell and Kirsten Newitt, 'Decent Work and Poverty Eradication: Literature Review and Two-Country Study' (2010) <https://www.ituc-csi.org/IMG/pdf/Decent-work-and-poverty-eradication-literature-review-and-two-country-study_Full-report.pdf> accessed 26 April 2020, 25 et seqq.

[153] ILO, *Independent Evaluation of the ILO's Strategy for Coherent Decent Work Policies* (n 139) xii.

[154] UN Joint Inspection Unit, 'Evaluation of Mainstreaming of Full and Productive Employment and Decent Work by the United Nations System Organizations – Full Report' (2015) UN Doc JIU/REP/2015/1, para 36.

concept among staff members was low.[155] Interestingly, the Joint Inspection Unit also found that, while UN System entities had increasingly shifted priorities closer to decent work,

> [t]hose shifts cannot be attributed directly to the Economic and Social Council resolutions on decent work. The underlying factor for the inclusion of social protection and employment/job creation in organizational activities is most likely due to the external environment (financial crisis) than the Council resolution.[156]

The general observation of mainstreaming's modest impact also applies to the World Bank in particular. For instance, studies on the implementation of the MDGs suggested that World Bank country planning through so-called Poverty Reduction Strategy Papers (PRSPs) referred to decent work aspects unevenly. Where they did, the emphasis was on employment, while the other strategic objectives of the Decent Work Agenda were treated more reticently.[157] For another example, it needs mention that the ILO's relative success in mainstreaming its Decent Work Agenda apparently did not have traceable influence on the World Bank's use of the EWI and the accompanying indirect and conflictual interactions with the ILO presented in Chap. 4. These examples showcase that the ILO's efforts to promote its agenda are limited, since the Bank still needs to embrace, internalize and fully implement the agenda thus promoted.

In addition, mainstreaming the Decent Work Agenda has not prevented new disagreements between the ILO and the Bank from arising. In late 2018, while the ILO was preparing its Centenary Declaration for the Future of Work, the World Bank published its 2019 World Development Report entitled "The Changing Nature of Work".[158] The report addresses some key issues the ILO sought to address in its Centenary Declaration, notably transformations in the world of work due to automation and technological progress. In preparing the report, the World Bank gave the ILO the opportunity to submit comments on the draft. Still, when the report was eventually published, it deviated far enough from the ILO's position that the International Labour Office publicly expressed concerns and questioned the Bank's approach to some of the key issues dealt with in the report.[159]

Finally, Maupain has pointed to a strategic risk for the ILO that is connected to the Decent Work Agenda's mainstreaming. The meaning of decent work needs to be concretized in order to be implemented. The ILO will have to invest significant

---

[155]ibid paras 37 et seqq. and 89 et seqq.

[156]ibid 41.

[157]Bell and Newitt (n 152) 27, with further references. This is reminiscent of the World Bank's traditionally more reserved stance to certain 'political' labour standards and to social dialogue.

[158]World Bank, *World Development Report 2019: The Changing Nature of Work* (World Bank 2019).

[159]ILO, 'International Labour Office Expresses Concern about World Bank Report on Future of Work' (*ILO Website, 12 October 2018*) <https://www.ilo.org/global/about-the-ilo/newsroom/statements-and-speeches/WCMS_646884/lang%2D%2Den/index.htm> accessed 26 April 2020.

attention and resources to this task in order to maintain its opportunity for exercising system-wide influence.[160] Moreover, the decent work concept, once streamlined, is not as evidently 'owned' by the ILO as it had been before. It is conceivable that the World Bank or other entities of the multilateral system will come up with their own readings of the concept.[161] Here, again, the inherent ambivalence of inter-organizational interactions becomes manifest.

3. Conclusion

Mainstreaming decent work in the UN System has resulted in considerable support for the ILO's Decent Work Agenda and its four strategic objectives, especially full and productive employment or social protection. As seen, the ILO's Decent Work Agenda also 'reached' the World Bank at a conceptual and programmatic level, inducing the Bank to engage in activities that are at least to some extent conducive to the ILO's model of labour governance. That being said, the results regarding the institutionalization and the operationalization of decent work are mixed.

II. The Weak Legal Framework for Promotion

The question remains whether the ILO can rely on the UN System's legal framework when promoting its agenda among the other UN System entities. To be sure, the issue here is not whether there was empirical causality between the existence of any legal provisions within the UN System and the level to which the ILO's actual promotional success.[162] Rather, the question is whether and to what extent the UN System's legal framework prescribes that such proliferation ought to occur, by endowing the ILO with promotional rights or by imposing corresponding obligations on the UN or the World Bank to follow suit. As will be seen in the following, this is hardly the case.

---

[160]Francis Maupain, 'A Second Century for What? The ILO at a Regulatory Crossroad' (n 113) 31 et seqq.

[161]ibid 33 et seqq.

[162]It is near illusory to empirically prove with any sufficient certainty any causal relation between the ILO's rights to participation in the UN System and the extent to which its promotional efforts have been successful. While the ILO of course advocated its agenda, its success might have simply been due to its persuasive capacity and 'moral' authority. In addition, the ILO's advocacy was supported by its member states and further actors. For instance, the aforementioned 2004 UNGA resolution that connected the World Commission on the Social Dimension of Globalization's final report to the Millennium Development Agenda (and thus made an important step for including decent work as a new target of MDG 1 in 2005) was sponsored by the Finnish and Tanzanian governments, the heads of which had previously co-chaired the World Commission and had gathered support for the UNGA resolution, Jenkins, Lee and Rodgers (n 117) para 21.

The UN-ILO contains several rights that enable the ILO to promote its model of labour governance. These rights are participatory rights (1.) and rights to propose agenda items to certain UN organs and bodies (2.).

1. Participatory Rights

Art. II(2)–(4) UN-ILO provide that the ILO shall be invited to meetings of UN bodies. The ILO may participate without vote in meetings of the ECOSOC and its commissions and committees, the UNGA and the UNGA's main committees.[163]

The language of these participatory rights is comparatively stronger than the one used in the ILO-CoE. The UN-ILO's participatory rights enable the ILO to play out its persuasive authority, one of its comparative strengths. What is more, given that the wording of Art. II(2) UN-ILO speaks of "meetings" in a non-specified manner, the ILO has a right to participate even in 'exclusive' meetings to which it has not been specifically invited by the ECOSOC.[164]

That being said, the participatory rights are still limited. Firstly, the access to meetings remains restricted: Meetings "of" the ECOSOC do not necessarily comprise meetings *with* other IOs, notably the annual high-level ECOSOC-Bretton Woods meeting with the World Bank, the IMF, the WTO and UNCTAD, in which the ILO does not participate.[165] Second of all, the right to participate without vote does not comprise important further rights, e.g. a right to propose amendments to draft resolutions.[166] Third of all, the right to participate does not imply that the UN has to adhere to the views the ILO might express. In fact, it does not prescribe any reaction whatsoever. Neither does the UN have to promote the ILO's position in the UN System. One could argue that, as a matter of fulfilling the UN-ILO in good faith (Art. 26 VCLT-IO), the UN has at least to consider the ILO's views and to take its position into account. However, beyond its right to participate, the ILO again depends on convincing the UN and other participating UN System entities.

---

[163]The ILO may also make written submissions, which must be distributed to all members of the bodies the ILO is entitled to participate in, Art. II(6) UN-ILO.

[164]Regarding the related issue of confidential meetings, it can be taken from the UN-ILO's *travaux* that it was intended to determine the ILO's right of participation on a case-by-case basis, Jenks, 'Coordination: A New Problem of International Organization' (n 6) 211.

[165]Volker Röben, 'Art. 62' in Bruno Simma and others (eds), *The Charter of the United Nations - A Commentary, vol II* (3rd edn, Oxford University Press 2013) para 48; Higgins and others (n 9) para 5.26.

[166]Rather, whether such proposals should be amended lies in the chairperson's discretion, Jenks, 'Coordination: A New Problem of International Organization' (n 6) 211.

2. The Right to Propose Agenda Items

Art. III UN-ILO provides that the ILO may propose agenda items for the ECOSOC and its commissions and committees. The latter must include them on their agendas.

Again, this right provides the ILO with an opportunity to play out its persuasive authority and to place its own topics at UN System level, which, politically, can be of significant relevance. However, the right is of limited scope. At the outset, the language ("subject to such preliminary consultation as may be necessary") is similarly reticent as in Art. 2 ILO-CoE. Here as there, there is no 'automatic' right that proposed items must be included in each and every case. Furthermore, the UN is again not required to do anything more than to address the item in good faith. It does not have to take any particular position on it, nor promote it in any way vis-à-vis the other UN System entities. Thus, again, the ILO depends on its capability to convince the UN and other entities to voluntarily follow the ILO's suggestions.

3. Conclusion

The ILO has only limited rights to be invited to, and to participate in, meetings of UN bodies, and to propose agenda items. These rights provide the ILO with opportunities to place topics at UN System level and to play out its persuasive authority there, one of its comparative strengths. In its relations to the World Bank, it can use these opportunities to gain support in order to induce the Bank to adjust its activities in a manner that is conducive to the ILO's model. However, beyond securing these opportunities, the UN System's legal framework does not contain any further legal provisions on which the ILO could rely when promoting its model.

III. Conclusion on Section C

This section has examined the UN System's potential as a legal framework on which the ILO can rely when actively promoting its model of labour governance. As seen, the ILO managed to gain considerable support, at least in principle, for its Decent Work Agenda. However, it has also been seen that this success was a political one. The UN System's pertinent legal provisions merely provide it with an opportunity to place topics within UN organs and bodies. Beyond that, there are no international legal provisions on which the ILO could rely when attempting to promote its positions among the UN and the other UN System entities.

D. Conclusion on Chap. 14

In sum, the UN System's legal framework provides machinery to facilitate cooperation if both parties are willing and able to cooperate. It is thus, like the ILO-CoE, a legal framework governing direct and cooperative interactions. By contrast, it hardly contains any international legal norms securing or promoting a certain role or relevance of the ILO's model regarding other forms of interactions with the World Bank.

First of all, the UN System's legal framework does not oblige the UN to step in and protect the ILO's model of labour governance against adverse influence from the World Bank. In any event, the existing machinery the UN has at its disposal does not oblige the World Bank to adhere to UN coordinative measures and change its conduct without its consent.

Second of all, the UN System only provides a rudimentary legal framework for promoting the ILO's model vis-à-vis the Bank. As per the example of mainstreaming the Decent Work Agenda, the ILO factually managed to use the UN System's legal framework to place topics and gain support. However, this success was hardly backed by inter-organizational legal mechanisms that would have reinforced the ILO's efforts. Thus, the success of promotion ultimately again depends on persuasion and the readiness of other IOs to cooperate.

All in all, the UN System only provides a loose legal framework, which is primarily oriented to facilitate political cooperation, but does not legally require or reinforce it. As aptly summarized by the UN Joint Inspection Unit in 1993:

> [t]he relationship agreements appear more like declarations of political intent than binding legal instruments containing specific rights and obligations with respect to coordination matters. However, they have provided a useful and flexible framework for the development of inter-organizational relationships. The general formulation of the agreements has thus provided broad scope for evolving coordination practices within the common system which have, over the years, lent concrete significance to some of the provisions of the agreements.[167]

At least regarding the regulation of ILO-World Bank interactions, this observation is still true today.

---

[167] UN Joint Inspection Unit, 'Relationship Agreements Between the UN and the Specialized Agencies: Review and Strengthening of Sections Pertaining to the Common System of Salaries, Allowances and Conditions of Service' (n 62) para 6.

15. Beyond Treaties: The Silence of Unwritten Inter-Organizational Law

As seen, inter-organizational treaties and the UN System's legal framework are limited to providing machinery for direct and cooperative interactions. They largely build on the expectation that the interacting IOs are willing and actively take steps to structure and order their interactions by themselves. This raises the question how inter-organizational law regulates cases of interactions in which the ILO, World Bank or CoE disagree or are not communicating at all. As their mutual inter-organizational treaties do not address this question, it is necessary to turn to other sources of inter-organizational law, namely customary inter-organizational law and general principles of law.

As a matter of principle, all examined IOs can be bound by customary law and general principles.[1] However, it remains an open question what precise rights and obligations stem from these sources. As things stand at present, customary inter-organizational law and general principles (of inter-organizational law) have not yet received much attention as a subject of legal analysis. As far as is apparent, there is no systematic survey of the field.[2] Rather, academic literature, insofar as it addresses the topic at all, confines itself to presenting and discussing certain instruments of

[1] *Interpretation of the Agreement of 25 March 1951 between the WHO and Egypt* (Advisory Opinion) [1980] ICJ Reports 73, 89 et seq.; *Reparation for Injuries Suffered in the Service of the United Nations* (Advisory Opinion) [1949] ICJ Reports 174, 179. There has been an ongoing and protracted debate on whether and to what extent IOs are bound by customary international law. For an overview see August Reinisch, 'The Sources of International Organizations' Law – Why Custom and General Principles Are Crucial' in Samantha Besson and Jean D'Aspremont (eds), *The Oxford Handbook on the Sources of International Law* (2017) 1016 et seqq.

[2] Early studies by Jenks and Dupuy, respectively, focus mostly on inter-organizational treaties and the UN System, Clarence Wilfred Jenks, 'Coordination: A New Problem of International Organization' 77 Recueil des Cours de l'Académie de Droit International 151; René-Jean Dupuy, 'Le Droit Des Relations Entre Les Organisations Internationales' (1960) 100 Recueil des Cours de l'Académie de Droit International 461.

H. Gött, *The Law of Interactions Between International Organizations*, Beiträge zum ausländischen öffentlichen Recht und Völkerrecht 299, https://doi.org/10.1007/978-3-662-62389-3_15

IOs' external relations, often without clear distinction as to whether these instruments are provided for by law or merely resemble inter-organizational political practice.[3] Other authors simply postulate that certain rights or obligations would emanate from the fact that IOs are international legal subjects.

Against this background, the analysis in this chapter necessarily has to address some more fundamental questions. Nevertheless, its principal aim is to expound the customary inter-organizational legal rules and any general principles of law that apply to the ILO's inter-organizational interactions with the World Bank and the CoE, in order to evaluate whether and to what extent these rules serve to protect or to promote the ILO's model of labour governance.

A. Moving Beyond the 'International Legal Personality Shortcut': The Need to Determine Specific Rights and Obligations

At the outset, it is necessary to set the proper analytical focus for pursuing this objective. As already indicated, it has repeatedly been argued that IOs have a certain right or obligation simply because they are international legal subjects (I.). As will be seen, this line of reasoning is insufficient (II.).

I. Invocations of International Legal Personality As a Basis for Rights and Obligations

International practice and legal scholars have repeatedly referred to IOs' international legal personality as a basis for assuming—usually by implication—that these IOs have certain international rights or obligations against non-members.[4] In a

[3]Henry G Schermers and Niels M Blokker, *International Institutional Law* (6th edn, Brill 2018) para 1742 et seqq. Whether an IO is legally bound to observe a norm of international law or whether it simply chooses to observe it as a matter of "sound policy" is a crucial difference, Rosalyn Higgins and others, *Oppenheim's International Law - United Nations* (Oxford University Press 2017) para 12.15.

[4]See e.g. Christian Tietje 'Global Governance and Inter-Agency Co-Operation in International Economic Law' (2002) 36 Journal of World Trade 501, 511; Geir Ulfstein, 'Institutions and Competences' in Jan Klabbers, Anne Peters and Geir Ulfstein (eds), *The Constitutionalization of International Law* (Oxford University Press 2009) 71. Some have also taken the recognition of international legal personality as a reason to demand greater accountability of IOs, see Reinisch (n 1) 1012 et seq.

manner of speaking, international legal personality is used as an argumentative 'shortcut': From the mere fact that an IO was recognized as a legal person, it is followed that it had certain specific rights or duties.

The ICJ's *Reparation for Injuries* opinion served as an important catalyst for such invocations of international legal personality as a source of rights and obligations against non-members. In that opinion, the ICJ established that the UN has international legal personality.[5] It further held that this personality was objective, i.e. it could be held against third states which were not UN members at the time. The Court concluded from the UN's objective legal personality that it had the capacity to bring international claims against non-member states.[6]

In the context of this study, rights and obligations vis-à-vis non-members emanating directly from international legal personality, as postulated by the ICJ in *Reparation for Injuries*, would be of great relevance. If an IO can have rights and duties towards non-member states, why not also vis-à-vis other IOs? One could contemplate, for instance, that the ILO's legal personality could entitle it to bring international claims for the protection of its interests against the Bank or the CoE, like the ICJ accepted *mutatis mutandis* for the UN in *Reparation for Injuries*. What is more, one could also consider primary rights and obligations emanating from legal personality, e.g. the right to demand respect for the integrity, the functioning or the output of a certain model of labour governance. Following this premise, the ILO might be able to demand respect for its policies, instruments and practice when, say, the World Bank drafts and publishes Doing Business reports, or when the ECtHR follows the CEACR's interpretations of labour conventions which are contested within the ILO.[7]

On a conceptual level, it has remained an open question if other IOs than the UN can be considered to have objective personality along the reasoning provided in *Reparation*.[8] The debate largely centred on the question whether an IO's

[5] *Reparation for Injuries Suffered in the Service of the United Nations* (n 1) 179.

[6] ibid 185. The acceptance of 'objective' personality is a departure from the *pacta tertiis* rule.

[7] One could feel tempted to consider this, considering the functionalist justification the ICJ and many scholars give for accepting IOs legal personality. After all, the effective achievement of organizational objectives by a separate entity would require certain rights safeguarding such efficacy.

[8] While affirming the objective personality of the UN has since been broadly accepted, the *Reparation* opinion sparked considerable uncertainty as to the personality of other IOs. The Court's reasoning in *Reparation* was utterly apodictic and did not provide much guidance in this respect. The Court confined itself to hold "that fifty States, representing the vast majority of the members of the international community, had the power, in conformity with international law, to bring into being an entity possessing objective international personality, and not merely personality recognized by them alone, together with capacity to bring international claims", *Reparation for Injuries Suffered in the Service of the United Nations* (n 1) 185. Thus, the Court seemingly modified the *pacta tertiis* rule by a 'vast majority approach', which it essentially left undefined. It never clarified if, and under which conditions, the *Reparation* criteria for objective personality would apply to other IOs. The Court's reasoning can be interpreted in various ways: 1) as stipulating a special rule only applicable to the UN, 2) as postulating a rule applying to all IOs founded by the 'vast majority', i.e. all IOs with a quasi-universal membership (in this direction Schermers and Blokker, *International Institutional Law* (n 3) para 1857), 3) as merely describing one out of many (unstated) ways

international legal personality needs to be recognized by non-member states. This discussion has its origins in the Cold War, when the Soviet Union rejected to deal with the EEC on the international plane.[9] The question was sustained during extensive debates both in the ILC and in legal literature and continues to linger today with no clear answer.[10]

In the context of this study, however, it is of no particular importance whether the recognition of an IO's legal personality is constitutive or not. Even if one accepted that IOs cannot have objective personality without a constitutive act of recognition by others, the relevance of this conceptual issue would be fused by the fact that the ILO, the World Bank and the CoE all recognize, in one way or the other, the respective others' existence as a legal person.[11] Therefore, none of them could

to attain objective personality or even 4) as resembling a general rule of the law of IOs. The question if other IOs had objective legal personality was most contentiously discussed during the Cold War era. The Soviet approach to IOs, cautious and restrictive in general, argued against objective personality, see e.g. Grigory Tunkin, 'International Law in the International System' (1975) 147 Recueil des Cours de l'Académie de Droit International 1, 165. In Western countries, the issue remained contentious, too. It even affected some of the ILC's draft conventions and rules, which in consequence included compromissory formulations both camps could support (for the VCLT-IO see Kirsten, Schmalenbach, 'Art. 6 VCLT' in Oliver Dörr and Kirsten Schmalenbach (eds), *Vienna Convention on the Law of Treaties: A Commentary* (2nd edn, Springer 2018) para 27). For instance, the issue was one of the most contentious points during the ILC's work on the the law of treaties between states and IOs or between IOs (galvanizing around the source of IOs' treaty-making power), Fernando Lusa Bordin, *The Analogy Between States and International Organizations* (Cambridge University Press 2019) 55 et seqq. Scholarly literature is divided as well: Pro Objectivity is Arnold D McNair, 'Treaties Producing Effects Erga Omnes', *Scritti di diritto internazionale in onore di Tomaso Perassi II* (Giuffrè 1957) 23. For a relative international legal personality, with recognition being constitutive, Hermann Mosler, 'Die Erweiterung des Kreises der Völkerrechtssubjekte' (1962) 22 Zeitschrift für ausländisches öffentliches Recht und Völkerrecht 1, 32, similar Marten Breuer, 'The Council of Europe and International Institutional Law – An Appraisal' in Stefanie Schmahl and Marten Breuer (eds), *The Council of Europe: Its Laws and Policies* (Oxford University Press 2017) 946, para 38.33, arguing that the *Reparation* case was a recognized exception. Similar James Crawford, *Brownlie's Principles of Public International Law* (8th edn, Oxford University Press 2012) 171; Christian Tomuschat, 'International Law: Ensuring the Survival of Mankind on the Eve of a New Century' (1999) 281 Recueil des Cours de l'Académie de Droit International 9, 128; Werner Meng, 'Art. 57' in Bruno Simma and others (eds), *The Charter of the United Nations - A Commentary, vol II* (3rd edn, Oxford University Press 2013) para 16; Eckart Klein and Stefanie Schmahl, 'Die internationalen und die supranationalen Organisationen' in Wolfgang Graf Vitzthum and Alexander Proelß (eds), *Völkerrecht* (de Gruyter 2013) para 96. In 2011, the ILC showed sympathy for expanding the objective personality approach to other IOs, ILC, 'Draft Articles on the Responsibility of International Organizations, with Commentaries' [2011] YILC Vol II Part Two 46, 50, albeit without giving further reasons. See also Reinisch (n 1) 1010.

[9]Hans M Blix, 'Contemporary Aspects of Recognition' (1970) 120 Recueil des Cours de l'Académie de Droit International 587, 621.

[10]For a recent account see Lusa Bordin (n 8) 53 et seqq.

[11]Much of the debate on objective personality has been led with regard to IOs' relations with non-member states. If one keeps this focus on non-member states, the question of objective international legal personality seems to lose importance. Among the IOs examined in this study, all except the CoE have attained quasi-universal membership, and the latter has been recognized by a large number of states and IOs, see Breuer (n 8) 38.34. See also Higgins and others (n 3) para

deny (nor would they) that the others have the capacity to posses rights or duties under international law, including vis-à-vis non-members.[12]

II. The Problem of Deriving Specific Rights and Obligations from Personality

The core problem, at least for present purposes, lies elsewhere: international legal personality, and its recognition by others, is not the same as the possession of specific rights and obligations. As will be shown in the following, international legal personality is a concept way too imprecise to pinpoint specific rights and obligations, safe for those rights and obligations that are already reasonably established and contoured by themselves.

1. From the ‘Capacity to Possess’ to Actual Possession of Rights and Obligations

It is often said that the general capacity of IOs to be bound by international law stems from their international legal personality.[13] This draws on the widespread definition of international legal personality as the *capacity of possessing rights or duties under international law*.[14] It is beyond question that the ILO, the ‘World Bank’ (i.e. IBRD and IDA) and the CoE all have this capacity and, in consequence, have international legal personality.

11.44. However, the focus of this study requires to consider the issue of objective personality in the context of inter-organizational legal relations. Each of the examined IOs is a non-member IO to the respective others, which is why the question of objective personality in principle remains valid. For a similar argument regarding recognition by non-member states see Gerhard Hafner, ‘The Legal Personality of International Organizations’ in August Reinisch and Ursula Kriebaum (eds), *The Law of International Relations - Liber Amicorum Hanspeter Neuhold* (Eleven 2007) 87.

[12]It is, at least today, in fact rather unlikely any IO would deny that with regard to any other IO.

[13]*Interpretation of the Agreement of 25 March 1951 between the WHO and Egypt* (n 1) 89 et seq.; Thomas Kleinlein, *Konstitutionalisierung im Völkerrecht* (Springer 2012) 591; Philippe Sands, Pierre Klein and David W Bowett, *Bowett's Law of International Institutions* (6th edn, Sweet & Maxwell 2009) 461, para 14–034.

[14]*Reparation for Injuries Suffered in the Service of the United Nations* (n 1) 179; Christian Walter, ‘Subjects of International Law’, *Max Planck Encyclopedia of Public International Law* (Oxford University Press 2007) para 1. Regarding many IOs, this capacity has been recognized by international and domestic jurisprudence, Sands, Klein and Bowett (n 13) 461 et seq., paras. 14-034 and 14-035, with references. On different variants see William Thomas Worster, ‘Relative International Legal Personality of Non-State Actors’ (2016) 42 Brooklyn Journal of International Law 207, 210 et seq.

However, generally affirming that IOs have the capacity to possess international rights and obligations by virtue of their international legal personality is insufficient. While such a conclusion is of course correct, it is in itself of little practical significance, because the mere statement that an entity *is capable of possessing* rights and obligations does not tell much about whether, and to what extent, it *actually does.*[15]

To begin with, it goes without saying that IOs are not bound by every single existing norm of international law simply by virtue of their general capacity to be bound by all sources of international law.[16] In fact, many international rights and obligations are explicitly reserved for states or other international legal subjects.[17] The ICJ, in a frequently cited passage from the *WHO/Egypt* opinion, supports this suggestion. This passage is mostly referred to as authority for IOs' general capacity to be bound by international law. However, the ICJ made an important qualification. It held that

> International organizations are subjects of international law and, as such, are bound by any obligations *incumbent upon them* under general rules of international law, under their constitutions or under international agreements to which they are parties.[18] (emphasis added)

Thus, it is not enough to establish that IOs can at all possess international rights and obligations by virtue of their legal personality. Rather, the true issue is *which* international rights and obligations an IO *actually possesses.*[19]

---

[15]Similar Crawford, *Brownlie's Principles of Public International Law* (n 8) 191; Dapo Akande, 'International Organizations' in Malcolm Evans (ed), *International Law* (Oxford University Press 2014) 279; Schermers and Blokker, *International Institutional Law* (n 3) para 1570; Karsten Nowrot, *Normative Ordnungsstruktur und private Wirkungsmacht* (BWV 2006) 574, with further references; Carolin Damm, *Die Europäische Union im universellen Völkergewohnheitsrecht* (Mohr Siebeck 2016) 58.

[16]Albert Bleckmann, 'Zur Verbindlichkeit des allgemeinen Völkerrechts für Internationale Organisationen' (1977) 37 Zeitschrift für ausländisches öffentliches Recht und Völkerrecht 107, 110 et seqq.; Kleinlein (n 13) 592; Dupuy (n 2) 530; Reinisch (n 1) 1020 et seq.; Higgins and others (n 3) para 11.16. Such an inference would not even hold true for states, which are bound by most, but not all international legal norms, for the sole reason that they do not fall within the personal scope of each and every international norm.

[17]Damm (n 15) 66 et seq; Lusa Bordin (n 8) 5.

[18]*Interpretation of the Agreement of 25 March 1951 between the WHO and Egypt* (n 1) 89 et seq. See also *Reparation for Injuries Suffered in the Service of the United Nations* (n 1) 179.

[19]Similar e.g. Hugo J Hahn, 'Euratom: The Conception of an International Personality' (1958) 71 Harvard Law Review 1001, 1045 et seq.; Philippe Gautier, 'The Reparation for Injuries Case Revisited: The Personality of the European Union' (2000) 4 Max Planck Yearbook of United Nations Law 331, 336 et seq. Definitions of legal subjectivity often speak of the capability to possess rights or obligations. 'Capable of possessing' is, of course, not meant as a distant possibility that, in the future, an actor will be able to attain international rights and obligations. Rather, as with states, the phrase means that an IO currently already possesses such rights and obligations. This includes rights to acquire new rights, e.g. by concluding a treaty (which is why the definition speaks of being 'capable').

2. Difficulties to Pinpoint Specific Rights and Obligations

This determination of rights and obligations deriving from IOs' international legal personality, however, has proven a difficult exercise. In its above-cited passage from *WHO/Egypt*, the ICJ enlists possible sources of IOs' obligations only in very general terms.[20] Those commentators who derive specific rights and obligations from IOs' international legal personality often tend to do so in two ways. They either focus on rights which are established and then present them as being adjuncts of international personality, such as the capacity to conclude treaties or to bring international claims. Or, they confine themselves to simply postulating, without further reasoning, that certain specific rights or obligations can be derived from IOs' international legal personality.

More systemic analyses are rare. Three possible avenues to determine specific rights and obligations will be discussed in the following, namely by approximation using a taxonomy of personalities (a), by externalizing the constitutional distribution of competences between the IO and its member states (b) and by assuming inherent rights emanating from 'organizationhood' (c).

a) Approximation Using a Taxonomy of Legal Subjectivity?

Traditional doctrine, drawing on occasional statements from international bodies,[21] has tried to concretize international legal personality by creating categories such as functional, partial or derivative legal personality for IOs (and, for that matter, other non-state international legal subjects).[22] These categories are meant to illustrate that non-state actors have legal personality, but do not possess the same kind and scope of rights and obligations as states.[23] Yet, this taxonomy achieves little more than juxtaposing states on the one side and all other international legal subjects on the other, regardless of how disparate and diverse these other subjects may be.[24] Thus, the taxonomy does not provide further assistance in the present, inter-organizational context.

---

[20]The reference to IOs' constitutions is rather straightforward. The term 'international agreements' may be assumed to cover all binding international treaties. The last category, "general international law", is so broad that it does not provide guidance, except the obvious point that international rights and obligations existing in inter-organizational relations which are not based on a treaty must be found in customary international law or in general principles, Jan Klabbers, 'The Paradox of International Institutional Law' (2008) 5 International Organizations Law Review 151, 165; Kristina Daugirdas, 'How and Why International Law Binds International Organizations' (2016) 57 Harvard International Law Journal 325, 326.

[21]See e.g. *Reparation for Injuries Suffered in the Service of the United Nations* (n 1) 179 et seq.

[22]See Walter 'Subjects of International Law' (n 14) para 23 et seqq.; Matthias Herdegen, *Völkerrecht* (17th ed, C H Beck 2018) ch 7, para 9 et seqq.

[23]Higgins and others (n 3) para 11.18.

[24]Klabbers, *An Introduction to International Organizations Law* (3rd edn, Cambridge University Press 2015) 41 et seq.

b) Externalizing the Constitutional Allocation of Competences?

Other commentators have suggested that the scope and content of an IO's international legal personality was a 'mirror image' to the scope and content of its competences under its institutional law.[25] Essentially, the argument goes as follows: since IOs have been endowed with legal personality by their members to perform certain tasks, (a) their legal personality is limited to these tasks and (b) this limited international legal personality also creates rights and obligations vis-á-vis non-member states, other IOs and other third parties. The consequence of this suggestion is that the distribution of competences between the IO and its member states has external legal effect.

It may of course always be that, on whatever legal basis, in a specific case, a specific IO is bound by a specific norm of general international law that plays a role in the exercise of its functions. As a general strategy for determining the scope of an IO's international legal personality vis-á-vis other IOs, however, the externalization of competences raises structural problems:

Firstly, as a practical matter, not all IOs' competences are regulated and delimited with sufficient clarity.[26] Externalizing these unclear allocations would expand this uncertainty to the inter-organizational plane.

Secondly, on a point of positive law, the externalization of the distribution of competences remains a postulate. IOs' competences (and these competences' limits) belong to the legal relationship between an IO and its member states. For example, a competence granted under an IO's institutional law to conclude treaties only means that the IO is entitled *vis-à-vis its member states* to conclude treaties with other IOs. This, however, does not in itself entitle the IO *vis-à-vis the contracting other IO*. IOs' institutional laws cannot delimit the scope of an IOs' rights and obligations vis-à-vis another IO, unless either the other IO has accepted the respective provisions (Arts. 34-36 VCLT-IO) or there is an inter-organizational legal norm pursuant to

---

[25]Dupuy (n 2) 532. For instance, IOs' treaty making power is sometimes simply derived from pertinent constitutional provisions in the IO's constituent instrument, Schmalenbach 'Art. 6 VCLT' (n 8) para 26, with further references. In a comparable manner, albeit not in the context of inter-organizational relations, the International Criminal Tribunal for Rwanda held in *Prosecutor v. Rwamakuba* derived from the UN Charter and from UN practice that the UN "as an international subject, is bound to respect rules of customary international law, including those rules which relate to the protection of fundamental human rights", *Prosecutor v. Rwamakuba* (Decision on Appropriate Remedy) ICTR-98-44C-T (25 October 2006) para 48. The Tribunal also relied on 'inherited' human rights obligations, ibid. Overall, the Tribunal, though emphasizing customary international law, eventually did not entirely clarify the normative basis for its assertion. Rather, the relevant passage of the decision (paras 39 et seqq.) relies on an argumentative conglomerate of customary international law, precedents of the ICTR's Appeals Chamber, international human rights instruments, the UN Charter, the inherent powers doctrine and practice of UN organs.

[26]A good example is the debate on whether the CoE had international legal personality, led in its early years of existence. As shown above, the CoE Statute is abundantly succinct. From this common starting point, different authors developed a whole continuum of diverging views, see Breuer (n 8) para 38.22, with further references.

which the internal distribution of competences between the IO and its member states is legally relevant in the inter-organizational relationship.[27] With regard to the capacity to conclude treaties, such an inter-organizational norm exists in customary law and is spelled out in Art. 6 VCLT-IO.[28] Beyond that, however, a general norm pursuant to which IOs' competences should also delimit their legal rights and obligations vis-à-vis other IOs is difficult to discern. In any event, whether any right or obligation of an IO laid down in its constituent instrument has external effect hinges on either acceptance or a respective inter-organizational norm, not on the IO's international legal personality.

c) Inherent Rights Emanating from 'Organizationhood'?

Finally, Finn Seyersted has developed a fundamentally different approach to determining the scope of rights and obligations deriving from IOs' international legal personality. He 'inverts' the starting position: Instead of positively identifying specific rights and obligations, he argues that IOs' international legal personality confers on them a general legal capacity, allowing them to act freely unless prohibited.[29] Although Seyersted does not discuss the inter-organizational

---

[27]These two alternatives correspond to Bordin's two conceptualizations of IOs, the "treaty conception" and a "subject conception", Lusa Bordin (n 8) 53 et seqq. For the 'acceptance' through recognition see also Ignaz Seidl-Hohenveldern and Gerhard Loibl, *Das Recht der Internationalen Organisationen* (7th edn, Heymann 2000) 47. By contrast, the mere "fact" (i.e. the social reality) that IOs have actually been founded is in itself insufficient to externalize their competences vis-à-vis third parties, because this would be an impermissible derivation of a normative proposition from a factual situation.

[28]Ulfstein, 'Institutions and Competences' (n 4) 71; Karl Zemanek, 'Vienna Convention on the Law of Treaties between States and International Organizations or between International Organizations - Introductory Note' (2009) United Nations Audiovisual Library of International Law <https://legal.un.org/avl/ha/vcltsio/vcltsio.html> accessed 26 April 2020, 2. Art. 6 VCLT-IO serves as a 'hinge norm' linking the regulation of treaty making powers in the inter-organizational legal relationship to each IO's constitutional treaty making competences, Schmalenbach, 'Art. 6 VCLT' (n 8) para 27. Despite this linkage, the differentiation between constitutional provisions and external norms in the VCLT-IO is not purely theoretical. For instance, a treaty can remain valid under the rules of the VCLT-IO although its conclusion exceeds the IO's constitutional treaty-making powers (Arts. 27 (2) and 46(2) VCLT-IO), Eckart Klein and Matthias Pechstein, *Das Vertragsrecht internationaler Organisationen* (Duncker & Humblot 1985) 25 et seqq.; Heribert Franz Köck and Peter Fischer, *Das Recht der Internationalen Organisationen* (3rd edn, Linde Verlag 1997) 574 et seq.; Thilo Rensmann, 'International Organizations or Institutions, External Relations and Co-Operation', *Max Planck Encyclopedia of Public International Law* (Oxford University Press 2009) para 16; Thilo Rensmann, 'Art. 46 VCLT' in Oliver Dörr and Kirsten Schmalenbach (eds), *Vienna Convention on the Law of Treaties - A Commentary* (2nd edn, Springer 2018) para 64.

[29]Seyersted draws on a passage in *Certain Expenses*, which he claims to implement one of his proposals, see Finn Seyersted, *Common Law of International Organizations* (Martinus Nijhoff Publishers 2008) 31. See also Finn Seyersted, *Objective Legal Personality of Intergovernmental Organizations – Do Their Capacities Really Depend Upon Their Constitutions?* (Copenhagen 1963) 21 et seqq.

constellation, it is evident that this proposal is of high relevance for the present study. Translating international legal personality into a general international capacity would, at least at first sight, render it unnecessary to attempt to determine specific rights or obligations from IOs' legal personality.

In his proposal, Seyersted reconceptualizes both the legal personality and the legal capacity of IOs. As to the former, he rejects the idea that IOs' legal personality depends on it being conferred by the IO's constituent treaty. Instead, he argues that IOs *ipso facto* obtain international legal personality if certain criteria of "organizationhood" are met, which he identifies as follows:

1) There is at least one international organ, i.e. an organ established by two sovereign communities,
2) this organ is not subject to the authority of other sovereign communities except its members acting jointly through the organ
3) the organ acts in its own name
4) the organ must be authorized to assume obligations for itself, i.e. not merely on behalf of its members.[30]

As to IOs' legal capacity, he concludes that

> all organizations which fulfil these criteria [of legal personality] are general subjects of international law, in the sense that they have the capacity to perform all types of international acts which they are in a practical position to perform, and which have not been precluded by any provision of their constitution (. . .).[31]

All IOs examined in this study fulfil Seyersted's criteria for international legal personality. Thus, applying his proposal would mean that all IOs have general international capacity, safe for any limitations enshrined in their constitutions that are relevant on the external plane.

However, Seyersted's inference of a general international legal capacity is not convincing.[32] As a fundamental methodological issue, his reliance on facts[33]—both as criteria for attaining legal personality and as a foundation for legal capacity—is

---

[30]ibid 64. Klabbers rightly points out that it was difficult to discern the "inherent" parts of organizationhood, Klabbers, *An Introduction to International Organizations Law* (n 24) 66.

[31]Seyersted, *Common Law of International Organizations* (n 29) 64.

[32]Seyersted rightly insists that a treaty is not a necessary requirement for the establishment of an IO. Nor is it necessary that the IO's capacities be laid down in its constituting document. That being said, it is noteworthy that Seyersted understands the implied powers doctrine narrowly to begin with. He seems to understand that doctrine as exclusively focusing on implying competences from the constituent instrument and neglecting practice. By contrast, the ICJ in *Reparation for Injuries* adopted a much more lenient approach, leaving room for institutional practice, when it held that "the rights and duties of an entity such as the Organization must depend upon its purposes and functions as specified or implied in its constituent documents and developed in practice", *Reparation for Injuries Suffered in the Service of the United Nations* (n 1) 180.

[33]Being sympathetic to realist conceptions of international law (Seyersted, *Common Law of International Organizations* (n 29) xi), he appears to understand these as 'facts' in the true sense of the word, i.e. as factual phenomena.

problematic. The mere fact that an IO *is* able to act in a certain way does not suffice to establish that it, as a matter of law, *ought* to act in this way.[34]

Moreover, Seyersted's inductive way of reasoning is contestable. Seyersted relies on comparatively recognized rights and obligations, including IOs' capacity to conclude treaties, the right to active and passive legation, the capacity to convene and to participate in international conferences and the capacity to become a member of other IOs.[35] However, inferring a general international capacity from these examples is premature. Firstly, these examples are not as straightforward as Seyersted presents them.[36] Secondly, Seyersted misses important aspects of IOs'

---

[34]Rather, there has to be an international legal norm stipulating that the respective factual situation ought to have the proposed legal consequences. As a matter of propositional logic, a normative proposition cannot, by way of a full syllogistic conclusion, be derived from facts, David Hume, *A Treatise of Human Nature* (1739), reprinted from the Original Edition in three volumes and edited, with an analytical index (Clarendon Press 1896), Book III, Part I, Section 1; Ulrich Klug, 'Die Reine Rechtslehre von Hans Kelsen und die Formallogische Rechtfertigung der Kritik am Pseudoschluß vom Sein auf das Sollen' in Salo Engel and Rudolf Métall (eds) *Law, State, and International Legal Order – Essays in Honor of Hans Kelsen* (University of Tennessee Press 1964) 153. Otherwise, his conclusion from the factual situation to a norm would be syllogistically incomplete. Seyersted provides the necessary norm only in parts and with regard to the proposed general scope of IOs' legal capacity, but not with regard to his proposed prerequisites of IOs' legal personality, i.e. that IOs ought to attain international legal personality upon fulfilment of the aforesaid criteria. Thus, with regard to the latter, his argument lacks a necessary element. Moreover, insofar as he refers to international norms to support IOs' general legal capacity, he mostly invokes customary law. This could provide a normative proposition which is in principle able to bridge the gap between is and ought. However, as will be shown in the next section (below, B.), his invocation of customary law only confirms what is anyways established. It does not provide a sufficient basis for assuming that IOs have a general international legal capacity.

[35]Seyersted, *Common Law of International Organizations* (n 29) 401 et seqq.

[36]To name but one example here, whereas IOs' treaty-making power as such is widely recognized, the scope of this power has been subject to intense debate for decades, Nicolas Levrat, 'Art. 6 VCLT-IO' in Olivier Corten and Pierre Klein (eds), *The Vienna Conventions on the Law of Treaties - A Commentary, vol 1* (Oxford University Press 2011) para 7 et seq. With references regarding the discussions in the ILC and academia, Klein and Pechstein (n 28) 23. At question was precisely the point if this treaty-making power depends on constitutional limitations or is an inherent competence conferred upon every IO by general international law. In a similar vein, states have also showed reluctance as to IOs' treaty making power regarding one of the potentially most important treaties to be concluded by IOs – the VCLT-IO itself. IOs did not participate in the Vienna Conference of 1986 on equal footing with the participating states. Rather, after the role of IOs had been controversially discussed in the run-up to the conference, only selected IOs were invited (UNGA Res 39/86 (13 December 1984) UN Doc A/RES/39/86, para 2 lit. c and e, and UNGA Res 40/76 (11 December 1985) UN Doc A/RES/40/76, para 3; Klein and Pechstein (n 28) 12). These IOs were not granted the status of full participants, but were merely invited as observers (see the Draft Rules of Procedure, annexed to UNGA Res 40/76 (11 December 1985) UN Doc A/RES/40/76 (1986 Vienna Conference Rules of Procedure), especially Rules 60 and 61). While certain of these IOs were granted specific enhanced procedural rights, none of the IOs present at the conference were given such important rights as the right to take part in votes (Rules 60 and 61 1986 Vienna Conference Rules of Procedure). This inferior position of IOs in the conclusion of a 'treaty on (their) treaties' is also reflected in the VCLT-IO itself. For example, pursuant to Art. 85(1) VCLT-IO, the convention's entry into force depends (only) on the ratification by at least 35 states. By contrast,

international legal capacity, which call into question his inductive conclusion that this capacity was general. His argument centres on only two aspects of international legal capacity: Firstly, IOs' right to commit certain specified international legal acts (to conclude treaties, to send and receive represenatives and to convene and participate in conferences), and, secondly, international responsibility, i.e. secondary rules on the consequences of an internationally wrongful act committed by an IO.[37] However, international legal capacity may comprise much more than that. Most relevantly, Seyersted does not address the question of IOs' primary international legal obligations vis-à-vis each other, such as possible obligations not to intervene into each other's functioning, or to take due account of each other's governance model.

Finally, his idea of general legal capacity crucially depends on this capacity being limited by existing bodies of law. As limits for IOs' general capacity, Seyersted names the IO's own institutional legal framework of substantive and procedural provisions, jointly established and controlled by the member states,[38] and the sovereignty of third states.[39] Neither, however, is directly relevant in inter-organizational legal relations. Other IOs cannot invoke sovereignty. Neither is it evident that another IO can rely on the acting IO's institutional legal framework of substantive and procedural provisions, as this framework only generates rights and obligations between the acting IO and its members.[40] In consequence, IOs' legal capacity to interact with each other would be virtually unlimited. IOs would thus be legally entitled to treat one another in almost any way they see fit, simply on the basis of their respective international legal personality. Thus, in the inter-organizational constellation, Seyersted's concept is devoid of its necessary limitations and, eventually, led *ad absurdum*.

---

again as a result of diverse previous discussions, IOs' acts of confirmation or accession have no influence on the VCLT-IO's entry into force; they are only relevant for their own status as party to the convention (Art. 85(3) VCLT-IO), Catherine Denis, 'Art. 85 VCLT-IO' in Olivier Corten and Pierre Klein (eds), *The Vienna Conventions on the Law of Treaties - A Commentary, vol 2* (Oxford University Press 2011) para 7 et seqq. The example illustrates that even as to widely recognized capacities such as IOs' capacity to conclude treaties, there are uncertainties which must not be easily put aside.

[37] Seyersted, *Common Law of International Organizations* (n 29) 401 et seqq.

[38] These provisions he considers relevant "if and to the extent that constitutional restrictions have external effect", i.e. insofar as *ultra vires* acts of an IO are invalid vis-à-vis third actors, ibid 64.

[39] The limits of this general international capacity are not listed consistently throughout Seyersted's work. At one point, he merely envisages constitutional limits, ibid, whereas in other passages, he also names state sovereignty, ibid 413. In another paragraph of the same page, he argues that IOs' acts must "not impose new obligations upon parties who are not subject to their jurisdiction", which is broader and could include other IOs. Yet, in his argument, Seyersted does not seem to contemplate inter-organizational relations in particular.

[40] Again, this would only be different insofar as there was an inter-organizational legal norm pursuant to which the rights and obligations emanating from an IO's relations with its members ought to create legal effect in that IO's inter-organizational relations.

3. The Methodological Issue: Personality As a Chiffre for Rights and Obligations

It is submitted here that the problem with deriving rights and obligations from international legal personality is—and arguably has always been—a methodological one: Personality is not the source of rights and obligations. On the contrary, international legal personality is a chiffre for certain established rights and obligations that are explicitly or implicitly associated with it.[41] International legal personality is a figurative term describing that an entity possesses certain rights and obligations under international law.

This cyphering is arguably due to the concept of legal personality historically being interlinked with state sovereignty and the rights and obligations associated with it. In 'Westphalian' conceptions of international law, legal personality was the 'entry ticket' to the international legal sphere—then understood as the law applying exclusively between sovereign entities.[42] As equals, all sovereign entities possessed the same set of basic legal rights and obligations as the others.[43] International legal personality could, therefore, safely be equated with sovereignty and the rights and obligations connected with it. However, this equation only works out if the nature and scope of the connected rights and obligations is reasonably clear.

In present times, this clarity arguably exists with regard to states. States are sovereign equals, and as such possess a certain set of basic rights and obligations which are the same for every state. By contrast, there is no comparable clarity with regard to IOs.[44] It is not surprising that international legal scholarship has struggled to fit IOs' limited and diverse sets of international rights and obligations into established categories of personality, resulting in the aforementioned categories of 'partial' or 'functional' personality. Neither is it a coincidence that, as seen, commentators only derive those rights from IOs' legal personality that are established in the first place.[45] Apart from these established rights, IOs' international legal personality is of little help when it comes to deriving specific rights or duties from it.[46]

IOs' international legal personality is not the origin of concrete rights and obligations of the examined IOs. On the contrary, personality *presupposes* that there is sufficient clarity regarding the rights and obligations allegedly flowing

[41] Dupuy (n 2) para 531 et seq. See further the discussion in Hermann Mosler, 'Die Erweiterung des Kreises der Völkerrechtssubjekte' (1962) 22 Zeitschrift für ausländisches öffentliches Recht und Völkerrecht 1, 19 et seqq.

[42] See e.g. Juliane Kokott, 'Souveräne Gleichheit und Demokratie im Völkerrecht' (2004) 64 Zeitschrift für ausländisches öffentliches Recht und Völkerrecht 517, 524.

[43] Dupuy (n 2) 530.

[44] See below, B. VI.

[45] Likewise, it is no coincidence that the question of how many and which rights a non-state actor must have in order to attain international legal personality is subject to debate, see with further references Worster (n 14) 211.

[46] Dupuy even argued that it was of no help at all, Dupuy (n 2) 531.

from it in the first place. This clarity can only be achieved by deriving specific rights and obligations from elsewhere, namely the sources of inter-organizational law.

III. Conclusion

This section has argued that the mere fact that an IO possesses international legal personality does not imply which inter-organizational rights and obligations it possesses. Such a 'shortcut' argumentation does not consider that international legal personality merely says whether or not an IO possesses *any* international rights or obligations *at all*, but not *which ones*. It is no coincidence that, as shown, attempts to isolate specific rights and obligations by concretizing IOs' legal personality do not yield convincing results. The reason for this is a methodological one: International legal personality is merely a chiffre for the entirety of the rights and obligations an IO possesses. Thus, such rights and obligations need to be ascertained with sufficient clarity in the first place. This can only be done by deriving them from the sources of inter-organizationa law.

B. Customary Inter-Organizational Law

In order to ascertain the ILO's, World Bank's and CoE's potential rights and obligations, it is necessary to look for specific rights and obligations in customary inter-organizational law. As will be seen in the following, customary inter-organizational law is a field with very few established norms. This is particularly true for potential customary inter-organizational rules governing other inter-organizational interactions than direct and cooperative ones. At this stage of the analysis, it would be too early to conclude that such norms do not exist at all. However, what can be constated is that they have hardly ever been explored to begin with. This calls for a genuine endeavour of normative 'discovery', with a particular focus on those few scholarly proposals that have been made.[47]

[47] At the outset, it deserves mention that some of these proposals were deliberately made 'en passant' and without being based on deeper analysis. However, given the overall scarcity of proposals, the proposals will be discussed as they have been made, without distinguishing between brief sketches and more elaborate arguments.

I. Preliminary Methodological Remarks

On a preliminary note, two methodological issues need to be addressed.

1. IOs As Adressees and Creators of Customary Inter-Organizational Law

The first issue is the distinction between IOs being bound by customary law on the one hand, and IOs being the creators of customary law on the other. In inter-state relations, both usually coincide, as states are both addressees and creators of customary international law.[48] By contrast, in the case of IOs, customary norm creation and norm subjugation can diverge.[49] Indeed, while it is recognized that IOs can be bound by norms of customary law, the question whether IOs can themselves create customary law through their own acts (as opposed to being facilitators of customary law creation by their member states) is still highly controversial.[50] In its 2018 Draft Conclusions on Identification of Customary International Law, the ILC concluded (albeit not with particular regard to inter-organizational constellations) that "in certain cases", the practice of IOs can contribute to the formation or expression of customary law.[51] On the other hand, it also reiterated

[48]At least following the established doctrine laid down in Art. 38(1) ICJ Statute, states are only bound by customary law if they consented to it (leaving aside the manifold theoretical and practical difficulties that this conceptualization entails).

[49]The IBRD has occasionally called into question that it is bound by general international law to which it has not consented, arguing that there is no explicit international legal norm stating that IOs are bound by general international law, Sabine Schlemmer-Schulte, 'International Bank for Reconstruction and Development (IBRD)', *Max Planck Encyclopedia of Public International Law* (Oxford University Press 2014), para 102. Taken literally, this would mean that norm creation and norm subjugation would always have to coincide. This argument, however, is not sustainable in this generality. Rather, the Bank's argument must be read as to oppose its subjugation to *certain* norms of general international law, e.g. customary human rights standards, see Reinisch (n 1) 1019 et seq. with further references.

[50]See e.g. Worster (n 14) 221, with further references. The International Law Commission has recently begun to tackle the question, see ILC, 'Report of the International Law Commission Seventieth Session' (2018) UN Doc A/73/10, 130 et seqq.; Daugirdas, 'How and Why International Law Binds International Organizations' (n 20) 327.

[51]ILC, 'Report of the International Law Commission Seventieth Session' (n 50) 130, Conclusion 4 (2). See also Ian Johnstone, 'Law-Making through the Operational Activities of International Organizations' (2008) 40 George Washington International Law Review 87; Michael Wood, 'International Organizations and Customary International Law (2014 Jonathan J Charney Distinguished Lecture in Public International Law)' (2015) 48 Vanderbilt Journal of Transnational Law 609; Michael Wood, 'The Present Position within the ILC on the Topic "Identification of Customary International Law": in Partial Response to Sienho Yee, Report on the ILC Project on "Identification of Customary International Law"' (2016) 15 Chinese Journal of International Law 3, 10.

that such practice must be general, meaning "widespread and representative, as well as consistent",[52] which, as the examples of inter-organizational interactions given above have shown, is hardly the case, safe for the comparatively uniform practice of concluding inter-organizational treaties.[53] Eventually, whatever position one might take on this issue, it is important to recall that IOs' existing or non-existing capacity to create customary law does not prejudice that they are bound by such norms, even if created not by them, but by states.[54]

2. The Role of Analogous Reasoning

The second issue is the method of identifying norms of customary inter-organizational law. The established (though not undisputed) approach is to search for "a general practice accepted as law" (Art. 38(1) lit. b ICJ Statute).[55]

There is certainly no lack of practice in inter-organizational relations. Nevertheless, the identification of customary inter-organizational law faces two additional challenges. The first challenge is the aforesaid persisting dispute over whether IOs can author customary law. Secondly, as to many topics, inter-organizational practice lacks consistency. Both challenges lead to an increased degree of uncertainty.

Against this background, both practitioners and scholars have relied on analogous reasoning, understood here as a form of systemic reasoning through which uncertainties regarding the law applying to one constellation are overcome by having

[52] ILC, 'Report of the International Law Commission Seventieth Session' (n 50) 135, Conclusion 8 (1).

[53] A frequent general concern in the context of customary international law is that those who are called to apply it do not examine practice and *opinio juris* in sufficient depth, sometimes leading to mere postulations of customary rules. A full-scale account of practice and opinion between the interacting IOs as well as their respective member states, as arguably required to remedy this critique, would exceed the scope of this study. Therefore, in terms of 'fact samples', the examples and case studies given throughout this study must suffice. That being said, the omission of a comprehensive survey is bearable in the present context, as the argument made in this chapter will be a conceptual one that does not necessarily depend on an exhaustive survey of practice.

[54] See e.g. *Prosecutor v. Sam Hinga Norman* (Decision on Preliminary Motion Based on Lack of Jurisdiction) SCSL-2004-14-AR72(E) (31 May 2004), para 22; Andrew Clapham, 'Human Rights Obligations of Non-State Actors in Conflict Situations' (2006) 88 International Review of the Red Cross 491, 497 et seq.; Daugirdas, 'How and Why International Law Binds International Organizations' (n 20) 334.

[55] James Crawford, *Brownlie's Principles of Public International Law* (n 8) 23 et seqq.; Andreas von Arnauld, *Völkerrecht* (3rd edn, C F Müller 2016) 104 et seqq.; Jan Klabbers, *International Law* (2nd edn, Cambridge University Press 2017) 29 et seqq.; Markus Krajewski, *Völkerrecht* (2nd edn, Nomos 2020) 92 et seqq. Critical Jean d'Aspremont, 'The Decay of Modern Customary International Law in Spite of Scholarly Heroism' in Giuliana Ziccardi Capaldo (ed), *The Global Community Yearbook of International Law and Jurisprudence 2015* (Oxford University Press 2016) 9; Matthias Lippold, 'Reflections on Custom Critique and on Functional Equivalents in the Work of Jean d'Aspremont' (2019) 21 International Community Law Review 257.

recourse to established norms applying to other, structurally similar constellations.[56]

The leading analogy that has become formative for inter-organizational law is the one between IOs and states. All bodies of inter-organizational law that can be considered reasonably established today have been decisively informed by analogies with international legal norms governing comparable aspects of inter-state relations.[57] Perhaps most visibly, the ILC heavily relied on the VCLT and its Articles on the Responsibility of States for Internationally Wrongful Acts when drafting the VCLT-IO and the DARIO, respectively.[58] Moreover, some international legal scholars have embraced analogous reasoning as a useful tool to develop international law applying to IOs.[59]

This openness to analogies hardly comes as a surprise. Firstly, analogies have a long tradition both in domestic and international legal reasoning.[60] Secondly, given the absence of established inter-organizational law beyond certain limited areas, there is simply not much else to turn to except international legal norms applying to inter-state relations. Thirdly, analogies seem to be intuitively plausible in light of certain structural similarities between states and IOs and their respective mutual relations. Both states and IOs are legally autonomous entities, i.e. they are capable of forming their respective own *volontés distinctes*. Moreover, both are capable of possessing international rights and obligations.[61]

Therefore, and in the light of the scarcity of established customary inter-organizational norms, this section will, where appropriate, extend the analytical scope to also examine proposals to apply international norms governing inter-state relations to inter-organizational interactions by way of analogy. However, it will do so mindful of the inherent limits of analogous reasoning: For one part, the relevance of analogies for the determination of positive law beyond bearing persuasive weight is highly disputed. Moreover, analogies depend on relevant structural similarities. As will be seen, while analogies can bear considerable persuasive weight, there is a limit to analogous reasoning when it comes to making propositions on the content of customary inter-organizational law.

---

[56]Lusa Bordin (n 8) 7.

[57]ibid.

[58]ibid 4. Jan Wouters and Jed Odermatt, 'Are All International Organizations Created Equal?' (2012) 9 International Organizations Law Review 7, 13.

[59]For example, in his recently published study on the analogy between states and IOs, Bordin argued that "analogy [between states and IOs] can provide a general justification for making propositions about the content of the public international law that applies to international organizations Lusa Bordin (n 8) 8.

[60]Silja Vöneky, 'Analogy in International Law', *Max Planck Encyclopedia of Public International Law* (Oxford University Press 2008). See e.g. Hersch Lauterpacht, *Private Law Sources and Analogies of International Law* (Longmans, Green and Co 1927). Regarding the inter-organizational law of treaties see JW Schneider, Treaty-Making Power of International Organizations (Droz/Minard 1959) 117 et seq.

[61]Lusa Bordin (n 8) 75 et seqq.

II. Shards of Customary Inter-Organizational Law: The VCLT-IO, DARIO and Others

Having clarified the aforementioned points of method, it is convenient to begin the analysis with those bodies of customary inter-organizational law that are relatively established. The first such body of law is the customary inter-organizational law of treaties, as spelled out in the VCLT-IO's substantive provisions. The second body is the law of responsibility of IOs, which however is still much more in flux – the ILC's attempt to codify this body of law in the DARIO continues to spark critical responses, not least from IOs themselves.[62]

Beyond these two areas, there are hardly any elements of recognizable customary inter-organizational law. Scholarly contributions addressing this matter tend to enumerate and briefly describe the different concepts, instruments and mechanisms that have emerged in IOs' external relations. They often do so without further differentiating the relevant legal bases and without differentiating between external relations with non-member states and external relations with other IOs. Apart from treaties and other agreements, these enumerations comprise

- unilateral acts,
- active and passive legation,
- the convening of and participation in international conferences,
- the recognition of other international legal subjects, and
- the registration of treaties and depository functions.[63]

Furthermore, the enumerations often include further aspects of IOs' external relations with other entities, such as the representation of states in IOs,[64] privileges

[62]See e.g. the comments by IOs on the DARIO reproduced in UN Secretary-General, 'Responsibility of International Organizations - Comments and Information Received from Governments and International Organizations, Report of the Secretary-General' (2017) UN Doc A/72/80, para 6 et seqq. See also Moshe Hirsch, *The Responsibility of International Organizations Toward Third Parties: Some Basic Principles* (Brill 1995); Alain Pellet, 'International Organizations are Definitely not States - Cursory Remarks on the ILC Articles on the Responsibility of International Organizations' in Maurizio Ragazzi (ed.), *Responsibility of International Organizations, Essays in Memory of Sir Ian Brownlie* (Martinus Nijhoff Publishers 2013) 41 et seqq.; Wouters and Odermatt (n 58) 7 et seqq.

[63]Seyersted, *Common Law of International Organizations* (n 29) 401 et seqq.; Rensmann, 'International Organizations or Institutions, External Relations and Co-Operation' (n 28) paras 11 et seqq.; Schermers and Blokker (n 3) paras 1742 et seqq.; Crawford, *Brownlie's Principles of Public International Law* (n 8) 179 et seqq.

[64]E.g. Krajewski (n 55) 191, referencing the Vienna Convention on the Representation of States in their Relations with International Organizations of a Universal Character (adopted 14 March 1975, not yet in force) UN Doc A/CONF.67/16.

and immunities[65] or the capacity to own property,[66] which are however not practically relevant in the present context.

The enumerated instruments and concepts vary in scope and character. Importantly, not all of them can be considered to have a firm basis in customary inter-organizational law.[67]

What is even more relevant for present purposes, however, is that the aforesaid instruments and concepts, even insofar as they can be considered to have an established basis in customary inter-organizational law, in any event almost exclusively apply in direct and cooperative inter-organizational interactions.[68] Thus, they hardly go beyond the timid regulation of inter-organizational interactions that was found in inter-organizational treaties.[69]

By contrast, they are of little practical use regarding other types of interactions, notably indirect or non-cooperative ones. Rules on concluding and performing treaties, for example, do not help much in cases in which two IOs are unwilling to settle their differences in the form of a binding treaty or in a case in which one IO influences another accidentally. The interactions between the ILO and the World Bank, described in Chap. 4, and between the ILO and the ECtHR described in Chap. 5, respectively, are cases in point. The only body of customary inter-organizational law that in principle also applies to other forms of interactions is the law of IOs' responsibility. However, as a set of secondary rules, these rules necessarily presuppose the existence of primary rights and obligations.[70]

Hence, what is yet missing is an established customary inter-organizational law establishing inter-organizational rights and obligations regarding such other types of inter-organizational interactions, notably indirect or non-cooperative ones.

---

[65]Lusa Bordin (n 8) 3.

[66]Crawford, *Brownlie's Principles of Public International Law* (n 8) 182.

[67]See Rensmann, 'International Organizations or Institutions, External Relations and Co-Operation' (n 28) para 47. For instance, it is doubtful whether there is a customary right of an IO to participate in international conferences convened by another IO (notwithstanding the fact that IOs actually do so and that they might be entitled to do so by virtue of particular inter-organizational treaties, other agreements or unilateral invitations). If at all, one might infer that there is a customary obligation to refrain from participating in other IOs' events without invitation, which would however be without any practical relevance. For another example, in the case of an IO being a treaty depository, the relevant legal basis for this status is usually a treaty, not customary law. In consequence, it remains doubtful whether these instruments resemble an accurate depiction of customary inter-organizational law in every instance.

[68]One could argue that certain elements of the customary law of inter-organizational treaties, such as the rules on the performance of treaties or on treaty interpretation, also apply to indirect and non-cooperative interactive conduct of IOs, e.g. in the case in which one IO, without any direct communication, misinterprets or violates one of its obligations under an inter-organizational treaty in a way that influences the conduct of the other contracting IO. However, it would still only do so with regard to existing inter-organizational treaties, which, as illustrated in Chapter 13, are sparse and tend to be vague.

[69]See Chapter 13 and Chapter 14.

[70]ILC, 'Draft Articles on the Responsibility of International Organizations, with Commentaries' (n 8) 46.

In the absence of consistent practice and articulated opinio juris, the main drivers of the development and systematization of such other rules have been scholarly contributions. Few proposals have been made, all of which strive to 'close the gap' by expounding additional norms of inter-organizational law that would, if established, arguably cover all types of inter-organizational interactions.

III. An Inter-Organizational Prohibition of Interference?

Some commentators propose that every IO has a sphere of jurisdiction which other IOs have to respect in inter-organizational interactions. Among others, Matthias Ruffert has proposed a prohibition of interference (*Störungsverbot*) to apply between IOs.[71]

1. The Proposal of a Prohibition of Interference

According to Ruffert, there is evidence of an emerging international norm according to which IOs must not interfere with another IO's scope of competences.[72]

Ruffert's main example are conflicts arising in situations in which two IOs apply and interpret the same international legal norm, e.g. the same treaty, in a diverging manner. While he notes that one IO's interpretation of a treaty is not formally binding on another, he acknowledges that one IO's interpretive activity might still cause "disturbances" within that other IO.[73] To address this issue, he suggests that there was an international legal norm *in statu nascendi* containing a prohibition of interference, pursuant to which IOs, especially their dispute settlement organs, must

[71] Ruffert suggests that the emergent duty to refrain from interferences was complemented by another emerging international legal norm, which required states to enable the IO to fulfil this duty. In this regard, an IO's member states had an obligation to respect the allocation of competences vis-à-vis other IOs when enacting secondary law and to formulate the mandate of their IO's dispute settlement mechanism in a way that prevents interferences with other IOs' scope of competences. As an example for the latter duty, Ruffert suggests that the narrow wording of Art. 7 WTO-DSU could violate that duty insofar it would affect the ILO Supervisory Bodies' competences, Matthias Ruffert, 'Zuständigkeitsgrenzen Internationaler Organisationen im institutionellen Rahmen der internationalen Gemeinschaft' (2000) 38 Archiv des Völkerrechts 129, 164; similar Jan Neumann, 'Die materielle und prozessuale Koordination völkerrechtlicher Ordnungen - Die Problematik paralleler Streitbeilegungsverfahren am Beispiel des Schwertfisch-Falls' (2001) 61 Zeitschrift für ausländisches öffentliches Recht und Völkerrecht 529, 559 et seqq. See also Erik Denters, 'New Challenges to IMF Jurisdiction' (1998) 29 Netherlands Yearbook of International Law 3, 10.

[72] ibid 160 et seqq.

[73] ibid 160 et seq. ("Störungen").

not interpret international legal norms in a way that interferes with the functioning of another IO.[74]

Ruffert derives this emerging rule from what he perceives as the role of IOs within the international community: to execute the tasks bestowed on them. The conferral of competences to an IO, he argues, is formally undertaken by the IO's member states.[75]

> In essence, however, it is the international community which constitutes itself for the joint execution of tasks in a certain subject area or region.[76]

Building on this idea of states acting on behalf of the international community, he further reasons that:

> [t]he concept of a joint execution of tasks by the international community must [...] reasonably have its institutional mirror image in the allocation of competences among the particular organizations, which (...) may exist in the said prohibition of interference.[77]

To achieve the allocation of competences among IOs, Ruffert suggests that the allocation of competences between an IO and its member states has external effect, i.e. can also be held against other IOs. Other IOs must not interfere in the exercise of competences an IO has been attributed by its member states.[78] As evidence of the emerging prohibition to interfere, he cites a variety of occasions in which IOs' member states have sought to minimise conflicts.[79]

Ruffert limits his approach, arguing that the prohibition to interfere resulted only in a negative duty to abstain from interferences. By contrast, it did not encompass a positive duty to cooperate with a view to minimize the risk of interferences.[80]

---

[74] ibid 161.

[75] Ruffert's concept of an IO's scope of competences is voluntarist in nature. He argues that the respective scopes are determined by the sovereign member states and the extent of their will to cooperate and integrate in a certain field, ibid 163.

[76] ibid 161 (translation by author).

[77] ibid 161 et seq. (translation by author).

[78] ibid 161.

[79] Relevant for the context of this study is especially his (debatable) invocation of the WTO's 1996 Singapore Declaration (WTO Ministerial Conference, Singapore Ministerial Declaration (13 December 1996) WT/MIN(96)/DEC), ibid 162.

[80] ibid 162 et seq. He also limits his proposal by arguing that his idea of a prohibition of interference only applied to IOs that are "on the same level" ('...die als Völkerrechtssubjekte gleichgeordnet in der Völkerrechtsordnung stehen.'), excluding those IOs which are members of other IOs, ibid 164. Neumann goes further and accepts a duty for international dispute settlement bodies to ask bodies established under other treaties about potential disturbances, Neumann, 'Die materielle und prozessuale Koordination völkerrechtlicher Ordnungen - Die Problematik paralleler Streitbeilegungsverfahren am Beispiel des Schwertfisch-Falls' (n 71) 567.

2. Discussion

Ruffert's proposal is highly relevant in the context of this study. His leading example of one IO causing interference by interpreting the law of another epitomizes the interactions between the ILO and the ECtHR presented in Chap. 5.[81] But even beyond interpretation, a general prohibition to interfere would arguably provide a basic element of a common inter-organizational legal standard governing inter-organizational interactions, and could serve as a safeguard for the ILO's model vis-à-vis the Bank or the CoE.

Nevertheless, the idea of a prohibition of interference also raises points of concern, which will now be addressed in turn.

a) Externalization of the Constitutional Allocation of Competences

Firstly, the proposal downplays the distinction between IOs' institutional laws and inter-organizational law by attributing external effect to IOs' institutional legal rules on competence allocation. However, as shown above, externalization requires either the other IO's consent or an inter-organizational norm pursuant to which the internal distribution of competences between the IO and its member states is legally relevant in the inter-organizational relationship.[82] The proposal presents neither. Instead, it presumes a 'masterplan' of the international community to constitute itself in separated institutional frameworks, the legal basis of which remains unclear.

b) The Ideal of Clear-Cut Competences and the Reality of Competencial Overlaps

Secondly, the idea of a prohibition of interference rests on the presumption of a planful and clear-cut separation of competences between IOs. However, this presumption is highly idealized. A reasonably clear-cut delimitation of issues and, accessory thereto, of institutional spheres of jurisdiction, is hardly possible in practice. From the start, there is much thematic overlap between "social justice/ decent work" (ILO), "development/poverty eradication" (World Bank) and "protection of human rights" (ECtHR/ECSR). Given these substantial and rather obvious overlaps, it is difficult to believe that a clear-cut separation of competences among IOs was intended.

---

[81] Moreover, it is reminiscent of the World Bank reviewing (and affirming) the compatibility of the EWI with ILO conventions, as described in Chapter 4 C. II. 3.

[82] See the discussion in Chapter 9 A.

Neither do the examined IOs' constituent instruments themselves presume a clear-cut separation of competences.[83] Rather, all three IOs' institutional laws envisage other IOs working on similar issues. Art. 12(1) ILO Constitution and Art. V(8) lit. a IBRD-AoA even explicitly speak of IOs working in "related fields". Art. 1 lit. c CoE Statute contains an explicit subsidiarity clause, Art. 35(2) lit. b ECHR envisages "substantially the same" cases being brought before other bodies, and the ESC widely covers matters falling within the ILO's purview and, for this reason, contains an institutional link and a working relationship with the International Labour Office.

Finally, each IO's mandate and competences can develop dynamically. Therefore, even if there was no overlap when the respective IOs were founded, it may appear later.

It is questionable if a prohibition to interfere would be viable in such situations of (dynamic) overlap. If one assumes that the international community has constituted itself in the form of different IOs to perform certain tasks, one would also have to assume that the thematic overlap is part of that plan. It remains open what, under these circumstances, the necessary threshold for a "disturbance" would be. This is particularly relevant because, as illustrated in Part I of this study, the very same conduct can be considered an orderly discharge of one IO's functions and a disturbance of another IO at the same time, depending on the perspective.

c) Delimiting Competences in the Inter-Organizational Constellation

Thirdly, and related to the problem of a dynamic overlap of competences, there is a conceptual problem with the idea of giving external effect to the competence allocation between an IO and its member states: In the legal relationship between the IO and its members, the IO's competences are delimited 'dialectically' by having recourse to member states' sovereignty.[84] This happens either 'formally', by insisting that IOs have only those competences which the states have consented to attribute to them (as the attributed powers doctrine suggests), or 'materially', by pondering the need to effective execution of the IO's mandate against states' sovereignty (as required under the implied powers doctrine).[85] Thus, because it is established that sovereignty protects an exclusive sphere of jurisdiction against

[83]Virginia A Leary, 'The WHO Case: Implications for Specialized Agencies' in Laurence Boisson De Chazournes and Philippe Sands (eds), *International Law, the International Court of Justice and Nuclear Weapons* (Cambridge University Press 1999) 119 et seq. Niels M Blokker, 'Proliferation of International Organizations: An Exploratory Introduction' in Niels M Blokker and Henry G Schermers (eds), *Proliferation of International Organizations* (Brill Nijhoff 2000) 28.

[84]*Nationality Decrees in Tunis and Morocco* (Advisory Opinion) PCIJ Rep Series B No 4, 24; Crawford, *Brownlie's Principles of Public International Law* (n 8) 189. Sometimes, this is explicitly provided for in the constituent instrument, e.g. in Art. 2(7) UN Charter.

[85]Even more, the implied powers doctrine, while being less protective of sovereignty, exists for the very reason that there is a need to justify limitations of sovereignty.

interference by the IO, and because the basic idea of this sphere and its scope is (reasonably) clear, IOs' competences can be defined 'dialectically', using member state sovereignty as a limiting counterposition.

By contrast, in the inter-organizational constellation, it proves difficult to identify a comparable exclusive right and, therefore, a counterposition for 'dialectically' delimiting two IOs' competences. The existence of any exclusive sphere of jurisdiction *that another IO is legally required to respect* is rather uncertain. In consequence, it remains unclear how IOs' competences should be delimited if they do not 'collide' with sovereignty, but with competences of another IO which are themselves in need of delimitation. Notably, an attempt at delimiting two IOs' implied powers, each based on considerations of effective achievement of the IOs' respective objectives, could easily result in an unfettered clash of effectivity rationales.[86] Ruffert's prohibition of interference presupposes that there is a solution for this issue and that IOs' spheres of competences can be delimited vis-à-vis each other with reasonable clarity. Thus, in a way, it avoids part of the problem altogether.

3. Conclusion

Ruffert's proposal is highly relevant for present purposes, Yet, it faces noteworthy conceptual problems. By externalizing IOs' provisions on competences, it diffuses the distinction between constitutional and inter-organizational norms. Furthermore, it relies on an idealized clear-cut separation of jurisdictional spheres between IOs, which often does not exist in reality. Finally, it leaves open how, and by which standard, IOs' competences should be delimited in the inter-organizational constellation.

A prohibition to interfere could arguably provide useful normative guidance if its implicit presumptions were given, i.e. if it was clear if and how IOs' jurisdictional spheres can be determined with external effect vis-à-vis other IOs, and if it was clear by which normative benchmark two IOs' jurisdictional spheres should be reconciled with each other. As will be seen further below, these two underlying issues are fundamental issues of inter-organizational law.

IV. A Law of Inter-Organizational Good-Neighbourliness?

A second strand of argument goes beyond delimitations of competences and seeks to apply customary rules that put IOs on 'good terms' with one another. In this manner, Niels Blokker proposes an "inter-organizational principle of good neighbourliness".

[86] See also the discussion in Chapter 18 A. I.

1. Blokker's Proposal of "Inter-Organizational Good-Neighbourliness"

Blokker's proposal is based on the observation that it was difficult to delimit IOs' competences at the time of their creation, notwithstanding occasional provisions in IOs' constituent instruments to this end.[87] As to the subsequent "life" of IOs, he observes that attempts to delimit competences mostly occurred on an ad hoc basis and were initiated either by powerful states or by IOs themselves.[88] In search for a more principled approach to inter-organizational coordination, Blokker suggests an inter-organizational principle of good-neighbourliness. He compares this principle to the principle of respect for the independence and sovereignty in inter-state relations,[89] arguing that,

> [a]s for states, it is often no longer possible for organizations to carry out their functions independently. In carrying out their tasks, international organizations should be aware of, and take into account, the tasks of organizations that are competent in a neighbouring field.[90]

Blokker suggests that inter-organizational good-neighbourliness would not, as in inter-state relations, be territory-based. Instead, since IOs' had usually been endowed with some degree of independence with regard to the fulfilment of a specific mandate, he argues that the inter-organizational principle of good-neighbourliness would be function-based.[91]

Blokker recognizes both a negative and a positive dimension of the principle. In its negative dimension, the principle prohibits interferences by one IO in the domain of another. Blokker describes this as a "hands-off principle" that would enable the "peaceful coexistence" between IOs.[92] The positive dimension aims at active cooperation between IOs for the pursuit of their objectives.[93]

2. Nature and Content of (Good-)Neighbourliness in International Law

Blokker's proposal draws on the existing inter-state customary law of neighbourliness/good-neighbourliness. Before discussing it, it is therefore convenient to briefly revisit the nature and contents of neighbourliness in international law.

[87] This, he argues, was particularly true for general organizations, as any ex ante delimitation would be "difficult to reconcile with the usual dynamics that a 'general' organization is expected to display", Blokker (n 83) 28.

[88] ibid 29.

[89] ibid 30. Drawing on earlier suggestions by Felice Morgenstern, *Legal Problems of International Organizations* (Grotius Publications 1986) 26.

[90] Blokker (n 83) 30.

[91] ibid.

[92] ibid 32.

[93] ibid.

a) Neighbourliness Between Contingent States

The law of neighbourliness is a body of law governing, at the outset, the relations of geographically proximate states, notably those sharing one border.[94] Its underlying rationale is to provide an adequate balance between each state's right to freely use its territory (a derivative of state sovereignty and the inviolability of borders), and the prohibition to cause damage to other states and their territories.[95] It comprises a set of international obligations. A state's territory, especially the border area, must not be used in a way that will cause damage to the neighbouring state, and hazardous use by third actors must not be tolerated or permitted.[96] When using its territory, a state must take into consideration the legitimate interests of neighbouring states and must prevent or mitigate transboundary harm.[97] This amounts to an obligation to exercise due diligence in order to ascertain whether a planned activity can cause transboundary harm, for example by carrying out impact assessments.[98] Neighbouring states must inform, notify and consult each other regarding potential

---

[94]The law of neighbourliness has gained particular relevance in international environmental law, where it found mention e.g. in the 1972 Stockholm Declaration on the Human Environment (UN, 'Report of the United Nations Conference on the Human Environment' (5-16 June 1972) UN Doc A/CONF.48/18/Rev.1, 3), Principles 7, 21, 22, and 24, the 1992 Rio Declaration on Environment and Development (UN, 'Report of the United Nations Conference on Environment and Development' (3-14 June 1992) UN Doc A/CONF.151/26 (Vol. I), 6), Principles 2, 13, 15, 18, and 19, and in a number of international treaties, e.g. the 1997 UN Convention on the Law of the Non-Navigational Uses of International Watercourses (adopted 21 May 1997, entered into force 17 August 2014) 2999 UNTS 1, preambular clause 6). In other treaties, the customary obligations are embodied in certain procedural and substantive provisions, e.g. in Arts. 7 et seqq. of the 1975 Statutes of the River Uruguay (adopted 26 February 1975, entered into force 18 September 1976) 1295 UNTS 331 (1975 Statute of the River Uruguay).

[95]As per the tribunal in the *Case Concerning Filleting in the Gulf of St. Lawrence*, "the law of neighbourliness is intended to enable neighbour States to avoid frictions, reconciling their divergent interests through a continuous cooperation in all activities comporting a necessary interpenetration between them", *Case Concerning Filleting within the Gulf of St. Lawrence (Canada v. France)* (Decision of 17 July 1986) (1990) XIX RIAA 225, 273; Laurence Boisson De Chazournes and Danio Campanelli, 'Neighbour States', *Max Planck Encyclopedia of Public International Law* (Oxford Universtiy Press 2006) 13; Elena Basheska, 'The Position of the Good Neighbourliness Principle in International and EU Law' in Dimitry Kochenov and Elena Basheska (eds), *Good Neighbourliness in the European Legal Context* (Brill 2015) 24.

[96]*Trail Smelter Arbitration (United States v. Canada)* (Award of 11 March 1941) (1941) III RIAA 1905, 1963; *Corfu Channel Case (United Kingdom v Albania)* (Merits) [1949] ICJ Reports 4, 22; Boisson De Chazournes and Campanelli (n 95) 11. See also *Lac Lanoux Arbitration (France v. Spain)* (1957) XII RIAA 281, 301.

[97]So-called principle of prevention, *Pulp Mills on the River Uruguay (Argentina v. Uruguay)* (Merits) [2010] ICJ Reports 14, 55 et seq.; *Certain Activities Carried Out by Nicaragua in the Border Area (Costa Rica v. Nicaragua) and Construction of a Road in Costa Rica along the San Juan River (Nicaragua v. Costa Rica)* [2015] ICJ Reports 665, para 104; Boisson De Chazournes and Campanelli (n 95) 11.

[98]*Certain Activities Carried Out by Nicaragua in the Border Area (Costa Rica v. Nicaragua) and Construction of a Road in Costa Rica along the San Juan River (Nicaragua v. Costa Rica)* (n 97) para 104.

or actual harm.[99] On the other hand, every state has to tolerate its neighbouring states' lawful activity carried out on their respective territory up to a certain threshold of gravity.[100]

b) Good-Neighbourliness As a Hesitant Conceptual Expansion

The concept of *good*-neighbourliness seeks to expand the scope of application of the law of neighbourliness's core rationale beyond the immediate context of territorial frontier zones.[101] Good-neighbourliness aims at maintaining and promoting friendly relations among states more generally, including the respect for sovereignty, territorial integrity and internal autonomy.[102] The rationale behind this expansion is to account for the growing interdependence among states.[103]

The concept of good-neighbourliness has remained less contoured than the abovementioned law of neighbourliness.[104] The concept's legal content is difficult to pinpoint. Efforts of the UNGA to enhance its contours have remained inconclusive.[105] One relatively established aspect of good-neighbourliness is the rejection of

---

[99] ibid.; Boisson De Chazournes and Campanelli (n 95) 11.

[100] Boisson De Chazournes and Campanelli (n 95) 11. This was also observed by the UNGA Sub-Committee on Good Neighbourliness as an obligation forming part of good neighbourliness, Basheska (n 95) 41.

[101] Boisson De Chazournes and Campanelli (n 95) 4 et seqq. For a synonymous use of both terms see Dimitry Kochenov and Elena Basheska, 'Introduction: Good Neighbourliness Inside and Outside the Union' in Dimitry Kochenov and Elena Basheska (eds), *Good Neighbourliness in the European Legal Context* (Brill 2015) 22.

[102] Jenks, writing during the Cold War, held that "[g]ood neighbourliness includes the obligation to respect the political independence and economic and social system of one's neighbour", Clarence Wilfred Jenks, *Law in the World Community* (Longmans 1967) 91.

[103] Basheska (n 95) 28.

[104] Drawing on a dictum by the ICJ in the 1951 *Haya de la Torre* case, the legal nature of good-neighbourliness has been called into dispute, *Haya de la Torre Case (Colombia v Peru)* [1951] ICJ Reports 71, 83. Given that good-neighbourliness is explicitly mentioned in Clause 5 of the Preamble of the UN Charter and in Art. 74 UN Charter, there is reason to believe that the concept has at least some legal-normative content, similar Ulrich Fastenrath, 'Art. 74' in Bruno Simma and others (eds), *The Charter of the United Nations - A Commentary, vol II* (3rd edn, Oxford University Press 2013) para 2. Still, its foundation remains unclear. Whereas some consider it to be rooted in customary international law, others perceive it as a general principle of law, Basheska (n 95) 34.

[105] In the early 1980s, the UNGA decided to draft an international instrument on good-neighbourliness. In 1981, following a Romanian initiative, the General Assembly decided to prepare a 'suitable international document' on good-neighbourliness. The UNGA's Sixth Committee even created a Sub-Committee on Good Neighbourliness to elucidate the meaning and the components of the concept. However, despite several years of work, the UNGA repeatedly missed the majority necessary to adopt the Sub-Committee's reports, until the Sub-Committee's work was finally discontinued in 1990, Iftene Pop, *Components of Good Neighbourliness between States* (Editura RAI 1991); Sompong Sucharitkul, 'The Principles of Good-Neighborliness in International Law' (1996) Golden Gate University School of Law Publications, Paper 559 <https://digitalcommons.law.ggu.edu/cgi/viewcontent.cgi?article=1559&context=pubs> accessed

zones of influence or domination,[106] which moves good-neighbourliness in the vicinity of sovereign equality, non-intervention and self-determination of states. Moreover, good-neighbourliness entails an element of good faith.[107] By way of a tentative conclusion, good-neighbourliness seems to aim for a 'good faith-use of sovereignty' in order to preserve other states' rights emanating from their own sovereignty.

c) Good-Neighbourliness in the Context of IOs

In the context of IOs, (good-)neighbourliness has hardly ever occurred in positive law. Insofar as it has played a role, two constellations can be distinguished: Firstly, IOs can be tasked to promote good-neighbourliness among states.[108] Secondly, an IO can itself be obliged to be a 'good neighbour'. The most important example for the latter is the EU's neighbourhood policy.[109]

That being said, both constellations concern good-neighbourliness between states. Even the EU's neighbourhood policy is both in law and in practice confined to the Union's relations with neighbouring *states*, while the EU treaties include

---

26 April 2020, 7. More recent UN practice has not produced greater clarity, see Boisson De Chazournes and Campanelli (n 95) 26 et seq.

[106]Sucharitkul (n 105) 8.

[107]For instance, the tribunal in the *Iron Rhine arbitration* referred to good-neighbourliness when determining whether the Netherlands could reasonably refrain from consulting with Belgium prior to the designation an area of its territory to which Belgium had contractual rights of transit as a nature reserve, *Arbitration Regarding the Iron Rhine ("Ijzeren Rijn") Railway (Belgium v. Netherlands)* (Decision of 24 May 2005) (2005) XXVII RIAA 35, 78.

[108]In some cases, IOs are mandated to fulfil some of the states' obligation stemming from the law of neighbourliness concerning the administration of frontier territory or specific territorial features. For example, under the 1975 Statute of the River Uruguay, the Administrative Commission of the River Uruguay (CARU) is endowed with certain regulatory, executive, administrative, technical and conciliatory competences, see *Pulp Mills on the River Uruguay (Argentina v. Uruguay)* (n 97) para 88. By their mandate and their capacities, IOs are frequently able to contribute to the promotion of good-neighbourliness among states. Similarly, the UNGA Legal Committee's Subcommittee on Good Neighbourliness contemplated actions of IOs, in particular regional and subregional IOs, in developing and strengthening good-neighbourliness, UNGA, Development and Strengthening of Good-Neighbourliness between States, Report of the Sub-Committee on Good-Neighbourliness' (1988) UN Doc A/C.6/43/L.11, 5. These considerations could be taken as an indicator that the concept of good-neighbourliness is expanding to include IOs and their mutual relations. Yet, nothing in the records indicates that the Subcommittee envisaged the existence or development of good-neighbourliness among IOs. Rather, both the Subcommittee's mandate and its reports explicitly referred to good-neighbourliness "between States". Even if one were to assume otherwise, the report indicates that the Subcommittee's members did not consider their work final but explicitly considered it provisional, with some delegations voicing doubts as to whether agreement was at all possible without further deliberations. Against this background, the contemplated role of IOs has been understood as promoting good-neighbourliness among states, not among each other.

[109]Building on political precursors, the neighbourhood policy was included in the EU's primary law by the Lisbon Treaty (see Art. 8 TEU), see Kochenov and Basheska (n 101) 10.

separate provisions on the EU's relations with other IOs, none of which relies on the law of good-neighbourliness.[110]

3. Discussion

The idea of inter-organizational good neighbourliness, although intended to be a brief scholarly proposal still to be developed, merits closer examination. Arguably the strongest reason for Blokker's idea is that the legal consequences it would trigger seem desirable. Inter-organizational good-neighbourliness would mean that IOs must not exercise their competences in a way that would cause damage to the 'neighbouring' IO. Every IO would have to take legitimate interests of others into account and exercise due diligence to avoid 'trans-functional harm'. They would have to inform, notify and consult each other if any such harm existed or was likely. Finally, each IO could demand others to tolerate its lawful behaviour up to a certain threshold of gravity. This legal consequence would have significantly helped to govern, say, the interactions between the ILO and the World Bank observed in Chap. 4. Arguably, under a paradigm of good-neighbourliness, the ILO could have demanded from the Bank to consider the EWI's implications on ILO standards and country initiatives, and perhaps even to consult with the ILO.

That being said, the idea to apply the law of good-neighbourliness among IOs seems to assume that the inter-organizational constellation is similar to the situation among states for which that body of law was developed and to which it is tailored. As will be seen in the following, however, there are important structural peculiarities to be considered.

a) The "Hands Off" Principle and the Distinction Between the 'Neighbours'

Firstly, good-neighbourliness aims at providing equitable middle ground in the coordination of *exclusive* spheres of jurisdiction. In doing so, it implicitly presupposes the existence of such exclusive spheres in the first place. The "hands off" principle mentioned by Blokker has its roots here.

However, as mentioned before, IOs' spheres of jurisdiction are virtually never exclusive to begin with.[111] Instead, functional overlap between IOs is the rule rather than the exception. In consequence, IOs may well be required—and perhaps also

[110]This comprises 'neighbouring' IOs like the CoE, the OSCE and the OECD (Art. 220(1) TFEU). Unlike Art. 8 TEU, Art. 220 TEU does not embody any reference to good-neighbourliness with regard to the relations between the EU and other IOs. The same is true for those provisions in the EU treaties governing the EU's relations with other, non-neighbouring states. Neither do the substantive, value-oriented provisions in the EU treaties which provide a general substantive framework for EU external relations (Art. 205 TFEU, Arts. 2 and 21 TEU) include a principle of good-neighbourliness that would extend to the EU's relations with other IOs.

[111]For a more comprehensive discussion, see below, VI. 1.

entitled—to exercise jurisdiction in their 'neighbour's' province. Even more, as to many tasks, IOs may find themselves being 'cohabitants' rather than 'neighbours'.

The lack of exclusive spheres of jurisdiction changes the context within which coordination and cooperation take place. Most importantly, Blokker's negative dimension of inter-organizational good-neighbourliness would arguably only apply to the extent that there is clearly no functional overlap whatsoever between two IOs. In other words, a "hands off" principle is hardly viable where there is no exclusive sphere of jurisdiction.

b) The Obligation to Cooperate and the Demarcation of the 'Neighbourhood'

Contrary to the "hands off" principle, the positive dimension of good-neighbourliness proposed by Blokker—the duty to cooperate—does not necessarily depend on exclusive jurisdictional spheres. However, for any neighbourly duty to cooperate, one would still have to identify who the obliged 'neighbours' are. Therefore, there is a need to ascertain which IOs are 'close enough' to one another in order to trigger neighbourly obligations and thus form part of the same 'neighbourhood'.

Despite the territorial origins of neighbourliness and good-neighbourliness,[112] neighbours in the legal sense do not necessarily have to be in close physical or geographical proximity to each other. Since the rationale of good-neighbourliness is to achieve a reconciliation of conflicting rights and interests, it is in principle conceivable that the protection extends to all those which are affected by conduct of one actor.

That being said, the existing law of neighbourliness between states is clearest where the demarcation is clearest as well—in the constellation of transboundary issues between adjacent states. The more one departs from this territorial context, the less defined the outer boundaries of the 'neighbourhood' become even in inter-state relations.

In inter-organizational relations, these outer boundaries are arguably even harder to determine. IOs' fields of work are, as Blokker rightly argues, not defined territorially, but functionally. Depending on the particular function, an IO's 'neighbourhood' may be significantly larger than any state's. To recall, the number of IOs engaging in multi-institutional labour governance alongside the ILO is

---

[112] At the outset, neighbourliness and good-neighbourliness have been, and remain today, "concepts of a basically territorial nature", Boisson De Chazournes and Campanelli (n 95) 8. The law of neighbourliness has evolved to adapt to new circumstances, including changes in the law. However, these developments have still always retained a territorial element, ibid 12; Sucharitkul (n 105) 9 et seq. Even in the context of the EU's neighbourhood policy, the neighbourhood is understood territorially. As the differences in wording between Art. 8 TEU and Art. 217 TFEU illustrate, good-neighbourliness applies only to the EU's neighbouring countries, not to other countries the EU associates itself with through agreements. In a similar vein Kochenov and Basheska (n 101) 11.

remarkably vast.[113] An inter-organizational principle of good-neighbourliness would thus have to deal with an inbuilt higher degree of uncertainty about which IOs can be considered 'neighbours' and thus to cooperate with each other.

c) The Unclear Legal Parameters for Cooperation

Finally, the proposed neighbourly duty to cooperate implicitly presumes that the legal parameters within which cooperation takes place is clear. These parameters are relevant because they define both the manner in which cooperation take place and the outer limits of cooperation, i.e. which items are (or may be left) 'off the table'.

Regarding neighbourly cooperation among states, the legal parameters are reasonably clear: States encounter each other on the basis of sovereign equality and its corollaries, including each state's *prima facie* exclusive jurisdiction over territory and its permanent population, the obligation to settle disputes by peaceful means, the prohibition of the use of force, the prohibition of intervention and the principle of equal rights and self-determination of peoples.[114] These parameters are further specified by other rules of international law applicable to the particular cooperating states' respective relations.

The legal parameters contour the process of cooperation and its possible outcome, as well as the content and the limits of states' duty to cooperate.[115] For example, while states are under an obligation to work towards an equitable solution, every state continues to have the right to political autonomy and territorial integrity. Similarly, in finding common ground, the interests of either side have to be considered to be of *prima facie* equal weight and value.[116]

By contrast, in the inter-organizational constellation, the legal parameters for cooperation are much less clear. IOs are not sovereign, they each have unique and widely diverging characteristics, their ambits widely overlap, and it is open whether they can claim from one another respect and non-interference regarding any part of their jurisdictional spheres.

---

[113] Chapter 3 A. I.

[114] Alfred Verdross and Bruno Simma, *Universelles Völkerrecht* (3rd edn, Duncker & Humblot 1984) 272 et seqq.; Kokott, 'Souveräne Gleichheit und Demokratie im Völkerrecht' (n 42) 520; Crawford, *Brownlie's Principles of Public International Law* (n 8) 447; von Arnauld (n 55) 129; Krajewski (n 55) 168 et seqq.

[115] The Declaration on Principles of International Law Concerning Friendly Relations and Co-Operation among States in Accordance with the Charter of the United Nations, UNGA Res 2625 (XXV) (24 October 1970) UN Doc A/RES/2625(XXV) (Friendly Relations Declaration) speaks of a "duty of States to co-operate with one another in accordance with the Charter" (principle (d)).

[116] E.g. resulting in the principle of equidistance, *North Sea Continental Shelf Cases (Federal Republic of Germany v. Denmark/Federal Republic of Germany v. Netherlands)* [1969] ICJ Reports 3, 47.

This, however, can make cooperation immensely more complex and difficult. This is already true *without* a duty to cooperate. It is one thing to cooperate to find a practical and satisfactory distribution of tasks, but it is quite another thing to incidentally negotiate general coordinates of the mutual relationship at the same time. For example, the ILO and the World Bank can agree to cooperate on individual projects and initiatives (which they have done and could also do in other instances). Yet, they will be reluctant to take steps that would indicate, say, the relative importance of labour governance through tripartite social dialogue as compared to removing regulatory obstacles for businesses. What is more, they would try to avoid the impression that issues that are vital to them are subject to negotiation, e.g. the Bank's obligation to abstain from political activity.

As the EWI episode showcases, there is no clear separation between technical and underlying 'political' issues. Instead, both dimensions are often inseparably intertwined, with fundamental questions flaring up even in the context of ostensibly technical matters. It may be suspected that the reluctance of the World Bank and the ILO to cooperate on a broader basis is in part fuelled by such complexities.

Against this background, assuming a neighbourly duty to cooperate would increase the urgency for the cooperating IOs to agree not only on specific issues, but also, incidentally, on the parameters of cooperation. At the same time, it would provide little normative guidance on how to do so. This is a significant structural issue: IOs engage in cooperation as 'functionally charged' actors: They each bring their own governance model to the fore, which they have to adhere to, not least to demonstrate their effectiveness and thus their continuing relevance to their constituents. Moreover, as seen in Part II, IOs' own institutional laws structurally prioritize the pursuit of their own agenda over the governance models, needs and demands of the respective other IOs. To ease the ensuing tension, normative guidance is required, e.g. as to the relative 'weight' of their mandates, standpoints and interests or issues that each IO can legitimately claim to be non-negotiable. Arguably, any inter-organizational duty to cooperate among 'neighbouring' IOs would only be viable if at the same time, greater clarity as to the legal parameters is achieved.

4. Conclusion

Blokker's proposal of inter-organizational good-neighbourliness is of high relevance for purposes of this study. Its intended legal consequences seem desirable. However, an inter-organizational law of good-neighbourliness relies on assumptions that need closer reflection. Similar to Ruffert's proposal, it does not sufficiently take into account that IOs' respective jurisdictional spheres are non-exclusive and overlap. In addition, the outer boundary of the 'neighbourhood', determining which IOs owe neighbourly obligations to each other, remains blurred. The same is true for the legal parameters for cooperartion between the 'neighbouring' IOs—and hence the normative backdrop against which an equitable reconciliation of interests is pursued.

To be sure, these findings do not mean that good-neighbourliness should be rejected as a principle to govern inter-organizational interactions. However, the mere desirability of the legal consequences alone cannot justify the transposition and application of the law of good-neighbourliness as it has developed between states. Further work has to be done to address the questions lying at the core of the proposal's implicit presumptions.[117]

*V. An Obligation to Cooperate in Good Faith (***Pactum de Negotiando***)?*

A duty to inter-organizational cooperation has also been derived from other normative bases than good-neighbourliness. Christian Tietje argues that IOs have a duty to cooperate with each other pursuant to an inter-organizational *pactum de negotiando*.[118] Despite the 'contractual' terminology, he understands this *pactum de negotiando*—the duty to cooperate with a view to reaching an agreement in the future—to exist irrespectively of an inter-organizational treaty providing for it.[119]

Tietje bases his argument on what he perceives as an inbuilt tension of international organization: On the one hand, IOs, being international legal subjects, (in his view) had an exclusive sphere of jurisdiction, conferred onto them by their constituent instruments, as well as the duty to fulfil their mandate effectively.[120] At the same time, there was an overlap of IOs' jurisdictional spheres. The combination of

---

[117] See Chapter 19.

[118] Tietje, 'Global Governance and Inter-Agency Co-Operation in International Economic Law' (n 4) 513 and Tietje, 'The Duty to Cooperate in International Economic Law and Beyond' in Jost Delbrück (ed) *International Law of Cooperation and State Sovereignty* (Duncker & Humblot 2001) 49 et seqq. On such duties to cooperate in general see *North Sea Continental Shelf Cases (Federal Republic of Germany v. Denmark/Federal Republic of Germany v. Netherlands)* (n 116) 47; *Case concerning Claims arising out of Decisions of the Mixed Graeco-German Arbitral Tribunal set up under Article 304 in Part X of the Treaty of Versailles (Greece v. Federal Republic of Germany) (Award of 26 January 1972)* (1974) XIX RIAA 27, 54 et seqq.; Ulrich Beyerlin, 'Pactum de contrahendo und pactum de negotiando im Völkerrecht?' (1976) 36 Zeitschrift für ausländisches öffentliches Recht und Völkerrecht, 407.

[119] It is not entirely clear whether Tietje understands the suggested duty to cooperate as an element of the inter-organizational legal relationship or as a duty under each IO's institutional law. If the latter is meant, such a duty might well be possible, but would have to be argued for each IO separately, and any successful establishment for one IO would not automatically have legal effects vis-à-vis other IOs. At several points, Tietje invokes IOs' constitutional provisions, e.g. the WTO agreement, Tietje, 'Global Governance and Inter-Agency Co-Operation in International Economic Law' (n 4) 513, which would indeed support the latter reading. On the other hand, he seems to derive this duty from a common principle of cooperation applicable among states, Christian Tietje, 'Die völkerrechtliche Kooperationspflicht im Spannungsverhältnis Welthandel/Umweltschutz und ihre Bedeutung für die europäische Umweltblume' [2000] Europarecht 285, 293.

[120] Tietje, 'Global Governance and Inter-Agency Co-Operation in International Economic Law' (n 4) 511.

exclusivity and overlap, Tietje argues, rendered inter-organizational cooperation a matter of necessity.[121]

As to the content of the duty to cooperate, Tietje argues that the *pactum de negotiando* encompassed

> more than an obligation to simply negotiate, but rather (...) a far-reaching obligation for international co-operation with the aim of achieving a mutually satisfactory solution. In order to fulfil the duty to co-operate in inter-agency relations, the respected organizations and their organs are thus obliged to conduct legal meaningful [sic], good faith efforts to solve the described problems of overlapping jurisdictions.[122]

Tietje's proposal has the advantage of embracing that there is an inherent and inevitable jurisdictional overlap between IOs. In this context, it desirably strengthens the case for cooperation among IOs.

Still, from the perspective of positive law, several issues remain open. Firstly, the necessity to cooperate mentioned in the proposal is not automatically a necessity *recognized by law*. In other words, there has to be a legal norm according to which coordination and the pursuit of goals shall be achieved through cooperation. It is, however, already questionable if a general international obligation to cooperate exists among states. While there are numerous treaties requiring cooperation in one or the other way, the existence of a general obligation has been controversially discussed for decades. Art. 1(3) UN Charter states it as one of the UN's purposes to "achieve cooperation in solving international problems of an economic, social, cultural, or humanitarian character." Arts. 55 and 56 UN Charter mention cooperation as a means to pursue the objectives named in these articles. The Friendly Relations Declaration does not specify the meaning of cooperation further. International practice has remained no less ambiguous and diffuse.[123] This has led a range of scholars to conclude that no general duty to cooperate exists among states.[124] Even if one were to take the opposite view, it would be difficult to isolate more specific contents of a general duty to cooperate, which requires not only to prove practice but also corresponding *opinio juris*. It would seem that the threshold to fulfil any general duty will be low: Not only may states reject cooperation requests from other states, they also may completely withdraw into isolation.[125]

Secondly, even assuming the existence of a duty to cooperate among, there would still be a need to establish why such a duty also exists among *IOs*. Contrary to what Tietje suggests, the conferral of competences on an IO does not in itself have

---

[121] ibid.

[122] ibid 511.

[123] On the one hand, states have repeatedly mentioned cooperation as a thematic backdrop e.g. for mutual assistance in disaster relief or even the creation of new IOs, such as the IFAD and UNIDO. On the other hand, states have shown great tolerance with states persistingly refusing to cooperate, Rüdiger Wolfrum, 'Art. 1' in Bruno Simma and others (eds), *The Charter of the United Nations - A Commentary, vol I* (3 edn, Oxford University Press 2012), para. 36.

[124] Rüdiger Wolfrum, 'Sources of International Law', *Max Planck Encyclopedia of Public International Law* (Oxford University Press 2011), paras 17 et seqq.; Krajewski (n 55) 191.

[125] Krajewski (n 55) 190 et seq.

external legal effects vis-à-vis other IOs.[126] Instead, the duty to cooperate, if not laid down e.g. in an inter-organizational treaty,[127] has to be identified within the pertinent sources of unwritten inter-organizational law. Insisting on this is more than legalistic pedantry: If this identification is not successful (or is omitted), IOs could always reject other IOs' requests for cooperation arguing that they were not legally obliged vis-à-vis these other IOs to cooperate.[128] The mere conviction that cooperation between IOs would be a desirable way to address inter-organizational interactions—however plausible it may appear—is not sufficient to establish (or substitute) a legal obligation to cooperate.

Tietje names two normative bases for an inter-organizational duty to cooperate, namely IOs' international legal personality and, secondly, an obligation to cooperate under customary international law as it applies between states.[129] However, as pointed out above, neither is IOs' international legal personality in itself a basis for specific rights and obligations, nor do IOs automatically 'inherit' their member states' obligations.[130] The legal basis of an inter-organizational *pactum de negotiando* thus remains open.

Thirdly, it is unclear if a *pactum de negotiando*—even if it existed in contemporary inter-organizational law—would always be a feasible way of regulating inter-organizational interactions. For example, a duty to agree on a mutually satisfactory result between the ILO and the ECtHR would have to remain limited in order to preserve the judicial independence of the Court, which can hardly be subject to another organization's consent.

Finally, even insofar as cooperation is feasible, the proposed duty to cooperate does not specify the legal parameters within which inter-organizational cooperation takes place. In consequence, the same questions that already flared up in the context of inter-organizational good-neighbourliness[131] resurface in the present context. There as here, the answer to these questions predetermines what a duty to cooperate in good faith actually means in every given case and where its limits lie.

To be sure, these points are not raised in order to make a case *against* cooperation between IOs. Inter-organizational cooperation is obviously happening, and sometimes with remarkable results, as the creation and implementation of the ESC discussed in Chap. 6 exemplifies. Moreover, cooperation is of course an indispensable element in regulating inter-organizational interactions. The point is rather that it

---

[126]See Chapter 9 A. III. and above, A. II. 2. b).

[127]On the duties to cooperate in the ILO-CoE and the treaties forming the UN System see Chapter 13 C. and Chapter 14.

[128]As an example, see the respective legal arguments brought forward by the World Bank in the abovementioned dispute with the UN over continued financial support to South Africa and Portugal, discussed above in Chapter 14 B. II. 2.

[129]Tietje, 'Die völkerrechtliche Kooperationspflicht im Spannungsverhältnis Welthandel/Umweltschutz und ihre Bedeutung für die europäische Umweltblume' (n 119) 293; Tietje, 'Global Governance and Inter-Agency Co-Operation in International Economic Law' (n 4) 511.

[130]See above, A.

[131]See above, B. IV. 3. c).

can hardly be the *only* element. As a complement to cooperation, there has to be sufficient clarity about the basic legal parameters of IOs' mutual relationships under inter-organizational law so that each IO can assess its rights and obligations independently of concrete instances of cooperation—or as a basis for them.

In sum, a duty to cooperate based on a *pactum de negotiando* lacks a sufficiently clear legal basis in inter-organizational law. What is more, like the duty to cooperate under an inter-organizational law of good-neighbourliness, it presumes that the legal parameters for cooperation are clear. As this is doubtful, it encounters the same underlying questions still in need for an answer.

VI. The Structural Peculiarities of the Inter-Organizational Constellation

All three proposals examined in the previous sections give valuable impulses for the development of customary inter-organizational law. At the same time, they leave important points unanswered, because they assume a certain structure of the inter-organizational constellation: Both the prohibition of interference and the "hands off" dimension of inter-organizational good-neighbourliness are based on the premise that IOs possess reasonably clear-cut spheres of jurisdiction that have an exclusionary external effect. Both the cooperative dimension of inter-organizational good-neighbourliness and the duty to cooperate under a *pactum de negotiando* assume that the legal parameters for cooperation are reasonably clearly defined. Thus, in essence, all proposals seem, at least implicitly, assume a structural comparability between the inter-organizational constellation and the inter-state constellation.

However, this comparability is not self-evident. In fact, the inter-organizational constellation has important structural peculiarities. Overlooking or downplaying these peculiarities diminishes the persuasiveness of the proposals discussed above, all of which essentially suggest applying certain norms from 'classic' international law to inter-organizational interactions. In the same manner, failure to duly acknowledge these peculiarities can misdirect future attempts to develop inter-organizational law beyond its present state.

Therefore, it is convenient at this point to reflect on the structural peculiarities of the inter-organizational constellation in closer detail. While a full-scale examination lies beyond the scope of this study, three of its structural peculiarities will be (re)addressed in the following:

1) the overlap between IOs' spheres of jurisdiction,
2) the unclarity as to whether, why and to what extent IOs' jurisdictional spheres have exclusionary external effect, and
3) the basic characterization of IOs' mutual relations, notably the question whether and to what extent one can assume a status of equality among IOs.

1. Jurisdictional Overlaps Among IOs

IOs' jurisdictional spheres typically overlap with those of one or more other IOs. This overlap has two dimensions: Firstly, at least in part, IOs deal with the same subject-matters (functional overlap). Secondly, IOs often do so regarding the same states and thus, at least indirectly, also for the same territories and population (membership overlap). For example, there is a functional overlap between the ILO and the CoE regarding the subject-matter of human rights at work and a membership overlap regarding the 47 European states which are members of both IOs.

a) The Ubiquity of Jurisdictional Overlaps

Why is jurisdictional overlap a peculiarity of the inter-organizational constellation? Jurisdictional overlaps can of course also appear between states. A state may, for example, in certain situations be entitled to exercise extraterritorial jurisdiction over the territory of another state. Moreover, in rare cases (and usually provided for by a specific treaty or other instrument), two or more states may exercise a *condominium* over a certain territory.[132] However, these instances are rather exceptional.[133] Moreover, in any event, it is established that every state retains an exclusive sphere of jurisdiction. Thus, the basic premise of the inter-state constellation remains that states' jurisdictional spheres are separated from each other. In the inter-organizational constellation, by contrast, a basic premise of separated jurisdictions would be at odds with the ubiquitous occurrence of overlaps, as exemplified by the many cases of multi-institutional labour governance mentioned in Chap. 3.[134]

b) No Overlaps of IOs' Organic Jurisdiction

Notwithstanding the ubiquity of overlaps, there are certain areas in which IOs' jurisdictional spheres are rather clearly separated. The main case in point is what has been termed IOs' organic jurisdiction, i.e. their competence to organize their internal affairs autonomously.[135] In this respect, Seyersted has pointed out that IOs

[132]See Joel Samuels, 'Condominium Arrangements in International Practice: Reviving an Abandoned Concept of Boundary Dispute Resolution' (2008) 29 Michigan Journal of International Law 727, with further references.

[133]Cedric Ryngaert, *Jurisdiction in International Law* (2nd edn, Oxford University Press 2015) 36 et seqq. and 142 et seqq., with further references.

[134]Chapter 3 A. I.

[135]Schermers and Blokker (n 3) para 1196. As far as the ILO, the Bank and the CoE are concerned, this right finds explicit mention, e.g. in Art. 7(8) ILO Constitution or Art. 16 CoE Statute.

> exercise legislative, administrative and judicial jurisdiction over their organs and the members hereof as such.[136]

The concept of organic jurisdiction was developed in the context of, and is primarily concerned with, the IO's relationship with its members.[137] Seyersted uses it to show that, within the scope of their organic jurisdiction, IOs' organs are not subject to the jurisdiction of their member states and can therefore form a *volonté distincte*.[138] Others have argued that the exclusivity of IOs' organic jurisdiction was also relevant in IOs' external relations.[139]

The observation that IOs' organic jurisdictions do not overlap appears to be accurate. The World Bank cannot decide how the ILO Governing Body should operate, and the ILO does not have a say in the internal organization of the ECtHR. As far as the free organization and operation of organs is concerned, the separation of IOs' jurisdictional spheres seems broadly comparable to the separation of states' organic jurisdictions in the inter-state constellation.

c) The Limited Relevance of This Exception

Why is the overlap of IOs' jurisdictional spheres still a relevant structural peculiarity? The answer is that organic jurisdiction is limited to the organization and functioning of an IO's organs. However, it does not reserve a certain subject-matter or a certain member state for one specific IO. Consequently, the aforesaid functional and membership overlaps remain.

This is markedly different in inter-state relations: States' jurisdictional spheres are separated from each other on a much more comprehensive scale: States may not only form a *volonté distincte*, they are also legally entitled to effectuate and execute it on their territory without interference from other states. Their jurisdiction is not limited to "exercise legislative, administrative and judicial jurisdiction over their organs and the members hereof as such." It rather also includes their territory and their 'members' properly (viz. their citizens and permanent inhabitants). Thus, widespread jurisdictional overlaps do not occur in the inter-state constellation; they remain a structural peculiarity of the inter-organizational constellation.

[136] Seyersted, *Common Law of International Organizations* (n 29) 97; Lusa Bordin (n 8) 75 et seqq.

[137] Its precise legal basis remains somewhat diffuse. Seyersted considers it 'inherent' in IOs, following his concept of inherent rights emanating from organizationhood, Seyersted, *Common Law of International Organizations* (n 29) 70 et seq.

[138] Lusa Bordin (n 8) 76.

[139] ibid.

2. Exclusionary External Effect of IOs' Jurisdictional Spheres?

A second structural peculiarity is the fundamental unclarity as to whether, why and to what extent IOs' jurisdictional spheres have exclusionary external effect.

The term 'exclusionary external effect' refers to the legal opposability vis-à-vis other actors. In the context of IOs' spheres of jurisdiction, exclusionary external effect means that an IO has a right against other IOs to non-interference with its jurisdictional sphere.

Between states, exclusionary external effect is a corollary of states' separated spheres of jurisdiction. It is rooted in the principle of sovereign equality and its sub-elements, notably the inviolability of a state's territory and political autonomy, the principle of non-intervention and the prohibition of the use of force.[140]

By comparison, the situation in the inter-organizational constellation is much more diffuse. To recall: An IO's jurisdictional sphere is defined in its constituent instrument.[141] However, as mentioned before, the constituent instrument only binds other IOs in two cases: Either the other IO accepts rights and obligations emanating from the constituent instrument, or there is an inter-organizational legal norm externalizing the rights and obligations laid down in the constituent instrument, making them legally binding on other IOs. Thus, to recall further, an IO's jurisdictional sphere only has exclusionary external effect if and to the extent that:

---

[140] Verdross and Simma (n 114) 272 et seqq.; Kokott, 'Souveräne Gleichheit und Demokratie im Völkerrecht' (n 42) 520; Crawford, *Brownlie's Principles of Public International Law* (n 8) 447; von Arnauld (n 55) 129; Krajewski (n 55) 168 et seqq.

[141] In this regard, certain IOs have been endowed by their members with exclusive jurisdiction over certain matters. As mentioned before, the EU has been endowed with exclusive competences in a number of subject-matters. By contrast, Art. 1 lit. d CoE Statute employs the 'opposite' model, stating that an IO is not competent for matters of defence. For another example, the ICJ has recognized a right of an IO to exercise conferred powers. In *Pulp Mills*, the ICJ observed with regard to CARU, the joint river commission of the Uruguay river created by Argentina and Uruguay, that "like any international organization with legal personality, CARU is entitled to exercise the powers assigned to it by the 1975 Statute and which are necessary to achieve the object and purpose of the latter (...)", *Pulp Mills on the River Uruguay (Argentina v. Uruguay)* (n 97) 53. In *Pulp Mills*, the question arose whether Argentina and Uruguay had to adhere to certain notification procedures which were laid down in the 1975 Statute of the River Uruguay and which involved the notification of planned uses of the river to CARU, a joint river commission established by both parties. Uruguay argued that CARU was not an autonomous body and that, consequently, the parties were entitled to deviate from the foreseen procedures as they wished, ibid 52. The Court invoked CARU's international legal personality and its mandate as established by the 1975 River Statute, including "the scale and diversity of the functions [the Parties] have assigned to CARU" (ibid 54) and eventually dismissed Uruguay's argument, ibid 60 et seqq. However, the protection of such acquired rights seems rather limited. The ICJ did not assume that Argentina and Uruguay were barred from assigning tasks to other mechanisms and 'sidelining' CARU: When addressing whether the parties had validly derogated from their procedural obligations under Arts. 7 – 12 of the 1975 Statute of the River Uruguay – which would have withdrawn functions from CARU and in favour of other mechanisms established by two subsequent additional agreements reached by the parties in the course of the dispute – the fact that CARU would have 'lost' its competence to deal with the matter was not considered by the Court.

– another IO accepts the exclusivity of the sphere, i.e. it accepts an obligation to respect that sphere and not to interfere with it, or
– there is an inter-organizational norm pursuant to which each IO's jurisdictional sphere has exclusionary external effect irrespective of other IOs' consent.[142]

As to the first alternative, it is conceivable but rather unlikely for an IO to recognize in a legally binding manner another IO's exclusive jurisdiction over a certain subject-matter.[143]

As to the second alternative, an inter-organizational norm to this effect is not established. When attempting to identify possible candidates for such a norm, two questions have to be distinguished:

1) Which part, if any, of an IO's jurisdictional sphere can or should be considered protected against exogenous interference by other IOs?
2) What is the inter-organizational legal basis for exclusionary external effect for any such reserved part?

As to the first question, IOs' organic jurisdiction may be a case in point. If no IO has any jurisdiction over others' internal organization and functioning, one could conclude that, in consequence, every IO can also legally demand from other IOs not to interfere with these matters.[144] The ICJ's *Reparation for Injuries* opinion points in this direction. The ICJ held that the UN possessed

> a right of functional protection in respect of its agents[145]

against non-member states. The Court reasoned that the damage before it was

> exclusively damage caused to the interests of the Organization itself, to its administrative machine, to its property and assets, and to the interests of which it is the guardian. It is clear that the Organization has the capacity to bring a claim for this damage.[146]

Besides organic jurisdiction, should also other parts of IOs' jurisdictional spheres be protected against interference by other IOs? The Court in *Reparation* seems to have contemplated the UN's protection against interference to reach beyond its organic jurisdiction *stricto sensu* by also including the "interests of which [the UN] is the guardian". The ICJ's opinion could thus be read as an (albeit faint)

[142] Chapter 9 A.

[143] If both IOs work on the same subject-matter, an IO recognizing exclusive jurisdiction of another IO will have to consider that it may no longer be able to fulfil its own mandate in respect of that subject-matter.

[144] This is a plausible, but not a necessary conclusion: If one IO interfered with another IO's organic jurisdiction, the interfering IO would overstep its own jurisdictional boundaries laid down in its constituent instrument. However, this would only mean that the interfering IO violated its international obligations – additionally, it would have to be shown that the injured IO had an inter-organizational legal claim, i.e. that the obligation not to overstep competences was *owed to that other IO*.

[145] *Reparation for Injuries Suffered in the Service of the United Nations* (n 1) 185.

[146] ibid 180.

indication of other protected parts of IOs' jurisdictional spheres. For the time being, however, it needs to be stressed that it was not even contemplated in *Reparation* whether the UN was similarly protected against influence by *other IOs*.[147] Moreover, as mentioned above, it remains an open question whether and to what extent the *Reparation* opinion applies to other IOs than the UN.

The second question—the inter-organizational legal basis for exclusionary external effect—is even more difficult to answer. It has already been shown above that IOs' international legal personality is not a suitable basis for exclusionary external effect of IOs' jurisdictional spheres. What can be said that, given the absence of written law or consistent practice, any such inter-organizational legal basis would have to be developed. Chapter 19 will offer more thoughts in this regard.[148] For now, the fundamental unclarity as to whether, why and to what extent IOs' jurisdictional spheres have exclusionary external effect, remains.

3. The Basic Character of IOs' Mutual Relations: A Principle of Inter-Organizational Equality?

The third structural peculiarity is that the basic character of IOs' mutual relations remains unclear. The basic character can e.g. be one of equality or of hierarchy between two IOs, it can be shaped by considerations of higher or lower relative 'weight', value or importance of one IO's governance model or the subject-matter it works on, by territorial or functional relations (universal v. regional; general vs. specialized mandate) etc.[149] This basic character may become a relevant factor in a number of ways, e.g. to determine undue interference between IOs or as a legal parameter for cooperative interactions.

As an empirical starting point, the diversity of IOs can hardly be overlooked. The ILO, the World Bank and the CoE—and with them virtually all other IOs—differ significantly as to their mandate and objectives, their organizational structure, their

[147] As to IOs' employees and civil servants, there is some practice indicating that IOs' right to set their own internal law can have third-party effect against its employees. For example, in *Gracia de Muniz v. FAO*, the ILOAT held that IOs are not bound to maintain their internal rules and structures regulating certain employment conditions of an employee. Rather, even if the internal law created rights or expectations of employees, the IO may at any time change or abolish such internal law, Judgment No 269 *Gracia de Muniz v. FAO* (ILO Administrative Tribunal, 36th session, 12 April 1976) [1976] United Nations Juridical Yearbook 142, 143. Schermers and Blokker, *International Institutional Law* (n 3) para 1200. However, in thr same case, the ILOAT also confirmed its jurisprudence that an IO is not entirely free to do so but has to observe certain legal limits.

[148] Chapter 19 C.

[149] It is duly acknowledged that 'basic character' is a simplifying term. Obviously, the nature of IOs' mutual relations is shaped by all kinds of factors, and the 'basic character' might depend not least on which factors one emphasizes over others. That being said, it may still be worthwhile to contemplate at least in a general manner what that 'basic character' of inter-organizational could be like, and how close it is to the (no less colourful) notion of 'sovereign equality' characterizing inter-state relations.

levels of integration and a whole range of other aspects. In their seminal treatise on international law, Verdross and Simma perceptively speak of the "individuality" of IOs.[150] Moreover, as seen in Part II of this study, IOs' constituent instruments tend to prioritize the own and relativize other IOs. In addition, many constituent instruments also draw distinctions between other IOs, indicating differences in importance.[151]

Accordingly, the comparability of different IOs became a focal point of discussion both in practice and academia. A seminal issue, recurrent to this day, is whether and to what extent IOs can be considered equal. As far as positions on the inter-organizational constellation can be extrapolated from these debates,[152] they remain diffuse: On the one hand, it seems to be broadly taken for granted that IOs encounter each other on the basis of equality—similar to states encountering each other on the basis of (sovereign) equality.[153] On the other hand, it is often readily conceded that there is no established general norm providing for equality among IOs.[154] Some

---

[150] Verdross and Simma (n 114) 594, para 944; ILC, 'Draft Articles on the Responsibility of International Organizations, with Commentaries' (n 8) 51, Art. 2 para. 15; PK Menon, *The Law of Treaties Between States and International Organizations* (Edwin Mellen 1992) 24.

[151] Some constituent instruments confine themselves to specifically mention certain IOs but not others: Art. III(5) WTO Agreement specifically mentions the IMF and the World Bank, while Art. V WTO Agreement concerns other IOs. Other IOs' constituent instruments go further and tie different legal consequences to different groups of other IOs. For example, the UN Charter envisages special relations with specialized agencies, defined in Art. 57 UN Charter as IOs "established by intergovernmental agreement and having wide international responsibilities, as defined in their basic instruments, in economic, social, cultural, educational, health, and related fields". This definition includes a wide range of IOs, but notably excludes regional organizations and organizations with a primarily military purview, Meng 'Art. 57' (n 8) 9 et seq. (the latter falling within the scope of Part VIII UN Charter and are not being coordinated by ECOSOC). Similar distinctions appear in the constituent instruments of further IOs: Art. XIV FAO Constitution contemplate the subjugation of certain other IOs under the authority of the FAO. As to other IOs, the FAO "shall" maintain relations with the UN, but "may" choose to enter into agreements with other IOs (Arts. XII and XIII FAO Constitution). In a similar manner, the IMO "shall" cooperate with the UN and its specialized agencies, but "may" do so with other IOs (Arts. 60 – 62 IMO Convention). The EU "shall establish all appropriate forms of cooperation" with the UN and its specialized agencies, the CoE, the OSCE and the OECD, but only "maintain such relations as are appropriate" with other IOs (Art. 220 (1) TFEU). These distinctions sometimes flattened out in practice, Nevertheless, they reflect that for every IO, certain other IOs are more relevant than others.

[152] In the pertinent discussions, as in other contexts, the inter-organizational constellation has mostly been treated together with (and in the shadow of) other actors.

[153] E.g. Tobias Winkler, *Die Vereinten Nationen im Gefüge der internationalen Organisationen – Eine rechtsdogmatische Untersuchung* (Nomos 2019) 62 et seqq.

[154] ILC, 'Sixth Report by Special Rapporteur Paul Reuter on the Question of Treaties Concluded Between States and International Organizations or Between Two or More International Organizations' [1977] YILC Vol II Part One 119, 120; Catherine Brölmann, 'International Organizations and Treaties: Contractual Freedom and Institutional Constraint' in Jan Klabbers and Åsa Wallendahl (eds), *Research Handbook on the Law of International Organizations* (Edward Elgar Publishing 2011) 292. It is important to highlight that the question is not whether the law must be applied equally to all its addressees. It is not disputed that, if a norm addresses all states (or all IOs, for that matter), it has to be applied to them equally. Rather, the question is whether the norm, if it addresses one category of legal subjects, needs to be applied to other categories alike, to the effect that a norm

authors even explicitly caution against characterizations of IOs as 'equal', given their palpable differences.[155]

a) The Debate Concerning Equal Rights and Obligations for All IOs

The issue materialized in the context of the ILC's work on the VCLT-IO and the DARIO. A vivid debate emerged on whether all IOs should be subject to the same international legal rights and obligations. Klabbers summarized the diverging views as follows:

> The first and dominant approach holds that even though there is great variety among international organisations in terms of their tasks and structures, nonetheless the law treats them (and should treat them) all alike. Yet there is also the recurring thought that this wide variety among organisations should somehow be reflected in their legal position and the extent of their rights and obligations under international law.[156]

The first approach is the one that ultimately prevailed within the ILC when it drafted the VCLT-IO and the DARIO. Consequently, these bodies of inter-organizational law create—for the respective subject-matter they govern—equal rights and obligations for IOs.

The way this is achieved is by providing a general and encompassing definition of 'International Organization'. For example, the VCLT-IO defines the term broadly as "an intergovernmental organization" (Art. 2(1) lit. i VCLT-IO). All entities fulfilling these criteria (the overwhelming majority of IOs, if not all), possess the same rights and obligations when it comes to the conclusion, interpretation, fulfilment, suspension, termination etc. of inter-organizational treaties.[157] Thus, by using a generously wide definition of IO, the VCLT-IO levels out IOs' uniqueness and diversity.

But does the VCLT-IO's and the DARIO's approach justify considering equality among IOs a principle of general application? Does it imply that IOs also possess the same set of basic rights and obligations vis-à-vis each other regarding other issues than treaties and responsibility?

To begin with, it does not seem that the ILC, when drafting the VCLT-IO and the DARIO, was purporting to incidentally establish a principle of general inter-

---

addressed to states has to be applied equally to IOs, Bleckmann (n 16) 115. Such an assertion is highly dubious.

[155]As Wouters and Odermatt argue, "from the viewpoint of public international law, states are identical legal entities irrespective of their culture, political system, or size. The same cannot be said of IOs, which, although they may have (some degree of) international legal personality, remain very heterogeneous legal entities", Wouters and Odermatt (n 58) 12.

[156]Jan Klabbers, 'Unity, Diversity, Accountability: the Ambivalent Concept of International Organisation' (2013) 14 Melbourne Journal of International Law 1, 2.

[157]See ILC, 'Tenth Report by Special Rapporteur Paul Reuter on the Question of Treaties Concluded between States and International Organizations or between Two or More International Organizations' [1977] YILC Vol II Part One 43, 46.

organizational equality.[158] Instead, the ILC's primary concern was to find a solution that, while being general, is nevertheless adequately tailored to the subject-matter proposed for codification. In this regard, it is worth noting that the definition of "International Organization" employed by the DARIO is similar, but not identical to the one in Art. 2(1) lit. i VCLT-IO. Instead, Art. 2 lit. a DARIO additionally requires that an IO must possess international legal personality. This deviation is based on a conscious decision following a prolonged debate withn the ILC, which concluded that different definitions were better suited for the different subject-matters of treaties and responsibility, respectively.[159] The practical impact of the deviation may be minor—most IOs will fall under both the VCLT-IO's and the DARIO's definitions. Still, it is of structural interest that even those bodies of law that are specifically concerned with laying down equal rights and duties for all IOs seem to have different conceptions on which entities are to be considered equal.

Moreover, in several instances, the VCLT-IO and the DARIO integrate rather than refute the idea that different IOs may have different rights and obligations. As mentioned, during the two instruments' drafting processes, intensive discussions ensued within the ILC as to whether there should be one general legal framework for all IOs or if certain distinctions between IOs were warranted.[160] While the choice mostly fell on the former, it is illuminating that some issues were not covered at all precisely because IOs were too diverse to find a general rule.[161]

Moreover, the debate left traces in the final texts. Several of the VCLT-IO's and DARIO's provisions recognize the differences between IOs in inter-organizational law and accordingly create rights and obligations of different scope by referring to IOs' respective internal (i.e. institutional) law. For example, pursuant to Art. 6 VCLT-IO, the capacity of every IO to conclude treaties "is governed by the rules of *that* organization" (emphasis added) and is therefore different for every IO.[162] To compare: no such reference to internal law exists in the case of states—

---

[158]Neither the VCLT-IO nor the DARIO claim that their respective definition of "IO" should be of general application, beyond the confines of the respective treaty or instrument, ILC, 'Draft Articles on the Responsibility of International Organizations, with Commentaries' (n 8) Art. 2, para. 1.

[159]See, for example, the reasons given by the ILC to adopt a definition in the DARIO which deviates from the one in the VCLT, ibid Art. 2, para. 3.

[160]The VCLT-IO's encompassing coverage was a deliberate choice made by the ILC upon the recommendation of Special Rapporteur Reuter, Lusa Bordin (n 8) 110 et seq. During the drafting of the DARIO, several IOs advocated for drafting separate rules for certain types of IOs. The issue was contemplated by the ILC, which however later decided in favour of a general approach, Wouters and Odermatt (n 58) 11.

[161]Such as a rule on ex officio representatives of IOs, Lusa Bordin (n 8) 97.

[162]See ILC, 'Draft Articles on the Law of Treaties between States and International Organizations or between International Organizations, with Commentaries' [1982] YILC Vol II Part Two 17, Art. 6, para. 4; Menon (n 150) 24 et seq. The rules of the organization differ widely among those IOs to which the VCLT-IO applies, as the discussion of the ILO's, the Bank's and the CoE's institutional laws in Part II illustrates. The selective equalization in treaty law is, therefore, an equalization in principle, which still provides ample room for inequalities to come to bear. What is more, the selective equalization of IOs in the law of treaties is one of form, but not necessarily of content. It

instead, irrespective of its constitutional peculiarities, "[e]very State possesses capacity to conclude treaties" (Art. 6 VCLT).

In a similar manner, Arts. 35 and 36(2) VCLT-IO and several provisions in the DARIO contain references to the 'rules of the organization'.[163] The DARIO also contains a dedicated *lex specialis* rule in Art. 64 DARIO, giving preference to any "special rules of international law". Again, these provisinos were conscious concessions to the empirical diversity of IOs.[164]

Remarkably, despite these efforts to take IOs' diversity into consideration, the ILC's general approach was still criticized. A range of scholars and some IOs noted with discontent that the DARIO were still 'too general' in nature.[165]

Besides the VCLT-IO and the DARIO, a range of inter-organizational treaties recognize the specific features of the contracting IOs and tailor their contractual rights and obligations accordingly. For example, the preamble of the ILO-CoE refers to each IO's "respective principles and objectives", which it spells out in remarkable detail in its first and second preambular clauses:

> Whereas the International Labour Organisation, as a universal organisation, attaches the greatest importance to the maintenance and advancement in the social and labour field of world standards based on the principles set forth in the Constitution of the International Labour Organisation and the Declaration of Philadelphia, and, while co-operating with the United Nations in the maintenance of international peace and security remains outside political controversy between nations or groups of nations, and is at the disposal of all its member nations to co-operate with them either severally or through regional organisations of which they are Members in implementing, in the light of the world standards evolved through the International Labour Organisation, the objectives for which the International Labour Organisation itself exists,
>
> and
>
> Whereas the Council of Europe is a regional organisation the aim of which is to achieve a greater unity between its Members for the purpose of safeguarding and realising the ideals and principles which are their common heritage and facilitating their economic and social progress, this aim being pursued through the organs of the Council by discussion of questions of common concern and by agreements and common action in economic, social, cultural, scientific, legal and administrative matters, and in the maintenance and further realisation of human rights and fundamental freedoms (...).

---

hardly needs mention that the IOs parties to a treaty, while concluding the treaty as equals, can perpetuate (or redefine) their legal inequality in the treaty by agreeing to rights and obligations that are unequal or take specific regards of each IO's distinct features.

[163] Wouters and Odermatt (n 58) 13.

[164] In the words of the ILC, "[t]here are very significant differences among international organizations with regard to their powers and functions, size of membership, relations between the organization and its members, procedures for deliberation, structure and facilities, as well as the primary rules including treaty obligations by which they are bound. Because of this diversity and its implications, the draft articles where appropriate give weight to the specific character of the organization (…)", ILC, 'Report of the International Law Commission, Sixty-third session' (2011) UN Doc A/66/10, 70, para 7.

[165] Wouters and Odermatt (n 58) 13.

The ILO-CoE's operative provisions, while containing a range of reciprocal obligatinos, reflect the unique features of each partner mentioned in the preamble. For example, Art. 3 ILO-CoE obliges (only) the ILO to convene regional tripartite meetings at the CoE's request. Art. 5 ILO-CoE obliges the ILO to provide specific technical assistance on labour matters to the CoE.

A similar tailoring of rights and obligations can be found in other inter-organizational treaties. Relationship agreements between the UN and the specialized agencies install the UN as the coordinating IO and thereby integrate this specific feature of the UN provided for in the UN Charter into an inter-organizational treaty. Moreover, different relationship agreements specify the roles of specialized agencies in different ways. For example, Art. I(2) UN-IBRD recognizes the World Bank's independence, based on the "nature of [the Bank's] international responsibilities and the terms of its Articles of Agreement"[166]—by comparison, other relationship agreements, such as the UN-ILO, do not preserve the autonomy of the specialized agency in such a far-reaching manner. More examples can be found in further agreements.[167]

This tailoring of rights and obligations in inter-organizational treaties reflects the functional diversification among IOs and is therefore hardly surprising. Yet, the point needs mention that IOs acknowledge each other's uniqueness and willingly tailor their contractual rights and obligations accordingly. The respective provisions may—as seen in Chaps. 12 and 13—mostly fail to regulate IOs' interactions. Still, the mentioned inter-organizational treaties integrate the uniqueness and diversity of every IO into inter-organizational law.

Thus, in sum, the situation remains ambiguous: On the one hand, the VCLT-IO and DARIO resemble two powerful attempts to 'equalize' IOs inter-organizational rights and obligations. On the other hand, the ILC's concessions to IOs' diversity, the persistent critique from IOs and scholar against general rules and IOs' own treaty practice indicate that it is not (yet?) established that all IOs share a basic set of inter-organizational rights and obligations.

b) The Unclear Basic Character of IOs' Mutual Relations

As the issue of equal rights and obligations exemplifies, the basic character of inter-organizational relations remains open and disputed. The question whether IOs are to be considered equal is thorny on several levels.

Methodologically, it needs to be emphasized that findings of equality or inequality presuppose a process of abstraction: To determine whether or not two items are equal, it must first be determined which of these items' respective characteristics

---

[166]See Chapter 14 B. II.

[167]See e.g. the preamble and No 1 of the 1992 ILO/UNIDO Working Arrangement (signed and entered into force 7 October 1991) LXXV ILO Official Bulletin Ser A 69. See also Art. I ILO-UNESCO and Art. I ILO-IMO.

shall be the relevant ones to compare.[168] Thus, equality requires a choice to highlight certain features and to ignore others. In the context of IOs, this means that the preselection of certain of their characteristics predetermines whether and to what extent they are to be considered equal.

As to the discussion's focal point, 'equality' is in itself an iridescent notion. In the context of equality of states, the term has been understood as, inter alia, equality before the law,[169] the judicial equality of all states,[170] the capacity to possess the same rights and obligations,[171] including respect for their postulated inherent dignity,[172] a safeguard for weaker states[173] or a prerequisite to ensuring the possibility of moral disagreement between states.[174] Others have considered the menaing of 'equality' to be contingent on the existence and structure of the international community at a given point in time.[175] Again others have considered it a redundant annex to sovereignty.[176]

A principle of inter-organizational equality would be just as open to different understandings. If one considers formal criteria as decisive, such as the absence of formal hierarchy or subjugation, most IOs would arguably have to be considered equal.[177] On the other hand, if one takes the diversity of governance models, the societal relevance of covered subject-matters (however determined) or other substantive criteria into account, the answer may well be different. The same may

[168] Pieter H Kooijmans, *The Doctrine of the Legal Equality of States* (A W Sythoff 1964) 7.

[169] Herbert Weinschel, 'The Doctrine of the Equality of States and Its Recent Modifications' (1951) 45 American Journal of International Law 417, 418.

[170] Declaration on Principles of International Law Concerning Friendly Relations and Co-Operation among States in Accordance with the Charter of the United Nations, UNGA Res 2625 (XXV) (24 October 1970) UN Doc A/RES/2625(XXV) (Friendly Relations Declaration); see already Art. 5 of the ILC's Draft Declaration on the Rights and Duties of States, ILC, 'Draft Declaration on Rights and Duties of States, with Commentaries' [1949] YILC 287.

[171] Edwin DeWitt Dickinson, *The Equality of States in International Law* (Harvard University Press 1920) 152.

[172] Verdross and Simma (n 114) 276.

[173] Juliane Kokott, 'States, Sovereign Equality', *Max Planck Encyclopedia of Public International Law* (Oxford University Press 2011) para 81.

[174] Brad R Roth, *Sovereign Equality and Moral Disagreement – Premises of a Pluralist International Legal Order* (Oxford University Press 2011) passim.

[175] Kooijmans (n 168) 42.

[176] Philip J Baker, 'The Doctrine of Legal Equality of States' (1923-1924) 4 British Yearbook of International Law 1, 3 et seq.

[177] The same would arguably true if one considered IOs to be of equal rank because their constitutent instruments were, Winkler (n 153) 94. The ILC used inductive reasoning to arrive at the conclusion of a formal equality when it held that the "general principle of consensualism, which constitutes the basis of any treaty commitment necessarily entails the legal equality of the parties", ILC, 'Tenth Report by Special Rapporteur Paul Reuter on the Question of Treaties Concluded between States and International Organizations or between Two or More International Organizations' [1977] YILC Vol II Part One 43, 46.

happen if one considers IOs to be mere instruments to pursue common goals or protect common fundamental values defined by the international community.

4. Conclusion

This section has reflected on structural peculiarities of the inter-organizational constellation that surfaced during the previous sections of this Chapter. Firstly, IOs' jurisdictional spheres regularly overlap with those of other IOs. Secondly, it is unclear whether and to what extent IOs' jurisdictional spheres have exclusionary external effect and are legally opposable to other IOs. Thirdly, the basic character of IOs' mutual relations remains unclear as well. Failure to duly acknowledge these peculiarities will likely impede attempts to develop customary inter-organizational law further.

VII. Conclusion on Section B

This section has endeavoured to identify customary legal norms applying to inter-organizational interactions between the ILO and other IOs. Customary inter-organizational law is piecemeal. Some fields of customary inter-organiaztional law can be considered relatively established, including the law of treaties between IOs and—to a lesser extent—the law of IOs' international responsibility. These bodies of law mostly govern direct and cooperative interactions. By contrast, there are no established customary inter-organizational legal norms governing indirect or non-cooperative interactions. Instead, several authors have made proposals for such norms, drawing on established customary international law applying between states. However, the analysis revealed that the transfer of customary norms developed in the context of inter-state relations comes with significant difficulties. Apart from lacking a legal basis in contemporary law, all examined proposals struggle to take into account the structural peculiarities of the inter-organizational constellation.

C. General Principles of (Inter-Organizational) Law

Given the demonstrated scarcity of other norms, general principles are the 'last resort' for the purposes of this study. Indeed, one of general principles' ascribed functions is to fill gaps in the international legal order, so as to avoid the law's 'incompleteness' and—as far as international adjudication is concerned—findings of *non liquet*.[178]

I. Methodological Issues Concerning General Principles of Inter-Organizational Law

Although in most cases, general principles have been identified and applied in interstate relations, there is evidence that they also apply to IOs.[179] That being said, general principles have hardly, if ever, been expressly relied on *between* IOs.

This does not come as a surprise. Already in the inter-state constellation, general principles of law pose significant conceptual and methodological challenges. When applying general principles of law in international legal relationships,

> an international tribunal chooses, edits, and adapts elements from other developed systems. The result is a body of international law which has been influenced by domestic law but still remains its own creation.[180]

As has repeatedly been observed (and criticized), this exercise, which mainly relies on analogous reasoning, almost inevitably requires incomplete evaluations of domestic legal orders, quantitative restrictions as to the number and variety of legal orders examined, simplifications, abstractions and often includes an element of norm creation.[181]

These methodological issues surrounding general principles of law aggravate in the inter-organizational constellation. As a first example, there is the question what the appropriate 'domestic analogy' is in the inter-organizational constellation. In inter-state relations, general principles are frequently (albeit not exclusively) derived

[178]*Legality of the Threat or Use of Nuclear Weapons* (Dissenting Opinion of Vice-President Schwebel) [1996] ICJ Reports 311, 323; von Arnauld (n 55) 112.

[179]E.g. the principle of *res judicata*, see *Effect of Awards of Compensation Made by the United Nations Administrative Tribunal* (Advisory Opinion) [1954] ICJ Reports 47, 53. Additionally, general principles have become relevant on a broader scale in individual IOs, notably the EU.

[180]Crawford, *Brownlie's Principles of Public International Law* (n 8) 35. See also *International Status of South-West Africa* (Separate Opinion by Sir Arnold McNair) [1950] ICJ Reports 146, 148.

[181]*Prosecutor v Tadić* (Appeals Chamber) ICTY-IT-94-1-A (15 July 1999), para 225; Giorgio Gaja, 'General Principles of Law', *Max Planck Encyclopedia of Public International Law* (Oxford University Press 2013) para 30. Fitzmaurice observed that "the concept of the general principles is so fluid that a quasi-legislative element would often be introduced into the Court's decisions by any 'bold' application of them, and (...) considerable harm might be done to the desideratum of increased resort to the Court unless a reasonable predictability as the basis of its decisions can be maintained", Gerald Fitzmaurice, 'The Future of Public International Law and of the International Legal System in the Circumstances of Today' in Institut de Droit International (ed), *Livre du centenaire 1873–1973: Evolution et perspectives du droit international* (Karger 1973) para 325.

by analogy from domestic private law.[182] It is, however, unclear if private law analogies are suitable in inter-organizational relations, given the special features of such relations. IOs are, by constitution, legally unique, diverse and often disparate entities. Modern private law and, for that matter, modern public law do not really resemble a legal framework for relations between actors which each have unique legal characteristics and encounter each other on a non-hierarchical footing. Against this background, particular care is warranted when deriving general principles for application in inter-organizational legal relationships.

A second special aspect of general principles lies in the 'source legal orders' from which general principles of inter-organizational law can be derived. In the context of IOs, general principles have time and again been derived from the domestic laws of the IO's member states. Famously, the CJEU, from its 1969 *Stauder* decision onwards, developed an elaborate body of EU fundamental rights as general principles of EU law, now laid down in Art. 6(3) TEU.[183]

However, the internal recognition of general principles for the internal legal order of one IO does not automatically imply that these general principles also apply to inter-organizational interactions with another IO. The EU example aptly illustrates that general principles can acquire much greater relevance in the institutional laws of regional IOs with a limited membership of constitutionally relatively homogeneous states.[184]

General principles of inter-organizational law would have to be derived not only from the domestic laws of selected states, but from all states, or at least from all domestic legal orders of both interacting IOs' member states. For instance, the EU's general principles derived pursuant to Art. 6(3) TEU will not automatically apply in the EU's legal relations with other IOs.[185]

In sum, there are methodological peculiarities surrounding general principles of inter-organizational law.

---

[182]See e.g. *International Status of South-West Africa* (Separate Opinion by Sir Arnold McNair) (n 180) 148 et seqq. For a counter-example, the Court of Justice of the European Coal and Steel Community derived principles from domestic administrative law, *Joined Cases 7/56, 3/57 to 7/57 Dineke Algera, Giacomo Cicconardi, Simone Couturaud, Ignazio Genuardi, Félicie Steichen v. Common Assembly of the European Coal and Steel Community* (ECLI:EU:C:1957:7) [1957] ECR 00039, para 55.

[183]Case 29/69 *Erich Stauder v. City of Ulm* (ECLI:EU:C:1969:57) [1969] ECR 00419, para 7; Case 11/70 *Internationale Handelsgesellschaft mbH v. Einfuhr- und Vorratsstelle für Getreide und Futtermittel* (ECLI:EU:C:1970:114) [1970] ECR 01125, para 3 et seq.; Case 4/73, Case 4/73 *J Nold, Kohlen- und Baustoffgroßhandlung v. Commission* (ECLI:EU:C:1974:51) [1974] ECR 00491, para 12 et seqq.; Case C-112/00, *Eugen Schmidberger, Internationale Transporte und Planzüge v. Austria* (ECLI:EU:C:2003:333) [2003] ECR I-05659, 70 et seqq.

[184]See August Reinisch, 'Securing the Accountability of International Organizations' (2001) 7 Global Governance 131, 135.

[185]While it is of course possible that the same or similar principles also apply in inter-organizational relations, an additional step for their identification is required.

II. The Irrelevance of Some General Principles in the Present Context

Regarding the identification of relevant general principles governing inter-organizational interactions between the ILO, the World Bank and the CoE, it quickly becomes apparent that the scope of possible candidates is limited from the beginning. Some general principles are simply not relevant in the present context. This is e.g. true for the principle of *res judicata*,[186] given the absence of any institutionalized inter-organizational dispute settlement mechanism between the ILO, the World Bank and the CoE. Other principles, like the obligation to give full compensation for injuries[187] presuppose the breach of primary obligations—the latter being precisely what this study is looking for.

III. The Accessory Nature of Good Faith and Its Corollaries

Other general principles do not create legal rights and obligations by themselves, but accessorily govern the exercise of rights or the performance of obligations deriving from other international legal norms. They hence require that an international right or obligation already exists. One important example is the principle of good faith.[188] Some of the pertinent issues of good faith have already been discussed before and do not need to be repeated here. Still, some further remarks are warranted.

1. The Contents of Good Faith

Good faith is a principle of fundamental importance for the international legal order. As the ICJ observed, it is

> one of the basic principles governing the creation and performance of legal obligations.[189]

Good faith comprises a number of sub-principles and is associated to others (the exact categorization varies). Such components include, for instance, the prohibition

---

[186] *Effect of Awards of Compensation Made by the United Nations Administrative Tribunal* (n 179) 53.

[187] See *Amco Asia Co v. Republic of Indonesia* ICSID Case No ARB/81/1, para 267.

[188] A noteworthy further example would be proportionality, if one considers it a general principle, see Ulf Linderfalk, 'What Are the Functions of the General Principles?' (2018) 78 Zeitschrift für ausländisches öffentliches Recht und Völkerrecht 1.

[189] *Nuclear Tests (Australia v France)* [1974] ICJ Reports 253, 268.

of abuse of rights, estoppel and the clean hands doctrine.[190] Many of these principles are intuitively relevant in the context of inter-organizational interactions.

2. The Accessory Nature of Good Faith

However, in order to unfold their relevance, good faith and its components require pre-existing norms, i.e. rights or obligations. As the ICJ held in *Border and Trans-border Armed Actions*,

> [good faith] is not in itself a source of obligation where none would otherwise exist.[191]

Instead, good faith and its components govern *how* pre-existing rights should be exercised or obligations should be fulfilled.[192]

This is more than just a formalistic and overly legalistic perspective. Rather, it is a necessary corollary of the principle itself. Whether conduct happens in good or bad faith depends on the context, and first and foremost on which right or obligation is at stake. The same is true for good faith's sub-principles. For instance, whether there is an abuse of rights can only be determined in a meaningful manner if it is clear which right has allegedly been abused.

In sum, good faith and its sub-principles are relevant for inter-organizational law in general and the legal protection of the ILO's model in inter-organizational interactions in particular. However, they require that the relevant rights and obligations, and their respective normative bases, are identified in the first place.

IV. The Vagueness of Other General Principles

Other general principles are not considered accessory.[193] However, they are almost inevitably too broad and vague to provide a normative framework for inter-organizational interactions just by themselves.[194] General principles can of course

[190] See Steven Reinhold, 'Good Faith in International Law' (2013) 2 UCL Journal of Law and Jurisprudence 40, 47 et seqq., with further references.

[191] *Border and Transborder Armed Actions (Nicaragua v Honduras)* (Jurisdiction and Admissibility) [1988] ICJ Reports 69, 105.

[192] ibid 105. See also *Land and Maritime Boundary between Cameroon and Nigeria (Cameroon v Nigeria)* (Preliminary Objections) [1998] ICJ Reports 275, para 39.

[193] E.g. a "general principle of cooperation", Tietje, 'Die völkerrechtliche Kooperationspflicht im Spannungsverhältnis Welthandel/Umweltschutz und ihre Bedeutung für die europäische Umweltblume' (n 119) 293.

[194] On the vagueness and the disagreement relating to general principles see generally Bin Cheng, *General Principles of Law as Applied by International Courts and Tribunals* (Cambridge University Press 1953) 2 et seqq. Other principles are only established in other contexts than jurisdictional limitation, see the discussion by Ryngaert (n 133) 152 et seqq.

inform inter-organizational relations, e.g. as fixpoints for interpretation of inter-organizational treaties, or, exceptionally, as an independent basis for claims, but do hardly provide a sufficiently elaborate legal framework that could provide guidance in the absence of treaties and customary rules.[195] As the name suggests, general principles do not provide more than an 'outer limit' for legality, leaving ample discretion for IOs to interact as they seem fit. It is conceivable that a more elaborate (customary or treaty-based) inter-organizational law could be developed around existing general principles. For the time being, however, the legal relevance of general principles as safeguards for the ILO's model in inter-organizational interactions is limited.

D. Conclusion

This chapter has examined whether and to what extent there are international legal norms in customary inter-organizational law or general principles of law protecting or promoting the ILO's model of labour governance in inter-organizational interactions.

As was demonstrated, customary inter-organizational law has not been systematically researched. Instead, a frequent approach is to enumerate the different instruments IOs use in their external relations, including the relations with other IOs. Whether and to what extent these instruments are provided for in norms of general inter-organizational law is an open question. In any event, such norms would be of limited relevance, as they would again mostly regulate direct and cooperative interactions, similar to the ILO's inter-organizational treaties examined in Chap. 13 and the rules of the UN System's legal framework discussed in Chap. 14.

In order to identify norms regulating also other types of interactions, the chapter has collected and evaluated proposals which have been made in this regard. As was seen, none of these proposals presented a convincing case for application of a customary international norm in the inter-organizational constellation. While details vary, they all struggle to accommodate the structural peculiarities of the inter-organizational constellation. These peculiarities boil down to two main aspects: (1) the demarcation of IOs' spheres of jurisdiction vis-à-vis other IOs, and (2) the basic character of the relation between two IOs.

Finally, this chapter has examined the relevance of general principles of law. It found that some principles, such as good faith and its component sub-principles, are relevant, but accessory to rights and obligations the existence of which is the very problem at hand. Other general principles are either irrelevant for inter-

[195]Daniel Bodansky, 'Non Liquet and the Incompleteness of International Law' in Laurence Boisson De Chazournes and Philippe Sands (eds), *International Law, the International Court of Justice and Nuclear Weapons* (Cambridge University Press 1999) 166.

organizational legal relations or are so vague that they do not resemble meaningful safeguards for the ILO's model.

All in all, there is virtually no established unwritten inter-organizational law that applies to the ILO's inter-organizational interactions with the World Bank and the CoE. Beyond the narrow scope of inter-organizational treaties, inter-organizational law remains overwhelmingly silent on IOs ought to conduct their interactions, and what role and relevance they ought to accord to the ILO and its model of labour governance.

16. The Undefined Inter-Organizational Legal Default Rule

The preceding chapters have highlighted that inter-organizational law regulates inter-organizational interactions only in a very rudimentary and piecemeal matter. Inter-organizational treaties are sparse, few established unwritten inter-organizational legal norms can safely be discerned, and proposed analogies struggle to cope with the structural peculiarities of the inter-organizational constellation. Against this background, further structural questions arise: how may (or must) the ILO and other IOs interact if no inter-organizational legal norm is discernible? Which IO, if any, has to bear the burden of legal uncertainty? Are IOs *in dubio* free to interact as they see fit, leaving other IOs with no legal claim whatsoever? In other words, what is the residual inter-organizational legal default rule?

A. Meaning and Relevance of the Inter-Organizational Legal Default Rule

At the outset, some remarks concerning the meaning and relevance of the concept of the inter-organizational legal default rule are warranted.

'Legal default rule' is used here as the most general positive legal norm applying to the legal relationship between two actors. Accordingly, 'inter-organizational legal default rule' refers to any such norm of positive inter-organizational law. As can be taken from this understanding, the notion refers to the *content* of a norm. It is

H. Gött, *The Law of Interactions Between International Organizations*, Beiträge zum ausländischen öffentlichen Recht und Völkerrecht 299, https://doi.org/10.1007/978-3-662-62389-3_16

therefore not to be confused with concepts concerned with the *validity* of norms, such as the concept of *Grundnorm* in the work of Hans Kelsen.[1]

Asking for a general (or a 'most general') norm is, of course, to some extent an artificial exercise. Still, for purposes of this study, it is not merely of theoretical interest. It is practically relevant because the default rule fulfils at least two functions:

- The first of these functions has already been named: The default rule, for example a general rule of unlimited freedom to act, steps in as a fall-back rule insofar as no specific inter-organizational legal norms exist.[2]
- Secondly, where more specific norms exist, the default rule may serve as a *leitmotif* shaping and predetermining the content and application of such more specific norms. The default rule can e.g. inform the interpretation of inter-organizational treaties.

On a practical note, one might ask why there is a need for identifying an inter-organizational default rule. After all, even insofar as no specific inter-organizational norms are in place, IOs will still have to observe their respective institutional laws. The answer is—again—that IOs' institutional laws do not have external legal effect. Neither would it suffice to derive a legal default rule from IOs' institutional laws: Whatever default rule, say, the World Bank could possibly derive from its constituent instrument, the ILO could still claim that it was not bound by that rule. Only an inter-organizational legal norm can establish a legal default rule that is equally binding on both interacting IOs.

On a methodological note, one could claim that an enquiry into the inter-organizational legal default rule was biased in favour of conceptions of international law as a coherent system, because the idea of a default rule presupposes (or at least recognizes the possibility) of the unity and completeness of international law in the inter-organizational sphere. Such a perspective, one could argue further, would neglect the possibility of a genuine normative gap in inter-organizational law.[3]

---

[1]Hans Kelsen, *Reine Rechtslehre - Einleitung in die rechtswissenschaftliche Problematik (Studienausgabe der 1. Auflage 1934) Hrsg. u. Eingel. v. Matthias Jestaedt* (Mohr Siebeck 2008) 74; William Ebenstein, 'The Pure Theory of Law: Demythologizing Legal Thought' (1971) 59 California Law Review 617, 638.

[2]Agreements and frameworks are always liable to insufficiencies, or are, as seen in Chaps. 13 and 14, restricted to certain types of inter-organizational interactions. Additionally, even if both IOs are willing and able, spelling out rules in a treaty might prove more difficult than having recourse to principles and, within their confines, allowing for progressive concretization through inter-organizational practice.

[3]It has been extensively debated whether there is a logical imperative that international law must be coherent and free of gaps, Eyal Benvenisti, 'The Conception of International Law as a Legal System' (2008) 50 German Yearbook of International Law 393, with further references. Critical e.g. Kelsen, Francois Rigaux, 'Hans Kelsen on International Law' (1998) 9 European Journal of International Law 325, 333. See also the discussion and references in Fernando Lusa Bordin, *The Analogy Between States and International Organizations* (Cambridge University Press 2019) 31 et seqq.

It is indeed true that an enquiry into the default rule would likely be futile if such a genuine normative gap was evident in inter-organizational law. That, however, would only be the case if there was not even the possibility of a general rule. Assuming the existence of such a gap would be premature at this point. As seen above, it is beyond question that certain bodies of inter-organizational law exist. The pertinent instruments themselves presuppose that these bodies of law are part of a wider framework of inter-organizational law.[4] Thus, an enquiry into the inter-organizational legal default rule is simply the consequential next step of enquiry into this framework.

B. The Inter-Organizational Default Rule: Possibilities and Contingencies

When it comes to identifying an inter-organizational legal default rule, one's first intuition might be that IOs are free to interact as they deem appropriate unless inter-organizational law provides otherwise. Conduct that is not prohibited under inter-organizational law, so it might seem, is legally permissible—a way of thinking inspired by traditional conceptions of international law applying between states.[5]

This conclusion, however, would be premature. The principal problem is that inter-organizational law is underdeveloped both from a conceptual and a practical point of view. In particular, there is no "negative residual rule"[6] to the effect that an IO's interactive conduct is legal as long as it is not prohibited by inter-organizational law, analogous of the residual rule famously relied on by the PCIJ in the *Lotus* case for inter-state constellations.[7]

---

[4]See e.g. Art. 3 VCLT-IO, which contemplates further legally binding agreements between IOs to which the VCLT-IO does not apply. Se further Art. 74(1) VCLT-IO and the VCLT-IO's ultimate preambular clause.

[5]*The Case of the S.S. Lotus (France v. Turkey)* PCIJ Rep Series A No 10.

[6]Julius Stone, 'Non Liquet and the Function of Law in the International Community' (1959) 35 British Yearbook of International Law 124, 135. On the concept of residual rule Ole Spiermann, 'Lotus and the Double Structure of International Legal Argument' in Laurence Boisson De Chazournes and Philippe Sands (eds), *International Law, the International Court of Justice and Nuclear Weapons* (Cambridge University Press 1999) 132 et seqq.

[7]*The Case of the S.S. Lotus (France v Turkey)* (n 5) 18. See also *Military and Paramilitary Activities in and against Nicaragua (Nicaragua v. United States of America)* (Merits) [1986] ICJ Reports 14, 135; *Legality of the Threat or Use of Nuclear Weapons* (Advisory Opinion) [1996] ICJ Reports 226; *Accordance with International Law of the Unilateral Declaration of Independence in Respect of Kosovo* (Advisory Opinion) [2010] ICJ Reports 403, 436 et seqq. On the nature of the 'Lotus statement' as a residual rule, rather than a presumption, see the instructive historical review by Spiermann (n 6). On the contemporary relevance of the Lotus rule see the discussion by Cedric Ryngaert, *Jurisdiction in International Law* (2nd edn, Oxford University Press 2015) 34 et seqq., with further references.

But why should the inter-organizational legal default rule not be similar to the one pronounced for the inter-state constellation in the PCIJ's seminal *Lotus* case? That is of course conceivable. However, it is also conceivable that the opposite is the case. Indeed, given the considerable practical and scholarly efforts to limit IOs' powers to those explicitly or implicitly conferred on them, a residual rule of unlimited freedom in inter-organizational relations would seem somewhat counterintuitive. Thus, one could also contemplate that in the absence of an inter-organizational norm saying otherwise, IOs must *not* interact with each other.[8] And, then, there is also the possibility that the inter-organizational default rule lies somewhere 'in between' these two poles. One could e.g. think of a residual rule of freedom to act under the condition of prior attempts to find cooperative solutions, a residual rule of freedom to act regarding certain essential functions etc.

Furthermore, it is unlikely that the inter-organizational legal default rule can be identified without also clarifying the other structural features of the inter-organizational constellation discussed in Chap. 15.[9] Any attempt to define that rule would necessarily have to take into account to what extent every IO can claim a jurisdictional sphere with exclusionary external effect, and, furthermore, what the basic character of IOs' mutual relations is.

In sum, as inter-organizational law stands at present, the inter-organizational legal default rule remains unclear.

C. Consequences for Regulating Interactions Between the ILO, the World Bank and the CoE

In the absence of a defined inter-organizational legal default rule, there is neither a residual fall-back rule nor a *leitmotif* informing more specific inter-organizational legal norms.

This has tangible consequences for the legal regulation of interactions between the ILO, the World Bank and the CoE. The compatibility of interactive conduct with inter-organizational law can only be determined in cases in which no fall-back rule and no *leitmotif* are needed. These are cases in which sufficiently specific inter-organizational norms exist—for example, if a sufficiently specific inter-organizational treaty is in place.[10] Yet, as is clear by now, such cases are hardly existing.

Without such specific norms, a legal assessment is often bound to remain inconclusive. If there is a need for a fall-back rule or a *leitmotif*, the lack of a defined

[8] On corresponding views with regard to inter-state relations Ryngaert (n 7) 34 et seqq.

[9] See Chap. 15 B VI.

[10] The application and interpretation of which would be guided by the customary inter-organizational law of treaties, as spelled out in the VCLT-IO.

default rule renders several outcomes possible at the same time. For example, it is conceivable that inter-organnizational law entitles the World Bank to interfere with ILO initiatives in common member states, as it is conceivable that it prohibits such interference. It is also possible that the ECtHR may take ILO supervisory practice into consideration as it sees fit, even if that contributes to a conflict among the ILO's constituents. But it is also possible that this is not permissible under inter-organizational law, or permissible only under certain conditions. Indeed, most interactive conduct observed in Part I could be either legal or illegal under inter-organizational law.

Thus, one is left with the conclusion that at the heart of inter-organizational law as it stands today, there lies a conundrum, a *non liquet*.[11]

D. Conclusion

Given the scarcity of established inter-organizational law, this chapter has enquired into the legal default rule in the inter-organizational legal relations between the ILO, the World Bank and the CoE.

An inter-organizational legal default rule would provide a fall-back rule in cases in which there are no more specific inter-organizational rules in place, and a *leitmotif* shaping and predetermining the content of such more specific norms insofar as they exist. In inter-organizational law, however, the default rule is undefined. In particular, it cannot simply be assumed that this default rule is an equivalent to the *Lotus* principle.

The absence of a defined legal default position has tangible consequences. Except in cases in which there are reasonably clear specific inter-organizational rules in place, it is often not possible to determine the legality or illegality of interactive conduct that has an effect on the ILO's model of labour governance.

E. Conclusion on Part III

The analysis conducted in this part has revealed a staggering absence of inter-organizational legal norms governing the ILO's inter-organizational interactions with the World Bank and the CoE.

The examination of bilateral inter-organizational treaties between the ILO and the other IOs, as well as the UN System's legal framework, has revealed that the

[11] On the different forms of *non liquet* and related concepts see Daniel Bodansky, 'Non Liquet and the Incompleteness of International Law' in Laurence Boisson De Chazournes and Philippe Sands (eds), *International Law, the International Court of Justice and Nuclear Weapons* (Cambridge University Press 1999) 152. In Bodansky's terminology, the form described here would qualify as an ontological *non liquet*. See further Stone (n 6).

pertinent treaties only contain few and sparse rules. Moreover, these rules almost exclusively concern direct and cooperative interactions. The treaties provide machinery to facilitate cooperation but presuppose that the interacting IOs are willing and able to cooperate in the first place. None of the examined treaties requires the contracting IOs to enhance the role and relevance of the ILO and its model of labour governance within their own laws and activities.

As to other types of interactions, virtually no established rules whatsoever could be identified, neither in treaties nor in customary inter-organizational law or general principles of law. On a structural level, there is not even a defined legal default rule between the ILO, the Bank and the CoE. Thus, in many instances, it will be difficult to ascertain whether, in the absence of specific inter-organizational legal norms, interactions are residually permissible or prohibited.

In sum, apart from the limited relevance of treaties, inter-organizational law hardly provides a common normative standard for inter-organizational interactions between the ILO, the World Bank and the CoE. By and large, there is a staggering absence of inter-organizational legal norms protecting or promoting the ILO's model of labour governance when engaging in inter-organizational interaction with other IOs.

Part IV
The Role of Law in the ILO's Inter-Organizational Interactions: An Evaluation

The legal analysis conducted in the preceding parts of this study has revealed how international law currently regulates inter-organizational interactions between the ILO, the World Bank and the CoE, and how (if at all) it protects and promotes the ILO's model of labour governance in such interactions. The results provide a basis for evaluating the role that positive international law currently plays in the ILO's inter-organizational interactions. The question is not merely how the legal status quo can properly be described, but also if that status quo is adequate.

17. The Current Role of Law in the ILO's Inter-Organizational Interactions

It is convenient to begin this evaluation by briefly recapitulating the preceding parts' results and reflecting on how international law currently regulates the ILO's inter-organizational interactions with other IOs.

A. The Legal Status Quo

As shown, inter-organizational interactions are of high factual relevance for the ILO and its model of labour governance. Moreover, they are ambivalent: For one part, inter-organizational interactions resemble opportunities to promote the ILO's model of labour governance and thereby to expand the organization's outreach to other IOs. At the same time, however, interactions also pose a challenge to the ILO's model, because they can have adverse repercussions on it. Given this ambiguity, the ILO finds itself in a dilemma: On the one hand, it can hardly avoid interactions, nor can it afford to let pass the opportunities that such interactions provide. On the other hand, as soon as it engages in such interactions, it exposes itself to the aforesaid challenge.

Against the background of this dilemma, this study has evaluated the role of international law in governing the ILO's inter-organizational interactions. It departed from the hypothesis that international law, given its general capacity to structure social conduct and to enhance predictability and certainty, could help to mitigate the ambivalence of inter-organizational interactions. The result, however, is sobering: Examining the ILO's, World Bank's and CoE's institutional laws has revealed a 'structural egocentrism' of these laws (I.). The analysis of the inter-organizational law applicable between the three IOs has shown that this structural egocentrism meets with a marked absence of inter-organizational legal norms functioning as a corrective (II.).

H. Gött, *The Law of Interactions Between International Organizations*, Beiträge zum ausländischen öffentlichen Recht und Völkerrecht 299, https://doi.org/10.1007/978-3-662-62389-3_17

I. IOs' 'Structurally Egocentric' Institutional Laws

If looking at the ILO's institutional law in isolation, one might be tempted to conclude that there is straightforward and unambiguous normative guidance for the ILO's inter-organizational interactions. However, as was seen in the further course of this study, the World Bank's and the CoE's institutional laws take different positions. Each examined IO's institutional law provides a distinct normative framework for its respective 'own' IO's interactive conduct, which however is legally disconnected from the other IOs' respective institutional laws. Moreover, each examined institutional law prioritizes its own IO and relativizes the respective other. This does not necessarily have to result in open conflict between the interacting IOs. Nevertheless, on a structural level, their institutional laws latently pit the examined IOs against each other. One could speak of a 'structural egocentrism'.

To be sure, 'structural egocentrism' is not necessarily unusual for legal instruments incorporating a legal person and providing institutional, procedural and substantive rules for its functioning. For instance, legal mechanisms prioritizing the 'own' and relativizing the 'other' can also be found in the domestic laws of states. There, legal concepts such as 'ordre public',[1] 'constitutional identity'[2] and others serve as justifications for not giving full regard to the law of other states or, for that matter, to inter- or supranational law.

II. The Absence of an Inter-Organizational Legal Corrective

However, the situation between the ILO, the World Bank and the CoE is structurally different from the one between states. If states choose to put their own interests over those of other states, they must still do so in a manner consistent with international law. Contemporary international law comprises an elaborate and established body of international legal norms requiring every state to respect other states' international legal rights and to honour all of its international obligations, irrespective of how much its own institutional law relativizes other states' interests in favour of its own. Constitutional limitations to international law, justified under the banner of 'constitutional identity' or similar ideas, may receive ample attention, but remain in many instances symbolic challenges to international law's normative propositions with eventually rather little practical significance.

By contrast, as Part III has shown, a normative corrective barely exists in the inter-organizational constellation. While the ILO and the other IOs must of course

[1]See e.g. Art. 6 Einführungsgesetz zum Bürgerlichen Gesetzbuche (BGBl I 1994, 2494).

[2]See e.g., with references to a range of cases from various states, *Outright Monetary Transactions* (Request for Preliminary Ruling) (ECLI:DE:BVerfG:2014:rs20140114.2bvr272813) BVerfGE 134, 366, 387, para 30.

also honour their treaty commitments vis-à-vis each other, such inter-organizational treaties are a rarity to begin with. Where they exist, they only contain rudimentary obligations that essentially provide machinery to facilitate direct and cooperative interactions. By contrast, they hardly regulate other types of interactions.

Beyond the scope of these treaties, inter-organizational law is virtually absent altogether. Not only are there no established unwritten inter-organizational obligations that the ILO, World Bank and CoE owe one another, but there is not even a defined international legal default rule that applies residually.[3]

III. Conclusion: The Underdeveloped Law of Inter-Organizational Interactions

It is not easy to find an adequate description for this legal status quo. Firstly, it would not be accurate to say that there was 'no' law regulating inter-organizational interactions: As seen, there are plenty of legal norms, primarily the examined provisions in the respective IOs' institutional laws, but also those few inter-organizational norms that could be determined.

Secondly, it would neither be entirely sufficient to say that the law was incoherent. It is true that there is a potential for incoherence between IOs' institutional laws, as their 'structural egocentrism' remains unmoderated by inter-organizational law. However, this potential for incoherence is not the result of different established bodies of law not interplaying well. Rather, inter-organizational law has never been systematically laid out in the first place. Thus, the legal incoherence results to a significant extent from the fact that one part of the law in question simply remains 'unknown'.

Thirdly, it would be inaccurate to conclude that the legal status quo was insufficient because it allowed IOs to act as they see fit. Inter-organizational law does not *allow* IOs to play out their agendas: just as there are no inter-organizational legal norms prohibiting or steering certain interactive conduct, there are also no inter-organizational legal norms permitting it.

Finally, it would also be inaccurate to say that it was unrealistic to expect that law could govern inter-organizational interactions in the first place. As seen, there is some inter-organizational law—inter-organizational relationship agreements and other treaties, the customary law of treaties between IOs, and some other fields—and these bodies of law are also being applied in practice.

[3]This situation is markedly different from the absence of special rules in inter-state relations (in which case sovereign equality applies as a fall-back position) or, for that matter, the absence of special norms between (public or private) entities at domestic level (in which domestic public and/or private law apply, each of which include either organizational hierarchies or rights and obligations erga omnes, e.g. property rights).

Instead of resorting to one of these explanations, it appears preferable to acknowledge that the legal status quo is of a *sui generis* nature which is arguably unprecedented in modern international law. One way to describe it could be to say that the law of inter-organizational interactions was underdeveloped. 'Underdeveloped' in this sense does not mean that there is law in need of change. Instead, 'underdeveloped' describes that the positive law of inter-organizational interactions, including even its most basic elements like the inter-organizational legal default rule, have never truly been conceptualized and 'explored' before.

B. Consequences for the Role of Law in the ILO's Inter-Organizational Interactions

The 'underdevelopment' described in the preceding section has significant implications for international law's current role regarding inter-organizational interactions in labour governance.

I. The Practical Relevance of Other Factors for Structuring Inter-Organizational Interactions

As a first implication, the absence of a 'developed' legal framework increases the practical relevance of other factors for ordering and structuring inter-organizational interactions. These factors include, for example, IOs' respective policy preferences, the resources available to them, and IOs' readiness and ability to reach arrangements with each other. Importantly, to a large extent, each IO's interactive conduct depends on what that IO can 'afford to do', constitutionally, politically, financially, administratively and reputationally. A relevant further factor is an IO's 'instinct of self-preservation', i.e. its inherent interest to cater to its constituents' interests as best as possible in order to prove its continued relevance.

To be sure, these non-legal factors give structure to interactions. The point is that they structure them in other ways. Apart from any existing shared policy preferences, they do not provide structure by reference to a common normative benchmark, like law does. Instead, the way non-legal factors shape interactions largely depends on each IO's political, financial, administrative or reputational power, and their willingness and ability to use it in a particular case.

The ILO is not particularly well-equipped to engage in such 'inter-organizational power plays'. Its overall political, financial and administrative leverage is modest. To name but one example, while the ILO can offer its members technical and other assistance, its financial power will always be outweighed by the World Bank's. The ILO's greatest asset is, besides its aggregated expertise on labour topics, its persuasive power emanating from universal tripartite social dialogue. As the observed interactions with the CoE illustrate, such persuasive power can have significant influence on the practice of other IOs. However, the other IO needs to be willing and able to be persuaded in the first place. As the observed interactions with the World Bank show, the ILO's persuasive power is mitigated if the other IO holds on to a different perception of how 'political' its own work is and should be, or if it relies on fundamentally different economic policy assumptions.

Moreover, even in an otherwise favourable environment, another IO's institutional features can dilute the ILO's persuasive power. As seen, even though the ECtHR chose to align its jurisprudence with ILO positions, it also invoked its judicial independence as justification for deviating from the ILO's positions and to decide autonomously on whether and how to take ILO instruments and practice into account.

In addition, one further factor can influence the way the ILO can wield its persuasive power: apart from the 'inter-organizational power play' just described, there is already another 'power play' taking place *inside* the ILO. The ILO's persuasive power rests on tripartite support for its positions and initiatives. Thus, the ILO depends on attaining the broadest possible consensus among its tripartite constituents. In consequence, it needs to deploy its resources on two fronts: On the one hand, it has to ensure that workers', employers' and governments' interests are satisfactorily and sustainably reconciled within its organs.[4] On the other hand, it has to ensure that its own model of labour governance, including its functioning and its output, is adequately protected and promoted vis-à-vis other IOs. The duality of an internal (even though regulated) 'power play of interests' and an external 'power play of institutions' makes inter-organizational interactions a particularly intricate topic for the ILO. This arguably puts a further strain on its capability to fully play out its persuasive power vis-à-vis other IOs.

II. Law as Potential Rhetoric Reinforcement

The legal status quo does not only render 'power plays' a prevalent factor for ordering inter-organizational interactions. Rather, it may even reinforce them. In the absence of a common inter-organizational legal standard, the observed 'structural egocentrism' of IOs' institutional laws can lead to entrenched positions. Notably, the ILO's relativization in the Bank's and CoE's institutional laws can rhetorically reinforce the position of these other IOs in their interactions with the ILO.

As seen, as long as the Bank and the CoE operate within the limits of their institutional legal framework, they can claim to act lawfully even if their conduct has

[4]Since, unlike other IOs such as the Bank or the CoE, the ILO places this 'power play of interests' at the heart of its model, it existentially depends on this power play leading to mutually acceptable results and to remain able to motivate all of its constituent groups to participate in the organization's work in a constructive manner. In the light of the post-2012 crisis, Maupain considered the latter one of the foremost challenges for the ILO to come, Francis Maupain, 'A Second Century for What? The ILO at a Regulatory Crossroad' (2019) 16 International Organizations Law Review 1, 22.

adverse influence on the ILO. This claim to 'be in the right' does perhaps not persuade the ILO, but it is a powerful argument vis-à-vis the World Bank's and CoE's own constituents, on which these IOs ultimately depend politically and financially. If the only available legal standard for the lawfulness of an IO's interactive conduct is the own institutional law, and if the Bank and the CoE faithfully adhere to this standard while interacting with the ILO, they have a strong case to show to their constituents that their influence on the ILO is appropriate and legitimate.

At the same time, the ILO is deprived of the opportunity to make a powerful counter-argument, namely to claim that another IO's conduct is *illegal*.[5] Thus, the ILO has to resort to other, non-legal arguments, e.g. by claiming that the conduct was politically unwise, economically unsound or morally unjust. Whether and to what extent such other arguments will pervade will depend on how other IOs react to them. In the case of self-perceivedly 'non-political' institutions like the World Bank, or a court of law like the ECtHR, it can be expected that political or moral critiques are somewhat less powerful than an argument of illegality.

Thus, in the absence of a counterbalancing inter-organizational legal standard, the plurality of IOs' institutional laws and their relativization of the respective other IOs may even serve as a rhetoric reinforcement to each IO's efforts to advocate and legitimize its own position.

C. Conclusion

The legal status quo regarding the ILO's inter-organizational interactions has two main characteristics. The first characteristic is the plurality of institutional laws, each of which takes a 'structurally egocentric' stance on interactions with other IOs. The second characteristic is the marked absence of inter-organizational law as a coherent and encompassing legal corrective. The best way to describe the legal status quo is to say that the law of inter-organizational interactions is underdeveloped, in the sense that large parts have never been conceptualized and 'explored'.

In consequence, the ILO's interactions with other IOs are, for better or worse, structured along non-legal factors in what could be termed 'inter-organizational power plays'. Existing law does not only fall short of orchestrating this 'power play' but may even cause IOs' positions to become (more) entrenched.

[5]The ILO is deprived of this argument both when criticizing the Bank or CoE themselves and when answering to its own constituents about how inter-organizational interactions with these IOs did (not) play out in the ILO's favour.

18. The Legal Status Quo: An Adequate Way of Regulating the ILO's Interactions?

How is this diminished and potentially 'partisan' role of international law to be assessed? As seen, the legal status quo leaves the ILO dependent on its (mostly persuasive) power. This puts the ILO in a fragile and potentially precarious position vis-à-vis other IOs. Still, this alone does not automatically imply that the law regulating (or not regulating) inter-organizational interactions is insufficient. Instead, whether or not the legal status quo is adequate is a question that requires closer consideration.

A. The Law of Inter-Organizational Interactions in Search for a Narrative

Assessing the adequacy of the legal status quo requires a yardstick for orientation. Such yardsticks could be found in international law narratives, i.e. theoretical and conceptual accounts that describe and assess phenomena and developments in international law.

In contemporary international legal scholarship, there is certainly no shortage of such narratives.[1] However, these narratives have remained markedly silent on the law of inter-organizational interactions, both in general and regarding labour

[1] Stoll has pointed to a "theoretical turn" in international legal scholarship, Peter-Tobias Stoll, 'Koordination, Kooperation und Konstitutionalisierung im Völkerrecht' in Werner Heun and Frank Schorkopf (eds), *Wendepunkte der Rechtswissenschaft - Aspekte des Rechts in der Moderne* (Wallstein Verlag 2014) 292.

H. Gött, *The Law of Interactions Between International Organizations*, Beiträge zum ausländischen öffentlichen Recht und Völkerrecht 299,
https://doi.org/10.1007/978-3-662-62389-3_18

governance in particular.[2] This silence is surprising, because many of the aspects arising in the context of inter-organizational interactions—the diversification and fragmentation of law, concerns about effectiveness and efficiency, unchecked power, hegemony and contestation, legitimacy of IOs and their conduct etc.—are familiar themes of international law narratives. Still, many narratives appear to have only limited explanatory potential for what has been observed in this study.

A comprehensive discussion of all accounts and variations would exceed the limits of this study. Still, some central points of concern regarding narratives of functionalism (Sect. 1.), fragmentation (Sect. 2.), constitutionalization (Sect. 3.), Global Administrative Law (Sect. 4.) and legal pluralism (Sect. 5.) will be flagged in the following.

I. The Permeation and the Limits of Functionalism

Functionalism, arguably the most influential theory of international organizations to date,[3] hardly if ever systematically addressed the phenomenon of inter-organizational interactions and the legal questions surrounding it.

1. The Permeation of Functionalist Thought in the Legal Status Quo

This abstinence is remarkable, because functionalist thought permeates the legal status quo revealed in this study.

First of all, functionalist thinking provides a conceptual basis for equipping IOs with 'structurally egocentric' institutional laws. The reason for this is that functionalism's perspective on IOs is state-centric:[4] Its central proposition is that states cooperate through IOs to pursue a defined objective in specific policy areas. This is seen as the reason why states establish IOs, confer competences on them, and contribute to their financial and other resources.[5] Functionalist thought conceptualizes IOs' activities as essentially administrative, technical and, therefore, apolitical.

[2]While some narratives barely address inter-organizational interactions at all, others touch on the topic but fail to grasp their factual or legal complexities and peculiarities. Again others blur the perspective by centring on interactions between 'regimes', glossing over the particular legal questions arising in the inter-organizational constellation.

[3]Jan Klabbers, *An Introduction to International Organizations Law* (3rd edn, Cambridge University Press 2015) 32; José E Álvarez, *International Organizations as Law-Makers* (Oxford University Press 2006) 17 et seqq. More cautious towards functionalism being a comprehensive theory and its dominance Guy Fiti Sinclair, 'The Original Sin (and Salvation) of Functionalism' (2015) 26 European Journal of International Law 965, 966 et seqq.

[4]See the discussion and the references in Jan Klabbers, 'The EJIL Foreword: The Transformation of International Organizations Law' (2015) 26 European Journal of International Law 9, 24 et seqq.

[5]Klabbers, *An Introduction to International Organizations Law* (n 3) 32.

This frames IOs as means to limit state power, pursue common objectives and cooperate jointly and peacefully for the common good.[6] Because of these positive connotations, functionalism has provided a powerful theoretical justification for generously reinforcing the standing of IOs in legal scholarship and practice.[7]

Second of all, functionalism offers a justification for relativizing 'external' actors and their interests. It may be suspected that functionalism inspired the pertinent constitutional provisions that require IOs to interact with others within the terms of their own institutional law. It may further be assumed that the staggering absence of safeguards for the governance models of other IOs is based on the idea that IOs are agents that are firmly controlled by their principals, i.e. their member states, which will take care of steering IOs' interactions in an appropriately coherent manner.[8]

Finally, functionalist thought also surfaces in inter-organizational law. It permeates the few inter-organizational agreements that exist. For instance, the ILO-CoE's 'cooperation for coordination' approach aims at achieving both IOs' goals more effectively. Similarly, the UN System's functionally decentralized architecture was designed for both effective and 'apolitical' (or at least less politicized) international cooperation.[9]

[6]Functionalists tend to present IOs and their activities in a positive light and, sometimes enthusiastically, see functional cooperation through IOs as means to overcome political divides and even to eventually achieve world peace, see e.g. Nagendra Singh, *Termination of Membership of International Organizations* (Frederick A Praeger 1958) vii ("salvation of mankind").

[7]Epitomizing example in *Application for Review of Judgment No 273 of the United Nations Administrative Tribunal* (Advisory Opinion) [1982] ICJ Reports 325, 347. On various occasions, functionalism has provided a rationale for IOs performing their functions in an undisturbed and effective manner. In this way, functionalism has served as justification e.g. for wide interpretations of IOs' competences (including the recognition of implied ones) or for accepting IOs' wide functional immunity before domestic courts.

[8]What is more, functionalist patterns appear in the examined IOs' practice, e.g. the ILO's concern to involve other IOs for its own agenda, or in the ECtHR's approach to render human rights protection under the ECHR "practical and effective" by including ILO instruments and practice where considered appropriate.

[9]John HE Fried, 'Relations Between the United Nations and the International Labor Organization' (1947) 41 The American Political Science Review 963. The vagueness and weakness of cooperative arrangements made in inter-organizational treaties are reinforcing the member states' position as 'principals', as they avoid that IOs' secretariats can sidestep member state control by creating (too) strong liaisons with other IOs at secretariat level, Mario Savino, 'Linkages Between Global Regimes and Interactions with Civil Society' in Sabino Cassese (ed), *Research Handbook on Global Administrative Law* (Edward Elgar Publishing 2016) 131, 135; Christian Tietje, 'Global Governance and Inter-Agency Co-Operation in International Economic Law' (2002) 36 Journal of World Trade 501, 507. The same explanation could be used for the vague provisions on inter-organizational interaction in IOs' institutional laws, as observed in Part II of this study.

2. Functionalism at Its Limits

However, although it permeates both IOs' institutional laws and inter-organizational law, functionalism fails to provide a convincing conceptual backdrop for the present legal status quo.

On a descriptive level, functionalism's state-centric perspective runs the risk of not even noticing inter-organizational law as a self-standing area of international law with own peculiarities. Firstly, conceptualizing member states as principals and IOs as agents downplays that, as a matter of law, even state-driven IOs are separate legal subjects having their own legal relationships to other IOs. In addition, the state-centric perspective also misses that inter-organizational interactions are often shaped by IOs' organs that are not composed of states. Furthermore, understanding IOs as apolitical administrators of the common good misses the variety and impact of inter-organizational interactions and is bound to underestimate the relevance of their legal regulation. This study's case studies exemplify that interactions between IOs can be highly political, and that they can be an expression of different conceptions of what the common good is and how it is to be achieved.

On a normative level, and perhaps most importantly for present purposes, functionalism's optimistic support for enhancing the effectiveness of IOs[10] may in fact lead to the exact opposite when it comes to inter-organizational interactions. While making the case for effectiveness, functionalism hardly explains when and why effectiveness should stand back in deference of other goals, rights or values.[11] This becomes especially problematic in the inter-organizational constellation, because here, one IO's strife for utmost effectiveness may be directly juxtaposed to another IO's. Thus, attempts to maximise IOs' effectiveness can result in an undamped collision of two IOs' respective effectivity rationales. Whenever one IO considers it necessary for the effective execution of its mandate, it can invoke functionalism as justification to influence another IO. And when another IO seeks to avert such influence in order to effectively safeguard or promote its governance model, it can rely on functionalism as well. For instance, the ILO could invoke the effective execution of its mandate when it promotes labour market reforms through tripartite social dialogue in its member states, just as the World Bank could argue that it effectively executes its mandate when it uses the EWI to demand business-friendly and 'economic' labour market deregulation without such 'political' dialogue. Advocating the effective execution of each IO's mandate under the paradigm of functionalism hence potentially justifies unfettered mutual influence among IOs, which,

[10]Klabbers, *An Introduction to International Organizations Law* (n 3) 35; Klabbers, 'The EJIL Foreword: The Transformation of International Organizations Law' (n 4) 64.

[11]This has provoked criticism in particular when the ideal of effectiveness was brought to bear against the sovereignty of non-member states or against human rights of individuals. Especially the latter calls into question whether an unequivocally positive image of IOs as apolitical agents of the common good was appropriate.

ironically, may even lead to an overall loss of effectiveness if the interacting IOs thwart each other's efforts.[12]

Functionalism's further conceptual assumption that the states as 'principals' will step in to coordinate 'their' agent IOs in a sound and coherent manner stands in stark contrast to the factual record, as exemplified in Part I of this study.

In consequence, it seems almost inevitable that assessments of inter-organizational interactions and their legal regulation need to move beyond established functionalist premises.

II. The Neglected Dimension(s) of Fragmentation

During the last decades, the diversification of the international legal order, including the proliferation of IOs, has widely been discussed under the banner of fragmentation of international law. The better part of the fragmentation debate, including on the fragmentation of international labour regulation, has centred on instances of conflicts between norms or 'regimes' (and how to overcome them).[13] By contrast, and quite surprisingly, the debate has by and large refrained from addressing inter-organizational interactions as such. Neither the ILC's work on fragmentation[14] nor most other contributions enquired into fragmentation's specific institutional dimension.[15]

---

[12]In consequence, functionalism almost inevitably will have to be developed further to explain how, in the inter-organizational constellation, a potential clash of IOs each relying on functionalist rationales should be accommodated.

[13]Margaret A Young, *Trading Fish, Saving Fish: The Interaction Between Regimes in International Law* (Cambridge University Press 2011) 52. Outstanding examples are the 'social clause' debate (see above Chap. 2 D. II), labour market deregulation requested by international financial institutions (see e.g. Chap. 4) and the status of labour rights in the EU, epitomized in the CJEU's case-law on the right to srike, Case C-438/05, *International Transport Workers Federation, Finnish Seamens Union v. Viking Line ABP and OÜ Viking Line Eesti* (ECLI:EU:C:2007:772) [2007] ECR I-10779, Case C-341/05, *Laval Un Partneri Ltd v. Svenska Byggnadsarbetareförbundet, Svenska Byggnadsarbetareförbundets Avdelning 1, Byggettan and Svenska Elektrikerförbundet* (ECLI: EU:C:2007:809) [2007] I-11767.

[14]Which deliberately did not address the institutional dimension of fragmentation. ILC, 'Fragmentation of International Law: Difficulties Arising from the Diversification and Expansion of International Law, Report of the Study Group of the International Law Commission, Finalized by Martti Koskenniemi' (2006) A/CN.4/L.682, paras 13 and 489. Moreover, those scholars who address the institutional dimension often focus on dispute settlement in specific areas of international law, Young, *Trading Fish, Saving Fish: The Interaction Between Regimes in International Law* (n 13) 14. Some earlier writers on the subject fully acknowledged the institutional dimension, e.g. Clarence Wilfred Jenks, 'The Conflict of Law-Making Treaties' (1953) 30 British Yearbook of International Law 401, 403.

[15]Some authors have taken a limited stance on institutions but focus on their impact at domestic level, deploring an asymmetry between 'hard' economic rules and 'soft' labour rules, see Adelle Blackett and Anne Trebilcock, 'Conceptualizing Transnational Labour Law' in Adelle Blackett and

As this study showcases, both the focus on conflicts and the insufficient consideration of the institutional dimension are shortcomings of the fragmentation debate. Firstly, focusing only on conflicts misses the manifold other types of interactions observed between the ILO and other IOs involved in labour governance. Secondly, focusing only on substantive law overlooks that international labour law is highly institutionalized, and that labour governance is significantly shaped by the plurality of IOs and the interactions between them.

As a consequence of this overly narrow focus, the 'solution strategies' often proposed for overcoming negative effects of fragmentation are in danger of missing the mark. This is especially true for systemic interpretation,[16] which is hardly more than one possible strategy (among others) to approximate IOs' structurally egocentric institutional laws. Moreover, it crucially depends on three factors:

a) the readiness of IOs to engage in systemic interpretation (that for instance the Bank in the EWI episode did not have),
b) the willingness of IOs not to use systemic interpretation exclusively at their respective own terms and discretion (which the ECtHR did not have), and
c) the readiness and the ability of the interpreting IO to properly accommodate the institutional peculiarities of the other IO (which the ECtHR was reluctant to do).

Finally, it has widely gone unnoticed by the fragmentation debate that IOs can develop their own special rules on interpretation, thus potentially corroding the common methodological ground for systemic interpretation. One could even consider this a third, 'methodological' dimension of fragmentation, complementing the substantive and institutional dimensions.

All in all, as the fragmentation debate did not 'ask the right questions' on inter-organizational interactions to begin with, it is bound to fall short of giving sufficient answers.

III. A Case of 'De-Constitutionalization'?

The third potential yardstick for assessing the legal status quo, constitutionalization narratives, provide an example of how focusing on one development can result in overlooking another.

Anne Trebilcock (eds) *Research Handbook on Transnational Labour Law* (Edward Elgar Publishing 2015) 5 et seq., with further references. Such a perspective is of course legitimate, but it remains silent on the particular inter-organizational aspects, notably the mutual influence on institutional governance models, and thus circumvents the pertinent questions of how these governance models are protected and how they relate to each other.

[16]See above, Chap. 11. The same applies for the recourse to the collision rules, see examples cited by Dirk Pulkowski, *The Law and Politics of International Regime Conflict* (Oxford University Press 2014) 318 et seqq.

At the heart of constitutionalization narratives lies the idea that international law either already contains or gradually develops elements that bear semblance of a constitution. Among these elements are individual rights and obligations, reformulated notions of sovereignty or the emergence of common fundamental values.[17] On a normative level, constitutionalization narratives usually welcome this development as a desirable turn away from power politics towards increased legal containment of power, accountability, legitimacy, and international integration.[18] Constitutionalists would typically assume a systemic unity of the international legal order, both as a description and as a normative postulate.[19]

When it comes to IOs' legal relations with their members and the relations between those members, constitutionalist narratives have provided powerful assessments. Against this background, it could be expected that the question whether the relations between 'constitutionalizing' IOs would 'constitutionalize' as well would be the natural next field of enquiry. However, so far, constitutionalization narratives have hardly if ever given sufficient attention to the inter-organizational constellation and the ensuing issues that surfaced in this study.[20]

What is more, many of the core propositions of constitutionalist narratives are called into question when applied to the observed interactions between the ILO, the World Bank and the CoE. This is, firstly, true for those strands that emphasize the emergence of common norms and values.[21] As has been seen, in the

---

[17] See e.g. Anne Peters, 'Rechtsordnungen und Konstitutionalisierung: Zur Neubestimmung der Verhältnisse' (2010) 65 Zeitschrift für Öffentliches Recht 3.

[18] Jan Klabbers, 'Setting the Scene' in Jan Klabbers, Anne Peters and Geir Ulfstein (eds), *The Constitutionalization of International Law* (Oxford University Press 2009) 4; Wouter Werner, 'The Never-Ending Closure: Constitutionalism and International Law' in Nicholas Tsagourias (ed), *Transnational Constitutionalism: International and European Perspectives* (Cambridge University Press 2007) 330.

[19] Andrea Bianchi, *International Law Theories* (Oxford University Press 2016) 48.

[20] Presumably, the enhanced visibility of intra-organizational constitutionalization processes is one reason for this, see Peters, 'Rechtsordnungen und Konstitutionalisierung: Zur Neubestimmung der Verhältnisse' (n 17) 30. For an exception, the allocation of functions among the UN System's component IOs and other entities has been woven into the constitutionalization narrative as an example of the law promoting systemic coherence and 'separation of powers', Geir Ulfstein, 'Institutions and Competences' in Jan Klabbers, Anne Peters and Geir Ulfstein (eds), *The Constitutionalization of International Law* (Oxford University Press 2009) 72, relying on the ICJ's *Nuclear Weapons in Armed Conflict* opinion.

[21] One strand of constitutionalization emphasizes the emergence of values operating as checks for global politics, Christian Tomuschat, 'International Law: Ensuring the Survival of Mankind on the Eve of a New Century' (1999) 281 Recueil des Cours de l'Académie de Droit International 9; Jost Delbrück, 'Prospects for a "World (Internal) Law"? Legal Developments in a Changing International System' (2002) 9 Indiana Journal of Global Legal Studies 401. See also Erika de Wet, 'The International Constitutional Order' (2006) 55 International and Comparative Law Quarterly 51. Such values are seen, for example, in the prohibition of the use of force or fundamental human rights, Klabbers, 'Setting the Scene' (n 18) 26. Their emergence is also seen in the rise of institutions and implementation mechanisms, such as the proliferation of international courts and tribunals, and in the formation of new IOs and the reconfiguration and reinvigoration of old ones, Nico Krisch, *Beyond Constitutionalism: The Pluralist Structure of Postnational Law* (Oxford

inter-organizational relations between the ILO, the World Bank and the CoE, it is already unclear to what extent there exists law at all. Even less, it can be said that there are common values in place.[22] Insofar as common goals are defined for inter-organizational cooperation (as in the case of the UN Millennium and Sustainable Development Goals), these goals presently rather seem to qualify as policy directives rather than genuine values, and in any event have not managed to surpass the egocentric stance of IOs' institutional laws. For the time being, their integrative dimension (insofar as it exists) remains political rather than 'constitutional'. It is conceivable that the definition of common political goals will 'harden' into legally relevant constitutional values in the future, e.g. surrounding the notion of sustainable development. However, it is too early to draw reliable conclusions in this regard.

In a similar vein, strands of constitutionalist thought focusing on emerging hierarchies or ordering principles[23] will struggle to catch on in the inter-organizational constellation. The reason for this is that, as seen, there are no legal hierarchies, virtually no established legal ordering principles and hardly any institutions and procedures in place that would predictably steer inter-organizational influence.

Descriptions of constitutionalization as a process[24] perhaps come closest to this study's findings. As seen, the few legal rules in place between the ILO and the other

---

University Press 2012) 32 et seq., with further references. On a more formal note, some authors point to some of these values being enshrined in norms with a higher hierarchical value, such as jus cogens and create obligations *erga omnes*, see Klabbers, 'Setting the Scene' (n 18) 26; Thomas Kleinlein, *Konstitutionalisierung Im Völkerrecht* (Springer 2012) 315 et seqq.; Bianchi (n 19) 50.

[22]One could argue that 'cooperation' was one such value. However, cooperation as such is hardly more than a shibboleth. Moreover, as shown, cooperation is understood and framed quite differently in each IO's institutional law and practice. Therefore, even though every IO would arguably subscribe to cooperation as a guiding idea, the existence of a truly *common* value seems questionable.

[23]Some constitutionalist contributions focus on the capacity of international law to give structure to the activities of international actors and the 'international community', Bianchi (n 19) 49. On the international community see Andreas L Paulus, *Die internationale Gemeinschaft im Völkerrecht* (C H Beck 2001). The international legal order is conceived as not only defining common values, but also allocating functions to actors, notably including states. Proponents of this strand of the constitutionalization narrative observe changes in the international legal order, towards an emergence of more constitutional structures which not only promote values, but also delimit power, Krisch, *Beyond Constitutionalism: The Pluralist Structure of Postnational Law* (n 21) 33 et seq., with further references. For an early example from practice, see e.g. *Competence of the General Assembly for the Admission of a State to the United Nations* (Dissenting opinion by Judge Álvarez) [1950] ICJ Reports 12, 13 et seqq. These structures can be expressed in values and norm hierarchies, but also in the emergence of ordering principles, such as the principle of subsidiarity, Bianchi (n 19) 54 et seqq.

[24]The starting point of this idea is different from the other strands. Proponents of this strand conceptualize 'constitution' less as a particular form or structure entrenching particular values than a continuous process allowing for discourse, contestation and recognition of differences, see e.g. Jo Shaw, 'Postnational Constitutionalism in the European Union' (1999) 6 Journal of European Public Policy 579. The proposed ideal is a transparent, inclusive and accountable constitutional discourse, sometimes conceptually fettered with the eventual aim of universality, Kleinlein (n 21)

examined IOs lay great emphasis on defining procedures for interaction.[25] On the other hand, however, it does not seem that the legalization of inter-organizational relations is traceably increasing. Beyond general relationship agreements like the UN-ILO, UN-IBRD or ILO-CoE, inter-organizational treaties seem to remain the exception rather than the rule. Thus, while there is a lot of interaction happening, this interaction is not in any discernible way moving towards 'more' constitutionalization between IOs.

Even more, the present body of established inter-organizational legal norms arguably even falls behind the degree of legalization that is usually associated with the classic 'non-constitutionalized' or 'Westphalian' international law between states.[26] Thus, one could even argue that the emergence of IOs, and the constitutionalization in their respective relations with their member states,[27] has been accompanied by a 'de-constitutionalization' in the relations between these IOs.

In sum, constitutionalization narratives mostly have refrained from genuinely addressing the phenomenon of inter-organizational interactions, both in labour governance and beyond. As many of constitutionalization's core premises are called into question, it is doubtful that it can serve as a conceptual backdrop at present.

IV. Global Administrative Law's Underestimation of Inter-Organizational Interactions

Other narratives take notice of inter-organizational interactions but underestimate their complexities. One case in point is Global Administrative Law (GAL). GAL's marvellous success story is all the more remarkable given that many of its central

700 et seq.; Krisch, *Beyond Constitutionalism: The Pluralist Structure of Postnational Law* (n 21) 34 et seq. With regard to the development of international law, some commentators propose institutional reforms to facilitate discourse while ensuring basic democratic principles, e.g. Kleinlein (n 21) 658.

[25] See above, Chaps. 13 and 14.

[26] On the different conceptualizations and categorizations of international law's development see Wolfgang Friedmann, *The Changing Structure of International Law* (Columbia University Press 1964); Stoll, 'Koordination, Kooperation und Konstitutionalisierung im Völkerrecht' (n 1).

[27] A number of constitutionalist writers contend that certain regimes or areas of international law, e.g. EU law or WTO law, are in a process of constitutionalization. See e.g. Eric Stein, 'Lawyers, Judges, and the Making of a Transnational Constitution' (1981) 75 American Journal of International Law 1; Florian Rödl, 'Regime-Collisions, Proceduralised Conflict of Laws and the Unity of the Law: On the Form of Constitutionalism Beyond the State' in Rainer Nickel (ed), *Conflict of Laws and Laws of Conflict in Europe and Beyond - Patterns of Supranational and Transnational Juridification* (ARENA 2009) 342; Surabhi Ranganathan, 'The Value of Narratives: The India-USA Nuclear Deal in Terms of Fragmentation, Pluralism, Constitutionalisation and Global Administrative Law' (2013) 6 Erasmus Law Review 17, 26.

conceptual elements have remained rather sketchy until today. The latter include the sources of GAL[28] and the concepts of 'global administration'[29] and 'global administrative space'.[30] The inter-organizational constellation examined in this study exposes the conceptually unfinished state of these elements. Firstly, even in the widest conceivable definition, 'global administration' does not comprise all types of inter-organizational interactions between the ILO, the Bank and the CoE examined in this study,[31] rendering it doubtful whether the specific focus on 'administration' is

[28]GAL focuses on the identification and analysis of principles and rules governing global administrative activities, both within and beyond the established sources of international law. GAL intentionally focuses only on procedural legal principles governing global administrative processes and purposefully refrains from analyzing substantive principles or values. These include rules on transparency and participation, rules requiring reasoned decisions or rules concerning review of decisions, Benedict Kingsbury and Megan Donaldson, 'Global Administrative Law', *Max Planck Encyclopedia of Public International Law* (Oxford University Press 2011) 3 and 28 et seqq., 41 et seqq. and 46 et seqq. The possible sources of such a GAL have remained a controversial issue (see e.g. the pronounced criticism by Klabbers, 'Setting the Scene' (n 18) 28. GAL proponents name as possible sources public international law, *ius gentium* (similar to the lex mercatoria), international public law, national administrative law or even autonomous norm creation by "functional communities", such as administrations themselves, through "repeated practice", Benedict Kingsbury and Megan Donaldson, 'Global Administrative Law', Max Planck Encyclopedia of Public International Law (Oxford University Press 2011) 21 et seqq. GAL has been defined as "mechanisms, principles, practices, and supporting social understandings that promote or otherwise affect the accountability of global administrative bodies, in particular by ensuring they meet adequate standards of transparency, participation, reasoned decision, and legality, and by providing effective review of the rules and decisions they make", Nico Krisch and Benedict Kingsbury, 'Introduction: Global Governance and Global Administrative Law in the International Legal Order' (2006) 17 European Journal of International Law 1, 17. Not all of these candidates are reconcilable with traditional sources doctrine. To approach this issue, Kingsbury has proposed that any norm which fulfils the criterion of 'publicness' forms part of GAL, Benedict Kingsbury, 'The Concept of "Law" in Global Administrative Law' (2009) 20 European Journal of International Law 23.

[29]The definition of global administration is suggested to comprise "rulemaking [in specific cases], administrative adjudication between competing interests, and other forms of regulatory and administrative decision and management", Benedict Kingsbury, Nico Krisch and Richard B Stewart, 'The Emergence of Global Administrative Law' (2005) 68 Law and Contemporary Problems 15, 17. They claim that global administrative action can be "distinguished from legislation in the form of treaties, and from adjudication in the form of episodic dispute settlement between states or other disputing parties", ibid.

[30]Global administration is considered to occur as a complex interplay between actors within a "global administrative space", transcending the boundaries between the national and international levels, as well as those between public and private spheres, Krisch and Kingsbury (n 28) 1; Bianchi (n 19) 61. The multitude of actors, some of which do not derive their authority form states, and the complexity of administrative processes is seen to blur the seemingly clear-cut doctrinal positions on sources and subjects of international law, which leads to concerns of legitimacy and accountability, Krisch and Kingsbury (n 28) 1.

[31]Notably the interactions between the ILO and the ECtHR appeared more on the stage of supervision and adjudication, as did the interactions between the ILO and the ECSR. Additionally, it is doubtful if interactions like those observed between the ILO and the World Bank would fully qualify as 'administration' either. One might ask, then, whether the focus on administration – difficult to define as it is anyway – is perhaps too narrow and would benefit from an expansion.

adequate to begin with. Secondly, the relations between the ILO and other IOs observed here do not easily match with the image of a 'global administrative space'.[32] It may not be a coincidence that those GAL contributions that actually address inter-organizational interactions tend to focus on direct or formal inter-organizational interactions, in which the opening of an administrative space is easiest to argue.

Those few GAL contributions that specifically address inter-organizational interactions[33] seem to assume that basic GAL premises developed for other constellations can simply be transposed to the inter-organizational constellation. In consequence, they tend to underestimate the dynamics and structural egocentrism of IOs' institutional laws demonstrated in this study. For instance, Stewart and Ratton Sanchez Badin propose that interacting IOs should review whether the respective other has observed GAL principles in its internal procedures when they incorporate the other IO's output into their own law.[34] However, if an IO proceeded as suggested, it would, firstly, inevitably apply its very own idea and interpretation of transparency, participation, review and further GAL principles, which would not necessarily be congruent with the other IO's interpretation.[35] Secondly, the

[32]Beyond terminological unclarities of that concept, the present study sheds light on aspects of it which have hardly been theorized before, see e.g. Savino (n 9). One such aspect is if, and how, the 'global administrative space' is created and maintained in inter-organizational interactions, given the broad variety of the latter. As seen, there is often no instituting act which would mark the 'opening' of the space, neither in a 'legislative' way (e.g. the creation of new rules via the conclusion of a treaty) nor in a factual-sociological way (e.g. by the emergence of inter-organizational communication or even the creation of a common 'system').

[33]The largest part of GAL contributions focuses on global administrative action transcending the 'vertical' boundaries between the international and national levels. For an exception see 'The World Trade Organization and Global Administrative Law' (2009) IILJ Working Paper 2009/7 (Global Administrative Law Series) <https://www.iilj.org/publications/the-world-trade-organization-and-global-administrative-law/> accessed 26 April 2020; Savino (n 9).

[34]The case under examination was the WTO's recognition of international regulatory standards created by other IOs and regulatory bodies. Pursuant to the SPS and TBT Agreements (WTO Agreement on the Application of Sanitary and Phytosanitary Measures (adopted 15 April 1994) 1867 UNTS 493 (SPS Agreement); WTO Agreement on Technical Barriers to Trade (adopted 12 April 1979, entered into force 1 January 1980) 1186 UNTS 276 (TBT Agreement)), member state regulations that are in conformity with such imported international standards are presumed to be consistent with these agreements (Art. 3.2 SPS Agreement and Annex A(3) lit. a – c SPS Agreement; Art. 2.4 and 2.5 TBT Agreement). Some of these standards are already enlisted in the agreements, but further ones can be added by the agreements' committees (Annex A(3) lit. d SPS Agreement). Having regard to such recognition, Stewart and Ratton Sanchez Badin argue that "it would be appropriate for [the WTO] to take into account the respective standard-setting organizations' decision-making processes, including the degree of openness, participation, reasons-giving and review. These GAL norms would help ensure that the standards were adopted through an open process allowing for fair consideration of affected interests and on the basis of reasoned justification", Richard B Stewart and Michelle Ratton Sanchez Badin, 'The World Trade Organization and Global Administrative Law' (2009) IILJ Working Paper 2009/7 (Global Administrative Law Series) <https://www.iilj.org/publications/the-world-trade-organization-and-global-administrative-law/> accessed 26 April 2020, 21.

[35]The importing IO could thus unilaterally choose to alter or abandon the application of GAL principles, like the ECtHR's unilateral decision to take ILO instruments and practice into account,

incorporating IO's unilateral decision would not necessarily take into account the other IO's model of governance.[36] It is symptomatic that the unilateral promotion of GAL principles by one IO is considered suitable to

> partially and indirectly but nonetheless significantly address concerns over factional capture, tunnel vision, and lack of accountability with respect to global regulatory bodies' decision making.[37]

In sum, it becomes apparent that GAL has not yet sufficiently problematized the questions which lie at the heart of this study.

V. The 'Factuality' of Legal Pluralism

A common main theme of (legal) pluralism is the idea that several legal orders—or other, non-legal, normative orders[38]—co-exist and apply to the same space or subject-matter in a heterarchical manner.[39] International law is conceived as encompassing several distinct and diverse legal regimes, which can overlap and even conflict. This pluralization of international law is emphasized to varying extents.[40] While some authors argue that the distinct areas of international law are

---

described in Chap. 5 above. Like the ECtHR, the WTO General Council would even have the competence to interpret its law authoritatively. The authors condone that "[t]he TBT Committee has already adopted a Decision on 'Principles for the Development of International Standards, Guide and Recommendations with relation to articles 2, 5 and Annex 3 of the Agreement', in which principles and procedures are provided in order to, inter alia, further transparency, openness, and impartiality and address the concerns of developing countries in the elaboration and adoption of international standards, guidelines and recommendations", ibid 22.

[36]The incorporating IO would thus be free to unilaterally impose its own interpretation of GAL principles regardless of the consequences this might have for the other IO. GAL seems to presuppose that its global administrative law principles are immutable and understood equally by all actors – an assumption which is highly questionable in the light of the results of this study. Even if there was such a thing as 'the' GAL principles, their imposition on another IO without due regard for the latter's constitutional peculiarities might come with unforeseen repercussions, as the interactions between the ECtHR and the ILO discussed in Chap. 5 illustrate.

[37]Stewart and Ratton Sanchez Badin (n 35) 24.

[38]Many pluralists suggest thinking beyond state-created international law. While this is a recurring and relevant aspect of legal pluralism in an international context, it is not further discussed here. For an overview see Nico Krisch, 'Pluralism in International Law and Beyond' (2015) <https://ssrn.com/abstract=2613930> accessed 26 April 2020, 9, with further references.

[39]Bianchi (n 19) 230 et seq.

[40]Krisch, *Beyond Constitutionalism: The Pluralist Structure of Postnational Law* (n 21) 71 et seqq.; André Nollkaemper, 'Inside or out: Two Types of International Legal Pluralism' in Jan Klabbers and Touko Piiparinen (eds), *Normative pluralism and international law: exploring global governance* (Cambridge University Press 2013) 94.

still interconnected and thus integrated into an encompassing legal system recognizing legitimate differences,[41] others challenge the idea of an overarching legal framework of the different areas and locate legal ordering principles within each system, much in the sense of conflict-of-laws rules in private law.[42]

Pluralist narratives have a comparatively greater explanatory potential for the status quo of the law of inter-organizational interactions than other narratives, as they centre on the interrelations between different areas of international law and pay greater attention to the interlinkages between norm complexes.[43] That being said, many pluralist accounts draw on politological or sociological concepts and in consequence, conceptualize conflicts or other interactions to occur between regimes[44] or even between societal rationalities.[45] Pluralism's fundamental empirical observation of separated sectors of law and the accompanying 'inside-outside dichotomy' is a valuable starting point, but it must nonetheless not blindly be adopted for an assessment of the law as a *normative* framework. The mere fact that the law is factually practiced in separate and contingent contexts does not in itself lead to the conclusion that IOs *ought to be* detached as a matter of law.[46] On the contrary, as this study has shown, there is *some* inter-organizational law in place after all—it just does not cover all types of inter-organizational interactions. Thus, legal pluralism can inform an assessment of this study's results (and some of its

[41]See Anne-Marie Slaughter, *A New World Order* (Princwton University Press 2004) 248. See Joost Pauwelyn, 'Bridging Fragmentation and Unity: International Law as a Universe of Inter-Connected Islands' (2004) 25 Michigan Journal of International Law 903, 915; William W Burke-White, 'International Legal Pluralism' (2004) 25 Michigan Journal of International Law 963, 977 et seq.; Bianchi (n 19) 232. Griffiths classifies this strand as 'weak' pluralism, John Griffiths, 'What Is Legal Pluralism?' (1986) 18 The Journal of Legal Pluralism and Unofficial Law 1, 8.

[42]See Krisch, 'Pluralism in International Law and Beyond' (n 38) 6. Krisch speaks of "interface norms" which regulate one system's approach to others, ibid 8. These ordering principles can be similar or even equivalent, but, due to their contingency, remain 'multisourced', Tomer Broude and Yuval Shany, 'The International Law and Policy of Multi-Sourced Equivalent Norms' in Tomer Broude and Yuval Shany (eds), *Multi-Sourced Equivalent Norms in International Law* (Hart Publishing 2011) 3 et seqq.

[43]As Krisch put it, "pluralism directs our doctrinal attention towards the interfaces between the orders. Responding to the increasing proximity of the different normative orders, it foregrounds the importance of norms long thought to be relatively marginal [, including] horizontally, regarding the place of norms of one area of international law in another (. . .). In a pluralist order, we can expect much of the action to lie at the margins, in these interfaces, and it is there that a major site of doctrinal construction should lie", Krisch, 'Pluralism in International Law and Beyond' (n 38) 16.

[44]See e.g. Paul Schiff Berman, *Global Legal Pluralism: A Jurisprudence of Law Beyond Borders* (Cambridge University Press 2012) 182 et seqq.; Pulkowski (n 16).

[45]Most prominently Gunther Teubner and Andreas Fischer-Lescano, 'Regime-Collisions: The Vain Search for Legal Unity in the Fragmentation of Global Law' (2004) 25 Michigan Journal of International Law 999. For the book-length version of the argument see Andreas Fischer-Lescano and Gunther Teubner, *Regime-Kollisionen. Zur Fragmentierung des globalen Rechts* (Suhrkamp 2006).

[46]As seen, whether the ILO (or any other IO) can claim a defined sphere of jurisdiction vis-à-vis other IOs is precisely one of the fundamental doctrinal questions to be answered.

suggestions will indeed be discussed in the following section), but it does not (and presumably does not intend to) replace a distinct legal doctrinal evaluation.

B. Is the Legal Status Quo Adequate? An Assessment of Selected Arguments

Given that pre-existing narratives have a certain tendency to 'pass over' the law of inter-organizational interactions, this section takes a different path. It focuses on evaluating selected key arguments with regard to the adequacy of the legal status quo.[47] The crucial question remains whether the ILO's relativization by other institutional laws, combined with the widespread absence of established inter-organizational law as a corrective, is an adequate legal status quo.

I. Moving Beyond (Ostensible) Pragmatism

At the outset, it is necessary to address two ostensibly pragmatic arguments that tend to conceal the normative character of the questions to be discussed in this section.

1. The Argument of 'Working' Interactions

The first of them is the argument of 'working' interactions. When asking whether the legal status quo is adequate, one could feel inclined to point to the factual record of the ILO's inter-organizational interactions: After all, despite undisputable setbacks, the ILO's inter-organizational interactions by and large seem to have 'worked' well. The same could arguably claimed for many other IOs and their mutual interactions. Thus, one could argue that the status quo is satisfactory.

Indeed, leaving repeated and prominent cases of inter-organizational conflict aside, it is true that there have been interactions that both the ILO and the respective other IO have considered successful, or at least reasonably satisfactory.

However, this can hardly be an argument to end further discussion. To begin with, whether or not interactions 'worked' crucially depends on how they *ought to* work. Everyone claiming that the ILO's interactions 'worked' necessarily presupposes, at least implicitly, a standard by which it can be determined under which conditions an interaction is to be considered successful. It is precisely that standard that needs to stand in the focus of attention if one endeavours to assess whether and to what extent interactions 'worked'.

---

[47]The intention is not to replace a fully-fledged theoretization of inter-organizational interactions, nor does it intend to come up with a new narrative. Such exercises deserve to be conducted in more detail in future treatises.

This study has shown that there is no established common inter-organizational legal standard beyond those few inter-organizational treaties that could be discerned. Therefore, the standard for how interactions ought to work can only be either each IO's institutional law (a legal standard) or the preferences of the involved actors (a non-legal, but political, moral or other normative standard).

As to the former, it was shown that different institutional laws take different perspectives on what role and relevance which IO should have in inter-organizational interactions. Consequently, the assessment of whether certain interactions 'worked' will vary depending on which institutional law is taken as a standard. This does not mean that the results will always diverge. However, taking also into account the evolutive dynamics of each IO's institutional law examined in Chap. 10, there is a chance that IOs' institutional legal standards will diverge at some point.

As to the latter, it needs to be recalled that in labour governance, not only the interacting IOs, but also the involved actors have their very own and often diametrically opposite conceptions of 'working' inter-organizational interactions. For instance, as seen in Chap. 4, employers took a way more conciliatory stance on the EWI than workers and trade unions. Reversely, as mentioned in Chap. 5, while employers criticized the adoption of CEACR positions on the right to strike by other international bodies, workers and trade unions welcomed the ECtHR's reversal of jurisprudence and its alignment to these very CEACR positions. And as seen in Chap. 6, while the ILO and the ECSR both lauded their mutual cooperation, the Norwegian government deplored that the ECSR sided with the CFA in criticizing the Norwegian practice of submitting labour disputes to compulsory arbitration.

Eventually, arguing that interactions 'worked' glosses over these underlying issues. By contrast, if one were to conduct a proper examination of whether interactions 'worked', this examination would inevitably lead back to the initial question of what an appropriate supra-partisan normative standard would be, and if the current standard is adequate.

2. The Legal Status Quo as a 'Normal' Situation?

Furthermore, one could raise the structural point that it is not untypical for international law to have certain incongruencies and gaps. Against this background, one could argue that the ILO's relativization in the other examined IOs' institutional laws and the absence of inter-organizational law as a corrective was 'normal' and therefore to be accepted as adequate.

However, whether or not one fundamentally accepts the possibility of gaps in international law,[48] such gaps are in any event not a *necessary* structural element of international law. In other words, even insofar as they exist, they do not *have to* exist. They can be removed, e.g. by clarifying, modifying or creating new international

[48]See Chap. 16 A.

legal norms. Hence, the real question is again a normative one, namely whether they *should* exist or not. The argument that the current underdeveloped legal status quo was adequate because it was 'normal' is tantamount to the normative argument that this status should be maintained.

Thus, the 'normality' argument leads again back to the initial question of whether the legal status quo is adequate and what an appropriate supra-partisan normative standard would be.

II. Voluntarist Arguments

Having dealt with ostensibly pragmatic answers, the discussion can now properly focus on the question whether the legal status quo is adequate. A first way to approach this normative question is by using the criterion of consent.

1. The Legal Status Quo as a Sovereign Choice of Member States?

In this vein, one could firstly argue that it is for states to decide how interactions between the ILO and other IOs involved in labour governance should be orchestrated by law, if at all. In this vein, the legal status quo could be regarded as an adequate depiction of states' preferences that have to be accepted.

From such a voluntarist perspective, IOs' member states as the principal international lawmakers have, by virtue of their consent, created and legitimized the situation of multi-institutional labour governance the ILO finds itself in. If they deemed it necessary, they could change it at any point in time.[49] Accordingly, so one could argue, inter-organizational interactions are appropriate and legitimate as long as the interacting IOs' behaviour stays within the scope of their member states' collective sovereign will, as expressed in the current state of positive international law.[50] What is more, on a realist note, parallel governance might even be considered to be of strategic use for states, which could promote their own interests through the

---

[49]See Ulfstein, 'Institutions and Competences' (n 20) 71. See e.g. the discussion on a World Environmental Organization, Steve Charnovitz, 'A World Environment Organization' (2002) 27 Columbia Journal of Environmental Law 323; Sebastian Oberthür and Thomas Gehring, 'Reforming International Environmental Governance: An Institutionalist Critique of the Proposal for a World Environment Organisation' (2004) 4 International Environmental Agreements: Politics, Law and Economics 359.

[50]See e.g. the focus on state sovereignty in Margaret Young's proposed "legal framework for regime interaction", Young, *Trading Fish, Saving Fish: The Interaction Between Regimes in International Law* (n 13) 267 et seqq. See also Margaret A Young, 'Regime Interaction in Creating, Implementing and Enforcing International Law' in Margaret A Young (ed), *Regime Interaction in International Law - Facing Fragmentation* (Cambridge University Press 2012) 94 et seqq.

selective activation of different institutions, their withdrawal from them, or the erection of new ones.[51]

However, leaving fundamental debates on voluntarism to one side, it is questionable that member states really favour the current status of law over an alternative that would lead to more concerted, predictable and reliable inter-organizational interactions. Firstly, historically, most states did not really have a choice to begin with, as the ILO, World Bank and the CoE, alongside many other IOs engaging in labour governance, were designed and erected way before the process of decolonization gained traction, in which a vast number of today's states first gained independence. While they could choose to become members of these IOs after becoming independent, multi-institutional labour governance as such had already been created beforehand.

Secondly, the IOs examined here were all intended to serve states' interests through international cooperation in an effective, de-politicized and administrative manner. However, as argued before, in the case of inter-organizational interactions, these functionalist objectives are in danger of being compromised, as inter-organizational interactions can be launched by IOs autonomously, may gain a political dimension, and may lead to the interacting IOs eventually hampering each other's effectiveness.[52] It would be hard to explain, and in fact be utterly ironic, if states made the immense effort of carefully designing, negotiating and establishing a plethora of IOs to cater to their interests and needs, only to let these IOs then influence each other in an almost entirely non-regulated manner, with hardly anything but their respective (and structurally egocentric) institutional laws as normative guidance. Against this background, it is reasonable to assume that states would not have wanted these contrary effects to appear.[53] This would also explain the numerous and repeated calls, supported by an overwhelming majority of governments, for increased policy coherence and coordination among the ILO and other IOs.[54]

Thirdly, the idea of strategically using institutional fragmentation should not be generalized too hastily. At the outset, even powerful states have historically

[51]Oran R Young, 'Institutional Linkages in International Society: Polar Perspectives' (1996) 2 Global Governance 1, 13; Eyal Benvenisti and George W Downs, 'The Empire's New Clothes: Political Economy and the Fragmentation of International Law' (2007) 60 Stanford Law Rev 595. In a similar direction Peter-Tobias Stoll, 'Global Public Goods: The Governance Dimension' in Volker Rittberger, Martin Nettesheim and Carmen Huckel (eds), *Authority in the Global Political Economy* (Palgrave Macmillan 2008) 121; Stoll, 'Koordination, Kooperation und Konstitutionalisierung Im Völkerrecht' (n 1) 295.

[52]See above, Sect. A. I.

[53]Indeed, while these states indeed designed each and every IO in a peculiar way, they also created at least vaguely defined competences and obligations to cooperate with others in the respective institutional laws.

[54]See e.g. UNGA Res 60/1 (16 September 2005) UN Doc A/RES/60/1, para 30; ECOSOC, Ministerial Declaration 'Creating an Environment at the National and International Levels Conducive to Generating Full and Productive Employment and Decent Work for All, and Its Impact on Sustainable Development' (5 July 2006) UN Doc E/2006/L.8, para 36 et seq.

struggled to keep control over IOs, and the ILO is no exception in this respect.[55] Moreover, some bodies, like the ECtHR and the ECSR, are structurally quite resilient against being strategically 'used' even by powerful states, because they operate as independent bodies to begin with.[56] In addition, even insofar as one single IO can be influenced strategically, the erratic character of inter-organizational interactions will make it difficult to predict how that IO will then interact with others—and how the others will react. Thus, it will be particularly difficult to exert strategic influence in a coherent and strategically sound manner across several IOs.[57] Against this background, a clearer regulation of inter-organizational interactions could even reinforce powerful states' attempts to strategically influence IOs (a point to be revisited below).

Eventually, it appears that the legal status quo, as identified in this study, is not in the presumed interest of states even from a voluntarist standpoint. It is more likely that states have simply underestimated the scale, dynamics and potential impact of inter-organizational interactions when deciding to erect the many IOs that, besides the ILO, are in one way or the other involved in multi-institutional labour governance.

The states of the world could in theory still come together and jointly change the law according to their collective will. Yet, it must be constated that there has not only been a constant lack of political momentum to do so, but also a lack of convincing and viable *leitmotifs* that could win the necessary majorities for such a large-scale reform. Against this background, it is prudent to assume that the conceptualization and formulation of a normative framework governing inter-organizational interactions in a more orderly manner would be in the well-understood interest of the ILO's and the other IO's member states.

2. The Legal Status Quo as a Choice Made by IOs Themselves?

In a related manner, one could also propose the 'IO-voluntarist' argument that the legal status quo was a legitimate expression of the collective will of the interacting IOs themselves. While IOs derive their competences and external capacities from

---

[55] For instance, even the USA's threat to withdraw in 1975 (and its subsequent actual withdrawal from 1977-1980), while putting a severe strain on the ILO's activities, could not induce the ILO to cease certain activities the USA considered 'politicized' at the time, see Chaps. 2 D. I. and 12 B. III. 3.

[56] It is perhaps no coincidence that the 2017 Danish CM chairmanship initiated a reform process of the European human rights system, one initial idea of which was to curtail the ECtHR's power to engage in dynamic and evolutive interpretation, Jacques Hartmann, 'A Danish Crusade for the Reform of the European Court of Human Rights' (*EJIL Talk!*, 14 November 2017) <https://www.ejiltalk.org/a-danish-crusade-for-the-reform-of-the-european-court-of-human-rights/> accessed 26 April 2020.

[57] On another note, strategy is not the exclusive province of states. It may as well be that IOs themselves strategically maintain their disconnection for their own interests, e.g. by deliberately refraining from cooperation or even from concluding a relationship agreement.

their member states, IOs have still been given the power to conclude inter-organizational treaties with each other within the terms of their respective own institutional legal rules. Therefore, one could argue that if the ILO and other IOs engaged in labour governance really intended to change the legal status quo, they could simply take matters in their own hands and regulate their inter-organizational matters by more, and more sophisticated, inter-organizational treaties.

However, to begin with, the mere absence of inter-organizational treaties cannot in itself be interpreted as an expression of a collective will of the interacting IOs not to enter into contractual relations. It may very well be, and has in fact occurred in practice,[58] that one IO is actually interested in intensifying and formalizing contractual relations, but another is unwilling or unable to do so.

Moreover, and in any event, solely pointing to the inactivity of IOs would ignore the position that the ILO and the other interacting IOs find themselves in under the legal status quo. Even if attempting to conclude a new inter-organizational treaty, both the ILO and other IOs would face the intricate task to ensure that the new treaty constrains their capability to effectively fulfil their mandate as little as possible, and at the same time expands their capabilities as much as possible. This situation of a 'staring contest' is perhaps one explanation for the overall scarcity and vagueness of current inter-organizational treaties, as well as for the emphasis of each IO's respective unique features and the discreteness of their respective mandates and objectives in such treaties, as this study has e.g. observed in the ILO-CoE and the UN-IBRD.

In sum, it seems problematic to argue that the legal status quo was adequate solely because the ILO and the other IOs have not undertaken to change it.

III. A Pluralist Argument: The Status Quo as a Counter-Hegemonic Opportunity for the ILO?

Finally, the question whether the legal status quo is adequate can be approached from a pluralist position: The legal status quo could be considered adequate and even desirable because the absence of a normative framework opened deliberative spaces that the ILO could use for counter-hegemonic contestation.

This argument is rooted in structural considerations by (mostly) pluralist authors. A number of these authors see the diversification of international law and international institutions as opportunities to promote diversity of concepts and ideas, as a chance for actors to pursue their interests in different fora and as an environment

[58]See for the situation between the ILO, the WTO and the Bretton Woods organizations see Francis Maupain, *The Future of the International Labour Organization in the Global Economy* (Hart Publishing 2013) 111 et seqq.

conducive to mutual contestation and critical reflection of viewpoints expressed and promoted in the various arenas of international governance.[59] From this perspective, a heterarchical structure can provide a comparative advantage over a unified law with a hierarchy of institutions.[60] The absence of a unified hierarchical structure for decision-making gives each IO the opportunity to complement, 'comment on', or contest the decision of another. Notably, it would give actors that are marginalized in one IO the opportunity to bring their points across in another IO, which then tries to influence the first IO. This in turn could promote mutual accountability and "pragmatic accommodation" within the heterarchical structure of governance that currently exists, ultimately enhancing the legitimacy of this structure as a whole.[61] In the context of labour governance, the absence of inter-organizational law could deprive powerful IOs of an important tool to hegemonically dominate the ILO. Moreover, the absence of law could open spaces for counter-hegemonic contestation and thereby enhance the legitimacy of labour governance as a whole. In this vein, Rittich has argued that

> a landscape of proliferating and divergent normative regimes and standards might be a good thing, or at least better than the alternative now on offer. Any unified approach in the current climate would be unlikely to reflect the aspirations of the ILO or enable workers to claim a greater share of the resources and power now circulating within workplaces and labour markets; rather, there is every reason to suppose the opposite.[62]

Ordering and structuring the ILO's inter-organizational interactions through law could compromise positive effects of the status quo, because law is a potential means for unifying and hierarchizing the heterarchical governance structure. Strengthening inter-organizational legal ties could narrow down the room for contestation that 'weaker' IOs currently have vis-à-vis more 'powerful' ones. Law could perpetuate power imbalances, inequalities and hegemonies on an inter-organizational level. Taking this argument even further, Koskenniemi has suggested that any attempt to coordinate and manage interactions through law would inevitably perpetuate each regime's innate aspiration for hegemony over other regimes and re-establish hegemony on an inter-regime level.[63] According to these arguments, a more defined inter-organizational law would only risk to further weaken the position the ILO currently has in its interactions with more powerful other IOs.

---

[59] See e.g. Paul Schiff Berman, 'A Pluralist Approach to International Law' (2007) 32 Yale Journal of International Law 301, 321; Ranganathan (n 27) 24.

[60] Krisch, *Beyond Constitutionalism: The Pluralist Structure of Postnational Law* (n 21) 78.

[61] See e.g. Nico Krisch, 'The Pluralism of Global Administrative Law' (2006) 17 European Journal of International Law 247, 276; David Kennedy, 'The Mystery of Global Governance' (2008) 34 Ohio Northern University Law Review 827, 859. Similar Martti Koskenniemi, 'Hegemonic Regimes' in Margaret A Young (ed), *Regime Interaction in International Law - Facing Fragmentation* (Cambridge University Press 2012).

[62] Kerry Rittich, 'The ILO: Challenges in Times of Crisis' (2015) 154 International Labour Review 85, 89.

[63] Koskenniemi, 'Hegemonic Regimes' (n 61) 317 et seqq.

It cannot be said that these arguments had no merit. In particular, they support a case against an 'overregulation' of inter-organizational interactions. That being said, any hope for enhancing accountability, pragmatic accommodation and legitimacy across the inter-organizational landscape is illusory if IOs may continue to influence each other randomly and only subject to their own institutional laws' imperatives. There is no gain in propositions and contestations without the realistic hope for reconciliation, synthesis and progress. Just as too onerous regulation, the entire absence or uncertain status of rules can promote and perpetuate hegemony and diminish opportunities for dialogue and contestation. And indeed, if the ILO faces a challenge, it is certainly not that inter-organizational law was so strict that it could not examine and contest what other IOs do. Rather, the major challenge for the ILO is that it remains unclear if and to what extent those other IOs are supposed to listen to what it has to say. If the pluralist model of 'inter-regime discourse' ought to be more than self-satisfied proposing, opposing and arguing, there has to be some basic common understanding of which voices are to be heard, 'how much' each of them counts, how, when and where they ought to be voiced and how suggestions made may or even must be followed.[64] As some pluralists themselves concede, a common understanding of inter-organizational legal parameters could help to channel and ultimately even reinforce such a process of proposition and contestation, to the ultimate benefit of all interacting IOs.[65]

As far as Koskenniemi's concerns about a perpetuation of hegemony through inter-organizational law are concerned, his argument that any regime-transcending law would inevitably set in stone the conditions for coordination and cooperation on the terms of one regime's rationale, is, at least in principle, arguably correct. However, this is not a specific issue of inter-organizational (or 'inter-regime') law. Rather, the embodiment and universalization of particular political, moral, technical or other rationales or preferences is a common feature of *all* law. By making one normative proposition, the law inevitably refrains from making another.[66] If this inherent 'hegemony of the normative' is seen as a problem, then every legal norm—national, international, and also inter-organizational—is affected by it. It is the price to pay, as it were, for taking advantage of law's potential to structure interactive conduct among IOs, or, for that matter, any social conduct whatsoever. One can of course legitimately oppose this inherent hegemonic potential of law. However, alternatively, one could also put up with it and focus on identifying counter-

[64]For instance, there is no point in the ILO contesting the World Bank's policies for labour market deregulation and demanding respect for its conventions and country initiatives if it remains unclear why and how the World Bank should listen, and, in consequence, whether, how, and how far it can be expected to adapt or cease its claims for labour market deregulation.

[65]In this vein, Krisch proposes "principles of mutual recognition, toleration, coherence, or inclusiveness of political communication" as the "benchmark for decision-making by all the constituencies relevant for global administration", Krisch, 'The Pluralism of Global Administrative Law' (n 61) 276 et seq.

[66]This almost inevitably leads to disagreement in reality, safe for the (hypothetical) case in which literally everyone agrees to the norm.

hegemonic safeguards, such as mechanisms enabling contestation and reversals of standpoints. In this respect, one might find comfort in the fact that legal norms governing inter-organizational interactions would not have to be 'objectively neutral' or entirely 'non-hegemonic': It would suffice if they managed to include mechanisms that would embed and temper potential hegemonic aspirations (of either IO), e.g. by defining how and to what extent each IO may strive to 'universalize' its own specific rationalities.[67]

Eventually, whether regulating the ILO's inter-organizational interactions by law will enhance or diminish hegemony, accountability and legitimacy will hardly depend on the existence of law as such, but on its content. In this respect, maintaining the benefits of counter-hegemonic contestation across IOs, as well as containing IOs' hegemonic potentials, are relevant aspects to be considered. They are of particular interest for the ILO and its comparatively vulnerable model of labour governance. That being said, the entire absence of law is likely to make it even more difficult to secure a proper environment for counter-hegemonic contestation, inter-regime discourse, as well as mutual accountability among IOs. Hence, from this perspective, a carefully 'dosed' and designed legal framework appears preferable to the legal status quo.

IV. Conclusion

This section has evaluated selected key arguments regarding the question whether the legal status quo is adequate. It must be emphasized that this section has not conducted a fully-fledged discussion of all conceivable arguments and counterarguments, which would have exceeded the confines of this study by far. Still, as a preliminary result of this section's discussion, the adequacy of the legal status quo is questionable. From a voluntarist perspective, it seems unlikely that the observed legal status quo is the result of planful and concerted legislative action by either the ILO's and other IOs' member states or these IOs themselves. Rather, it appears that there is a lack of political momentum, arguably aggravated by a lack of a sound legal concept, to reshape the ILO's inter-organizational interactions in a more ordered fashion. Considering a pluralist perspective, an inter-organizational space for dialogue and contestation needs at least some basic rules that define this space, lest inter-organizational interaction will drown in cacophony.

[67]That being said, even the conceptualization of such a 'hegemony-conscious' law would still require translating the peculiarities of the inter-organizational constellation into the language of legal concepts, such as the lack of defined jurisdictional spheres (if any) or the basic character of IOs' mutual relations (see Chap. 15 B. VI.), because they form essential framework conditions for any desired landscape of pluralist diversity and counter-hegemonic contestation.

C. Conclusion on Chap. 18

This chapter has undertaken to assess the current diminished role of international law in the context of the ILO's inter-organizational interactions. First of all, it has noted that the ILO's inter-organizational interactions and their legal regulation have largely remained in the 'slipstream' of major contemporary international law narratives. In consequence, this chapter has proceeded by examining selected key arguments. As was seen, the legal status quo is more likely to be the result of historical developments and the profound difficulty of systemic legal reform than of states' or IOs' planful, concerted and conscious decisions. Moreover, even if one embraces the current heterarchical institutional structure of multi-institutional labour governance, the marked absence of inter-organizational legal regulation of interactions runs the risk of compromising some of the benefits that such a structure can have. All in all, the legal status quo does not regulate the ILO's inter-organizational interactions in an adequate manner.

Part V
Developing the Law of Inter-Organizational Interactions

The preceding discussion suggests that it is worthwhile to address how the role of law in orchestrating inter-organizational interactions in labour governance and beyond could be enhanced. Thus, this final part will look at the potential of law as a normative framework for inter-organizational interactions, and how the law of inter-organizational interactions could be developed beyond its present stage.

19. Perspectives for Law as a Normative Framework for Inter-Organizational Interactions

This final chapter sets out to address the aforesaid questions. At the outset, it enquires into law's realistic potential and cautions against both overly pessimistic and overly enthusiastic visions (A.). It then sketches the road towards developing the law of inter-organizational interactions according to this potential (B.). Finally, it walks first steps on this road by proposing an inter-organizational duty not to compromise accomplished or ongoing work (C.).

A. The Potential of Governing the ILO's Inter-Organizational Interactions Through Law

To be clear from the start, this chapter does not call for unconditional inter-organizational regulation at any price. While the preceding chapter has indicated that a more defined legal regulation of the ILO's inter-organizational interactions could be beneficial, there is certainly no need for blind regulatory enthusiasm. Neither is there a realistic prospect that law could entirely eliminate the ambivalence of inter-organizational interactions and their repercussions on the ILO's model of labour governance. Therefore, contemplating the proper role of law in this respect first means to ask what the realistic potential of law is.

H. Gött, *The Law of Interactions Between International Organizations*, Beiträge zum ausländischen öffentlichen Recht und Völkerrecht 299, https://doi.org/10.1007/978-3-662-62389-3_19

I. Fragmented Societal Rationalities as a Structural Limit?

In this respect, one might deny, as occasionally has been done in the literature, that law could regulate inter-organizational interactions in any meaningful manner to begin with.

Some authors have expressed doubts whether international law was capable of promoting coherence among the diversified elements of global governance. For example, Gunther Teubner and Andreas Fischer-Lescano, influenced by Niklas Luhmann's systems theory, suggest that law is not capable of providing an effective framework. They claim that the fragmented areas of law were inextricably linked to an underlying fragmentation of societal subsystems with distinct societal rationalities.[1] Suggesting that each of the fragmented areas of law follows its respective social subsystem's own rationalities, they claim that legal fragmentation is irreversible, and that organizational and doctrinal unity were out of reach.[2] In their view,

> much would already have been achieved [if law was] able to furnish forms of legal guarantees for autonomy in the face of totalizing tendencies and domination by one system.[3]

This dire conclusion, however, may be premature. At the outset, it needs to be recalled that there is a difference between law as an empirical social fact and law as a normative proposition, the former being a factual (i.e. ontic), the other a normative (i.e. deontic) phenomenon. Law as an empirical social fact, i.e. the status and effects it has in societal reality, may indeed be so closely connected to societal rationalities that achieving a unified understanding of legal norms in reality is difficult to achieve. A trade union representative at the ILO will perhaps never have the exact same understanding of freedom of association as a financial policy expert at the World Bank. However, this perspective on law as an empirical social fact is just one side of

---

[1]In their view, the diversification of international law is merely a symptom of a broader and much more fundamental fragmentation of society into autonomous subsystems of societal sectors, which has occurred in the course of globalization. Each of these subsystems is conceived to produce its own law and, even further, its own conception of law. Consequently, in this model, there is not one, but many autopoietic legal systems, regulating the fractured subsystems of society. Each of these sectorial bodies of law are conceptualized as 'structurally coupled' to the respective societal sector's inherent and independent logic (in the theory of (autopoietic) systems, 'structural coupling' enables a system to communicate with its environment), Gunther Teubner and Andreas Fischer-Lescano 'Regime-Collisions: The Vain Search for Legal Unity in the Fragmentation of Global Law' (2004) 25 Michigan Journal of International Law 999; Andreas Fischer-Lescano and Gunther Teubner, *Regime-Kollisionen. Zur Fragmentierung des globalen Rechts* (Suhrkamp 2006) passim.

[2]"Any aspiration to the organizational and doctrinal unity of law is surely a chimera", Teubner and Fischer-Lescano (n 1) 1017.

[3]ibid 1046 et seq. Similar Koskenniemi, who argues that a 'neutral' position was unattainable, at best, one could hope for a coordinative law ("*Koordinationsrecht*"), Martti Koskenniemi, 'Hegemonic Regimes' Regimes' in Margaret A Young (ed), *Regime Interaction in International Law - Facing Fragmentation* (Cambridge University Press 2012) 305, 325.

the coin. A legal norm as a *normative proposition* can always surpass factually existing societal frictions, because it is a deontic concept.[4] What is more, the normative proposition of a legal norm can resemble a reference point in social reality around which, over time, societal rationalities can converge as they develop. Examples such as the gradual inclusion of ILO instruments by the ECtHR, the use of the ILO-CoE in drafting the ESC, the mainstreaming of the ILO's Decent Work Agenda throughout the UN System and even the limited accommodation of labour standards in the World Bank show that regime-specific rationalities can be surmounted, and rationalities can converge in reality. Law may not be the sole or the principal driver of convergence, but it may reinforce an approximation of societal systems, and lawyers can take an active position in it.

II. The Risk of Overestimating Law's Potential

On the other hand, law's potential for ordering the ILO's interactions with other IOs must not be overestimated and assessed unrealistically. At the risk of repeating a truism, law is not a panacea, and one must not fall for unbalanced regulatory activism. Especially in an inherently contentious and conflict-ridden field like labour governance, the goal cannot be to depoliticize interactions by muting them through legal regulation. Rather, the foremost goal is that interactions occur in a less ad hoc and unilateral and instead in a principled and more predictable manner. To pursue this goal (inter alia) by law seems possible and also desirable.[5]

---

[4]Even if societal rationalities do not converge in reality, a legal prescription can still pose the same demands to all actors and require them to behave in a way that approximates or reconciles these rationalities. The normative character and content of a legal norm is hardly ever called into question by factually existing societal frictions. These norms may not be effective or 'as effective' as required, but that does not impair their prescriptive character, safe perhaps for exceptional situations. This is no less true in the inter-organizational constellation. In fact, norm complexes like the VCLT-IO or the UN System's legal framework normatively 'connect' the laws of IOs.

[5]The potentials to achieve this goal are larger or smaller depending on the situation and the type of inter-organizational interaction involved. As seen in this study, some rules for direct and cooperative interactions already exist. By contrast, an example for a particularly difficult case for finding suitable legal standards are informal and indirect interactions at the stage of interpretation of law, i.e. interactions in which one IO or one of its bodies interprets its own law in the light of ILO's instruments and practice, as illustrated by the ECtHR's reception of ILO instruments and practice in Chap. 5. Arguably, defining a common inter-organizational standard for such interpretative recourse is reaching the limits of what is possible and expedient, given that a) it is difficult to prescribe a particular interpretation to begin with, and b) IOs usually depend on retaining a certain margin of interpretative flexibility. Positively prescribing certain interpretations might therefore be too onerous. That being said, law can still have a structuring and legitimizing effect if leaving margins for the interpreter. Giving deference to other IOs is not something that is alien to current interpretative rules, whether under the general rules (Art. 31(3) lit. c VCLT) or in some of the observed special approaches, e.g. the ECtHR's living instrument approach as applied in *Demir and Baykara*, discussed in Chap. 5 above. More specific guidance can also be achieved by negative

Neither would it be appropriate to give one-sided preference to one of the interacting IOs. In this vein, the result cannot be that the ILO 'dominates' all other IOs engaging in labour governance, or vice versa. Instead, the aim must be to find suitable mechanisms that accommodate the political dimension of interactions in an adequate manner, while also having regard to each IO's mandates, governance models, peculiarities and limitations.

III. Realistic Perspectives for Law

To illustrate what this could mean in particular, it is convenient at this point to name some realistic potential applications for law, without any claim of exhaustiveness.

As seen, at the level of IOs' institutional laws, increasing the ILO's role and relevance is first and foremost a policy choice of each IO.[6] Still, such a policy choice could be informed by legal concepts. To make but one suggestion, one such element could be to mitigate other IOs' relativization by increasing the flexibility of the wider institutional legal framework in which each IO's competences to interact with others is embedded.

Under some domestic constitutions, the constitutional legal ties for external action of the state are relaxed in order to allow flexibility for international cooperation. This result is not achieved by constitutional amendments, but solely via interpretation of the existing institutional law.[7] One could contemplate to transpose this concept of relaxed constitutional ties to IOs' institutional laws, with the possible

---

interpretative rules, defining how law should not be understood, e.g. Art. 53 ECHR or Art. 19 (8) ILO Constitution.

[6]As seen, other IOs are not legally obliged to enhance the ILO's role and relevance in their own institutional laws. Hence, for better or worse, the call for increased awareness and mutual regard is a call on these other IOs to adapt their policies. Yet, within the legal margin of discretions, IOs can have recourse to legal concepts that have been developed in other contexts. They could choose such legal concepts as guidance when interpreting, applying, or even amending their own institutional laws.

[7]In this vein, a number of constitutional courts have exercised judicial self-restraint and have accepted that some state activities with an external dimension – for instance the ratification of treaties – only have to be consistent with core elements of the constitution instead of each and every constitutional norm. For the case of Germany, see e.g. *Storage of Chemical Weapons* (ECLI:DE:BVerfG:1987:rs19871029:2BvR62483) BVerfGE 77, 170, 231; *Treaty of Lisbon* (ECLI:DE:BVerfG:2009:es20090630.2bve000208) BVerfGE 123, 267 339 et seqq.; *ESM Treaty* (ECLI:DE:BVerfG:2012:rs20120912.2bvr139012) BVerfGE 135, 317398 et seqq.; *European Arrest Warrant II* (ECLI:DE:BVerfG:2015:rs20151215.2bvr273514) BVerfGE 140, 317.

result that, say, the World Bank may give greater regard to the ILO's activities even if that would not resemble a perfectly non-political and purely economic exercise.[8]

At inter-organizational level, attempts to order and structure interactions between the ILO and other IOs would benefit from giving clearer conceptual contours to the unwritten parts of inter-organizational law. For example, as seen in Part III and notably Chap. 15, the transposition of the law of good-neighbourliness and other norms applying between states currently struggles to come to terms with the structural peculiarities of the inter-organizational constellation. To overcome these hurdles, it will be necessary to address the fundamental uncertainties regarding whether and to what extent IOs have a legally protected sphere of jurisdiction and within which legal parameters a reconciliation of such spheres ought to be conducted.

This calls for a further development and gradual refinement of the underlying fundamental concepts and principles of inter-organizational law, including the inter-organizational legal default rule. The aim is to conceptualize, i.e. to construct, analyze, debate and refine, elements of an inter-organizational law of labour governance that builds on existing law where possible.[9]

B. The Road Ahead

In the light of the foregoing, it becomes apparent that much will depend on the approach that is taken to address the further development of the law of inter-organizational interactions.

[8]That being said, 'importing' constitutional ideas from domestic constitutions is a delicate exercise. Both the ILO and the IOs it interacts with depend on adhering to their constitutional mandate. From the start, IOs may only exercise those powers which have explicitly or implicitly been conferred onto them and may not exceed their powers. Moreover, whether or not IOs abide by their own institutional law is also an important criterion for holding IOs accountable and assessing the legitimacy of their actions. Relaxing the constitutional ties of, say, the World Bank or the CoE in order to give more deference to the ILO and its model of labour governance may conflict with these other IOs' legitimate interest to abide by their institutional laws to the fullest extent. It would thus take a reason and a standard by which it could be determined why and to what extent a relaxation of constitutional ties would be permissible. Moreover, giving (more) regard to other IOs hinges on the expectation of reciprocity. Each IO can only influence how much room it itself gives to other IOs—it must count on the other IO's goodwill to do the same in return. As the examples provided in this study have illustrated, this hope has been fulfilled in some cases but frustrated in others. What could facilitate such reciprocity would again be a common understanding among IOs why, when, and to what extent such reciprocity ought to be given.

[9]As to direct and cooperative interactions, there is already the comparatively established law of inter-organizational treaties, which can be integrated. However, remain other instances which arguably will never be exhaustively governed by treaties, including both informal cooperation and non-cooperative interactions. For all these other cases, the task is to conceptualize norms defining the ILO's legal status and the rights and obligations vis-à-vis other IOs involved in labour governance.

I. The Creative Role of Conceptual, 'Political' and De Lege Ferenda Debates

With large parts of the law of inter-organizational interactions still being underdeveloped, it will inevitably be necessary to explore additional legal norms (or to soundly transpose existing ones by way of analogy). This task is, at least to a certain extent, a creative one.

Still, it would be insufficient to engage only in conceptual or political debates on which norms would be desirable. If law ought to function as a supra-partisan normative framework for inter-organizational interactions, conceptual and policy proposals need to be sufficiently rooted in (or connected to) pre-existing legal norms.

Nor would it be enough to lead *de lege ferenda* debates about how to cast policy conceptions of better inter-organizational coordination and coherence into concrete legal provisions. It is true that, hypothetically, IOs' constituent instruments could be amended, or new or 'better' inter-organizational treaties be concluded.[10] However, such debates do not address the issues in full. Leaving aside that large-scale treaty reforms are rather unrealistic to begin with, any such reform would be in need of a conceptual backdrop and legal parameters that provide, for instance, a basic understanding of how to determine IOs' spheres of jurisdiction and how to set them into relation. What, then, would the backdrop and the parameters for amendments of constituent instruments and new inter-organizational treaties be? Even in the scenario of a concerted systemic reform, there would still be a need to systematically define fundamental elements of inter-organizational law.[11]

---

[10]Provisions could be included in which IOs define and recognize each other's governance models and include elaborate rules on managing their mutual influence on these models. Indeed, there have been ambitious proposals to promote coherence and systemic unity by amending IO's constituent instruments (see Geir Ulfstein, 'Institutions and Competences' in Jan Klabbers, Anne Peters and Geir Ulfstein (eds), *The Constitutionalization of International Law* (Oxford University Press 2009) 45, 71), by erecting new IOs (e.g. the discussion on the erection of a central international environmental organization, see Julie Ayling, 'Serving Many Voices: Progressing Calls for an International Environmental Organisation' (1997) 9 Journal of Environmental Law 243; Steve Charnovitz 'A World Environment Organization' (2002) 27 Columbia Journal of Environmental Law 323; Sebastian Oberthür and Thomas Gehring, 'Institutional Interaction in Global Environmental Governance: The Case of the Cartagena Protocol and the World Trade Organization' (2006) 6 Global Environmental Politics 1), by erecting inter-organizational treaty frameworks between the ILO and its interacting counterparts (See in general Ulfstein, 'Institutions and Competences' (n 10) 74, with respect to the ILO e.g. Kofi Addo, *Core Labour Standards and International Trade* (Springer 2015) 320 et seqq.) or by merging existing bodies, Ulfstein, 'Institutions and Competences' (n 10) 72.

[11]Otherwise, such reforms would almost inevitably remain piecemeal and reactive, i.e. they could only remedy concrete instances of identified disharmony but could not establish a system of inter-organizational coordination and cooperation that, from the point of its inauguration onwards, would in principle 'run by itself', without the constant need of supervision and correction.

II. The Additional Task of Developing a Normative Scaffold for Inter-Organizational Law

Therefore, it is also necessary to address inter-organizational interactions from the specific perspective of legal doctrine. The task is to simultaneously develop the normative scaffold, i.e. the basic legal concepts defining IOs' inter-organizational status and serving as legal parameters for their mutual relations. Not least, this requires embracing the structural peculiarities of the inter-organizational constellation, as discussed in Chap. 15.[12]

In the absence of a sufficient international legislative momentum, developing this scaffold is a task for international legal scholarship.[13] Given the scarcity of written law, it is likely to be an exercise of doctrinal construction rather than one of norm interpretation.[14]

This task should not be mistaken for a purely technical one. It necessarily entails making a range of substantive choices, e.g. as to the scope and level to which IOs' interests should be protected, the relative 'weight' of their governance models, and so on. Therefore, it will require sound reconnection to existing norms, or a legitimizing legislative decision in due time. Until then, those engaging in the task will inevitably infuse their respective political, economic, moral and other perspectives and preferences, which is why methodological sincerity and transparency will be of particular relevance here.

C. Walking First Steps

To walk some first steps along this path, some initial thoughts shall be provided here on how certain aspects of the law of inter-organizational interactions could be developed further.

Arguably, one of the most central issues regarding the inter-organizational level will be to find appropriate rules that govern indirect or non-cooperative interactions. To recall: during indirect interactions, IOs influence each other, either intentionally

---

[12]Chapter 15 B. VI.

[13]See *mutatis mutandis* Peter-Tobias Stoll, 'Koordination, Kooperation und Konstitutionalisierung im Völkerrecht' in Werner Heun and Frank Schorkopf (eds), *Wendepunkte der Rechtswissenschaft - Aspekte des Rechts in der Moderne* (Wallstein Verlag 2014) 273, 277; Henner Gött, 'Interactions between International Organizations - Approaching a Neglected Governance Dimension' (2020) 17 International Organizations Law Review 75, 96 et seqq.

[14]On interpretation and construction as elements of legal doctrinal scholarship see Jannis Lennartz, *Dogmatik Als Methode* (Mohr Siebeck 2017) 32 et seqq. and 189 et seqq. This exercise includes to ascertain the sources of law in relation to which the doctrinal concepts are to be developed. This study has deliberately confined itself to the canonic trias of sources – treaties, custom and general principles. However, this trias is not exhaustive, and moreover subject to intense debate as far as IOs are concerned.

or accidentally, without direct communication. During conflictual interactions, IOs are unwilling or unable to agree on the appropriate shape and form of mutual influence.[15] In both cases, one solution could be to define a protected area for each IO that the respective other must respect.

I. A Duty Not to Compromise Accomplished and Ongoing Work

One step towards this solution is to engage in the abovesaid creative task of exploring additional inter-organizational rights and obligations. As seen, a structural peculiarity of the inter-organizational constellation—and a particular challenge for defining protected areas—is the fact that IOs' jurisdictions overlap. This overlap has a 'functional' and a 'membership' dimension.[16] In light of this overlap, it proves difficult to conceptualize exclusive spheres of jurisdiction beyond every IO's organic jurisdiction.[17] As to functional overlap, it would not be adequate to simply 'reserve' a certain subject-matter for one IO, thereby excluding others.[18] For example, it would be inappropriate if the ILO could demand from the World Bank or the CoE not to address any labour issues. Vice versa, it would be equally inappropriate if the Bank or the CoE could require the ILO not to address issues of economic

---

[15] See Chap. 3 B. II.

[16] Chapter 15 B. VI. 1.

[17] Chapter 15 B VI. 1. b).

[18] There are few instances where the ILO and other IOs themselves have attempted to do so. For instance, the ILO and the UNESCO have attempted to allocate competences regarding their activities in technical and vocational education and training, in order to implement UN development goals, see the 2014 Memorandum of Understanding between the International Labour Organization (ILO) and the United Nations Educational, Scientific and Cultural Organization (UNESCO) (signed and entered into force 8 July 2014) <https://www.ilo.org/wcmsp5/groups/public/%2D%2D-dgreports/%2D%2D-jur/documents/genericdocument/wcms_434545.pdf> accessed 26 April 2020 (ILO-UNESCO-MoU), concluded as a supplementary agreement according to Art. VIII(1) 1947 ILO-UNESCO, notably No. 2.2.2 (delimitation of "primary concerns") and No. 2.2.3 (division of labour; partnerships and inter-agency coordination). The 1987 Agreement between the International Labour Organisation and the United Nations Industrial Development Organization (adopted and entered into force 14 September 1987) LXX ILO Official Bulletin 195 (ILO-UNIDO) contains a mutual pledge for respect of each other's competence, Art. 1 ILO-UNIDO. Another example is UNAIDS, in which the ILO and the other cosponsoring IOs have inter alia agreed on a division of labour, Mario Savino, 'Linkages Between Global Regimes and Interactions with Civil Society' in Sabino Cassese (ed), *Research Handbook on Global Administrative Law* (Edward Elgar Publishing 2016) 131. However, as the examples already shows, such an agreement will likely be of a high degree of specificity. What is more, it might not even be in either IO's interest to allocate jurisdiction on a basis of exclusivity to begin with. In many instances, both interacting IOs can benefit from the respective other's work on a similar field. The ILO has repeatedly made explicit that it would welcome if other IOs, namely the economic and financial ones, would increase their efforts in the field of labour. In other words, exclusive jurisdiction also implies exclusive responsibility.

development or of human rights. As to membership overlap, it would be inappropriate if any IO could require the others to abstain from working in a common member state.

Instead, it seems more promising to presume that every IO is *prima facie* entitled to perform its own tasks according to its own governance model. This would imply that one IO's governance model should be protected vis-à-vis other IOs with overlapping ambits.

How would this protection be framed in legal rights and obligations? One could first think of a duty to cooperate. Influence of one IO on another would then trigger a duty of both IOs to find a mutually satisfactory solution. However, turning cooperation into a duty would face—besides the difficulties discussed in Chap. 15—the practical difficulty that reticent IOs would be 'carried to the hunt', i.e. forced to cooperate against their will, which may have an adverse impact on the success of the cooperation. Moreover, it may be expected that IOs willing to cooperate would do so even without being obliged.

A possible alternative could therefore be to formulate an inter-organizational obligation, incumbent on every IO, to respect that another IOs acts in accordance with its (i.e. that other IO's own) governance model. This would imply, as a minimum, a duty not to compromise each other's accomplished and ongoing work. Thus, every IO would have to omit or cease any acts having that effect. Failure to comply with this duty would resemble an internationally wrongful act vis-à-vis the other IO.

Such a duty not to compromise other IOs' accomplished and ongoing work has to accommodate two practical concerns. Firstly, inter-organizational interactions are not always intentional and not even always apparent for the acting IO.[19] Secondly, there may be a dispute as to whether one IO's conduct compromises the accomplished or ongoing work of another IO. To recall: the World Bank's initial response to the EWI's critics was to claim that the EWI was compatible with all ILO conventions—which the ILO emphatically rejected.[20]

In both constellations, the crucial question is who decides whether an IO's work has been compromised. Who decides under which conditions a particular work may be deemed compromised, and whether these conditions are met in a given situation?

At the outset, it would be every IO's own responsibility to evaluate the situation and to ensure that it does not compromise other IOs' work. However, these other IOs are in a far better position to determine whether their work has been compromised. Therefore, to achieve greater legal certainty, it could be considered that an influenced IO may explicitly object to the influencing IO's conduct. Together with this

[19]In some cases, it might be overly onerous for one IO to assess whether its actions exert influence on another IO. For example, in the case of the ILO-ECtHR interactions discussed in Chap. 5, the ECtHR may not have anticipated which repercussions of aligning its jurisprudence with ILO supervisory practice might have on the ILO.

[20]See Chap. 4 C. II. 3.

objection, the influenced IO would have to specify how the incriminated conduct compromises its own work.[21] Such an explicit objection could be treated as an important, if not decisive, criterion for establishing that its work has been compromised.[22] On the other hand, the lack of an objection could be treated as indicating the influenced IO's consent.[23] In any event, the possibility of an objection could reinvigorate IOs' preventive efforts not to compromise each other's work, and may set an incentive for cooperation.

If an IO becomes aware that its conduct compromises another IO's work, it would have several options to proceed:

(1) to try to find a mutually satisfactory solution by seeking a dialogue with the other IO,
(2) not to take any further action beyond ceasing the conduct in question, or
(3) to review and to change its conduct in a way that does not compromise the other IO's work anymore. If the other IO has raised an explicit objection, this objection and the reasons given therein may serve as guidance.

Applied to the cases of indirect or non-cooperative interactions examined in Part I, the duty to respect other IOs' accomplished or ongoing work would tentatively play out as follows:

In the EWI episode, the World Bank would have been under an obligation to ensure that the EWI and its use do not compromise the ILO's work taking place in the countries included in the Doing Business rankings. It is difficult to reconstruct whether and to what extent the Bank had actually done so before it conceptualized and employed the EWI for the first time. However, in any event, the ILO could have raised an explicit objection, pointing out how the EWI and surrounding World Bank activities hampered its reform initiative in Nepal,[24] its supervisory practice regarding

---

[21]This objection would not necessarily be the same as a claim made pursuant to Art. 4 DARIO. Depending on the situation, it could also be considered a mere 'warning' to make the other IO aware of circumstances and thus to reduce uncertainties about the wrongfulness of the conduct.

[22]The influencing IO thus would have to establish atypical circumstances, or an abuse of rights by the objecting IO. Some authors, writing about the inter-state constellation, are sceptical whether the (lack of) protest is an adequate indicator, arguing that a state will only defer to protests by another state if there is a credible threat that the protesting state is in a position to otherwise resort to retaliation that actually have an impact on the acting state, see e.g. Cedric Ryngaert, Jurisdiction in international Law (2nd edn, Oxford University Press 2015) 41 et seq. In the inter-organizational constellation, however, the threat of direct retaliation of one IO against another is generally much lower than among states. At the same time, all IOs crucially depend on maintaining the impression that they adhere to international law and do not exceed their competences. It may therefore be questioned if the prospect of retailiatory harm by a protester plays the same role in the inter-organizational constellation.

[23]According to Art. 20 DARIO, valid consent precludes wrongfulness. Depending on the circumstances, the influenced IO may also lose its claim pursuant to Art. 46 DARIO. In inter-state relations, diplomatic protest (or the absence thereof) has been considered an important indicator of whether one state has overstepped its jurisdiction, Michael Akehurst, 'Jurisdiction in International Law' (1972-3) 46 British Yearbook of International Law 145, 176; Ryngaert (n 22) 39 et seqq.

[24]Chapter 4 C. I. 1.

Georgia[25] or other aspects of its accomplished or ongoing work. The ILO's objection would have been an important, if not decisive, criterion for establishing that the World Bank's conduct compromised the ILO's work.[26] The Bank would thus have been obliged to omit further steps that would compromise the ILO's efforts. Apart from this obligation, the Bank would have remained free to unilaterally review its activities (e.g. by modifying the EWI), to enter into a dialogue with the ILO to pursue a consensual solution, or to simply discontinue the use of the EWI and take no further action.

In the case of the ECtHR referencing ILO supervisory practice, the Court may not have anticipated that its change of jurisprudence would fuel the ILO's internal crisis. Moreover, one might legitimately question whether the Court actually would have violated the CoE's obligation not to compromise the ILO's work simply by referencing ILO practice. On the other hand, this uncertainty would have been reduced—if not eliminated—if in 2012, the ILO had explicitly objected to further references and pointed to the difficulties that had arisen. The objection would have established that the Court had—at least at that point in time—compromised the ILO's ongoing work.

This solution may appear overly rigid for the CoE, and open to abuse by the objecting ILO. It is freely admitted that careful further examination is needed to assess whether and on what grounds an objection should be rebuttable. In any event, however, there would have been a range of options for the Court (or the CoE as a whole) to react: for example, the Court could have revisited the way it referenced ILO practice. Moreover, it could also have stopped further ILO references—the Court would have remained free to rely on other arguments and arguably could even have arrived at the same conclusion as before. The Court could also have invited the ILO to make submissions or participate in hearings for pending cases, pursuant to Art. 36(2) ECHR. Finally, the CoE's main organs could have facilitated a dialogue under the ILO-CoE to clarify the matter. The example shows that even in cases of uncertainty, the proposed duty and the tool of an explicit objection could help to facilitate a solution.

II. Establishing a Normative Scaffold for the Duty

As mentioned before, it is insufficient to simply postulate a duty to respect other IOs' accomplished or ongoing work. Rather, there is a need to establish the relevant normative scaffold, i.e. to determine on what legal basis such a duty could be based.

The critical point is to soundly justify why one IO's accomplished or ongoing work should be legally relevant for—and thus respected by—another IO. Every IO works pursuant to its governance model, which is decisively shaped by its own

[25] Chapter 4 C. I. 2.

[26] Whether and under which circumstances this would be rebuttable is left open here.

institutional law. Yet, as mentioned before, one IO's institutional law is not legally binding on another IO. Pursuant to the *pacta tertiis* rule, it is *res inter alios acta*. Therefore, if one IO's governance model should be of any legal relevance for another, one way to proceed would be to consider whether the rigidity of the *pacta tertiis* rule can be surpassed in a doctrinally sound manner.

In the context of IOs' international legal personality, it has been argued that there was a customary international rule of incorporation, pursuant to which all states had the right to create IOs as new legal persons with objective legal personality.[27] This proposal could be expanded to a customary right to create (and a corresponding duty to respect) specific governance models. However, as the proponents of a rule of incorporation themselves concede, it is difficult to identify sufficient state practice of a norm at this level of abstraction.[28]

Another avenue could be to further explore the potential of the *lex specialis* rule embodied in Art. 5 VCLT. To recall, pursuant to Art. 5 VCLT, any 'rule of the organization' is *lex specialis* to the VCLT's provisions. Art. 5 VCLT unconditionally refers to all VCLT provisions. Thus, it also refers to Arts. 34-38 VCLT—the provisions containing the *pacta tertiis* rule.

Against this background, one could argue that IOs' constituent instruments (or parts thereof) modify the *pacta tertiis* rule and create certain obligations for non-members, including other IOs.[29] This construction could provide a basis for endowing provisions in IOs' constituent instruments with external legal effect vis-à-vis other IOs.

Using Art. 5 VCLT to soften the *pacta tertiis rule* is of course a bold argument. It is unlikely that the ILC and the 1968 Vienna Conference had this application in mind when they drafted and adopted Art. 5 VCLT.[30] Moreover, it might still be necessary to identify sufficient state practice and *opinio juris* supporting this application.[31]

On the other hand, using Art. 5 VCLT to soften the *pacta tertiis* rule is supported by the provision's unconditional wording. Moreover, it would not be entirely new to inter-organizational law to endow IOs' institutional laws with certain external

[27] Fernando Lusa Bordin, *The Analogy Between States and International Organizations* (Cambridge University Press 2019) 55 et seqq.

[28] ibid 62.

[29] Some commentators have considered Art. 5 VCLT to apply regarding the *pacta tertiis* rule, Kirsten Schmalenbach, 'Art. 5 VCLT' in Oliver Dörr and Kirsten Schmalenbach (eds), *Vienna Convention on the Law of Treaties: A Commentary* (2nd edn, Springer 2018) Art. 5, para. 19.

[30] The issue of exceptions to the *pacta tertiis* rule was repeatedly debated during the drafting process, see for an overview Alexander Proelß, 'Art 34 VCLT' in Oliver Dörr and Kirsten Schmalenbach (eds), *Vienna Convention on the Law of Treaties - A Commentary* (2nd edn, Springer 2018) Art. 34 para 35 et seqq. See also the discussion in Chap. 9 A. III.

[31] Regarding an obligation of other IOs, it would probably not be enough to argue that, because Art. 5 VCLT is a treaty norm, no further evidence of customary law is necessary. Art. 34-38 VCLT only protect third states, not third IOs. On the other hand, Art. 34-38 VCLT-IO, which protect third IOs, do not apply to IOs constituent instruments, which are not covered by the VCLT-IO but the VCLT (see Art. 5 VCLT and Art. 5 VCLT-IO). Therefore, whether a constituent instrument of an IO could modify the pacta tertiis rule vis-à-vis other IOs remains a question of customary law.

legal effects vis-à-vis other IOs. As seen in Part III, there are some inter-organizational legal norms already externalizing certain aspects of IOs' institutional laws.[32]

As far as supporting practice is concerned, IOs' institutional laws mirror states' desire to let IOs interact smoothly, but also with due regard for their respective own governance model. A pertinent example are provisions obliging IOs to enter into relations with each other, but requiring them to do so "within the terms" of their respective own constituent instrument.[33] As far as IOs' own practice is concerned, it appears that, even in conflictual interactions, IOs do not entirely disregard or reject other IOs' accomplished and ongoing work. As seen in Part I, the World Bank and the ECtHR ultimately decided to prioritize their own approach to labour governance. Yet, neither denied that the ILO was entitled to work on labour topics in accordance with its own governance model, too. In fact, the ECtHR went to great lengths to align its jurisprudence with ILO supervisory practice, and even the Bank attempted to argue that the EWI was fully consistent with all ILO conventions.[34]

All these aspects indicate that overcoming the *pacta tertiis* rule via Art. 5 VCLT may not be as far-fetched as it may seem at first. By virtue of Art. 5 VCLT, the definition of IOs' governance models in their respective constituent instruments could become legally relevant vis-à-vis other IOs.[35] This again might form a basis for an inter-organizational duty not to compromise accomplished or ongoing work.

[32]See Chap. 15. One example is Art. 6 VCLT-IO regarding the capacity to conclude treaties.

[33]E.g. those examined in Chaps. 8 and 9.

[34]Chapter 4 C. II. 3. and Chap. 5 B. III.

[35]The scope of this externalization will still have to be defined. It could in fact depend on the particular constituent instrument at hand. Art. 5 VCLT gives precedence to the rules of *a specific* IO over the general rules of the VCLT. The extent to which Art. 5 VCLT surpasses the *pacta tertiis* rule could therefore depend on the shape and form of every IO's institutional law (which again would allow more tailored and flexible solutions than a one-size-fits-all customary rule).

20. Final Remarks

For the foreseeable future, the ILO will continue to engage in labour governance alongside other IOs with different objectives, different political, professional and ideational starting points, and different means to achieve their goals. The ILO will continue to interact with these IOs, and these interactions will play out in all their diversity and ambivalence.

The systemic importance of structuring and ordering these interactions is perhaps greater than ever before. In its 2019 final report, the Global Commission on the Future of Work, incepted by the current ILO Director-General to provide the analytical basis for recalibrating the ILO's agenda at the occasion of its centenary, observed that

> the multilateral system confronts serious questioning of its very effectiveness and legitimacy. The two are not coincidental. Multilateralism is under such pressure precisely because of doubts about its capacity to deliver credible responses to the global challenges of the day. Demonstrating that by working together in full coherence the system is able to provide such responses will do much to win back the political support that it needs to operate to its full potential.[1]

The Commission observed further that

> [t]he ILO has a unique role to play (. . .), guided by its rights-based, normative mandate and in full respect of its tripartite character. The ILO can become a focal point in the international system (. . .).

It recommended that

[1]Global Commission for the Future of Work, 'Work for a Brighter Future' (ILO 2019) 55.

H. Gött, *The Law of Interactions Between International Organizations*, Beiträge zum ausländischen öffentlichen Recht und Völkerrecht 299, https://doi.org/10.1007/978-3-662-62389-3_20

all relevant organizations in the multilateral system explore ways to strengthen substantive joint work[2]

With a view to these observations and recommendations, it is crucial to ensure that inter-organizational interactions occur in a way that advances the causes of all interacting IOs and benefits those for whose ultimate gain they work, including their member states, but also workers, employers and society as a whole. With particular regard to the ILO, it is essential that its model of labour governance is adequately protected and promoted, so that the ILO can play out its "unique role" among the IOs engaged in labour governance.

Given the ubiquity and potential impact of inter-organizational interactions on the ILO and its model of labour governance, social ordering techniques like international law are of increasingly high interest. This study's in-depth and systematic analysis of the legal dimension of inter-organizational interactions has revealed the rather modest role that international law plays at present. As per now, the ILO can hardly (if ever) rely on international law to protect or promote its model of labour governance in inter-organizational interactions. Instead, it has to rely, for better or worse, on its persuasive power and a number of non-legal factors which are often beyond its control and anticipation. It is, of course, to a large extent a question of policy and preference whether to keep it that way. However, if the goal is to reduce the ambivalence of inter-organizational interactions and to channel their repercussions on the ILO's model of labour governance, it will be worthwhile to re-evaluate the role that law can play in this regard. This study has expounded the complexities that such an undertaking will face. Exploring, articulating and refining what could become a more developed law of inter-organizational interactions is an intricate and ambitions task. Yet, pursuing it would not only be of structural relevance for labour governance, but for inter-organizational interactions as a whole. This is a genuine contribution for international legal scholarship to make, and it is to be hoped that more attention will be devoted to it in the future.

---

[2]It recommended "in particular the establishment of more systemic and substantive working relations between the WTO, the Bretton Woods institutions and the ILO.", ibid 56. This recommendation was picked up in the ILO's 2019 Centenary Declaration, Part F.

Table of Treaties

- Additional Protocol to the European Social Charter (adopted 5 May 1988, entered into force 3 September 1992) CETS No 128
- Additional Protocol to the European Social Charter Providing for a System of Collective Complaints (adopted 9 November 1995, entered into force 1 July 1997) CETS No 158
- Agreement between the EFTA States on the Establishment of a Surveillance Authority and a Court of Justice (signed 2 May 1992, entered into force 1 January 1994) [1994] OJ L 344/3
- Agreement between the International Labour Office and the United International Bureaux for the Protection of Intellectual Property (entered into force 9 June 1969) LII ILO Official Bulletin No 1 331 (ILO-WIPO)
- Agreement between the International Labour Organisation and the Council of Europe (entered into force 23 November 1951) XXXV ILO Official Bulletin 380 (ILO-CoE)
- Agreement between the International Labour Organisation and the Intergovernmental Maritime Consultative Organisation (entered into force 16 January 1959) XLII ILO Official Bulletin 261 (ILO-IMO)
- Agreement between the International Labour Organisation and the United Nations Educational, Scientific and Cultural Organization (entered into force 15 December 1947) 18 UNTS 346 (ILO-UNESCO)
- Agreement between the International Labour Organisation and the United Nations Industrial Development Organization (adopted and entered into force 14 September 1987) LXX ILO Official Bulletin 195 (ILO-UNIDO)
- Agreement between the International Labour Organization and the Food and Agriculture Organization of the United Nations (entered into force 11 September 1947, 18 UNTS 335 (ILO-FAO)

H. Gött, *The Law of Interactions Between International Organizations*,
Beiträge zum ausländischen öffentlichen Recht und Völkerrecht 299,
https://doi.org/10.1007/978-3-662-62389-3

- Agreement between the Secretariat General of the Council of Europe and the Secretariat of the United Nations (exchange of letters between Mr JC Paris and Mr Trygve Lie 15 December 1951) UN Doc SG 324/080 <https://rm.coe.int/CoERMPublicCommonSearchServices/DisplayDCTMContent?documentId=090000168059acd8> accessed 26 April 2020
- Agreement between the United Nations and the International Bank for Reconstruction and Development (adopted 15 November 1947, entered into force 13 April 1948) 16 UNTS 341 (UN-IBRD)
- Agreement between the United Nations and the International Labour Organization (adopted 30 May 1946, entered into force 14 December 1946) XXIX ILO Official Bulletin 385 (UN-ILO)
- Agreement on Cooperation and Relationship between the United Nations and the International Tribunal for the Law of the Sea (signed 18 December 1997, entered into force 8 September 1998) 2000 UNTS 467 (UN-ITLOS)
- Agreement on the European Economic Area (signed 2 May 1992, entered into force 1 January 1994) [1994] OJ L1/3
- Arrangement between the International Labour Organisation and the Council of Europe on the Creation and Activities of the International Vocational Training Information and Research Centre (adopted and entered into force 8 December 1960) 398 UNTS 291 (ILO-CoE 1960 Arrangement)
- Arrangement on Co-operation and Liaison between the Secretariats of the United Nations and the Council of Europe (exchange of letters of 19 November 1971) <https://rm.coe.int/CoERMPublicCommonSearchServices/DisplayDCTMContent?documentId=090000168059acd9> accessed 26 April 2020
- Articles of Agreement of the International Bank for Reconstruction and Development (adopted at the UN Monetary and Financial Conference, Bretton Woods, New Hampshire, 22 July 1944, entered into force 27 December 1945) 2 UNTS 134 (IBRD-AoA)
- Articles of Agreement of the International Development Association (approved for submission to Governments by the Executive Directors of the International Bank for Reconstruction and Development on 26 January 1960, entered into force 24 September 1960) 439 UNTS 249 (IDA-AoA)
- Articles of Agreement of the International Finance Corporation (entered into force 20 July 1956) 264 UNTS 117 (IFC-AoA)
- Articles of Agreement of the International Monetary Fund (adopted at the UN Monetary and Financial Conference, Bretton Woods, New Hampshire, 22 July 1944, entered into force 27 December 1945) 2 UNTS 39 (IMF-AoA)
- Charter of the Organization of American States (signed 30 April 1948, entered into force 13 December 1951) 119 UNTS 3
- Charter of the United Nations (adopted 26 June 1945, entered into force 24 October 1945) 1 UNTS XVI (UN Charter)
- Comprehensive Economic and Trade Agreement between Canada, of the one part, and the European Union and its Member States, of the other part (adopted 28 October 2016) [2017] OJ L11/23 (CETA)

- Constitution of the International Labour Organization (adopted 1 April 1919, entered into force 28 June 1919) 15 UNTS 40 (ILO Constitution)
- Constitution of the United Nations Educational, Scientific and Cultural Organization (adopted 16 November 1945, entered into force 4 November 1946) 4 UNTS 275 (UNESCO Constitution)
- Convention establishing the Multilateral Investment Guarantee Agency (adopted 11 October 1985, entered into force 12 April 1988) 1508 UNTS 99 (MIGA Convention)
- Convention for the Protection of Human Rights and Fundamental Freedoms (adopted 4 November 1950, entered into force 3 September 1953) CETS No 5 (ECHR)
- Convention on the Elimination of All Forms of Discrimination against Women (adopted and opened for signature, ratification and accession by General Assembly resolution 34/180 of 18 December 1979, entered into force 3 September 1981) 1249 UNTS 13 (CEDAW)
- Convention on the International Maritime Organization (adopted 6 March 1948, entered into force 17 March 1958) 289 UNTS 3 (IMO Conventio
- Convention on the Law of the Non-Navigational Uses of International Watercourses (adopted 21 May 1997, entered into force 17 August 2014) 2999 UNTS 1
- Convention on the Rights of the Child (adopted 20 November 1989, entered into force 2 September 1990) 1577 UNTS 3 (CRC)
- Covenant of the League of Nations (signed 28 June, entered into force 10 January 1920) 225 CTS 195 (LoN Covenant)
- European Code of Social Security (adopted 16 April 1964, entered into force 17 March 1968) CETS No 46 (ECSS)
- European Code of Social Security (revised) (adopted 6 November 1990, not yet in force) CETS No 139 (Revised ECSS)
- European Social Charter (adopted 18 October 1961, entered into force 26 February 1965) CETS No 35 (ESC)
- European Social Charter (Revised) (adopted 3 May 1996, entered into force 1 July 1999) CETS No. 163 (RESC)
- Executing Agency Agreement between the United Nations Development Programme (UNDP) and the International Labour Organization (ILO) (entered into force 8 July 1993) LXXVI ILO Official Bulletin Ser A 218
- ILO Abolition of Forced Labour Convention, 1957 (No 105) (adopted 25 June 1957, entered into force 16 January 1959) 320 UNTS 291
- ILO Contracts of Employment (Indigenous Workers) Convention, 1947 (No 86) (adopted 11 July 1947, entered into force 13 February 1953, abrogated by decision of the International Labour Conference at its 107th Session (2018)) 161 UNTS 113
- ILO Discrimination (Employment and Occupation) Convention, 1958 (No 111) (adopted 25 June 1958, entered into force 15 June 1960) 362 UNTS 31
- ILO Employment Policy Convention, 1964 (No 122) (adopted 9 July 1964, entered into force 15 July 1966) 569 UNTS 65

- ILO Equal Remuneration Convention, 1951 (No 100) (adopted 29 June 1951, entered into force 23 May 1953) 165 UNTS 303
- ILO Forced Labour Convention, 1930 (No 29) (adopted 28 June 1930, entered into force 1 May 1932) 39 UNTS 55
- ILO Freedom of Association and Protection of the Right to Organise Convention, 1948 (No 87) (adopted 9 July 1948, entered into force 4 July 1950) 68 UNTS 17
- ILO Hours of Work (Industry) Convention, 1919 (No 1) (adopted 28 November 1919, entered into force 13 June 1921) 38 UNTS 17
- ILO Indigenous and Tribal Peoples Convention, 1989 (No 169) (adopted 27 June 1989, entered into force 5 September 1991) 1650 UNTS 383
- ILO Labour Inspection (Agriculture) Convention, 1969 (No 129) (adopted 25 June 1969, entered into force 19 January 1972) 812 UNTS 87
- ILO Labour Inspection Convention, 1947 (No 81) (adopted 11 July 1947, entered into force 7 April 1950) 54 UNTS 3
- ILO Labour Inspectorates (Non-Metropolitan Territories) Convention, 1947 (No 85) (adopted 11 July 1947, entered into force 26 July 1955) 214 UNTS 33
- ILO Labour Relations (Public Service) Convention, 1978 (No 151) (adopted 27 June 1978, entered into force 25 February 1981) 1218 UNTS 87
- ILO Labour Standards (Non-Metropolitan Territories) Convention, 1947 (No 83) (adopted 11 July 1947, entered into force 15 June 1974) 943 UNTS 104
- ILO Minimum Age Convention, 1973 (No 138) (adopted 26 June 1973. entered 19 June 1976) 1015 UNTS 297
- ILO Night Work Convention, 1990 (No 171) (adopted on 26 June 1990, entered into force on 4 January 1995), 1846 UNTS 418
- ILO Protection of Workers' Claims (Employer's Insolvency) Convention, 1992 (No 173) (adopted on 23 June 1992, entered into force on 8 June 1995), 1886 UNTS 1
- ILO Right of Association (Non-Metropolitan Territories) Convention, 1947 (No 84) (adopted 11 July 1947, entered into force 1 July 1953) 171 UNTS 329
- ILO Right to Organise and Collective Bargaining Convention, 1949 (No 98) (adopted 1 July 1949, entered into force 18 July 1951) 96 UNTS 257
- ILO Social Policy (Non-Metropolitan Territories) Convention, 1947 (No 82) (adopted 11 July 1947, entered into force 19 June 1955) 218 UNTS 345
- ILO Social Security (Minimum Standards) Convention, 1952 (No 102) (adopted 28 June 1952, entered into force 27 April 1955) 210 UNTS 131
- ILO Termination of Employment Convention, 1982 (No 158) (adopted 22 June 1982, entered into force 23 November 1985) 1412 UNTS 1
- ILO Tripartite Consultation (International Labour Standards) Convention, 1976 (No 144) (adopted 17 June 1976, entered into force 16 May 1978) 1089 UNTS 354
- ILO Workers with Family Responsibilities Convention, 1981 (No 156) (adopted 23 June 1981, entered into force 11 August 1983) 2029 UNTS 297
- ILO Workers' Representatives Convention, 1971 (No 135) (adopted 23 June 1971, entered into force 30 June 1973) 883 UNTS 111

- ILO Worst Forms of Child Labour Convention, 1999 (No 182) (adopted 17 June 1999, entered into force 19 November 2000) 2133 UNTS 161
- ILO/UNIDO Working Arrangement (signed and entered into force 7 October 1991) LXXV ILO Official Bulletin Ser A 69
- International Convention on Standards of Training, Certification and Watchkeeping for Seafarers, 1978 (adopted 7 July 1978, entered into force on 28 April 1984) 1361 UNTS 2 (STCW Convention)
- International Convention on the Elimination of All Forms of Racial Discrimination (adopted and opened for signature and ratification by General Assembly resolution 2106 (XX) of 21 December 1965, entered into force 4 January 1969) 660 UNTS 195 (CERD)
- International Convention on the Protection of the Rights of All Migrant Workers and Members of Their Families (adopted by General Assembly resolution 45/158 of 18 December 1990, entered into force 1 July 2003) 2220 UNTS 3 (ICMW)
- International Covenant on Civil and Political Rights (adopted and opened for signature, ratification and accession by General Assembly resolution 2200A (XXI) of 16 December 1966, entered into force 23 March 1976) 999 UNTS 171 (ICCPR)
- International Covenant on Economic, Social and Cultural Rights (adopted and opened for signature, ratification and accession by General Assembly resolution 2200A (XXI) of 16 December 1966, entered into force 3 January 1976) 993 UNTS 3 (ICESCR)
- Maritime Labour Convention (adopted by the International Labour Conference at its 94th (Maritime) Session (2006) entered into force 20 Aug 2013) 2951 UNTS 1
- Optional Protocol to the Convention on the Rights of the Child on the involvement of children in armed conflict (adopted and opened for signature, ratification and accession by UNGA resolution A/RES/54/263 of 25 May 2000, entry into force 12 February 2002) 2173 UNTS 222
- Optional Protocol to the Convention on the Rights of the Child on the sale of children, child prostitution and child pornography (adopted and opened for signature, ratification and accession by UNGA resolution A/RES/54/263 of 25 May 2000, entered into force 18 January 2002) 2171 UNTS 227
- Protocol amending the European Social Charter (adopted 21 October 1991) CETS No 142
- Standard Agreement on Operational Assistance (with Annex) between the United Nations (including the United Nations Industrial Development Organization and the United Nations Conference on Trade and Development), International Labour Organisation, Food and Agriculture Organization of the United Nations, United Nations Educational, Scientific and Cultural Organization, International Civil Aviation Organization, World Health Organization, International Telecommunication Union, World Meteorological Organization, International Atomic Energy Agency, Universal Postal Union, Inter-Governmental Maritime Consultative Organization and International Bank for Reconstruction and Development, and Central African Republic (signed 13 January 1972) 807 UNTS 284

- Statute of the Council of Europe (adopted 5 May 1949, entered into force 3 August 1949) CETS No 1 (CoE Statute)
- Statutes of the River Uruguay (adopted 26 February 1975, entered into force 18 September 1976) 1295 UNTS 331 (1975 Statute of the River Uruguay)
- Treaty of Peace between the British Empire, France, Italy, Japan and the United States (the Principal Allied and Associated Powers), and Belgium, Bolivia, Brazil, China, Cuba, Czechoslovakia, Ecuador, Greece, Guatemala, Haiti, the Hedjaz, Honduras, Liberia, Nicaragua, Panama, Peru, Poland, Portugal, Roumania, the Serb-Croat-Slovene State, Siam, and Uruguay, and Germany (signed 28 June, entered into force 10 January 1920) 225 CTS 195 (Treaty of Versailles)
- Treaty on European Union (Consolidated Version 2016) [2016] OJ C202/01
- Treaty on the Functioning of the European Union (Consolidated Version 2016) [2016] OJ C202/47 (TFEU)
- Vienna Convention on the Law of Treaties (adopted 23 May 1969, entered into force 27 January 1980) 1155 UNTS 331 (VCLT)
- Vienna Convention on the Law of Treaties between States and International Organizations or between International Organizations (adopted 21 March 1986, not yet in force) A/CONF.129/15 (VCLT-IO)
- Vienna Convention on the Representation of States in their Relations with International Organizations of a Universal Character (adopted 14 March 1975, not yet in force) UN Doc A/CONF.67/16
- WTO Agreement on Technical Barriers to Trade (adopted 12 April 1979, entered into force 1 January 1980) 1186 UNTS 276 (TBT Agreement)
- WTO Agreement on the Application of Sanitary and Phytosanitary Measures (adopted 15 April 1994) 1867 UNTS 493 (SPS Agreement)

Table of Official Documents and Publications

1. Council of Europe

1.1 Resolutions, Decisions and Recommendations

- CM, Decision Relating to the Application of the 1991 Amending Protocol (467th meeting of the Ministers' Deputies, 11 December 1991) CM/Del/Dec(1991)467
- CM, Resolution (8th session, 3 May 1951) CETS No 8 (Statutory Resolution (51) 30)
- CM, Statutory Resolution (93) 26 on Observer Status (92nd session, 14 May 1993) <https://search.coe.int/cm/Pages/result_details.aspx?ObjectID=09000016804e42f6> accessed 26 April 2020 (Statutory Resolution (93) 26)
- CM, Statutory Resolution (93) 28 on Partial and Enlarged Agreements (92nd session, 14 May 1993) https://search.coe.int/cm/Pages/result_details.aspx?ObjectID=0900001680534828 accessed 26 April 2020
- PACE, Recommendation 839 (1978) on the Revision of the European Social Charter (30th session, 28 September 1978)
- PACE, Resolution 1202 (1999) 'Rules of Procedure of the Assembly (consolidated version of July 2019)' (4 November 1999)
- PACE, Resolution 1442 (2005) 'The Right to Strike in Essential Services: Economic Implications' (6 June 2005)

H. Gött, *The Law of Interactions Between International Organizations*, Beiträge zum ausländischen öffentlichen Recht und Völkerrecht 299, https://doi.org/10.1007/978-3-662-62389-3

1.2 Other Documents and Publications

- CM, 'Programme of Work of the Council of Europe' Communication of the CM (6th session (first part), 20 May 1954) PACE Doc 238
- CM, Rules of Procedure of the Committee of Ministers of the Council of Europe (9th session, August 1951)
- CoE, 'Explanatory Reports to the 1995 Protocol' in CoE (ed), *European Social Charter - Collected Texts* (7th edn, Council of Europe Publishing 2015) 145
- CoE, 'Explanatory Reports to the Additional Protocol of 1988' in CoE (ed), *European Social Charter - Collected Texts* (7th edn, Council of Europe Publishing 2015) 129
- CoE, 'Explanatory Reports to the Revised European Social Charter' in CoE (ed), *European Social Charter - Collected Texts* (7th edn, Council of Europe Publishing 2015) 153
- CoE, 'Form for the Reports Submitted in Pursuance of the European Social Charter (1961) and the Additional Protocol of 1988' in CoE (ed), *European Social Charter - Collected Texts* (7th edn, Council of Europe Publishing 2015) 216
- CoE, 'Form for the Reports to Be Submitted in Pursuance of the European Social Charter (Revised) Adopted by the Committee of Ministers on 26 March 2008' in CoE (ed), *European Social Charter - Collected Texts* (7th edn, Council of Europe Publishing 2015) 268
- CoE, 'Participation of International Organizations and Institutions in Council Of Europe Bodies' (2017) DER/INF(2017)4
- CoE, 'Preparatory Work on Article 4 of the Convention' (1962) DH (62) 10
- CoE, 'Report of the Committee of Experts' (16 March 1950) CM/WP 1 (50) 15; A 924, IV TP 2–55
- CoE, 'Warsaw Action Plan' (2005) CM(2005)80
- CoE, Warsaw Declaration, Adopted the Third Summit of Heads of State and Government of the Council of Europe (Warsaw, 16-17 May 2005) <https://www.coe.int/t/dcr/summit/20050517_decl_varsovie_EN.asp> accessed 26 April 2020
- ECtHR, Rules of Court (2020) (adopted 4 November 2019, entered into force 1 January 2020) (ECtHR Rules of Court)
- PACE, 'Opinion No 57 (1971) on the Application of the European Social Charter' in CoE (ed), *European Social Charter - Collected Texts* (7th edn, Council of Europe Publishing 2015) 337

2. European Free Trade Area

- European Free Trade Area, '57th Annual Report of the European Free Trade Association' (2017)

3. European Union

- Council Decision 2010/427/EU of 26 July 2010 Establishing the Organisation and Functioning of the European External Action Service [2010] OJ L201/30

4. League of Arab States

- League of Arab States (Council) Res No 2102 d/43 (21 March 1965)

5. International Labour Organization

5.1 Declarations of the International Labour Conference

- Centenary Declaration for the Future of Work (International Labour Conference, 108th session, 21 June 2019) <https://www.ilo.org/wcmsp5/groups/public/%2D%2D-ed_norm/%2D%2D-relconf/documents/meetingdocument/wcms_711674.pdf> accessed 26 April 2020
- Declaration Concerning the Aims and Purposes of the International Labour Organisation (International Labour Conference, 26th session, 10 May 1944) 15 UNTS 104 (Declaration of Philadelphia).
- Declaration Concerning the Policy of "Apartheid" of the Republic of South Africa (International Labour Conference, 48th session) (1964) XLVII ILO Official Bulletin Ser A 1 (Apartheid Declaration)
- Declaration on Equality of Opportunity and Treatment for Women Workers (1975) LVIII ILO Official Bulletin Ser A 96
- Declaration on Fundamental Principles and Rights at Work and its Follow-up (Labour Conference, 86th session, 18 June 1998) (Annex revised 15 June 2010) LXXX ILO Official Bulletin Ser A 73 (1998 Declaration)
- Declaration on Social Justice for a Fair Globalization (International Labour Conference, 97th session, 10 June 2008) XCI ILO Official Bulletin Ser A No 2 58 (2008 Declaration)
- Tripartite Declaration of Principles concerning Multinational Enterprises and Social Policy (amended in 2000 and 2006) and revised in 2017) (1977) reproduced in ILO, *Tripartite Declaration of Principles Concerning Multinational Enterprises and Social Policy* (ILO 2017) 1 (MNE Declaration)

5.2 Recommendations

- Income Security Recommendation, 1944 (No 67) (adopted 12 May 1944) XXVI ILO Official Bulletin 4
- Medical Care Recommendation, 1944 (No 69) (adopted 12 May 1944) XXVI ILO Official Bulletin 29
- Social Protection Floors Recommendation, 2012 (No 202) (adopted 14 June 2012) XCV ILO Official Bulletin Ser A No 2 64
- Working Environment (Air Pollution, Noise and Vibration) Recommendation, 1977 (No 156) (1977) LX ILO Official Bulletin Ser A Vol 3 146

5.3 Resolutions of the International Labour Conference

- International Labour Conference (105th session) Resolution on Advancing Social Justice through Decent Work (9 June 2016) XCIX ILO Official Bulletin Ser A No 2 30
- International Labour Conference (40th session) Resolution concerning the Abolition of Anti-Trade Union Legislation in the States Members of the International Labour Organisation (26 June 1957) XL ILO Official Bulletin No 1 30
- International Labour Conference (54th session) Resolution Concerning Trade Union Rights And Their Relation To Civil Liberties (25 June 1970) LIII ILO Official Bulletin No 3 287
- International Labour Conference (97th session) Resolution on Strengthening the ILO's Capacity to Assist Its Members' Efforts to Reach Its Objectives in the Context of Globalization (10 June 2008) XCI ILO Official Bulletin Ser A No 2 66

5.4 Standing Orders etc.

- Standing Orders of the Governing Body, reproduced in ILO, *Compendium of Rules Applicable to the Governing Body of the International Labour Office* (ILO 2016) 14 (GB Standing Orders)
- Standing Orders of the International Labour Conference https://www.ilo.org/dyn/normlex/en/f?p=NORMLEXPUB:62:0::NO::P62_LIST_ENTRIE_ID:3088520, accessed 26 April 2020 (International Labour Conference Standing Orders)
- Staff Regulations (April 2019) HRPOL-190401-1-En
- Statute of the Administrative Tribunal of the International Labour Organization, (adopted by the International Labour Conference on 9 October 1946 and amended by the Conference on 29 June 1949), reprinted in ILO, *Statute and Rules of the Administrative Tribunal* (ILO 2019)

5.5 Reports, Meeting Documents and Records of the International Labour Conference and Committees

- 'Final List of Delegations, Supplement to the Provisional Record' (International Labour Conference, 106th session, June 2017) <https://www.ilo.org/ilc/ILCSessions/previous-sessions/106/lang%2D%2Den/index.htm> accessed 26 April 2020
- 'Provisional Record' (International Labour Conference, 85th session, 13 June 1997) <https://www.ilo.org/public/english/standards/relm/ilc/ilc85/wolf.htm> accessed 26 April 2020
- 'Report of the Committee on Constitutional Questions to the 27th Session of the International Labour Conference' (1945) XXXVIII ILO Official Bulletin 64
- 'Report of the Committee on the Application of Standards Part One: General Report' (International Labour Conference, 101st Session May-June 2012) Provisional Record 19(Rev.) Part I
- 'Report of the Committee on the Application of Standards: Submission, Discussion, and Approval, Record of Proceedings' (International Labour Conference, 101st Session, 2012) No 27

5.6 Reports, Meeting Documents and Records of the Governing Body and Committees (incl. CEACR and Commissions of Inquiry)

- 'Collective Bargaining in the Public Service: A Way Forward, General Survey of the Committee of Experts on the Application of Conventions and Recommendations Concerning Labour Relations and Collective Bargaining in the Public Service' (2013) ILC.102/III/1B
- 'Giving Globalization a Human Face, General Survey on the Fundamental Conventions Concerning Rights at Work in Light of the ILO Declaration on Social Justice for a Fair Globalization', Report of the Committee of Experts on the Application of Conventions and Recommendations (International Labour Conference, 101st Session, 2012) ILC.101/III/1B
- 'ILO Relations with the Bretton Woods Institutions' (Governing Body, 279th session, November 2000) GB.279/ESP/1
- 'Minutes of the 300th Session of the Governing Body of the International Labour Office' (2007) GB.300/PV
- 'Report of the Commission Appointed under Article 26 of the Constitution of the ILO to Examine the Complaint Filed by the Government of Ghana Concerning the Observance by the Government of Portugal of the Abolition of Forced Labour Convention, 1957' (1962) XLV ILO Official Bulletin 1
- 'Report of the Committee of Experts on the Application of Conventions and Recommendations, General Survey on Freedom of Association and Collective

Bargaining' (International Labour Conference, 81st Session, 1994), Report III (Part 4B)
- 'Report of the Committee of Experts on the Application of Conventions and Recommendations' (International Labour Conference, 43rd Session, 1959) Part I, Report III
- 'Report of the Committee of Experts on the Application of Conventions and Recommendations: General Report and Observations Concerning Particular Countries' (International Labour Conference, 104th Session, 2015) ILC.104/III (1A)
- 'Report of the Committee of Experts on the Application of Conventions and Recommendations: General Report and Observations Concerning Particular Countries' (International Labour Conference, 106th Session, 2017) ILC.106/III (1A)
- 'Report of the International Organizations Committee of the Governing Body' (Governing Body, 141st Session, 10-13 March 1959) GB.L41/Ll/22
- 'The ILO and the Multilateral System' (Governing Body, 303rd Session, 2008) GB.303/6
- 'The Standards Initiative: Follow-up to the 2012 ILC Committee on the Application of Standards' (2014) GB.322/INS/5
- 'The Standards Initiative: Follow-up to the 2012 ILC Committee on the Application of Standards, Revised Draft Decision Following the Governing Body Debate Held on 11 November 2014' (2014) GB.322/INS/5(Add.2)
- 'The Standards Initiative' (2015) GB.323/INS/5
- 'Working Party on the Social Dimensions of the Liberalization of International Trade, Future of the Working Party' (1999) GB.276/ WP/SDL/1
- 'World Bank Doing Business Report: The Employing Workers Indicator' (2007) GB.300/4/1

5.7 Reports of the International Labour Office and the Director-General

- 'Changing Patterns in the World of Work, Report of the Director-General' (International Labour Conference, 95th session, 2006) Report 1(C)
- 'The Cost of Coercion, Global Report Under the Follow-up to the ILO Declaration on Fundamental Principles and Rights at Work' (International Labour Conference, 98th Session 2009) Report I(B)
- 'Towards the ILO Centenary: Realities, Renewal and Tripartite Commitment, Report of the ILO Director-General' (International Labour Conference, 102nd session, June 2013) ILC.102/I(A)
- 'Report on the High Level Mission to Greece' (2011) https://www.ilo.org/wcmsp5/groups/public/@ed_norm/@normes/documents/missionreport/wcms_170433.pdf accessed 26 April 2020

- 'Third-Party Monitoring of Measures against Child Labour and Forced Labour during the 2016 Cotton Harvest in Uzbekistan - A Report Submitted to the World Bank by the International Labour Office' (2017) <https://www.ilo.org/wcmsp5/groups/public/%2D%2D-ed_norm/%2D%2D-ipec/documents/publication/wcms_543130.pdf> accessed 26 April 2020
- 'Third-Party Monitoring of Measures against Child Labour and Forced Labour during the 2017 Cotton Harvest in Uzbekistan - A Report Submitted to the World Bank by the International Labour Office' (2018) <https://www.ilo.org/wcmsp5/groups/public/%2D%2D-ed_norm/%2D%2D-ipec/documents/publication/wcms_617830.pdf> accessed 26 April 2020

5.8 Memoranda of Understanding, Exchanges of Letters etc. with Other Institutions

- ILO and European Investment Bank, Memorandum of Understanding between the European Investment Bank and the International Labour Organization (16 July 2015) <https://www.ilo.org/global/about-the-ilo/how-the-ilo-works/departments-and-offices/jur/legal-instruments/WCMS_442247/lang%2D%2Den/index.htm> accessed 26 April 2020
- ILO and FAO, Memorandum of Understanding between the International Labour Organization (ILO) and the Food and Agriculture Organization of the United Nations (FAO) (2004) <https://www.ilo.org/wcmsp5/groups/public/%2D%2D-dgreports/%2D%2D-jur/documents/genericdocument/wcms_434511.pdf> accessed 26 April 2020
- ILO and ICAO, Memorandum of Understanding between the Director-General of the International Labour Office and the President of the Council of the International Civil Aviation Organisation (Proposed Joint Civil Aviation Commission) (1954) XXXVII ILO Bulletin 402
- ILO and UN HABITAT, Memorandum of Understanding Concerning Co-operation between the International Labour Organisation and the United Nations Centre for Human Settlements (HABITAT) (1984) LXVII ILO Official Bulletin Ser A 74 (ILO-UN HABITAT-MoU)
- ILO and UNCTAD, Memorandum of Understanding between the International Labour Organization and the United Nations Conference on Trade and Development (signed 4 December 2014) <https://www.ilo.org/wcmsp5/groups/public/%2D%2D-dgreports/%2D%2D-jur/documents/genericdocument/wcms_433858.pdf> accessed 26 April 2020 (ILO-UNCTAD-MoU)
- ILO and UNDCP, Memorandum of Understanding for cooperation between the United Nations International Drug Control Programme and the International Labour Organization (signed 15 August 1994) <https://www.ilo.org/wcmsp5/groups/public/%2D%2D-dgreports/%2D%2D-jur/documents/genericdocument/wcms_433887.pdf> accessed 26 April 2020

- ILO and UNESCO, Memorandum of Understanding between the International Labour Organization (ILO) and the United Nations Educational, Scientific and Cultural Organization (UNESCO) (signed and entered into force 8 July 2014) <https://www.ilo.org/wcmsp5/groups/public/%2D%2D-dgreports/%2D%2D-jur/documents/genericdocument/wcms_434545.pdf> accessed 26 April 2020 (ILO-UNESCO-MoU)
- ILO and UNOPS, Memorandum of Understanding between the International Labour Organization and the United Nations Office for Project Services (signed 10 December 2015) <https://www.ilo.org/wcmsp5/groups/public/%2D%2D-dgreports/%2D%2D-jur/documents/genericdocument/wcms_458165.pdf> accessed 26 April 2020
- ILO and World Bank, Memorandum of Understanding Between the World Bank and the International Labour Organization (17 November 2016) <http://www.worldbank.org/en/projects-operations/products-and-services/brief/procurement-new-framework#un> accessed 26 April 2020
- ILO, 'Letter of the Director-General of the International Labour Office to the Secretary-General of the Council of Europe of 19 March 1952' (1952) XXXV ILO Official Bulletin 384
- ILO, Instrument of the Adhesion of the International Labour Organization to the Memorandum of Understanding on a Joint and Cosponsored United Nations Programme on HIV/AIDS (2001) LXXXIV ILO Official Bulletin Ser A No 3 153

5.9 Other Documents and Publications

- Global Commission for the Future of Work, *Work for a Brighter Future* (ILO 2019)
- ILO and World Bank, 'A Shared Mission for Universal Social Protection - Concept Note' (2015) <https://www.ilo.org/wcmsp5/groups/public/%2D%2D-dgreports/%2D%2D-dcomm/documents/genericdocument/wcms_378996.pdf> accessed 26 April 2020
- ILO, 'Notice of Withdrawal Required Under Article 1, Paragraph 5 of the Constitution of the International Labour Organisation From Any State Member Intending to Withdraw From the Organisation - Question Whether an Extension of the Notice Is Legally Permissible' [1977] United Nations Juridical Yearbook 248
- ILO, 'Protocol Concerning the Entry into Force of the Agreement between the United Nations and the International Labour Organization' (1946) XXIX ILO Official Bulletin 383
- ILO, 'The ILO Standards Initiative – Joint Statement of Workers' & Employers' Groups' (23 February 2015) TMFAPROC/2015/2
- ILO, 'Work in Fishing Convention and Recommendation, 2007 - Action Plan 2011-2016', <http://www.ilo.org/wcmsp5/groups/public/@ed_dialogue/@sector/documents/publication/wcms_161220.pdf> accessed 11 April 2020

- ILO, 'Working Party on Policy Regarding the Revision of Standards (Cartier Working Party)' (2002) - Information Note on the Progress of Work and Decisions Taken Concerning the Revision of Standards' (2002) <https://www.ilo.org/wcmsp5/groups/public/%2D%2D-ed_norm/%2D%2D-normes/documents/genericdocument/wcms_125644.pdf> accessed 26 April 2020
- ILO, 'World Bank President Cites Growing Ties with ILO on Globalization and Decent Work Agenda, Welcomes "Partnership Through Dialogue"' (Press Release, 17 March 2008) (2008)
- ILO, *Compendium of Rules Applicable to the Governing Body of the International Labour Office* (ILO 2016)
- ILO, *Digest of Decisions and Principles of the Freedom of Association Committee of the Governing Body of the ILO* (5th edn, ILO 2006)
- ILO, *Handbook of Procedures Relating to International Labour Conventions and Recommendations (Revised Edition)* (ILO 2012)
- ILO, *ILO Declaration on Social Justice for a Fair Globalization* (ILO 2008)
- ILO, *ILO Law on Freedom of Association - Standards and Procedures* (Alberto Odero and Horacio Guido eds, ILO 1995)
- ILO, Instrument for the Amendment of the Constitution of the International Labour Organisation (1946) XXIX ILO Official Bulletin 203
- ILO, *International Labour Conference, 97th Session, June 2008, Conference Committee on the Application of Standards, Extracts from the Record of Proceedings* (ILO 2008)
- ILO, Report of the UN Secretary-General on Oceans and Law of the Sea, 2014 (Submission by ILO) (2014) <http://www.un.org/Depts/los/general_assembly/contributions_2014/ILO.pdf> accessed 11 April 2017
- ILO, *Toolkit for Mainstreaming Employment and Decent Work - Country Level Application* (ILO 2008)
- ILO, *Tripartite Conference Convened by the International Labour Organization at the Request of the Council of Europe, Strasbourg 1-12 December 1958, Record of Proceedings* (ILO 1959)
- World Commission on the Social Dimension of Globalization, *A Fair Globalization - Creating Opportunities for All, Final Report* (ILO 2004)

6. International Monetary Fund

- IMF, 'Communiqué of the Interim Committee of the Board of Governors of the International Monetary Fund' *IMF Press Release No 95/51, 8 October 1995* <www.imf.org/external/np/sec/pr/1995/pr9551.htm> accessed 26 April 2020

7. MERCOSUR

- MERCOSUR, 'Declaración Sociolaboral del MERCOSUR' (10 December 1998)
- MERCOSUR, 'Declaración Sociolaboral del MERCOSUR 2015' (17 July 2015)

8. Organization for Economic Co-operation and Development

- OECD, *Guidelines for Multinational Enterprises on Employment and Industrial Relations* (OECD Publishing 2011)

9. Southern African Development Community

- SADC, 'Charter of the Fundamental Social Rights in SADC' (1 August 2003). Reprinted in SADC, *Charter of Fundamental Social Rights in SADC* (SADC 2003).

10. United Nations

10.1 Resolutions and Decisions of the General Assembly

- Dec 42/450 (17 December 1987) UN Doc A/DEC/42/450
- Res 1386 (XIV) (20 November 1959) UN Doc A/RES/14/1386
- Res 1510 (XV) (12 December 1960) UN Doc A/RES/1510(XV)
- Res 1514 (XV) (14 December 1960) UN Doc A/RES/1514(XV)
- Res 1597 (XV) (13 April 1961) UN Doc A/RES/1597(XV)
- Res 1598 (XV) (13 April 1961) UN Doc A/RES/1598(XV)
- Res 1654 (XVI) (27 November 1961) UN Doc A/RES/1654(XVI)
- Res 1779 (XVII) (7 December 1962) UN Doc A/RES/1779(XVII)
- Res 1780 (XVII) (7 December 1962) UN Doc A/RES/1780(XVII)
- Res 2054 (XX) (15 December 1965) UN Doc A/RES/2054(XX)
- Res 2105 (XX) (20 December 1965) UN Doc A/RES/2105(XX)
- Res 2107 (XX) (21 December 1965) UN Doc A/RES/2107(XX)
- Res 217 A (III) 'Universal Declaration of Human Rights' (10 December 1948) UN Doc A/RES/3/217 A (UDHR)

- Res 2184 (XXI) (12 December 1966) UN Doc A/RES/2184(XXI)
- Res 2202 (XXI) (16 December 1966) UN Doc A/RES/2202(XXI)
- Res 2307 (XXII) (13 December 1967) UN Doc A/RES/2307(XXII)
- Res 2426 (XXIII) (18 December 1968) UN Doc A/RES/2426(XXIII)
- Res 2625 (XXV) 'Declaration on Principles of International Law Concerning Friendly Relations and Co-Operation among States in Accordance with the Charter of the United Nations' (24 October 1970) UN Doc A/RES/2625(XXV) (Friendly Relations Declaration)
- Res 39/86 (13 December 1984) UN Doc A/RES/39/86
- Res 40/76 (11 December 1985) UN Doc A/RES/40/76
- Res 55/2 (8 September 2000) UN Doc A/RES/55/2
- Res 58/587 (23 December 2003) UN Doc A/RES/58/587
- Res 59/57 (2 December 2004) UN Doc A/RES/59/57
- Res 60/1 (16 September 2005) UN Doc A/RES/60/1
- Res 63/230 (19 December 2008) UN Doc A/RES/63/230
- Res 64/135 (18 December 2009) UN Doc A/RES/64/135
- Res 65/185 (21 December 2010) UN Doc A/RES/65/185
- Res 66/125 (19 December 2011) UN Doc A/RES/66/125
- Res 72/266 (24 December 2017) UN Doc A/RES/72/266
- Res 73/342 (16 September 2019) UN Doc A/RES/73/342

10.2 Resolutions of the Security Council

- Res 1132 (1997) (8 October 1997) UN Doc S/RES/1132(1997)
- Res 181 (1963) (7 August 1963) UN Doc S/RES/181(1963)
- Res 748 (1992) (31 March 1992) UN Doc S/RES/748(1992)

10.3 Resolutions, Declarations and Decisions of the Economic and Social Council

- Dec 2001/321 (24 October 2001) UN Doc E/DEC/2001/321
- Res 1994/24 (26 July 1994) UN Doc E/RES/1994/24
- Res 2007/2 (17 July 2007) UN Doc E/RES/2007/2
- Res 2008 (LX) (14 May 1976) UN Doc E/RES/2008(LX)
- Res 2008/18 (24 July 2008) UN Doc E/RES/2008/18
- Res 920 (XXIV) (3 August 1962) UN Doc E/RES/920(XXIV)
- Ministerial Declaration 'Creating an Environment at the National and International Levels Conducive to Generating Full and Productive Employment and Decent Work for All, and Its Impact on Sustainable Development' (5 July 2006) UN Doc E/2006/L.8

- Ministerial Declaration 'Promoting Productive Capacity, Employment and Decent Work to Eradicate Poverty in the Context of Inclusive, Sustainable and Equitable Economic Growth at All Levels for Achieving the Millennium Development Goals' (9 July 2012) UN Doc E/2012/L.10

10.4 Reports of the Secretary-General

- 'Responsibility of International Organizations, Comments and Observations Received from International Organizations, Report of the Secretary-General' (2004) UN Doc A/CN.4/545
- 'Note to the Assistant Secretary-General for Peacekeeping Operations Regarding the United Nations Mission in Kosovo and the Protection of Cultural Heritage' [2004] United Nations Juridical Yearbook 350
- 'Promoting Productive Capacity, Employment and Decent Work to Eradicate Poverty in the Context of Inclusive, Sustainable and Equitable Economic Growth at All Levels for Achieving the Millennium Development Goals, Report of the Secretary-General' (2012) UN Doc E/2012/63
- 'Repositioning the United Nations Development System to Deliver on the 2030 Agenda: Our Promise for Dignity, Prosperity and Peace on a Healthy Planet, Report of the Secretary-General' (2017) UN Doc A/72/684
- 'Responsibility of International Organizations - Comments and Information Received from Governments and International Organizations, Report of the Secretary-General' (2017) UN Doc A/72/80

10.5 International Law Commission

- ILC, 'Draft Articles on the Law of Treaties between States and International Organizations or between International Organizations, with Commentaries' [1982] YILC Vol II Part Two 17
- ILC, 'Draft Articles on the Responsibility of International Organizations [2011] UN Doc A/CN.4/L.778 (DARIO)
- ILC, 'Draft Articles on the Responsibility of International Organizations, with Commentaries' [2011] YILC Vol II Part Two 46
- ILC, 'Draft Declaration on Rights and Duties of States, with Commentaries' [1949] YILC 287
- ILC, 'Fourth Report on the Law of Treaties, by Sir Humphrey Waldock, Special Rapporteur' (1965) UN Doc A/CN.4/177
- ILC, 'Fragmentation of International Law: Difficulties Arising from the Diversification and Expansion of International Law, Report of the Study Group of the International Law Commission, Finalized by Martti Koskenniemi' (2006) A/CN.4/L.682

- ILC, 'Report of the International Law Commission to the General Assembly' (1966) 16 YILC, Vol II 169
- ILC, 'Report of the International Law Commission, Seventieth session' (2018) UN Doc A/73/10
- ILC, 'Report of the International Law Commission, Sixty-third session' (2011) UN Doc A/66/10
- ILC, 'Sixth Report by Special Rapporteur Paul Reuter on the Question of Treaties Concluded Between States and International Organizations or Between Two or More International Organizations' [1977] YILC Vol II Part One 119
- ILC, 'Tenth Report by Special Rapporteur Paul Reuter on the Question of Treaties Concluded between States and International Organizations or between Two or More International Organizations' [1977] YILC Vol II Part One 43

10.6 Rules of Procedure and Regulations

- Committee for Programme and Coordination, Terms of Reference, contained in UNGA Res 2008 (LX) (14 May 1976) UN Doc E/RES/2008(LX), Annex (CPC Terms of Reference)
- Regulations and Rules Governing Programme Planning, the Programme Aspects of the Budget, the Monitoring of Implementation and the Methods of Evaluation (2018) UN Doc ST/SGB/2018/3
- Rules of Procedure of the General Assembly (September 2016) UN Doc A/520/Rev.18 (UNGA Rules of Procedure)

10.7 UN Funds, Programmes etc.

- Social Protection Interagency Cooperation Board, '1st Social Protection Inter-Agency Cooperation Board Meeting' (2-3 July 2012) Report <https://www.ilo.org/wcmsp5/groups/public/%2D%2D-dgreports/%2D%2D-nylo/documents/genericdocument/wcms_226913.pdf> accessed 26 April 2020
- UN and World Bank, United Nations-World Bank Partnership Framework for Crisis-Affected Situations (signed 22 April 2017) <https://www.un.org/peacebuilding/sites/www.un.org.peacebuilding/files/documents/un-wb_partnership_framework_for_crisis-affected_situations_signed_april_22_2017.pdf> accessed 26 April 2020
- UN Department of Economic and Social Affairs and UNDP, 'Employment and Decent Work' (4 June 2013) TST Issues Brief <https://sustainabledevelopment.un.org/content/documents/18331106tstissuesemploywork.pdf> accessed 26 April 2020

- UN Joint Inspection Unit, 'Evaluation of Mainstreaming of Full and Productive Employment and Decent Work by the United Nations System Organizations – Full Report' (2015) UN Doc JIU/REP/2015/1
- UN Joint Inspection Unit, 'Relationship Agreements Between the UN and the Specialized Agencies: Review and Strengthening of Sections Pertaining to the Common System of Salaries, Allowances and Conditions of Service' (1993) UN Doc JIU/REP/93/3
- UNAIDS and ILO, Cooperation framework between the Joint United Nations Programme on HIV/AIDS (UNAIDS) and the International Labour Organization (ILO), reproduced in ILO, 'Instrument of the Adhesion of the International Labour Organization to the Memorandum of Understanding on a Joint and Cosponsored United Nations Programme on HIV/AIDS' (2001) LXXXIV ILO Official Bulletin Ser A No 3 153, Annex II
- UNAIDS, Memorandum of Understanding on a Joint and Cosponsored United Nations Programme on HIV/AIDS (1996), reproduced in ILO, 'Instrument of the Adhesion of the International Labour Organization to the Memorandum of Understanding on a Joint and Cosponsored United Nations Programme on HIV/AIDS' (2001) LXXXIV ILO Official Bulletin Ser A No 3 153, Annex I (UNAIDS-MoU)
- UNDP, *Human Development Report 2015 - Work for Human Development* (UNDP 2015)

10.8 UN Conference Reports and Records

- UN, 'Report of the United Nations Conference on Environment and Development' (3-14 June 1992) UN Doc A/CONF.151/26 (Vol. I)
- UN, 'Report of the United Nations Conference on the Human Environment' (5-16 June 1972) UN Doc A/CONF.48/18/Rev.1
- UN, 'Report of the World Summit for Social Development' (6-12 March 1995) UN Doc A/CONF.166/9
- UN, Summary Records of the Plenary Meetings and of the Meetings of the Committee of the Whole, United Nations Conference on the Law of Treaties (1st session, Vienna, 26 March-24 May 1968) Official Records (1969) UN Doc A/CONF.39/11

10.9 Other Documents and Publications

- CEB, 'The Global Financial Crisis and Its Impact on the Work of the UN System' (1 April 2009) <http://www.unsystem.org/content/ceb-issue-paper-global-financial-crisis-and-its-impact-work-un-system> accessed 26 April 2020

- Commission on Global Governance, *Our Global Neighbourhood: Report of the Commission on Global Governance* (Oxford University Press 1995)
- Independent Team of Advisors to the ECOSOC Bureau, ‘The Future We Want, the UN System We Need - Papers by the Independent Team of Advisors to the ECOSOC Bureau’ (2016) <https://www.un.org/ecosoc/sites/www.un.org.ecosoc/files/files/en/qcpr/ecosoc-dialogue-publication.pdf> accessed 26 April 2020
- UN, ‘Article 63’ in Repertory of Practice of United Nations Organs Vol IV (Supplement No 10, 2000–2009)
- UN, *Independent Evaluation of “Delivering as One” - Main Report* (UN 2012)
- UNGA, Development and Strengthening of Good-Neighbourliness between States, Report of the Sub-Committee on Good-Neighbourliness’ (1988) UN Doc A/C.6/43/L.11

11. United Nations Educational, Scientific and Cultural Organization

- UNESCO, *Strategy for Technical and Vocational Education and Training (TVET) (2016-2021)* (UNESCO 2016)

12. World Bank Group

12.1 Resolutions by the Board of Governors

- IBRD Board of Governors Res No 24 (16 September 1947) <http://documents.worldbank.org/curated/en/532521468149674407/International-Bank-for-Reconstruction-and-Development-IBRD-Board-of-Governors-resolution-no-24-agreement-between-the-United-Nations-and-the-Bank> accessed 26 April 2020

12.2 World Development Reports

- *World Development Report 1995: Workers in an Integrating World* (World Bank 1995)
- *World Development Report 2013: Jobs* (World Bank 2012)

- *World Development Report 2019: The Changing Nature of Work* (World Bank 2019)

12.3 Doing Business Reports

- *Doing Business 2005 - Removing Obstacles to Growth* (World Bank 2004)
- *Doing Business 2006 - Creating Jobs* (World Bank 2005)
- *Doing Business 2007 - How to Reform* (World Bank 2006)
- *Doing Business 2008* (World Bank 2007)
- *Doing Business 2009* (World Bank 2008)
- *Doing Business 2010 - Reforming Through Difficult Times* (World Bank 2009)
- *Doing Business 2012 - Doing Business in a More Transparent World* (World Bank 2011)
- *Doing Business 2014 - Understanding Regulations for Small and Medium-Size Enterprises* (World Bank 2013)
- *Doing Business 2018 - Reforming to Create Jobs* (World Bank 2017)
- *Doing Business 2020* (World Bank 2019)
- *Doing Business in 2004 - Understanding Regulation* (World Bank 2003)

12.4 Other Reports

- '2015 Development Policy Financing Retrospective: Results and Sustainability' (2015) <http://pubdocs.worldbank.org/en/420441457100264616/DevelopmentPolicyRetrospective2015.pdf> accessed 26 April 2020
- 'Colombia Labor Market Adjustment, Reform and Productivity: What Are the Factors That Matter? (In Two Volumes), Volume I: Issues and Policy Brief November 2005' (2005) Report No 32068-CO
- 'Country Partnership Framework for the Republic of Belarus for the Period FY 18-22' (2018) Report No 123321-BY
- 'Doing Business Employing Workers Consultative Group Final Report' (25 April 2011) <https://www.doingbusiness.org/content/dam/doingBusiness/media/Miscellaneous/Final-EWI-CG-report-2011.pdf> accessed 26 April 2020
- 'Doing Business: An Independent Evaluation - Taking the Measure of the World Bank-IFC Doing Business Indicators' (2008) Report No 44995
- 'Independent Panel Review of the Doing Business Report' (2013) http://pubdocs.worldbank.org/en/237121516384849082/doing-business-review-panel-report-June-2013.pdf accessed 26 April 2020 24
- 'Nepal - First Poverty Reduction Support Credit Project' (Implementation Completion Report, 28 March 2006) Rep No 35462 (IDA-38300)

12.5 By-laws, Terms of Reference etc.

- By-laws of the International Bank for Reconstruction and Development, as amended by IBRD Board of Governors Res No 360 (26 September 1980) <https://www.worldbank.org/en/about/leadership/directors/by-laws> accessed 26 April 2020
- World Bank, 'Engaging with Citizens for Improved Development Results Strategic Framework for Mainstreaming Citizen Engagement in World Bank Group Operations, Expert Advisory Council, Terms of Reference' (2014) <https://consultations.worldbank.org/Data/hub/files/consultation-template/engaging-citizens-improved-resultsopenconsultationtemplate/materials/ce_advisory_group_tor_final_04072014.pdf> accessed 26 April 2020
- Terms of Appointment of David R Malpass as President of the International Bank for Reconstruction and Development (2019) http://documents.worldbank.org/curated/en/665771554752513452/Terms-of-Appointment-of-David-R-Malpass-as-President-of-the-International-Bank-for-Reconstruction-and-Development accessed 26 April 2020

12.6 Press Releases

- IFC, 'World Bank and USAID Honor Reformers of Business Environment: Zurab Nogaideli, Prime Minister of Georgia, Recognized as Top Reformer of the Year' *IFC Press Release, 13 April 2007* <https://ifcextapps.ifc.org/ifcext/pressroom/ifcpressroom.nsf/1f70cd9a07d692d685256ee1001cdd37/57dc18e02affaecb852572bc004fb5f7> accessed 26 April 2020
- World Bank, 'Doing Business 2005: Poor Nations Struggle to Reduce Red Tape for Business, Miss Large Growth Opportunities' *World Bank News Release No 2005/69/S* (Washington, DC, 8 September 2005)
- World Bank, 'Economies Perform Better in Coordinated Labor Markets' *World Bank Press Release No. 2003/211/S* <http://web.worldbank.org/WBSITE/EXTERNAL/NEWS/0,,contentMDK:20091655~menuPK:34463~pagePK:34370~piPK:34424~theSitePK:4607,00.html> accessed 26 April 2020

12.7 Other Documents and Publications

- World Bank, 'Guidance Note for World Bank Group Staff on the Use of the Doing Business Employing Workers Indicator for Policy Advice' (2009)

- World Bank, List of Observers - 2018 Annual Meetings (2018) <http://www.worldbank.org/content/dam/meetings/external/annualmeeting/2018-AMs-Observers-Final.pdf> accessed 26 April 2020

13. World Health Organization

- WHO (World Health Assembly), 'Workers' Health: Global Plan of Action' (2007) WHA60.26

14. World Trade Organization

- WTO Ministerial Conference, Singapore Ministerial Declaration (13 December 1996) WT/MIN(96)/DEC

15. World Tourism Organization

- UNWTO, *World Tourism Report 2017* (UNWTO 2018)

16. Domestic Legislation and Documents

- Einführungsgesetz zum Bürgerlichen Gesetzbuche (Germany), BGBl I 1994, 2494
- Grundgesetz für die Bundesrepublik Deutschland (Germany), BGBl 1949, 1
- United States Department of State, 'Proceedings and Documents of the United Nations Monetary and Financial Conference, Vol. I' (United States Government Printing Office 1948)
- United States House of Representatives, Amendment in the Nature of a Substitute to H.R. 6306 (2008)

Table of Cases and Supervisory Practice

ILO Committee of Experts on the Application of Conventions and Recommendations

- Direct Request (CEACR) Freedom of Association and Protection of the Right to Organise Convention, 1948 (No. 87) - Georgia (Ratification: 1999) https://www.ilo.org/dyn/normlex/en/f?p=1000:13100:0::NO:13100:P13100_COMMENT_ID:2277861 accessed 26 April 2020
- Observation (CEACR) Abolition of Forced Labour Convention, 1957 (No. 105) - Uzbekistan (Ratification: 1997) Report of the Committee of Experts on the Application of Conventions and Recommendations (2013) ILC.105/III(1A) 216
- Observation (CEACR) Freedom of Association and Protection of the Right to Organise Convention, 1948 (No. 87) - United Kingdom (Ratification: 1949) Report of the Committee of Experts on the Application of Conventions and Recommendations (2008) ILC.97/III(1A) 187
- Observation (CEACR) Freedom of Association and Protection of the Right to Organise Convention, 1948 (No. 87) - United Kingdom (Ratification: 1949) Report of the Committee of Experts on the Application of Conventions and Recommendations (2010) ILC.99/III(1A) 209
- Observation (CEACR) Freedom of Association and Protection of the Right to Organise Convention, 1948 (No. 87) - United Kingdom (Ratification: 1949) Report of the Committee of Experts on the Application of Conventions and Recommendations (2011) ILC.100/III(1A) 186
- Observation (CEACR) Freedom of Association and Protection of the Right to Organise Convention, 1948 (No. 87) - Sweden (Ratification: 1949) Report of the Committee of Experts on the Application of Conventions and Recommendations (2013) ILC.102/III(1A) 176

H. Gött, *The Law of Interactions Between International Organizations*, Beiträge zum ausländischen öffentlichen Recht und Völkerrecht 299, https://doi.org/10.1007/978-3-662-62389-3

ILO Committee on Freedom of Association

European Court of Human Rights and European Commission of Human Rights

- Bosphorus Hava Yollari Turizm ve Ticaret Anonim Sirketi v. Ireland ECHR 2005–VI 107
- Case Relating to Certain Aspects of the Law on the Use of Languages in Education in Belgium (1967) Series A No 5
- Chapman v. United Kingdom ECHR 2001–I 41
- Christine Goodwin v. United Kingdom ECHR 2002–VI 1
- CN and V v. France App No 67724/09 (ECtHR, 11 October 2012)
- Danilenkov and Others v. Russian Federation ECHR 2009–III 365
- Demir and Baykara v. Turkey ECHR 2008–V 395
- Emonet and Others v. Switzerland App No 39051/03 (ECtHR, 13 December 2007)
- Enerji Yapi-Yol Sen v. Turkey App No 68959/01 (ECtHR, 21 April 2009)
- Federation of Offshore Workers Trade Unions and Others v. Norway ECHR 2002–VI 301
- Golder v. United Kingdom (1975) Series A No 18
- Graziani-Weiss v. Austria App No 31950/06 (ECtHR, 18 October 2011)
- Gustafsson v. Sweden (Revision) ECHR 1998–V 483
- Hrvatski Liječnički Sindikat v. Croatia App No 36701/09 (ECtHR, 27 November 2014)
- Ireland v. United Kingdom (1978) Series A No 25
- James and Webster v. United Kingdom (1979) Series B No 39 (Commission Report)
- Karlheinz Schmidt v. Germany (1994) Series A 291-B
- Kaya and Seyhan v. Turkey App No 30946/04 (ECtHR, 15 September 2009)
- Kjeldsen, Busk Madsen and Pedersen v. Denmark (1976) Series A No 23
- Lithgow and Others v. United Kingdom (1986) Series A No 23
- Loizidou v. Turkey (Preliminary Objections) (1995) Series A No 310
- Loizidou v. Turkey ECHR 1996–VI 2220
- Mamatkulov and Askarov v. Turkey ECHR 2005–I 293
- Manole and "Romanian Farmers Direct" v. Romania App No 46551/06 (ECtHR, 16 June 2015)
- Marckx v. Belgium (1979) Series A No 31
- Micallef v. Malta ECHR 2009–V 289
- MSS v. Belgium and Greece ECHR 2011–I 255
- National Union of Belgian Police v. Belgium (1975) Series A No 19
- National Union of Rail, Maritime and Transport Workers v. United Kingdom ECHR 2014–II 1
- OAO Neftyanaya Kompaniya Yukos v. Russian Federation App No 14902/04 (ECtHR, 20 September 2011)
- Özcan v. Turkey App No 22943/04 (ECtHR, 15 September 2009)
- Pini and Others v. Romania ECHR 2004–V 297
- POA and Others v. United Kingdom App No 59253/11 (ECtHR 21 May 2013)
- Saadi v. United Kingdom ECHR 2008–I 31
- Sabeh El Leil v. France App No 34869/05 (ECtHR, 29 June 2011)
- Schmidt and Dahlström v. Sweden (1976) Series A No 21

- Scoppola v. Italy (No. 2) App No 10249/03 (ECtHR, 17 September 2009)
- Sergey Zolotukhin v. Russian Federation ECHR 2009–I 291
- Sibson v. United Kingdom (1993) Series A No 258-A
- Sigurður A Sigurjónsson v. Iceland (1993) Series A No 264
- Siliadin v. France ECHR 2005–VII 333
- Sindicatul "Păstorul Cel Bun" v. Romania ECHR 2013–V 41
- Soering v. United Kingdom (1989) Series A No 161
- Sørensen and Rasmussen v. Denmark ECHR 2016–I 24
- Stummer v. Austria ECHR 2011–V 1
- Svenska Lokmannaförbundet v. Sweden (1974) Series B No 18 (Commission Report)
- Swedish Engine Drivers' Union v. Sweden (1976) Series A No 20
- Tănase v. Moldova ECHR 2010–III 361
- Trade Union of the Police in the Slovak Republic and Others v. Slovakia App No 11828/08 (ECtHR, 25 September 2012)
- Tyrer v. the United Kingdom (1978) Series A No 26
- Unison v. United Kingdom ECHR 2002–I 491
- van der Mussele v. Belgium (1983) Series A No 70
- Veniamin Tymoshenko and Others v. Ukraine App No 48408/12 (ECtHR, 2 October 2014)
- Vörður Ólafsson v. Iceland ECHR 2010–III 281
- Waite and Kennedy v. Germany ECHR 1999–I 393
- Wilson, National Union of Journalists and Others v. United Kingdom ECHR 2002–V 49
- Winterwerp v. Netherlands (1979) Series A No 47
- Young, James and Webster v. United Kingdom (1981) Series A No 55

European Committee of Social Rights (incl. Committee of Independent Experts)

Conclusions

- ECSR, Conclusions 2006, Ireland - Article 5
- ECSR, Conclusions 2006, Sweden - Article 5
- ECSR, Conclusions 2014, Lithuania, Article 4-1
- ECSR, Conclusions 2014, Norway, Article 6-4
- ECSR, Conclusions 2014, Russian Federation, Article 6-4
- ECSR, Conclusions 2014, Serbia, Article 5
- ECSR, Conclusions 2014, Serbia, Article 6-2
- ECSR, Conclusions 2014, Serbia, Article 6-4
- ECSR, Conclusions 2014, Ukraine, Article 6-4

- ECSR, Conclusions 2016, Ukraine, Article 24
- ECSR, Conclusions I (1969), Norway, Article 12-2
- ECSR, Conclusions I (1969), Statement of Interpretation, Article 5
- ECSR, Conclusions I (1969), United Kingdom, Article 5
- ECSR, Conclusions IX-1 (1987-90), Norway, Article 6-4
- ECSR, Conclusions IX-2 (1985-86), Italy, Article 1-2
- ECSR, Conclusions VII (1981), United Kingdom, Article 5
- ECSR, Conclusions VIII (1984) "Dissenting Opinion" by Prof. Zanetti Concerning the Application of Article 5 by the United Kingdom
- ECSR, Conclusions X-2 (1987-90), Ireland, Article 4-1
- ECSR, Conclusions XII-1 (1991-92), Norway, Article 6-4
- ECSR, Conclusions XIII-1 (1993-97), Norway, Article 6-4
- ECSR, Conclusions XIII-3, France, Article 5
- ECSR, Conclusions XIII-3 (1993-97), Norway, Article 6-4
- ECSR, Conclusions XIV-1, Iceland, Article 5
- ECSR, Conclusions XIV-1 (1998), Denmark, Article 5
- ECSR, Conclusions XIV-1 (1998), Norway, Article 6-4
- ECSR, Conclusions XIV-1 (1998), United Kingdom, Article 6-4
- ECSR, Conclusions XIV-1, Volume 2 (1998-2000), Norway, Article 6-4

Collective Complaint Procedures

- European Trade Union Confederation (ETUC) Centrale Générale Des Syndicats Libéraux de Belgique (CGSLB) and Others v. Belgium Collective Complaint No 59/2009 (ECSR, 13 September 2011)
- Finnish Society of Social Rights v. Finland Collective Complaint No 107/2014 (ECSR, 6 September 2016)
- General Federation of Employees of the National Electric Power Corporation (GENOP-DEI) / Confederation of Greek Civil Servants Trade Unions (ADEDY) v. Greece Collective Complaint No 65/2011 (ECSR, 23 May 2012)
- General Federation of Employees of the National Electric Power Corporation (GENOP-DEI) / Confederation of Greek Civil Servants Trade Unions (ADEDY) v. Greece Collective Complaint No. 66/2011 (ECSR, 23 May 2012)
- Pensioners Union of the Athens-Piraeus Electric Railways (ISAP) v. Greece, Collective Complaint No. 78/2012 (ECSR, 7 December 2012)
- Swedish Trade Union Confederation (LO) and Swedish Confederation of Professional Employees (TCO) v. Sweden Collective Complaint No 85/2012 (ECSR, 3 July 2013)

Inter-American Court of Human Rights

- Case of the Ituango Massacres v Colombia (2006) IACtHR Series C No 148

African Commission of Human Rights

- Luke Munyandu Tembani and Benjamin John Freeth v. Angola and Thirteen Others, Communication 409/12 (African Commission on Human and Peoples' Rights, 30 April 2014)

Committee on Economic, Social and Cultural Rights

- 'General Comment No 18: The Right to Work (Art. 6 of the Covenant)' (6 February 2006) E/C.12/GC/18

UN Committee on Migrant Workers

- 'General Comment No 1 on Migrant Domestic Workers' (23 February 2011) CMW/C/GC/1
- 'General Comment No 2 on the Rights of Migrant Workers in an Irregular Situation and Members of Their Families' (28 August 2013) CMW/C/GC/2

UN Committee on the Elimination of Discrimination Against Women

- 'General Recommendation No. 13, Equal Remuneration for Work of Equal Value' (Eighth Session) [1989] UN Doc. A/44/38

UN Committee on the Rights of the Child

- 'General Comment No. 16 on State Obligations Regarding the Impact of the Business Sector on Childrens' Rights' (17 April 2013) CRC/C/GC/16

UN Human Rights Committee

- 'Concluding Observations on Uzbekistan' (114th Session, 29 June–24 July 2015) UN Doc CCPR/C/UZB/CO/4

International Criminal Tribunal for Rwanda

- Prosecutor v. Rwamakuba (Decision on Appropriate Remedy) ICTR-98-44C-T (25 October 2006)

International Criminal Tribunal for the Former Yugoslavia

- Prosecutor v. Simić et al (Decision on Motion for Judicial Assistance) ICTY-IT-95-9-PT (18 October 2000)
- Prosecutor v Tadić (Appeals Chamber) ICTY-IT-94-1-A (15 July 1999)

Special Court for Sierra Leone

- Prosecutor v. Sam Hinga Norman (Decision on Preliminary Motion Based on Lack of Jurisdiction) SCSL-2004-14-AR72(E) (31 May 2004)

International Court of Justice

- Accordance with International Law of the Unilateral Declaration of Independence in Respect of Kosovo (Advisory Opinion) [2010] ICJ Reports 403
- Aegean Sea Continental Shelf (Greece v. Turkey) [1978] ICJ Reports 3
- Application for Review of Judgment No. 273 of the United Nations Administrative Tribunal (Advisory Opinion) [1982] ICJ Reports 325
- Arrest Warrant of 11 March 2000 (Democratic Republic of the Congo v. Belgium), Separate Opinion of President Guillaume [2002] ICJ Reports 35
- Border and Transborder Armed Actions (Nicaragua v. Honduras) (Jurisdiction and Admissibility) [1988] ICJ Reports 69
- Case Concerning Certain Questions of Mutual Assistance in Criminal Matters (Djibouti v. France) [2008] ICJ Reports 177
- Case Concerning the Right of Passage over Indian Territory (Portugal v. India) (Preliminary Objections) [1957] ICJ Reports 125

- Certain Activities Carried Out by Nicaragua in the Border Area (Costa Rica v. Nicaragua) and Construction of a Road in Costa Rica along the San Juan River (Nicaragua v. Costa Rica) [2015] ICJ Reports 665
- Certain Expenses of the United Nations (Article 17, Paragraph 2 of the Charter) (Advisory Opinion) [1962] ICJ Reports 151
- Competence of the General Assembly for the Admission of a State to the United Nations (Dissenting Opinion by Judge Álvarez) [1950] ICJ Reports 12
- Conditions of Admission of a State to Membership in the United Nations (Article 4 of the Charter) (Advisory Opinion) [1948] ICJ Reports 57
- Corfu Channel Case (United Kingdom v. Albania) (Merits) [1949] ICJ Reports 4
- Delimitation of the Maritime Boundary in the Gulf of Maine Area (Canada v. United States) (Constitution of Chamber, Order) [1982] ICJ Reports 3
- Effect of Awards of Compensation Made by the United Nations Administrative Tribunal (Advisory Opinion) [1954] ICJ Reports 47
- Haya de La Torre Case (Colombia v. Peru) [1951] ICJ Reports 71
- International Status of South-West Africa (Separate Opinion by Sir Arnold McNair) [1950] ICJ Reports 146
- Interpretation of the Agreement of 25 March 1951 between the WHO and Egypt (Advisory Opinion) [1980] ICJ Reports 73
- Land and Maritime Boundary between Cameroon and Nigeria (Cameroon v Nigeria) (Preliminary Objections) [1998] ICJ Reports 275
- Legality of the Threat or Use of Nuclear Weapons (Advisory Opinion) [1996] ICJ Reports 226
- Legality of the Threat or Use of Nuclear Weapons (Dissenting Opinion of Vice-President Schwebel) [1996] ICJ Reports 311
- Legality of the Use by a State of Nuclear Weapons in Armed Conflict (Request of the World Health Organization) (Advisory Opinion) [1996] ICJ Reports 66
- Maritime Delimitation and Territorial Questions between Qatar and Bahrain (Qatar v. Bahrain) (Jurisdiction and Admissibility) [1994] ICJ Reports 112
- Military and Paramilitary Activities in and against Nicaragua (Nicaragua v. United States of America) (Jurisdiction and Admissibility) [1984] ICJ Reports 392
- Military and Paramilitary Activities in and against Nicaragua (Nicaragua v. United States of America) (Merits) [1986] ICJ Reports 14
- North Sea Continental Shelf Cases (Federal Republic of Germany v. Denmark/ Federal Republic of Germany v. Netherlands) [1969] ICJ Reports 3
- Nuclear Tests (Australia v. France) [1974] ICJ Reports 253
- Pulp Mills on the River Uruguay (Argentina v. Uruguay) (Merits) [2010] ICJ Reports 14
- Reparation for Injuries Suffered in the Service of the United Nations (Advisory Opinion) [1949] ICJ Reports 174
- Reparation for Injuries Suffered in the Service of the United Nations, Dissenting Opinion by Judge Hackworth [1949] ICJ Reports 196

- Reservations to the Convention on the Prevention and Punishment of the Crime of Genocide (Written Statement of the International Labour Organization) [1951] ICJ Pleadings 216
- Territorial Dispute (Libyan Arab Jamahiriya/Chad) [1994] ICJ Reports 6

Permanent Court of International Justice

- Competence of the International Labour Organization to Regulate, Incidentally, the Personal Work of the Employer (Advisory Opinion) PCIJ Rep Series B No 13
- Competence of the ILO to Examine Proposal for the Organization and Development of the Methods of Agricultural Production (Advisory Opinion) PCIJ Rep Series B No 3
- The Case of the S.S. Lotus (France v. Turkey) PCIJ Rep Series A No 10
- Designation of the Workers Delegate for the Netherlands at the Third Session of the International Labour Conference (Advisory Opinion) PCIJ Rep Series B No 1
- Competence of the ILO in Regard to International Regulation of the Conditions of the Labour of Persons Employed in Agriculture (Advisory Opinion) PCIJ Rep Series B No 2
- Interpretation of the Greco-Turkish Agreement of 1 December 1926 (Final Protocol, Article IV) (Advisory Opinion) PCIJ Rep Series B No 16
- Nationality Decrees in Tunis and Morocco (Advisory Opinion) PCIJ Rep Series B No 4
- The Mavrommatis Palestine Concessions (Greece v. United Kingdom) PCIJ Rep Series A No 2
- Legal Status of Eastern Greenland (Denmark v. Norway) PCIJ Rep Series A/B No 53
- Delimitation of the Polish-Czechoslovakian Frontier (Question of Jaworzina) (Advisory Opinion) PCIJ Rep Series B No 8
- Jurisdiction of the European Commission of the Danube (Advisory Opinion) PCIJ Rep Series B No 14

International Tribunal for the Law of the Sea

- MOX Plant Case (Ireland v. United Kingdom) (Provisional Measures, Order of 3 December 2001) ITLOS Reports 2001, 95

World Trade Organization

- Argentina—Measures Affecting Imports of Footwear, Textiles, Apparel and Other Items, Report of the Appellate Body (27 March 1998) WT/DS56/AB/R
- European Communities—Approval and Marketing of Biotech Products, Panel Report (29 September 2006) WT/DS291-3/R
- European Communities and Certain Member States—Measures Affecting Trade in Large Civil Aircraft, Report of the Appellate Body (18 May 2011) WT/DS316/AB/R

Decisions in Inter-State Arbitrations

- Arbitration Regarding the Iron Rhine ("Ijzeren Rijn") Railway (Belgium v. Netherlands) (Decision of 24 May 2005) (2005) XXVII RIAA 35
- Case concerning Claims arising out of Decisions of the Mixed Graeco-German Arbitral Tribunal set up under Article 304 in Part X of the Treaty of Versailles (Greece v. Federal Republic of Germany) (Award of 26 January 1972) (1974) XIX RIAA 27
- Case Concerning Filleting within the Gulf of St. Lawrence (Canada v. France) (Decision of 17 July 1986) (1990) XIX RIAA 225
- Island of Palmas (Netherlands v. United States) (1928) 2 RIAA 829
- Lac Lanoux Arbitration (France v. Spain) (1957) XII RIAA 281
- Trail Smelter Arbitration (United States v. Canada) (Award of 11 March 1941) (1941) III RIAA 1905

Court of Justice of the European Union (incl. Predecessors)

- Case 11/70 Internationale Handelsgesellschaft mbH v. Einfuhr- und Vorratsstelle für Getreide und Futtermittel (ECLI:EU:C:1970:114) [1970] ECR 01125
- Case 230/81 Luxembourg v. European Parliament (ECLI:EU:C:1983:32) [1983] ECR 00255
- Case 29/69 Erich Stauder v. City of Ulm (ECLI:EU:C:1969:57) [1969] ECR 00419
- Case C-112/00, Eugen Schmidberger, Internationale Transporte und Planzüge v. Austria (ECLI:EU:C:2003:333) [2003] ECR I-05659
- Case 4/73 J Nold, Kohlen- und Baustoffgroßhandlung v. Commission (ECLI:EU:C:1974:51) [1974] ECR 00491
- Case C-246/07 Commission v. Sweden (ECLI:EU:C:2010:203) [2010] ECR I-03317
- Case C-25/94 Commission v. Council (ECLI:EU:C:1996:114) [1996] ECR I-01469

- Case C-301/08 Irène Bogiatzi, Married Name Ventouras v Deutscher Luftpool and Others (ECLI:EU:C:2009:649) [2009] ECR I-10185
- Case C-308/06 International Association of Independent Tanker Owners (Intertanko) et Al. v. Secretary of State for Transport (ECLI:EU:C:2008:312) [2008] ECR I-04057
- Case C-341/05 Laval Un Partneri Ltd v. Svenska Byggnadsarbetareförbundet, Svenska Byggnadsarbetareförbundets Avdelning 1, Byggettan and Svenska Elektrikerförbundet (ECLI:EU:C:2007:809) [2007] ECR I-11767
- Case C-438/05 International Transport Workers Federation, Finnish Seamens Union v. Viking Line ABP and OÜ Viking Line Eesti (ECLI:EU:C:2007:772) [2007] ECR I-10779
- Case C-45/07 Commission v. Greece (ECLI:EU:C:2009:81) [2009] ECR I-00701
- Case C-399/12 Federal Republic of Germany v. Council (ECLI:EU: C:2014:2258)
- Case T-315/01 Yassin Abdullah Kadi v. Council and Commission (ECLI:EU: T:2005:332) [2005] ECR II-03649
- Case C-188/07 Commune de Mesquer v. Total France SA and Total International Ltd (ECLI:EU:C:2011:864) [2008] ECR I-04501
- Joined Cases 21-24/72 International Fruit Company NV and Others v. Produktschap Voor Groenten En Fruit (ECLI:EU:C:1972:115) [1972] ECR 01219
- Joined Cases 281, 283, 284, 285 and 287/85, Federal Republic of Germany and Others v. Commission (ECLI:EU:C:1987:351) [1987] ECR 03203
- Opinion 1/94 Competence of the Community to Conclude International Agreements concerning Services and the Protection of Intellectual Property (ECLI:EU: C:1994:384) [1994] ECR I-05267
- Opinion 2/91 Convention No 170 of the International Labour Organization concerning Safety in the Use of Chemicals at Work (ECLI:EU:C:1993:106) [1993] ECR I-01061
- Ruling 1/78 Draft Convention of the International Atomic Energy Agency on the Physical Protection of Nuclear Materials, Facilities and Transports (ECLI:EU: C:1978:202) [1978] ECR 02151
- Case 8/55 Fédération Charbonnière de Belgique (ECLI:EU:C:1956:11) [1956] ECR 00292
- Joined Cases 7/56, 3/57 to 7/57 Dineke Algera, Giacomo Cicconardi, Simone Couturaud, Ignazio Genuardi, Félicie Steichen v. Common Assembly of the European Coal and Steel Community (ECLI:EU:C:1957:7) [1957] ECR 00039

Decisions in International Investment Disputes

- Amco Asia Co v. Republic of Indonesia ICSID Case No. ARB/81/1
- Asian Agricultural Products, LTD (AAPL) v. Sri Lanka ICSID Case No ARB/87/3

- Industria Nacional de Alimentos, S.A. and Indalsa Perú, S.A. v. Peru (Decision on Annulment) ICSID Case No ARB/03/4

Administrative Tribunal of the International Labour Organization

- Judgment No 269 Gracia de Muniz v. FAO (ILO Administrative Tribunal, 36th session, 12 April 1976) [1976] United Nations Juridical Yearbook 142
- Judgment No 17 Duberg v. UNESCO (ILO Administrative Tribunal, 5th session, 26 April 1955)

Domestic Courts

- Bundesverfassungsgericht, ESM Treaty (ECLI:DE:BVerfG:2012:rs20120912.2bvr139012) BVerfGE 135, 317
- Bundesverfassungsgericht, European Arrest Warrant II (ECLI:DE:BVerfG:2015:rs20151215.2bvr273514) BVerfGE 140, 317
- Bundesverfassungsgericht, Outright Monetary Transactions (Request for Preliminary Ruling) (ECLI:DE:BVerfG:2014:rs20140114.2bvr272813) BVerfGE 134, 366
- Bundesverfassungsgericht, Solange II (ECLI:DE:BVerfG:1986:rs19861022:2BvR19783) BVerfGE 73, 339
- Bundesverfassungsgericht, Storage of Chemical Weapons (ECLI:DE:BVerfG:1987:rs19871029:2BvR62483) BVerfGE 77, 170
- Bundesverfassungsgericht, Treaty of Lisbon (ECLI:DE:BVerfG:2009:es20090630.2bve000208) BVerfGE 123, 267
- Supreme Court of Canada, Saskatchewan Federation of Labour v. Saskatchewan [2015] 1 SCR 245

Table of Websites

- CoE, 'Chart of Signatures and Ratifications of Treaty 158 - Additional Protocol to the European Social Charter Providing for a System of Collective Complaints' (*CoE Website*) <https://www.coe.int/en/web/conventions/full-list/-/conventions/treaty/158/signatures?p_auth=fCQiWTQl> accessed 26 April 2020
- CoE, 'Chart of Signatures and Ratifications of Treaty 163 - European Social Charter (Revised)' (*CoE Website*) <https://www.coe.int/en/web/conventions/full-list/-/conventions/treaty/163/signatures> accessed 26 April 2020
- CoE, 'Directorate of External Relations (DER)' (*CoE Website*) <https://rm.coe.int/16805970bf> accessed 26 April 2020
- CoE, 'Lists of Agreements Concluded by the Council of Europe with Other International Intergovernmental Organisations or Public International Institutions' (*CoE Website*) <https://www.coe.int/en/web/conventions/bi-or-multilateral-agreements> accessed 26 April 2020
- CoE, 'The Council of Europe's Relations with the United Nations' (*CoE Website*) <https://www.coe.int/en/web/der/united-nations> accessed 26 April 2020
- Food and Agriculture Organization of the United Nations, 'Child Labour in Agriculture' (*FAO Website*) <http://www.fao.org/childlabouragriculture/en/> accessed 26 April 2020
- ILO, 'ILO Cooperation Agreements with Other International Organizations' (*ILO Website*) <https://www.ilo.org/global/about-the-ilo/how-the-ilo-works/departments-and-offices/jur/legal-instruments/WCMS_442247/lang%2D%2Den/index.htm> accessed 26 April 2020
- ILO, 'International Labour Conference, Address by Mr. James D. Wolfensohn, President of the World Bank, 13 June 1997' (*ILO Website*) <https://www.ilo.org/public/english/standards/relm/ilc/ilc85/wolf.htm> accessed 26 April 2020
- ILO, 'International Labour Office Expresses Concern about World Bank Report on Future of Work' (*ILO Website, 12 October 2018*) <https://www.ilo.org/

H. Gött, *The Law of Interactions Between International Organizations*, Beiträge zum ausländischen öffentlichen Recht und Völkerrecht 299, https://doi.org/10.1007/978-3-662-62389-3

global/about-the-ilo/newsroom/statements-and-speeches/WCMS_646884/lang%2D%2Den/index.htm> accessed 26 April 2020

- ILO, 'International Labour Office' <https://www.ilo.org/global/about-the-ilo/who-we-are/international-labour-office/lang%2D%2Den/index.htm> accessed 26 April 2020
- ILO, 'Jobs and Livelihoods at the Heart of the Post-2015 Development Agenda - ILO Concept Note on the Post-2015 Development Agenda' (2013) <https://www.ilo.org/global/about-the-ilo/newsroom/statements-and-speeches/WCMS_193483/lang%2D%2Den/index.htm> accessed 26 April 2020
- ILO, 'Joint ILO/UNESCO Committee of Experts on the Application of the Recommendations Concerning Teaching Personnel (CEART)' (*ILO Website*) <https://www.ilo.org/global/industries-and-sectors/education/WCMS_364850/lang%2D%2Den/index.htm> accessed 26 April 2020
- ILO, 'Joint IMO/ILO Activities on Seafarers' (*ILO Website*) <https://www.ilo.org/global/standards/maritime-labour-convention/text/WCMS_162318/lang%2D%2Den/index.htm> accessed 26 April 2020
- ILO, 'Keynote Address by Greg Vines, ILO Deputy Director-General, at the Fourth Session of the Open Working Group on Sustainable Development Goals' (17 June 2013) https://www.ilo.org/newyork/speeches-and-statements/WCMS_216335/lang%2D%2Den/index.htm accessed 26 April 2020
- ILO, 'Member States' (*ILO Website*) https://www.ilo.org/global/about-the-ilo/how-the-ilo-works/member-states/lang%2D%2Den/index.htm accessed 26 April 2020
- ILO, 'Millennium Development Goals (MDGs) Employment Indicators' (*ILO Website*) <https://www.ilo.org/empelm/what/WCMS_114244/lang%2D%2Den/index.htm added in 2005> accessed 26 April 2020
- ILO, 'Monitoring and Implementation Tools for the Maritime Labour Convention, 2006' (*ILO Website*) <https://www.ilo.org/global/standards/maritime-labour-convention/monitoring-implementation-tools/lang%2D%2Den/index.htm> accessed 26 April 2020
- ILO, 'Partnering for Development' (*ILO Website*) <https://www.ilo.org/pardev/lang%2D%2Den/index.htm> accessed 26 April 2020
- ILO, 'Ratifications for Palau' (*ILO Website*) <https://www.ilo.org/dyn/normlex/en/f?p=1000:11200:0::NO:11200:P11200_COUNTRY_ID:2466492> accessed 26 April 2020
- ILO, 'Ratifications for Poland' (*ILO Website*) <https://www.ilo.org/dyn/normlex/en/f?p=NORMLEXPUB:11200:0::NO::P11200_COUNTRY_ID:102809> accessed 26 April 2020
- UN Women, 'Employment and migration' (*UN Women Website*) <http://www.unwomen.org/en/what-we-do/economic-empowerment/employment-and-migration> accessed 26 April 2020
- UN, 'Inter-Agency Coordination Mechanisms' (*UN Website*) <https://www.unsystem.org/iacms> accessed 26 April 2020

- UN, 'Promoting the MDGs: The Role of Employment and Decent Work', *XLIV UN Chronicle No 4 (December 2007)* https://unchronicle.un.org/article/promoting-mdgs-role-employment-and-decent-work accessed 26 April 2020
- UN, 'United Nations Chief Executives Board for Coordination' (*UN Website*) <https://www.unsystem.org/content/who-we-are> accessed 26 April 2020
- UNICEF, 'Factsheet Child Labour' (*UNICEF Website*) <https://data.unicef.org/topic/child-protection/child-labour/> accessed 26 April 2020
- World Bank, 'Changes to the Methodology, 2005 - 2017' (*Doing Business Website*) <http://www.doingbusiness.org/en/methodology/changes-to-the-methodology> accessed 26 April 2020
- World Bank, 'Doing Business' (*World Bank Website*) <http://www.doingbusiness.org> accessed 26 April 2020
- World Bank, 'Joint Statement by World Bank Group President Jim Yong Kim and ILO Director General Guy Ryder' (*World Bank Website*) <http://www.worldbank.org/en/news/press-release/2015/06/30/joint-statement-world-bank-group-president-ilo-director-general-guy-ryder> accessed 26 April 2020
- World Bank, 'Member Countries' (*World Bank Website*) https://www.worldbank.org/en/about/leadership/members#1 accessed 26 April 2020
- World Bank, 'Who we are' (*World Bank Website*) <https://www.worldbank.org/en/who-we-are> accessed 26 April 2020
- World Bank, 'World Bank Advisory Council on Gender and Development' (*World Bank Website*) <http://www.worldbank.org/en/topic/gender/publication/world-bank-advisory-council-on-gender-and-development> accessed 26 April 2020
- World Bank, 'World Bank Group President Jim Yong Kim: Discrimination by Law Carries a High Price' (*World Bank Website*) <http://www.worldbank.org/en/news/opinion/2014/02/28/world-bank-group-president-jim-yong-kim-discrimination-law-price> accessed 26 April 2020

Bibliography

Abel Patrick, 'Comparative Conclusions on Arbitral Dispute Settlement in Trade-Labour Matters Under US FTAs' in Henner Gött (ed), *Labour Standards in International Economic Law* (Springer 2018) 153

Addo Kofi, *Core Labour Standards and International Trade* (Springer 2015)

Agustí-Panareda Jordi, Ebert Franz Christian and LeClercq Desirée, 'Labour Provisions in Free Trade Agreements: Fostering Their Consistency with the ILO Standards System' (2014) Background Paper Social Dimensions Of Free Trade Agreements <https://www.ilo.org/wcmsp5/groups/public/%2D%2D-dgreports/%2D%2D-inst/documents/genericdocument/wcms_237940.pdf> accessed 26 April 2020

Akande Dapo, 'International Organizations' in Malcolm Evans (ed), *International Law* (Oxford University Press 2014) 248

Akehurst Michael, 'Jurisdiction in International Law' (1972-3) 46 British Yearbook of International Law 145, 176

Alcock Antony Evelyn, *History of the International Labour Organization* (Palgrave Macmillan 1971)

Aleksynska Mariya and Cazes Sandrine, 'Comparing Indicators of Labour Market Regulations Across Databases: A Post Scriptum to the Employing Workers Debate' (ILO 2014) 50

Alois Paul, 'Lessons for Effective Governance: An Examination of the Better Work Program' (2018) 24 Global Governance 139

Alston Philip, '"Core Labour Standards" and the Transformation of the International Labour Rights Regime' (2004) 15 European Journal of International Law 457

—— 'The United Nations' Specialized Agencies and Implementation of the International Covenant on Economic, Social and Cultural Rights' (1979) 18 Columbia Journal of Transnational Law 79

Álvarez José E, *International Organizations as Law-Makers* (Oxford University Press 2006)

—— 'Constitutional Interpretation in International Organizations' in Jean-Marc Coicaud and Veijo Heiskanen (eds), *Legitimacy of International Organizations* (United Nations University Press 2001) 104

Amerasinghe Chittharanjan Felix, *The Law of the International Civil Service: (as Applied by International Administrative Tribunals), vol I* (Clarendon Press 1994)

—— *Principles of the Institutional Law of International Organizations* (Cambridge University Press 2005)

Angbie Antony, 'International Financial Institutions' in Christian Reus-Smit (ed), *The Politics of International Law* (Cambridge University Press 2004) 217

H. Gött, *The Law of Interactions Between International Organizations*, Beiträge zum ausländischen öffentlichen Recht und Völkerrecht 299, https://doi.org/10.1007/978-3-662-62389-3

Anner Mark and Caraway Teri, 'International Institutions and Workers' Rights: Between Labor Standards and Market Flexibility' (2010) 45 Studies in Comparative International Development 151

Arato Julian, 'Subsequent Practice and Evolutive Interpretation: Techniques of Treaty Interpretation over Time and Their Diverse Consequences' (2011) 9 Law and Practice of International Courts and Tribunals 443

Asrani-Dann Sheetal and Dann Philipp, 'International Finance Corporation (IFC)', *Max Planck Encyclopedia of Public International Law* (Oxford University Press 2014)

Aston Jurij Daniel, *Sekundärgesetzgebung Internationaler Organisationen zwischen mitgliedstaatlicher Souveränität und Gemeinschaftsdisziplin* (Duncker & Humblot 2005)

Aust Anthony, 'Vienna Convention on the Law of Treaties (1969)', *Max Planck Encyclopedia of Public International Law* (Oxford University Press 2008)

Ayling Julie, 'Serving Many Voices: Progressing Calls for an International Environmental Organisation' (1997) 9 Journal of Environmental Law 243

Babb Sarah and Kentikelenis Alexander, 'International Financial Institutions as Agents of Neoliberalism' in Damien Cahill and others (eds), *The SAGE Handbook of Neoliberalism* (SAGE Publishing 2018) 16

Baker Philip J, 'The Doctrine of Legal Equality of States' (1923-1924) 4 British Yearbook of International Law 1

Bakvis Peter, 'The World Bank's Doing Business Report: A Last Fling for the Washington Consensus?' (2009) 15 Transfer: European Review of Labour and Research 419

—— 'How the World Bank & the IMF Use the Doing Business Report to Promote Labour Market Deregulation in Developing Countries' (2006) https://library.fes.de/pdf-files/gurn/00171.pdf accessed 26 April 2020

Barnard Catherine, 'Viking and Laval: An Introduction' (2008) 10 Cambridge Yearbook of European Legal Studies 463

Barnett Michael and Finnemore Martha, 'The Power of Liberal International Organisations' in Michael Barnett and Raymond Duvall (eds), *Power in Global Governance* (Cambridge University Press 2005) 161

Barry Christian and Reddy Sanjay G, *International Trade and Labor Standards: A Proposal for Linkage* (Columbia University Press 2008)

Basheska Elena, 'The Position of the Good Neighbourliness Principle in International and EU Law' in Dimitry Kochenov and Elena Basheska (eds), *Good Neighbourliness in the European Legal Context* (Brill 2015) 24

Bauer Paul J, 'The Maritime Labour Convention: An Adequate Guarantee of Seafarer Rights, or an Impediment to True Reforms?' (2008) 8 Chicago Journal of International Law 643

Becker Ulrich, 'European Social Charter', *Max Planck Encyclopedia of Public International Law* (Oxford University Press 2007)

Bedjaoui Mohammed, 'For a "World Charter of Human Labour and Social Justice"' in International Labour Office (ed), *Visions of the Future of Social Justice: Essays on the Occasion of the ILO's 75th Anniversary* (ILO 1994) 25

Beigbeder Yves, 'Civil Service, International', *Max Planck Encyclopedia of Public International Law* (Oxford University Press 2007)

—— 'The United States' Withdrawal from the International Labor Organization' (1979) 34 Relations industrielles / Industrial Relations 223

Bell Stuart and Newitt Kirsten, 'Decent Work and Poverty Eradication: Literature Review and Two-Country Study' (2010) <https://www.ituc-csi.org/IMG/pdf/Decent-work-and-poverty-eradication-literature-review-and-two-country-study_Full-report.pdf> accessed 26 April 2020

Bellace Janice R, 'The ILO and the Right to Strike' (2015) 153 International Labour Review 29

Benoît-Rohmer Florence and Klebes Heinrich, *Council of Europe Law: Towards a Pan-European Legal Area* (Council of Europe Publishing 2005)

Benvenisti Eyal, 'The Conception of International Law as a Legal System' (2008) 50 German Yearbook of International Law 393

—— and Downs George W, 'The Empire's New Clothes: Political Economy and the Fragmentation of International Law' (2007) 60 Stanford Law Rev 595

Berg Janine and Cazes Sandrine, *The Doing Business Indicators: Measurement Issues and Political Implications* (ILO 2007)

—— 'Policymaking Gone Awry: The Labor Market Regulations of the Doing Business Indicators' (2008) 29 Comparative Labour Law and Policy Journal 349

Berliner Daniel and others, *Labor Standards in International Supply Chains: Aligning Rights and Incentives* (Edward Elgar Publishing 2015)

Berman Paul Schiff, 'A Pluralist Approach to International Law' (2007) 32 Yale Journal of International Law 301

—— *Global Legal Pluralism: A Jurisprudence of Law Beyond Borders* (Cambridge University Press 2012)

Bernhardt Rudolf, 'Interpretation and Implied (Tacit) Modification of Treaties. Comments on Arts 27, 28, 29 and 38 of the ILC's 1966 Draft Articles on the Law of Treaties' (1967) 27 Zeitschrift für ausländisches öffentliches Recht und Völkerrecht 491

Beyerlin Ulrich, 'Pactum de contrahendo und pactum de negotiando im Völkerrecht?' (1976) 36 Zeitschrift für ausländisches öffentliches Recht und Völkerrecht, 407

Bianchi Andrea, *International Law Theories* (Oxford University Press 2016)

Biermann Rafael and Koops Joachim A, 'Studying Relations Between International Organizations in World Politics: Core Concepts and Challenges' in Rafael Biermann and Joachim A Koops (eds), *Palgrave Handbook on Inter-Organizational Relations in World Politics* (Palgrave Macmillan 2017) 1

Blackett Adelle and Trebilcock Anne, 'Conceptualizing Transnational Labour Law' in Adelle Blackett and Anne Trebilcock (eds) *Research Handbook on Transnational Labour Law* (Edward Elgar Publishing 2015) 3

Blanchard Francis, *L'Organisation Internationale Du Travail - De La Guerre Froide à Un Nouvel Ordre Mondial* (Seuil 2004)

Blanke Hermann-Josef, 'Art. 4' in Hermann-Josef Blanke and Stelio Mangiameli (eds), *The Treaty on European Union (TEU) - A Commentary* (Springer 2013)

Blanpain Roger, *European Labour Law* (11th edn, Kluwer Law International 2008)

Bleckmann Albert, 'Zur Verbindlichkeit des allgemeinen Völkerrechts für internationale Organisationen' (1977a) 37 Zeitschrift für ausländisches öffentliches Recht und Völkerrecht 107

—— 'Zur Feststellung und Auslegung von Völkergewohnheitsrecht' (1977b) 37 Zeitschrift für ausländisches öffentliches Recht und Völkerrecht 504

Bleicher Samuel A, 'UN v. IBRD: A Dilemma of Funcationalism' (1970) 24 International Organisation 31

Blix Hans M, 'Contemporary Aspects of Recognition' (1970) 120 Recueil des Cours de l'Académie de Droit International 587

Blokker Niels M, 'Proliferation of International Organizations: An Exploratory Introduction' in Niels M Blokker and Henry G Schermers (eds), *Proliferation of International Organizations* (Brill Nijhoff 2000) 1

Blome Kerstin and others, 'Contested Collisions: An Introduction' in Kerstin Blome and others (eds), *Contested Regime Collisions - Norm Fragmentation in World Society* (Cambridge University Press 2016) 1

—— and Markard Nora, '"Contested Collisions": Conditions for a Successful Collision Management – The Example of Article 16 of the Rome Statute' (2017) 29 Leiden Journal of International Law 551

Bodansky Daniel, 'Non Liquet and the Incompleteness of International Law' in Laurence Boisson De Chazournes and Philippe Sands (eds), *International Law, the International Court of Justice and Nuclear Weapons* (Cambridge University Press 1999) 152

Boisson De Chazournes Laurence, 'Relations with Other International Organizations' in Jacob Katz Cogan, Ian Hurd and Ian Johnstone (eds), *The Oxford Handbook of International Organizations* (Oxford University Press 2016) 691

—— and Campanelli Danio, 'Neighbour States', *Max Planck Encyclopedia of Public International Law* (Oxford University Press 2006)

Bonet Pérez Jordi, 'The European Social Charter' in Felipe Gómez Isa and Koen de Feyter (eds), *International Human Rights Law in a Global Context* (University of Deusto 2009) 689

Botero Juan C and others, 'The Regulation of Labor' (2004) 119 Quarterly Journal of Economics 1339

Boudahrain Abdellah, *The Arab Labour Organization* (Kluwer Law International 1996)

Bradlow Daniel D, 'Developing Countries Debt Crises, International Financial Institutions and International Law: Some Preliminary Thoughts' (2009) Washington College of Law Research Paper No. 2009/01

—— 'The World Bank, the IMF, and Human Rights' (1996) 6 Transnational Law & Contemporary Problems 47

—— 'International Law and the Operations of the International Financial Institutions' in Daniel D Bradlow and David Hunter (eds), *International Financial Institutions and International Law* (Kluwer Law International 2010) 1

Breuer Marten, 'The Council of Europe and International Institutional Law – An Appraisal' in Stefanie Schmahl and Marten Breuer (eds), *The Council of Europe: Its Laws and Policies* (Oxford University Press 2017) 946

Brölmann Catherine, 'International Organizations and Treaties: Contractual Freedom and Institutional Constraint' in Jan Klabbers and Åsa Wallendahl (eds), *Research Handbook on the Law of International Organizations* (Edward Elgar Publishing 2011) 285

—— *The Institutional Veil in Public International Law: International Organisations and the Law of Treaties* (Hart Publishing 2007)

—— 'Specialized Rules of Treaty Interpretation: International Organizations' in Duncan B Hollis (ed), *The Oxford Guide to Treaties* (Oxford University Press 2012) 507

Broude Tomer and Shany Yuval, 'The International Law and Policy of Multi-Sourced Equivalent Norms' in Tomer Broude and Yuval Shany (eds), *Multi-Sourced Equivalent Norms in International Law* (Hart Publishing 2011) 1

Brown Weiss Edith and Sornarajah Ahila, 'Good Governance', *Max Planck Encyclopedia of Public International Law* (Oxford University Press 2013)

Brown Bartram Stewart, *The United States and the Politicization of the World Bank: Issues of International Law and Policy* (Kegan Paul International 1992)

Brownlie Ian, 'The Responsibility of States for the Acts of International Organizations' in Maurizio Ragazzi (ed), *International Responsibility Today: Essays in Memory of Oscar Schachter* (Martinus Nijhoff Publishers 2005) 355

—— 'Problems Concerning the Unity of International Law', *Le droit international à l'heure de sa codification. Études en l'honneur de Roberto Ago, vol I (Giuffrè 1987)*

Brummer Klaus, *Der Europarat: Eine Einführung* (Springer VS 2008)

Burke-White William W, 'International Legal Pluralism' (2004) 25 Michigan Journal of International Law 963

Cabrera Ormaza Maria Victoria, *The Requirement of Consultation with Indigenous Peoples in the ILO: Between Normative Flexibility and Institutional Rigidity* (Brill Nijhoff 2018)

Calliess Christian, Kahl Wolfgang and Puttler Adelheid, 'Art. 4 EUV' in Christian Calliess and Matthias Ruffert (eds), *EUV/AEUV - Das Verfassungsrecht der Europäischen Union mit Europäischer Grundrechtecharta, Kommentar* (5th edn, C H Beck 2016)

Carstens Karl, *Das Recht des Europarats* (Duncker & Humblot 1956)

Charnovitz Steve, 'A World Environment Organization' (2002) 27 Columbia Journal of Environmental Law 323

—— 'The International Labour Organization in Its Second Century' (2000) 4 Max Planck Yearbook of United Nations Law 147

Cheng Bin, *General Principles of Law as Applied by International Courts and Tribunals* (Cambridge University Press 1953)

Chiu Hungdah, *The Capacity of International Organizations to Conclude Treaties, and the Special Legal Aspects of the Treaties so Concluded* (Martinus Nijhoff 1966)

Ciorciari John D, 'The Lawful Scope of Human Rights Criteria in World Bank Credit Decisions: An Interpretive Analysis of the IBRD and IDA Articles of Agreement' (2000) 33 Cornell International Law Journal 331

Cissé Hassane, 'Should the Political Prohibition in Charters of International Financial Institutions Be Revisited? The Case of the World Bank' (2012) 3 World Bank Legal Review 59

Clapham Andrew, 'Human Rights Obligations of Non-State Actors in Conflict Situations' (2006) 88 International Review of the Red Cross 491

CoE, *The Implementation of Judgments of the European Court of Human Rights* (Council of Europe Publishing 2018)

Collins English Dictionary - Complete & Unabridged (13th edn, Harper Collins Publications 2018) entry 'model'

Committee on the Accountability of International Organizations, 'Final Report of the Committee on the Accountability of International Organizations' in International Law Association Report of the Seventy-First Conference (Berlin 2004) (International Law Association 2004) 4

Cradden Conor, 'The True Cost of Doing Business' [2011] *Global Labour Column* 1

Crawford James, *Brownlie's Principles of Public International Law* (8th edn, Oxford University Press 2012)

Cremona Marise, 'Member States as Trustees of the Union Interest: Participating in International Agreements on Behalf of the European Union' in Anthony Arnull and others (eds), *Constitutional Order of States: Essays in EU Law in Honour of Alan Dashwood* (Oxford University Press 2011) 435

Cropper Steve and others, 'Introducing Inter-Organizational Relations' in Steve Cropper and others (eds), *Oxford Handbook on Inter-Organizational Relations* (Oxford University Press 2009) 1

Cryer Robert, 'Immunities and International Criminal Tribunals' in Alexander Orakhelashvili (ed), *Research Handbook on Jurisdiction and Immunities in International* Law (Edward Elgar Publishing 2015) 468

Damm Carolin, *Die Europäische Union im universellen Völkergewohnheitsrecht* (Mohr Siebeck 2016)

Dañino Roberto, 'The Legal Aspects of the World Bank's Work on Human Rights' (2007) 41 The International Lawyer 21

Darrow Mac, *Between Light and Shadow - The World Bank, The International Monetary Fund and International Human Rights Law* (Hart Publishing 2003)

Daugirdas Kristina, 'How and Why International Law Binds International Organizations' (2016) 57 Harvard International Law Journal 325

—— 'Reputation and the Responsibility of International Organizations' (2014) 25 European Journal of International Law 991

de Baere Geert and Roes Timothy, 'EU Loyalty as Good Faith' (2015) 64 International and Comparative Law Quarterly 829

de Waele Henri, *Legal Dynamics of EU External Relations* (2nd edn, Springer 2017)

de Wet Erika, 'The International Constitutional Order' (2006) 55 International and Comparative Law Quarterly 51

Deacon Bob and others, 'Globalisation and the Emerging Regional Governance of Labour Rights' (2011) 32 International Journal of Manpower 334

Delbrück Jost, 'Prospects for a "World (Internal) Law"? Legal Developments in a Changing International System' (2002) 9 Indiana Journal of Global Legal Studies 401

Denis Catherine, 'Art. 85 VCLT-IO' in Olivier Corten and Pierre Klein (eds), *The Vienna Conventions on the Law of Treaties - A Commentary, vol 2* (Oxford University Press 2011)

Denters Erik, 'New Challenges to IMF Jurisdiction' (1998) 29 Netherlands Yearbook of International Law 3

Deshman Abigail C, 'Horizontal Review Between International Organizations: A Rejoinder to Rosa Raffaelli' (2013) 24 European Journal of International Law 1201

Desierto Diane A, *Public Policy in International Economic Law: The ICESCR in Trade, Finance, and Investment* (Oxford University Press 2015)

Dethier Jean-Jacques, 'Producing Knowledge for Development: Research at the World Bank' (2007) 13 Global Governance 469

Dicke Klaus, *Effizienz und Effektivität Internationaler Organisationen* (Duncker & Humblot 1994)

Dickinson Edwin DeWitt, *The Equality of States in International Law* (Harvard University Press 1920)

Diller Janelle M, 'Pluralism and Privatization in Transnational Labour Regulation: Experience of the International Labour Organization' in Adelle Blackett and Anne Trebilcock (eds), *Research Handbook on Transnational Labour Law* (Edward Elgar Publishing 2015) 329

Dillon Conley Hall, *International Labour Conventions: Their Interpretation and Revision* (University of North Carolina Press 1942)

Djeffal Christian, *Static and Evolutive Treaty Interpretation - A Functional Reconstruction* (Cambridge University Press 2015)

Dombois Rainer, 'Sozialklauseln Im US-Freihandelsabkommen: Ein Wirksames Mittel Internationaler Arbeitsregulierung?' (2006) 13 Industrielle Beziehungen 238

—— Hornberger Erhard and Winter Jens, *Internationale Arbeitsregulierung in der Souveränitätsfalle - Das Lehrstück des NAALC* (LIT Verlag 2004)

Dörr Oliver, 'Art. 31 VCLT' in Oliver Dörr and Kirsten Schmalenbach (eds), *Vienna Convention on the Law of Treaties - A Commentary* (2nd edn, Springer 2018)

Dorssemont Filip, 'The Right to Take Collective Action: The Prospects of the Accession to the European Convention on Human Rights. How the European Court on Human Rights Gave Us Enerji to Cope with Laval and Viking' in Marie-Ange Moreau (ed), *Before And After The Economic Crisis* (Edward Elgar Publishing 2011)

Dunoff Jeffrey L, 'Mapping a Hidden World of International Regulatory Cooperation' (2015) 78 Law and Contemporary Problems 267

—— 'How to Avoid Regime Collisions' in Kerstin Blome and others (eds), *Contested Regime Collisions - Norm Fragmentation in World Society* (Cambridge University Press 2016) 49

Dupuy René-Jean, 'Le Droit Des Relations Entre Les Organisations Internationales' (1960) 100 Recueil des Cours de l'Académie de Droit International 461

Dzehtsiarou Kanstantsin, 'European Consensus and the Evolutive Interpretation of the European Convention on Human Rights' (2011) 12 German Law Journal 1730

Ebenstein William, 'The Pure Theory of Law: Demythologizing Legal Thought' (1971) 59 California Law Review 617

Ebert Franz Christian, 'Labour Standards and the World Bank. Analysing the Potential of Safeguard Policies for Protecting Workers' in Henner Gött (ed), *Labour Standards in International Economic Law* (Springer 2018) 273

—— 'International Financial Institutions' Approaches to Labour Law: The Case of the International Monetary Fund' in Adelle Blackett and Anne Trebilcock (eds), *Research Handbook on Transnational Labour Law* (Edward Elgar Publishing 2015) 124

—— 'Kohärenz der Politik der Weltbank mit den arbeitsrechtlichen Mindeststandards der Internationalen Arbeitsorganisation' in Wolfgang Däubler and Reingard Zimmer (eds), *Arbeitsvölkerrecht - Festschrift für Klaus Lörcher* (Nomos 2013a) 72

—— and La Hovary Claire, 'International Labour Law', *Max Planck Encyclopedia of Public International Law* (Oxford University Press 2013b)

—— and Martin Oelz, 'Bridging the Gap Between Labour Rights and Human Rights: The Role of ILO Law in Regional Human Rights Courts' (2012) IILS Discussion Paper 212/2012

—— and Posthuma Anne, 'Labour Standards and Development Finance Institutions: A Review of Current Policies and Activities' (2010) IILS Discussion Paper No 204 <http://www.oit.org/wcmsp5/groups/public/%2D%2D-dgreports/%2D%2D-inst/documents/publication/wcms_192837.pdf> accessed 26 April 2020

Eeckhout Piet, *EU External Relations Law* (2nd edn, Oxford University Press 2011)
Engel Norbert Paul, 'Status, Ausstattung und Personalhoheit des Inter-Amerikanischen und des Europäischen Gerichtshofs für Menschenrechte' (2003) 30 Europäische Grundrechte-Zeitschrift 122
European Commission (Directorate-General for Economic and Financial Affairs), 'The Economic Adjustment Programme for Greece' Occasional Papers No. 61 (2010)
Evju Stein, 'The Right to Collective Action under the European Social Charter' (2011) 2 European Labour Law Journal 196
—— 'The European Social Charter and the International Labour Organisation – Interlinks Past and Present' in Wolfgang Däubler and Reingard Zimmer (eds), *Arbeitsvölkerrecht - Festschrift für Klaus Lörcher* (Nomos 2013) 146
Ewing Keith D, 'The Implications of Wilson and Palmer' (2003) 32 Industrial Law Journal 1
Fassbender Bardo, 'Art. 2(1)' in Bruno Simma and others (eds), *The Charter of the United Nations - A Commentary, vol I* (3 edn, Oxford University Press 2012)
—— 'The United Nations Charter as Constitution of the International Community' (1998) 36 Columbia Journal of Transnational Law 529
Fastenrath Ulrich, 'Art. 74' in Bruno Simma and others (eds), *The Charter of the United Nations - A Commentary, vol II* (3rd edn, 2013)
Ferri Marco, 'Coordination between the EU and its Member States', in Christina Kaddous (ed), *The European Union in International Organisations and Global Governance* (Hart Publishing 2017) 77
Fischer-Lescano Andreas and Teubner Gunther, *Regime-Kollisionen. Zur Fragmentierung des globalen Rechts* (Suhrkamp 2006)
Fitzmaurice Gerald, 'The Future of Public International Law and of the International Legal System in the Circumstances of Today' in Institut de Droit International (ed), *Livre du centenaire 1873–1973: Evolution et perspectives du droit international* (Karger 1973) 196
Freedland Mark R and Prassl Jeremias (eds), *Viking, Laval and Beyond* (Hart Publishing 2016)
Freeman R Edward, *Strategic Management: A Stakeholder's Approach* (Pitman 1984)
Fried John HE, 'Relations Between the United Nations and the International Labor Organization' (1947) 41 The American Political Science Review 963
Friedmann Wolfgang, *The Changing Structure of International Law* (Columbia University Press 1964)
Gadkowski Andrzej, 'The Doctrine of Implied Powers of International Organizations in the Case Law of International Tribunals' (2016) 6 Adam Mickiewicz University Law Review 45
Gaja Giorgio, 'General Principles of Law', *Max Planck Encyclopedia of Public International Law* (Oxford University Press 2013)
Gardiner Richard, *Treaty Interpretation* (2nd edn, Oxford University Press 2017)
Gautier Philippe, 'The Reparation for Injuries Case Revisited: The Personality of the European Union' (2000) 4 Max Planck Yearbook of United Nations Law 331
Ghazi Bahram, *The IMF, The World Bank Group and the Question of Human Rights* (Transnational Publishers 2005)
Ginther Konrad, 'Mitgliedschaft in Internationalen Organisationen - Grundfragen' in Konrad Ginther and Thomas Oppermann (eds), *Grundfragen der Mitgliedschaft in Internationalen Organisationen - Referate und Diskussion der 14. Tagung der Deutschen Gesellschaft für Völkerrecht* (C F Müller 1978) 7
Giubbioni Stefano, 'The Rise and Fall of EU Labour Law' (2018) 24 European Law Journal 7
Golsong Heribert, *Das Rechtsschutzsystem der Europäischen Menschenrechtskonvention* (1958)
Gött Henner, '"Legitimation durch den, den es angeht?" - Die Einbindung der Zivilgesellschaft in die Transatlantische Regulierungszusammenarbeit aus demokratischer Perspektive' in Sinthiou Buszewski, Stefan Martini and Hannes Rathke (eds), *Freihandel vs. Demokratie* (Nomos 2016) 199
—— 'Art. 6 RESC' in Eduardo Ales and others (eds), *International and European Labour Law - Article by Article Commentary* (Nomos 2018a) 286

—— 'An Individual Labour Complaint Procedure for Workers, Trade Unions, Employers and NGOs in Future Free Trade Agreements' in Henner Gött (ed), *Labour Standards in International Economic Law* (Springer 2018b) 185

—— 'Interactions between International Organizations - Approaching a Neglected Governance Dimension' (2020) 17 International Organizations Law Review 75

Graf Vitzthum Wolfgang, 'Begriff, Geschichte und Rechtsquellen des Völkerrechts' in Wolfgang Graf Vitzthum and Alexander Proelß (eds), *Völkerrecht* (8th edn, de Gruyter 2019) 1

Grant Thomas D, *Admission to the United Nations - Charter Article 4 and the Rise of Universal Organization* (Martinus Nijhoff Publishers 2009)

Griffiths John, 'What Is Legal Pluralism?' (1986) 18 The Journal of Legal Pluralism and Unofficial Law 1

Guder Leonie, 'International Development Association (IDA)', *Max Planck Encyclopedia of Public International Law* (Oxford University Press 2011)

Haas Ernst B, *Beyond the Nation State: Functionalism and International Organization* (Stanford University Press 1964)

Haas M Peter, 'Epistemic Communities and International Policy Coordination' 46 International Organization 1

Hafner Gerhard, 'The Legal Personality of International Organizations' in August Reinisch and Ursula Kriebaum (eds), *The Law of International Relations - Liber Amicorum Hanspeter Neuhold* (Eleven 2007) 81

Hagen Katherine A, 'Policy Dialogue between the International Labour Organization and the International Financial Institutions: The Search for Convergence' (2003) FES Occasional Papers No 9 <http://library.fes.de/pdf-files/bueros/genf/50035.pdf> accessed 26 April 2020

Hahn Hugo J, 'Euratom: The Conception of an International Personality' (1958) 71 Harvard Law Review 1001

Halberstam Daniel and Stein Eric, 'The United Nations, the EU, and the King of Sweden: Economic Sanctions and Individual Rights in a Plural World Order' (2009) 46 Common Market Law Review 13

Hartmann Jacques, 'A Danish Crusade for the Reform of the European Court of Human Rights' (EJIL Talk!, 14 November 2017) <https://www.ejiltalk.org/a-danish-crusade-for-the-reform-of-the-european-court-of-human-rights/> accessed 26 April 2020

Harris David John, *The European Social Charter* (Transnational Publishers 1984)

Hasan Sharina Farihah and others, 'ASEAN Economic Community: The Potential Impacts of Labour Mobility on the Economy and Construction Industry' (2016) 3 Journal of Scientific Research and Development 144

Hassel Anke, 'The Evolution of a Global Labor Governance Regime' (2008) 21 Governance 231

Helleiner Eric, 'Incremental Origins of Bretton Woods' in Orfeo Fioretos, Tulia G Falleti and Adam Sheingate (eds), *The Oxford Handbook of Historical Institutionalism* (Oxford University Press 2016) 617

Hendrickx Frank and others, 'The Architecture of Global Labour Governance' (2016) 155 International Labour Review 339

Herdegen Matthias, *Völkerrecht* (17th edn, C H Beck 2018)

Hexner Ervin P, 'Interpretation by Public International Organizations of Their Basic Instruments' (1959) 53 American Journal of International Law 341

Heywood Anderson David, 'Art. 5 VCLT-IO' in Olivier Corten and Pierre Klein (eds), *The Vienna Conventions on the Law of Treaties - A Commentary, vol 1* (Oxford University Press 2011)

Higgins Rosalyn and others, *Oppenheim's International Law - United Nations* (Oxford University Press 2017)

Hirsch Moshe, *The Responsibility of International Organizations Toward Third Parties: Some Basic Principles* (Brill 1995)

Holterhus Till Patrik, 'EWR' in Horst-Günther Krenzler, Christoph Herrmann and Marian Niestedt (eds), *EU-Außenwirtschafts- und Zollrecht Vol II* (14th edn, C H Beck 2019) 1

Hosanee Nivedita M, *A Critical Analysis of Flag State Duties As Laid Down Under Article 94 of the 1982 United Nations Convention on the Law of the Sea* (UN 2009)

Hughes Stephen and Haworth Nigel, *The International Labour Organization: Coming in from the Cold* (Routledge 2011)

Humbert Franziska, *The Challenge of Child Labour in International Law* (Cambridge University Press 2009)

Hume David, *A Treatise of Human Nature* (1739), reprinted from the Original Edition in three volumes and edited, with an analytical index (Clarendon Press 1896)

ILO, *Assessment of Labour Provisions in Trade and Investment Arrangements* (ILO 2016)

—— *Independent Evaluation of the ILO's Strategy for Coherent Decent Work Policies* (ILO 2014)

—— *The Social Dimensions of Free Trade Agreements* (ILO 2013)

—— and World Bank, *Export to Jobs - Boosting the Gains from Trade in South Asia* (ILO and World Bank 2019)

—— UNICEF and World Bank, 'Understanding Trends in Child Labour' (2017) <https://cocoainitiative.org/wp-content/uploads/2019/04/Understanding-Child-Labour-Trends-2017.pdf> accessed 26 April 2020

ITUC, '2007 Annual Survey of Violation of Trade Union Rights' (2007) https://www.ituc-csi.org/annual-survey-of-violations-of?lang=en accessed 26 April 2020

ITUC/Global Unions, 'The IFIs' Use of Doing Business to Eliminate Workers' Protection: Analysis of Doing Business 2008 and New Country Evidence' (2007) <https://www.ituc-csi.org/IMG/pdf/doing_business.pdf> accessed 26 April 2020

Janik Cornelia, *Die Bindung Internationaler Organisationen an internationale Menschenrechtsstandards* (Mohr Siebeck 2012)

Janse Ronald, '(Why) Was the World Bank Supposed to Be a Nonpolitical Organization? An Interpretation of the Original Meaning and Rationale of Article 4(10) of the Articles of Agreement of the International Bank for Reconstruction and Development, 1941–1948' (2014) 16 Journal of the History of International Law / Revue d'histoire du droit international 113

Jenkins Hamish, Lee Eddy and Rodgers Gerry, *The Quest for a Fair Globalization Three Years On - Assessing the Impact of the World Commission on the Social Dimension of Globalization* (ILO 2007)

Jenks Clarence Wilfred, 'Coordination: A New Problem of International Organization' 77 Recueil des Cours de l'Académie de Droit International 151

—— 'The Significance for International Law of the Tripartite Character of the International Labour Organisation' (1936) 22 Transactions of the Grotius Society 45

—— *The International Protection of Trade Union Freedom* (Stevens and Sons 1957)

—— *Law in the World Community* (Longmans 1967)

—— 'The Conflict of Law-Making Treaties' (1953) 30 British Yearbook of International Law 401

Johnstone Ian, 'Law-Making through the Operational Activities of International Organizations' (2008) 40 George Washington International Law Review 87

Jönsson Christer, 'IR Paradigms and Inter-Organizational Theory: Situating the Research Program Within the Discipline' in Rafael Biermann and Joachim A Koops (eds), *Palgrave Handbook on Inter-Organizational Relations in World Politics* (Palgrave Macmillan 2017) 49

Jurje Flavia and Lavenex Sandra, 'ASEAN Economic Community: What Model for Labour Mobility?' (2015) NCCR Trade Working Paper No 2015/02 http://www.nccr-trade.org/fileadmin/user_upload/nccr-trade.ch/wp4/NCCR_working_Paper_ASEAN_Jurje_Lavenex.pdf accessed 26 April 2020

Kang Suzan, 'Labor and the Bank: Investigating the Politics of the World Bank's Employing Workers' Index' (2009) 14 Journal of Workplace Rights 481

Kapur Devesh, Lewis John P and Webb Richard C, *The World Bank: Its First Half Century, vol 1* (Brookings Institution Press 1997)

Karl Wolfram, *Vertrag und spätere Praxis im Völkerrecht* (Springer 1983)

Kaufmann Christine, *Globalisation and Labour Rights. The Conflict Between Core Labour Rights and International Economic Law* (Hart Publishing 2007)

Kearney Richard D and Dalton Robert E, 'The Treaty on Treaties' (1970) 64 American Journal of International Law 495

Kelsen Hans, *Reine Rechtslehre - Einleitung in die rechtswissenschaftliche Problematik (Studienausgabe der 1. Auflage 1934) Hrsg. u. Eingel. v. Matthias Jestaedt* (Mohr Siebeck 2008)

Kennedy David, 'The Mystery of Global Governance' (2008) 34 Ohio Northern University Law Review 827

Kerhuel Anne-Julie and Fauvarque-Cosson Bénédicte, 'Is Law an Economic Contest? French Reactions to the Doing Business World Bank Reports and Economic Analysis of the Law' (2009) 57 American Journal of Comparative Law 811

Kern Christoph A, 'Die Doing-Business-Reports der Weltbank - Fragwürdige Quantifizierung rechtlicher Qualität?' (2009) 64 Juristenzeitung 498

Kicker Renate and Möstl Markus, *Standard-Setting Through Monitoring? The Role of Council of Europe Expert Bodies in the Development of Human Rights* (Council of Europe Publishing 2013)

Kingsbury Benedict, 'The Concept of "Law" in Global Administrative Law' (2009) 20 European Journal of International Law 23

Kingsbury Benedict and Donaldson Megan, 'Global Administrative Law', *Max Planck Encyclopedia of Public International Law* (Oxford University Press 2011)

Kingsbury Benedict, Krisch Nico and Stewart Richard B, 'The Emergence of Global Administrative Law' (2005) 68 Law and Contemporary Problems 15

Klabbers Jan, *An Introduction to International Organizations Law* (3rd edn, Cambridge University Press 2015a)

—— 'On Human Rights Treaties, Contractual Conceptions and Reservations' in Ineta Ziemele (ed), *Reservations to Human Rights Treaties and the Vienna Convention Regime: Conflict, Harmony or Reconciliation* (Martinus Nijhoff Publishers 2004) 149

—— *International Law* (2nd edn, Cambridge University Press 2017)

—— 'Interpretation as the Continuation of Politics by Other Means' (*Opinio Juris*, 2 March 2009a) <http://opiniojuris.org/2009/03/02/continuation/> accessed 26 April 2020

—— 'The EJIL Foreword: The Transformation of International Organizations Law' (2015b) 26 European Journal of International Law 9

—— 'The Paradox of International Institutional Law' (2008) 5 International Organizations Law Review 151

—— 'Setting the Scene' in Jan Klabbers, Anne Peters and Geir Ulfstein (eds), *The Constitutionalization of International Law* (Oxford University Press 2009b) 1

—— 'Unity, Diversity, Accountability: the Ambivalent Concept of International Organisation' (2013) 14 Melbourne Journal of International Law 1

Klamert Marcus, *The Principle of Loyalty in EU Law* (Oxford University Press 2016)

Klebes Heinrich, 'Die Rechtsstruktur des Europarats und insbesondere der Parlamentarischen Versammlung' (Europa-Institut 1996) https://europainstitut.de/fileadmin/schriften/340.pdf accessed 26 April 2020

Klein Eckart, 'United Nations, Specialized Agencies', *Max Planck Encyclopedia of Public International Law* (Oxford University Press 2006)

—— and Pechstein Matthias, *Das Vertragsrecht internationaler Organisationen* (Duncker & Humblot 1985)

—— and Schmahl Stefanie, 'Die internationalen und die supranationalen Organisationen' in Wolfgang Graf Vitzthum and Alexander Proelß (eds), *Völkerrecht* (8th edn, de Gruyter 2019) 237

Kleinlein Thomas, *Konstitutionalisierung Im Völkerrecht* (Springer 2012)

Klug Ulrich, 'Die Reine Rechtslehre von Hans Kelsen und die Formallogische Rechtfertigung der Kritik am Pseudoschluß vom Sein auf das Sollen' in Salo Engel and Rudolf Métall (eds), *Law,*

State, and International Legal Order – Essays in Honor of Hans Kelsen (University of Tennessee Press 1964) 153

Kneller Robert W, 'Human Rights, Politics, and the Multilateral Development Banks' (1980) 6 Yale Studies in World Public Order 361

Kochenov Dimitry and Basheska Elena, 'Introduction: Good Neighbourliness Inside and Outside the Union' in Dimitry Kochenov and Elena Basheska (eds), *Good Neighbourliness in the European Legal Context* (Brill 2015) 3

Köck Heribert Franz and Fischer Peter, *Das Recht der Internationalen Organisationen* (3rd edn, Linde Verlag 1997)

Koebele Michael, 'World Trade Organization, Enforcement System', *Max Planck Encyclopedia of Public International Law* (Oxford University Press 2011)

Köhler Gabriele, 'The Challenges of Delivering as One: Overcoming Fragmentation and Moving Towards Policy Coherence' (2011) ILO Policy Integration Department Working Paper No 100 <https://www.ilo.org/wcmsp5/groups/public/%2D%2D-dgreports/%2D%2D-integration/documents/publication/wcms_153043.pdf> accessed 26 April 2020, 5 et seqq.

Kokott Juliane, 'Souveräne Gleichheit und Demokratie im Völkerrecht' (2004) 64 Zeitschrift für ausländisches öffentliches Recht und Völkerrecht 517

—— 'States, Sovereign Equality', *Max Planck Encyclopedia of Public International Law* (Oxford University Press 2011)

Koliev Faradj and Lebovic James H, 'Selecting for Shame: The Monitoring of Workers' Rights by the International Labour Organization, 1989 to 2011' (2018) 62 International Studies Quarterly 437

Kooijmans Pieter H, *The Doctrine of the Legal Equality of States* (A W Sythoff 1964)

Kopela Sophia, 'Climate Change, Regime Interaction, and the Principle of Common but Differentiated Responsibility: The Experience of the International Maritime Organization' (2014) 24 Yearbook of International Environmental Law 70

Koskenniemi Martti, 'Hegemonic Regimes' in Margaret A Young (ed), *Regime Interaction in International Law - Facing Fragmentation* (Cambridge University Press 2012) 305

Koukiadaki Aristea and Grimshaw Damian, *Evaluating the Effects of the Structural Labour Market Reforms on Collective Bargaining in Greece* (ILO 2016)

Krause Rüdiger, 'The Promotion of Labour Standards Through International Framework Agreements' in Henner Gött (ed), *Labour Standards in International Economic Law* (Springer 2018) 319

Krajewski Markus, *Völkerrecht* (2nd edn, Nomos 2020)

Krisch Nico, 'Pluralism in International Law and Beyond' (2015) <https://ssrn.com/abstract=2613930> accessed 26 April 2020

—— *Beyond Constitutionalism: The Pluralist Structure of Postnational Law* (Oxford University Press 2012)

—— 'The Pluralism of Global Administrative Law' (2006a) 17 European Journal of International Law 247

—— and Kingsbury Benedict, 'Introduction: Global Governance and Global Administrative Law in the International Legal Order' (2006b) 17 European Journal of International Law 1

Krylov Serge M, 'Les Notions Principales Du Droit Des Gens: La Doctrine Soviétique Du Droit International' (1947) 70 Recueil des Cours de l'Académie de Droit International 407

Kryvoi Yaraslau, 'The World Bank and the ILO: Two Visions of Employment Regulation' in Roger Blanpain and Claire Grant (eds), *Fixed-Term Employment Contracts - A Comparative Study* (Vanden Broele Publishers 2009) 47

—— 'Discrimination and Security of Employment in a Post-Soviet Context' (2006) 22 The International Journal of Comparative Labour Law and Industrial Relations 5

Kuijper Pieter Jan and others, *The Law of EU External Relations - Cases, Materials, and Commentary on the EU as an International Legal Actor* (2nd edn, Oxford University Press 2015)

Kyloh Robert, 'Poverty and Reform in the Magical Kingdom: Nepal's PRSP' in International Labour Office (ed), *Trade Unions and Poverty Reduction Strategies* (ILO 2004) 31

—— *From Conflict to Cooperation: Labour Market Reforms That Can Work in Nepal* (ILO/Academic Foundation India 2008)
La Hovary Claire, 'A Challenging Ménage À Trois? Tripartism in the International Labour Organization' (2015a) 12 International Organizations Law Review 204
—— 'Showdown at the ILO? A Historical Perspective on the Employers' Group's 2012 Challenge to the Right to Strike' (2013) 42 Industrial Law Journal 338
—— 'The ILO and the Interpretation of Fundamental Rights at Work: A Closer Look at Establishing a Tribunal under Article 37(2)' in Paul van der Heijden (ed), *Ensuring Coherence in Fundamental Labor Rights Case Law: Challenges and Opportunities* (SJEC 2016)
—— 'The 2015 ILC and the Right to Strike: Business as Usual?' (2015b) 22 International Union Rights 16
—— 'The ILO's Mandate and Capacity: Creating, Proliferating and Supervising Labour Standards for a Globalized Economy' in Henner Gött (ed), *Labour Standards in International Economic Law* (Springer 2018) 38
—— 'The ILO Supervisory Bodies' 'Soft Law Jurisprudence'' in Adelle Blackett and Anne Trebilcock (eds), *Research Handbook on Transnational Labour Law* (Edward Elgar Publishing 2015c) 316
Lambert-Abdelgawad Elisabeth, 'The Court as a Part of the Council of Europe: The Parliamentary Assembly and the Committee of Ministers' in Andreas Føllesdal, Birgit Peters and Geir Ulfstein (eds), *Constituting Europe. The European Court of Human Rights in a National, European and Global Context* (Cambridge University Press 2013) 263
Landelius Torsten, *Workers, Employers and Governments: A Comparative Study of Delegations and Groups at the International Labour Conference, 1919–1964* (Norstedt & Söner 1965)
Lang Andrew TF, 'Legal Regimes and Regimes of Knowledge: Governing Global Services Trade' LSE Law, Society and Economy Working Papers 15/2009 (2009)
Langille Brian A, 'Consistency, Consensus, or Coherence? Legal Interpretation of Fundamental Labor Rights' in Social Justice Expertise Center (ed), *Ensuring Coherence in Fundamental Labor Rights Case Law: Challenges and Opportunities* (SJEC 2016) 60
—— 'The Curious Incident of the ILO, Myanmar and Forced Labour' in Adelle Blackett and Anne Trebilcock (eds), *Research Handbook on Transnational Labour Law* (Edward Elgar Publishing 2015) 519
Lasslett Kristian and Gstrein Vanessa, 'Measuring Forced Labour in an Authoritarian Context: An Evaluation of ILO Third Party Monitoring in Uzbekistan' (The Corruption and Human Rights Initiative 2018) <https://pure.ulster.ac.uk/ws/files/77749500/isci_ilo_tpm_report_2018.pdf> accessed 26 April 2020
Lauterpacht Hersch, *Private Law Sources and Analogies of International Law* (Longmans, Green and Co 1927)
Lavelle Jennifer (ed), *The Maritime Labour Convention 2006: International Labour Law Redefined* (Routledge 2013)
Lavelle Kathryn C, 'American Politics, the Presidency of the World Bank, and Development Policy' (2013) Policy Research Working Paper No. 6377 https://elibrary.worldbank.org/doi/pdf/10.1596/1813-9450-6377 accessed 26 April 2020
Le Blanc David, 'Towards Integration at Last? The Sustainable Development Goals as a Network of Targets' (2015) 23 Sustainable Development 176
Leary Virginia A, 'The WHO Case: Implications for Specialized Agencies' in Laurence Boisson De Chazournes and Philippe Sands (eds), *International Law, the International Court of Justice and Nuclear Weapons* (Cambridge University Press 1999) 112
—— 'The WTO and the Social Clause: Post-Singapore' (1997) 8 European Journal of International Law 118
LeClercq Desiree, 'Sea Change: New Rulemaking Procedures at the International Labour Organization' (2015) 22 ILSA Journal of International & Comparative Law 105

Lee Sangheon, McCann Deirdre and Torm Nina, 'The World Bank's "Employing Workers" Index: Findings and Critiques – A Review of Recent Evidence' (2008) 147 International Labour Review 416
Lennartz Jannis, *Dogmatik als Methode* (Mohr Siebeck 2017)
Letsas George, *A Theory of Interpretation of the European Convention of Human Rights* (Oxford University Press 2007)
Levrat Nicolas, 'Art. 6 VCLT-IO' in Olivier Corten and Pierre Klein (eds), *The Vienna Conventions on the Law of Treaties - A Commentary, vol 1* (Oxford University Press 2011)
Liivoja Rain, 'The Scope of the Supremacy Clause of the United Nations Charter' (2008) 57 International and Comparative Law Quarterly 583
Linderfalk Ulf, 'What Are the Functions of the General Principles?' (2018) 78 Zeitschrift für ausländisches öffentliches Recht und Völkerrecht 1
—— 'Who Are "The Parties"? Article 31, Paragraph 3 (c) of the 1969 Vienna Convention and the "Principle of Systemic Integration" Revisited' (2008) 55 Netherlands International Law Review 343
Lörcher Klaus, 'Interpretation' in Niklas Bruun and others (eds), *The European Social Charter and the Employment Relation* (Hart Publishing 2017) 52
—— 'The New Social Dimension in the Jurisprudence of the European Court of Human Rights (ECtHR): The Demir and Baykara Judgment, Its Methodology and Follow-Up' in Filip Dorssemont, Klaus Lörcher and Isabelle Schömann (eds), *The European Convention on Human Rights and Employment Relation* (Hart Publishing 2013) 3
Lorenz Edward C, 'The Search for Constitutional Protection of Labor Standards, 1924-1941: From Interstate Compacts to International Treaties' (2000) 23 Seattle University Law Review 569
Lusa Bordin Fernando, *The Analogy Between States and International Organizations* (Cambridge University Press 2019)
Mackay Fergus, 'Universal Rights or a Universe Unto Itself? Indigenous Peoples' Human Rights and the World Bank's Draft Operational Policy 4.10 on Indigenous Peoples' (2002) 17 American University International Law Review 527
Mantouvalou Virginia, 'Labour Rights in the European Convention on Human Rights: An Intellectual Justification for an Integrated Approach to Interpretation' (2013) 13 Human Rights Law Review 1
Marek Krystyna, 'Thoughts on Codification' (1971) 31 Zeitschrift für ausländisches öffentliches Recht und Völkerrecht 489
Marx Axel, Ebert Franz Christian and Hachez Nicholas, 'Dispute Settlement for Labour Provisions in EU Free Trade Agreements: Rethinking Current Approaches' (2017) 5 Politics and Governance 49
Matz Nele, *Wege zur Koordinierung völkerrechtlicher Verträge* (Springer 2005)
Maul Daniel Roger, 'The ILO, Asia and the Beginnings of Technical Assistance, 1945–60' in Jill M Jensen and Nelson Lichtenstein (eds), *The ILO from Geneva to the Pacific Rim: West Meets East* (Palgrave Macmillan 2016) 110
—— *Human Rights, Development and Decolonization: The International Labour Organization, 1940-70* (Palgrave Macmillan 2012)
Maupain Francis, 'A Second Century for What? The ILO at a Regulatory Crossroad' (2019) 16 International Organizations Law Review 1
—— *The Future of the International Labour Organization in the Global Economy* (Hart Publishing 2013a)
—— 'The ILO Regular Supervisory System: A Model in Crisis?' (2013b) 10 International Organizations Law Review 117
—— 'New Foundation or New Façade? The ILO and the 2008 Declaration on Social Justice for a Fair Globalization' (2009) 20 European Journal of International Law 823
McCann Deirdre, 'Labour Law on the Plateau: Towards Regulatory Policy for Endogenous Norms' in Alan Bogg and others (eds), *The Autonomy of Labour Law* (Hart Publishing 2015) 397

McConnell Moira L, Devlin Dominick and Doumbia-Henry Cleopatra, *The Maritime Labour Convention 2006 - A Legal Primer in an Emerging Regime* (Martinus Nijhoff Publishers 2011)
McGrady Benn, 'Fragmentation of International Law or "Systemic Integration" of Treaty Regimes: EC-Biotech Products and the Proper Interpretation of Article 31(3)(c) of the Vienna Convention on the Law of Treaties' (2008) 42 Journal of World Trade 589
McInerney-Lankford Siobhán, 'Human Rights and Development: Regime Interaction and the Fragmentation of International Law' (2012) 3 World Bank Legal Review 123
McLachlan Campbell, 'The Principle of Systemic Integration and Article 31(3)(c) of the Vienna Convention' (2005) 54 International and Comparative Law Quarterly 279
McNair Arnold D, 'Treaties Producing Effects Erga Omnes', *Scritti di diritto internazionale in onore di Tomaso Perassi II* (Giuffrè 1957) 23
—— 'The Functions and Differing Legal Character of Treaties' (1930) 11 British Yearbook of International Law 100
—— *The Law of Treaties* (Clarendon Press 1961)
Meardi Guglielmo and Marginson Paul, 'Global Labour Governance: Potential and Limits of an Emerging Perspective' (2014) 28 Work, Employment and Society 651
Mégret Frédéric and Hoffmann Florian, 'The UN as Human Rights Violator? Some Reflections on the United Nations Changing Human Rights Responsibilities' (2003) 25 Human Rights Quarterly 314
Meng Werner, 'Art. 57' in Bruno Simma and others (eds), *The Charter of the United Nations - A Commentary, vol II* (3rd edn, Oxford University Press 2013a)
—— 'Art. 58' in Bruno Simma and others (eds), *The Charter of the United Nations - A Commentary, vol II* (3rd edn, Oxford University Press 2012)
—— 'Art. 60' in Bruno Simma and others (eds), *The Charter of the United Nations - A Commentary, vol II* (3rd edn, Oxford University Press 2013b)
—— 'Art. 62' in Bruno Simma and others (eds), *The Charter of the United Nations - A Commentary, vol II* (3rd edn, Oxford University Press 2013c)
—— 'Art. 63' in Bruno Simma and others (eds), *The Charter of the United Nations - A Commentary, vol II* (3rd edn, Oxford University Press 2013d)
Menon PK, *The Law of Treaties Between States and International Organizations* (Edwin Mellen 1992)
Merhof Katrin, *Der internationale und innerstaatliche Schutz von Arbeitnehmerrechten in der kolumbianischen Blumenindustrie* (Mohr Siebeck 2014)
Merills John, 'International Adjudication and Autonomy' in Richard Collins and Nigel D White (eds), *International Organizations and the Idea of Autonomy - Institutional Independence in the International Legal Order* (Routledge 2011) 160
Merry Sally Engle, Davis Kevin E and Kingsbury Benedict (eds), *The Quiet Power of Indicators: Measuring Governance, Corruption, and Rule of Law* (Cambridge University Press 2015)
Meyer-Ladewig Jens and Peters Birgit, 'Art. 35' in Jens Meyer-Ladewig, Martin Nettesheim and Stefan von Raumer (eds), *Europäische Menschenrechtskonvention* (4th edn, Nomos 2017)
Michaels Ralf, 'Comparative Law by Numbers? Legal Origins Thesis, Doing Business Reports, and the Silence of Traditional Comparative Law' (2009) 57 American Journal of Comparative Law 765
Milman-Silvan Faina, 'Freedom of Association in Deliberative Spaces: The ILO Credentials Committee' in Adelle Blackett and Anne Trebilcock (eds), *Research Handbook on Transnational Labour Law* (Edward Elgar Publishing 2015) 204
Mohr Manfred, 'The Turin Protocol of 22 October 1991: A Major Contribution to Revitalizing the European Social Charter' (1992) 3 European Journal of International Law 362
Mola Lorenza, 'Governance of Financial Crises: A Role for the International Protection of Economic and Social Rights?' in Photini Pazartzis and Maria Gavouneli (eds), *Reconceptualizing the Rule of Law in Global Governnce, Resources, Investment and Trade* (Hart Publishing 2016) 105

Möldner Mirka, 'Responsibility of International Organizations – Introducing the ILC's DARIO' (2012) 16 Max Planck Yearbook of United Nations Law, 281

Möllers Christoph, *Gewaltengliederung: Legitimation und Dogmatik im Nationalen und Internationalen Rechtsvergleich* (Mohr Siebeck 2005)

Morgenstern Felice, *Legal Problems of International Organizations* (Grotius Publications 1986)

Morsink Johannes, *The Universal Declaration of Human Rights: Origins, Drafting, and Intent* (University of Pennsylvania Press 1999)

Mosler Hermann, 'Die Erweiterung des Kreises der Völkerrechtssubjekte' (1962) 22 Zeitschrift für ausländisches öffentliches Recht und Völkerrecht 1

Murphy Hannah, 'The World Bank and Core Labour Standards: Between Flexibility and Regulation' (2014) 21 Review of International Political Economy 399

Neframi Eleftheria, 'The Duty of Loyalty: Rethinking Its Scope Through Its Application in the Field of EU External Relations' (2010) 47 Common Market Law Review 323

Neumann Jan, 'Die materielle und prozessuale Koordination völkerrechtlicher Ordnungen - Die Problematik paralleler Streitbeilegungsverfahren am Beispiel des Schwertfisch-Falls' (2001) 61 Zeitschrift für ausländisches öffentliches Recht und Völkerrecht 529

Nollkaemper André, 'Inside or out: Two Types of International Legal Pluralism' in Jan Klabbers and Touko Piiparinen (eds), *Normative pluralism and international law: exploring global governance* (Cambridge University Press 2013) 94

Nolte Georg, 'Jurisprudence Under Special Regimes Relating to Subsequent Agreements and Subsequent Practice' in Georg Nolte (ed), *Treaties and Subsequent Practice* (Oxford University Press 2013) 210

Novitz Tonia, 'Core Labour Standards Conditionalities: A Means by Which to Achieve Sustainable Development?' in Julio Faundez and Celine Tan (eds), *International Economic Law, Globalization and Developing Countries* (Edward Elgar Publishing 2010) 234

—— *International and European Protection of the Right to Strike* (Oxford University Press 2003)

—— 'The Restricted Right to Strike: "Far-Reaching" ILO Jurisprudence on the Public Sector and Essential Services' (2017) 38 Comparative Labor Law and Policy Journal 353

Nowrot Karsten, *Normative Ordnungsstruktur und private Wirkungsmacht* (BWV 2006)

Nunner Michael, *Kooperationen internationaler Gerichte - Lösung zwischengerichtlicher Konflikte durch herrschaftsfreien Diskurs* (Mohr Siebeck 2009)

Nußberger Angelika, 'Auswirkungen Der Rechtsprechung des Europäischen Gerichtshofs für Menschenrechte auf das Deutsche Arbeitsrecht' [2012] Recht der Arbeit 270

—— 'The ECtHR' Use of Decisions of International Courts and Quasi-Judicial Bodies' in Amrei Müller and Hege Elisabeth Kjos (eds), *Judicial Dialogue and Human Rights* (Cambridge University Press 2017) 419

Oberthür Sebastian and Gehring Thomas, 'Reforming International Environmental Governance: An Institutionalist Critique of the Proposal for a World Environment Organisation' (2004) 4 International Environmental Agreements: Politics, Law and Economics 359

—— 'Conceptual Foundations of Institutional Interaction' in Sebastian Oberthür and Thomas Gehring (eds), *Institutional Interaction in Global Environmental Governance. Synergy and Conflict among International and EU Policies* (MIT Press 2006a) 19

—— 'Institutional Interaction in Global Environmental Governance: The Case of the Cartagena Protocol and the World Trade Organization' (2006b) 6 Global Environmental Politics 1

Olmos Giupponi María Belén, 'Free Trade and Labour and Environmental Standards in MERCOSUR' (2014) 81 Colombia Internacional 67

Orbie Jan, Putte Lore van den and Martens Deborah, 'Civil Society Meetings in European Union Free Trade Agreements: The Purposes Unravelled' in Henner Gött (ed), *Labour Standards in International Economic Law* (Springer 2018) 135

Orakhelashvili Alexander, 'Art. 30 VCLT-IO' in Olivier Corten and Pierre Klein (eds), *The Vienna Conventions on the Law of Treaties - A Commentary, vol 1* (Oxford University Press 2011)

Osieke Ebere, *Constitutional Law and Practice in the International Labour Organization* (Martinus Nijhoff Publishers 1985)

Oxford Living Dictionaries English (Oxford University Press 2018) entry 'interaction'
Pahle Simon, 'The Rise and Demise of the "Social Clause" Proposal in the 1990s: Implications of a Discourse Theoretical Reading' (2010) 51 Labor History 389
Pasquet Luca, 'Dialogue or Interaction? A Non-Cosmopolitan Reading of Transjudicial Communication' in Amrei Müller and Hege Elisabeth Kjos (eds), *Judicial Dialogue and Human Rights* (Cambridge University Press 2017) 467
Paulus Andreas L, *Die Internationale Gemeinschaft Im Völkerrecht* (C H Beck 2001)
—— 'The International Legal System as a Constitution' in Jeffrey L Dunoff and Joel P Trachtman (eds), *Ruling the World? Constitutionalism, International Law, and Global Governance* (Cambridge University Press 2009) 69
—— and Johann Ruben Leiß, 'Art. 103' in Bruno Simma and others (eds), *The Charter of the United Nations - A Commentary, vol II* (3rd edn, Oxford University Press 2013)
Pauwelyn Joost, 'Typology of Multilateral Treaty Obligations: Are WTO Obligations Bilateral or Collective in Nature?' (2003a) 14 European Journal of International Law 907
—— 'Bridging Fragmentation and Unity: International Law as a Universe of Inter-Connected Islands' (2004) 25 Michigan Journal of International Law 903
—— *Conflict of Norms in Public International Law: How WTO Law Relates to Other Rules of International Law* (Cambridge University Press 2003b)
Pellet Alain, International Organizations are Definitely not States - Cursory Remarks on the ILC Articles on the Responsibility of International Organizations, in Maurizio Ragazzi (ed.), *Responsibility of International Organizations, Essays in Memory of Sir Ian Brownlie* (Martinus Nijhoff Publishers 2013) 41
Peters Anne, 'Das Gründungsdokument Internationaler Organisationen als Verfassungsvertrag' (2013) 68 Zeitschrift für Öffentliches Recht 1
—— 'Rechtsordnungen und Konstitutionalisierung: Zur Neubestimmung der Verhältnisse' (2010) 65 Zeitschrift für Öffentliches Recht 3
—— 'The Refinement of International Law: From Fragmentation to Regime Interaction and Politicization' (2017) 15 International Journal of Constitutional Law 671
Peters Christopher, 'Subsequent Practice and Established Practice of International Organizations: Two Sides of the Same Coin?' (2011) 3 Goettingen Journal of International Law 617
—— *Praxis Internationaler Organisationen - Vertragswandel und völkerrechtlicher Ordnungsrahmen* (Springer 2016)
Pfaff-Czarnecka Joanna, 'No End to Nepal's Maoist Rebellion' (2005) 46 Focaal, European Journal of Anthropology 158
Polakiewicz Jörg, 'Alternatives to Treaty-Making and Law-Making by Treaty and Expert Bodies in the Council of Europe' in Rüdiger Wolfrum and Volker Röben (eds), *Developments of International Law in Treaty Making* (Springer 2005) 245
—— 'Council of Europe (COE)', *Max Planck Encyclopedia of Public International Law* (Oxford University Press 2013)
—— *Treaty-Making in the Council of Europe* (Council of Europe Publishing 1999)
Politakis George P, 'Deconstructing Flexibility in International Labour Conventions' in Jean-Claude Javillier, Bernard Gernigon and George P Politakis (eds), *Les Normes Internationales du Travail: Un Patrimoine pour l'Avenir: Mélanges en l'Honneur de Nicolas Valticos* (ILO 2004) 463
Pons-Deladrière Geneviève, 'European Union Participation and Cooperation in ILO Institu-tions and Activities: An ILO Perspective', in: Christina Kaddous (ed), *The European Un-ion in International Organisations and Global Governance* (Hart Publishing 2017) 93.
Pop Iftene, *Components of Good Neighbourliness between States* (Editura RAI 1991)
Portela Clara and Orbie Jan, 'Sanctions under the EU Generalised System of Preferences and Foreign Policy: Coherence by Accident?' in Maurizio Carbone and Jan Orbie (eds), *The Trade-Development Nexus in the European Union: Differentiation, Coherence and Norms* (Routledge 2016) 63
Portmann Roland, *Legal Personality in International Law* (Cambridge University Press 2010)

Proelß Alexander, 'Art 34 VCLT' in Oliver Dörr and Kirsten Schmalenbach (eds), *Vienna Convention on the Law of Treaties - A Commentary* (2nd edn, Springer 2018)

Pulkowski Dirk, *The Law and Politics of International Regime Conflict* (Oxford University Press 2014)

Rachovitsa Adamantia, 'The Principle of Systematic Integration in Human Rights Law' (2017) 66 International and Comparative Law Quarterly 557

Ragazzi Maurizio, 'World Bank Group', *Max Planck Encyclopedia of Public International Law* (Oxford University Press 2014)

Ranganathan Surabhi, 'The Value of Narratives: The India-USA Nuclear Deal in Terms of Fragmentation, Pluralism, Constitutionalisation and Global Administrative Law' (2013) 6 Erasmus Law Review 17

Reed Austina and Yates Charlotte, 'The ILO Declaration on Fundamental Principles and Rights at Work: The Limitations to Global Labour Standards' in Maureen Irish (ed), *The Auto Pact: Investment, Labour, and the WTO* (Kluwer Law International 2004) 243

Reinhold Steven, 'Good Faith in International Law' (2013) 2 UCL Journal of Law and Jurisprudence 40

Reinisch August, 'Securing the Accountability of International Organizations' (2001) 7 Global Governance 131

—— 'The Sources of International Organizations' Law – Why Custom and General Principles Are Crucial' in Samantha Besson and Jean D'Aspremont (eds), *The Oxford Handbook on the Sources of International Law* (2017) 1007

Rensmann Thilo, 'Art. 46 VCLT' in Oliver Dörr and Kirsten Schmalenbach (eds), *Vienna Convention on the Law of Treaties - A Commentary* (2nd edn, Springer 2018)

—— 'International Organizations or Institutions, External Relations and Co-Operation', *Max Planck Encyclopedia of Public International Law* (Oxford University Press 2009)

Ress Georg, 'Die Organisationsstruktur internationaler Gerichte, insbesondere des neuen Europäischen Gerichtshofs Für Menschenrechte' in Alfred Rest and others (eds), *Liber Amicorum Professor Ignaz Seidl-Hohenveldern* (Brill 1998) 541

Riegner Michael, *Informationsverwaltungsrecht Internationaler Organisationen. Dargestellt am Entwicklungsverwaltungsrecht der Weltbank und der Vereinten Nationen* (Mohr Siebeck 2018)

—— 'Measuring the Good Governance State: A Legal Reconstruction of the World Bank's "Country Policy and Institutional Assessment"' (2016) 19 Journal of International Economic Law 1

Rigaux Francois, 'Hans Kelsen on International Law' (1998) 9 European Journal of International Law 325

Rittberger Volker and others, 'Inclusive Global Institutions for a Global Political Economy' in Volker Rittberger, Martin Nettesheim and Carmen Huckel (eds), *Authority in the Global Political Economy* (Palgrave Macmillan 2008) 21

Rittich Kerry, 'The ILO: Challenges in Times of Crisis' (2015) 154 International Labour Review 85

Röben Volker, 'Art. 62' in Bruno Simma and others (eds), *The Charter of the United Nations - A Commentary, vol II* (3rd edn, Oxford University Press 2013)

Robertson Arthur Henry, *Constitutional Developments in the Council of Europe* (Institut d'Études Européennes 1964)

—— *The Council of Europe: Its Structure, Functions and Achievements* (Stevens & Sons 1956)

—— *The Relations Between the Council of Europe and the United Nations* (UNITAR 1972)

Rödl Florian, 'Regime-Collisions, Proceduralised Conflict of Laws and the Unity of the Law: On the Form of Constitutionalism Beyond the State' in Rainer Nickel (ed), *Conflict of Laws and Laws of Conflict in Europe and Beyond - Patterns of Supranational and Transnational Juridification* (ARENA 2009) 341

Rolin Henri, 'Les principes de droit international public' (1950-II) 77 Recueil des Cours de l'Académie de Droit International 305

Rosenne Shabtai, *Developments in the Law of Treaties 1945–1986* (Cambridge University Press 1989)

Roth Brad R, *Sovereign Equality and Moral Disagreement – Premises of a Pluralist International Legal Order* (Oxford University Press 2011)
Ruffert Matthias, 'Zuständigkeitsgrenzen Internationaler Organisationen im institutionellen Rahmen der internationalen Gemeinschaft' (2000) 38 Archiv des Völkerrechts 129
—— and Walter Christian, *Institutionalisiertes Völkerrecht* (2nd edn, C H Beck 2015)
Rüthers Bernd, *Rechtstheorie* (10th edn, C H Beck 2018)
Ryngaert Cedric, *Jurisdiction in International Law* (2nd edn, Oxford University Press 2015)
Samuels Joel, 'Condominium Arrangements in International Practice: Reviving an Abandoned Concept of Boundary Dispute Resolution' (2008) 29 Michigan Journal of International Law 727
Sands Philippe, Klein Pierre and Bowett David W, *Bowett's Law of International Institutions* (6th edn, Sweet & Maxwell 2009)
Santos Alvaro, 'Labor Flexibility, Legal Reform and Economic Development' (2009) 50 Virginia Journal of International Law 43
Sauer Heiko, 'International Labour Organization', *Max Planck Encyclopedia of Public International Law* (Oxford University Press 2014)
Saunders Imogen, 'General Principles of Law and a Source-Based Approach to the Regulation of International Security Institutions' in Hitoshi Nasu and Kim Rubenstein (eds), *Legal Perspectives on Security Institutions* (Cambridge University Press 2015) 123
Savino Mario, 'Linkages Between Global Regimes and Interactions with Civil Society' in Sabino Cassese (ed), *Research Handbook on Global Administrative Law* (Edward Elgar Publishing 2016) 131
Schabas William A, *The European Convention on Human Rights - A Commentary* (Oxford University Press 2015)
Scharpf Fritz Wilhelm, 'Economic Integration, Democracy and the Welfare State' (1997) 4 Journal of European Public Policy 18
—— *Governing in Europe: Effective and Democratic?* (Oxford University Press 1999)
Schermers Henry G, 'The Legal Bases of International Organization Action', in: René-Jean Dupuy (ed), *A Handbook on International Organizations* (Martinus Nijhoff Publishers 1998) 401
—— and Blokker Niels M, 'International Organizations or Institutions, Membership', *Max Planck Encyclopedia of Public International Law* (Oxford University Press 2008)
———, *International Institutional Law* (6th edn, Brill 2018)
Schill Stephan W, 'Multilateral Investment Guarantee Agency (MIGA)', *Max Planck Encyclopedia of Public International Law* (Oxford University Press 2014)
Schlemmer-Schulte Sabine, 'International Bank for Reconstruction and Development (IBRD)', *Max Planck Encyclopedia of Public International Law* (Oxford University Press 2014a)
—— 'International Monetary Fund, Structural Adjustment Programme (SAP)', *Max Planck Encyclopedia of Public International Law* (Oxford University Press 2014b)
Schmahl Stefanie, 'The Council of Europe Within the System of International Organizations' in Stefanie Schmahl and Marten Breuer (eds), *The Council of Europe: Its Laws and Policies* (Oxford University Press 2017) 875
Schmalenbach Kirsten, 'Art. 5 VCLT' in Oliver Dörr and Kirsten Schmalenbach (eds), *Vienna Convention on the Law of Treaties: A Commentary* (2nd edn, Springer 2018a)
—— 'Art. 6 VCLT' in Oliver Dörr and Kirsten Schmalenbach (eds), *Vienna Convention on the Law of Treaties - A Commentary* (2nd edn, Springer 2018b)
Schneider JW, *Treaty-Making Power of International Organizations* (Droz/Minard 1959)
Schreuer Christoph, 'International Centre for Settlement of Investment Disputes (ICSID)', *Max Planck Encyclopedia of Public International Law* (Oxford University Press 2013)
Schueth Sam, 'Assembling International Competitiveness: The Republic of Georgia, USAID, and the Doing Business Project' (2011) 87 Economic Geography 51
Schwebel Stephen M, 'The Prescience and Pertinence of the ILO' in International Labour Office (ed), *Visions of the Future of Social Justice: Essays on the Occasion of the ILO's 75th Anniversary* (ILO 1994) 257

Schweißfurth Theodor, 'International Treaties and Third States' (1985) 45 Zeitschrift für ausländisches öffentliches Recht und Völkerrecht 653
Seidl-Hohenveldern Ignaz and Loibl Gerhard, *Das Recht der Internationalen Organisationen* (7th edn, Heymann 2000)
Servais Jean-Michel, *International Labour Law* (4th edn, Kluwer Law International 2014)
Seyersted Finn, *Common Law of International Organizations* (Martinus Nijhoff Publishers 2008)
—— *Objective Legal Personality of Intergovernmental Organizations – Do Their Capacities Really Depend Upon Their Constitutions?* (Copenhagen 1963)
Shaw Jo, 'Postnational Constitutionalism in the European Union' (1999) 6 Journal of European Public Policy 579
Shaw Malcolm N, *International Law* (8th edn, Cambridge University Press 2017)
Shihata Ibrahim FI, 'The Creative Role of the Lawyer – Example: The Office of the World Bank's General Counsel' (1999) 48 Catholic University Law Review 1041
—— *The World Bank Legal Papers* (Springer 2000)
—— *The World Bank in a Changing World* (Springer 1991)
Shotwell James T, *The Origins of the International Labour Organization, Volume 1: History* (Columbia University Press 1934)
Simma Bruno, 'From Bilateralism to Community Interest in International Law' (1994) 250 Recueil des Cours de l'Académie de Droit International 217
—— and Kill Theodore, 'Harmonising Investment Protection and International Human Rights: First Steps towards A Methodology' in Christina Binder and others (eds), *International Investment Law for the 21st Century* (Oxford University Press 2009) 678
Sinclair Guy Fiti, 'The Original Sin (and Salvation) of Functionalism' (2015) 26 European Journal of International Law 965
Singh Nagendra, *Termination of Membership of International Organizations* (Frederick A Praeger 1958)
Skogly Sigrun, *The Human Rights Obligations of the World Bank and the IMF* (Cavendish Publishing 2001)
Slaughter Anne-Marie, *A New World Order* (Princeton University Press 2004)
Spiermann Ole, 'Lotus and the Double Structure of International Legal Argument' in Laurence Boisson De Chazournes and Philippe Sands (eds), *International Law, the International Court of Justice and Nuclear Weapons* (Cambridge University Press 1999) 131
Ssenyonjo Manisuli, 'The Applicability of International Human Rights Law to Non-State Actors: What Relevance to Economic, Social and Cultural Rights?' (2008) 12 The International Journal of Human Rights 725
Stahn Carsten, 'The ICC, Pre-Existing Jurisdictional Treaty Regimes, and the Limits of the Nemo Dat Quod Non Habet Doctrine - A Reply to Michael Newton' (2016) 49 Vanderbilt Journal of Transnational Law 443
Standing Guy, 'The ILO: An Agency for Globalization?' (2008) 39 Development and Change 355
Steffek Jens, 'The Output Legitimacy of International Organizations and the Global Public Interest' (2015) 7 International Theory 263
Stein Eric, 'Lawyers, Judges, and the Making of a Transnational Constitution' (1981) 75 American Journal of International Law 1
Stewart Richard B and Ratton Sanchez Badin Michelle, 'The World Trade Organization and Global Administrative Law' (2009) IILJ Working Paper 2009/7 (Global Administrative Law Series) <https://www.iilj.org/publications/the-world-trade-organization-and-global-administrative-law/> accessed 26 April 2020
Stokke Olav Schram, 'The Interplay of International Regimes: Putting Effectiveness Theory to Work' (2001) FNI Report 14/2001
Stoll Peter-Tobias, 'Global Governance and the Private Sector' in Joachim Ahrens, Rolf Caspers and Janina Weingarth (eds), *Good Governance in the 21st Century Conflict, Institutional Change, and Development in the Era of Globalization* (Edward Elgar Publishing 2011a) 263

—— 'Global Public Goods: The Governance Dimension' in Volker Rittberger, Martin Nettesheim and Carmen Huckel (eds), *Authority in the Global Political Economy* (Palgrave Macmillan 2008) 116

—— 'Koordination, Kooperation und Konstitutionalisierung im Völkerrecht' in Werner Heun and Frank Schorkopf (eds), *Wendepunkte der Rechtswissenschaft - Aspekte des Rechts in der Moderne* (Wallstein Verlag 2014a) 273

—— 'International Economic and Social Dimensions: Divided or Connected?' in Henner Gött (ed), *Labour Standards in International Economic Law* (Springer 2018a) 11

—— 'The World Trade Organization as a Club: Rethinking Reciprocity and Common Interest' in Ulrich Fastenrath and others (eds), *From Bilateralism to Community Interest: Essays in Honour of Bruno Simma* (Oxford University Press 2011b) 172

—— 'World Trade Organization, Dispute Settlement', *Max Planck Encyclopedia of Public International Law* (Oxford University Press 2014b)

—— Gött Henner and Abel Patrick, 'A Model Labour Chapter for Future EU Trade Agreements' in Henner Gött (ed), *Labour Standards in International Economic Law* (Springer 2018b) 381

Stone Julius, 'Non Liquet and the Function of Law in the International Community' (1959) 35 British Yearbook of International Law 124

Sucharitkul Sompong, 'The Principles of Good-Neighborliness in International Law' (1996) Golden Gate University School of Law Publications, Paper 559 <https://digitalcommons.law.ggu.edu/cgi/viewcontent.cgi?article=1559&context=pubs> accessed 26 April 2020

Supiot Alain, 'A Legal Perspective on the Economic Crisis of 2008' (2010) 149 International Labour Review 151

Suy Erik, 'The Status of Observers in International Organizations' (1978) 160 Recueil des Cours de l'Académie de Droit International 75

Swepston Lee, 'Human Rights Law and Freedom of Association: Development Through ILO Supervision' (1998) 137 International Labour Review 169

Szasz Paul C, 'The Complexification of the United Nations System' (1999) 3 Max Planck Yearbook of United Nations Law 1

Teubner Gunther and Fischer-Lescano Andreas, 'Regime-Collisions: The Vain Search for Legal Unity in the Fragmentation of Global Law' (2004) 25 Michigan Journal of International Law 999

Thomann Lars, 'The ILO, Tripartism, and NGOs: Do Too Many Cooks Really Spoil the Broth?' in Jens Steffek, Claudia Kissling and Patrizia Nanz (eds), *Civil Society Participation in European and Global Governance. A Cure for the Democratic Deficit?* (Palgrave Macmillan 2008) 71

Tietje Christian, 'Die völkerrechtliche Kooperationspflicht im Spannungsverhältnis Welthandel/Umweltschutz und ihre Bedeutung für die Europäische Umweltblume' [2000] Europarecht 285

—— 'Global Governance and Inter-Agency Co-Operation in International Economic Law' (2002) 36 Journal of World Trade 501

—— 'The Duty to Cooperate in International Economic Law and Beyond' in Jost Delbrück (ed) *International Law of Cooperation and State Sovereignty* (Duncker & Humblot 2001) 45

Tikriti Abdul-Karim, *Tripartism and the International Labour Organization* (Almqvist & Wiksell International 1982)

Tomuschat Christian, 'International Law: Ensuring the Survival of Mankind on the Eve of a New Century' (1999) 281 Recueil des Cours de l'Académie de Droit International 9

Trebilcock Anne, 'The Maritime Labour Convention 2006: Breathing Life into Art. 94 of UNCLOS' (2010) 1 LOS Reports 1

—— 'The International Labour Organization' in Michael J Bowman and Dino Kritsiotis (eds), *Conceptual and Contextual Perspectives on the Modern Law of Treaties* (Cambridge University Press 2018) 848

Tsangalis Rologas Amanda, 'Fisheries Subsidies under the Trans-Pacific Partnership: Towards Positive Outcomes for Global Fisheries Sustainability and Regime Interaction under International Law' (2016) 17 Melbourne Journal of International Law 445

Tunkin Grigory, 'International Law in the International System' (1975) 147 Recueil des Cours de l'Académie de Droit International 1
UIA, 'Arab Labour Organization (ALO)' (*UIA Open Yearbook*, 2015)
Ulfstein Geir, 'Evolutive Interpretation in the Light of Other International Instruments: Law and Legitimacy' in Anne van Aaken and Iulia Motoc (eds), *The European Convention on Human Rights and General International Law* (Oxford University Press 2018) 83
—— 'Institutions and Competences' in Jan Klabbers, Anne Peters and Geir Ulfstein (eds), *The Constitutionalization of International Law* (Oxford University Press 2009) 45
Valticos Nicolas and von Potobsky Geraldo W, *International Labour Law* (2nd edn, Kluwer 1995)
van Aaken Anne, 'Defragmentation of Public International Law through Interpretation: A Methodological Proposal' (2009) 16 Indiana Journal of Global Legal Studies 483
van Daele Jasmien, 'Engineering Social Peace, Peace: Networks, Ideas, and the Founding of the International Labour Organization' (2005) 50 International Review of Social History 435
van der Kooy Henne, 'What is the Substance of Tripartism in the International Labour Organisation?: Criteria for the Verification of Credentials at the International Labour Conferences' (1977) 8 Netherlands Yearbook of International Law 73
van Damme Isabelle, 'Treaty Interpretation by the Appellate Body' (2010) 21 European Journal of International Law 605
van Genugten Willem, *The World Bank Group, the IMF and Human Rights - A Contextualised Way Forward* (Intersentia 2015a)
—— 'Tilburg-GLOTHRO Guiding Principles on the World Bank Group, the International Monetary Fund and Human Rights', *The World Bank Group, the IMF and Human Rights: A Contextualised Way Forward* (Intersentia 2015b) 55
van Reenen Willem, 'Rules of Reference in the New Convention on the Law of the Sea, in Particular in Connection with the Pollution of the Sea by Oil from Tankers' (1981) 12 Netherlands Yearbook of International Law 3
Veldman Albertine, 'The Protection of the Fundamental Right to Strike within the Context of the European Internal Market: Implications of the Forthcoming Accession of the EU to the ECHR' (2013) 9 Utrecht Law Review 104
Verdirame Guglielmo, *The UN and Human Rights: Who Guards the Guardians?* (Cambridge University Press 2011)
Verdross Alfred and Simma Bruno, *Universelles Völkerrecht* (3rd edn, Duncker & Humblot 1984)
Villiger Mark Eugen, 'Art. 5' in Mark Eugen Villiger (ed), *Commentary on the 1969 Vienna Convention on the Law of Treaties* (Brill 2009a)
—— 'Art. 31' in Mark Eugen Villiger (ed), *Commentary on the 1969 Vienna Convention on the Law of Treaties* (Brill 2009b)
—— 'Art. 34' in Mark Eugen Villiger (ed), *Commentary on the 1969 Vienna Convention on the Law of Treaties* (Brill 2009c)
Vogt Jeffrey, 'A Little Less Conversation: The EU and the (Non)Application of Labour Conditionality in the Generalized System of Preferences (GSP)' (2015) 31 The International Journal of Comparative Labour Law and Industrial Relations 284
von Arnauld Andreas, *Völkerrecht* (3rd edn, C F Müller 2016)
von Bogdandy Armin, 'General Principles of International Public Authority: Sketching a Research Field' (2008) 9 German Law Journal 1909
von der Decken Kerstin, 'Art 30 VCLT' in Oliver Dörr and Kirsten Schmalenbach (eds), *Vienna Convention on the Law of Treaties - A Commentary* (2nd edn, Springer 2018)
Vöneky Silja, 'Analogy in International Law', *Max Planck Encyclopedia of Public Interna-tional Law* (Oxford University Press 2008)
Waeyenberge Elisa van, 'Selectivity at Work: Country Policy and Institutional Assessments at the World Bank' (2009) 21 European Journal of Development Research 792
Walter Christian, 'Interpretation and Amendments of the Founding Treaty' in Stefanie Schmahl and Marten Breuer (eds), *The Council of Europe: Its Laws and Policies* (Oxford University Press 2017) 23

—— 'International Law in a Process of Constitutionalization' in Janne E Nijman and André Nollkaemper (eds), *New Perspectives on the Divide Between National and International Law* (Oxford University Press 2007a) 191

—— 'Subjects of International Law', *Max Planck Encyclopedia of Public International Law* (Oxford University Press 2007b)

Wassenberg Birte, *History of the Council of Europe* (Council of Europe Publishing 2013)

Watzlawick Paul, Beavin Janet H and Jackson Don D, *Menschliche Kommunikation. Formen, Störungen, Paradoxien* (11th edn, Huber 2007)

Weaver Catherine, 'The World's Bank and the Bank's World' (2007) 13 Global Governance 492

Weaver Jane D and Wilcox-Staats Ann, 'The World Bank Group' (1986) 1 American University International Law Review 391

Weinschel Herbert, 'The Doctrine of the Equality of States and Its Recent Modifications' (1951) 45 American Journal of International Law 417

Weiss Friedl, 'Trade and Labor I' in Patrick FJ Macrory, Arthur E Appleton and Michael G Plummer (eds), *The World Trade Organization: Legal, Economic and Political Analysis Vol II* (Springer 2005) 571

Werner Wouter, 'The Never-Ending Closure: Constitutionalism and International Law' in Nicholas Tsagourias (ed), *Transnational Constitutionalism: International and European Perspectives* (Cambridge University Press 2007) 329

Wetzel Ralf Günther and Rauschning Dietrich, 'Waldock Report IV' in Ralf Günther Wetzel and Dietrich Rauschning (eds), *Commentary on the 1969 Vienna Convention on the Law of Treaties, Travaux préparatoires* (Metzner 1978) 90

White Nigel D, *The Law of International Organizations* (2nd edn, Juris Publishing 2005)

Wildhaber Luzius, 'The European Convention on Human Rights and International Law' (2007) 56 International and Comparative Law Quarterly 217

Williams Douglas, *The Specialized Agencies and the United Nations – A System in Crisis* (Hurst 1987)

Winkler Tobias, *Die Vereinten Nationen im Gefüge der internationalen Organisationen – Eine rechtsdogmatische Untersuchung* (Nomos 2019)

Wisskirchen Alfred, 'The Standard-Setting and Monitoring Activity of the ILO: Legal Questions and Practical Experience' (2005) 144 International Labour Review 253

Wittinger Michaela, *Der Europarat: Die Entwicklung seines Rechts und der 'Europäischen Verfassungswerte'* (Nomos 2005)

Wittreck Fabian, *Die Verwaltung der dritten Gewalt* (Mohr Siebeck 2006)

Woeste Peter and Thomma Thomas, 'Art. 17' in Bruno Simma and others (eds), *The Charter of the United Nations - A Commentary, vol I* (3rd edn, Oxford University Press 2012)

Wolfrum Rüdiger, 'Art. 1' in Bruno Simma and others (eds), *The Charter of the United Nations - A Commentary, vol I* (3 edn, Oxford University Press 2012)

—— 'Sources of International Law', *Max Planck Encyclopedia of Public International Law* (Oxford University Press 2011)

Wood Michael, 'International Organizations and Customary International Law (2014 Jonathan J Charney Distinguished Lecture in Public International Law)' (2015) 48 Vanderbilt Journal of Transnational Law 609

—— 'The Present Position within the ILC on the Topic "Identification of Customary International Law": in Partial Response to Sienho Yee, Report on the ILC Project on "Identification of Customary International Law"' (2016) 15 Chinese Journal of International Law 3

World Bank, *A Guide to the World Bank* (3rd edn, World Bank 2011)

World Bank and OECD, *Integrating Human Right into Development* (2013)

Worster William Thomas, 'Relative International Legal Personality of Non-State Actors' (2016) 42 Brooklyn Journal of International Law 207

Wouters Jan and Odermatt Jed, 'Are All International Organizations Created Equal?' (2012) 9 International Organizations Law Review 7

Young Margaret A, *Trading Fish, Saving Fish: The Interaction Between Regimes in International Law* (Cambridge University Press 2011)

———, 'Regime Interaction in Creating, Implementing and Enforcing International Law' in Margaret A Young (ed), *Regime Interaction in International Law - Facing Fragmentation* (Cambridge University Press 2012a) 85

———, *Regime Interaction in International Law - Facing Fragmentation* (Cambridge University Press 2012b)

———, 'Introduction: The Productive Friction between Regimes' in Margaret A Young (ed), *Regime Interaction in International Law - Facing Fragmentation* (Cambridge University Press 2012c) 1

Young Oran R, 'Institutional Linkages in International Society: Polar Perspectives' (1996) 2 Global Governance 1

Zelenev Sergei, 'Universal Social Protection: The World Bank Group and ILO Join Forces in Launching the Universal Social Protection Initiative' (2015) 58 International Social Work 840

Zemanek Karl, *Das Vertragsrecht der Internationalen Organisationen* (Springer 1959)

—— 'Vienna Convention on the Law of Treaties between States and International Organizations or between International Organizations - Introductory Note' (2009) United Nations Audiovisual Library of International Law <https://legal.un.org/avl/ha/vcltsio/vcltsio.html> accessed 26 April 2020

Zwanenburg Marten C, *Accountability Of Peace Support Operations* (Martinus Nijhoff Publishers 2005)

Index

H. Gött, *The Law of Interactions Between International Organizations*, Beiträge zum ausländischen öffentlichen Recht und Völkerrecht 299,
https://doi.org/10.1007/978-3-662-62389-3

Max-Planck-Institut für ausländisches öffentliches Recht und Völkerrecht

Beiträge zum ausländischen öffentlichen Recht und Völkerrecht

Hrsg.: A. von Bogdandy, A. Peters

Bde. 27–59 erschienen im Carl Heymanns Verlag KG Köln, Berlin (Bestellung an: Max-Planck-Institut für Völkerrecht, Im Neuenheimer Feld 535, 69120 Heidelberg); ab Band 60 im Springer-Verlag GmbH

299 Henner *Gött*: **The Law of Interactions Between International Organizations**. 2021. XXIII, 523 Seiten. Geb. € 149,99 zzgl. landesüblicher MwSt.

298 Armin *von Bogdandy*, Piotr *Bogdanowicz*, Iris *Canor*, Christoph *Grabenwarter*, Maciej *Taborowski*, Matthias *Schmidt* (eds.): **Defending Checks and Balances in EU Member States**. 2021. X, 480 Seiten. Geb. € 49,99 zzgl. landesüblicher MwSt. Open Access

297 Valentina *Volpe*, Anne *Peters*, Stefano *Battini* (eds.): **Remedies against Immunity?**. 2021. XXXIV, 425 Seiten. Geb. € 49,99 zzgl. landesüblicher MwSt. Open Access

296 Björnstjern *Baade*, Dana *Burchardt*, Prisca *Feihle*, Alicia *Köppen*, Linus *Mührel*, Lena *Riemer*, Raphael *Schäfer* (eds.): **Cynical International Law?**. 2021. XVI, 369 Seiten. Geb. € 139,99 zzgl. landesüblicher MwSt.

295 Layla Kristina *Jaber*, Stefanie *Lüer*, Anne-Marie *Thévenot-Werner* (Hrsg.): **Rechtsweggarantie im vergleichenden Verwaltungsrecht**. 2021, XIV, 247 Seiten. Geb. € 99,99

294 Desirée C. *Schmitt*: **Familienzusammenführung und Rechtsschutz in Deutschland und den USA**. 2020. XXIV, 719 Seiten. Geb. € 129,99

H. Gött, *The Law of Interactions Between International Organizations*, Beiträge zum ausländischen öffentlichen Recht und Völkerrecht 299,
https://doi.org/10.1007/978-3-662-62389-3

293 Andrej *Lang*: **Die Verfassungsgerichtsbarkeit in der vernetzten Weltordnung**. 2020. XXVII, 646 Seiten. Geb. € 119,99

292 Raffaela *Kunz*: **Richter über internationale Gerichte?**. 2020. XIV, 275 Seiten. Geb. € 53,49. Open Access

291 Adele *Kirschner*: **Grenzüberschreitende Implikationen eines Menschenrechts auf Wasser?**. 2020. XVIII, 257 Seiten. Geb. € 89,99

290 Anne *Peters* (ed.): **Studies in Global Animal Law**. 2020. VIII, 183 Seiten. Geb. € 49,99 zzgl. landesüblicher MwSt. Open Access

289 Oliver *Strank*: **Common Concern of Humankind im Völkerrecht**. 2019. XXVIII, 666 Seiten. Geb. € 119,99

288 Alix *Schlüter*: **Beweisfragen in der Rechtsprechung des Europäischen Gerichtshof für Menschenrechte**. 2019. XVIII, 500 Seiten. Geb. € 119,99

287 Martin Philipp *Sommerfeld*: **Staatensouveränität und ius cogens**. 2019. XVI, 424 Seiten. Geb. € 99,99

286 Laura *Hering*: **Fehlerfolgen im europäischen Eigenverwaltungsrecht**. 2019. XXI, 385 Seiten. Geb. € 99,99

285 Marten *Breuer* (ed.): **Principled Resistance to ECtHR Judgments - A New Paradigm?**. 2019. XVIII, 350 Seiten. Geb. € 109,99 zzgl. landesüblicher MwSt.

284 Stephan G. *Hinghofer-Szalkay*: **Verfassungsrechtsentwicklung aus rechtstatsächlicher Perspektive**. 2019. XVII, 383 Seiten. Geb. € 109,99

283 Arthur *Brunner*: **Subsidiaritätsgrundsatz und Tatsachenfeststellung unter der Europäischen Menschenrechtskonvention**. 2019. XVI, 188 Seiten. Geb. € 53,49. Open Access

282 María Pía *Carazo Ortiz*: **Das Länderberichtsverfahren der Interamerikanischen Kommission für Menschenrechte**. 2019. XX, 475 Seiten. Geb. € 109,99.

281 Romy *Klimke*: **Schädliche traditionelle und kulturelle Praktiken im internationalen und regionalen Menschenrechtsschutz**. 2019. XVIII, 530 Seiten. Geb. € 99,99

280 Elisabeth Veronika *Henn*: **International Human Rights Law and Structural Discrimination**. 2019. XVI, 237 Seiten, € 89,99 zzgl. landesüblicher MwSt.

279 Eike *Blitza*: **Auswirkungen des Meeresspiegelanstiegs auf maritime Grenzen**. 2019. XIII, 294 Seiten. Geb. € 89,99

278 Anna Katharina *Struth*: **Hassrede und Freiheit der Meinungsäußerung**. 2019. XV, 472 Seiten. Geb. € 109,99

277 Franziska *Sucker*: **Der Schutz und die Förderung kultureller Vielfalt im Welthandelsrecht**. 2018. XXIV, 635 Seiten. Geb. € 109,99

276 Clemens *Mattheis*: **Die Konstitutionalisierung des Völkerrechts aus systemtheoretischer Sichtweise**. 2018. XXIV, 557 Seiten. Geb. € 109,99

275 Aydin *Atilgan*: **Global Constitutionalism**. 2018. X, 312 Seiten. Geb. € 114,99 zzgl. landesüblicher MwSt.

274 Andreas *Kolb*: **The UN Security Council Members' Responsibility to Protect**. 2018. XXI 624 Seiten. Geb. € 199,99 zzgl. landesüblicher MwSt.

273 Matthias *Goldmann*, Silvia *Steininger* (eds.): **Democracy and Financial Order: Legal Perspectives**. 2018. V, 230 Seiten. Geb. € 114,99 zzgl. landesüblicher MwSt.

272 Jochen *Rauber*: **Strukturwandel als Prinzipienwandel**. 2018. XXXIV, 970 Seiten. Geb. € 159,99

271 Anja *Höfelmeier*: **Die Vollstreckungsimmunität der Staaten im Wandel des Völkerrechts**. 2018. XX, 356 Seiten. Geb. € 89,99

270 Rudolf *Bernhardt*, Karin *Oellers-Frahm*: **Das Max-Planck-Institut für ausländisches öffentliches Recht und Völkerrecht**. 2018. XII, 344 Seiten. Geb. € 89,99

269 Philine *Wehling*: **Wasserrechte am Nil**. 2018. XVI, 351 Seiten. Geb. € 84,99

268 Katharina *Berner*: **Subsequent Agreements and Subsequent Practice in Domestic Courts**. 2018. XLV, 298 Seiten. Geb. € 114,99 zzgl. landesüblicher MwSt.

267 Josephine *Asche*: **Die Margin of Appreciation**. 2018. XII, 255 Seiten. Geb. € 84,99

266 Nele *Yang*: **Die Leitentscheidung**. 2018. XI, 362 Seiten. Geb. € 84,99

265 Roya *Sangi*: **Die auswärtige Gewalt des Europäischen Parlaments**. 2018. XV, 179 Seiten. Geb. € 69,99

264 Anna *Krueger*: **Die Bindung der Dritten Welt an das postkoloniale Völkerrecht**. 2018. XII, 434 Seiten. Geb. € 89,99

263 Björnstjern *Baade*: **Der Europäische Gerichtshof für Menschenrechte als Diskurswächter**. 2017. XVIII, 543 Seiten. Geb. € 99,99

262 Felix *Lange*: **Praxisorientierung und Gemeinschaftskonzeption**. 2017. XIV, 403 Seiten. Geb. € 94,99

261 Johanna Elisabeth *Dickschen*: **Empfehlungen und Leitlinien als Handlungsform der Europäischen Finanzaufsichtsbehörden**. 2017. XIX, 277 Seiten. Geb. € 84,99

260 Mohamed *Assakkali*: **Europäische Union und Internationaler Währungsfonds**. 2017. XV, 516 Seiten. Geb. € 99,99

259 Franziska *Paefgen*: **Der von Art. 8 EMRK gewährleistete Schutz vor staatlichen Eingriffen in die Persönlichkeitsrechte im Internet**. 2017. XV, 220 Seiten. Geb. € 69,99

258 Tim René *Salomon*: **Die internationale Strafverfolgungsstrategie gegenüber somalischen Piraten**. 2017. XXXII, 743 Seiten. Geb. € 129,99

257 Jelena *Bäumler*: **Das Schädigungsverbot im Völkerrecht**. 2017. XIX, 379 Seiten. Geb. € 89,99

256 Christopher *Peters*: **Praxis Internationaler Organisationen - Vertragswandel und völkerrechtlicher Ordnungsrahmen**. 2016. XXVIII, 498 Seiten. Geb. € 99,99

255 Nicole *Appel*: **Das internationale Kooperationsrecht der Europäischen Union**. 2016. XVIII, 608 Seiten. Geb. € 109,99

254 Christian *Wohlfahrt*: **Die Vermutung unmittelbarer Wirkung des Unionsrechts**. 2016. XIX, 300 Seiten. Geb. € 84,99

253 Katja *Göcke*: **Indigene Landrechte im internationalen Vergleich**. 2016. XVII, 818 Seiten. Geb. € 139,99

252 Julia *Heesen*: **Interne Abkommen**. 2015. XXI, 473 Seiten. Geb. € 94,99

251 Matthias *Goldmann*: **Internationale öffentliche Gewalt**. 2015. XXIX, 636 Seiten. Geb. € 109,99

250 Isabelle *Ley*: **Opposition im Völkerrecht**. 2014. XXIII, 452 Seiten. Geb. € 94,99

249 Matthias *Kottmann*: **Introvertierte Rechtsgemeinschaft**. 2014. XII, 352 Seiten. Geb. € 84,99

248 Jelena *von Achenbach*: **Demokratische Gesetzgebung in der Europäischen Union**. 2014. XVI, 522 Seiten. Geb. € 94,99

247 Jürgen *Friedrich*: **International Environmental "soft law"**. 2014. XXI, 503 Seiten. Geb. € 94,99 zzgl. landesüblicher MwSt.

246 Anuscheh *Farahat*: **Progressive Inklusion**. 2014. XXIV, 429 Seiten. Geb. € 94,99

245 Christina *Binder*: **Die Grenzen der Vertragstreue im Völkerrecht**. 2013. XL, 770 Seiten. Geb. € 119,99

244 Cornelia *Hagedorn*: **Legitime Strategien der Dissensbewältigung in demokratischen Staaten**. 2013. XX, 551 Seiten. Geb. € 99,99

243 Marianne *Klumpp*: **Schiedsgerichtsbarkeit und Ständiges Revisionsgericht des Mercosur**. 2013. XX, 512 Seiten. Geb. € 94,99

242 Karen *Kaiser* (Hrsg.): **Der Vertrag von Lissabon vor dem Bundesverfassungsgericht**. 2013. XX, 1635 Seiten. Geb. € 199,99

241 Dominik *Steiger*: **Das völkerrechtliche Folterverbot und der "Krieg gegen den Terror"**. 2013. XXX, 821 Seiten. Geb. € 139,99

240 Silja *Vöneky,* Britta *Beylage-Haarmann,* Anja *Höfelmeier,* Anna-Katharina *Hübler* (Hrsg.): **Ethik und Recht - Die Ethisierung des Rechts/Ethics and Law - The Ethicalization of Law**. 2013. XVIII, 456 Seiten. Geb. € 94,99

239 Rüdiger *Wolfrum,* Ina *Gätzschmann* (eds.): **International Dispute Settlement: Room for Innovations?** 2013. XIV, 445 Seiten. Geb. € 94,95 zzgl. landesüblicher MwSt.

238 Isabel *Röcker*: **Die Pflicht zur rahmenbeschlusskonformen Auslegung nationalen Rechts**. 2013. XXIII, 410 Seiten. Geb. € 89,95

237 Maike *Kuhn*: **Die Europäische Sicherheits- und Verteidigungspolitik im Mehrebenensystem**. 2012. XIII, 325 Seiten. Geb. € 79,95

236 Armin *von Bogdandy,* Ingo *Venzke* (eds.): **International Judicial Lawmaking**. 2012. XVII, 509 Seiten. Geb. € 94,95 zzgl. landesüblicher MwSt.

235 Susanne *Wasum-Rainer,* Ingo *Winkelmann,* Katrin *Tiroch* (eds.): **Arctic Science, International Law and Climate Change**. 2012. XIX, 374 Seiten. Geb. € 84,95 zzgl. landesüblicher MwSt.

234 Mirja A. *Trilsch*: **Die Justiziabilität wirtschaftlicher, sozialer und kultureller Rechte im innerstaatlichen Recht**. 2012. XIX, 559 Seiten. Geb. € 99,95

Printed by Printforce, the Netherlands